Managing Financial Institutions

Cases within the Financial Services Industry

Managing Financial Institutions

Cases within the Financial Services Industry

Samuel L. Hayes, III

Jacob H. Schiff Professor of Investment Banking
Harvard University

David M. Meerschwam

Harvard University

The Dryden Press

Harcourt Brace Jovanovich College Publishers

Fort Worth   Philadelphia   San Diego   New York   Orlando   Austin
San Antonio   Toronto   Montreal   London   Sydney   Tokyo

Acquisitions Editor: Rick Hammonds
Manuscript Editor: Robert H. Watrous
Designer: James Hughes
Art Editor: Elizabeth Banks
Production Manager: David Hough

ISBN: 0-15-527542-9

Library of Congress Catalog Number: 91-75065

Printed in the United States of America

Preface

The challenge of presenting a relevant course in the management of financial service organizations is daunting in the contemporary capital market environment. The only "constant" seems to be the persistence of change. We have spent much time and resources at the Harvard Business School in adapting and updating our second-year MBA course entitled "Management of Financial Services Organizations." This casebook represents our effort to share these materials and our experience in teaching them to students from different educational backgrounds.

Because this casebook presents teaching materials for a full 28-session course, it spans a variety of different financial service organizations, product lines, and national market settings.

Part 1 of the casebook presents six cases that look at different "segments" of the financial services industry. While we sought cases that deal with organizations closely identified with the segments, we found that one of the essential characteristics of the industry in the 1980s has been (and will continue to be in the 1990s) the blurring of boundaries between these segments as a result of new regulatory freedoms and strategic moves by financial firms. In the United States, for example, a "commercial" bank that is engaged in asset-backed lending and then reselling those loans thus generated utilizes marketing and distribution skills traditionally identified with the underwriting activity of an investment bank. This is contrary to the lending expertise historically associated with a U.S. commercial bank. Similarly, the "bridge-loan" financing technique developed by investment banks has more in common with the traditional lending activity of the commercial bank than with the pure intermediary function historically associated with the investment bank. Despite the reality of this blurring of boundaries, the cases presented in Part 1 set the stage for class discussions that can familiarize students with the basic market segments that prevail both in the United States and in the international marketplace.

Part 2 of the casebook presents five examples of strategies that relate to gaining entry into new markets. Here the importance of strategic choice comes to the fore as loosened regulatory constraints have allowed financial firms to choose what to do, and where to do it, as an outcome of strategic evaluation rather than of regulated direction. The primary focus of this section is international strategies, but ample opportunity is also provided to discuss the general issues of new-product market entry.

The financial and organizational consequences of new strategic directions are discussed in Part 3. These three cases were selected to highlight the cost of strategic redirection under market pressures. Here students have an opportunity to apply standard corporate financial analysis to the business strategies of financial rather than non-financial corporations.

The seven cases of Part 4 look at the segments of the financial *product* market.

All business firms ultimately create value through the products and services they offer to their clients; therefore, these cases examine the "ingredients" for success by analyzing the activities of the firms in generating these products and services. The cases consider such diverse issues as complex pricing considerations, restructuring techniques, and new-product development.

Part 5, the last section of the casebook, is particularly important given the new choices available to participants in the global financial services industry, and the ever-more centralized role of information, trust, and direction. The final three cases focus on the management of a financial firm's corporate responsibility. We have often found this to be the most challenging and rewarding part of the course. By this point in the curriculum, students have developed a sense of how the financial firms operate and, thus, are in a good position to consider just how firms use their power.

Our choice of cases and the suggested order of presentation reflect our belief that the constancy of change and the growing complexity of the decision-making process no longer allow for the simple structure an earlier casebook might have permitted. Products are more complicated, a sometimes bewildering set of new choices for issuers and investors exists, deregulation has widened the set of feasible activities for the financial service vendors, and markets have become internationalized. More simply, we could argue that two decades ago financial strategy was of relatively low priority for business corporations because the choices in finance were highly restricted by a web of government regulations. Business strategy was highly restricted for financial service firms because of the regulatory-defined environment. This casebook presents a different financing environment. On one side, there are almost limitless financial products and service choices for issuers and for investors; on the other side (the major focus of this casebook), financial service vendors face complex choices about how to position themselves within these markets.

We hope that instructors will feel comfortable about experimenting with the materials provided here. As is well known, case studies are usually written not to illustrate "right" or "wrong" managerial responses to business problems, but rather to develop an approach to analyzing the components of those problems. Thus, these cases are designed to build the student's skills in asking the right *questions* in order to illuminate the problem's anatomy. That is often the most difficult but also the most important step in the process of managerial decision making. These cases should stimulate broad discussion and, although some are more technical than others (and some require sophisticated financial analysis), we believe that the myriad of issues they raise are proving to be the important ones in the current financial market environment. Even though teaching notes that present our own thinking about these cases are available to instructors, we do not suggest that those notes are exhaustive; we would be delighted to expand our own understanding through questions and suggestions from you, the users.

As we mentioned, the cases can be used together in the order they are presented. As such, they offer an integrated course on the management and strategy formulation of financial service organizations. Since most cases are designated for a single hour-and-twenty-minute class discussion, a semester-long course would be required to cover them all. Alternatively, selected cases can be used either to design a shorter course or to supplement already established courses, not only those dealing with the financial service organizations but also those focused on banking, corporate finance, and monetary policy's interaction with financial institutions.

▼ ■

Acknowledgments

We are indebted to many who have helped us in producing this casebook. Our research associates contributed to much of the case materials. They included Michael Baldwin, Jack Cave, Bill Allen, and Steve Percoco. Our Harvard Business School colleagues Dwight Crane, Robert Eccles, Scott Mason, and Lynn Sharp Paine were kind enough to let us include some of their materials. The Anchor Savings Bank case was written by Florence Langford under the supervision of Crane and Mason, the Cumberland National Corporation case by Paige Manning under the supervision of Crane, and the Bankers Trust New York Corporation case by Susan Crevoor under the supervision of Crane and Eccles. The Cameron case was written at George Washington University by Paine and Rivoli. We are also grateful to numerous other colleagues who have made valuable comments and suggestions about the cases during their development.

Special thanks are due to the business firms which generously gave us access to internal documents and to their executives who were willing to take the time to talk with us. The interviews we conducted at many of the firms were critical to the shape of the final teaching materials. Some of the cases were based on public sources only, and many published materials served either to supplement the field-based cases or to build other cases around.

The environment of the Harvard Business School is especially well suited to produce the materials we present here. It provides a remarkable link between academe and the corporate world and makes available financial support sufficient to produce in-depth case studies. Dean John McArthur deserves special mention for stimulating this case-development effort.

Finally we are indebted to our students. They served not only as a rigorous quality control mechanism, but also spurred us on to develop new materials through their questions and suggestions. Most important, however, they were a challenging group of promising individuals for whom it was a pleasure to write and rewrite draft after draft of these cases.

Samuel L. Hayes
David A. Meerschwam

Contents

PART 4

PART 5

Managing Financial Institutions

Cases within the Financial Services Industry

PART 1

Segments of the Financial Services Industry

Salomon Brothers' Strategic Review: 1987

During the week of October 5, 1987, John Gutfreund, the chairman and CEO of Salomon Inc., met several times with his two top executives to discuss the future of the company. Earnings at Salomon Brothers, the firm's investment banking subsidiary, had declined precipitously in late 1986 and 1987, and Gutfreund had initiated a broad study of Salomon's strategy and cost structure. The study was now complete. It recommended cutting hundreds of jobs, disbanding several business units (including municipal finance and commercial paper) and placing a new emphasis on investment banking activities far removed from Salomon's roots as a trading firm. Gutfreund and his deputies needed to decide whether to take the study's advice and, if so, how to implement it.

Salomon Brothers[1]

Salomon Brothers was founded in 1910 when Arthur, Herbert, and Percy Salomon, armed with $5,000 in capital, left their father's money brokerage business to set up their own partnership. The brothers were immediately successful in the business of raising short-term bank loans for brokerage houses, and soon expanded their efforts to dealing in bankers' acceptances and acting as intermediaries between institutional clients that wanted to buy or sell corporate bonds. While they lacked the elite social status that was then required to underwrite corporate bonds, this did not prevent them from entering the government bond business. In 1915 the firm began underwriting and dealing in foreign bonds, and in 1917 it became the second authorized dealer of U.S. government securities. By the early 1920s the firm was well established in its fixed income businesses, and money brokerage formed only a minor part of its operations.

Salomon's core businesses remained essentially unchanged for many years. By the late 1950s, however, new management initiatives and changes in the national economy were beginning to transform Salomon into a more powerful firm which participated in a wider range of businesses. Salomon had historically concentrated on dealing with institutions, mainly out of necessity since an over-

This case was prepared by Michael Baldwin under the supervision of Assistant Professor David M. Meerschwam.

whelming majority of its employees lacked the social credentials that were a pre-requisite for selling securities to wealthy investors in the years before the Second World War.[2] While this institutional focus was originally something of a handi-cap, it put the firm in a strong position after the war, when institutions such as pension and mutual funds began managing an ever greater share of the nation's wealth.

The initiative that laid the groundwork for much that followed was con-ceived by Percy's son, William, who became part of a ruling troika in 1957 and managing partner in 1963. Billy Salomon saw that the firm would need capital to expand, and in 1958 he pushed through new rules that placed stringent limits on the partners' salaries and their ability to withdraw capital from the firm. The new rules played a crucial role as Salomon's capital expanded from $7.5 million in 1958 to almost $236 million in 1980.

Salomon's growing capital base enabled it to undertake several new initia-tives. In 1960, for example, the firm hired Sidney Homer to start a bond research department. Homer and his young associates (one of whom was Henry Kauf-man) were given generous resources to build a world-class fixed-income research organization. Another initiative of the early 1960s developed from Billy Salomon's conviction that the firm should be able to serve its institutional clients' growing appetite for equities. The firm accordingly borrowed $6.5 million to finance the development of a prominent block trading desk. Salomon undertook yet another major initiative in 1962, when it joined Merrill Lynch, Lehman, and Blyth in forming an underwriting group to compete with the elite firms that dom-inated corporate underwriting. Salomon was the most aggressive member of the group, which muscled its way into prominence by cutting spreads. John Gut-freund, who became manager of Salomon's syndicate department in 1962, recalled: "We were joined by almost no one on the first deals. We made outsized commitments, and were at the mercy of the markets."[3] By 1964 the firm had more than tripled its underwriting volume and moved from thirteenth to sixth place in the league tables.

Gutfreund spearheaded the firm's move into domestic underwriting. In the early 1970s, he also oversaw Salomon's successful effort to build a major presence in European trading and underwriting by duplicating the aggressive tactics that had proven so successful in the U.S. One competitor recalled: "He was the first to realize that the power to distribute securities would become the power to under-write them."[4] When Billy Salomon retired in September 1978, Gutfreund became the new managing partner.

The Salomon Brothers of 1978 had progressed far beyond its former status as a small bond house. It had 52 partners, 1,600 employees and $300 million in annual revenue. Its role in helping New York City out of a fiscal crisis in the mid-1970s had demonstrated its arrival as part of Wall Street's establishment. Still, some areas needed strengthening. Although Salomon had a star dealmaker in J. Ira Harris, it was the regular investment banker for only 10 of the top 500 U.S. cor-porations, and the organizational structure of its 10-year-old corporate finance department was weak. Gutfreund recalled Salomon's client relationships: "We had great initial penetration, but then we forgot about them until the time came for the next transaction. We had no system in place to make sure that we got to understand all their business, to become *simpatico* with the top executives."[5] In 1977, Salomon hired James Wolfensohn away from Schroders to head an effort to strengthen the corporate finance department. Wolfensohn reorganized the department and then launched a major effort to win new underwriting clients. Between 1978 and 1980, Salomon captured 12 of the 30 major corporations that switched underwriters without losing any clients of its own. By 1981, however, some of the firm's investment bankers were complaining that Wolfensohn was spending too much time on the Chrysler bailout, and not enough time on his broader duties.

Organizational stresses continued to accumulate in spite of the firm's success. Some of the problems revolved around compensation. Salomon's need to retain capital severely limited the incomes of the partners, especially the younger ones. There was a persistent dilemma concerning the question of how to compensate the growing numbers of vice presidents. Finally, the retired partners wanted higher incomes. Another set of problems involved the firm's management and organizational structure. Gutfreund saw a need to bring more centralized management to the firm without driving away the entrepreneurial talent that had made it successful in the first place. Gaining control over the firm's executive committee, however, was not an easy task. One former partner commented: "Johnny hates confrontations and tries to please them all, but he can't because they're either fighting or going off in different directions."[6] Finally, some of the partners saw the need for more capital. By 1981, as William Voute recalled: "We saw the needs of the market expanding and the U.S. Treasury needs expanding. We had only in the neighborhood of $300 million in capital, and it was felt that this wasn't enough to bring us into the next century."[7]

The firm continued to grow, and profits reached record heights. By 1981, Salomon had 62 partners, 2,500 employees, over $700 million in annual revenue, and about $100 million in annual aftertax profits. The mounting strains within the firm, however, were beginning to produce a high level of infighting and executive turnover. Several key partners left between 1978 and 1980. The turnover accelerated in 1981 as seven partners, including Wolfensohn, announced plans to resign.

The Sale

On Friday, July 31, 1981, Salomon's general partners reported to an unusual weekend-long meeting at the Tarrytown Conference Center, where they were informed that the firm's executive committee had negotiated a tentative merger agreement with the Phibro Corporation. The agreement called for Salomon's partners to withdraw their equity (which was roughly $233 million as of March 31) and additional 1981 earnings (which would be at least $70 million after taxes by the time the merger took effect on October 1). Phibro would then replace the partners' capital with $300 million of its own. Phibro would also give the general partners $250 million in bonds, which would pay 9% and could be converted into Phibro stock at $27.78 over the course of five years. The seven members of the executive committee would share $75 million worth of bonds. The biggest payout went to Gutfreund, who received $32 million in capital and bonds even before the distribution of 1981 profits. Limited partners, who collectively owned about a third of the firm, would not receive any bonds. (Billy Salomon, for example, received less than $10 million before his share of the year's earnings.)

At less than twice book value, the price was not as high as for some of the brokerage mergers that occurred earlier in 1981. American Express paid 3.4 times book value for Shearson, and Prudential paid over twice book value for Bache. Nevertheless, by 10 AM Sunday, all of the general partners had agreed to sell the firm. Salomon would become an autonomous part of Phibro, which would soon change its name to Phibro-Salomon. Phibro's current chairman would be the CEO of the merged firms, but John Gutfreund would continue to run Salomon and serve as co-chairman of Phibro-Salomon.

The Phibro Corporation

Phibro was a huge commodities trading firm which had its roots in a metals trading business begun by Oscar and Julius Philipp late in the nineteenth century. By 1981 the firm traded over 150 commodities from 60 offices in 45 countries. It had 4,600 employees and almost $1.7 billion in capital. Phibro had expanded rapidly into new commodities in the 1970s. (By 1980, the oil trading business it started in the early 1970s accounted for about 50% of its revenue.) In 1980 Phibro earned $466.8 million on revenues of $23.7 billion, compared to earnings of $26.8 million on revenues of $1.2 billion in 1971. In the first half of 1981, however, Phibro's earnings had plunged by 50% as commodity prices fell.

Phibro's chairman, David Tendler, believed that Salomon's financial capabilities would enhance Phibro's ability to make deals all over the world. The two companies would function autonomously, but Tendler saw many opportunities for them to use each others' contacts and skills and, perhaps, create "the world's leading merchant bank."[8] He remarked: "We are creating a unique company in the world of trading, be it commodities or money. There is a limitless area in which we can both expand."[9] Still, some wondered how Salomon would fare in the combination. Phibro was renowned as a tough competitor in a tough business, and many observers predicted that Tendler would come out on top after a struggle with Gutfreund. As Henry Jarecki of Mocatta Metals told a Salomon partner: "They will chew you up and spit out the bones."[10]

The Boom Years

The years following the merger were good for Wall Street in general, and for Salomon in particular. By 1983, the firm had captured the largest market share in the rapidly growing underwriting business. Salomon's preeminence was primarily based upon dominance in underwriting debt securities, but by 1985 it had also become a top equity underwriter. In 1985, the firm's most profitable year, it lead-managed eight of the largest ten securities issues.

Part of Salomon's success was due to constant innovation. In 1981, the firm started a group which attempted to link the needs of corporate finance clients with the needs of institutional investors. One example of the many products created by this "capital markets group" (which was soon imitated by other firms) was the hugely successful debt-for-equity swap. Salomon did twenty debt-for-equity swaps within four months of the product's introduction, reaping high profits while other firms scrambled to obtain a share of the market. Salomon also introduced or helped pioneer many other new products, including original issue discount bonds, zero coupon bonds synthesized from Treasury securities, and bonds backed by automobile loans. The firm was a pioneer in quantitative research, and by 1985 it had about 40 Ph.D.'s at work analyzing markets, creating new securities, and developing new trading techniques.

The firm also benefitted when regulatory innovation allowed customers to register securities far in advance of the date of issue, enabling them to approach a number of underwriters shortly before an offering in an effort to obtain the best possible terms. The skills developed through generations of taking large positions to eke out small profits proved well-suited for this popular new approach to underwriting. The market shares of the largest underwriters almost doubled after the introduction of the new "shelf registration" procedures, which accounted for almost 40% of issue volume in 1983, their first full year of operation. Salomon immediately became the leading underwriter of shelf-registered securities.

The firm competed fiercely for business. Nowhere was this more evident than in the municipal securities business, especially from 1985 onward. Sherman Lewis, a vice chairman at Shearson Lehman Brothers, complained: "Salomon had a conscious policy to drive other people from the business by cutting out the management fees on deals; they drove the margins into the ground so nobody made money."[11] Salomon was one of a handful of leading municipal bond underwriters, which was a particularly impressive achievement since it did not have a retail operation to serve the individual investors who accounted for a substantial fraction of purchases even before the 1986 tax reforms. Nevertheless, competitors claimed that Salomon's municipal bond unit was not particularly profitable. One rumor put the unit's operating profits at a mere $8 million in 1986.[12]

Salomon's success in the mortgage-backed securities market epitomized the results the firm obtained by combining trading skills, persistence, and innovation. Salomon virtually invented the market in the 1970s, and continued to expand its mortgage operations even when other firms abandoned the business in the wake of the 1979 housing crash. When the business began to boom again in 1981, Salomon had a valuable franchise with more depth and breadth than any of its competitors. As competitors became more serious, the franchise began to erode, and spreads on some mortgage-backeds narrowed to amounts commensurate with Treasuries. Nevertheless, Salomon held 40% of the market even in the mid-1980s. In 1983, its 135-person MBS unit traded over $250 billion, commonly took positions of $1 billion or more, and employed more equity capital than some of Salomon's leading competitors. A number of observers claimed that the unit was responsible for 40% of the firm's profits during its most profitable years. (A Salomon spokesman later suggested that 25% would be closer to the truth.) In 1986 Gutfreund remarked that Lewis Ranieri, the entrepreneurial executive who was responsible for much of the unit's success, was a potential candidate to be his successor as CEO.

Salomon's aggressive, opportunistic style was exemplified by a transaction it completed in August 1984. After the U.S. repealed a law which required 30% interest withholding for foreign investors, Salomon led a syndicate which purchased $1.7 billion of 30-year Treasury bonds. It used the bonds to back $7 billion of CATS (Certificates of Accrual on Treasury Securities), each of which embodied a single payment of interest or principal. The CATS were sold to both foreign and domestic investors, with foreign investors receiving bearer securities. Because such a Euro-issue could offer lower yields than those on the underlying Treasuries (a fact which most observers attributed to the inherent potential for tax avoidance offered by bearer securities) Salomon created a profitable arbitrage for itself. One day later, the Senate passed a non-binding resolution asking the Treasury to prohibit selling bearer securities backed with government securities to foreigners. The Treasury complied early in September. Salomon's outstanding CATS, however, were not affected by the Treasury's decision.

While Salomon's market expertise was undisputed, many competitors downplayed its skills in corporate finance. John Whitehead, the former co-chairman of Goldman Sachs, remarked: "It's an interest rate shop, period." He went on to say that "most of Salomon's emphasis is placed on offering the best terms to a client once that company has already decided what to do."[13] Salomon's corporate finance and mergers and acquisitions areas were, in fact, smaller than those of its major competitors. Salomon's M&A unit, which in 1985 had about 40 investment bankers generating over $100 million in fees, was only about one-fourth the size of the M&A units at First Boston, Goldman Sachs, and Morgan Stanley. In 1986, Salomon advised on 130 deals worth a total of $32.5 billion, which made it the fifth ranking adviser in terms of dollar volume. (Goldman Sachs, which advised on 181 deals worth $68.1 billion, placed first.) Salomon advised on two of *Institutional Investor*'s thirteen "most noteworthy" deals of 1986, earning $5.2 million in fees. James Wolfensohn, who had started his own investment banking boutique after leaving Salomon, also advised on two of these thirteen deals. He earned $9.75 million in fees. Goldman Sachs advised on five of the thirteen deals, earning $44.5 million in fees on the three whose terms were made public.

Culture and Management at Salomon Brothers

Salomon's approach to the securities business was mirrored in its internal culture. As Henry Kaufman described the firm: "We're tough winners, sore losers and the question always is: What are we going to do tomorrow?"[14] When a group of trainees asked John Gutfreund for the secret of how to succeed at Salomon, he reportedly answered: "You've got to be in shape. And I don't mean jogging and all that crap. You've got to be ready to bite the ass off a bear every morning."[15]

Throughout the years of rapid expansion, Salomon Brothers retained much of the loose horizontal structure of its partnership days. The firm was run by Gutfreund, who spent much of his time at his desk on the trading floor, and an executive committee composed of Gutfreund and eight other senior managers. Much operating authority was delegated to lower level managers. Executives complained, however, that top management was sometimes slow to make big decisions. Gutfreund admitted that occasionally things moved slowly: "I'm too paternalistic. My problem is that I am too deliberate on people issues."[16] The deliberate approach could lead to problems. One executive gave an example: "The munis area was very poorly managed. We all knew that. It never made as much money as it should have. It was a people problem. And John can be very slow to make people decisions."[17]

Phibro and Salomon

Although Salomon Brothers prospered after the merger, Phibro continued to suffer from broad downturns in commodity markets. Phibro's Ludwig Jesselson commented: "You know how long I have been with Phibro? Forty-five years. And I have *never* experienced as disastrous a situation in our commodities as I've experienced in the last two years."[18] Phibro and Salomon had made few attempts to achieve any operating synergies, but executives began talking about how the two parts of the company would complement each other at different points of the business cycle. Tendler commented: "The synergy was the merger."[19]

With Salomon accounting for the largest portion of Phibro-Salomon's profits, Gutfreund campaigned for power equal to Tendler's, and was promoted to co-CEO in September 1983. Faced with what Gutfreund recalled as a "two-headed monster," Tendler attempted to buy Philipp Brothers, Phibro's non-energy commodities operations.[20] When the attempt failed, Gutfreund began pressuring the board for status as sole CEO. Soon after the board agreed in August 1984, Tendler resigned.

In 1985, Gutfreund made sweeping changes at Philipp Brothers. He assigned two 32-year-old sugar traders to manage the unit, and accelerated the gradual cost cutting that Tendler had begun in 1982. Many of the facilities that dealt with physical commodities were sold, and Philipp Brothers reduced the number of commodities it handled to about 40 that were traded on exchanges. Restructuring plans called for reducing the staff from over 3,000 to about 1,000. Finally, in 1986, Phibro-Salomon was renamed Salomon Inc.

The End of the Boom

Salomon Brothers expanded rapidly in 1986. The firm's staff grew to about 6,000, a 40% increase within the space of a year. The London office grew to 700 employees, up from 200 only two years earlier. The volume of securities that Salomon lead-managed grew nearly 58% from 1985, to $53.6 billion. The firm's net interest revenue increased by 76%, to $471 million, and investment banking revenue increased by 45%, to $524 million. Total revenues grew by almost 26%. Unfortunately, however, Salomon Brothers' revenues did not grow as fast as its expenses. Pretax expenses grew by almost 30%. Pretax earnings plunged 33% in the fourth quarter. Salomon Brothers' annual pretax earnings grew by less than 4%. Pretax earnings for Salomon Inc as a whole fell 16% after a poor year at the commodities units.

By October 1986, Gutfreund had decided that the firm's management structure was outdated: "Our problem is symptomatic of Wall Street's problem. The business has grown faster than our ability to manage it."[21] As he admitted later: "Central control was lacking."[22] Gutfreund moved to restructure Salomon Brothers' management, effectively diluting the power of some of the firm's older executives. He created an "Office of the Chairman" consisting of himself, a president, and two vice chairmen. He promoted ten younger executives to a new board of directors, which would share power with the existing executive committee. He formed two committees to monitor Salomon's investments and balance sheet. The structural changes continued into the next year. In early 1987, over Ranieri's objections, Gutfreund began consolidating control over Salomon's taxable fixed income areas, and in March 1987 he appointed Salomon's first chief financial officer.

The reorganization seemed to signify the resolution of a longstanding internal dispute over the firm's approach to investment banking. A number of top managers (Kaufman and Ranieri, for example) were philosophically opposed to abandoning Salomon's roots as a trading and underwriting house and rushing into the sort of merchant banking and buyout activity that had generated large profits for other investment banks. Kaufman's opposition to merchant banking and high-yield financing was particularly vehement. By late 1986, however, Gutfreund saw the need to expand the firm's investment banking capabilities. In particular, he wanted to increase the size of the M&A area and place more emphasis on merchant banking. Gutfreund's decision was reflected in the reorganization. Kaufman relinquished his position as vice chairman, and the head of corporate finance was replaced by the founder and head of Salomon's M&A unit. Still, Gutfreund planned to approach the new areas with caution: "Just because other firms make a fortune in high-yield bonds or buyouts doesn't mean we should recast ourselves to make that a priority. The issue is how to get ourselves into a competitive mode without risking our entire firm on bridges that might turn out to be bridges to nowhere."[23]

Gutfreund's choice of top aides also attracted speculation. Salomon's first president would be Tom Strauss, who had risen through government bond sales to become head of governments, money markets, foreign exchange, and the firm's international effort. The two vice chairmen would be Ranieri and William Voute, the head of corporate bond trading. All three men had been viewed as contenders for the CEO's position, and some observers claimed that Strauss's appointment as president could mark the beginning of a new management style at Salomon Brothers. Strauss was renowned as a controlled, team-oriented manager who was very different from the explosive, individualistic Salomon Brothers stereotype. Gutfreund remarked: "The time has come in our industry for those with Tommy's characteristics to emerge as leaders. Wall Street has to move from a partnership culture to corporate management."[24] Another executive wondered about what the choice meant for the future: "Tommy can undoubtedly run a ruthlessly well-oiled, low-cost machine. But is that in fact what the future will look like?"[25]

The firm's problems didn't stop its expansion. It proceeded with plans to construct a new headquarters complex in midtown Manhattan. It injected $300 million of new capital into the Tokyo office, increasing the unit's capitalization by a factor of 10 and making it the fifth biggest securities firm in Japan. It continued to hire new people, and by August 1987 the employment rolls had increased to over 6,500.

Salomon's performance continued to suffer in 1987. The firm had lost market share in underwriting in both 1985 and 1986, and in the first quarter of 1987 the dollar volume of securities it lead-managed slipped as well. (Some analysts attributed the decline to the firm's relative weakness in offering securities tied to buyouts and acquisitions.) Trading and underwriting spreads were under pressure in many of its markets. Interest rates rose unexpectedly in the spring, and several fixed income areas accumulated large losses. The municipal bond area, which had positions in a number of illiquid securities, was said to have been especially hard hit. Analysts estimated that it had lost $50 to $100 million by autumn. (Gutfreund commented, in retrospect: "The trading management was not as prudent as it might have been."[26]) Widespread defections struck the London office, whose staffers had often complained about lack of autonomy and a management style not suited for Europe. Some observers claimed to see a more general malaise. A top executive at another firm remarked: "An unusually large number of people have left recently or are looking to leave. I sense a certain instability over there."[27] Pretax profits plunged 22% from 1986 levels in the first quarter, and 68% in the second quarter.

In July, Gutfreund moved to reorganize the mortgage-backed securities area, which Ranieri had run as what some observers called a "separate fiefdom" of 400 employees. The unit had recently suffered from declining margins, increased competition, and a reported lack of coordination between traders. After discussions among Salomon's highest-ranking executives, Ranieri and his top aide left the firm. Strauss explained Ranieri's departure: "He was better at building businesses, and the transition into management was more difficult."[28] Gutfreund then split the mortgage-backed securities department in half as he proceeded with a broader plan to consolidate most of the firm's trading and finance units into two large trading and finance departments.

In August, with the markets once again going against Salomon Brothers, Gutfreund froze hiring and initiated a review of the firm's strategy. The review would examine both the firm's cost structure and some of its weaker units. One official described these weak spots as "Anything that a bank sells."[29] Particular attention would be devoted to the firm's commercial paper and municipal finance areas. Completion of the review was scheduled for October.

Municipal Finance

Municipal securities were securities issued by state or local governments (or related entities) to serve some public purpose. Interest on such securities was generally exempt from federal taxes and state and local taxes in the states where they were issued. As the needs of municipal issuers had become more specialized, investment banks had set up separate units to serve them.

Municipal bonds could be broadly divided into general obligation and revenue bonds. General obligation bonds were backed by government taxing power, while revenue bonds were backed by revenue from specific projects. General obligation bonds were often assigned to investment banks on the basis of competitive bids. Revenue bond issuers often selected an underwriter and then negotiated a price after the issue had been structured. Commercial banks could underwrite general obligation bonds and certain types of revenue bonds. A number of major banks were adept at private placements, which enabled them to circumvent the restrictions on underwriting revenue bonds.

The municipal bond business grew rapidly and changed dramatically in the 1980s. A typical year in the late 1970s might have seen the issuance of $45 billion in long-term municipal bonds. Volume expanded greatly in the 1980s, peaking at $204 billion in 1985. More and more financing ($77 billion in 1985) seemed tied to "private purpose" bonds which were only marginally related to the public good. Finally, issuers and their bankers became much more innovative. Among the innovations were floating-rate debt (1981), floating-rate demand obligations (1983), and municipal bond index futures (1985). Growing use of information technology encouraged ever more complex financings and more efficient markets as traders got quick access to prices. A few investment banks experimented with merging parts of their taxable and tax-exempt bond units as municipal issuers took greater advantage of techniques developed in the taxable areas. (Salomon, for example, experimented with limited consolidation of its taxable and tax-exempt units in housing, health care and resource recovery financing.)

The tax reforms of August 1986 had a major impact on the municipal bond business. New guidelines limited the volume and uses of funds raised with tax-exempt securities. One industry study estimated that, if the guidelines anticipated for 1991 had existed in 1984, 41% of the tax-exempt bonds issued in that year would not have been eligible for tax exemption. Private purpose bonds were particularly hard hit. The guidelines limited issuance of private purpose bonds to $21.3 billion in 1987, and less thereafter.

Tax reform affected purchasers as well as issuers. Some municipal bond interest would have to be included in calculating alternative minimum taxes. Property and casualty insurers would have their loss deductions reduced by 15% of the tax-exempt interest they earned on newly acquired securities. Most importantly, the reform largely eliminated financial institutions' ability to deduct most of the interest costs they incurred to carry newly acquired tax-exempt bonds. The reform therefore accelerated a trend in municipal bond ownership patterns that was already underway. Historically, banks had been the largest holders of municipal bonds. (In 1978, for example, banks owned 44% of outstanding municipals.) In 1982, banks owned 38% of outstanding municipal bonds, individuals and mutual funds owned 35%, and insurance companies owned 23%. By 1986, banks owned 28%, individuals and mutual funds owned 55%, and insurance companies owned 14%. Mutual funds owned about 19% of outstanding municipals in 1986, up from virtually nothing in 1980.

Volume peaked in 1985 as issuers rushed to refinance debt incurred earlier at much higher rates, and to raise money before anticipated tax reforms went into effect. Volume began to fall in 1986, and competition for business grew ferocious. By 1987 issue volume had collapsed to about $100 billion, and underwriters were slashing prices. Spreads fell from 1984's level of $22.70 per $1,000 worth of bonds to $12.62 in 1987. The average amount that Salomon received for underwriting $1,000 worth of bonds fell from over $17 in 1985 to $7.62 in 1987.

In spite of the current crisis, some experts saw better days ahead in the municipal finance business. Some thought that municipalities would greatly increase the amount of taxable bonds they issued. There was also a growing recognition that much of the nation's crumbling infrastructure would need to be replaced. One respected study saw the need for about $1 trillion in infrastructure financing by the year 2000. Other estimates were even higher.

Commercial Paper

Commercial paper was unsecured short-term debt. Issuers generally avoided the need to register their paper with the SEC by setting the maturity to 270 days or less. They frequently planned to refund their paper with the proceeds of another issue, and would arrange lines of credit at banks to serve as backup sources of funds in the event of adverse developments in the commercial paper market. Industrial firms accounted for 30% to 40% of commercial paper volume, with banks and other financial companies accounting for the remainder. Large financial corporations typically sold their paper directly to investors, while industrial firms and some smaller financial organizations issued their paper through dealers. Commercial paper issued through dealers generally matured in one to three months.

Commercial paper dealers bought paper from issuers and sold it to investors. They also stood ready to make a market in the paper of their clients. A handful of dealers accounted for much of the $190 billion of dealer paper outstanding in the fall of 1987. The biggest dealer was Merrill Lynch, with $60 billion of paper outstanding. Shearson Lehman was the second biggest, with $50 billion of paper outstanding. Salomon, with about $30 billion of paper outstanding, was the fourth largest dealer. A number of commercial banks were also making efforts to strengthen their presence as dealers. Some already had a major presence in the overseas markets.

Spreads in the commercial paper market, as in all of the money markets, were quite thin. A dealer might obtain a spread of 10 basis points (quoted on an annual basis) in buying and selling commercial paper. In spite of the low spreads, many saw commercial paper dealing as a necessary adjunct to more profitable businesses. The head of Merrill Lynch's money market unit, for example, commented: "It really is difficult for us to comprehend being in the taxable-debt business without having a presence in the short-term maturities."[30] An executive at Morgan Guaranty commented that the commercial paper business required a "daily dialogue" with issuers, and that it had helped Morgan build its investment banking business. While Morgan's commercial paper unit was profitable, he said, "You sell not for the high profit of commercial paper, but for the relationship and opportunity to sell other services."[31] Nevertheless, some analysts were skeptical that dealing commercial paper could help generate much corporate finance business. One commented: "It's a routine financial activity, a middle-level business. You probably aren't dealing with the chief financial officer, or treasurer."[32] Salomon, observers claimed, had not been notably successful in using its commercial paper expertise to generate other corporate finance business.

Late September: The Takeover Threat

As the strategic review drew to a close, Salomon faced a new problem. Gutfreund knew that Salomon's largest shareholder, Harry Oppenheimer's Minerals & Resources Corporation, had been interested in selling its 14% stake for several months. On September 23, he learned that Minorco was in the final stages of negotiation with Ronald Perelman of Revlon. Perelman had offered Minorco $809 million for its 21.282 million shares. (Minorco would therefore receive $38 per share at a time when the market price was $32.) Gutfreund recalled: "I was shocked. Perelman was just a name to me, but I felt that the structure of Salomon Brothers, in terms of our relationships with our clients, their trust and confidence, would not do well with our having a bond with someone deemed to be a corporate raider."[33]

Gutfreund and his top managers quickly concluded that they would not work for Perelman, and Gutfreund contacted Warren Buffet, a billionaire investor who had been interested in purchasing part of Salomon for some time. They arranged a deal which would enable Salomon to repurchase Minorco's stake for $809 million. The purchase would be financed by selling $700 million worth of preferred stock to Buffet. The preferred stock could be converted to common at $38 per share in three years. If it wasn't converted by October 1995, Salomon had to redeem it at the original purchase price over the course of five years. It would give Buffet a 12% voting stake in Salomon and would pay dividends of $63 million annually. (Salomon's common stock, in contrast, paid a dividend of $0.64 per share.) Buffet got two seats on the board, and agreed not to raise his stake above 20%.

On September 28, Gutfreund and other top managers met with the board. They informed the board that they would resign rather than work for Revlon. The board approved the Buffet deal. Perelman kept up his threats, first offering better terms than Buffet for the preferred stock, then purchasing $6.5 million worth of stock in the open market. Observers were divided as to whether Perelman was serious about wanting to take over Salomon. In any event, however, Gutfreund saw the possibility of similar threats in the future. He remarked: "If we don't get our act together over the next year, we'll be threatened again. And we should be!"[34]

The Results of the Strategic Review

Early in the week of October 5, Salomon Brothers' board released the results of the strategic study to the office of the chairman. The study called for broad measures to cut and control costs, exit from two unprofitable businesses, and a new focus on high-margin investment banking activities. The study estimated that Salomon could save $150 million annually by cutting 800 jobs. About 200 of these jobs would come from the municipal finance unit, which would be disbanded. Another 80 would come from the commercial paper unit, which would also be disbanded. Although Salomon had been the leading municipal underwriter in the first nine months of 1987, and was the fourth largest commercial paper dealer with $30 billion of paper outstanding, the executives had calculated that neither business was profitable. The firm would also leave its other money markets businesses (including dealing in bankers' acceptances and certificates of deposit), eliminating about 120 jobs. About 100 people would be trimmed from the London office, and an additional 300 jobs would be cut throughout the firm, mainly from the ranks of support personnel and the corporate bond sales staff. The restructuring and associated severance pay would cost $60 million to $70 million in the fourth quarter.

As Gutfreund, Strauss, and Voute met to consider the results of the study, they knew that Salomon Brothers' third quarter income had fallen to $49 million before taxes, almost 80% less than the $225 million earned before taxes in the third quarter of the previous year.

▶ Endnotes

1. The casewriter relied heavily upon Robert Sobel's *Salomon Brothers* (1986) when describing the firm's history from its founding to the late 1970s.
2. See, for example, Sobel, pp. 33 and 64–65.
3. Sobel, p. 94.
4. *Business Week*, December 9, 1985, p. 101.
5. *Business Week*, April 3, 1978, p. 84.
6. *Institutional Investor*, December 1981, p. 48.
7. Sobel, p. 174.
8. *Economist*, August 8, 1981, p. 63.
9. *Business Week*, August 17, 1981, p. 24.
10. *Institutional Investor*, December 1981, p. 53.
11. *New York Times Magazine*, January 10, 1988, p. 24.
12. *Investment Dealers' Digest*, October 19, 1987, p. 22.
13. *Institutional Investor*, March 1986, p. 69.
14. *Wall Street Journal*, September 17, 1984, p. 31.
15. *Wall Street Journal*, September 17, 1984, p. 37.
16. *New York Times Magazine*, January 10, 1988, p. 24.
17. Ibid.
18. *Fortune*, January 10, 1983, p. 74.
19. *Fortune*, January 10, 1983, p. 78.
20. *Business Week*, December 9, 1985, p. 102.
21. *Business Week*, April 20, 1987, p. 72.
22. *New York Times Magazine*, January 10, 1988, p. 24.
23. *Business Week*, April 20, 1987, p. 73.
24. *Institutional Investor*, October 1987, p. 226.
25. *Institutional Investor*, October 1987, p. 230.
26. *Business Week*, October 26, 1987, p. 30.
27. *Business Week*, April 20, 1987, p. 73.
28. *Wall Street Journal*, July 27, 1987, p. 1.
29. *Wall Street Journal*, October 10, 1987, p. 44.
30. *Business Week*, October 26, 1987, p. 31.
31. *Pensions & Investment Age*, November 23, 1987, p. 14.
32. Ibid.
33. *New York Times Magazine*, January 10, 1988, p. 26.
34. *Wall Street Journal*, October 2, 1987, p. 22.

Exhibit 1

Consolidated Balance Sheets for Salomon Inc.
($ millions)

	September 30,		December 31,					
Assets	1987	1986	1985	1984	1983	1982	1981	1980
Cash	$ 696	$ 1,224	$ 931	$ 345	$ 432	$ 268	$ 451	$ 468
Inventories:								
Securities owned:								
U.S. Government and Federal agencies	NA	25,611	30,253	21,586	10,667	14,690	NA	NA
Bankers acceptances, certificates of deposit, and commercial paper	NA	2,628	3,494	4,035	3,183	3,585	NA	NA
Corporate debt	NA	7,768	8,110	4,256	2,478	2,564	NA	NA
Mortgages	NA	3,008	5,360	2,359	—	—	—	NA
Equities, municipal debt, and other	NA	2,309	1,932	1,100	1,505	523	NA	NA
Bonds and CP issues for General Motors	—	—	—	—	—	864	—	—
Total	NA	41,324	49,149	33,336	17,833	22,226	10,705	311
Commodities	NA	1,138	631	902	1,233	1,339	1,019	2,059
Total	27,246	42,462	49,780	34,238	19,066	23,565	11,724	2,370
Securities purchased under agreements to resell	32,800	18,797	22,424	16,368	16,471	10,121	9,045	—
Loans and receivables	11,986	10,972	11,343	6,771	5,100	4,663	3,806	1,986
Property, plant and equipment	344	311	140	107	120	170	242	126
Assets securing collateralized mortgage obligations	3,860	6,506	3,333	—	—	—	—	—
Oil and gas properties	—	—	—	—	307	323	312	307
Other	791	812	650	541	521	559	570	151
Total assets	$77,723	$78,164	$88,601	$58,370	$42,017	$39,669	$26,150	$5,407

NA = Not available.

Note: Consolidated balance sheets give data for both Phibro and Salomon beginning in 1981. Only Phibro data are given for 1980.

Source: Annual reports, Salomon Inc.

Exhibit 2

Consolidated Balance Sheets for Salomon Inc.
($ millions)

	September 30,				December 31,			
Liabilities	1987	1986	1985	1984	1983	1982	1981	1980
Securities sold under agreements to repurchase	$25,263	$31,140	$37,959	$33,746	$23,159	$25,669	$12,463	$ —
Short-term borrowings:								
Banks	NA	7,469	8,844	4,787	3,144	2,991	2,897	434
Commercial paper	NA	3,993	4,294	1,125	908	629	591	707
Total	11,475	11,462	13,138	5,912	4,052	3,620	3,488	1,141
Securities sold but not yet purchased:								
U.S. Government and Federal agencies	NA	15,397	18,543	7,677	NA	NA	NA	—
Corporate debt	NA	1,218	685	808	NA	NA	NA	—
Equities, municipal debt, and other	NA	314	400	229	NA	NA	NA	—
Total	20,628	16,929	19,268	8,714	6,922	3,534	4,543	—
Payables and accruals	11,681	10,360	10,683	6,912	4,933	4,297	3,313	2,564
Collateralized mortgage obligations	3,847	3,574	3,322	—	—	—	—	—
Deferred taxes	—	—	—	—	—	—	24	9
Long-term debt	1,315	1,245	917	680	711	780	842	441
Total liabilities	74,209	74,710	85,647	55,964	39,777	37,900	24,673	4,155
Redeemable preferred stock	700	—	—	—	—	—	—	—
Common stockholders' equity								
Common stock at par	153	153	149	146	144	70	69	69
Additional paid-in capital	NA	264	211	158	121	126	82	80
Retained earnings	NA	3,055	2,635	2,158	2,024	1,627	1,354	1,126
Cumulative translation adj.	NA	(11)	(29)	(36)	(23)	(13)	—	—
Treasury stock	NA	(7)	(12)	(20)	(26)	(41)	(28)	(23)
Total common equity	2,814	3,454	2,954	2,406	2,240	1,769	1,477	1,252
Total liabilities and equity	$77,723	$78,164	$88,601	$58,370	$42,017	$39,669	$26,150	$5,407

Source: Annual reports, Salomon Inc.

Exhibit 3

Consolidated Statement of Income for Salomon Inc.
($ millions, except per share amounts)

| | 9 Months Ended September 30, | | Year Ended December 31, | | | | | | |
	1987	1986	1986	1985	1984	1983	1982	1981	1980
Revenues	$ 4,674	$ 5,062	$ 6,789	$ 5,701	$ 4,039	$ 3,087	$ 2,887	$ 1,309	$1,084
Interest expense	(2,946)	(3,317)	(4,484)	(3,622)	(2,504)	(1,685)	(1,680)	(572)	(221)
Selling, general, and administrative expenses	(1,351)	(1,081)	(1,512)	(1,132)	(875)	(785)	(773)	(439)	(273)
Special items	—	—	—	(4)	(400)	—	—	—	—
Pretax income	377	664	793	943	260	617	434	298	590
Income taxes	(161)	(229)	(277)	(386)	(48)	(147)	(97)	(9)	(123)
Net income	$ 216	$ 435	$ 516	$ 557	$ 212	$ 470	$ 337	$ 289	$ 467
Cash dividends	$ 73	$ 72	$ 96	$ 80	$ 78	$ 73	$ 64	$ 62	$ 63
Primary earnings per share ($)	1.42	2.91	3.45	3.78	1.48	3.35	2.48	2.11	3.44
Cash dividends per share ($)	0.48	0.48	0.64	0.54	0.54	0.52	0.47	0.47	0.45

Note: Salomon Brothers' earnings are consolidated beginning on October 1, 1981. Only Phibro's earnings are shown prior to that date. Revenue figures have been restated to show gross profits, and hence are not consistent with the early revenue figures for Phibro given in the text. (Before 1986, commodities revenues were broken down into total sales and cost of sales. Salomon Inc. switched to a net revenue basis in 1986.)

Exhibit 4

Breakdown of Salomon Inc's Assets by Business Segment
($ millions)

| | December 31, | | | | | | |
Business unit	1986	1985	1984	1983	1982	1981	1980
Salomon Brothers	$71,997	$81,003	$53,185	$36,061	$33,867	$20,984	$ —
Salomon Commercial Finance*	2,536	2,356	1,854	NA	NA	NA	NA
Phibro Energy & Philipp Brothers	3,549	5,208	3,297	5,956	5,802	5,166	5,407
General corporate	82	34	34	NA	NA	NA	NA
Total assets	$78,164	$88,601	$58,370	$42,017	$39,669	$26,150	$5,407

*Note: Assets of Salomon Commercial Finance are included in assets of Phibro Energy and Philipp Brothers before 1984.

Source: Annual reports, Salomon Inc.

Exhibit 5

Breakdown of Salomon Inc.'s Pretax Earnings by Business Segment
($ millions)

BUSINESS UNIT	Nine Months Ended September 30,		Year Ended December 31,						
	1987	1986	1986	1985	1984	1983	1982	1981	1980
Salomon Brothers	$ 351	$ 661	$ 787	$ 760	$ 557	$ 463	$ 421	$ 80	$ —
Salomon Commercial Finance	111	132	173	182	179	142	NA	NA	NA
Phibro Energy	66	18	33	119	66	98	NA	NA	NA
Philipp Brothers*	10	19	19	38	13	107	222	364	619
Phibro Resources**	—	—	—	—	—	(58)	(40)	(28)	2
General corporate	(161)	(166)	(219)	(173)	(155)	(135)	(109)	(68)	(31)
Special items***	—	—	—	17	(400)	—	(60)	(50)	—
Total pretax earnings	$ 377	$ 664	$ 793	$ 943	$ 260	$ 617	$ 434	$ 298	$ 590

Note: Salomon Brothers' earnings are included beginning on October 1, 1981.

*Includes results for Salomon Commercial Finance and Phibro Energy until 1983.

**Phibro Resources bought and sold natural resources and engaged in various industrial operations. Most of Phibro Resources was sold at the end of 1983.

***Special items are mainly writeoffs and restructuring expenses for Phibro and Philipp Brothers.

Source: Annual reports, Salomon Inc.

Exhibit 6

Income Statements for Salomon Brothers
($ millions)

	9 Months Ended September 30,		Year Ended December 31,		
	1987	1986	1986	1985	1984
REVENUES					
Interest and dividends	$3,001	$3,563	$4,746	$3,663	$2,324
Principal transactions	655	NA	869	848	NA
Investment banking*	410	NA	524	361	NA
Commissions	219	NA	202	179	NA
Total revenues	4,285	4,732	6,341	5,051	3,415
EXPENSES					
Interest	2,766	3,162	4,275	3,396	2,224
Compensation & benefits	730	608	838	588	429
Other	438	301	441	307	205
Total expenses	3,934	4,071	5,554	4,291	2,858
Pretax earnings	$ 351	$ 661	$ 787	$ 760	$ 557

*Revenues from underwriting were $212 million in 1985, $307 million in 1986, and between $244 and $262 million in the first nine months of 1987.

Source: Annual reports, Salomon Inc.

Exhibit 7

Salomon's Secondary Market Trading Volume
(\$ trillions)

Type of security	1986	1985	1984	1983	1982	1981	1980
Treasury notes and bonds	\$1.500						
Treasury bills	0.500						
Commercial paper	0.734						
Currencies	0.332						
Certificates of deposit	0.067						
Bankers' acceptances	0.025						
Federal agencies	0.667						
Corporate bonds	0.265						
Municipal bonds	0.116						
Equities	0.181						
Total	\$4.387	\$3.3	\$2.4	\$2.0	\$1.6	\$1.2	\$0.9

Note: Full sets of subtotals are not available for years before 1986.

Source: Annual reports, Salomon Inc.

Exhibit 8

Industry Average Underwriting Fees
(gross spread as percent of issue)

Type of security	Year			
	1987	1986	1985	1984
Debt				
Investment grade	0.65%	0.68%	0.65%	0.62%
Non-investment grade	3.05	3.07	2.99	2.86
Convertible	3.01	2.36	2.13	1.64
Mortgage-related	0.67	0.67	0.87	0.98
Common stock				
Publicly traded	5.62	3.94	3.79	4.49
Initial public offering	7.86	6.49	6.70	7.09
Preferred stock				
Straight	2.81	2.25	3.51	2.48
Money market	NA	1.65	1.60	1.60
Convertible	1.53	3.70	3.83	3.92

Source: *Investment Dealers' Digest*, various issues.

Exhibit 9

Gross Spreads from Domestic Corporate Underwriting in 1986

Book manager	Total gross spread ($ millions)
Drexel Burnham Lambert	927
Salomon Brothers	547
Merrill Lynch	524
Morgan Stanley	437
First Boston	434
Goldman Sachs	401
Shearson Lehman Brothers	336
Kidder Peabody	190
Prudential Bache	166
Paine Webber	139

Note: The total gross spread is the revenue to all investment banks participating in an issue. The gross spread includes a management fee for the issue's manager, an underwriting fee for the members of the underwriting syndicate, and a selling concession for all the firms that sell the issue. Typical management and underwriting fees would each account for 20% of the gross spread, with the selling concession accounting for the remaining 60%. (Other arrangements, however, are not uncommon.) The table above assigns the entire gross spread to the lead manager. The amounts in the table are therefore related (but not identical) to the revenue that each firm derived from underwriting.

Source: *Investment Dealers' Digest*, February 16, 1987.

Exhibit 10

Securities Underwritten in the United States
for Corporate and Foreign Issuers

Year	Total Securities Underwritten ($ billions)	Securities Underwritten by Salomon*		
		Amount ($ billions)	Share (%)	Rank
1982	$ 62.566	$ 9.337	14.9%	3
1983	97.104	15.760	16.2	1
1984	82.435	21.237	25.8	1
1985	138.288	30.898	22.3	1
1986	285.332	51.028	17.9	1

*Full credit to lead manager.

Note: The table above includes issues in the U.S. markets for U.S. and foreign businesses and foreign governments.

Source: Salomon's underwriting amounts for 1982 and 1983 are from *Euromoney*. All other dollar figures are from *Investment Dealers' Digest*. The figures reflect net proceeds. Amounts for 1982 and 1983 are somewhat different from those originally reported by *Investment Dealers' Digest*.

Exhibit 11

Long-term Municipal Bond Issues in the United States

Year	Bonds issued ($ billions)	Total refunding* ($ billions)	Lead-managed by Salomon		
			Amount ($ billions)	Share ($)	Rank
1978	$ 46.215	$ 9.284	NA	NA	NA
1979	42.261	1.872	NA	NA	NA
1980	47.133	1.650	NA	NA	NA
1981	46.134	1.192	NA	NA	NA
1982	77.179	4.044	NA	NA	NA
1983	83.348	13.047	NA	NA	NA
1984	101.882	11.389	NA	NA	NA
1985	203.954	57.867	$11.494	5.8%	5
1986	142.544	56.063	13.642	9.2	1
1987**	74.409	32.649	7.558	9.7	1

*Also included in "Bonds issued."

**January through September. Refunding amount is estimate made as of October 1987.

Note: Exhibit includes bonds with maturities over 12 months.

Source: Bonds issued and total refundings are from *Credit Markets*. Salomon's volume, market share and rank are from *Investment Dealers' Digest*. As the two sets of statistics are not entirely consistent, the market share appearing in the table is slightly different from the market share that would be computed with the dollar amounts in the table.

Exhibit 12

Underwriting Rankings: Securities Underwritten in the United States for Corporate and Foreign Issuers

Manager	Six Months Ended June 30, 1987			Six Months Ended June 30, 1986		
	Amount ($ billions)	Share (%)	Rank	Amount ($ billions)	Share ($)	Rank
Salomon Brothers:						
Mortgage-related debt	$ 10.296	21.1%	1	$ 6.941	32.9%	1
Total Salomon Brothers	23.737	15.4	1	28.689	20.0	1
First Boston	20.281	13.2	2	20.077	14.0	2
Merrill Lynch	18.798	12.2	3	13.929	9.7	6
Goldman Sachs	17.016	11.1	4	14.965	10.4	5
Morgan Stanley	16.086	10.5	5	15.736	10.9	4
Drexel Burnham Lambert	11.246	7.3	6	18.035	12.5	3
Industry total	$153.876	100.0%	—	$143.790	100.0%	—
Subtotal:						
Mortgage-related debt	$ 48.465	31.5%	—	$ 21.102	14.7%	—

Note: The table above includes issues in the U.S. markets for U.S. and foreign businesses and foreign governments. Full credit is given to the lead manager.

Source: *Investment Dealers' Digest*.

Exhibit 13

Underwriting Activity: Salomon Brothers

Product	6 Months Ended June 30, 1987			6 Months Ended June 30, 1986			Year Ended December 31, 1986		
	Amount ($ billions)	Share (%)	Rank	Amount ($ billions)	Share (%)	Rank	Amount ($ billions)	Share (%)	Rank
Debt:									
Mortgage & asset backed	$11.779	22.7%	1	$ 6.941	29.5%	1	$17.787	26.6%	2
Total non-convertible	21.914	19.4	1	23.900	22.4	1	44.057	20.2	1
Convertible	0.435	5.5	8	0.085	1.2	17	0.270	2.7	9
Non-investment grade	0.703	5.4	5	0.375	2.4	7	2.424	7.5	3
Eurobonds	3.210	3.5	8	4.888	5.2	4	8.362	4.6	7
Municipal bonds							13.516	9.4	2
Equity:									
Common	0.913	3.7	10	3.249	13.9	1	4.101	9.5	3
Preferred	0.475	6.1	8	1.455	22.0	2	2.600	18.6	2
IPOs	0.239	1.6	12	0.242	2.7	10	0.799	3.6	11

Note: Salomon is given credit for issues it lead-managed. All figures except Eurobonds are for U.S. capital markets.

Source: *Investment Dealers' Digest.* 1986 Eurobond total from *Euromoney.*

Exhibit 14

Commercial Paper Outstanding in U.S. Market
($ billions)

Year	Total commercial paper	Dealer-placed paper
1980	$124.4	$ 56.5
1981	165.5	83.7
1982	166.2	82.0
1983	187.7	90.6
1984	237.6	127.0
1985	300.9	165.4
1986	331.0	178.6
1987*	357.0	191.7

*1987 figures are amounts outstanding at the end of September.

Note: Figures are seasonally adjusted.

Source: Board of Governors of the Federal Reserve System, *Annual Statistical Digest*, various editions.

Exhibit 15

Revenue Breakdown for Selected Firms in 1986
(Expressed as percent of total)

| | Firm | | | |
Source of revenue	Morgan Stanley	First Boston	Salomon Brothers	Merrill Lynch
Net interest revenue	2%	8%	23%	5%
Investment banking	46	51	25	14
Principal activities	33	30	42	15
Commissions	15	9	10	31
Other	4	1	—	35
Total	100%	100%	100%	100%
Total revenue ($ million)	$1,428	$1,310	$2,066	$6,908

Source: Annual reports.

Exhibit 16

Revenues and Expenses per Employee
for Selected Firms in 1986
($ thousands)

| | Firm | | | |
	Morgan Stanley	First Boston	Salomon Brothers	Merrill Lynch
Revenue per employee	269	292	347	144
Expenses per employee	209	237	215	128
Compensation & benefits per employee	131	157	141	73
Employees	5,300	4,493	5,957	47,900

Note: The revenue and expense figures used in this exhibit are net of interest expense.

Source: Annual reports, Harvard Business School case 288–024.

Exhibit 17

Return on Average Common Equity for Brokerage Firms

Firm	1986	1985	1984	1983	1982
First Boston	21.7%	22.3%	18.8%	24.4%	39.6%
E. F. Hutton	—	1.6	8.6	22.1	22.7
Merrill Lynch	17.5	10.2	5.0	13.2	24.7
Morgan Stanley	36.8	38.0	27.5	27.1	33.8
Paine Webber	14.2	8.5	3.9	35.8	25.2
Salomon Inc.	16.1	20.8	9.1	23.4	20.7
Shearson Lehman	24.9	18.9	12.7	27.6	26.8

Exhibit 18

Return on Average Assets for Brokerage Firms

Firm	1986	1985	1984	1983	1982
First Boston	0.3%	0.4%	0.4%	0.4%	0.7%
E. F. Hutton	—	0.2	0.3	1.1	1.5
Merrill Lynch	0.9	0.6	0.3	1.0	1.6
Morgan Stanley	0.8	0.7	0.6	0.8	1.3
Paine Webber	0.5	0.3	0.1	1.5	0.9
Salomon Inc.	0.6	0.8	0.4	1.1	1.0
Shearson Lehman	0.7	0.7	0.7	2.3	2.3

Note: Revenue in exhibit is *not* net of interest expense.

Exhibit 19

Return on Revenue for Brokerage Firms

Firm	1986	1985	1984	1983	1982
First Boston	5.5%	5.3%	4.0%	5.4%	6.7%
E. F. Hutton	—	0.4	1.9	5.1	4.8
Merrill Lynch	4.7	3.1	1.6	4.0	5.9
Morgan Stanley	8.2	5.9	4.6	6.0	7.0
Paine Webber	3.0	1.8	0.8	5.9	3.0
Salomon Inc.	7.6	9.8	5.2	15.2	11.7
Shearson Lehman	6.9	6.2	4.6	9.6	9.4

Source: Most information on this page is taken from Standard & Poor's Insurance and Investment Industry Survey (December 31, 1987). The Salomon figures, however, have been adjusted to reflect the firm's 1986 change in accounting for commodity transactions. In addition, some other figures have been corrected using information in annual reports.

Exhibit 20

Yields on Corporate and Municipal Bonds (%)

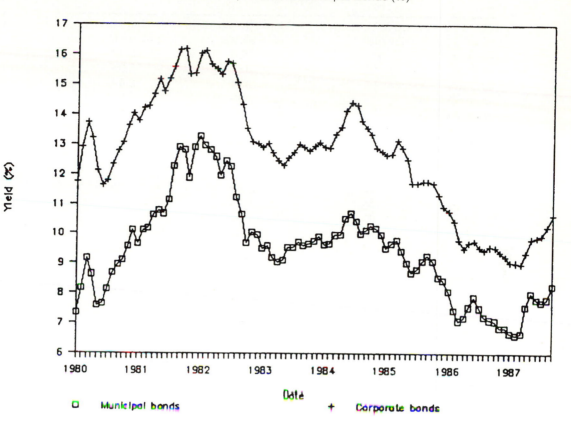

Corporate index: Monthly average of yields on seasoned long-term bonds for a variety of industries.

Municipal index: Monthly average of yields for *Bond Buyer* series of twenty 20-year general obligation bonds of various ratings.

Source: Board of Governors of the Federal Reserve System, *Annual Statistical Digest,* various editions.

Exhibit 21

Salomon Inc. Common Stock History

Date	Price at Month-end ($)	Shares Outstanding (millions)	Earnings per Share*($)
Dec. 1981	$13	136	$2.32
Dec. 1982	25	137	2.36
Mar. 1983	35	137	2.49
Jun. 1983	38	139	3.01
Sep. 1983	30	139	3.37
Dec. 1983	32	142	3.21
Mar. 1984	32	142	3.35
Jun. 1984	27	142	3.35
Sep. 1984	32	142	3.25
Dec. 1984	32	143	3.25
Mar. 1985	38	145	3.03
Jun. 1985	43	145	1.60
Sep. 1985	35	147	1.87
Dec. 1985	44	148	1.98
Mar. 1986	57	148	3.78
Jun. 1986	49	148	4.10
Sep. 1986	39	150	3.88
Dec. 1986	38	150	3.80
Mar. 1987	39	150	3.45
Jun. 1987	33	152	3.15
Sep. 1987	36	152	2.64

*The table shows earnings per share for the most recently reported 12-month period (as opposed to earnings per share for the most recent 12 months).

Source: Standard & Poor's Corporation, *Daily Stock Price Record,* various editions.

Bankers Trust
New York Corporation

By early 1985, Bankers Trust had made significant progress in its shift from traditional commercial banking to its goal of becoming an international merchant bank. This progress was reflected in its performance over the past few years. Earnings grew at an average rate of 26% during the prior five years, resulting in a 1984 return on equity of 16.2%, the highest of the major money center banks. In keeping with its change in strategy, Bankers Trust's net income per employee rose to more than double the average of the nine other largest banks. (Financial information is provided in Exhibits 1–3.)

Alfred Brittain III, Chairman and Chief Executive Officer, commented on the changes underway:

> Bankers Trust will combine the on-balance-sheet capability and service breadth of a commercial bank with the intermediary skills and entrepreneurial spirit of an investment bank. We call that worldwide merchant banking. . . .
>
> Ultimately, we will have a group of relationship managers that originate transactions, and a variety of specialists that distribute the products generated to other institutions, as well as to our own organization. I do not believe that merchant banking will create misfits among our account officers except for those unwilling to think of using others' balance sheets as a home for assets.

International merchant banking represented a major change from traditional commercial banking. As practiced in the United States, commercial banks normally invested their own capital and that of their depositors in loans and other assets held on the banks' books. Conversely, U.S. investment banks generally facilitated transactions in which assets were placed on balance sheets other than their own. Merchant banking, as seen in the United Kingdom and some other countries, was somewhere in between these two banking worlds. It combined the deposit taking and loan making functions and the broad relationship list of a commercial bank with the origination and distribution functions of an investment bank. This was the model Bankers Trust had adopted for its strategic thrust.

Given the cost structure and lending culture of a large commercial bank, some

---

This case was prepared by Susan Crevoor under the supervision of Professors Dwight B. Crane and Robert G. Eccles.
Copyright © 1985 by the President and Fellows of Harvard College. Harvard Business School case 9-286-005.

important changes were clearly required to implement the merchant banking strategy. Indeed, several major changes had already been made or were well underway by early 1985:

▶ The business thrusts of Bankers Trust had been redirected to large corporations, financial institutions and governments.

▶ Corporate finance capabilities had been substantially strengthened.

▶ The bank had in place and had actively used an ability to originate and place commercial loans with other institutional investors.

▶ A 20% return on equity had been adopted as a corporate goal and measurement systems were in place to monitor risk-adjusted returns throughout the organization.

▶ The organizational structure had been changed to encourage more profit-oriented management of the firm's various activities.

▶ Incentive compensation programs were in place to encourage individuals, including commercial loan officers, to generate profits that related to corporate goals.

Underlying these organizational changes was the desire to achieve a cultural change in which officers of the bank would be more entrepreneurially driven, and would identify and take advantage of opportunities at an early stage. It was also important, though, for the various units of the bank to work together to provide coordinated, high quality service to customers. To help spread these attitudes, Al Brittain promoted the theme, "Excellence through common purpose." Another phrase that had caught on and was heard frequently in the organization expressed a different aspect of the cultural change underway: "Fewer, better, higher paid officers."

Many observers gave the banking company high marks for its efforts to date. One financial analysts said, for example, ". . . its bold and unprecedented innovation places the company in the forefront of the financial services revolution." However, even this analyst noted that the jury was still out. He felt that challenges remained with regard to management of credit quality, funding, and customer acceptance.[1]

Background

Al Brittain joined the bank after graduating from Yale in 1946 and by 1966 had worked his way up to the presidency. When William Moore retired in 1975, Brittain was appointed Chairman and Chief Executive Officer of Bankers Trust New York Corporation and its principal commercial bank subsidiary, Bankers Trust Company.

Bankers Trust was the seventh largest bank in the country when Brittain took over, but the recession underway at the time was taking its toll. Like many other major banks that expanded their real estate lending in the early 1970s, loan losses became a significant problem as a result of the high interest rates in 1973–74 and the subsequent downturn in the economy. Thus, in Brittain's early years, significant attention was given to solving problems rather than planning new strategic moves.

As the loan problems were brought under control, management turned its attention to the development of a strategy for the future. With capital and resource constraints the bank could not serve all markets effectively. Thus, a decision was made to focus on four core businesses related to the wholesale or corporate market, rather than the retail or consumer sector. Bankers Trust had a substantial consumer business with over a hundred branches in the New York Metropolitan area and it owned some upstate banks with another 100 branches, but deregulation of interest rates on consumer deposits was making this source of funds more expensive. Furthermore, it was becoming clear that retail banking would require substantial investment in new technology, such as automatic teller machines and computer systems. These capital investments would raise the fixed costs of retail banking and thereby make it more difficult for banks with relatively small market shares to compete on a cost-effective basis with the largest New York City banks. Bankers Trust was only the fifth largest in the NYC retail market.

Thus, Bankers Trust decided to exit retail banking and began to sell its NYC branches and upstate banking subsidiaries. For a time, it negotiated for the sale of its branches to the Bank of Montreal. However, when negotiations broke down in 1979, it began to sell groups of branches to a variety of other banks, mostly foreign owned. For example, Barclay's Bank of New York, a subsidiary of the well known English bank, bought 31 branches. This process was completed by 1984, resulting in a total sales price significantly more than that being discussed with the Bank of Montreal.

While the sale of branches was underway, the bank also sold its retail credit card business to the First National Bank of Chicago, further diminishing its investment in retail banking. In addition, the bank agreed to sell most of its lower middle market business (companies typically having $10 to $30 million in sales) to National Westminster Bank U.S.A. in 1984.

With the phaseout of consumer and lower middle market banking, Bankers focused its attention on four core wholesale banking businesses: commercial banking, corporate finance, resources management, and fiduciary. The company was reorganized around these functions, each headed by an Executive Vice President that reported to a newly created Office of the Chairman. (See Exhibit 4 for an organization chart.) This Office included Charles S. Sanford, Jr., who was appointed President in January 1983; Carl M. Mueller, Vice Chairman; and, Brittain. Also formed was a broader Management Committee that included (in 1984) the Office of the Chairman and the heads of the banking and fiduciary functions, Philip M. Hampton and Edward A. Lesser, respectively.

The Fiduciary Function Becomes ProfitCo.

Although the fiduciary or trust business had been one of the most traditional of the core businesses, it was not immune to the change in focus of the bank. In late 1984 and early 1985, Fiduciary was reorganized into ProfitCo., so that it no longer resembled a conventional bank trust department. As explained by George Vojta, Executive Vice President and head of strategic planning, this reorganization was tied closely to the bank's new operating philosophy of decentralizing staff functions. In this decentralization, some staff areas were shifted to a line function and given the responsibility of earning a profit on their services. Each of these functions became, in effect, a business whose performance could be compared to outside firms.

The new ProfitCo. contained four departments that reported to Ed Lesser, Executive Vice President. The Fiduciary and Securities Services Department contained groups engaged in businesses that were relatively normal for bank trust departments. The Investment Management Group, for example, managed pools of funds for pensions, trust funds and other large pools of capital. Similarly, the Employee Benefit Group performed traditional non-investment services, such as administrative and recordkeeping services for pension and employee benefit plans; and, the Trust and Agency Group served as a trustee for public bond issues, among other services. The important departure from some other trust departments, though, was that all securities processing activities were also included in this department in its Securities Processing Group. This group was expected to earn a profit comparable to outside processing companies.

An even more dramatic departure from other banks was the inclusion of the Global Operations and Information Services Department in ProfitCo. Placing it under Lesser brought almost all of the bank's processing into one function and, more importantly, separated it from the commercial banking function. It offered non-credit services such as deposit and payment services (e.g., cash management) to corporations, institutions, and governments worldwide. In many banks, these services were provided and delivered in part by banking officers, with profits from customer deposits credited to the banking units. However, in keeping with its philosophy of motivating each business to be profitable, Bankers Trust set up this group as a separate business with its own sales force (drawn primarily from the loan officer corps) and product management capabilities. Earnings on customer deposits were credited to this group rather than the banking units, unless the deposits were explicitly part of the compensation for credit or related banking services.

ProfitCo. also included Private Clients Banking. This department was basically a combination of traditional trust services and other commercial banking services for wealthy and high-income individuals. It was formed to target the upscale customers that Bankers Trust wanted to serve and to provide a full range of fiduciary, banking and investment services. Private Clients Banking assumed responsibility for the few carefully selected branch offices that were retained for use by the bank's upscale customers. These branches numbered six in New York City, one in suburban New York (White Plains), and another in Florida for trust customers.

Resources Management: Money and Securities

While the 1985 organizational changes in the Fiduciary Function illustrated the continuing evolution of Bankers Trust, much of the early stages of the strategy occurred in the Resources Management Department (RMD). RMD was located on Wall Street and was actively involved in the "Wall Street" kind of activities, including trading and underwriting of securities. Thus, it was in active competition with investment banking firms, both in its business activities and in its competition for good people. Given RMD's location, the nature of its business, and its importance to the successful funding of the bank, it was perhaps not surprising that this department was the first to break with bank tradition in terms of compensation packages and other issues.

The origins of Resources Management could be roughly traced to the establishment of the Bond Department in 1919. The bond business was so successful that Bankers Trust expanded it to include the underwriting and distributing of all classes of investment securities, only to be forced to contract it again once the Glass-Steagall Act came into effect in 1931. This Act prohibited banks from underwriting corporate securities, but the bank was still able to underwrite and deal in

U.S. Government securities, as well as general obligation bonds issued by state and local governments.

During the next three decades, the forerunner of Resources Management continued to underwrite allowable securities and it managed the bank's own holdings of U.S. Government and municipal securities. This portfolio made up a significant share of the bank's assets prior to the late 1960s and it served as a major source of liquidity. The bank was also in the business of trading securities and money instruments for its own account as well as for its corporate and individual customers.

The role of this department within the bank became more important in the late 1960s when Bankers Trust and other large banks began to rely more on short-term borrowed funds, such as negotiable certificates of deposit, bankers acceptances and commercial paper. The department took on the job of issuing these and other securities to fund the bank, as regular demand and time deposits declined in importance as a source of funds. Traditional portfolio management became a less important problem as Treasury and municipal securities became a smaller share of bank assets and short-term liabilities became the major source of funding and liquidity of the bank.

Recognizing the growing importance of the money markets, the department was expanded and renamed the Resources Management Department in 1967. Charlie Sanford joined the department from the lending side of the bank at that time and was put in charge two years later. He set to work to bring the department to a level where it could compete on a par with investment banking firms. He hired traders and other professionals with Wall Street experience and expertise, and he introduced incentive compensation opportunities parallel to those offered by NYC's major securities firms. By the early 1980s Sanford believed he had developed a trading capability comparable to the best of the Wall Street firms.

One of Sanford's innovations was a new system of measurement and control called "Risk Adjusted Return on Capital," or RAROC. In this system, a risk factor was assigned to each category of assets based upon the volatility of its market price. A CD trader who ended the day with a long position in 60-day CDs, for example, would be assigned a risk-adjusted amount of capital based upon the risk factor for this maturity. Performance would then be assessed by dividing his or her profit by the amount of capital allocated.

In addition, Sanford similarly strengthened the marketing side of the business by developing an institutional sales force and regional office system. Through these offices, both domestic and international, the bank developed and maintained contact with a large number of short-term investors. An important purpose of this marketing effort was to assure a ready market for Bankers Trust's own securities (and for the sale of commercial loans discussed later), since the funding of the bank depended heavily on the sale of CDs and other short-term paper. However, the trading and sales force handled a wide range of short-term instruments including those issued by competitors.

As part of its strategy, Sanford believed that Bankers Trust should offer a wide range of financial services on a global basis to corporations and institutions. An important step in the expansion of services in the U.S. was Sanford's decision to enter the commercial paper business in 1978, positioning Bankers Trust as an agent for corporations that issued commercial paper. Although commercial paper traditionally had been viewed by many as the domain of investment bankers, Sanford believed that the way the business was conducted, commercial bankers could perform the service.

Bankers Trust maintained that commercial paper was basically a short-term loan, not a security, as defined by the Glass-Steagall Act, and that Bankers' role was that of agent, not underwriter. For example, the bank offered to place paper issued by its customers with short-term investors, but did not take this paper into its own portfolio if it could not be sold. The Federal Reserve concurred with this opinion and in 1984, Bankers Trust was handling approximately $3 billion in outstandings, ranking it sixth among U.S. paper dealers. The bank earned fee income on this business and more importantly, it broadened the services provided to corporate customers and expanded the line of securities that the RMD sales force could offer short-term investors.[2]

Bankers Trust also moved to take advantage of the development of the futures and options markets in the U.S. BT Futures Corp. was only the second subsidiary of a banking company to receive full certification as a futures commission merchant. It provided innovative hedging programs to customers, writing contracts in 1984 for more than $400 billion in value in the interest rate, currency and precious metals markets.

Internationally, Bankers Trust also expanded the services it provided. The process was helped in 1979 when its money and securities market activities outside the U.S. were made part of the Resources Management Department. This organizational change provided for an integrated approach to the funding of the bank. It also encouraged the development of products and services that supported Bankers' international merchant banking strategy. Foreign exchange services were expanded, for example, so that the bank could provide worldwide 24-hour market-making capability with 10 geographic locations. In 1984, foreign exchange transactions reached a daily average of $3 billion. Another example was provided by the syndications function in the bank which expanded its role in the global syndicated loan and Euronote market, ranking Bankers Trust sixth among the top lead managers in 1984.

John Tritz, the former Deputy Department Head, took over RMD when Sanford became President in 1983. The department continued to prosper under his direction; for example, Bankers Trust was one of the five largest primary dealers in U.S. Government securities in 1984.

Corporate Finance Department

As Bankers Trust shifted its focus to the wholesale corporate and institutional market, it recognized the need to develop a significant corporate finance capability. Carl Mueller rejoined the bank in 1977 to help in this effort after a 17-year stay at Loeb Rhoades & Co. Mueller began his recruiting drive by hiring David Beim, who came to Bankers after heading the project finance group at the First Boston Corporation and then serving as Executive Vice President of the U.S. Export-Import Bank.

Beim was appointed Executive Vice President and head of Corporate Finance in 1979. He proceeded to form a new team, hiring people with experience in each of the principal areas of business of the department. Beim's strategy was to search out the best talent in the marketplace and "to pay whatever we have to pay for quality people." His strategy led to significant profits for the bank. Corporate Finance activities contributed (after tax) about $15 million (or 6%) to 1983 net income, up from $5 million the year before. This number reach $36 million in 1984, accounting for 12% of the bank's total.

With Beim's arrival, the department was organized into five principal business lines: capital markets, lease financing, venture capital, public finance, and mergers and acquisitions (see Exhibit 5). The Capital Markets Group acted as a financial advisor or agent for corporations in the private placement of their securities with insurance companies, pension funds and other financial institutions. Services extended over the full range of maturities from commercial paper to long-term bonds. In 1984, Bankers Trust was eighth largest private placement agent (the largest among banks) with over $2 billion of transactions. The group, often in liaison with its London merchant bank, Bankers Trust International, also handled interest rate and foreign currency swaps. In fact, it was recognized as one of the leaders in swaps, completing 350 transactions that totalled $7.3 billion in 1984. The bank's international participation also included a significant role as a trader and underwriter of Eurosecurities. It led or co-led 17 issues in 1984, putting Bankers Trust among the top fifteen.

The Lease Financing Group acted like an investment banking unit, arranging big ticket leases and placing the assets with other institutions and with Bankers Trust. It acted as an advisor to the lessor and/or lessee in transactions with a total asset value of more than $2.5 billion in 1984. This accounted for 16.5% of the market and placed Bankers Trust ahead of all other advisors.

The Venture Capital Group made equity and other investments for the holding company (Bankers Trust New York Corporation). Most of the investments were part of leveraged buyouts, expansion financing, and similar transactions, rather than start-up situations. In fact, Bankers Trust developed a special product niche in structuring leveraged buyouts. The group invested $27.5 million in 10 deals in 1984, bringing its total investment to $63.8 million by year end.

Bankers' Public Finance Group had achieved a major position in the marketplace. The group acted as financial advisor, underwriter, or sales agent in tax-exempt financings for public and corporate issuers. David Dougherty, group head, was recruited from a major Wall Street firm. He was a developer of the variable rate demand note, a tax exempt security placed with investors and then later remarketed by the bank. This kind of obligation called TENR^R (Tax Exempt Note Rate) by Bankers, grew in popularity. It typically carried a nominal maturity of 30 years, but its variable interest rate was set on a weekly basis.

The advantages of this instrument accrued to both the issuer and the investor. The issuer paid only a floating short-term rate that was usually much lower than a fixed 30-year rate. At the same time the investor made only a short-term commitment because Bankers Trust agreed to remarket the security on demand. The demand feature was backed by a letter of credit from a major bank, usually not Bankers Trust. In order to maintain its competitive edge in the market, Dougherty doubled the size of his staff from eight to sixteen in 1984. With this capability, Bankers Trust served as managing underwriter or placement agent on 167 variable rate demand note transactions totaling $25 billion in 1984. At year-end, it was serving as remarketing agent on 260 transactions, more than any other investment or commercial bank.

In early 1985, David Dougherty's responsibilities were shifted as he took over the Mergers and Acquisitions Group. This group of eight professionals had been quite active, serving as a financial advisor in fifteen transactions in 1983 and ten in 1984. However, the transactions tended to be with smaller companies and the group had not yet achieved the penetration thought possible by senior management.

The merger and acquisition business was probably the most difficult corporate finance business for a commercial bank to crack. Charlie Sanford noted, "It is relatively easy to do M&A business with smaller companies. However, large companies tend to think of only a few investment bankers for M&A transactions. The key is to attract good, smart people. There is a suspicion of investment bankers in the field, but they are regarded as smarter than commercial bankers." Carl Mueller agreed that people were the key. He reported, "It was difficult to hire the best people in our early stages, but now we can hire better hitters."

Dean Miltimore, a Vice President in the M&A group, believed that Bankers Trust had a number of strengths. The M&A group had worked to build credibility with the account officers so that they were an active source of leads. M&A officers also sought leads on their own. Miltimore described an example in which he learned that a major industrial firm was interested in selling its chemical subsidiary. Working with one of the bank's relationship managers, a selective search was performed for a buyer within the chemical industry. Miltimore approached the buyer targeted from the search. Negotiations proceeded successfully, in spite of competition from the firm's regular investment banker, and the bank put together a deal that included buyer financing.

As he took over the M&A group, Dougherty planned to make more effective use of the leads generated by the commercial banking officers. By building upon the relationships that Bankers Trust already had established with existing customers, he believed that the M&A officers could more successfully penetrate large company transactions.

Commercial Banking Function

Although the shift to merchant banking was requiring substantial changes throughout the Bankers Trust organization, the break from traditional culture was probably most felt in the commercial banking or lending function. Account officers accustomed to serving primarily as a lender to companies were asked to play quite different roles. The new roles covered a variety of functions including manager of customer relationships and originator of loans for resale. This shift was encouraged by a significant increase in incentive compensation. In addition, the organization of commercial banking was substantially changed to promote the development of merchant banking and to provide a strengthening of the credit management function in which credit authority was shifted somewhat from banking officers to credit officers.

Organization

Like many other large banks, the lending side of Bankers Trust had been organized into a domestic and an international department. This was changed in 1984 when four banking departments were created, two with an international focus. The international departments were the Europe/Middle East/Africa Department headed by Executive Vice President Jan R. Brumm and the Latin American/Asia Pacific Department headed by William S. Epstein, also an Executive Vice President. These departments provided services to foreign financial institutions, foreign governments and their agencies, worldwide multinational corporations and major indigenous foreign corporations.

The major domestic banking unit was the North America Department that provided financial services to multinational corporations, large and medium domestic corporations and financial institutions, and local, state and federal agencies in the U.S. and Canada. This department was headed by Ralph L. MacDonald, Jr., Executive Vice President. The fourth department, Credit Policy, performed several functions. As a lending unit it served several credit-intensive businesses including commercial real estate and shipping, and it provided asset based lending services. The Credit Policy Department also provided credit services to the bank, including industry and economic research, and loan administration and operations. It also included a loan workout group. Joseph A. Manganello, Jr., an Executive Vice President, was the head of Credit Policy and the chief credit officer of the bank.

Exhibit 6 illustrates the basic organization of the banking *function* by concentrating on the North America *Department*. It was organized into geographic *groups*, such as Eastern, Central and so forth, although one specialty group (Energy) was also included. Each group was further divided into *divisions*, such as the Eastern Division II that included New York and New England. Finally, each division consisted of several *teams* of two or three professionals. The North America Department in total included 335 officers, 250 of which were account officers that called on customers.

Role of Banking Officers

Two professional paths were developing in the banking function. One was the role of relationship manager that was receiving increased emphasis in the bank. These relationship managers moved up the corporate ladder based upon their product and market knowledge and their ability to manage client relationships effectively. The other professional path was the more traditional route up the bank management ladder, that of administrative responsibility for divisions, groups and so forth. Robert M. Bysshe, Vice President and head of Eastern Division II, illustrated the bank management path, while Paul Cambridge, a Vice President and team leader within this division, was an example of a relationship manager.

Bysshe helped participate in customer calling programs at the senior corporate level, but his primary responsibility was the management of the division. He was responsible for its profitability and other aspects of the division's performance, including the degree of cooperation between his officers and other units within the bank. The sale of corporate finance products contributed significantly to the performance of his division, since profits from these transactions were attributed both to the Corporate Finance Department and the banking unit involved. This double counting of profits was used for performance evaluation to promote cooperation between the corporate finance and banking departments.

Paul Cambridge was a team leader responsible for twelve large multinational firms, most of which were headquartered in Connecticut. He described the changing nature of his job as a relationship manager:

Formerly, my main focus was the sale of credit and other banking services to corporations. Now my job requires substantially more knowledge of corporate financial concepts along with products and services that the bank can deliver in this area. I am expected to have a general handle on each of the products and be capable of managing the transaction to a successful conclusion.

The emphasis today is on the financial advisory role combined with the selective use of the bank's balance sheet. As a result, the nature of my calling has changed. It is much less credit driven. Given our compensation system, I am more willing to say no to a thinly priced credit deal. It is clearly better to utilize corporate finance products to meet the client's needs than to simply offer a bank loan.

In developing each client relationship, considerably more effort is expended in tailoring or directing the calling effort to the perceived needs of the client. With some of my clients, we have a major credit relationship in which we are a top-tier bank that provides traditional credit and other services. In these situations we continue to manage our relationship in a traditional sense, but in addition leverage the relationship to develop a total merchant banking role. In other cases the relationship is based on our ability to deliver non-traditional services. With one customer known for thinly priced credit arrangements, our relationship is built on leveraged-lease transactions. In another situation, we are a major provider of project finance.

In discussing corporate finance, Cambridge stated that the coordination was working out reasonably well. He said that there were occasional "fights" about who received credit for a transaction, but the discussion occurred after the transaction, not before. Cambridge also stated his perception that the double counting of profits was not a major factor in gaining the cooperation of the relationship managers in generating corporate finance business. The real factor was a perception that management knew who was generating the business.

One of the important issues that Bankers Trust faced with the relationship management concept was that not all corporate customers generated enough business to justify the cost of this approach. Andrew Forrester, Senior Vice President and head of the Eastern Group, commented on this issue:

The relationship management concept started in the 1970s when spreads were still high. As spreads started to narrow in the late-70s, companies still wanted to be managed on a relationship basis, but it was becoming harder to justify in some cases from the standpoint of the bank's cost and the profit potential.

Forrester went on to say that if major companies wanted a relationship, Bankers Trust would provide it. However, the bank was paying more attention to the actual and potential profits from customers. Some companies preferred to be dealt with on a transaction by transaction basis and this frequently made more sense. In this situation, account officers were to look actively for opportunities to help with individual transactions, but they would not call on these companies as regularly as those managed on a relationship basis.

Senior Relationship Managers

Bankers Trust emphasized the importance of relationship management in mid-1984 when it appointed two Senior Relationship Managers (SRMs). Forrester explained that these officers, both Senior Vice Presidents, acted as the equivalent of partners in an investment banking firm. The new SRMs, Michael Dacey and Roger Vincent, both had a proven ability to originate and close corporate finance deals, as well as extensive credit experience. Unlike other Senior Vice Presidents in the bank, they did not have administrative responsibility beyond their own group of professionals.

When Dacey was appointed a Senior Relationship Manager, he helped identify the set of fifteen major multinational customers for which he and his group would take responsibility. He and his team of four professionals (ranging from a junior officer to a Vice President) worked as generalists to provide a full range of financial services to these U.S. and European companies. They had access to Bankers Trust specialists as needed for particular transactions, including corporate finance transactions that were an important part of the services needed by these companies. As Dacey explained, these major companies did relatively little bank borrowing. The aggregate borrowings outstanding for the fifteen companies taken together was typically under $200 million.

Unlike Dacey, whose customers covered a variety of industries, Vincent and his team were responsible for the automobile industry worldwide. The team included ten officers in New York and other relationship officers in industrial centers in Europe and Japan, reflecting the geographic spread and needs of the automobile companies.

Vincent and his group actively managed the bank's relationships with these companies. For example, the equivalent of five to six officers were assigned full-time to one of the major auto companies, not including specialists used on particular transactions. Vincent believed that managing these relationships was key:

> Relationships and transactions are highly complementary. Good relationships lead to good transactions and vice versa. We don't need to go after every deal, but we do need to insure that we are highly professional in every deal we go after.

Dacey and Vincent both had a high degree of autonomy. They used the term, "self-managed." For administrative purposes they coordinated with a corresponding Group Head, Andrew Forrester of the Eastern Group in Dacey's case and Tim Miller of the Central Group for Vincent, but they did not report to these officers. For policy matters or important work-related issues they talked with Ralph MacDonald, the North America Department head.

Credit Policy

As Bankers Trust implemented its merchant banking strategy, the bank substantially strengthened its credit management process. Previously the bank had a relatively loose "two-signature system" in which two account officers could approve a credit, so long as one of the two officers had been given sufficient authority to approve loans of that size. In the new system, two signatures were still required but one of the two signatures on sizeable loans had to be a credit officer. In addition, the organization and staffing of the credit function had been improved.

A new credit organization was created to parallel the banking function. Thus, there was a department credit officer corresponding to each department and a group credit officer for each group. Terence Mogan, for example, was the credit officer for the North America Department and Deborah Baxter, who reported to him, was the credit officer for the Eastern Group within North America. Mogan reported to the head of the North America Department, Ralph MacDonald, but he also had a reporting relationship to Joe Manganello, chief credit officer for the bank.

Manganello explained the credit approval process:

> The credit approval process is owned by line management. Each department writes a credit policy statement and specifies lending authority for its line officers and credit officers. For example, division managers are given a credit approval limit. Loan amounts within this limit can be approved with the signatures of an account officer and the division manager. Larger loans require the signature of the group credit head and the loan officer. Loans larger than the group credit officer's limit go to the department credit officer and those exceeding $200 million require the signature of the department head or the chief credit officer. Thus, all loans above the division manager's limit, require a credit officer's signature (or the department head).

> The credit officers are "staff" officers. However, they are very high quality people and are generally recognized for their credit expertise by the loan officers.

Mogan, the North America Department credit officer, explained the job of the credit officer, "The line loan officers are responsible for the analysis of each credit and they make a recommendation for each loan, including the structure of the deal. It is the job of the credit officer to make sure all the bases are covered." He went on to explain there are a number of checks in the credit management process, including a loan rating system. In addition, each division head was asked to identify the division's five weakest loans each quarter, regardless of their ratings.

Loan Sales

As illustrated by the difficulties at the Continental Illinois Bank in Chicago in 1983 and 1984, maintenance of strong credit quality was particularly important at money-center banks that relied heavily on short-term money market borrowings. Bankers Trust was certainly in this category with its focus on wholesale customers. Credit quality at Bankers, though, was even more critical because it planned to be an active seller of loans. It had already sold a substantial volume, more than $7 billion of loans in 1984, and the bank planned to expand this activity as part of its merchant banking strategy.

An important part of the rationale was the bank's desire to improve its return on equity by paying careful attention to the return provided by its assets. The bank believed that it could achieve higher returns in some cases by originating and selling loans than by holding the assets on its own books. In addition, the ability to originate and sell large loans would allow it to provide more service to major corporations, handling larger financings than would otherwise be supported by the size of its capital base. Finally, Bankers Trust planned to maintain substantial liquidity by having a large share of its loans in a saleable or liquid form, and by the development of a ready market for these loans.

Carl Roark, Senior Vice President in charge of loan syndications, helped develop the loan sale activity of the bank. By early 1985, groups of asset product managers and sales officers had been put in place in New York, London and Hong Kong. Roark explained the role of these individuals:

> The asset product management group works closely with account officers to design loan structures and related documentation so that the loans will be readily marketable. Many companies, such as the major oil firms, need substantial funds and broad access to the financial markets. Working with relationship managers, the asset product managers can recommend financing programs that improve the market access of such companies. Often product specialists from corporate finance are also involved, so that the bank provides relationship and credit knowledge, technical product skills, and "selling knowledge" when it works with customers to structure financing arrangements.

> The asset product management group is a cost center and it receives no profit when a loan arrangement is structured.

> The sales officers maintain contact with the investors that buy loans from the bank. Loans, if they choose to market them, are sold primarily to regional and foreign banks, insurance companies and pension funds. Selling these assets is much more complicated than the normal securities sold by traders. Sometimes it takes weeks of education to make sure new investors understand the loan sales program and have approved the credit. Frequently they need special approval to buy loans. These loans are not securities, in the common use of the term, and Bankers Trust does not provide guarantees.

> We have a significant share of our loans in liquid form now and in five years from now, we hope to have over 75% of our loan portfolio liquid.

Michael Schraga, a Vice President and relationship manager in the Central Group, was actively involved in the loan program. Revolving credits and other loan arrangements were regularly structured and documented by his team, so that they could be sold. He reported that there was little customer resistance to the loan sale program, except for major corporations which wanted to make sure that Bankers Trust would not be selling loans into the same marketplace that the company wanted to tap for its commercial paper sales. Schraga felt that the ability to sell loans made it easier for him to help customers. He could arrange financing for a BBB credit, for example, even though the spread might be too low to justify making the loan if it were only going to be held on Bankers Trust books.

The head of asset trading, Joe Wood, explained that regional and foreign banks were the major purchasers of these loans. In selling them a loan participation, Bankers was able to offer them a slightly higher yield than they could obtain in the Federal Funds market or by placing funds with banks in the Euromarket. It was Wood's job to stay in close touch with the money markets, as well as the U.S. loan market, so that he could quote prices to loan officers on proposed deals and suggest loan structures that could be readily sold.

The bank's policy for loan sales was set by the Tactical Asset and Liability Management Committee chaired by Joe Manganello. This committee met weekly to decide the quantity and pricing of loan sales. In these decisions, it took into account the overall credit exposure of the bank including industry concentrations, the liquidity position of the bank and current market conditions. As the committee saw opportunities in the marketplace, it also tried to direct the loan origination function to take advantage of these situations.

Philip Hampton, who headed the Banking Function, saw the loan sale program as an integral part of the bank's lending strategy. He noted that the movement of the processing function and related corporate deposit balances to ProfItCo. correctly removed a profit "annuity" from the lending side of the bank. Without the annuity from the earnings credit on these deposits, the banking function would better understand the profitability of its customer relationships and see the need to "earn its money every day."

Hampton believed that the bulk of the banking function profits came from a relatively small share of its customers, about 20%. As the bank continued to implement its strategy, he felt that these customers and others with high profit potential would be served on a relationship management basis. Other customers would be served on a product basis. Some of the products would be corporate finance products, but lending and loan products would also be important. He went on to break the loan products into two types, "value-added" products, such as project finance, and "commodity" products, such as commercial paper-type loans. Lenders in the first example would have the job of creating the value that could be incorporated in the price, while with commodity products the job of the lender would be to originate a stream of deals that could be sold into the market.

Compensation

Bankers Trust had broken with traditional bank compensation practices to attract new people and to provide incentive for its officers to generate profitable business for the organization. In the commercial banking area, for example, the bank had raised salary levels to be at the top of the New York City commercial banks. Incentive compensation programs had also been adopted in each of the functions of the firm.

Incentive compensation was first used in the Resources Management Department. Traders were compensated for achieving a high risk-adjusted rate of return on capital and there was no policy limiting maximum compensation. Large bonuses of 100% or more were received by only the top few performers, but like other Wall Street firms, a very successful trader could (and did) receive compensation that exceeded the Chairman's.

As Bankers developed its Corporate Finance Department, it moved to a compensation system competitive with investment banking firms so that it could attract similar people. One important difference, though, was that bonuses were based not only on the profitable business brought into the bank, but also on the degree to which the officer cooperated with others in the organization. Individual performance ratings and bonuses of Corporate Finance officers were reviewed with Hampton, head of the Banking Function, to make sure that the bonuses took into account cooperation with commercial banking officers. This was one of the ways that the bank reinforced its desire to achieve "excellence through common purpose."

The Fiduciary Function also adopted an incentive program, rewarding investment portfolio managers for superior risk-adjusted performance. However, the most dramatic departure from traditional banking practice occurred in the commercial banking function. Bonuses had been awarded in the past, but the maximum bonus had been limited to 50% of salary until 1983. In that year and in 1984, about one percent of the commercial banking officers received bonuses that exceeded their salaries. Overall, about one-third of the banking officers received bonuses in 1983 and 1984, with the typical bonus in the range of 20–30% of base salary.

In the bonus-setting process, line managers in the banking function were asked to rank the officers reporting to them, starting at the team leader level, and to make a bonus recommendation. These evaluations were based upon an explicit specification of each officer's contribution to incremental profits obtained through new lending business, sale of fee-generating business, and so forth. This naturally provided some incentive to generate corporate finance business since the profit potential was often higher than lending to high quality companies.

In the rankings no more than 15% could be given the top ranking of "one" and at least 5% had to rank in the bottom category. Ones and twos had a high probability of receiving a bonus, with the size based upon the volume of incremental profits produced. Since senior people had greater opportunities to bring in substantial business, their bonus participation rates and the size of their bonuses tended to be higher than those for junior officers.

The size of the bonus pool available to each department was tied to the profits generated by the department. Bonuses available to commercial banking officers, however, depended in principle upon the total profits generated within the corporation with the exception of the specialty areas. However, in 1983 and 1984 the Office of the Chairman approved some shifts in bonus pools to increase the pool of the Banking Function.

Finally, there was a "long-term bonus plan" for senior management in addition to the incentive program described above. This plan for Executive Vice Presidents and more senior officers was based on total corporate performance over a three-year period. Bonuses were paid, for example, if earnings growth and return on equity exceeded a standard set at the beginning of the three-year period. The amount of the bonus increased with better performance, but in no event could the bonuses of these officers exceed 200% of salary.

Conclusions

Brittain, Sanford and other members of senior management were pleased with the progress that Bankers Trust had made over the past few years. However, all agreed that the bank still faced important issues, including the evolving culture of the organization and the development of the relationship concept. The "excellence through common purpose" culture was working and achieving results, but it would take a few years to know if the new culture had really been adopted by the organization. Similarly, the relationship manager concept was still being implemented. Brittain and Sanford envisioned relationship managers that would be "generalists" with excellent origination skills. These persons would ultimately come from both the corporate finance and commercial banking parts of the bank, but not all relationship managers were ready yet to be corporate finance generalists and not all of the corporate finance generalists were ready to originate credit products.

▶ Endnotes

1. Raphael Soifer, Brown Brothers Harriman & Co., "Basic Reports: Bankers Trust," September 1984.

2. The Securities Industry Association sued Bankers Trust and the Federal Reserve, eventually taking the case to the U.S. Supreme Court. In 1984, the Court overruled the Federal Reserve and decided that commercial paper was a security and asked the Federal Reserve to reconsider whether Bankers was acting as agent (in compliance with Glass-Steagall) or as underwriter (in violation of the Act). In June 1984, the Federal Reserve ruled that Bankers Trust was acting as an agent.

Exhibit 1

Selected Performance Measures

	1984	1983	1982	1981	1980
Income and Expense as % of Assets					
Net Interest Income	1.95%	2.05%	2.06%	1.88%	2.12%
Noninterest Income	1.41	1.11	0.95	0.93	1.05
Noninterest Expense	1.91	1.98	1.93	1.89	1.86
Net Income (ROA)*	0.68	0.64	0.60	0.51	0.64
Assets/Equity	23.84	25.06	28.70	31.08	34.92
Return on Equity	16.20	16.16	17.35	16.00	22.27
Number of Employees	10,409	11,653	11,906	12,397	11,827
Net Income/Employee	$28,149	$21,231	$18,915	$14,044	$16,910

*Net income to common shareholders as a percent of assets.

Exhibit 2

Consolidated Statement of Income
($ millions)

			Year Ended December 31,			
	1984	1983	1982	1981	1980	1979
INTEREST INCOME						
Loans	$2,912	$2,363	$2,721	$2,850	$2,209	$1,753
Interest-bearing deposits with banks	662	574	955	878	689	437
Federal funds sold and securities purchased under resale agreements	208	190	227	295	168	129
Trading account assets	363	196	186	128	116	89
Investment securities						
Taxable	44	70	126	144	132	78
Exempt from federal income taxes	38	39	42	44	50	31
Total interest income	4,227	3,432	4,256	4,338	3,363	2,516
INTEREST EXPENSE						
Deposits						
In domestic offices	494	440	752	767	410	303
In foreign offices	1,535	1,146	1,700	1,771	1,357	961
Short-term borrowings	1,299	1,016	1,006	1,141	905	671
Long-term debt	58	44	32	24	26	27
Total interest expense	3,386	2,646	3,489	3,704	2,699	1,961
Net Interest Income	842	786	767	635	664	555
Provision for loan losses	230	80	114	60	90	48
Net interest income after provision for loan losses	612	706	653	575	574	509
NONINTEREST INCOME						
Trading account profits and commissions	66	42	81	39	50	27
Foreign exchange trading income	68	28	46	31	23	17
Trust and custodian income	153	118	91	75	63	61
Fees and commissions	204	142	126	107	82	69
Investment securities gains (losses)	(1)	(1)	(66)	(5)	(1)	(2)
Gain on sales of branches, upstate banks and credit card, net	57	6	38	—	54	—
Gain on reacquisition of long-term debt	—	—	—	6	12	1
Other	58	92	39	59	45	37
Total noninterest income	$607	$426	$354	$313	$329	$209

(Exhibit 2 continues on next page.)

Exhibit 2 (continued)

	Year Ended December 31,					
	1984	1983	1982	1981	1980	1979
NONINTEREST EXPENSES						
Salaries	$435	$387	$368	$311	$284	$239
Employee benefits	72	80	76	72	66	60
Occupancy expense, net	91	78	71	63	61	55
Furniture and equipment expense	47	47	38	29	27	23
Other	178	167	166	163	146	136
Total noninterest expenses	825	759	719	638	584	512
Income before income tax expense and extraordinary item	394	373	288	249	320	204
Income tax expense	87	116	65	61	106	90
Income before extraordinary item	307	257	223	188	214	114
Gain on reacquisition of long-term debt, tax free	—	4	16	—	—	—
Net income	$307	$261	$239	$188	$214	$114
Net income applicable to common stock	$293	$247	$225	$174	$200	$100
Earnings per common share Income before extraordinary item	$ 10	$ 8	$ 8	$ 7	$ 9	$ 5
Net income	$ 10	$ 9	$ 8	$ 7	$ 9	$ 5
Cash dividends declared per common share	$ 3	$ 2	$ 2	$ 2	$ 2	$ 2
Average common shares outstanding (in millions)	31	29	27	25	23	21

Exhibit 3

Consolidated Balance Sheet
($ millions)

	December 31,					
	1984	1983	1982	1981	1980	1979
ASSETS						
Cash and due from banks	$ 1,864	$ 1,679	$ 2,735	$ 1,994	$ 3,993	$ 4,798
Interest-bearing deposits with banks	6,905	5,110	5,909	4,970	5,117	4,177
Federal funds sold and securities						
purchased under resale agreements	1,466	2,278	2,411	2,425	1,586	581
Trading account assets, net	6,015	1,656	2,488	894	852	1,306
Investment securities	1,118	1,086	1,755	1,961	2,315	1,805
Loans	23,513	23,651	21,330	19,109	17,576	16,184
Less, allowance for loan losses	(365)	(268)	(232)	(211)	(191)	(157)
Net loans	23,149	23,383	21,099	18,898	17,386	16,026
Premises and equipment, net	365	336	301	237	222	226
Due from customers on acceptances	2,538	3,052	2,452	1,551	1,629	1,179
Accrued interest receivable	639	481	528	579	479	418
Other assets	1,148	941	749	705	624	438
Total	$45,208	$40,003	$40,427	$34,213	$34,202	$30,953
LIABILITIES						
Deposits*						
Noninterest-bearing						
In domestic offices	$ 4,551	$ 4,485	$ 4,684	$ 4,782	$ 7,432	$ 8,237
In foreign offices	186	207	230	232	220	259
Interest-bearing						
In domestic offices	4,511	4,628	6,446	5,670	4,939	3,428
In foreign offices	16,311	13,509	13,100	12,660	11,226	10,514
Total deposits	25,559	22,829	24,493	23,345	23,816	22,407
Short-term borrowings	12,476	10,967	10,489	6,332	6,447	5,259
Acceptances outstanding	2,540	3,055	2,458	1,588	1,634	1,182
Accrued interest payable	358	311	362	435	313	266
Other liabilities	1,395	629	629	916	534	546
Long-term debt	776	422	440	266	298	335
Total liabilities	$43,104	$38,213	$38,871	$32,882	$33,042	$30,024
Redeemable Preferred Stock	—	—	150	150	150	150
Stockholders' Equity						
Preferred stock	$ 150	$ 150	$ —	$ —	$ —	$ —
Common stock	320	297	282	262	247	108
Capital surplus	350	272	226	184	154	221
Cumulative translation adjustments	(14)	(12)	(5)	—	—	—
Retained earnings	1,298	1,083	903	735	609	449
Total stockholders' equity	2,104	1,790	1,406	1,181	1,110	779
Total	$45,208	$40,003	$40,427	$34,213	$34,202	$30,953

*Deposits by foreign depositors in domestic offices at the end of 1984 amounted to $1.4 billion and ranged from $.9 billion to $1.4 billion at the end of 1979 to 1983.

Exhibit 4

Organization Chart

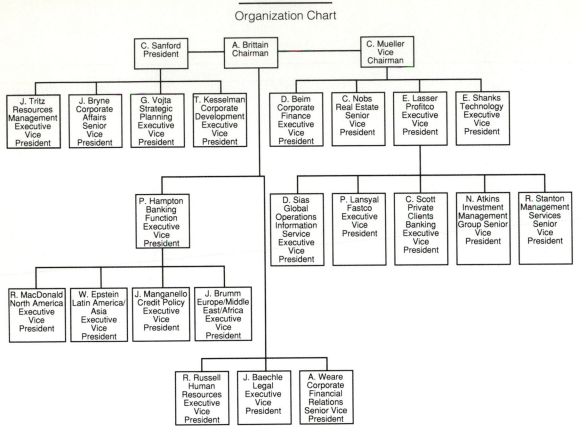

Exhibit 5

Corporate Finance Department

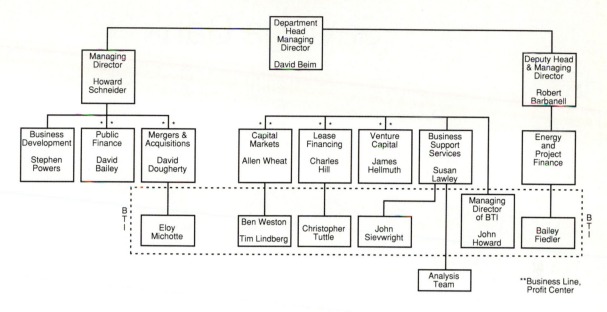

**Business Line, Profit Center

Exhibit 6

Structure of the Banking Function*

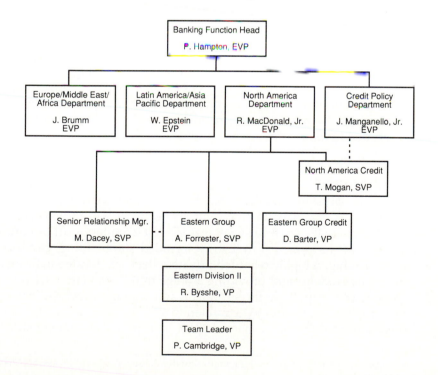

*A partial organization chart.

Anchor Savings Bank

Anchor Savings Bank in Portland, Maine resulted from a consolidation between Berkshire Savings Institution and Port County Bank in April 1981. Berkshire's president, Richard Harding, became CEO of the new bank. He had certainly known more prosperous, and less turbulent times as Berkshire's president than he had experienced since taking over at Anchor Savings. While Berkshire Savings had been profitable and had managed a difficult 1980, Anchor (by the end of 1982) had lost nearly $1.5 million in its brief twenty-one month history (see Exhibits 1 and 2 for financial statements). In addition, Anchor was losing deposit market share despite the recent decision to aggressively price its new Money Market Accounts (see Exhibit 3).

In view of the operating losses and deposit experience, a number of Anchor's directors had suggested serious consideration of recent merger overtures. However, other directors had argued that Anchor should remain independent and requested that senior management develop an operating plan to accomplish this goal. One director had inquired about the possibility of converting the bank to a stock organization and going public through a sale of shares. Harding's inclination was for Anchor Savings Bank to survive as an independent organization, but he needed to think through the options carefully.

Background

Both Berkshire and Port had had long and successful histories. Berkshire Savings was organized in 1858, with its head office in Brunswick, Maine. With a population of 17,366, Brunswick was located 27 miles north of Portland, Maine's largest city. Its principal industries included shipbuilding, clothing, shoes, and papermaking. A highly regarded private college was located in Brunswick, attracting many students and providing a bulge to the population each year. Berkshire Savings grew rapidly in the 1970s as it added four branches in nearby towns and increased its assets from $32.2 million to $79.5 million. As of 1980, the bank held a dominant deposit market share of 28.3% in its primary banking market.

This case was prepared by Florence Langford under the supervision of Professors Dwight B. Crane and Scott P. Mason.
Copyright © 1984 by the President and Fellows of Harvard College. Harvard Business School case 9-284-051.

Port Savings was organized in 1860, with its head office in Biddeford, Maine (1980 population 19,638). The town had a large and stable French Canadian population. Its industries consisted of textiles, wearing apparel, shoes and automotive parts. Port Savings was located 15 miles south of Portland, and served primarily the banking market of Port County, in which it held a 16.2% deposit market share. Like Berkshire, Port Savings opened five of its branches in the 1970s, during which its assets reached $57.1 million, up from $19 million in 1973.

Harding explained that the two banks merged to achieve economies of scale. A larger bank, Harding believed, could (1) establish itself in the Portland market, (2) more effectively compete for and attract better personnel, and (3) realize operating cost savings. Both banks were interested in entering the Portland market to stimulate and sustain long-term growth. The banks and their respective branches bracketed Portland geographically. At their closest point, the two banks' markets were 20 miles apart. Neither bank was represented in the Portland banking market, which already contained the head offices of three commercial banks, two savings banks, and a large savings and loan association, each of which was larger than the new Anchor Savings Bank. Two smaller S&Ls were also located there.

During merger negotiations, the issues of the new entity's location, name, and senior management were confronted. First, the two banks' markets were split by Portland, a market which each had intended to tap. Thus a headquarters (including a branch) was established in Portland. Second, a new name, Anchor, was chosen since neither bank would be dominating. Third, Port's president and CEO, Lawrence Grantly, assumed the chairmanship of the new board, while Berkshire's president and CEO, Harding, became Anchor's president and CEO. In addition, all members of each board of directors were retained, as well as all officers and staff.

Operating Experience

Anchor could not have picked a more difficult banking environment for its debut. At the beginning of the 1980s, loan demand was low as rates rose to new highs, e.g., the prime rate exceeded 20%. Subsequently, Anchor's loan portfolio shrank by 2.25% between 1981 and 1982. Savings institutions generally were suffering as they were caught in the squeeze between a rising cost of funds and low, fixed-interest rates on their mortgage portfolio. About 60% of Anchor's mortgage portfolio had interest rates of 10% or below, at a time when new funds were costing the bank 14% to 15% (see Exhibit 5). The cost of funds was rising because short-term rates were rising and customers were shifting their money from regular savings to accounts with market-determined rates. Low interest rate savings accounts declined from 38.7% of assets in 1980 to 32.4% in 1982 (see Exhibits 6 and 7).

In comparison with its peer group, Anchor's composition of assets and liabilities was favorable. As shown in Exhibit 7, Anchor still had more regular savings than its peer group average in 1982. The bank also had more loans than the others, but earned a slightly lower yield on them, as shown in Exhibits 8 and 9. However, operating costs were a problem, increasing 7.5% in 1981. They remained higher than Anchor's peer group average in 1982, despite efforts to trim the organization. Anchor's 1982 total operating expenses amounted to 2.61% of average deposits, as opposed to the 2.23% of its peer group average (see Exhibit 10). The bank reduced the number of employees from 98 to 81, including a reduction of ten officers. This brought the ratio of deposits per employee in line; however, Anchor still experienced relatively high overhead, perhaps because its deposits per office were smaller than those of the peer group (see Exhibit 11). The net result was a loss of $800,000 in Anchor's first nine months, and of $690,000 in 1982.

Harding stated that it was a difficult time for everyone associated with Anchor Savings. Many customers were disappointed that the focus of their community bank had shifted to Portland. This impression was reinforced by empty offices in the old headquarter buildings in Biddeford and Brunswick, as bank employees were transferred to the new headquarters. As a result, deposits at these offices fell, contributing substantially to Anchor's total deposit loss of 3.7% in 1981. The bank recovered somewhat in 1982 as the active promotion of its new money market deposit accounts in December of that year attracted close to $13 million; however, Anchor still lost market share.

Some board members suggested merging with another bank. In 1981 Anchor was approached by five different banks regarding a merger, including two large Maine savings banks, and other in- and out-of-state organizations. All of these institutions were significantly larger than Anchor, and therefore would have been the surviving entity in any merger. Partly for this reason, other directors wanted to remain independent. They believed that Anchor could become profitable without the help of another organization.

Current Environment

As Harding was thinking through Anchor's situation, he realized he had a number of major decisions to make, in addition to providing the board with a plan to deal with the bank's problems. The regulatory environment was changing dramatically as the Garn-St. Germain Depository Institutions Act of 1982 had just been passed. It expanded asset and liability powers for thrifts, as well as gave added authority to federal regulators to deal with financially weak institutions. This act allowed savings banks like Anchor to grant commercial loans and to increase their personal loans as a percent of total assets. Such legislation helped thrifts reduce their traditional dependence on mortgage lending. In addition, the act authorized thrifts to offer deposit accounts that would be competitive with money market mutual funds.

Changes in regional banking laws had also come into effect, which Harding had to consider. Federal law did not strictly prohibit interstate banking. While the McFadden Act prohibited interstate bank branching, the Bank Holding Company Act allowed interstate ownership of banks by holding companies, so long as state law permitted it. In 1975, Maine passed the first New England reciprocal interstate banking law, which allowed out-of-state bank holding companies to acquire or establish banks in Maine, provided Maine holding companies were given similar privileges in other states. New York passed a similar bill in June of 1982.

New England regional banking gained headway in 1983 when Massachusetts, Connecticut, and Rhode Island also passed reciprocal banking statutes. A key feature of these laws was that the reciprocity was limited to the six New England states. Moreover, these laws prohibited (temporarily in the case of Rhode Island) "leapfrogging." For example, a Maine bank owned by a New York banking company could not acquire a Massachusetts bank. This legislation gave New England banks an opportunity to consolidate before being exposed to acquisition by large organizations from New York or other areas.

Alternatives

Clearly, one option open to Harding was to suggest a merger with another bank. Potential economies of scale from the merger could provide cost savings and enable the bank to compete better for well-qualified personnel. Also, the surviving institution would have access to larger and perhaps more attractive markets. However, by merging, Anchor would lose its identity and control since it would be the smaller of the two entities.

Should Anchor reject the merger idea, its managers would need to develop a plan to improve profitability. Such a plan could include taking advantage of the new commercial lending option available to savings banks. Commercial lending would enable Anchor to reduce its dependence on mortgage lending and would give the bank more assets with floating instead of fixed rates of interest. Harding believed that the present officers at Anchor with commercial lending experience would ease entry into this activity. The issue was whether Anchor could attract and administer a sufficient volume of quality loans to cover fixed costs and earn an attractive return.

A third option which Harding considered was the aggressive marketing of Anchor's Money Market Accounts (MMA). The bank had introduced the MMAs after the new accounts were allowed in December 1982, and marketed them at an initial rate higher than that of its competitors in order to build market share. However, Harding wondered whether to keep this aggressive posture. It was expensive money, and the strategy risked a speedier erosion of Anchor's large regular savings deposit base.

Harding also had to decide whether Anchor would benefit from keeping all of its branches open. Operating expenses related to the number of employees and offices were higher for Anchor than for its peer group average, probably because its deposits per office were lower than the other banks in the group. Such statistics indicated to Harding that Anchor's eleven-branch network was expensive. He reviewed the branches individually to see which, if any, were candidates for closing (see Exhibit 12). However, he realized that the locations of these branches had been carefully chosen by both the Berkshire and Port County banks, because they were locations with growth potential. Although Automatic Teller Machines (ATMs) might ultimately reduce the value of branches, it wasn't clear to Harding that ATMs could capture the potential of these communities. (Anchor had not yet introduced ATMs, but did actively promote a point-of-sale check-cashing card.)

Anchor's board had also discussed the possibility of making a public offering of its shares to raise capital. A major investment banking firm had suggested to Harding that Anchor could sell approximately 1 million shares at $10 each. By rebuilding its capital base, Anchor would increase its ability to take advantage of future opportunities. In addition, it could indirectly benefit depositors and the community by allowing these individuals to profit (as shareholders) from the bank's progress. The downside to going public was the possible loss of some control and increased vulnerability to outside parties. In addition, a public offering would expose Anchor to a potential acquisition, which again required considering the attractiveness of a merger.

Harding needed to develop an action plan that would satisfactorily reconcile the divergent interests of the board, as well as the best interests of Anchor, its employees and the communities in which it operated.

Exhibit 1

Income and Expense Report
($ thousands)

	9 Months Ending December 31, 1981	12 Months Ending December 31, 1982
Income		
Income on Securities		
U.S. Govt. & Agencies	$ 1,756	$ 1,141
Other Bonds	569	511
Money Market Instruments	669	1,348
Dividends on Stocks	411	378
Total	3,405	3,378
Interest on Loans		
Real Estate Mortgage Loans	8,407	8,712
Personal Loans	1,386	1,384
Total	9,793	10,096
Other Income		
Origination & App. Fees	233	331
Income from Service Oper.	221	252
Income Rentals	16	19
Total	470	602
Total Current Operating Income	$13,669	$14,075
Expenses		
Current Operating Expenses	$ 3,368	$ 3,609
Dividends Paid & Accrued		
Regular Savings	2,732	2,573
Certificates of Deposit	8,723	8,525
Less Penalties on Cert. of Dep.	(156)	(66)
Christmas Clubs	23	14
NOW Accounts	183	194
Total	14,873	14,849
Total Operating Income Before Taxes	(1,205)	(775)
Net Gain on Securities Plus Other Non-Recurring Items	139	85
Net Current Income	$ (1,066)*	$(690)

*The actual loss for April–December 1981 was $800,000, which represents an annual rate of $1,066,000.

Exhibit 2

Comparative Statements of Condition
($ thousands)

Assets	April 1, 1981	December 31, 1981	December 31, 1982
Cash & Due from Banks	$ 2,643	$ 3,908	$ 1,987
Securities			
U.S. Govt. & Agency Issues	17,769	12,476	10,510
Corporate Bonds	7,080	6,019	5,351
Money Market Instruments	3,866	6,486	15,188
Corporate Stocks	4,794	6,054	3,628
Total	33,509	31,035	34,677
Loans			
Real Estate Mortgages	90,610	89,131	88,638
Personal Loans	10,550	9,742	10,780
Less Loan Loss Reserve	—	—	70
Total	101,160	98,873	99,348
Banking Premises, etc.	2,702	2,676	2,439
Other Real Estate Owned	69	116	183
Other Assets	1,299	1,021	2,219
Total Assets	$141,382	$137,628	$140,853
Liabilities			
Savings			
Money Market	—	—	$ 12,824
Regular Savings	$ 53,088	$ 47,256	45,527
6-Month Certificates	38,078	36,627	32,385
Other Certificates (under $100,000)	32,080	33,094	30,672
Large Certificates (over $100,000)	—	1,415	1,062
Total Savings	123,246	118,392	122,470
Club Deposits	298	122	106
Demand Deposits	1,509	1,699	1,914
NOW Accounts	3,570	3,697	3,445
Total Deposits	128,624	123,911	127,936
Borrowed Funds	867	867	250
Repurchased Agreement Cert.	—	1,303	1,012
Other Liabilities	694	1,149	1,914
Total Liabilities	130,185	127,230	131,112
Total Reserves & Undivided Profits	11,198	10,398	9,741
Total Liabilities & Reserves	$141,382	$137,628	$140,853

Exhibit 3

Deposit Growth Trends

| | Percent Change from Prior Year | | |
Year	Anchor Savings Bank	Seven Other Peer Group Banks	Anchor's Deposits as a Percent of Eight Bank Total
1977	+15.2%	+13.0%	7.5%
1978	+7.9	+8.7	7.4
1979	+5.5	+8.8	7.2
1980	+4.5	+7.3	7.1
1981	–3.7	+2.3	6.7
1982	+3.1	+5.5	6.5

Note: Anchor deposits include Berkshire and Port Savings for years prior to the merger. A similar procedure was used for other peer group banks which merged.

Exhibit 4

Mortgage Characteristics
($ thousands)

Interest Rate Structure (12/31/82)

Rate	Amount
Under 5%	$ 9
5–6	1,216
6–7	1,782
7–8	8,258
8–9	19,819
9–10	23,140
10–11	9,937
11–12	5,334
12–13	3,613
13–14	7,442
14–15	3,866
15 and above	4,222
Total	$88,638

Types of Mortgages

Conventional	$72,723
F.H.A.	2,367
V.A.	13,549
Total	$88,638

Exhibit 5

Savings Balances
($ thousands)

| | December 31, | |
	1981	1982
Regular Savings	$ 47,256	$ 45,527
Money Market Accounts	—	12,824
Certificates of Deposit		
Rates Set Under Previous Regulations		
6.50%	155	112
6.75%	296	268
7.50%	5,494	5,057
7.75%	7,263	6,547
8.00%	1,576	1,524
Total	14,784	13,508
Market Determined Rates		
91-day CDs	—	240
6-month CDs	36,628	32,385
2½-year CDs	14,999	15,108
4-year	802	795
All Savers Cert.	2,509	1,021
Large CDs (over $100,000)	1,415	1,062
Total	56,353	50,611
Repurchase Agreement Certificates	1,303	1,012
Total Certificates	72,440	65,131
Total Savings	$119,696	$123,482

Exhibit 6

Composition of Liabilities
(percent of total assets)

	Berkshire Savings 1980	Port Savings 1980	Anchor Savings Bank			Peer Group Average 1982
			Pro forma 1980	Actual 1981	Actual 1982	
NOW Accounts	1.96%	3.69%	2.69%	2.69%	2.45%	2.84%
Regular Savings	40.13	36.79	38.73	34.34	32.35	27.19
Money Mkt. Deposit Accts.	—	—	—	—	9.10	5.73
6-Month MM Certificates	22.79	28.86	25.34	26.61	22.99	29.25
30-Month Certificates				10.90	12.93	13.28
Other Time under $100,000	24.81	20.72	23.09	13.15	8.82	7.98
Other Time over $100,000	.12	—	.07	1.03	.75	1.32
Demand Deposits	1.09	.89	1.01	1.23	1.36	1.03
Other Deposits	.10	.15	.12	.55	.89	.29
Total Deposits	91.00	91.10	91.05	90.50	91.64	88.90
Repurchase Agreements	—	—	—	.94	.72	2.25
Other Liabilities	1.35	.79	1.11	1.00	.72	2.26
Total Liabilities	92.35	91.89	92.16	92.44	93.08	93.41
Total Surplus	7.65	8.11	7.84	7.56	6.92	6.59
Total Liabilities & Surplus	100.00%	100.00%	100.00%	100.00%	100.00%	100.00%

Exhibit 7

Composition of Assets
(percent of total assets)

	Berkshire Savings 1980	Port Savings 1980	Anchor Savings Bank			Peer Group Average 1982
			Pro forma 1980	Actual 1981	Actual 1982	
Cash & Due from Banks	1.92%	1.94%	1.93%	4.71%	7.84%	3.86%
U.S. Obligations	3.83	7.51	5.38	4.21	3.02	8.78
Mortgage-backed Securities	4.90	4.22	4.61	4.64	4.45	2.28
Corporate & Other Bonds	2.68	8.44	5.10	4.37	3.80	6.47
State & Local Govt. Securities	—	.20	.08	—	—	.09
Corporate Stock	1.39	4.28	2.60	4.40	2.58	3.19
Fed. Funds Sold & Sec. Purchased	4.38	7.01	5.48	2.84	4.36	3.80
Real Estate Mortgages	69.08	57.95	64.41	64.76	62.93	59.67
All Other Loans	9.45	5.36	7.73	7.30	7.61	8.24
Other Assets	2.37	3.09	2.67	2.77	3.44	3.60
Total Assets	100.00%	100.00%	100.00%	100.00%	100.00%	100.00%

Exhibit 8

Earnings Rate on Assets
(as a percent of average holdings)

	Berkshire Savings 1980	Port Savings 1980	Anchor Savings Bank		Peer Group Average 1982
			Actual 1981	Actual 1982	
Interest:					
U.S. Securities	8.49%	8.74%	10.42%	9.65%	11.90%
Other Securities	9.18	9.24	9.43	9.07	10.32
Dividends on Stock*	6.63	9.37	7.56	7.55	8.15
Total Security Income	8.38	9.08	9.67	10.63	12.10
Interest Fees:					
Mortgage Loans	9.07	9.36	9.57	10.21	10.27
Other Loans	11.79	11.99	13.34	15.04	14.65
Total Loans	9.38	9.59	9.97	10.69	10.75
Federal Funds					
FHLB Overnight	14.35	11.15	18.07	13.69	14.04
CDs, Commercial Paper & Acceptances	8.43	—	11.17	12.49	9.86
Total Operating Income	9.57%	9.66%	10.30%	11.05%	11.28%

*Includes call option income.

Exhibit 9

Income and Expense as a Percent of Average Deposits

| | Berkshire Savings 1980 | Port Savings 1980 | Anchor Savings Bank | | | Peer Group Average 1982 |
			Pro forma 1980	Actual 1981	Actual 1982	
INTEREST INCOME	10.09%	10.15%	10.12%	10.77%	11.09%	11.91%
Dividend & Int. Expense						
Deposits	7.38	7.76	7.54	8.85	8.86	9.31
Repurchase Agreements	—	—	—	.05	.14	.40
Other Borrowings	.11	.19	.14	.08	.07	.18
Cost of Money	7.49	7.95	7.68	8.98	9.07	9.89
Net Interest Income	2.60	2.20	2.44	1.79	2.02	2.02
EXPENSES						
Salaries	.77	1.09	.90	.96	.91	.81
Pensions & Other Benefits	.17	.20	.18	.20	.20	.18
Net Occupancy	.23	.26	.24	.30	.26	.22
Furniture and Equipment	.15	.19	.17	.19	.21	.13
Provision for Loan Losses	.04	.11	.07	.02	.08	.05
Advertising & Marketing	.07	.11	.09	.11	.09	.09
Professional Fees	.16	.04	.11	.20	.10	.07
Elect. Data Processing	.18	.16	.17	.22	.24	.15
Other Operating Expenses	.29	.63	.43	.38	.52	.54
Total Operating Expenses	2.06	2.79	2.36	2.58	2.61	2.23
Income Before Tax & Gains	.54	(.59)	.07	(.79)	(.59)	(.21)
Taxes	.15	—	.09	—	—	.09
Income Before Net Gains	.39	(.59)	(.02)	(.79)	(.59)	(.12)
Net Gains	(.10)	.12	(.01)	.07	.03	—
Net Income	.29%	(.47%)	(.03%)	(.72%)	(.59%)	(.12%)

Exhibit 10

Branch Office and Employee Efficiency
(end of year data)

	Berkshire Savings 1980	Port Savings 1980	Anchor Savings Bank*			Peer Group Average** 1982
			Pro forma* 1980	Actual 1981	Actual 1982	
Total Deposits ($ millions)	$ 73.9	$ 54.6	$ 128.5	$ 123.9	$ 128.0	$ 244.7
Number of Offices	4	6	10	11	11	11
Deposits per Office ($ millions)	$ 18.5	$ 9.1	$ 12.9	$ 11.3	$ 11.6	$ 22.2
Full-Time Employees						
Officers	11	12	23	22	13	25
Non-Officers	34	41	75	74	68	113
Total	45	53	98	96	81	138
Officers as % of Total	32%	23%	24%	23%	16%	18%
Deposits per Employee (incl. part-time) ($ thousands)	$1,540	$1,071	$1,298	$1,328	$1,670	$1,682

*1980 Pro forma data for Anchor Savings Bank based on a combination of Berkshire and Port County Savings Bank data.
**Average of eight Maine savings banks, including Anchor. Anchor was fifth largest in 1982.

Exhibit 11

Banking Office Analysis

	Total Deposits (12/31/82) ($ thousands)	Growth from Prior Year (%)	Average Balance per Account	Deposits per Employee	Regular Savings as % of Total	Installment Loans (12/31/82) ($ thousands)
Main St., Brunswick	$42,394	−4.3%	$4,722	$4,248	38.6%	$1,888
Main St., Biddeford	24,979	−9.3	4,389	3,910	47.8	1,268
Saco	11,663	1.7	3,447	1,542	22.8	300
Freeport	10,713	−1.9	2,875	2,079	36.1	1,443
Cook's Corner, Brunswick	9,800	3.0	3,361	2,628	41.8	388
Kennebunk	6,341	19.1	3,574	1,989	25.4	619
Kezar Falls	4,223	10.7	1,934	1,253	35.22	255
Forest Ave., Portland*	5,731	270.9	3,849	3,256	1.4	3,889
Alfred Rd., Biddeford	3,174	15.2	4,330	1,527	5.0	63
Woolwich	2,511	15.6	3,223	1,434	28.0	444
Hollis	$ 2,153	15.4%	$1,592	$ 562	32.5%	$ 223

*Located at corporate headquarters.

Population Growth: 1970–1980	
Brunswick	−1.7%
Biddeford	1.1
Saco	10.6
Freeport	4.6
Kennebunk	19.2
Kezar Falls	NA
Portland	−5.4
Woolwich	26.1
Hollis	85.4

Prudential Capital Corporation: 1989

In the summer of 1989 Ken MacWilliams, chairman and CEO of the Prudential Capital Corporation (PCC) was preparing for a meeting with several senior managers at PCC. MacWilliams and Homer Rees, the President of the company, would be joined by three of PCC's ten SVPs; Robert Hanlon, John Hannon, and Robert Hoke (see Exhibit 3).

Hannon, a 23-year veteran from The Prudential and head of the national marketing group, had only joined a year ago. Hoke, the chief credit officer, had arrived at Prudential Capital in late 1988 after a consulting (McKinsey) and banking (Citicorp and Royal Bank of Canada) career. Hanlon, in charge of the investment management group, had come to Prudential Capital at the very beginning and had risen through the organization to reach his current position. Homer Rees (MBA, 1961), the president of PCC, had joined The Prudential in 1982 from Morgan Guaranty. Most in the industry considered him the "dean" of the private placement markets. He had been with PCC since 1988.

While a regional network had been in place at The Prudential since 1948, after several reorganizations PCC was formed in 1981 to function as a direct origination capability of The Prudential. MacWilliams (MBA, 1962) had been with Prudential Capital since 1982 and became CEO in May 1987. He was also a senior vice president of The Prudential. PCC had undergone rapid growth since its formation. From originating $400 million in transactions in 1984, now more than $3.9 billion of placements were made through Prudential Capital Corporation.

With most senior managers located in offices next to one another, and frequent contacts each day, MacWilliams wanted to use the meeting to discuss some of the general issues that faced the organization. The senior managers felt that to remain as successful as the group had been over the last few years, they had to identify the possible weaknesses in the organization and to consider if any changes were required to deal with a changing business climate in the future.

Prudential Capital Corporation

Prudential Capital Corporation (PCC) is one of many wholly owned subsidiaries of The Prudential Insurance Company of America (The Prudential). In

This case was prepared by Assistant Professor David M. Meerschwam.
Copyright © 1990 by the President and Fellows of Harvard College. Harvard Business School case N9-291-001.

1989, The Prudential was the largest insurance company in the U.S. The activities of The Prudential cause it to have large investment appetites each year, and the firm has various ways to invest the funds it gathers through the sale of its insurance products. All of The Prudential's investment activities are organized through the Prudential Investment Corporation (PIC) and its subsidiaries (see Exhibit 4). Portfolio managers determine rate, maturity and asset quality guidelines for new investments.

In 1989, The Prudential held a total of $153 billion in assets (and managed another $63 billion). Due to net increases in assets and maturation of existing assets, more than $15 billion in permanent investments were made each year. Private placements, which are not publicly traded and involve the sale of securities directly to an institutional investor, such as an insurance company, were an important investment outlet for The Prudential. Originally various units were charged with buying the private placements for the parent company, but by the late 1970s the units had been reorganized, which led to two different outlets: (1) Prudential Capital Corporation, which was responsible for direct origination through its own sales force organized around regional offices (for the original organization of PCC see PruCapital (A), HBS case 9-283-077); and (2) the Corporate Finance group, which participated in transactions originated by investment banks (including Pru-Bache, formed after The Prudential acquired Bache).

PCC had 307 employees: 130 were employed in the regional offices, 177 in the Newark, N.J., headquarters of the company, where The Prudential also had its headquarters. After some reorganizations in 1988 and 1989, several new groups were formed at PCC. The Central Credit group, under Hoke, provided one level of credit control from Newark and was also actively involved in assisting the regional offices in risk identification and price structuring of new transactions, originated by the regional offices. Furthermore, both the regional offices and the Central Credit group monitored the credit quality of the existing portfolio.

The Central Financial Services group also closely cooperated with the regional offices; its function was to supply sophisticated corporate finance advice and analysis to support the transactions originated by the business developers in the regional offices (the Regional Financial Services groups). The Central Financial Services group consisted of industry and transactions specialists, mostly MBAs.

The SouthWest/Energy group, a regional office located in Dallas, Texas, was specialized in dealing with gas and oil investments. It was expected to originate about $1.2 billion in transactions in 1989 in the SouthWest region in these oil and gas deals, as well as in general corporate finance transactions.

The National Marketing group, under Hannon, was primarily responsible for helping identify the target markets for, and developing the marketing skills of, the business developers. These business developers operated from 12 regional offices (one of which was Dallas).

The Special Investments group, located in Newark, was involved in troubled transactions and work-outs. Also located in Newark was the Investment Management group. Hanlon oversaw its operations. It was responsible for the "back-office" operations (7 were active in Human Resources, 9 in Strategic Planning and Systems and 75 in Accounting, Investment Administration and Office Services). Recently Hanlon had been charged with increasing the productivity of his group. Senior managers at PCC and at The Prudential had noted that revenue growth had lagged expense increases and decided to hold the staff size at current levels and push instead for greater productivity.

In 1988, Prudential Asset Sales and Syndications (PASS), formerly a part of

PCC, was made into a separate subsidiary of The Prudential (see below). The activities of PCC that related primarily, but not exclusively, to project financings of utilities were placed in another separate group, Prudential Power Funding Associates (PPFA). Still, both units continued to have links with PCC. For example, both used (and paid for) the services of the operational support group (part of Hanlon's investment management group).

The Origination Process at PCC

The central activity of PCC was to originate opportunities that led to investment transactions. This was accomplished through business developers who targeted and contacted new business prospects and existing portfolio customers on a direct basis from 12 regional field offices across the country. Typically a business developer, after having established a corporate client relationship, would suggest possible financing transactions with that client. The business developer, after determining a risk category for the client, would consult a rate matrix available from the portfolio managers at The Prudential. The matrix would link risk classes with rate requirements, subject to frequent updating and dependent upon the particular investment needs of The Prudential.

Having identified a client's needs and the approximate rate from the matrix, a combination of informal and formal meetings, which would include senior members of the regional office, the responsible line senior vice president and some specialists in Newark, would refine the proposal while further credit analysis was applied. Then, a "Pricing Committee Meeting" would take place to consider approval for the proposal, subject to approval of the Finance Committee of the Board of Directors of The Prudential, and a final quality rating and price (interest rate) were set, depending on the current matrix structure. At the Pricing Committee Meeting at least three members of senior management would be present, typically MacWilliams or Rees, Hoke and the line senior vice president in charge of the regional office. The transactions varied in size from $10 to $20 million to several hundred million dollars. On average, PCC originated transactions with a value of $53 million.

This process meant that PCC, in effect, combined the activities that were required of Prudential's Corporate Finance group and an outside investment bank. It also meant that PCC had to support a regional network. Of course, such a network carried costs. One manager noted:

> It is quite expensive to run the regional offices. They have to look nice, people fly back and forth to Newark and there is a real telephone bill! Of course, these offices are essential for our success, but the portfolio managers can't make any allowance in the matrix for who brings the investment opportunity to them. Our regional costs won't find an easy "off-set" on the revenue side. Anyway, we are lucky that there is so much good business and that we have been able to grow well.

Most of the private placements would be put on the balance sheet of The Prudential, even though a portion could be resold to other investors through another unit of The Prudential (PASS) while PCC could also use its own balance sheet, although this was small by comparison.

PASS

Prudential Asset Sales and Syndications, Inc., was another wholly owned subsidiary created by The Prudential. It was responsible for all non-registered asset sales that took place. Especially in 1989, attention was focussed on this unit since a possible change in regulation, SEC Rule 144A, could facilitate the secondary market trading of private placements tremendously.

Historically, private placements, once made, were difficult to trade due to regulatory restrictions and the lack of full disclosure. (Since the placements were typically made by sophisticated institutional investors, the securities regulators had not insisted on broad disclosure, such as a public prospectus —it was thought that in contrast to publicly traded securities the investment professionals did not need the protection of mandatory disclosure.) Rule 144A would now significantly facilitate sales and syndication of private placements among institutional investors, despite the lack of full disclosure.

PASS would, the more active it became, not only compete with investment banks but also start to compete with a fairly recent activity of commercial banks—asset sales. For these banks, asset sales had become a very popular way to increase corporate RoA and RoE. In particular, the burgeoning market for asset backed financing and highly leveraged financing (LBOs) had created a market where the banks placed (or "sold down") most of the loans they originated in these transactions.

PCC's Future Role

In determining the future of PCC, MacWilliams and his managers all saw continued opportunities for the firm, but several different issues still needed some attention. MacWilliams noted that:

> This is a very interesting group. When we started we had to go through various reorganizations and since The Prudential has so many related activities it always is difficult to exactly figure out "who you are." That matters, since unless you know that, you can't determine what success is. Now our function is becoming really clear. Our mission is to provide The Prudential with a continuous flow of directly originated, attractive, investment opportunities. Also, our customers know that The Prudential has a long term interest in them. We don't have a typical trading mentality that is "here today, gone tomorrow."

> The other advantage of this set up is that The Prudential is now not competing through the same organization with the investment bankers. If Goldman Sachs has a deal for which it wants financing, it can go to Prudential's Corporate Finance group and get the same rate quoted from the Matrix as we would quote. The competition is "clean."

> We have had some pressures to reduce the overhead, but overall we have done really well—the growth was produced, we priced our deals to meet the matrix, we made some very profitable deals and we have had a very low loan-loss experience.

An example of the profitable deals MacWilliams referred to was a much publicized transaction in which PCC had originated a $700 million LBO of CBS magazines group that had generated $300 million in profits for The Prudential and a private investor in less than 9 months. Such deals showed the corporate finance ability of the group and reminded industry participants that The Prudential had often been in the forefront of "innovative transactions." For example, in 1978 The Prudential had helped invent the "strip-financing" concept for the Congoleum LBO, whose $470 million price tag had been the largest in history to that date.

One senior manager, much involved in the complex corporate finance transactions at PCC believed that the corporate finance ability at PCC was absolutely on par with that of the major investment banks:

Our people are just as good as those anywhere else. We hire many of the best MBAs, but we have a couple of additional advantages. Quite a few very bright MBAs want to work here because they know that while we are just as aggressive as any other major investment bank, this place has a different culture. You can really go for a long-term perspective and if you have some real good ideas, you can get a lot of deals done—financing in place and the whole show. Also, we get a whole lot of clients that like us better. They know that if they transact with an investment bank they will likely get some Prudential involvement anyway or that of another large investor. If they come to us, they get it direct and there is much less risk of possible conflicts of interest. Now, with PASS becoming so visible we can really compete with any investment bank. They all say they want to become merchant banks; in many respects we have a unique ability through combining all the units of The Prudential to act as a merchant bank; we have a continued interest in the transactions.

Hannon, in charge of marketing, believed that the direct marketing field force was the real asset of the firm.

When I was offered this job I had spent a whole career in the (group) insurance business. There is a kind of duality at The Prudential. One set of people thinks about the marketing of the insurance products. Then you have the investment side —very talented people who know how to invest. At first I really didn't understand why they needed me here. Actually, I think that some people here also didn't quite understand it. But now that I have been here a little while, I really see how this fits. The role of the business developers in the regional offices is central. They have to build relationships with prospective customers and sell our product.

Look, we can't compete in coverage with the large banks and investment banks. But we don't have to. We should be able to identify the most likely prospective customer for the kind of deals we want to do. Don't forget, we are a direct placement arm of The Prudential and have a different mission from the Corporate Finance group. There the investment banks send a memo to Corporate Finance and perhaps another 10 or 15 possible suppliers of finance. It is then up to Corporate Finance to negotiate a deal and to make a bid or not in light of the matrix structure at the time. We have 150,000 possible companies. First we narrowed that down to 40,000. Next we looked more closely at this group and brought it down to 1,600 companies. Those are our potential clients and we have approximately 80 business developers. Each of them is asked to identify the 20 most likely prospects and to develop and sustain an ongoing relationship. The list changes and we cultivate it, but the size of the list and the intensity of the relationship development effort doesn't.

When I came here, there were still some business developers who counted transactions with companies that went through the Corporate Finance group as "their" business. But that is changing. I think the message is getting really clear. And even if not all the business developers really understood what was required and what was compensated, I think that this is now much better communicated. People are really doing a great job. They have generated terrific growth and have been compensated for that. Bonuses can account for 50% or even more of total compensation and it is becoming much more clear what will generate a bonus.

Hoke, the Chief Credit Officer, saw opportunities for PCC in various areas:

I have not been here that long and there are many things we haven't fully explored. With PASS coming more on line, the opportunities for different deals increase. If we work more like a merchant bank and use PASS to lay off part of our positions, there is a whole set of deals we could do, unrelated to the investment appetite of The Prudential. Not too long ago someone used a metaphor that PCC should generate a river of deals and The Prudential stands on the banks with buckets—let it dip in if it wants to do so, but if not, we'll use other investors. We have the competence to generate good deals; we have showed it in the past and can do it again. Still, The Prudential will always play the primary role.

But you know, there are some problems as well. Since we have The Prudential right behind us, there is almost a natural tendency to think that there are no resource constraints —think about it, a company which has to invest more than $100 million per day! Customers may tend to think that we can provide unlimited, "one-stop" financing. On the other hand the appetites of the portfolio managers have shown a high degree of variability and they tend to communicate by pricing us either on or off the market. In addition we have a history of demanding stringent terms and conditions. It can be a real problem for our business developers. On top of that, I wonder about the future of some of our most successful products—LBO's are going to be tougher in the future and they have already been so this year.

Hanlon's group (strategy planning, human resources and operations support) was well regarded, not only at PCC but widely in The Prudential. While The Prudential, and many of its units, had their own operations support groups, PCC's group held advantages. A senior manager said:

I go out and get some terrific MBA's. Now I know that some of these people don't want to spend the rest of their careers on the operations side, but PCC offers unique opportunities. It can be a feeder area to the investment side of the company. You come here, do a great job and you move on to other things that you find interesting. In few other operations groups can you achieve the same. Some may argue that having inside The Prudential several operations groups may be inefficient, but there is no way that, for example, PCC could get all the "tailor made" services we provide or that we could hire the kind of people we do, if all the operations support was centralized. Of course, you may think that there would be some cost savings—those are always easy to identify. But how do you account for the value added of the higher quality we provide; how do you measure the value of being able to hire really good people? That PASS and PPFA stayed with us shows you that we really can deliver a first rate product.

Managers in the Strategic Planning group, which also reported to Hanlon, were responsible for suggesting performance measures for the Company which were then reviewed and refined by senior managers in PCC and The Prudential. The actual performance relative to these measures affected the amount available for the bonus plan for the year. Strategic planning had to balance various views held inside the corporation. It was clear that PCC's premier objective so far had been to satisfy the growing investment appetite of The Prudential. The Prudential had established PCC for this purpose and it had succeeded, better than many had thought, as the growth record showed (from the $400 million to $3.9 billion in origination). Historically, compensation relied much on the employee's ability to generate transaction volume without sacrificing stringent credit control. While each had a base salary, bonuses could play an important role. The total resources for bonus allocation came from a pool made available by The Prudential. Due to the complex internal relationships among the "members of the Pru-family," it was not a foregone conclusion how much of this pool would go to PCC. PCC's actual performance was reviewed in light of the performance measures and a determination was made about the amount that would be available for PCC. Once determined, this amount had to be distributed among the PCC employees. This allocation was done by a rigorous, time-intensive process managed by PCC's Senior Management. Both objective and subjective measures were used. As the company's performance measures grew to include more than transaction volume, so did the measures against which each professional was evaluated.

"The staff knows that each of us is responsible for contributing to the company's objectives and our success is tied to our compensation," mentioned Valerie Mauriello, VP, the manager responsible for the Strategic Planning group,

> We ask the individuals to complete a self appraisal indicating how much they have contributed to company performance, have their supervisors comment, and then bonus allocation is determined by senior Management of PCC. Everyone knows the specific performance criteria, these are distributed early in the year. Total compensation is very competitive and while perhaps not as high as on the Street, virtually all people think that the combination of compensation, corporate culture and opportunities, make this a really great place.

Homer Rees, the President of Prudential Capital, considered the opportunities and difficulties for PCC in the context of overall changes in the financial industry. In an April 1989 article in the *United States Banker* he was quoted as saying:

> The result [of all the changes in the financial industry] is that we now pay more for insurance money, we get less for our investments, and time horizons are shorter. This squeeze means that our traditional function—buying and holding assets—has grown riskier and less profitable.

Looking at PCC itself, Rees remarked:

> Our real advantage is going to be the kind of service we can offer to the clients. The way we do business, the quality of the work, the notion that if you do business with PCC we are a long term investor, all these distinguish us. Even if PASS plays a more active role we still will only deal with participations; The Prudential will keep a significant portion of each transaction on its own books. PASS allows us to take on deals that we can syndicate and creates liquidity for the portfolio managers.

Measuring PCC's Success

Since PCC was a wholly owned subsidiary of The Prudential (itself a mutual, rather than publicly traded, company) and because over 80% of PCC's assets were actually housed elsewhere in The Prudential, some at PCC found it difficult to define the firm's bottom line. In addition, the corporate level performance measures focussed on the expense/asset ratio. Many felt that a lack of a corporate methodology for evaluating all asset origination units on a consistent basis was a major problem. While PCC provided all the usual financial information (though this information was not publicly available), interpreting the numbers was not obvious. Some wondered what the correct cost of funds was, others were not sure what reasonable return requirements would look like. As mentioned before, several at PCC considered that, by the nature of the organization, it would always be faced with a higher cost structure than the Corporate Finance group, yet would typically be compared to that department in terms of performance, since both were "in the business of making private placements for The Prudential."

One internal document had bluntly stated that:

> We must demonstrate an ability to achieve sufficiently superior returns to offset the incremental costs of PCC. As one of a number of entities to which the portfolio

managers of The Prudential look to place funds, we must be able to demonstrate the total value added by PCC to The Prudential.

The Meeting

Just before MacWilliams walked into the meeting with his top team, he got a phone call from Jim Stevens, an EVP of Prudential Investment Corp, the insurance company's investment arm, to whom MacWilliams reported. Stevens congratulated MacWilliams on PCC's performance so far and in particular on the increases in productivity. But he also mentioned that the portfolio managers now forecast that, at least for 1990, the direct placement requirement from PCC would probably remain substantially the same as it had been in 1989. No growth in investible funds could be expected for the year.

Exhibit 1

Consolidated Balance Sheet*
(as of Dec. 31; $ thousands)

ASSETS	1988	1987
Cash	$ 3,159	$ 3,549
Short-term investments	12,394	50,102
Net investments in		
Loans	710,886	1,699,620
Leases	551,652	654,815
Mortgages	0	588,041
Stock	62,812	102,520
Supply contracts	0	78,193
Property under operating leases	20,876	8,446
Other	71,013	72,546
	1,417,238	3,174,181
Allowance for losses	(48,685)	(68,968)
Total net investments	1,368,553	3,105,213
Investments in affiliate's stock	600,000	600,000
Other assets	39,943	43,820
Total Assets	$2,024,049	$3,802,684
LIABILITIES AND STOCKHOLDER EQUITY		
Short-term notes	$1,204,454	$3,016,875
Long-term notes	279,754	269,498
Total senior debt	1,484,208	3,286,373
Taxes payable	44,035	24,416
Other liabilities	95,790	94,049
Total senior liabilities	1,624,033	3,404,838
Deferred taxes	47,932	28,861
Deferred asset sale gain due to affiliates	28,593	2,810
Junior subordinated notes	50,000	50,000
Common stock	17,586	17,586
Retained earnings	255,905	298,589
Stockholder equity	273,491	316,175
Total liabilities and stockholder equity	$2,024,049	$3,802,684

*All figures in the balance sheet have been disguised. The figures are only indicative of the position of PCC.

Exhibit 2

Consolidated Income Statement*
(as of Dec. 31; $ thousands)

	1988	1987
Investment revenue	$238,635	$264,175
Dividends from affiliate	38,912	41,620
Total revenue	277,548	305,795
Interest expense	174,535	224,249
Investment income	103,013	81,546
Provision for losses	29,653	32,256
Net investment income	73,359	49,290
General and administrative expenses	57,478	32,416
Income from operations	15,882	16,874
Other income	149,518	90,254
	165,400	107,129
Taxes	59,544	38,566
Net income	$105,856	$ 68,562

*All figures in the balance sheet have been disguised. The figures are only indicative of the position of PCC.

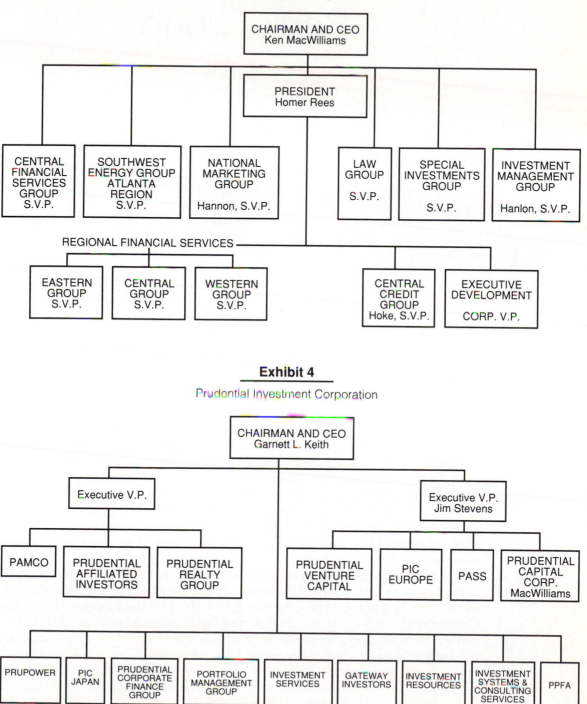

Exhibit 3

Prudential Capital Corporation

CHAIRMAN AND CEO
Ken MacWilliams

PRESIDENT
Homer Rees

CENTRAL FINANCIAL SERVICES GROUP
S.V.P.

SOUTHWEST ENERGY GROUP ATLANTA REGION
S.V.P.

NATIONAL MARKETING GROUP
Hannon, S.V.P.

LAW GROUP
S.V.P.

SPECIAL INVESTMENTS GROUP
S.V.P.

INVESTMENT MANAGEMENT GROUP
Hanlon, S.V.P.

REGIONAL FINANCIAL SERVICES

EASTERN GROUP
S.V.P.

CENTRAL GROUP
S.V.P.

WESTERN GROUP
S.V.P.

CENTRAL CREDIT GROUP
Hoke, S.V.P.

EXECUTIVE DEVELOPMENT
CORP. V.P.

Exhibit 4

Prudential Investment Corporation

CHAIRMAN AND CEO
Garnett L. Keith

Executive V.P.

Executive V.P.
Jim Stevens

PAMCO

PRUDENTIAL AFFILIATED INVESTORS

PRUDENTIAL REALTY GROUP

PRUDENTIAL VENTURE CAPITAL

PIC EUROPE

PASS

PRUDENTIAL CAPITAL CORP.
MacWilliams

PRUPOWER

PIC JAPAN

PRUDENTIAL CORPORATE FINANCE GROUP

PORTFOLIO MANAGEMENT GROUP

INVESTMENT SERVICES

GATEWAY INVESTORS

INVESTMENT RESOURCES

INVESTMENT SYSTEMS & CONSULTING SERVICES

PPFA

Deutsche Bank Group

It was early April 1990 and the managing board of Deutsche Bank was assembled for one of its regular weekly meetings at its imposing glass headquarters complex at 6000 Frankfurt am Main in the heart of Frankfurt's financial district.

Events had been moving so rapidly in Germany and in eastern Europe that there was a persistent need to be updated on developments affecting various of the huge bank's worldwide activities. Mr. Hilmar Kopper, the board's recently appointed "speaker" to replace Alfred Herrhausen who had been assassinated by terrorists at the end of the previous November, was constantly besieged by the national and the international newsmedia concerning the bank's attitudes and plans in a variety of its product and geographic markets. Two of the most pressing queries related to important developments taking place both to the east and the west of the Federal Republic's strategic location in the heart of Europe.

The piercing of the infamous Wall separating East from West Germany in the autumn of 1989 had coalesced a powerful set of forces for reunification on both sides of that barrier. The Germany which had been defeated in World War II had been overwhelmed by Allied forces composed of the very European and North American countries which were now West Germany's most important economic and military collaborators. To the east, the rapid-order collapse in 1989 of Communist Poland, Hungary, Czechoslovakia, and Rumania were further momentous developments with which West Germany—and Deutsche Bank—had to come to terms.

To the west, the European economic collaboration which had its foundations in the European Coal and Steel Community after World War II had gathered such momentum by the spring of 1990, that the prospect for the European Economic Community (EEC) establishing an almost irreversible integration in the economic, monetary, and even political spheres was now much more realistic than the distant dream of some of the earlier European planners such as Robert Schumann. In no sector was this advancing integration more evident than in the increasingly linked and interdependent European and other Free World capital

This case was prepared by Professor Samuel L. Hayes III.
Copyright © 1990 by the President and Fellows of Harvard College. Harvard Business School case N9-290-036.

markets. The prospective removal of many tariff and other intra-EEC commercial barriers in 1992 promised to further alter those financial markets. In this context, Deutsche Bank's recently announced purchase of the prestigious British merchant bank, Morgan Grenfell, was particularly notable.

The West German Banking Market

The banking system in the Federal Republic was made up of three large sectors, differing from each other in their legal form, ownership structure, and goals, but competing with each other as universal banks in all sections of the financial market. The three sectors included:

1. Private and commercial banks

2. Public banks, especially the public banks and the central giro institutions (i.e. regional central institutions of the savings banks)

3. Credit cooperatives

The group of commercial and private banks, in turn, embraced four types: large commercial banks, regional banks, private banking firms, and the branches of foreign banks. They were private law corporations under the ownership of private individuals or firms, and profit-oriented in their operations. Savings banks and their central giro institutions, on the other hand, were public law institutions under state ownership and basically pursued a public welfare goal. The individual savings banks were restricted in the business they could do, both by geographic region and by being prevented from engaging in certain types of business. But the institutions with which they were associated at the "Land" level, the central giro institutions and the Landesbanken, were not subject to such restrictions and thus could—and did—compete in all markets as universal banks. The credit cooperatives originated as public self-help organizations for agriculture and crafts, but had likewise joined together to form large, full-service banks. Their customers were also their shareholders so that their operating policies were most particularly geared to the customers' interests.

Because West Germany did not have any regulatory or custom-determined product or market segmentation of its banking industry, the banks in West Germany engaged in the broadest possible array of commercial banking and securities-related financial services to individuals, institutions and corporations. The West German financial markets were dominated by three large banks—Deutsche Bank, Dresdner Bank, and Commerzbank—and they and a few others were fiduciaries for huge amounts of individuals' and institutional savings (in the form of securities and other investments) and also held important equity investments in key German industrial concerns. The nation's ten largest banks owned strategically important blocks of equities in 27 of the 32 largest West German industrial concerns, by some estimates.[1] And while no precise figures are available, the banks were believed to have a substantial equity stake in nearly all of the country's top 50 companies.

West Germany was a different but alluring market for foreign banks. The size and buoyancy of the economy, the strength of the Deutschemark, and its role as the fourth most important international investment and borrowing currency were immensely attractive. West Germany was moving to liberalize its financial markets, but some controls were retained for fear of undermining monetary policy.

Only since 1985 had local subsidiaries of foreign banks been allowed to lead-manage Euro-Dm issues (and only since Oct. 1987 had this been the case for Japanese banks). The underwriting consortium for government bonds had similarly been widened to include foreign banks. But the Bundesbank still required Euro-Dm issues to be lead-managed from West Germany, and foreign banks without a presence in West Germany were still excluded from a lead manager role, thus strengthening the Bundesbank's influence over the course of new securities offerings.

With some 4,500 banks of one description or another, West Germany was one of the world's most "overbanked" markets. The retail market was crowded, the wholesale market was expensive, and the corporate banking market was dominated by "house-bank" relationships and a growing surplus of cash among German companies. In sum, the 270 foreign banks (with 4.4% of the banking assets) operated only at the fringe of West German banking and profitability was marginal.

The West German Securities Market

Trading in stocks and bonds took place on the eight regional stock exchanges in Berlin, Hamburg, Bremen, Düsseldorf, Frankfurt, Hanover, Munich and Stuttgart, with the universal banks acting in the role of stockbrokers. The role played by the securities markets in the flow of funds had been less important in the Federal Republic than in many other western countries. However, because of the rise in public sector borrowing in recent years, the market for fixed income securities was now growing. Leaving aside financings made abroad, the public debt securities market could be divided into three segments:

1. Bonds issued by public authorities, including the Federal Government, the Federal Railways, the Federal Post Office, and the "Lander" and Local Authorities. The Federal Government was by far the largest issuer, utilizing the Bundesbank and the banking system as distribution channels.

2. Bonds issued by banks (essentially mortgage banks and Landesbanken/central giro institutions) which mainly issued mortgage bonds and local authority bonds.

3. Industrial Bonds, issued by larger corporations. Typically, the whole of the new issue was first taken up by a consortium of banks, which then resold them to the public, oftentimes into trust accounts which the banks managed on behalf of individuals.

Profile of Deutsche Bank

Deutsche Bank was founded in Berlin in 1870 by industrialist George Siemens to pursue a general-purpose banking business both domestically and in other European and overseas markets. Offices in Bremen and Hamburg were established in 1871–1872, in Shanghai and Yokohama in 1872 and in London in 1873. In subsequent decades the bank played an important role in financing such growth industries as electrical utilities, railways and mining.

The decade and a half following Imperial Germany's defeat in the First World War was characterized by great political instability: between 1919 and 1933, Germany had 20 different cabinets as well as runaway inflation; this paved the way for the assumption of power by Adolph Hitler and his Nazi party. Deutsche Bank weathered this period via a series of mergers and acquisitions.

Following Germany's defeat in World War II, the three big banks (Deutsche

Bank, Dresdner Bank, and Commerzbank) were split up by the Allied occupying powers into 30 successor institutions. Each was allowed to do business in only one of the federal states. In 1952 a partial reconsolidation was legislated and in 1956 the final reunification of the big banks was permitted.

It was Deutsche Bank which reputedly coined the phrase "universal bank" as part of an advertising campaign to publicize the scope of its activities and capabilities both within Germany and in the international community. With assets of Dm 305 billion ($166 billion) at the end of 1988, it was one-third larger than second-place Dresdner Bank (see Exhibits 1 and 2).[2]

Deutsche Bank (DB) had 1,640 branches around the world, with the bulk located within West Germany, where savers had proved remarkably loyal to their local bank branches. DB dominated trading on West Germany's eight stock exchanges and in recent years had been the lead underwriter for 40% of all new stock issues. Acknowledging its leading role in the country's public securities markets at the time of the October 1987 stockmarket crash, the bank made a valiant effort to prop up West German securities with heavy buying at the cost of billions of marks in securities losses.

The bank's clout was also evident the day after the East Germans began pouring through the Berlin Wall in October 1989, seeking to buy everything from toasters to bananas with their nearly worthless currency. Hesitant West Berlin merchants turned for guidance to Deutsche Bank, which promptly declared that it would guarantee them an exchange rate of one Deutsche mark to ten East German marks.

DB's executives sat on the boards of numerous German corporations. The bank's equity stakes among the giants of German industry included a 28% holding in Daimler-Benz AG and a 10% interest in Allianz AG, Europe's largest insurance company. To many of these companies, Deutsche Bank served in the comprehensive roles of lender, underwriter and financial adviser, akin to the relationships that long existed between Japan's city banks and that country's leading industrial concerns. Investors often viewed DB and the other leading German universal banks as de facto investment companies (e.g., mutual funds) because of their huge ownership holdings in German industry.

The bank had not hesitated to use its influence when necessary. When in 1988 Kloeckner & Co., a trading company, was poised on the brink of bankruptcy after having gotten caught with huge open positions in oil futures in an unfavorable market, DB rushed in with a rescue plan. By announcing its support for Kloeckner, DB assured that thousands of international trade contracts were fulfilled and that there was no ripple effect from a failure of a major international trading house. In the process, it temporarily assumed control of West Germany's largest trading group with some 30,000 employees. Once the problems had been resolved, DB sold its position to another German company.

In the recently approved acquisition of the aerospace concern Messerschmitt-Bolkow-Blohm G.m.b.H. by Daimler-Benz A.G., DB also played a key role. Daimler was already the nation's largest industrial concern, with annual sales of $39 billion. Alfred Herrhausen, then the head of Deutsche Bank and also chairman of Daimler's supervisory board, played a highly visible role in reshaping the maker of Mercedes cars and trucks into an aerospace and technology conglomerate.

Despite its global aspirations, Deutsche Bank's domestic operations produced 83% of its operating profits on 62% of its business volume. About 13% of earnings came from Europe, 2% from North and South America, and 2% from Asia and Australia. Although after-tax return on assets was a meager (by international banking standards) .39% in 1988, this was nonetheless the highest rate of profitability among the German banks (see Exhibits 3 and 4). In 1988 Deutsche Bank earned 10.8% after-tax on its equity; this was better than its two leading German rivals but less than the 14% which was reportedly its target.

Deutsche Bank possessed a substantial capital base (see Exhibit 4). Perhaps with an eye on the new Bank for International Settlements (BIS) capital standards,[3] Deutsche Bank further increased its equity base with a rights offering in 1989, which raised Dm 1.28 billion ($687 million). (Dresdner Bank followed soon after with its own equity rights offering for approximately the same amount.) DB's capital strength was also believed to be buttressed by substantial hidden reserves not reflected on its balance sheet.

Given these evidences of domestic economic power, it was not too surprising that there had been recent calls from some quarters within West Germany for the enactment of legislative curbs on the big universal banks. The country's parliament had begun studying steps to limit the banks' shareholdings in other companies, as well as their seats on corporate boards and their influence on corporate decisionmaking. Critics of German banking contended that the current system, originally set up to give the nation's war-shattered economy strong banks to finance the post-war recovery, had outlived its usefulness. Today, said some politicians and economists, this structure resulted in too great a concentration of economic power and an inefficient allocation of financial resources.

Otto Graf Lambsdorff,[4] the head of the Free Democratic Party (a junior partner in Chancellor Helmut Kohl's ruling coalition), contended that the banks were making the economy less efficient. Lambsdorff wanted to limit a bank's holdings in a company to 15% of the company's equity capital. He also favored curbing a bank's use of proxy shares (shares which the bank holds in safekeeping for its customers), arguing that this gave the bank too much control over companies and diminished the power of the other stockholders. The opposition Social Democratic Party agreed, but wanted to go even further by limiting banks' equity holdings to only 5% of a company's capital.

The Social Democrats also wanted changes in the proxy rules, and would like to reduce the maximum number of supervisory board seats to five from the ten now permitted. Mr. Kohl's Christian Democratic Union favored less drastic measures, although the party had not yet offered a unified position on the issue of bank power. Most banking experts and other observers believed that the range of proposals made a compromise inevitable, but the precise shape of such a compromise was hard to predict. While there had been some talk of legislation being enacted before the next national elections in the fall of 1990, some observers considered this unlikely, given the West German government's understandable preoccupation with more pressing concerns surrounding reunification.

German bankers and most business executives, on the other hand, generally defended the banking system as a major positive element in their nation's continuing economic success. They contended that the arrangement provided German companies with secure and stable financing that freed managements from short-term pressures to please fickle investors and worry about gyrating stock markets. Instead, these business enterprises could safely concentrate on long-term growth.

Internal Organization of Deutsche Bank

Historically, DB had been organized as a series of seventeen semi-autonomous regional "universal" banks (in essence, branches with a great deal of autonomy) based on the precepts of relationship banking and shared responsibility. Former board speaker Dr. F. Wilhelm Christians let his local staff do their business as though they were private bankers. As a result, today's DB was a confederation of autonomous regional universal banks where all business was managed under one roof. The only exceptions were the "Going Public" and the "Mergers and Acquisitions" areas, which were managed from central headquarters in Frankfurt.

Industry observers attributed DB's past success within Germany to its marketing power, high-quality customer services, and operating efficiencies. Nevertheless, Speaker Herrhausen had frequently expressed uneasiness over the bank's organizational structure, particularly in light of the European economic integration slated for 1992. In his view, the bank would not only require new strategic plans, but also the formulation of a new corporate culture and a new way of fostering communication both within and outside the bank.

To this end, Herrhausen had hired two teams of management consultants—McKinsey and Roland Berger—to undertake a study to determine what adjustments in corporate organizational structures would be required to facilitate the bank's broader strategic objectives. After an eight-month-long investigation, the consultants produced a set of recommendations for DB's managing board that would effect far-reaching changes in the organization. They proposed a new vertical organization structure defined by clients and products rather than by the traditional geographic regions. Consequently, the proposal would call for the regional offices to lose much of their autonomy and status as profit centers, and the seventeen existing head offices would be reduced to seven.

In line with Herrhausen's oft-stated goals of positioning DB as a universal bank in Europe and an investment bank throughout the rest of the world, the consultants noted that, like other universal banks, DB did not really know where many of its costs originated or where it made its money; the bank managed its business based on the overall results of the regional head offices.

The consultants defined four future "pillars" or business segments within the bank:

► Retail banking

► Wholesale banking (e.g., corporations and institutional investors)

► Trading (e.g., currency, securities) and asset management (high net worth individuals)

► Services and logistics (personnel, back office)

While the studies' conclusions and recommendations were supposed to remain confidential until the managing board felt the time was right to announce them internally, the business journal *Manager Magazine* somehow obtained a copy of the consultants' report and published their findings in June of 1989[5] (see Exhibit 5 for some further details). The premature leakage of this information caused some consternation among the DB executive ranks.

At the top of the bank's internal organizational structure was the Supervisory Board, akin to the board of directors of a U.S. corporation. Under German law, 50% of its membership was composed of company employees who had been elected by their fellow employees. The Supervisory Board was charged with approving appointments to the Board of Managing Directors (although the candidates were nominated by the Board of Managing Directors) and for approving all major actions taken by the Bank, such as the purchase of Morgan Grenfell. The

Board of Managing Directors (the "Vorstand") was composed of thirteen top executives, who essentially ran the bank. All Vorstand members were equals, each with one vote. Decisions were implemented only with a unanimous favorable vote. This "consensus" style of decisionmaking also filtered down to lower levels of management. Thus, the decision process had much in common with that typically associated with Japanese organizations.

Normally, two "Spokesmen" were elected from this board to represent it to both internal and external constituencies and to serve as de facto co-chairmen of the managing board and initiators of new policies. Alfred Herrhausen was only the second *sole* spokesman to be named in the entire post-World War II period,[6] a reflection of the very high regard in which he was held both inside and outside the bank. Following his tragic assassination at the end of November 1989, it was widely anticipated that there would be two spokesmen named as his successors, in keeping with the past tradition of the bank. It was therefore something of a surprise when Hilmar Kopper, already a prime candidate for one of the leadership slots, was named sole spokesman as the successor to Herrhausen.

Kopper, 55, was the first in the long and distinguished list of spokesmen who had spent his entire career with DB. Born to a farming family in 1935 in what was then Polish Oslanin, he and his family were dislocated by the war to the Lower Rhine Region where, at the age of 19, Kopper joined DB in 1954 as an apprentice. While much of his work in those early years was, in his view, "stupid manual chores to which I could see no connection at all to banking,"[7] advancement in the post-war years was relatively rapid because of the depleted senior management ranks as a consequence of the war. Kopper also spent two years as a trainee with the Henry Schroder Bank in New York but then returned to DB to work in the Foreign Department of the Düsseldorf Head Office. It was not long before he became manager of the Foreign Department in the Leverkusen branch, which handled the large Bayer account. And in 1969 he became manager of the entire Leverkusen branch.

Three years later Kopper moved to Hamburg to take a seat on the Board of the Deutsche-Asiatische Bank, which later became the Euras-Bank. In 1975 he was appointed Executive Vice President of the Deutsche Bank with offices in Düsseldorf. The Supervisory Board appointed Kopper to the DB Board of Managing Directors in 1977 and in more recent years he had been in charge of the bank's securities underwriting and syndication business, its activities in the Cologne business area as well as in North America, and various investment banking subsidiaries. He was, for instance, instrumental in DB's acquisition of Morgan Grenfell.

In assuming the function of spokesman, Kopper took on responsibility for Group planning. Since his appointment as spokesman, Kopper had emphasized that "the good ship Deutsche Bank" would remain on the course which Herrhausen and the rest of the Board had earlier set. He had also been quoted as saying that the bank must move towards an even more open and unconstrained internal dialogue that transcended all hierarchical boundaries.[8]

Opportunities in the West

In recent years DB, under Herrhausen's leadership, had moved aggressively through a series of mergers and acquisitions to build its presence across the face of Europe and thereby anticipate the likely consequences and opportunities that would flow from the removal of trade and regulatory barriers within the EEC in 1992. As already mentioned, Deutsche Bank had frequently articulated its goal of being a leading force in three areas: retail banking across all of Europe, investment banking on a global basis, and a broad array of other finance-related services, initially within Germany, but ultimately abroad, as well.

In the commercial banking arena, for instance, DB bought Bank of America's Italian subsidiary in 1986 and Spain's Banco Commercial Transatlantico in 1989. In addition, DB set up a variety of new branches and financial service units in European financial centers. However, it had thus far been frustrated in Britain and, especially, in France, where the government wasn't inclined to privatize banks that DB wanted to buy. France was a particularly important target for Deutsche Bank's expansion because it was both a large domestic banking market as well as West Germany's major trading partner.

In the securities sector, DB made acquisitions in Portugal (1987), Holland (1988), Canada (1988), Australia (1988) and Italy (1989). Perhaps its most dramatic move was to purchase the prestigious, 151-year-old London merchant banking firm of Morgan Grenfell in late 1989. This was an important move, not just because of the $1.5 billion price tag, but because it provided DB with important supplemental coverage. With the exception of bond trading, DB had no significant investment banking operation in London. In 1988, for instance, Morgan Grenfell ranked second in handling takeovers of British companies. Morgan also had strong historic connections in Eastern Europe, where DB itself had strong interests.

Like a handful of other foreign banks, DB enjoyed an exemption from the Glass-Steagall Act, prohibiting banks within the United States from underwriting most corporate securities. And the bank engaged in a variety of different financing activities. In 1987, for example, DB coordinated efforts by two commercial banking units—a leasing subsidiary in Deerfield, Illinois as well as DB's New York branch—to enable the Southeastern Pennsylvania Transport Authority to lease $56 million worth of West German buses.

In 1987, Deustche Bank became the first foreign bank in Japan to be allowed to open a securities unit, and in 1989, the bank raised capital of $422 million in a share offering in Tokyo.

The Potential to the East

As DB looked eastward, it drew a sharp distinction in its thinking between East Germany and the other countries which had made up the post-war Soviet bloc. In some ways, West and East Germany were like identical twins who had been forcibly separated at an early age. Each twin had grown up in radically different home environments, but there nonetheless remained common ties, language and heritage that made the prospect of reunification much different with respect to its competitive position in the West (see Exhibit 6) from the outlook for renewed and expanded economic ties with the rest of eastern Europe.

Economically, the commerce that flowed between the two parts of Germany was important to both. East Germany imported three times as much from West Germany in 1988 as from all the other eleven countries of the EEC combined. And the prospects for further growth were truly impressive. Some analysts believed that East German imports of capital goods could reach a massive DM 184.9 billion. It was expected that priority would be given to products for cleaning up the heavily polluted environment, electrifying the railways, modernizing the telecommunication system and improving industrial efficiency. On the consumer goods side (where imports could reach DM 5 billion), household appliances and quality food would probably be a first priority.

East German banks were predominately branches of the Staatsbank central bank. Thus, with East Germany lacking any real retail banking industry, the leading West German banks were moving in to establish beachheads. DB already had 10 offices and 50 employees in East Germany and planned a 300-branch network with a staff of 5,000. Dresdner Bank, which now had 9 offices, including one in the city where it first opened for business in 1872, reportedly had plans for an initial 35 branches with a longer-term goal of a full-branch network.

In the commercial sector, it was the Japanese banks who were currently the largest lenders to East Germany, with an exposure of approximately $4 billion. By comparison, the West German banks' loans totaled roughly $3.1 billion. But with a large number of West German companies migrating back to their prewar geographic locations and market niches in East Germany, there was little doubt that the West German banks—and DB prominently among them—would be massively stepping up their lending activities there, too.

All kinds of structural impediments had to be surmounted by western banks and commercial businesses wanting to do business in East Germany. There was, for instance, the problem of all the property that was expropriated by the government 40 years ago; Chase Bank still had a claim to a house on East Berlin's Unter den Linden. And then there were such questions as the ownership of the large farms once held by Prussian landowners. Even if East Germany abandoned its ban on private ownership of property, how much trouble would it be for a Western company to get a clear title to land for building a factory? One positive element was that East Germany still had a "company law" that had survived from the prewar era and which gave significant powers to the chief executive of a company. That law might prove useful in the transition from state ownership to private enterprise.

In the rest of Eastern Europe, West German bank lending exposure varied country-by-country. In October 1989, DB was the first German bank to be allowed by the Hungarian Ministry of Finance to open a representative office in Budapest. This step reaffirmed the traditionally strong linkage of DB to the Hungarian economy, as well as reflected a positive attitude towards the changing economic structures and an expected increase in German-Hungarian trade relations. DB was currently expecting permission to open a representative office in Warsaw as well.

DB had enjoyed a close relationship with the Soviet Union. Former DB speaker Dr. Christians' business links with Moscow went back to 1969, just preceding the "Ostpolitik" drive initiated by West German Chancellor Willy Brandt. In succeeding years DB negotiated a series of major credit deals with Moscow, including the controversial natural gas pipeline project between the U.S.S.R. and western Europe. Dr. Christians was the first senior western businessman to be received by Mikhail Gorbachev in Moscow following his appointment as the Soviet leader. In 1986, DB also became the first foreign bank whose representative office was permitted to occupy a separate and permanent building in Moscow. After a thirteen-year stay in the Metropol Hotel, the bank held a gala inauguration of its new office at which, in addition to "Speaker" Dr. Christians, Mr. Hilmar Kopper officiated in his role as board member in charge of East bloc businesses.

The opportunities for further lending were enormous, with the major drawbacks being the credit and security surrounding various financing proposals (see Exhibits 7, 8 and 9). Bankers were trying to determine appropriate standards for extending loans to specific private enterprises as well as to countries' state-owned businesses. With the sad default experience with earlier loans to Latin America and other less-developed countries (LDCs) fresh on their minds, there was an understandable air of caution in some quarters. How, for instance, would lending or investing terms differ in the case of Eastern Europe as compared to western Europe? To answer that question, DB and other leaders would have to develop more extensive credit research facilities that could be specifically directed at these eastern European countries with their long histories of centrally controlled economies. There was even the prospect of issues of publicly offered securities on behalf of some of these enterprises. Would DB's investment banking arm be willing and able to actively participate as underwriters and distributors? And would DB be predisposed to consider placing some of those newly issued bonds and stocks in various of the trust accounts which they managed for individuals and institutions?

Rainer Emil Gut, the chairman of Credit Suisse, was quoted as disclaiming an interest in bankrolling Eastern Europe at this point. He drew attention to the Zurich bankers' traditional reservations about the East, except in special circumstances, such as sales of Russian gold! He further expressed the opinion that it would be government entities which would have to put up the money for the fundamental rebuilding of Eastern Europe.[9] Nonetheless, there seemed little doubt that as West German (and other foreign) companies focussed attention on business opportunities in Eastern Europe, their banking connections would inevitably follow right along with their customers.

The Managing Board's Task

As DB's managing board sorted through the myriad factors and forces that were at work to influence the bank's future well-being, there was a sense that, at this juncture in 1990, something of a watershed had been reached. For the bank, for Germany and for other nations, the relatively stable and predictable political and economic order of the post-World War II era was being irreversibly altered. The bank would now have to plot its strategy in the face of a number of uncertainties—as well as exciting possibilities—unprecedented in the careers of the current senior management. Assigning priorities and weights to the various factors involved would not be easy.

▶ Endnotes

1. *New York Times,* November 11, 1989.

2. At the end of 1989, DB's assets totaled Dm 344 billion ($200 billion).

3. These standards required international banks to finance their assets with a minimum of 4% of pure equity by the end of 1992 and a minimum of 8% of equity plus subordinated debt.

4. "Graf" is the German word for "Count." Despite the formal abolition of the nobility, class distinctions nonetheless persisted and a title was considered an asset to an individual in operating within Germany.

5. "Einer Knacht die Bank," *Manager Magazine,* June 1989.

6. The first was Hermann I. Abs, who was instrumental in rebuilding DB following World War II.

7. *International Forum Magazine,* January 1990.

8. Ibid.

9. *Wall Street Journal,* February 20, 1990.

Exhibit 1

Largest Capitalized Banks Worldwide—Selected Data

Size by Capital	Bank Name Statement Date	Capital ($ millions)	Assets ($ millions)	C/A Ratio	Pretax Profits ($ millions)	Return on Assets %	Return on Assets Rank
1	Sumitomo Bank 3/31/90	$13,357	$372,101	3.59	$2,343	0.63%	478
2	Dai-Ichi Bank 3/31/90	12,322	408,025	3.02	1,916	0.47	588
3	Fuji Bank 3/31/90	11,855	366,745	3.23	1,974	0.54	534
4	Crédit Agricole 12/31/89	11,802	241,992	4.88	1,266	0.52	547
5	Sanwa Bank 3/31/90	11,185	357,760	3.13	2,042	0.57	507
6	Mitsubishi Bank 3/31/90	10,900	364,100	2.99	1,719	0.47	584
7	Barclays Bank 12/31/89	10,715	204,907	5.23	1,111	0.54	528
8	National Westminster Bank 12/31/89	9,761	186,559	5.23	649	0.35	684
9	Deutsche Bank 12/31/89	8,462	202,263	4.18	2,081	1.03	316
10	Industrial Bank of Japan 3/31/90	8,184	259,860	3.15	1,015	0.39	663
11	Union Bank of Switzerland 12/31/89	8,150	113,854	7.16	784	0.69	438
12	Citicorp 12/31/89	7,319	227,037	3.22	1,538	0.68	444
13	Comp. Finan. de Paris 12/31/89	6,968	138,668	5.02	1,225	0.88	362
26	Dresdner Bank 12/31/89	5,105	147,001	3.68	796	0.54	530
47	Commerzbank 12/31/89	3,803	112,825	3.37	221	0.55	523

Source: *The Banker*, London, July 1990.

Exhibit 2

The Big Three Parent Banks (DM millions)

	Deutsche			Dresdner			Commerzbank		
	1988	1987	1986	1988	1987	1986	1988	1987	1986
ASSETS									
Claims on customers	103,817	86,668	79,690	63,808	55,458	51,563	59,138	48,716	46,198
Claims on banks	56,140	44,661	46,098	36,929	31,845	28,104	32,124	31,189	24,795
Bonds and notes	8,544	7,549	9,773	7,940	8,850	10,298	9,068	7,331	7,017
Securities	4,730	5,086	4,637	2,403	1,818	2,053	1,100	769	767
Others	18,776	21,234	19,730	15,646	13,686	13,389	13,826	13,103	12,030
LIABILITIES									
To customers	94,790	82,245	82,420	77,449	68,916	63,384	68,671	60,145	53,912
To banks	65,728	55,027	52,360	28,333	24,093	23,837	34,002	28,583	23,647
Bonds and notes	7,696	7,305	5,561	7,379	7,393	7,478	3,526	4,101	4,983
Capital	1,773	1,773	1,623	1,474	1,312	1,243	1,131	1,040	1,038
Reserves	8,404	8,004	6,658	4,835	4,082	4,081	3,241	2,903	2,834
Others	13,616	10,844	11,306	7,256	5,861	5,384	4,685	4,336	4,393
Balance sheet total	192,007	165,198	159,928	126,726	111,657	105,407	115,256	101,108	90,807
Total Income	14,961	12,660	12,827	9,263	8,352	8,352	8,308	7,148	6,679
Total Expenses	12,707	11,688	10,760	8,507	7,703	7,616	7,662	6,619	6,147
Taxes	1,429	547	1,243	384	317	368	301	240	244
Net income	825	425	824	372	332	368	345	289	288

Note: Unconsolidated financial statements.

Source: *Asian Finance,* September 15, 1989.

Exhibit 3

Deutsche Bank
Comparative Consolidated Income Accounts, Years Ending December 31
(DM billions)

	1988	1987	1986	1985	1984	1983	1982
REVENUE							
Interest and disc.	13.4	11.5	10.5	11.5	12.6	11.8	14.0
Investment income	1.6	1.6	2.6	1.5	1.4	1.2	1.1
Commissions, fees	2.5	2.0	1.9	1.7	1.4	1.3	1.1
Other income	7.2	6.4	6.0	6.4	5.5	5.3	5.0
Total Revenue	24.7	21.5	21.0	21.7	20.9	19.6	21.2
OPERATING EXPENSES							
Interest, etc.	13.3	11.8	11.1	11.9	12.8	11.8	14.2
Write-offs	0.2	0.7	0.9	0.8	1.3	1.5	1.7
Comm. fees paid	0.1	0.1	0.1	0.1	0.1	φ	0.1
Salaries and wages	3.1	2.9	2.7	2.4	2.3	2.1	1.9
Social Security and benefits	1.0	1.0	0.8	0.8	0.8	0.7	0.6
Other administrative expenses	1.6	1.4	1.3	1.1	1.0	0.9	0.8
Depreciation and adjustments	1.6	1.3	1.0	0.8	0.6	0.6	0.5
Taxes	2.0	1.0	1.6	1.7	1.2	1.2	1.0
Reserves and provisions	0.3	0.1	0.1	φ	φ	φ	φ
Other expenses	0.3	0.5	0.4	0.4	0.1	0.1	0.1
Total Operating Expenses	23.5	20.8	20.0	20.0	20.2	18.9	20.9
Net Income	1.2	0.7	1.0	1.1	0.7	0.7	0.3

Note: Accounts maintained, prepared, and reported in conformity with West German accounting principles.
Symbol φ indicates item too small for inclusion.

Source: Deutsche Bank Group.

Exhibit 4

Deutsche Bank
Comparative Consolidated Balance Sheets, as of December 31
(DM billions)

	1988	1987	1986	1985	1984	1983	1982
ASSETS							
Loans	126.9	109.2	99.4	96.1	100.2	88.1	81.0
Cash, checks, banks	5.2	8.8	7.3	8.3	7.0	6.6	6.7
Notes discounted	2.3	2.2	2.0	2.2	2.5	2.6	2.1
Finance institutions	68.8	53.2	51.7	43.7	42.7	40.0	43.3
Treasury bills	3.9	3.1	2.3	2.0	1.2	1.4	1.2
Bonds, etc.	15.8	13.0	15.1	14.4	13.5	11.2	8.4
Additional securities/participants	8.3	8.0	9.1	3.9	3.2	2.8	2.3
Mortgage loans	62.6	61.6	59.3	55.8	52.3	48.4	45.1
Equalization claims	0.2	0.2	0.2	0.3	0.3	0.3	0.3
Trust loans	1.2	1.2	1.4	1.6	1.2	1.0	1.0
Affiliates' bonds	1.7	1.5	1.5	0.8	0.6	0.6	0.6
Land, bldg. equipment	6.0	4.4	3.5	3.2	2.6	2.4	2.3
Other assets	1.9	2.4	4.2	4.8	4.7	4.6	4.8
Deferred items	0.5	0.2	0.2	0.1	0.3	0.2	0.1
Total assets	305.3	268.3	257.2	237.2	232.3	210.2	199.2
LIABILITIES							
Capital	1.8	1.8	1.6	1.6	1.5	1.4	1.4
Free reserve	8.4	8.0	6.7	6.1	4.8	4.3	4.0
Consol. reserve	1.1	0.9	1.4	1.3	1.1	0.9	0.8
Group profit	0.7	0.6	0.7	0.6	0.5	0.4	0.4
Minority interest	0.2	0.2	0.3	0.4	0.4	0.4	0.3
Due institutions	66.4	55.0	57.8	57.4	60.8	56.8	56.8
Debentures	84.1	78.5	71.7	64.0	60.4	54.6	50.8
Long-term mortgage loans	2.5	2.3	2.0	1.6	1.4	1.3	1.3
Deposits	121.6	106.0	100.1	90.3	88.4	78.3	72.8
Acceptances and notes	4.7	3.1	2.8	2.2	2.4	2.0	1.4
Trust loans (contra)	1.2	1.2	1.4	1.6	1.2	1.0	1.0
Provisions	7.4	6.4	6.6	5.9	5.2	4.6	3.9
Spec. leg. reserves	0.3	0.1	φ	φ	φ	0.1	0.1
Sundry liabilities	2.5	2.5	2.5	2.4	2.2	2.1	2.0
Deferred items	2.4	1.7	1.6	1.8	2.0	2.1	2.2
Total Liabilities	305.3	268.3	257.2	237.2	232.2	210.2	199.2

Note: Accounts maintained, prepared, and reported in conformity with West German accounting principles. Symbol φ indicates item too small for inclusion.

Source: Deutsche Bank Group.

Exhibit 5

Deutsche Bank
Summary of Consultants' Report on DB's Strategic Position

Strengths	Weaknesses
GENERAL ASPECTS	
High domestic customer potential,	but weak customer base in Europe, United States, and Japan.
Strong domestic market position,	but a high percentage of small unprofitable clients.
Highly qualified, loyal management, excellent operational management,	but not enough internationally-oriented managers.
Conservative, careful business policies,	but weak entrepreneurship especially in the main office (weak image for innovations).
High continuity in leadership,	but mediocre ability to integrate employees from outside.
High reputation,	but tendency to arrogance (internal and external).
STRUCTURE AND CONTROL	
All the advantages of a universal bank,	but complex, inflexible organization "collective responsibility."
High motivation and higher than average growth through regional organization,	but coordination problems among the head offices and also between head offices and central office; dense coordination through committees.
RETAIL BUSINESS	
Germany's #1 in many areas, high reliability,	but too complicated procedures, underutilization of technology.
"Allfinanz" with all consulting qualities,	but not enough cross-selling, directioning problems (i.e., three mortgage banks).
WHOLESALE BUSINESS/INVESTMENT BANKING	
Excellent relationship with larger firms,	but weak impact on mid-size firms.
High market share in Germany with export clients,	but low share within Europe.
Strong in foreign currency payments, credits, and with financing of imports and exports,	but relatively weak with demanding, intelligent products such as corporate finance (i.e., M&A).
#1 in the German issuing business, leading in Euromarket,	but weak in the most important capital markets and currencies (U.S. dollar, Yen, Swiss francs and pounds).
Strong, profitable position in the Germany securities business,	but inferior position in trading with international stocks.
Strong position in capital investment,	but a high degree of unexploited potential with high net worth individuals.

Source: "Einer Knackt die Bank," *Manager Magazine,* June 1989.

Exhibit 6

Comparisons of United Germany, U.S. and Japan in 1989
(U.S. $)

	United Germany	United States	Japan
Per Capita GNP	$14,910	$21,018	$22,879
Total GNP (billions)	$ 1,373	$ 5,233	$ 2,820
Exports (billions)	$ 428	$ 624	$ 413
Gross Investment (as % of GNP)	20%	15%	32%
Compensation per hour	$ 17.72	$ 14.51	$ 12.42

Source: DRI/McGraw-Hill.

Exhibit 7

The Eastern European Economies in 1989

(Country ranked by population)	Population (million)	Area (sq. km. 000)	Labor Force (millions)	Per capita income[a] (EC = 100)
USSR	288	22,402	156	50
Poland	38	313	19	40
Yugoslavia	24	256	10	45
Rumania	23	238	11	35
GDR	16	108	9	75
Czechoslovakia	16	128	8	70
Hungary	11	93	5	55
Bulgaria	9	111	4	45
Eastern Europe (total)	425	23,649	222	50
(for comparison: EC)	(325)	(2,261)	(145)	(100)

[a]Estimates at near market exchange rates based on purchasing power parity. These do not allow adequately for differences in quality. The eastern European countries lag even further.

	Employment in agriculture (%)	Electricity generation (TWh)	Petroleum production (million tons)	Primary energy demand per capita (tons, oil equivalent)
USSR	18	1,720	608	5.0
Poland	28	144	0.1	3.5
Yugoslavia	22	83	3.5	2.0
Rumania	28	70	9.0	3.0
GDR	10	119	0.1	6.0
Czechoslovakia	13	81	0.1	5.0
Hungary	19	30	2.0	2.5
Bulgaria	19	45	0.3	4.5
Eastern Europe (total)	19	2,292	623.0	5.0
(for comparison: EC)	(7)	(1,700)	(115)	(3.5)

Exhibit 8

The Industrial Structure of Eastern Countries (shares of selected segments in 1987 according to PlanEcon as % of gross value of output)

Country	Food processing	Textiles, clothing, leather, shoes	Metals	Chemicals (including oil refining)	Mechanical and electrical engineering	Others
USSR	15	14	10	11	24	26
Poland	18	11	11	12	22	26
Yugoslavia	15	12	10	14	20	29
Rumania	12	14	10	16	24	24
GDR	15	9	9	20	26	21
Czechoslovakia	15	8	12	14	27	24
Hungary	17	9	8	19	24	23
Bulgaria	23	9	6	14	27	21

Source: Deutsche Bank Economics Department publication entitled "Special Eastern Europe," February 1990.

Exhibit 9

Foreign Debt of Comecon Countries (year end 1989)

Country	Hard currency debt (net, $ billion)	Debt ratio (in years)
USSR	37	1.4
Poland	38	3.2
Rumania	0	0.0
GDR	13	1.3
Czechoslovakia	5	0.7
Hungary	19	2.1
Bulgaria	9	2.7
Yugoslavia	14	0.9
Total[a]	126	1.6

[a]Includes liabilities by Comecon banks which cannot be more closely allocated.

Source: Deutsche Bank Economics Department publication entitled "Special Eastern Europe," February 1990.

The Nomura Securities Company, Ltd. (A)

By the beginning of the 1990s, The Nomura Securities Co., Ltd. of Japan had, over the previous decade, comfortably settled into a role of being an international phenomenon. For, not only was it recognized as the leading securities firm in Japan, it had also flexed its muscles in the London Euro-markets where it is well known that it seized the Eurobond underwriting lead from long-established leader Credit Suisse First Boston in 1987. Now, Nomura's far-flung financial services empire reached throughout the Far East (including the Republic of China), Europe and North and South America. Nomura's worldwide profits in its fiscal year ending March 31, 1990, were some US$1.8 billion—about ten times that of Merrill Lynch, its closest counterpart and rival, who reported US$192 million at its fiscal year ending December 1990.

Despite such evidences of success, Nomura was still struggling to transform itself from a domestic Japanese stockbroker, with only secondary links to the Japanese corporate community, into a full-service investment bank in the tradition of comparable U.S. firms. Progress had been slow and Nomura was being hounded by new potential competitors. Both Japanese commercial banks and foreign securities firms were clamoring for regulatory approval to expand their involvement in the Tokyo home securities markets and the Ministry of Finance had recently circulated a plan for deregulation that would do just that. Moreover, the market environments abroad were more unsettled and Nomura's position in places like London and New York were not that secure.

Early History

There is no denying that Nomura had come a long way from its humble beginnings. The firm's early history was primarily the story of Tokushichi Nomura.[1] Born in 1878, he was the adopted first son of a modestly successful moneychanger in Osaka, then the major center of domestic commerce and finance in Japan. Since there was not a national currency, moneychangers played a key role in all commercial activities. Nevertheless, changers were considered to be the lowest-ranked and socially least respectable class in Japan.

This case was prepared by Professor Samuel L. Hayes, III.
Copyright © 1991 by the President and Fellows of Harvard College. Harvard Business School case N9-291-035.

In 1904, the young Nomura joined the family firm, which had turned its attention toward stock trading. (With the appearance of a national currency after the Meiji Restoration in 1868, most of the large money changers had gone into national banking, while the smaller firms gravitated toward the stock exchanges.) Although the stock market was on the periphery of the financial system, Japan's success in the 1904 war against Russia in Manchuria acted as a powerful stimulus to the market, and the Nomura firm profited and grew along with it.

Securities underwriting, which guaranteed to the issuer that an entire offering would be successfully sold, dated only from the 1890s in Japan and had been the exclusive domain of the national banks. Beginning in 1910, securities firms had sought also to act as primary underwriters of major Japanese government bond and corporate equity issues; however, they could obtain only positions subordinate to the large banks. By World War I, Nomura's business had broadened to include some underwriting, trading, and sales of fixed-income as well as equity securities, but it remained primarily a retail-oriented stockbroker.

Tokushichi Nomura was not averse to taking big risks. He timed the market correctly in 1917 and scored record-breaking trading gains. Despite a string of successes, he was painfully conscious of the superior status accorded the national banks in Japan's financial system and envied the close relationships between securities firms and commercial banks in other countries. As a result, the Osaka Nomura Bank[2] was founded in 1918 not only to edge into the commercial banking sphere but also to handle the underwriting and sales of government bonds and corporate debentures—areas dominated by the national banks.

The move towards bonds was fortuitously timed. In the early 1920s, the Japanese government responded to a slump in the equity market by attempting to revitalize the dormant government bond market. Like other banks controlled by securities firms, the Osaka Nomura Bank reaped the benefits of this expanding market.

Nomura Securities Founded

The bond business was on a roll, and by 1922 it had become evident that a separate organization would be needed for servicing. The result was The Nomura Securities Co., Ltd., headquartered in Osaka, in December 1925. The new firm was originally chartered primarily to underwrite and distribute government bonds, corporate bonds, and stocks, and to trade already issued public and corporate bonds, but it soon encompassed all kinds of securities activities. Nomura, along with the Osaka Nomura Bank and several other family-controlled enterprises, was part of a nascent *zaibatsu* (a centrally-controlled group of business and financial institutions) controlled by Nomura Company, a holding company, established in 1922.

The next twenty years were extremely difficult for Japan's securities industry. The Great Kanto earthquake in 1923 devastated Tokyo. There were massive financial panics in Japan in 1927 and again in 1929. Many securities firms folded and, prodded by the Ministry of Finance, the securities industry began a dramatic process of consolidation that lasted through the end of World War II. During this period, Nomura continued to grow, establishing eight domestic branch offices by the late 1920s. In March 1927, Nomura also opened a New York representative office to act primarily as an agent for the sales and related clearing functions of dollar-denominated Japanese government bonds. But the U.S. depression seriously eroded the demand for foreign bonds, and the New York office was closed in December 1936.

The early 1930s were years of political uncertainty in Asia, and Japan prepared for military conflict, which erupted in full-scale war in 1937. Like other parts of the private sector, securities firms and national banks were mobilized by the government in support of the war effort. The Ministry of Finance instituted regulatory changes in 1938 that forced further consolidation in the securities industry. By the end of the decade, only eight firms qualified as securities underwriters. Although not the largest, Nomura was a powerful and respected member of the group. While this development enabled Nomura and other members of the securities oligarchy to expand their role in the business of underwriting and distributing government bonds, the market remained dominated by the big national banks. The government had come to rely more and more heavily on the *zaibatsu* and their affiliated banks. These major national banks, along with the Industrial Bank of Japan, thus occupied preeminent positions as capital market vendors, counselors and strategists for the Japanese corporate establishment.

The climate was nonetheless favorable for stock brokering. With increasing government control of the bond market and the rise in inflation resulting from the wartime economy, investors turned their attention to stocks, and Nomura profitably stepped up its activities in secondary-market trading.

A major new business with far-reaching implications was created in 1941 when the Ministry of Finance authorized the establishment of equity investment trusts, patterned after those in Britain and similar to present-day U.S. mutual funds. These trusts served to bolster prices (and civilian morale) on the stock market and thus assisted the war effort. Nomura successfully offered the first Japanese investment trust and took the unusual step of guaranteeing that investors would suffer only a limited capital loss if the securities in the trust declined in value. Other securities firms were quick to follow.

The year 1945 was devastating for both Japan and Nomura. During the final months of World War II, Nomura lost over half of its domestic branch offices as a result of Allied bombing, including the new head office that had been moved from Osaka to Tokyo during the war. Almost half the staff had taken temporary leave to join the armed forces, many never to return. The Nomura *zaibatsu's* investments in the fallen Japanese colony of Manchuria were lost, and many critical documents were destroyed in fires from the bombing. The measurable losses incurred by Nomura totalled ¥25 million—more than twice its total capital.

Postwar Rebuilding

As part of the reforms instituted by the occupation forces after the war, the Nomura *zaibatsu* and holding company were dissolved, separating Nomura from its banking affiliate. Several of the group's senior officers and directors were forced to resign. Nomura, like some other securities firms, avoided having to change its name by procrastinating on the implementation of this Allied order, thus preserving its associated and valuable retail customer franchise.

Article 65

Then, in 1948, the Allied occupation instituted a number of financial reforms, including Article 65, the Japanese equivalent of the U.S. Glass-Steagall Act. The separation of investment from commercial banking gave the surviving securities firms—including what came to be known as the Big Four (Yamaichi, Nomura, Nikko, and Daiwa)—the exclusive privilege of underwriting new issues of corporate bonds and equity. After decades of playing second fiddle to the national banks, the franchise was perceived to be a rich prize indeed. And while a number of the occupation administration's reforms were dropped or substantially modified following the signing of the peace treaty in 1952, the separation of public securities business from commercial banking business was retained by the Ministry of Finance, perhaps in recognition of the historically weak position of Japanese securities firms vis-à-vis the commercial banks and the Ministry's desire to achieve a better future balance between the two groups of financial intermediaries.

The period of the occupation and its reforms resulted in a shift in share ownership. As the *zaibatsu* were dismembered, their share holdings were more broadly distributed. This development played to the strength of retail brokers. Nomura responded to the revitalization of the retail market by re-establishing and expanding its branch networks across the country. "Investment consultant centers" were opened throughout Japan in department stores and other locations, and the firm's capital base was also increased. With these moves, Nomura firmly established itself as a major postwar retail force among Japan's securities firms.

Cultivating Investors

Spurred initially by the economic expansion engendered by the nearby internal Korean War, the 1950s and early 1960s were generally years of prosperity and growth for Japan. At the same time, the accompanying boom in its securities markets accelerated activity among individual shareholders. Nomura, through its promotion of investment trusts, assorted savings schemes, and investment seminars, was in the vanguard of the movement. Equity investment trusts had been reintroduced in 1951 and were heavily marketed by the major firms to individual investors. Nomura had soon established a network of 620 agencies, called "service stations," across Japan to accept applications for investment trust and bond subscriptions from individual savers. An important factor in Nomura's success with investment trusts was its development of various savings plans. One such scheme, the "Million Ryo Savings Chest," was launched in 1950.[3] Small cash boxes were lent to individuals who used them like piggy banks. The catch was that Nomura retained the key and employed a staff of 150 women as collectors. In exchange for a full box, the customer received an investment trust certificate. Over a million chests were distributed through the plan, which continued until 1962.

Nomura also increased retail securities sales through investment seminars, investors clubs, and publications. In the mid-1950s, Nomura adopted a policy of identifying and recommending growth stocks. Remarkably accurate predictions, considered by some critics to be a result of price manipulation, further enhanced the firm's image among investors and kept up the flow of an incoming stream of money.

With business brisk at home, Nomura began looking beyond its borders for new opportunities. Restrictions on the sale of Japanese equities to foreign investors were loosened in 1951 and sales to nonresidents became increasingly important. In March 1953, Nomura became the first Japanese securities firm after the Korean War to open a branch in New York. In 1959, the Japanese government issued its first foreign currency-denominated bonds in twenty-eight years, and Nomura participated in the underwriting syndicate with several major U.S. securities firms, lead-managed by First Boston. About that time, Nomura also began to send some personnel to be trained by Merrill Lynch in the United States.

The interest shown by foreigners in Japanese securities enabled Sony Corporation to issue the first Japanese-American depository receipts (ADRs) in the United States in 1961.[4] Nomura co-managed the deal along with the American firm of Smith Barney & Co. and, over the next few years, was involved in several other ADRs for Japanese companies. At the same time, Nomura helped underwrite Japanese corporate bonds in New York. A 1962 convertible issue for Mitsubishi Heavy Industries, for instance, was co-managed by Nomura, with First Boston running the books.

Relationships and Regulation

Back in the home market of Tokyo, however, corporate capital fund raising was sparse in the public markets. As mentioned earlier, the corporate community remained closely wedded to their main commercial banks, relying on them for both financing and advice on matters of corporate finance. It is no wonder that Japanese securities firms viewed with envy the more favorable corporate relations enjoyed by their U.S. investment banking counterparts.

Other regulatory changes did have an important positive influence on Nomura's growth. Government and corporate bond trading on the Tokyo and Osaka exchanges was officially restarted in April 1956. In 1961, corporate bond syndication procedures were revised. Previously, the Big Four securities firms each underwrote 20% of every issue. Now the lead manager's share was increased to 23%, and the other three firms were allotted 19%. Nomura, as a frequent lead manager, benefitted substantially from this change. As to the equity markets, "second sections"[5] were added to the Tokyo, Osaka, and Nagoya stock exchanges in 1961, making it easier for medium-sized companies to be publicly traded. This move also served to expand the base of business for firms like Nomura.

Nomura's strong financial position served it well through the major recession and depressed markets of 1965. In contrast, several of Nomura's competitors, including the largest—Yamaichi Securities—had to be rescued with government-secured loans. As a result, Nomura emerged for the first time as the undisputed leading securities firm in Japan.

The disasters of World War II had left Japan's economy starved for capital. While the Ministry of Finance was pleased to open the door to capital that "wanted in," the door was closed for capital outflows during the decades of economic recovery. The early 1970s saw the beginning of two-way capital flows in and out of Japan. In 1970, the Ministry of Finance authorized, for the first time, the purchase of foreign securities by Japanese investment trusts. A few years later, restrictions were lifted on the purchase of foreign securities by individual Japanese investors, and foreign securities were approved for listing on the Tokyo Stock Exchange (TSE). Foreign investment trusts also started to be actively sold in Japan. Nomura profited from the Japanese appetite for foreign securities and, in 1973, established Fund America of Japan, Inc., an investment trust jointly managed with Merrill Lynch.

Fixed Income Financing

The 1970s were a boom time in the issuance of Japanese government bonds, particularly after the government undertook extensive infrastructure development as an antidote to the shock of the massive oil price increases in 1974 and 1979. New issues, along with reduced restrictions on sales of secondary market government bonds by financial institutions, turned up the heat on trading volume. With their tradition in trading, securities firms made the most of this opportunity, although Japanese commercial banks were by far the largest holders of government bonds in their own portfolios. Nomura scored impressive successes, partly through its door-to-door efforts that employed 2,500 women to sell the securities the way Avon sold beauty products to U.S. housewives.

Bond trading was also facilitated by official recognition of *gensaki* transactions, the Japanese equivalent of U.S. Treasury securities-repurchase agreements (repos). In this type of arrangement, bonds were sold with an agreement to repurchase them at a fixed future date, perhaps in one day or one week, at a price slightly higher than the original sale. Nomura and the other securities firms, seeking an inexpensive and convenient way of funding their bond-trading positions, played a significant role in such transactions. However, government bonds continued to be underwritten by a fixed syndicate dominated by the commercial banks, and so the securities firms' (and Nomura's) share of that underwriting volume remained comparatively small.

Euromarket Underwriting

Also in the 1990s, some Japanese corporations (like their counterparts in Europe and the United States) were becoming less reliant on bank loans, as both their external financing needs diminished and their access to lower-cost, publicly traded bonds increased. In particular, the Eurobond markets provided attractively priced financing opportunities. Nomura, as has been mentioned earlier, and the other big securities firms, had become active as underwriters in this London-based market and therefore benefitted substantially from this trend.

Nomura was instrumental in the development of the samurai bond market, the name given to yen-denominated bonds issued publicly in the domestic Japanese market by foreign borrowers, such as other overseas governments, supranational organizations, and a limited number of well-known foreign corporations. The first samurai bond deal was led by Nomura in 1970, and the firm quickly seized a large part of this market.

Other important changes served to strengthen the position of the securities firms relative to the commercial banks. By the mid-1970s, unsecured corporate bonds had gained some acceptance. Without the need to keep track of collateral, the role of the banks acting as commissioned agents in bond underwriting was diminished. At the same time, small and medium-sized financial institutions, as well as individuals, (both prime sales targets for the securities firms) increased their absorption of new government and corporate bond issues, relative to purchases made by the big commercial banks for their own portfolios.

Nomura, with its vast retail sales network, benefitted from the growing pool of individual investors in Japan, many of whom had a special interest in bonds. Meanwhile, institutional investors were becoming a growing factor in the equity markets. In 1949, individual investors owned 70% of the listed shares in Japan. This figure fell to 32% by 1972 and decreased even further to about 25% by the mid-1980s, forcing Nomura to pay increasing attention to equity sales to institutions and companies in addition to its traditional commitment to individual investors.

Thus, by the end of the 1970s, Nomura was already the undisputed leader among the Big Four Japanese securities firms as well as a major player, along with the commercial banks, in the domestic financial markets. However, its strength was still primarily in selling stocks and bonds to Japanese investors. Ahead lay struggles to improve the balance of its service mix, particularly to increase its corporate finance capabilities, and to position itself as a leader in the increasingly global financial marketplace.

Entering the 1990s

Nomura came into the limelight as a truly international firm in the 1980s. Historically, its overseas network in the 1950s and early 1960s consisted primarily of branch and representative offices that were largely extensions of Tokyo. With the increasing internationalization of capital flows, Nomura decided to expand its foreign subsidiaries and give them greater autonomy in local decision-making. Reorganizations took place in New York (1969), London and Amsterdam (1972), Frankfurt (1973), and Paris (1979). New representative offices were opened in Bahrain and Sydney (1980), and a number of joint ventures were established in Southeast Asia, Australia, and the Middle East.

In 1981, Nomura Securities International, Inc., now the official name of its major U.S. broker-dealer subsidiary, became a member of the New York Stock Exchange, the first Japanese securities firm to be admitted. At the same time, Nomura International (Hong Kong) Limited was formed. Securities operations were established in Canada following that country's regulatory reform (dubbed "Little Bang") in 1987. New representative offices were also established in Bejing, Brussels, Lugano, Kuala Lumpur, and other locations. The Nomura network, by 1990, had grown to 146 domestic and 52 overseas offices.

Through its extensive domestic branch network and overseas operations, Nomura was active in securities underwriting, sales, trading, brokerage, and research in practically every major market around the world. Further, it was strongly trying to enhance its international corporate finance activities. This was evidenced by the acquisition of a minority position in U.S.-based Wasserstein Perella Group, Inc., a M&A boutique.

By the beginning of the 1990s, the preponderance of the company's earnings were still generated from operations within Japan. Only 20% of Nomura's total revenues were coming from overseas operations—with 13% coming from Europe and 4% and 3% respectively from the United States and Asia.

Perhaps its most impressive international presence was in the London Euromarkets. Nomura International PLC, originally a small branch office established in London in 1964, was chartered in 1981 to act as the center of the firm's European operations. With the growth of Japanese issuers in the Eurobond market, as well as Nomura's placing power for aggressively priced Eurodollar bonds among Japanese investors, Nomura steadily climbed in the underwriting league tables. As a result of an opportunity opened by Britain's Big Bang, a deregulatory move in 1986, Nomura became a member of the International Stock Exchange (earlier the London Stock Exchange) and was granted a commercial bank charter. In 1987, Nomura supplanted Credit Suisse First Boston as the top-ranked Eurobond underwriter, a ranking it was able to hold onto through the end of the decade.

By the early 1990s, Nomura was the largest and most profitable securities firm in the world. Revenues (see Exhibit 1) in 1990 totaled ¥1,201 billion (US$7.9 billion), and net income was ¥276 billion (US$1.8 billion). Shareholders' equity (see Exhibit 2) approached ¥1,900 billion (almost US$12.3 billion), dwarfing by comparison the major investment banks and securities firms from other countries. But, as competing global investment banks were quick to point out, size was not everything. Nomura's international successes, especially in the Eurobond market, were built primarily on its strong domestic franchise with Japanese investors. Critics pointed out that the firm still lacked entrée into top-ranked multinational corporate boardrooms, and even among Japanese corporate issuers, Nomura and the other large Japanese securities firms were still struggling to dislodge the commercial banks form their long-standing roles as primary corporate financial counselors, especially in the area of mergers and acquisitions.

Securities sales continued to dominate the firm's activities. Commission income from securities brokerage, primarily in Japan, recently had accounted for just about half of Nomura's total revenues.[6] Although there were over 200 securities firms in Japan, the Big Four dominated trading on the TSE. Directly, they handled more than half of the daily volume; indirectly, including the trading of their affiliates, they controlled approximately 70%. Of this amount, Nomura and its affiliates accounted for about 30%. However, with the growth of smaller Japanese firms and the appearance of foreign brokers, the proportion of trading handled directly by the Big Four did decline somewhat during the 1980s, in a weakening Japanese market where market values dropped 19% in 1989.

Nomura's past trading strength in brokerage had led to the further expansion not only of its extensive retail distribution network but also its control of a substantial number of investment trusts and investment funds. The firm's almost five million customer accounts, most of whom purchased at least some investment trusts, were serviced by an army of sales people, including door-to-door saleswomen,[7] operating out of over 100 locations in Japan. Of the total of over ¥42 trillion ($300 billion) of outstanding investment trusts in Japan, Nomura's share accounted for about one-quarter. In addition, assets totaling ¥14 trillion ($100 billion) were managed by its subsidiary, Nomura Investment Management Co., Ltd.

The Nomura culture over the years demanded hard work, dedication, and relentless selling. Young sales people were exhorted to follow in the tradition of President Tabuchi, who apocryphally had made at least 100 calls a day and wore out a pair of shoes a week during his years as a broker. But some market participants accused the Japanese brokers of abusing the trust of small investors through churning—the execution of unnecessary trades in a client's account to generate large commissions. The practice appeared to be more widespread in Japan than in the United States and to have been largely ignored by the authorities.

Securities trading in which Nomura has acted as a principal represented about one-eighth of total revenues. In the important secondary market for Japanese government bonds, Nomura's share usually represented twice the volume of any other firm. In equities, Nomura had been just as dominant; in fact, its competitors complained that Nomura could move the markets strictly on the basis of rumor! Nonetheless, Nomura remained cautious about committing its own capital to trading positions, despite its enormous capital base. This contrasted markedly with the aggressive positioning adopted by a number of U.S. securities firms.

Although fixed-commission rates were reduced in Japan for large trades following upon London's Big Bang, there was continuing pressure for further liberalization. Institutional investors, who accounted for roughly three-quarters of the total Japanese market volume, were particularly vocal. However, it appeared that the TSE, backed by the government, was committed to maintaining fixed-commission rates for the present, ostensibly to maintain order in the markets, but practically to protect the revenue streams of the politically powerful smaller Japanese brokerage houses with higher cost structures. Fixed rates also had the effect of preserving the lucrative revenue streams of the leading brokerage firms. Nevertheless, the Ministry of Finance indicated its intention to periodically review commission rates with the aim of maintaining Tokyo's relative competitiveness with other major markets around the globe.

Nomura also had a sizable domestic underwriting business, which, along with Eurobond activity, accounted for about 23% of revenues in 1990. It led the league tables for both domestic Japanese equity share and bond issues.

Nomura's revenues from merger- and acquisitions-related business were, however, still nominal in relation to its overall operations, reflecting a number of factors. Historically, Japanese corporations had not paid for counseling services, which were extended in large part free of charge by their main banks, which counted on the revenue from the total relationship to compensate for an array of counseling and other unbilled services. Thus, it had been difficult for the Japanese securities firms, striving for access to Japanese corporate boardrooms, to charge fees in addition to gross spreads earned on occasional public financing. Then, too, the volume of mergers and acquisitions in Japan was much smaller than either the United States or Europe, and tended to involve small to medium-sized companies with strong ties to their main bank, which usually had its own staff of M&A specialists.

The most important potential source of M&A fees was from cross-border activities, typically involving a Japanese purchaser and a foreign (often American) seller. In these instances, Japanese corporate executives would typically turn to U.S. investment banks or British or continental merchant banks with an internationally recognized expertise and franchise in the field. Only in recent years had Nomura focused its attention on penetrating the M&A market, and it recognized that a key to achieving that objective domestically was to demonstrate its full-service investment banking capabilities offshore with a variety of foreign corporate clients. The Wasserstein-Parella joint venture was an obvious building block in that strategy.

Nomura's profits had grown to the point where, in 1987, it was believed to be the most profitable Japanese company in *any* industry. Further, its capital position (see Exhibit 2) was, among securities firms, probably the strongest in the world. This was the case whether one looked at total funds available or at the capital as a fraction of total assets.[8]

Yet, despite these impressive statistics, Nomura's leadership was uneasy at the outset of the 1990s. For fiscal 1991, profits were expected to be down 60% from the previous year and Nomura's position both inside and outside of Japan was under some competitive pressure.

Domestically, the Ministry of Finance was pushing steadily forward with a plan of market liberalization which would provide other vendors easier access to the Japanese securities market sector which Nomura had long dominated so profitably. In fact, this assault on Nomura's domestic hegemony presented quite a philosophical dilemma for Yoshihisa Tabuchi and the rest of the senior management. While on the one hand they had worked assiduously to instill new thinking in the firm's 16,000 personnel, they were at the same time strenuously resisting the efforts to liberalize the Tokyo financial markets, the source of Nomura's fundamental power.

Abroad, Nomura was finding the pickings quite slim. While in 1990 it still retained its number one position in the Euromarkets for the fourth straight year, its market share was, nonetheless, slashed in half, to less than 9%. In the United States, a number of market forces had conspired to thwart Nomura's ambition to become a significant factor in the domestic U.S. capital markets [see Nomura (B)]. Its latest remedial move was to hire the former head of a well-regarded U.S. investment bank, Max Chapman, to serve as co-chairman of the penetration. Mr. Chapman also became the first outsider to be invited to join the parent company's board in Tokyo.

In a March 1991 interview with *The New York Times'* Tokyo correspondent James Sterngold, Nomura's Tabuchi was quite frank about the challenge that faced Nomura in the 1990s:

> Over the years, we may have overemphasized the positive side of all the changes taking place. There was a relatively small amount of discussion of the negative side, the limits that we would face. . . ."

Determining how to best capitalize on Nomura's enormous strengths and avoid the pitfalls of such a rapidly changing domestic and international market was an obvious priority for the firm's top management during the 1990s.

▶ Endnotes

1. The material in this first section has been drawn largely from *Beyond the Ivied Mountain: The Origin and Growth of a Japanese Securities House, Nomura: 1872–1985* (Tokyo: The Nomura Securities Co., Ltd., 1986). See also Hayes and Hubbard, "Investment Banking: A Tale of Three Cities" (Boston: Harvard Business School Press, 1989).

2. It was later renamed the Daiwa Bank (no relation to the present-day Daiwa Securities Company).

3. The ryo was an ancient Japanese unit of currency. The expression "I'd like to have a million ryo" was commonly used to indicate an ambition to be wealthy.

4. An ADR is a certificate, denominated in dollars, and traded in the United States that represents a specific number of shares of a non-U.S. company, denominated in a foreign currency and traded in the overseas market. The foreign shares underlying the ADR, while not actually traded, are normally held in trust by either an overseas or U.S. bank.

5. Roughly equivalent to the NASDAQ over-the-counter market in the United States.

6. In 1990, securities commissions accounted for 41% of Nomura's global revenues (see Exhibit 1) compared to 15% for Merrill Lynch and 2% for Salomon Brothers.

7. Referred to as "middies" because they were typically middle-aged housewives who took on the job to supplement the family income.

8. Its capital was almost double that of second-place Daiwa Securities and four and one-half times as large as that of Merrill Lynch. Capital-to-assets was roughly 30% for Nomura and only about 7% for Merrill Lynch.

Exhibit 1

Consolidated Income Statements, 1984–1990 (¥ millions and U.S. $ millions except per-share figures)

	1984	1985	1986	1987	1988	1989[a,b]	1990	1990[b]
REVENUES								
Commissions	¥212,480	¥275,694	¥503,651	¥ 583,253	¥459,031	¥269,119	¥ 489,033	$3,217
Underwriting and distribution	55,141	82,042	106,476	176,452	184,872	94,512	277,133	1,823
Net gain on trading	58,664	86,301	138,365	128,998	135,000	107,089	141,033	928
Interest and dividends	107,071	142,500	191,046	176,494	173,128	111,408	286,548	1,885
Other	3,599	3,058	2,026	7,810	7,764	2,538	7,518	50
	436,955	589,595	941,564	1,073,007	959,795	584,666	1,201,265	7,903
EXPENSES								
Compensation and benefits	89,109	100,539	115,480	137,055	144,419	75,033	148,931	980
Commissions/floor brokerage	11,558	16,700	20,124	24,205	19,215	10,349	28,459	187
Communications	11,000	11,907	13,773	16,436	19,025	9,705	20,932	138
Interest	60,873	90,987	127,649	98,412	85,485	59,508	161,536	1,063
Rental and maintenance	21,775	24,837	26,745	30,364	34,504	19,071	42,451	279
Advertising and publicity	6,791	5,425	7,496	10,902	9,878	5,447	10,937	72
Taxes other than income taxes	18,005	25,656	39,466	75,284	67,158	41,072	58,046	382
Other operating expenses	53,667	63,957	95,122	96,822	109,446	63,363	140,897	927
	272,778	340,008	445,855	489,480	489,130	283,548	612,189	4,028
Income before taxes	164,177	249,587	495,709	583,527	470,665	301,118	589,076	3,875
Income taxes	91,106	138,691	274,853	315,437	256,528	163,588	312,956	2,059
Net income	73,071	110,896	220,856	268,090	214,137	137,530	276,120	1,816
Net income per 1,000 shares	42,711	64,324	118,070	141,613	112,024	71,782	141,160	929
Dividends per 1,000 shares	7,209	7,824	9,737	12,211	13,132	7,254	15,024	99

[a]In 1989, the fiscal year was changed from 9/30 to 3/31. These are six-month figures.
[b]Exchange rate translation at ¥152 = US$1.

Source: Moody's Bank and Finance Manual; company annual report, 1990.

Exhibit 2

Consolidated Balance Sheets, 1984–1990 (¥ millions and U.S. $ millions)

	1984	1985	1986	1987	1988	1989[a,b]	1990	1990[b]
ASSETS								
Cash	¥ 83,144	¥ 69,166	¥ 116,057	¥ 66,635	¥ 82,989	¥ 233,893	¥ 122,209	$ 804
Time deposits	358,017	534,137	544,732	827,667	1,004,207	928,476	1,076,313	7,081
Deposits related to securities transactions	25,309	38,248	41,884	75,118	62,960	69,289	80,264	528
Lease deposits	44,983	45,941	51,348	59,495	68,256	72,689	84,369	555
Loans and receivables	558,374	560,385	906,855	1,299,387	1,466,653	1,549,321	2,357,457	15,510
Securities owned	389,743	827,398	1,136,848	988,208	1,112,822	1,264,608	1,805,849	11,881
Investments	—	—	—	—	185,517	229,219	289,885	1,907
Affiliated companies	6,305	4,214	3,710	10,756	24,439	24,943	26,001	171
Net properties, plant and equipment	35,605	41,317	47,911	64,708	79,648	91,381	101,098	665
Other assets	40,142	57,020	77,144	93,696	119,100	137,663	216,847	1,428
Total	1,541,622	2,177,826	2,926,489	3,485,670	4,206,591	4,601,482	6,160,292	40,528
LIABILITIES								
Bank loans	217,219	281,416	189,995	215,397	221,692	258,574	499,930	3,289
Other loans, bonds, etc.	217,859	400,563	484,820	570,446	794,533	874,778	1,366,405	8,990
Customer deposits	259,589	313,482	481,704	516,694	620,958	601,690	881,113	5,797
Other accounts payable	206,565	391,764	629,825	792,518	961,494	971,063	1,222,345	8,042
Accruals	106,900	153,879	304,718	281,180	296,601	330,760	323,724	2,130
Stockholders' equity	533,490	636,722	835,427	1,109,435	1,311,313	1,564,617	1,866,775	12,280
Total	1,541,622	2,177,826	2,926,489	3,485,670	4,206,591	4,601,482	6,160,292	40,528

[a]In 1989, the fiscal year was changed from 9/30 to 3/31. These are six-month figures.

[b]Exchange rate translation at ¥152 = US$1.

Source: Moody's Bank and Finance Manual; company annual report, 1990.

The Nomura Securities Company, Ltd. (B)

Nomura Securities, the largest of the "Big Four" Japanese securities firms (see *The Nomura Securities Co.* [*A*]), had a longer presence in the United States than any of its Japanese competitors. It had seen its New York-based operations grow from a handful of people to more than 500 employees at the beginning of the 1990s. But, while the operations of its U.S. subsidiary, Nomura Securities International, Inc., (hereinafter called Nomura [U.S.]) were profitable and had supported some of the elements of the firm's global strategy, Nomura had not as yet achieved its objective of becoming a wide-ranging competitor in the domestic U.S. securities marketplace, the largest such national marketplace in the world. Management was considering what strategy it should pursue in order to achieve those domestic U.S. objectives and to this end, had just put in charge of its U.S. operations, Max C. Chapman, Jr.,—an American with an impeccable investment banking background.[1]

U.S. Operations

Nomura's post-World War II American operations, dating back to 1953, were originally involved with facilitating the importation into Japan of capital through the sale of Japanese securities to foreign investors. However, because most of these sales went through London or Hong Kong, one senior manager at Nomura (U.S.) labeled the early New York operations as merely a "tourist bureau." It was not until the mid-1980s that the American subsidiary was positioned to play a substantial role in Nomura's global aspirations.

The Federal Reserve's designation in 1986 of both Nomura and Daiwa Securities as primary dealers in government securities was an important Japanese breakthrough and marked a first major business penetration of the Japanese securities firms into the United States. Nomura's New York operations grew rapidly from under 200 employees in 1986 to a peak of over 600 in late 1987. By early 1988, however, total employment at Nomura (U.S.) had fallen to about 500 through attrition and layoffs, in reaction to the crash of 1987. This is a level which exists to the present day.

An important goal for Nomura—and for the dozen or so other Japanese secu-

---

This case was prepared by Professor Samuel L. Hayes, III.
Copyright © 1991 by the President and Fellows of Harvard College. Harvard Business School case N9-291-036.

rities firms with New York operations, including the other Big Four—was to Americanize operations by hiring U.S. professionals. The Japanese term for this, "dochaku-ka," is roughly translated as "becoming deeply rooted" or "homesteading." At Nomura (U.S.), only about 12 percent of the staff in 1988 represented Japanese who were on loan from the Tokyo office, and the percentage had fallen from over 20 percent just a few years before. Presently, however, roughly 10% and 60% of senior management and department heads positions, respectively, were held by Japanese personnel. Daiwa had earlier achieved a similar ratio, although Nikko, Yamaichi, and some smaller firms had a comparatively larger percentage of Japanese in New York. One senior executive at Nomura (U.S.) stated a belief that only after his firm had become a truly American securities firm, with a substantial business in U.S. securities with U.S. issuers and investors, would the parent Nomura be able to achieve its goal of becoming a globally preeminent investment bank.

Despite Nomura's success in Japan and in the Euromarkets, New York was still considered the weak link in its global network. Until mid-1989, Masaaki Kurokawa, the head of Nomura (U.S.), had talked about increasing the contribution from New York to Nomura's profits, estimated at only about 4 percent of Nomura's 1990 worldwide total. To do this, he noted, "We aim to be a solid member of the Wall Street Clan!"[2] Until recently, the U.S. operation had relied primarily on the strength of its U.S. government-bond sales to Japanese investors. However, former Nomura (U.S.) chairman, Yoshio Terasawa, noting that the firm did not want to get stuck as a niche player, once commented, "We don't want to be a Japanese restaurant in New York serving only sushi and sukiyaki."[3]

Throughout the mid-1980s and up until the crash of October 1987, equity sales and trading grew in importance for the New York firm. By the late 1980s, Nomura (U.S.) derived about 50 percent of its revenues from the sales and trading of fixed-income securities, 10 percent from the sales and trading of equity securities, and 10 percent from investment banking. Although officials at Nomura (U.S.) stated that all three areas were equally targeted for expansion, Nomura appeared especially sensitive to the underweighting of investment banking revenues. The following sections discuss the various operations of Nomura (U.S.) in more detail.

Treasury Securities

Sales and trading of U.S. Treasuries, especially with Japanese investors, were the most important targeted growth areas for Nomura (U.S.) beginning in the mid-1980s. Following the repeal of U.S. withholding taxes in 1984, and Nomura's success in selling Treasury issues within Japan, the firm made a major commitment to this market that culminated in primary-dealer status in 1986. Starting with only a handful of sales people, a U.S. government-securities dealing operation had been put in place that, by the late 1980s, comprised about a dozen traders and over 20 salespeople. The present head of this group, Thomas Gribbon, and the majority of staff were Americans. Sales and trading of U.S. government bonds in the recent past had contributed three-quarters of the revenues from fixed-income sales and trading, or about 35 percent of the U.S. operation's total revenues.

The Big Four Japanese firms had at times accounted for roughly 20 percent of the $100-billion-per-day, long-term U.S. government-bond secondary-market turnover.[4] Although officially kept as nonpublic information, Nomura's market share had been believed to be well above the 3/4 percent minimum share required by the Federal Reserve for primary dealership. Some observers estimated that at times in the past, Nomura had ranked 15 out of the then roughly 40 primary dealers in terms of transaction volume. Further, Nomura (U.S.) reportedly had in the past won as much as 10 percent of some auctions of new U.S. government bonds.[5]

At first, most of this business was in selling 10- and 30-year Treasury bonds to Japanese institutions. However, with Japanese participation crucial at U.S. Treasury auctions, U.S. institutions began to contact Nomura to get the Japanese investor's perspective on the Treasury market before making their own moves. As a consequence, by the late 1980s, one source estimated that as much as 75 percent of the Japanese Big Four's government-bond transactions in New York were with major U.S. investors compared to less than one-third barely two years before.[6] With Nomura and Daiwa Securities battling neck and neck in this market, it was not clear who would be the winner. Some observers believed that, despite Nomura's tremendous capital backing and investor franchise in Tokyo, its network of institutional investors in the United States lagged behind that of Daiwa.[7]

To avoid problems with profit allocation, Nomura historically maintained separate dealing books in New York, Tokyo, and London. Unlike some other global investment banks, particularly some of the American firms, there was no single integrated book (or portfolio of outstanding securities positions) encompassing the profits and losses on U.S. Treasuries trading worldwide on a 24-hour basis. Instead, each Nomura location passed its book to the next location with strict instructions for defensive trading. For example, when the New York market closed, Tokyo watched over the American subsidiary's positions, mindful of the New York desk's established loss limits for various positions; it used only the Tokyo book for its own market-making activities. The Tokyo book was so large that several traders from the home office were stationed in New York just to trade Tokyo's positions during the American work day.

One important ingredient in Nomura's success with U.S. government bonds may have been the high quality of its professional staff, including some well-known experts from the Street and government. For example, Nomura (U.S.) had been able to recruit John J. Neihenke, the former deputy assistant secretary of the Treasury who handled U.S. Treasury auctions, for Nomura's sales force. However, other Japanese firms in the United States had also attracted top names. Scott E. Pardee, a vice chairman at Yamaichi, was formerly with the New York Federal Reserve Bank. Nikko vice chairman Stephen H. Axilrod had been the Fed's staff director under Paul Volker. And Mary R. Clarkin, as Nikko's bond-sales manager, was formerly the New York Fed's chief domestic-securities trader. Nomura was quick to add that it did not "buy" talent. On the contrary, many of its stars were hired at relatively low guaranteed salaries, but with higher potential earnings from bonuses and commissions than they had been paid by their former employers.

Nomura (U.S.) believed it had a unique compensation system for securities firms that encouraged the cooperation of bond traders and sales people. Traders were paid a salary plus bonus, determined by departmentwide profits. The wrinkle was, however, that the traders took home only two-thirds of their bonus—the rest was paid over to the sales staff. The sales staff were paid on straight commission, but one-third of this was also withheld and given to the traders. It was hoped that the mix would enhance the chances of success of future marketing efforts for product-line extensions, such as T-bills and derivative products (including bond futures and options), targeted at U.S. institutional investors as well as central banks in Central and South America.

Other Fixed-Income Securities

In addition to U.S. government securities, Nomura (U.S.) was actively involved in the sales and trading of a wide range of other fixed-income securities, contributing perhaps another 15 percent of its total revenues. In the past, a dozen professionals, only one of whom was Japanese, traded U.S. and Canadian corporate bonds, Eurodollar bonds, mortgage-backed securities, Japanese government bonds, and Euroyen bonds. The same sales staff that handled U.S. Treasuries also sold these other fixed-income products, mostly to U.S. institutions.

Nomura's U.S. corporate bond-trading business, a relatively small operation that had been developed only recently, began to be profitable by the late 1980s. A big push was underway into mortgage-backed sales and trading, because Nomura had fallen behind Daiwa as the first Japanese securities firm to venture into this area. Also, Nomura (U.S.) was considering expanding its coverage to include municipal bonds and medium-term notes. To handle the growth in fixed-income securities business, Nomura (U.S.) planned to double its current sales and trading staff over the next few years. Fixed income derivatives, such as interest rate futures and options were also being added to their offered services.[8]

Equity Securities Sales and Trading

Equity sales, including selling Japanese stocks to U.S. investors and American stocks to both Japanese and U.S. investors, was an increasingly important growth area for Nomura (U.S.)—at least until the October 1987 market crash. A strong point for Nomura (U.S.) had always been selling Japanese stocks to U.S. investors, contributing historically about 30 percent of the New York operation's total revenues. Nomura (U.S.) estimated that it controlled about half of all Japanese equities sold by the Big Four securities houses in the United States. However, these revenue flows were still low compared to London, where there were more internationally oriented portfolios. In the United States, Nomura contacted about 90 institutions per day, while the London office had over 300 on its call list. Eventually, as U.S. portfolio managers became more international, this business was expected to grow.

In contrast, Nomura's (U.S.) sales of U.S. equities to both Japanese and U.S. institutions was estimated to represent only about 10% of total revenues but was considered a potential hot new growth area. Nomura estimated in the past that its share of the trading on the NYSE was normally 1/2–1% about the same as the American firm Merrill Lynch had on the TSE. On certain days, Nomura (U.S)'s share was considerably larger because of its involvement in "macho trading" of million-share blocks to execute dividend capture strategies for some of its Japanese customers.[9]

Nomura (U.S.) believed at that time that it controlled 20–25% of the Japanese capital flowing into U.S. equities, with the other major Japanese securities firms and some American investment banks with strong Tokyo operations handling the rest.

The equity sales staff increased from just over 10 in 1986 to over 50 by 1989; most of the growth reflected the emphasis on the sale of U.S. equities to U.S. institutions. Nine Japanese sales people sold U.S. equities to Japan. Another group of nine professionals was involved in selling Japanese securities to U.S. investors.

All position trading was done through the dozen or so traders located in New York, the majority of whom were Americans, though department heads tended to be Japanese.[10] Nomura (U.S.), having first obtained a seat on the Boston Stock Exchange in 1970, gained a coveted seat on the New York Stock Exchange in 1981.

By the early 1990s, Nomura (U.S.) had expanded its exchange memberships to include the American and Pacific Stock Exchanges, the two major futures markets in Chicago, and New York Futures Exchange, the Chicago Board of Trade, the Chicago Mercantile, the Midwest Stock Exchange, the National Association of Security Dealers, and the Philadelphia Stock Exchange.

The real emphasis for the future, the New York office believed, would be in selling U.S. equities to U.S institutional investors. Yoshitaka Yamashita, executive vice president who at one point was in charge of equities at the U.S. operations, hoped "to capture five to six percent of the U.S. institutional equity business by 1990, up from a minor share today."[11] Nomura, he believed, was in an excellent position to capitalize on the large volume of the flow of two-way deals between the United States and Japan. American investors would be interested in dealing with Nomura (U.S.) primarily to learn the appetite of Japan for U.S. equities. Also, with its trans-Pacific connections, Nomura was often able to arrange large block trades (that is, large institutional-investor transactions, usually in excess of 10,000 shares) between U.S. and Japanese institutions.

Another potential advantage for Nomura (U.S.) in dealing with American investors was its international equity research, a part of Nomura Research Institute, formed in 1965 as a think tank along the lines of the Stanford Research Institute. Five Japanese analysts initially followed about 120 blue-chip U.S. firms in several industries and prepared reports for Japanese investors in a format familiar and comfortable to them. Another eight analysts, all American, reported on selected U.S. firms and supported the equity sales effort to U.S. institutions. Nomura was selective in its industry coverage, following companies in industries where Japan had a particular strength, such as the automotive, banking, electronics, and telecommunications fields.

Expanding this business had proven a difficult task, however.[12] First, Nomura was in tough competition with the other Japanese firms, especially Daiwa. Further, the Japanese selling effort in the United States had to overcome an unfavorable reputation that lingered from the early days. In the past, U.S. institutional clients were often put off by what was sometimes characterized as Nomura's "hucksterism." One U.S. fund manager commented, "Nomura's research is workmanlike, but its salesmen are incompetent. I keep telling them they can't talk to us as though we were a retail customer in Yokohama. We're not interested in the stock of the week."[13] This statement echoed the often heard criticism that foreign securities firms in the United States, including the Japanese, had, in some cases, been burdened with second-rate talent that had not been able to make the grade at premier American firms.

Underwriting

Despite a remarkable success in the Euromarkets, where it retained a number one ranking in 1990 for the fourth straight year, Nomura had been able to make only limited headway in investment banking activities in the United States. Furthermore, although it maintained its Euromarket lead, its market share was slashed almost in half to less than 9% in 1990. At the end of the 1980s, Nomura's New York investment banking staff numbered about 50 professionals, roughly a threefold increase from the 1984 levels. About 18 corporate finance specialists, of which four were Japanese, called on U.S. corporations and public sector enterprises in search of business. Another six, five of whom were Japanese, worked with the U.S. subsidiaries of Japanese firms. In addition, the investment banking group included syndication, merger-and-acquisitions, new products, and swap professionals. Corporate finance professionals covered the top 200 U.S. companies. With a planned doubling of its corporate finance staff over the next few years, Nomura (U.S.) at that time stated a hope to be able eventually to call on the entire *Fortune 500*. More recently, however, Chairman Chapman expressed a preference to especially target mid-sized U.S. companies with a global expansion potential.[14]

Nomura, however, had barely made a dent in the domestic U.S. underwriting-league tables. It was a co-manager for 140 underwritings in 1990, moving up from a rank of 21 in 1989 to 14 in 1990. Although most of the issues it co-managed in the early and mid-1980s were for Japanese firms or their U.S. subsidiaries, by the late 1980s Nomura (U.S.) had become involved in deals for several major borrowers such as General Electric and the Federal Home Loan Mortgage Corporation as well as several U.S. utility firms. Unlike in the Euromarket, U.S. investment banks did not feel the need to invite Nomura (U.S.) into domestic offerings as co-managers. Rather, Nomura usually was only a syndicate member, albeit as a "major-bracket" participant, a real step up from the past. What Nomura brought to these deals was Japanese distribution: normally, half its syndicate allocation was sold in Japan.

The fact that Nomura had captured only one lead management—that for General Electric Credit Corporation (GECC) in the fall of 1986—was at that time a sore point with top management in Tokyo. And other participants alleged unusually aggressive price undercutting in the deal with GECC. The then head of investment banking at Nomura (U.S.) admitted, "There were about 10 basic points between our bid and the next one. It took us a month to sell, and half of it went to Japan. We took a loss on it."[15] In addition to the problem of establishing relationships with U.S. borrowers, Nomura also had to overcome an earlier perception by many market participants that it lacked creativity and innovativeness. "Their product scope is limited. They're pretty provincial," quipped another competitor.[16]

Still, Nomura continued with the advantage of being able to place what many considered to be very leanly priced securities with its relatively unsophisticated and cash-heavy retail customers in Japan. As one U.S. investment banker once complained, "Nomura was the single largest institution with the dumbest customers. And they're using their customers to subsidize their entry into international corporate finance."[17] But Nomura was not the only firm to be criticized in this respect. Daiwa, in its first U.S. domestic-bond underwriting for Rockwell, faced basically the same circumstances.[18]

Nomura's performance in equity underwriting was even less spectacular. The co-management with Goldman, Sachs of a 1986 initial public offering (IPO) for EXAR, the California subsidiary of a Japanese firm, was its first success. In 1987, it was co-manager, with L.F. Rothschild Unterberg Towbin, of a small $3.8 million IPO for Plant Genetics, a U.S. firm.

The strategy for the corporate finance group was to try to leverage off Nomura's impressive Eurobond and samurai bond (foreign bonds denominated in Japanese yen) underwriting successes to establish relations with U.S. companies and win U.S. domestic underwriting mandates. Another technique used in relationship-building was to get American firms to list their stock on the Tokyo Stock Exchange. By the end of 1987, Nomura had sponsored 36 of the 88 listed American companies. Still, it was not clear how long—if ever—it would take before Nomura's New York operation would regularly get the nod from U.S. corporations to lead-manage domestic issues. Within Nomura, the possibility of acquiring a well-established U.S. firm with strong origination business had been mentioned, and there had been rumors in the past of preliminary talks between Nomura and both E.F. Hutton and Kidder, Peabody, prior to their acquisitions by Shearson Lehman and General Electric, respectively.

Real Estate

As a small nation with a dense population, Japan commanded some of the highest real estate prices on earth. In view of its stratospheric property prices, it is little wonder that cash-rich Japanese investors were drawn to the U.S. real estate market. Properties in New York, San Francisco, and Los Angeles—whose prices made even free-spending Americans blanch—were inviting to Tokyo's investors. The continuing strength of the yen made them even more appealing.

Real estate had been a growth business area within Nomura's investment banking operations. In 1987, for instance, it handled Japanese purchases of U.S. real estate of about $10 billion. As Japanese money increasingly poured in, such famous landmarks as the Tiffany building in Manhattan were bought. Nomura (U.S.) entered the leveraged leasing and real estate business in the United States in 1986 by entering into a cooperative agreement with Babcock and Brown, a U.S.-based leveraged leasing specialist. Then in 1986, it acquired a 50 percent stake in Eastdil, a premier real estate finance firm of the 1970s, for $50 million. In this venture, Nomura brought to the table a strong capital base in addition to contacts with Japanese investors, while Eastdil had the ability to design imaginative financing techniques. If the partnership remained amiable, observers thought that Eastdil could leap once again into the forefront of real estate finance along-side the American investment banks.

Mergers and Acquisitions

The merger and acquisitions team, which at Nomura was referred to as the corporate strategy and services group, was a small part of the investment banking group. Three professionals—two Japanese and one American—worked closely with the corporate finance officers calling on Japanese corporations in Tokyo and at the U.S. offices of their U.S. subsidiaries. Nomura had not been involved in any American-style hostile takeover, preferring to work with Japanese companies who, particularly with a strong currency, were casting their nets for friendly acquisitions, licensing arrangements, and joint ventures in the United States.

Japanese financial institutions, including Nomura, were latecomers to the M&A field for several reasons. Merger and acquisitions were much smaller in Japan than in the United States and represented a radically different service matrix.[19] Historically, counsel and assistance in this area had been provided free by the commercial banks, the traditional financial advisers to the Japanese companies. Hostile takeovers just were not done. In the international arena, Japanese companies traditionally preferred to build up overseas operations from scratch rather than acquire existing operations in order to avoid buying troubled, over-priced companies. With the accumulation of experience in operating foreign environments, this reticence to acquire had only recently begun to change, thereby offering potential opportunities to the Japanese securities firms.

Although a couple of Japanese commercial banks, Sanwa Bank and Long-Term Credit Bank, had taken an early lead in assisting Japanese companies investing in U.S. firms, the securities houses, including Nomura, were determined to leap to the forefront. In 1988, Nikko Securities purchased a minority interest in Blackstone Group (a Lehman Brothers spinoff), and Yamaichi securities purchased a similar interest in Lodestone Group, a boutique started by a former senior merger and acquisition banker from Merrill Lynch. For its part, Nomura tied in with Wasserstein, Perella.

The Wasserstein Perella Deal

In August 1988, Nomura announced the purchase for $100 million of a 20 percent equity interest in a new start-up mergers and acquisitions boutique, Wasserstein, Perella. Bruce Wasserstein and Joseph Perella were both Harvard Business School graduates who, as co-heads, had catapulted First Boston into a leading role in the lucrative and rapidly growing mergers and corporate-restructurings area. Disgruntled in part by First Boston's tolerance for large losses in the trading area, and convinced that the appropriate strategy for a firm with First Boston's profile was to fortify a specialized niche position in the global M&A area, they resigned from First Boston in December 1987 and within a few weeks hung out their "Wasserstein, Perella" shingle (soon jocularly referred to in the industry as "Wasserella"), with the intent of implementing their M&A boutique strategic concept.

Because both men had high public profiles and personal followings that were unusual even by Wall Street standards, they were able to get off to a running start by signing up some impressive companies for monthly retainers in exchange for M&A and strategy counseling. Within a few months, they closed their first billion dollar leveraged buyout. But because their initial equity was small, without a big partner they were limited in their ability to exploit the corporate-restructuring investment opportunities that were coming their way.

They talked with a number of potential outside capital sources and, not surprisingly, their quest took them to Tokyo. They quickly learned that it had been a mistake to have printed their Japanese-language calling cards identifying themselves as "securities brokers." It was made clear to them that in Japan, stockbrokers were historically identified with shady business practices. They made out much better with new cards explicitly associating themselves with M&A activity, which was then attracting a great deal of favorable interest in the Japanese financial and business community.

Their resultant deal with Nomura, which placed a total value of some $500 million on "Wasserella" after only a few months in business, caused a sensation in international investment banking circles. There was active speculation as to just how the two parties intended to collaborate to realize benefits from the hookup, which included jointly owned subsidiaries in Tokyo and London to service the M&A potential in those regions. From Wasserstein and Perella's viewpoint, the benefits were obvious: an enormous infusion of capital, a spectacular "market" valuation for the firm, and a partner with very deep pockets and the muscle to open doors in the Far East and elsewhere.

From Nomura's perspective, immediate payoffs would likely come from shared U.S. and foreign M&A deals and the opportunity for both the parent and the Nomura (U.S.) organizations to edge into the potentially lucrative merchant banking business as co-venturers with Wasserstein, Perella.

The Talent Challenge

More than almost any industry, the securities business runs on human energy and talent. Because its products are intangible, the output of a securities firm's human resources is paramount. It is in this area that Nomura and other Japanese firms faced their greatest challenge. For all their success in product development, management, manufacturing, and foreign trade, Japan's corporations had not been notably effective in reproducing clones of themselves on foreign soil. As management consultant and observer Kenichi Ohmae had noted, the failure of Japan's overseas subsidiaries to fully empower their indigenous talent—always reserving key decision-making authority for native Japanese—constituted a major roadblock to successful internationalization.[20] Nowhere, perhaps, was this challenge greater than in the international securities industry.

The cultures of Wall Street and Japan's securities firms could not be more different. Wall Street was practically a caricature of American frontier values, strangely transported through time and space to the canyons of Manhattan. Its youthful gunslinger traders and investment bankers brashly confronted each other across the deal table, confident of success and rewards that pushed the limits of common sense. Talent was for hire. In recent years, personal allegiance was to one's craft, not to a firm. This ambience was a far cry from the culture of Japan's security industry, which, like that nation's corporate mentality in general, honored the virtues of teamwork, subordination of individual agendas to those of the group, a get-rich-slowly attitude, and the "good soldier."

With so much of Nomura's future strategy in the United States dependent on the quality of its professional staff, the firm took measures to strengthen its human resources management. Stan Lomax, an American, was hired early in 1986 from a competing U.S. investment bank to establish a human resources department. According to Lomax, Nomura, even at that early date, gave him considerable freedom to establish policies that were appropriate in New York but at odds with those in Tokyo. More significantly, in early 1990, Nomura welcomed Max C. Chapman, who had had a remarkable career in investment banking in the United States, as co-chairman of Nomura (U.S.). Also, in a history-setting precedent, he was invited to join the parent company's board in Tokyo.

Salary, bonus, and commission arrangements that were competitive in New York contrasted sharply with lower pay, primarily in the form of salaries, for Japanese professionals both in Tokyo and on temporary assignment in New York. It was difficult to get a handle on these differences, however, since the Japanese in New York were paid housing allowances and other perks for living abroad. Nomura, along with the other Japanese securities firms, rationalized these differences by emphasizing the employment guarantees implicit for Japanese professionals. In fact, the layoffs at Nomura (U.S.) in early 1988 affected only Americans. (When Nikko Securities and Sumitomo Bank made earlier similar decisions to lay off Americans in New York, fired employees filed a class-action suit against them, charging discrimination.) But the pay differentials did not go unnoticed. Several of Nomura's key Japanese professionals in New York, who were suspected of resenting the higher earnings of their American counterparts, defected to American competitors, where they were offered top jobs with the Tokyo offices of Morgan Stanley and Merrill Lynch. Over time, Nomura believed that salaries for the Japanese would rise. In fact, Yoshihisa Tabuchi, the president of the parent Nomura in Tokyo, publicly admitted that he expected some employees in the future to earn more than he did—quite a radical concession for a Japanese firm that historically based pay on seniority.

At the same time, many American employees of the Japanese securities firms had regularly complained of limited autonomy and excessive direction from Tokyo. Nomura's New York subsidiary was hurt by the resignation of 34 Ameri-

▼ ■

can traders, analysts, and salespeople in 1986 and 1987 over disputes involving pay and differing U.S. and Japanese management styles.[21]

Perhaps the greatest personnel problem facing Nomura and all Japanese securities firms in the United States had been the nationality and tenure of senior management. There was a certain lack of continuity of senior management sent from Japan. Japanese management in most Japanese firms usually came from Tokyo or other overseas posts on assignments of three to six years. Nomura's normal overseas posting for a Japanese executive was at the short end of that range— about three years. When Terasawa, the former head of the New York operation, was replaced in late 1986, there was some hope within the firm that he would be succeeded by an American. But, for reasons that were never made clear, he was not. As one ex-employee of a Japanese securities house commented, "Even if you get on marvelously with the present regime, you just don't know who's coming through the door the next time." In that light, the appointment of Max Chapman as co-chairman in 1990 was seen as an important step forward.

Conclusion

Nomura was determined to succeed as a player in the U.S. financial marketplace. While New York had declined in relative importance as the capital markets had become increasingly global, it seemed destined to remain an important source of financing business for the foreseeable future. The question was: how to position Nomura so as to best capitalize on its strengths and avoid the pitfalls of its weaknesses?

▶ Endnotes

1. "Can Chapman Build U.S. Presence for Japan's Nomura?" *Wall Street Journal*, May 14, 1990, p. C1.

2. "Yen Power: Nomura Flexes its Global Financial Muscle," *Time*, August 8, 1988, p. 46.

3. *The Wall Street Journal*, April 1, 1987, p. 1.

4. "Japan on Wall Street," *Business Week*, September 7, 1987, p. 82.

5. Bernard Wysocki, Jr., "Big Dealer: Tough Japanese Firm Grows in Importance in Securities Markets," *The Wall Street Journal*, April 1, 1987, p. 1.

6. "Japan on Wall Street," p. 84.

7. "Nomura's Three Major Japanese Rivals," *The Wall Street Journal*, April 1, 1987, p. 24.

8. The Nomura Securities Co., Ltd., Annual Report 1990, p. 4.

9. For a time, Japanese institutions, particularly insurance companies, were keen to receive the high current income from dividends, since such funds had special advantages for their own dividend-paying programs. Therefore, they bought high-yielding U.S. stocks on the dividend date of record, with firm agreements to resell them immediately when the stock went ex-dividend.

10. Securities Industry Yearbook, p. 528, Securities Industry Association, New York, N.Y.

11. "Foreign Firms Are Easier to Capture Bigger Chunk of U.S. Equity Market," *The Wall Street Journal*, February 16, 1988, p 51.

12. "Can Chapman Build U.S. Presence for Japan's Nomura?" *Wall Street Journal*, May 14, 1990, p. C1.

13. Lee Smith, "Japan's Brokerage Giant Goes International," *Fortune*, March 19, 1984, p. 70.

14. Ibid.

15. "Investments Flood Into U.S. Markets," *Euromoney Special Supplement*, September 1987, p. 38.

16. "Mighty Nomura Tries to Muscle in on Wall Street," *Business Week*, December 16, 1985, p. 76.

17. Ibid., p. 77.

18. "Investments Flood Into U.S. Markets," *Euromoney Special Supplement*, September 1987, p. 38.

19. "Mergers and Acquisitions in Key National Markets," *Mergers & Acquisitions*, July/August 1987, p. 58.

20. Kenichi Ohmae, *Beyond National Borders: Reflections on Japan and the World* (Homewood, Ill: Dow Jones-Irwin, 1987).

21. "It Won't Stop with the Shearson Deal," *Business Week*, April 6, 1987, p. 36.

PART 2

Entering New Markets

Morgan Stanley: The Tokyo Branch

John Wadsworth, managing director, prepared for his new responsibilities as head of investment banking at the Tokyo office of Morgan Stanley, beginning in September 1987. He, and the other managing directors, would have to manage further growth at the office, which already had grown from fewer than 20 employees only five years ago to over 440. Even more important, these managers faced the task of determining what kind of business Morgan Stanley would ultimately conduct in Japan. Luckily, there was no immediate problem to be solved; yet the management team in Tokyo needed to make a general strategic assessment of both the risks and the opportunities for Morgan Stanley in Tokyo. This assessment had to be consistent with the notion of a global financial network envisioned by the management committee in New York.

In Japan, it was obvious that foreign and domestic securities firms played very different roles. And even within the group of foreign firms, there were noticeable differences. Some foreign firms used their Tokyo offices mostly as centers for gathering information and helping their clients do business in Japan. Others were attempting to carve a niche for themselves in particular areas of the Japanese market by, for example, trying to enter the Japanese government bond market.

Wadsworth and the Tokyo management team realized that Morgan Stanley planned to be a broadly based investment bank in Japan, with a commitment to play a significant role in the Japanese domestic market. If the firm were to continue growing, the managing directors would have to decide which markets appeared most promising and which invited their efforts. The exact role which any foreign firm—in particular, Morgan Stanley—could play in a financial market that had long been closed to non-Japanese, first by regulation and later by custom, remained unclear. But somehow the traditional strengths of Morgan Stanley had to be used as stepping stones to achieve additional success in Japan. Only such a resolution could give practical meaning to the firm's professed goal of becoming a leading global investment bank.

This case was prepared by Assistant Professor David M. Meerschwam.
Copyright © 1987 by the President and Fellows of Harvard College. Harvard Business School case 9-288-024.

Morgan Stanley

Morgan Stanley Group Inc. is a publicly held holding company, headquartered in New York, with international offices in London, Tokyo, Frankfurt, Melbourne, Sydney, Toronto, and Zurich, and several regional offices in the U.S. At the end of 1986, the firm employed approximately 5,300 persons; total assets stood at $29.2 billion; long-term debt was $381 million, and total equity $798 million. Net income stood at $210 million (eps of $8.42) after $695 million paid out in compensation and benefits. Of the firm's revenues (net of interest expense) of $1.4 billion, 46% was generated by investment banking, 33% through principal transactions, 15% through commissions, and 6% through other activities.

The activities of Morgan Stanley are organized into six divisions: (1) Investment Banking, (2) Equities, (3) Taxable Fixed Income, (4) Tax-Exempt Fixed Income, (5) Asset Management, and (6) Finance, Administration, and Operations.

The Investment Banking Division provides advice to, and raises capital worldwide for, domestic and international clients through underwriting various types of securities. In 1986, financial advisory activities (dominated by the Mergers and Acquisitions group) contributed 62% of the total revenues of the division (71% in 1985). Underwriting fees accounted for the remaining 38% (29% in 1985). Total Investment Banking revenue was $656 million in 1986. Morgan Stanley often entered new product areas through the Investment Banking Division. In 1982, it entered the Commercial Paper market, and, in 1984, the mortgage-backed securities business and short- and medium-term notes in the Euromarkets.

Equities, Taxable Fixed Income, and Tax-Exempt Fixed Income transactions are made through sales and trading, supported by research activities. Morgan Stanley enters into both principal and agent transactions. In 1986, principal transactions generated revenues of $473 million, while commissions in agency transactions produced revenues of $216 million. Inventories of securities, required for sales and trading, are held by Morgan Stanley and marked-to-market. Gains and losses on these inventories are attributed to principal transactions. Apart from direct trading for its own account, Morgan Stanley also contains a risk arbitrage group. Since 1983, the firm has been active in foreign exchange transactions. It entered the Commodities markets in 1985.

Equity sales and trading in the U.S. are carried out by approximately 350 salesmen and traders. Fixed-income trades and sales are separated into taxable and tax-exempt. Within the taxable group, Morgan Stanley is one of 36 primary dealers in U.S. government securities. Also, in 1984, the firm had entered the "high-yield" fixed-income market. After an initial embarrassment when OXOCO Inc.—one of Morgan Stanley's first high-yield underwritten issues—defaulted after six months, the firm renewed its commitment to this area and remained active in the market.

Asset Management, which had produced revenues of less than $10 million in 1981 (or less than 3% of revenue net of interest), grew to $49 million in 1986 (3.4% of revenue net of interest). As an investment advisor, Morgan Stanley emphasizes a global strategy. In 1986, total funds under management were $9 billion.

Annual Report 1986

Morgan Stanley's first annual report as a publicly held corporation noted how different the financial marketplace of the 1980s had become, in contrast to the one in which the firm operated during the 1970s:

We are now witnessing the emergence of a global securities market. This market has few national boundaries and is open to virtually all investors, issuers, borrowers or savers. Price is established by supply and demand from around the world rather than a single domestic market and transactions often take place on a twenty-four hour basis. Morgan Stanley operates in these global markets on an integrated worldwide basis.

Morgan Stanley has had an active presence in Europe for nearly 20 years, and opened its office in London in 1976. Today we have a London staff of over 700 people. Morgan Stanley continues to be a leader in the management and distribution of public offerings of debt and equity securities in the Euromarket, the business that drew the firm to London originally. . . .

Based on our trading volume in equity and convertible securities we are now the leading non-Japanese broker on the Tokyo Exchange. . . . In our Tokyo fixed-income activities, we have expanded trading beyond Eurodollar, U.S. Treasury and U.S. federal agency securities to include yen bonds, floating rate notes, and U.S. corporate bonds. The Tokyo office increased its activity in arranging complex interest rate transactions for Japanese investors and almost doubled its volume of foreign exchange transactions. We have also remained a leader in mergers and acquisitions for Japanese companies, particularly those investing in the U.S. We continue to be a major dealer in foreign equities for Japanese investors through our Tokyo office. For international investors interested in purchasing Japanese stocks, we have put in place in Tokyo a sizeable Japanese equity research staff.

Morgan Stanley's strategy, as enunciated in the annual report, was taken seriously by several observers. In a July 1987 survey of Wall Street firms, *The Economist* noted that Morgan Stanley was

[a] more formal (some would say stuffy) organization than Salomon, where traders dominate senior management in a kind of creative anarchy. . . . It actually indulges in formalized "planning," . . . Morgan Stanley's planning mechanism represents an attempt to try to formalize the never-ending entrepreneurial process of generating new business. A plan is submitted that details the pros and the cons of a new product. . . . The plan, if approved, becomes a budget. This stipulates the resources needed, from the number of people right down to the amount of square feet of office space to be allocated.

Several market participants argued that this more formal approach to planning had actually protected Morgan Stanley from the large losses taken by several competitors, either when products did not perform well or a lack of proper management control failed to prevent unexpected trading losses.

On the other hand, a more formal structure meant that producer-driven profits could be stifled by too many layers of management. In fact, for all Wall Street firms including Morgan Stanley, as they grew rapidly in both personnel and capital, the trade-off between the advantages of being small-scale entrepreneurs and the disadvantages of being large global players was becoming increasingly complex.

Investment Analyst Report on Morgan Stanley

After Morgan Stanley went public, it was closely followed by analysts. One, Michael W. Blumstein of the First Boston Corporation, rated its stock a long-term buy. At the end of 1986, he argued:

The largest investment banks are sometimes difficult to differentiate, but Morgan Stanley differentiates itself in a few respects. . . . First and foremost, the firm is less market share driven than some competitors. Morgan Stanley is usually not the first player to enter a new business, and management's stated philosophy is that the firm should have a "market presence" in all areas, perhaps ranking among the "top half-dozen" players in each one. . . . It is among the more tightly run firms. . . . The strong culture is particularly noteworthy in this time of rapid growth when so many new employees need to be indoctrinated so quickly. . . . [T]he international push that seems so promising was obviously not done on a whim. . . . Morgan Stanley seems well positioned among investment banks because it recognized the globalization of the financial markets early and aggressively began building its capacity . . .

Morgan Stanley in Tokyo

Morgan Stanley was one of the first U.S. investment banks to establish a presence in Tokyo. As early as 1970, the firm opened a representative office with a modest staff of only two. By 1980, that staff had grown to 14; and by 1987, 425 people were employed in Tokyo. As a senior managing director commented:

> I think that what distinguishes Morgan Stanley from many other investment banks is that we showed very early a real commitment to developing our Tokyo presence. When we looked, during the late 1970s, as part of the planning process at the possible size of the Japanese market we were actually surprised by what our numbers showed. We all expected the market to be big, but it was even bigger than most thought would be possible. It was clear that we wanted to be in that market, that we needed to be in, because of the interactions with the markets in New York and London. The difficulty is to set the limits to your expansion so that you have profitable growth. What are the capital, credit, technology and processing implications of the Tokyo presence? What are the personnel problems and costs?

Morgan Stanley—in contrast to several other U.S. investment banks in Japan—pursued a broadly based strategy during the first phase of its growth. In the Tokyo office, one managing director explained:

> We want to enter into all aspects of investment banking in Japan. It is not Morgan Stanley's style to do only one thing spectacularly well. We want to be in all the Japanese markets. And we want to be a real factor in those markets. Morgan Stanley is not a niche player. We want to build this thing carefully through excellence in services and not just by throwing capital onto the market. Some people think that to gain presence you have to buy your way in. That may hold for Japanese in the U.S. but it doesn't hold for business in Japan and it doesn't hold for Morgan Stanley. Our strength comes through our reputation and ability to do good, solid work. Also our relationship with the New York and London offices, with whom we work very closely, is central. We won't organize this office as a profit center that has to throw off cash in and of itself. Sure we are profitable over here, but it is the interaction with New York that matters.

Meanwhile, another managing director and member of the six-person management committee stressed the central importance of the links between all of Morgan Stanley's offices around the world:

> Morgan Stanley does not have a separate international division. This creates for the branches something akin to, but far less personalized than, a matrix structure. The business managers carry out strategy and plans that are those of their worldwide divisions, but in consultation with the branch head. Since we at Morgan Stanley spend a lot of time on developing a plan, with input from many managers, there is a "shared" vision. That allows us to make use of this "matrix-like" system. I think that this ability to develop an integrated worldwide approach allowed Morgan Stanley to anticipate and prepare for the emergence of the global financial market well before its competitors.

The main areas in which Morgan Stanley, Tokyo did business were defined as: (1) Investment Banking (underwriting, mergers and acquisitions); (2) Fixed-Income Trading (U.S. governments, Eurobonds, futures); (3) Equity (U.S. stocks, Japanese stocks, convertible bonds and warrants, stock index futures); and (4) foreign exchange transactions. This product line represented a significant extension of that which had been offered in the late 1970s. At that time, the principal business of Morgan Stanley's Tokyo operation was to help in off-shore underwriting and to deal in U.S. government securities for Japanese investors. By 1984, branch status had been conferred on the office. In 1985, the Tokyo Stock Exchange (TSE) announced that it would be willing to receive applications from foreign firms to enter its exchange. Morgan Stanley was awarded one of the seats because of its high share of turnover of TSE transactions, and the seat on the exchange further enhanced its prestige in the market.

Like other foreign firms that operated in Tokyo, Morgan Stanley employed both foreign and Japanese personnel. In particular, 75% of all employees were Japanese and, except for some members of the operations group, all spoke English. Of the 446 employees, approximately 325 were Japanese nationals. Yet the cost of employing the 100 or so foreigners remained high; one report estimated that, on average, every dollar in compensation paid actually cost a foreign investment bank three dollars. Of the six managing directors in Tokyo, two were Japanese. One of these, David S. Phillips (whose English name was the result of adoption after WW II), had been with Morgan Stanley in Tokyo since the opening of the office. The other, Kenji Munemura, had been with the firm since the early 1970s. Of the nine executive directors, six were Japanese. It was intended that the office in Japan would increasingly be managed by Japanese, which supported the objective of the firm, to become a "real presence in the domestic Japanese securities market." A managing director in Tokyo explained:

> We can service our clients well and make good money, just by being agents that facilitate international capital transactions. Our knowledge of various markets, through offices in various places and especially New York would give us information that can be used in the international flow business. But the real value added comes from being a major presence in the markets here. Not only do we service our clients here, because of the way Morgan Stanley is organized, we allow people in New York or London to do better business too. When it was decided that Tokyo would not be a profit center it really reflected the way business is done in this firm. You don't bicker about where and by whom the profits are made.

In spite of a generally anticipated continuation of liberalization and internationalization in financial markets, many knowledgeable observers did not think that the specifically Japanese nature of the investment banking business in Japan would change much. As one senior U.S. investment banker in Tokyo remarked: "No matter what will happen here, the *gaijin* (non-Japanese) will remain *gaijin*. In a way the worst thing is that you might think you have become accustomed to the market but in reality you are still out there, a *gaijin* securities firm." In evaluating the Japanese market, then, foreign investment bankers had to identify the distinct challenges presented by the Japanese culture. In conversations, these bankers frequently reflected on "a Japanese style of doing business" and the "consensus-driven" nature of Japanese investors, whose behavior displayed a "herd instinct." They also observed how many intricate relationships and interests across companies ruled Japanese business life. Still, most bankers recognized that change, however slow, was occurring and that even the leading Japanese firms were entering more complex and sophisticated product markets while, at the same time, loosening some of their traditional ties.

The so-called "herd instinct" also showed in the transactions of Japanese investors in the U.S. government bond market. During the summer of 1985, many U.S. securities firms lost very substantial sums of money (rumor placed the total at several hundred million dollars) when Japanese investors took—en masse—positions not anticipated by the American firms. At Morgan Stanley, managers hoped that the herd instinct would disappear, and that product innovation and price deregulation would continue. One managing director noted that "the only real chance of having true domestic success" would emerge "if we can use our financial technology advantage over the Japanese firms." For example, if an active options market developed, Morgan Stanley could use its experience in creating complex hedging products by offering superior services compared to any offered by less experienced competitors. At the same time, another managing director noted that Japanese firms were rapidly learning from foreign firms such as Morgan Stanley, both by looking at the firm's transactions in Tokyo in the newer markets as well as by seeing what happened in New York, through the offices of the Japanese securities houses there: "We have the technology advantage now in some products and some clients think that we can do better in complex products that we bring over from abroad, but that is only a temporary advantage."

To Morgan Stanley, of course, the evolution of the Japanese market into a truly international market represented a matter of central importance. In the current environment, foreign firms already had increased their presence dramatically, and many new products that increased price-driven transactions had begun to appear; yet the overall presence of foreign securities firms anywhere except in the Japanese government securities market still remained small. At the same time, the profitability of foreign firms appeared difficult to measure; indeed, it was even difficult to determine cost centers, and once identified, those centers could show only a short history to base projections on. In particular, future performance seemed certain to improve, as the initial costs of entering a new environment were absorbed. On the other hand, it was possible that expansion from almost no presence—which had taken place in a relatively short period of time—had proved much easier than would expansion to the next stage. For Morgan Stanley, the next stage would be reached by about 1990. At that time, the firm expected to employ 600-700 employees in Japan, as well as capital of around $150 million up from the current $60 million. This business growth would come from the markets in which Morgan Stanley was already active, such as equities, fixed income, corporate finance, M&A, and foreign exchange transactions.

Foreign Exchange Activities

In Japan, Morgan Stanley was not allowed to deal in foreign exchange, since no securities firm could do so. Only authorized banks could deal in these markets. In the U.S., on the other hand, securities firms could trade in foreign exchange markets, even though the largest foreign exchange dealers were the commercial banks. Overall, the foreign exchange market had become increasingly deep; on an average day, a total of $100–200 billion could turn over, worldwide. Spreads had, according to traders, significantly narrowed as volume had increased.

In Tokyo, Morgan Stanley could legally make foreign exchange transactions in support of securities transactions. For example, a Eurodollar issue by a Japanese issuer could be managed by the firm. If the proceeds had to be sold into yen, the American securities firm was allowed to do so—even though the issuer could, and often did, use another bank for the foreign exchange transaction. Morgan Stanley estimated that some 90% of the time Japanese banks were invited to make the foreign exchange transaction.

Apart from doing the business associated with securities denominated in different currencies, the Tokyo office also acted as an agent for New York. Five dealers and traders, as well as one salesman, worked in this area after 1985.

The value of Morgan Stanley's foreign exchange capability in Tokyo—irrespective of actual business with Japanese clients—derived from information gathering and from the role Tokyo played in a network of global financial centers. One dealer noted:

> Foreign exchange is a really global market. Not only do you want to know what the various markets do from the newspapers. If New York wants to trade they have to phone us and we talk about what the market did during the day in Tokyo. Of course we run separate books, but our input is crucial to them, as is theirs to us. Also we hear a lot about what the Japanese companies do in the market. There is no way you really can get a sense for the market without being here. And the way foreign exchange markets are linked you can't have a gap in the second biggest market. Also, once we can start dealing here as an authorized foreign exchange dealer, so that we really can position, our volume is going to double. You know, we also have the opportunity to supply the Japanese companies with a view different from what the Japanese dealers suggest. Everyone knows that we have a foreign view and that we know the New York and London market well. Of course there are also the U.S. commercial banks. . . .

Mergers and Acquisitions

Morgan Stanley's involvement with M&A in Japan began in the early 1970s, when one of the firm's partners who had been involved in the earliest M&A deals between Japanese and U.S. companies visited Japan and "preached" M&A. Still, by 1982, with about 14 people in the Tokyo offices, there were still very few M&A transactions, in contrast to the U.S., where M&A had become for several of the most prestigious firms on Wall Street the largest profile generator outside the U.S. M&A had not spread much. In Japan especially, takeovers (in particular, unfriendly ones) remained most unusual.

By 1987, Morgan Stanley employed five full-time professionals in the M&A business. A Japanese national trained in the U.S. and a veteran from Morgan Stanley's New York office managed them, and together they represented the largest M&A group of any foreign securities firm in Japan. Virtually all their deals related to Japanese investors purchasing foreign companies. In 1987, five transactions were completed, with a total market value of $650 million. These acquisitions were friendly and often structured as cash deals. Also, Morgan Stanley, Tokyo, cooperated closely in the deals with other groups in the Tokyo office, as well as with Morgan Stanley, New York.

For Morgan Stanley, its reputation as an acknowledged leader in M&A on Wall Street proved helpful in gaining access to the Japanese deal flow. "One thing Japanese people really care about is to deal with the best. Reputation is very important here," noted one M&A expert. Almost 90% of all M&A activity done by Morgan Stanley in Japan involved a Japanese buyer and a U.S. seller. Most deals were demand driven; only a few were supply determined. Five percent of the deals involved Japanese and European companies, while what remained were deals within Japan. Most of the total were "specialty deals." For example, a merger between two U.S. companies, both with interests in Japan might, for antitrust reasons, lead to a divestiture inside Japan. Also, some joint ventures had been organized within the country.

Since 1983, most of the deals done by Morgan Stanley were "execution-driven," meaning that the deals came to Morgan Stanley without that firm having to spend much time on "business development"—the active pursuit of potential clients for the purpose of getting into the deal flow. According to the M&A group, this fact distinguished Morgan Stanley from the other foreign investment banks. Here, because Morgan Stanley entered into the M&A business in Japan early, execution-driven deals had been available; but in the future, business development would become increasingly important.

Looking at the M&A market in Japan in general, the group leader remarked:

> It is difficult to predict what kind of local M&A market you will get in Japan. There are many conflicting signals. Some foreigners say that a M&A market will never develop in Japan because of cultural reasons. Others say that because there are so many relationships between the various firms with cross stockholding, an active (hostile) market can never develop. But actually mergers and acquisitions are not that foreign to Japan. How do you think that the *zaibatsus* were formed? Also as more and more investors become performance oriented the long-term shareholders may become more short term focussed. So you don't know. But there are some clear obstacles. For example, you don't have the legal infrastructure that you need for the M&A market. There are no "M&A lawyers."

Another U.S. participant in the Japanese M&A market noted that additional M&A activity might show up in the near future, as some Japanese companies began to face a more difficult business environment. He reasoned that Japan's export success could not continue forever, and that a worsening of business conditions could lead to corporate restructurings and other M&A-related activities.

Fixed Income

The Japanese fixed-income market was dominated by Japanese government bonds. In this market, the four large Japanese securities firms played a commanding role, although recently banks were allowed to trade in government securities. Traditionally, new issues had to be absorbed by a syndicate of banks and securities houses at regulated prices, even though in recent times several maturities were sold at auction. In this market, Salomon Brothers attained a large presence. As in the U.S., it occasionally bid for a large share of a new placement and, accordingly, most participants considered it a major force. Here, Morgan Stanley seemed a much less important player, although it did enter the government market, for both Japanese and U.S. clients.

In the corporate fixed-income market, Morgan Stanley played no role in Japan. Since the overall market was small, this was not seen as a major problem. In the Eurobond market, where Japanese issues were increasingly done with either convertible features or in combination with a warrant issue, Morgan's share was significant in both underwriting and trading. While the dominant share of underwriting was lead-managed and co-managed by Japanese houses, Morgan Stanley's underwriting share stood at approximately 4% (using the full credit to lead-manager method). The fixed-income business in Europe profited from the syndicated Euroyen market, which developed as early as 1977, when Morgan Stanley became one of the early entrants in Europe.

Fixed income developed slowly in Tokyo. By 1979, although only four professionals were employed in the area, Morgan Stanley represented the largest U.S. player in this field. As Eurosecurities started to play a more important role, Morgan Stanley was able to retain a significant position in this market. Again, Morgan Stanley hoped to expand its position in the Japanese government bond market; as the large government issues of 1976 and afterward had to be refinanced, the authorities would likely rely increasingly on auction markets.

Equity Market

The rationale for Morgan Stanley's attaining a seat on the Tokyo Stock Exchange rested on the fact that among foreign securities firms, it was a leader in generating commissions on the TSE through its dealings with the Japanese houses. Seats were also awarded to Merrill Lynch, Goldman Sachs, Jardine Fleming, S.G. Warburg, and Vickers da Costa. With the seat, acquired at a direct cost of $5.5 million, came potentially lucrative (fixed) commissions. Of course, fixed commissions could be abolished in the future, though. By 1987, however, Morgan Stanley had become the foreign securities firm with the largest share of transactions on the TSE, a share that varied between 0.5 and 1.0%.

On the TSE itself, Morgan Stanley traded in both Japanese and U.S. securities. In all, 53 U.S. firms were listed on the TSE. Japanese investors who traded in these securities used U.S. brokers more often than their Japanese counterparts, because of research from New York. The foreign firms' client base displayed various motivations in dealing in Japanese securities. A Japanese institutional investor's trading with one of the big four houses could lead to problems of confidentiality, so it was believed that a foreign firm, with fewer relationships to handle, would be better able to keep transactions confidential. Also, Morgan Stanley could be expected to offer a different view on any particular stock, and many Japanese clients liked to have a foreign perspective, rather than just another echo of the big four Japanese firms. In fact, some traders argued that this foreign view could be particularly important because of the peculiar nature of the Japanese stock market, which both foreign and Japanese participants termed "managed." These traders described how a stock (or a sector of stocks) was picked in Tokyo as "stock-of-the-month." Then the local securities firms, in happy unison, would drive that choice to unusual heights in the market. Also so-called "election stocks" were driven up by the firms in order to support particular securities positions of favored political candidates. Officially, of course, the market did not acknowledge such abuses, and, for the client, it was difficult to separate fact from fiction. Thus, the foreign perspective could prove invaluable.

In underwriting Japanese securities, Morgan Stanley showed little success. While there were no legal obstacles to foreign firms co-leading (or leading) an issue, no positions of co-leadership had been offered. Even when Nippon Telephone & Telegraph (NTT) went public (an issue with a market value of $300 billion issued in eight tranches) the Ministry of Finance (MOF), acting for the issuer, decided not to allocate a share of the issue to foreign securities firms. Foreign observers noted that this kind of treatment was usual: "Sometimes I wish there was some law that was unfair. Then you can at least fight. But now you don't really know who and where to fight, all you know is why!" About the NTT deal, the American-born equity dealer in Morgan Stanley's Tokyo office declared:

You can't imagine what the TSE is like. Take the NTT issue. Right now all is allocated to the Japanese firms and the *gaijin* cry murder. So what will happen is that the MOF will think and think, and will say that they are studying it. If by the time they do the next tranche of the issue the market has slipped away and the deal isn't that rich anymore for the Japanese firm, the foreign firms will all murder themselves for a piece of the action and we will wave good-bye to the profitable part as we get into it too late.

The attraction of trading in the Japanese market remained large. Such trading could be valuable to Morgan Stanley in several different ways: One was related to Morgan Stanley's growing asset management service and its global portfolio advice. Again, as more and more performance-oriented investors populated the Japanese market, the opportunities increased for Morgan Stanley to be involved in security transactions, because U.S.-type research would become more acceptable and a performance orientation of Japanese investors would lead them to dissolve their current cozy relationships with the Big Four. As an example of this trend, many traders cited the development of the so-called Tokkin funds, allowed by the MOF since 1985.

These Tokkin funds were basically unconsolidated subsidiaries, which allowed for portfolio management without reference to the stocks that had been purchased early. Tokkin funds provided a response to the Japanese law that had forced firms to compute capital gains taxes based on the price of the securities held longest in the portfolio and on the price of the last sale. Since all firms in Japan kept securities on their books at historical costs—rather than mark-to-market method—the attraction of actively managing one's portfolio was reduced, even when the stock market rose. Of course, other opportunities for performance investing were also anticipated as more sophisticated markets and products developed. These included a stock index and a futures market.

Future Market Opportunities

Between 1983 and 1987, Morgan Stanley grew rapidly in Japan; and the firm expected that, by the end of the decade, it would be employing approximately 600 people. Even at that size, however, Morgan Stanley would represent merely a small presence in the Japanese market—compared to major Japanese firms. In fact, the period 1983–1987 demonstrated an almost "natural" growth and expansion, as some closed markets opened up to create a need for office expansion. Yet, in reality, Morgan Stanley's strategy differed markedly from the plans pursued by many of its competitors. For even though everyone argued the same intention to build a strong, broad investment banking base in Japan, most firms seemed to focus only on one or two business activities. Here, Morgan Stanley saw a window of opportunity.

After the initial phase in which most areas of investment banking were pursued, Morgan Stanley knew that some evaluation of long-term opportunities in Tokyo had to be made. As one managing director commented:

We have to decide, or find out, whether we will be an American firm with a presence in Japan with an American culture in our office, or is it going to be some sort of bilingual culture or are we going to become really Japanese? Is one office here going to be just a link in a "global" network, or one of three legs? It makes a lot of difference in managing an office and firm like this one. But you can't really decide on that, without deciding what the market opportunity will be . . . .

Another pointed out that

> Morgan Stanley has to become a fully Japanese firm in Tokyo. This is the most exciting, exploding, new market in the world and we can be a real presence here. What has to happen is that the government bond allocation system changes into a fully competitive auction. Also we have to be given a fair share in underwriting. The restrictions on foreign exchange dealing have to go. And, finally, deregulation has to continue. If all that happens Morgan Stanley can really expand its position. And then we can truly become a player in the Japanese markets. Our strength is the ability to use our U.S. expertise and integrate it with a Japanese environment.

Still, some other executives were less sanguine about Morgan Stanley's ability to become a real force in the domestic Japanese markets:

> Surely we have a role to play here and we can do it well. But we can never really play against Nomura or Daiwa in the Japanese markets. Perhaps we can play with them or behind them. We have to really carefully evaluate in which markets we can become a factor and what is needed to do it. Also we have to understand the importance of the Tokyo office as a link. Not so much as a way to penetrate the Japanese market itself, but as a way to help New York and London.

Given this diversity of views, the firm had to make a number of decisions about managing the Tokyo expansion. Also, any plan for growth in the Tokyo office would have to be managed against the background of rapid growth in the New York office (and in U.S. investment banking in general). Already some observers had started to voice warnings about the continued growth of the U.S. investment banking industry; in the fall of 1987, one prominent firm, Salomon Brothers, imposed a hiring freeze.

In fact, there were additional complications in Morgan Stanley's decision making on Tokyo: Not merely an evaluation of the pace of deregulations in Japan had to be made—but also a careful calculation of Morgan Stanley's ability to penetrate various market segments. Here, it was necessary to consider the likelihood that the Japanese officials and public would allow foreign firms to become a real—rather than merely a marginal—factor. For this evaluation, the history of deregulation did offer some help, as did an understanding of recent developments in the product markets. One important issue would certainly be the ability of Morgan Stanley to offer services that were unique to Japan. Furthermore, Morgan Stanley had to decide just how "Japanese" its office should be in all its activities, and then how to establish that degree of nativity.

The firm also had to decide how to focus its product market strategy. Here it must consider the potential to develop various markets and products in Japan for the "Japanese" market, and identify the markets and products that would be important primarily because of interaction with products in the U.K. or the U.S. (The Appendix provides three examples and shows some of the interrelationships that exist.)

Finally, Morgan Stanley (like all other foreign investment banks operating in Japan) would have to evaluate how profitable its Tokyo office was and what local profits meant to a truly international investment bank. If the Tokyo office served only to get information for the global network, was it really necessary to operate in that fairly expensive location? Office space in Tokyo, for example, cost approximately twice as much as comparable space did in New York.

Jack Wadsworth and the management team in Tokyo knew that Morgan Stanley's intention was to become a major factor in the most rapidly growing and second largest capital market in the world. As he sat down with the other managing directors in one of the conference rooms of the Otemachi Center Building in the Marunouchi district of Tokyo, someone remarked that these Morgan Stanley offices looked like the familiar New York surroundings. But a glance outside confirmed that Japan's financial district did not resemble Wall Street in the least. As the managers began to generate a general strategic assessment for Morgan Stanley's Tokyo office, the contrast seemed symbolic.

APPENDIX
Morgan Stanley: The Tokyo Branch

Debt Offering of a Japanese Company in the Euromarket

1. Japanese company calls Morgan Stanley, New York to get a bid on a three-year $150 million issue.

2. A team is created, composed of Morgan Stanley staff members in New York, London, and Tokyo. The New York corporate bond trading desk obtains Eurobond price information from the London office. The swap group in New York and the Investment Banking Division in Tokyo begin a search for a bank to provide the accompanying interest rate swap.

3. Tokyo finds a bank, "close" to the Japanese company, willing to participate in a swap at low cost. This is called a "Harakiri" swap. (The Japanese bank is willing to enter into the swap in order to further develop its relationship with the Japanese company that is doing the issue.)

4. The bid is put together. This includes: bond price, swap level, and timing recommendation (as coordinated with Tokyo and London). New York puts the package together through its Japanese coverage and Eurobond desk.

5. Timing is coordinated with London to assure that no other issue of the Japanese client will interfere.

6. Bid is placed in New York, and Japanese client selects Morgan Stanley.

7. Phone conversations at time of issue—7:00 a.m. London, 2:00 a.m. New York, 3:00 p.m. Tokyo—to discuss market conditions. If market in London has a "window," issue is launched, with several co-managers: U.S., European, and Japanese investment banks and brokers.

8. After deal is launched, three weeks of close contact are required to provide documentation among New York, London, Tokyo and company (offering circular, agreement among underwriters, opinions, etc.).

9. Parties from New York, London and Tokyo (company) meet to close the deal.

International Equity Trading

1. London   Client orders one million of shares in Japanese firm, Japan. Morgan Stanley sells client one million of Japan shares short at ¥1375 (including 2% net markup). Stock trading at 1350. Morgan Stanley buys an equivalent amount of U.S. dollars while the yen is at 141.5 and receives $9.3 million.

2. New York Dollar strengthens in New York. Japanese blue chip trade up, and Morgan Stanley does not cover its position because Japan has traded up to 1375. Morgan Stanley waits for Tokyo to open and hopes that Japan will decline.

3. Tokyo Market remains steady. Morgan Stanley buys Japan in Tokyo at 1375. However, firm sells dollars and purchases yen to pay for stock. The yen is now trading at 143.5, and the purchase is valued at $9.1.

Summary Firm profits from currency move on what is a slightly better than break-even trade.

International Interest Rate Swap

1. Morgan Stanley sales force team in Tokyo identifies investment strategy for clients, and markets securities to fit their investment needs.

2. A group of Japanese insurance companies is interested in purchasing an investment which has coupons in Australian dollars and principal redemption in U.S. dollars. The Japanese are willing to assume foreign exchange risk on the principal in U.S. dollars in order to maximize current yield.

3. Tokyo sales force contacts Morgan Stanley New York swap desk. Finds that a U.S. bank is interested in raising floating rate U.S. dollars. Issuer has a fixed-rate liability, which it wants to convert through a swap.

4. A New York and Tokyo swap team structure an acceptable blue print, where an issuer issues a Eurobond documented in London to meet needs of the Japanese investor, i.e., Australian dollar coupon.

5. New York, Tokyo, and London all engage in hedging at the level of the issue where Australian dollar coupons are converted by forward foreign exchange contracts. In these transactions, the issuer buys the Australian dollars and sells U.S. dollars.

6. Net effect for the issuer is that borrowing cost is 6 month LIBOR minus 0.5%, which represents a saving of 1/2 to 3/8 over other financing alternatives.

Exhibit 1

Morgan Stanley: Consolidated Balance Sheets ($ millions)

	1986	1985	1984	1983	1982	1981
ASSETS						
Cash and Interest-bearing Equivalents	$ 385	$ 173	$ 62			
Deposits with Clearing Organizations	74	27	16			
Securities and Commodities Owned						
U.S. Gov. and Federal Agencies	3,109	1,751	1,223			
Comm. Paper, CDs, Bks. Accept.	1,474	436	1,285			
Corporate Debt	2,677	1,630	444			
Corporate Equities	1,391	776	913			
State and Municipal	802	348	134			
Commodities	59	74	109			
Securities Purch. under Agreement to						
Resell	14,189	5,733	7,229			
Receivables from Brokers and Dealers	2,910	3,416	1,075			
Receivables from Customers	1,506	998	301			
Other Assets	615	432	263			
Total Assets	$29,190	$15,794	$13,054	$7,442	$4,869	$3,184
LIABILITIES AND STOCKHOLDERS' EQUITY						
Short-term Borrowings	$ 4,246	$ 1,810	$ 1,215			
Sec.'s & Commod.'s Sold (Not Yet Purchased)						
U.S. Government and Agencies	1,710	1,407	825			
Corporate Debt	516	262	107			
Corporate Equities	1,041	627	492			
Commodities & Other	256	230	266			
Sec's Sold Under Agreement to						
Repurchase	15,828	6,950	8,083			
Payables to Brokers and Dealers	1,974	2,261	842			
Payables to Customers	1,423	1,028	392			
Long-Term Borrowings	539	358	243			
Other Liabilities	861	546	351			
Total Liabilities	28,393	15,480	12,815	7,235	4,698	3,055
Stockholders' Equity						
Common Stock	25	20				
Paid-in Capital	284	—				
Retained Earnings	473	282				
Other	15	12				
Total Stockholders' Equity	798	314	238	207	171	129
Total Liabilities and Stockholders' Equity	$29,190	$15,794	$13,054	$7,442	$4,869	$3,184

Note: Complete Balance Sheet data unavailable before 1984.

Source: Morgan Stanley Annual Report 1986; prospectuses, various issues.

Exhibit 2

Morgan Stanley Group, Inc.: Consolidated Income Statement ($ millions)

	1986	1985	1984	1983	1982	1981
Revenues						
Investment Banking	$ 656	$ 424	$ 267	$212	$173	$159
Principal Transactions	473	243	122	78	75	45
Commissions	216	154	130	131	96	77
Interest and Dividends	1,063	938	795	415	363	345
Asset Management	49	35	25	21	16	9
Other	6	1	2	1	2	1
Total Revenues	$2,463	$1,795	$1,340	$860	$725	$637
Expenses						
Interest	$1,035	$ 900	$ 748	$391	$336	$323
Compensation and Benefits	695	421	305	254	191	146
Brokerage, Clearing and Exch. Fee	70	45	31	23	14	10
Other	342	244	151	106	92	68
Total Expenses	2,141	1,612	1,235	773	633	547
Income Before Taxes	323	183	106	86	93	90
Income Taxes	121	77	45	35	42	42
Net Income	$ 201	$ 106	$ 61	$ 51	$ 51	$ 48

Source: Morgan Stanley Annual Reports and prospectuses, various issues.

Exhibit 3

Morgan Stanley: Detail of Revenues ($ millions)

	1986	1985	1984	1983	1982	1981
Investment Banking	$ 656 (49%)	$424 (52%)	$267 (51%)	$212 (50%)	$173 (50%)	$159 (57%)
Underwriting and Financing	250 (19%)	123 (15%)	67 (13%)	106 (25%)	71 (21%)	50 (18%)
Financial Advisory	406 (30%)	300 (37%)	200 (39%)	107 (25%)	102 (30%)	109 (39%)
Principal Transactions	473 (35%)	243 (30%)	122 (23%)	78 (19%)	75 (22%)	45 (16%)
Fixed Income	327 (24%)	133 (16%)	83 (16%)	60 (14%)	73 (21%)	50 (18%)
Equity	96 (7%)	78 (10%)	24 (5%)	12 (3%)	4 (1%)	−6 (−2%)
For. Exch. & Commodities	50 (4%)	32 (4%)	15 (3%)	7 (2%)	−3 (−1%)	2 (1%)
Brokerage Commissions	216 (16%)	154 (19%)	130 (25%)	131 (31%)	96 (28%)	77 (27%)
Fixed Income	15 (1%)	4 (0%)	1 (0%)	1 (0%)	0 (0%)	1 (0%)
Equity	195 (15%)	145 (18%)	127 (24%)	127 (30%)	94 (27%)	75 (27%)
For. Exch. & Commodities	6 (0%)	5 (1%)	2 (0%)	3 (1%)	1 (0%)	1 (0%)
Total Identified Revenue	$1,345	$821	$519	$422	$344	$281

Note: Percentages represent item as a percent of total identified revenue.

Source: Morgan Stanley prospectuses, various issues.

Exhibit 4

Securities Firms: Selected Data 1986

	Morgan Stanley	First Boston	Salomon Brothers (Inv. Bank)	Merrill Lynch	Nomura	Yamaichi	Daiwa	Nikko
Employees	5300	4493	5957	47900	9455	7512	8540	8398
Revenue[1,a]	$ 1,428	$ 1,310	$ 2,066	$ 6,909	$ 4,963	$ 2,405	$ 3,202	$ 2,815
Rev./Employee	$269,434	$291,565	$346,819	$144,238	$524,907	$320,154	$374,941	$335,199
Tot. Expenses[1,b]	$ 1,106	$ 1,065	$ 1,279	$ 6,134	$ 1,941	$ 1,120	$ 1,353	$ 1,348
Exp./Employee	$208,679	$237,035	$214,705	$128,058	$205,288	$149,095	$158,431	$160,514
Compensation & Benefits[1]	$ 695	$ 706	$ 838	$ 3,473	$ 704	$ 470	$ 500	$ 466
C&B/Employee	$131,132	$157,133	$140,675	$ 72,505	$ 74,458	$ 62,567	$ 58,548	$ 55,489
Net Income before taxes	$ 323	$ 245	$ 787	$ 773	$ 3,023	$ 1,263	$ 1,802	$ 1,420
Net Income[1]	$ 201	$ 181	NA	$ 454	$ 1,347	$ 515	$ 728	$ 541
Total Assets[1]	$ 29,190	$ 48,618	$ 78,164	$ 53,013	$ 17,844	$ 13,246	$ 20,253	$ 12,750
Cash[1]	$ 385	$ 115	$ 1,224	$ 1,871	$ 4,285	$ 1,819	$ 3,881	$ 2,159
Sec. Owned[1]	$ 9,511	$ 18,337	$ 41,324	$ 15,515	$ 6,932	$ 4,261	$ 4,780	$ 2,853
Sec. Repo[1]	$ 14,189	$ 20,017	$ 18,797	$ 21,405	$ 5,530[4]	$ 2,790[4]	$ 11,057[4]	$ 7,247[4]
Other[1]	$ 5,105	$ 10,149	$ 16,819	$ 14,222	$ 1,097	$ 4,376	$ 535	$ 491
Equity[1]	$ 798	$ 958	$ 3,454	$ 2,876	$ 5,094	$ 2,217	$ 2,958	$ 2,750
Revenue – Int. Exp.[1]	$ 1,428	$ 1,310	$ 2,066	$ 6,909	$ 4,963	$ 2,405	$ 3,202	$ 2,815
%Investment banking	46[2]	51	20	14	13	23	18	17
%Principal	33	30	57[6]	15	17	5	14	11
%Brokerage Commissions	15	9	c	31	62	61	56	60
%Other	6	9	23	39[3]	8	12	12	12

[1]Million $U.S.

[2]Approximately 70% of which is due to Mergers and Acquisitions. Thus 32% of total revenues generated through M&A.

[3]Real Estate, Insurance and Asset Management contributed 65% of this.

[4]Refers to "secured loans."

[5]Not separately reported, included in "Other."

[6]Includes underwriting.

[a] Excludes interest expense.

[b] Excludes interest expense.

[c] Included under "Other."

Source: Annual Reports.

Exhibit 5

Employee Count of Foreign Securities Firms in Japanese Branches

		Number of Employees			Compound Growth
		6/86	12/86	6/87	12/87[1]	Rate 6/86–12/87
1	Morgan Stanley International, Ltd.	208	300	404	500	34.0%
2	Merrill Lynch Japan, Inc.	290	322	373	410	12.2%
3	Salomon Brothers Asia, Ltd.	112	173	270	350	46.2%
4	Goldman Sachs (Japan) Corp.	107	162	259	320	44.1%
5	Vickers da Costa, Ltd.	174	182	245	270	15.8%
6	First Boston (Asia), Ltd.	78	103	164	220	41.3%
7	Jardine Fleming (Securities), Ltd.	105	122	150	180	19.7%
8	Shearson Lehman Brothers Asia, Inc.	70	91	142	180	37.0%
9	S. G. Warburg Securities (Japan), Inc.	74	89	133	178	34.0%
10	Smith Barney, Harris Upham Intl., Ltd.	80	75	115	130	17.6%
	Total for Top Ten	1,298	1,619	2,255	2,738	28.2%
	Total All Foreign Securities Firms	1,925	2,501	3,692	4,667	

[1]1987 estimate.
Source: Morgan Stanley.

Exhibit 6

Top Twenty Foreign Exchange Dealers:
Rank by Market Share

	Rank			Estimated Market Share		
	1987	1986	1985	1987	1986	1985
Citibank[1]	1	1	1	8.3%	6.5%	6.9%
Chemical	2	3	4	3.4	3.7	5.4
Barclays	3	2	2	3.3	5.5	5.9
Chase	4	4	3	3.1	3.5	5.6
Morgan Guaranty	5	7	7	2.2	1.6	3.3
Bank of America	6	5	6	2.0	2.5	4.1
First Chicago	7	9	—	1.8	1.4	—
Westpac	8	—	—	1.6	—	—
Royal Bk. of Canada	9	12	16	1.4	0.9	1.2
Bankers Trust	10	8	5	1.2	1.5	4.5
Manufacturers Hanover	11	19	8	1.1	0.6	3.2
Midland	12	13	—	1.1	0.8	—
Nat. Westminster	13	—	—	1.1	—	—
Lloyds	14	15	—	1.0	0.8	—
Security Pacific	15	—	—	0.9	—	—
Irving Trust	16	—	19	0.8	—	0.8
Skandinaviska Enskilda	17	17	11	0.6	0.7	3.0
Australia & New Zealand	18	11	—	0.6	1.0	—
Standard Chartered	19	10	14	0.6	1.1	1.4
Goldman Sachs	20	16	—	0.6	0.7	—
Combined Share of Top Twenty[2]				36.7	36.6	59.4

[1]Citibank 1986 Foreign Exchange Revenue was $412 million.

[2]1986 and 1985 totals include banks which were in the top twenty in those years but are not included in the current list.

Source: *Euromoney,* May 1987.

Exhibit 7

Foreign Securities Dealers in Japan: Pre-Tax Profit[1]
(U.S. $ thousand[2])

	1986	1985	1984
Salomon Brothers	10,076	1,128	720
Jardine Fleming	8,278	1,379	2,429
Merrill Lynch	3,276	1,794	(63)
Bache	2,925	(319)	998
Morgan Stanley	2,397	(256)	(379)
W. I. Carr	2,243	428	NA
First Boston	2,047	(268)	NA
S. G. Warburg	991	25	NA
Vickers da Costa	979	344	1,305
Kidder Peabody	398	138	(446)
Smith Barney	225	29	59
Goldman Sachs	(421)	17	(63)

[1]Pre-tax profits for fiscal year ending in September.

[2]Dollar value calculated using average exchange rates.

Source: *Financial Times*, February 16, 1987. *International Financial Statistics*, various issues.

Exhibit 8

Exchange Rate: Yen per Dollar

	Average Annual Rate	Annual % Change
1981	220.54	
1982	249.08	12.94%
1983	237.51	−4.65%
1984	237.52	0.00%
1985	238.54	0.43%
1986	168.52	−29.35%

Source: *International Financial Statistics*, IMF.

Exhibit 9

Composition of Japanese Company Financing (Yen billion)

	1981	1982	1983	1984	1985	1986	Compound Growth Rate 1981–1986
Loans	18,761	20,560	19,290	23,258	20,778	26,295	7%
Securities Issues	5,025	3,970	4,425	5,998	6,518	9,553	14%
In Domestic Markets[1]	72%	64%	54%	53%	50%	54%	8%
Stocks	36%	26%	19%	14%	10%	7%	−19%
Bonds	36%	38%	35%	39%	40%	48%	20%
In Foreign Markets	28%	36%	46%	47%	50%	46%	25%
Stocks	6%	2%	2%	1%	0%	0%	−71%
Bonds	22%	35%	44%	47%	50%	46%	31%
Security and Loan Financing	23,786	24,530	23,716	29,255	27,296	35,848	7%
Securities	21%	16%	19%	21%	24%	27%	
Loans	79%	84%	81%	79%	76%	73%	

[1]Rates computed from the underlying values, not the percentages.

Source: *Manual of Securities Statistics 1987*, Nomura Research Institute. *International Financial Statistics*, IMF. *Economic Statistics Monthly*, June 1987, Bank of Japan.

Exhibit 10

Euromarket Rankings of Securities Firms

Lead Managers to Japanese Borrowers

1985 Rank		1985 Amount (U.S.$ M)	Share	1984 Rank	Share	1983 Rank	Share	1982 Rank	Share
1	Nomura Securities	$ 1,311	9.3%	1	1.2%	2	8.9%	1	16.8%
2	Daiwa Securities	897	6.4%	6	5.3%	16	2.0%	2	10.1%
3	Salomon Brothers	814	5.8%	4	6.0%	6	6.0%	17	2.0%
4	Yamaichi Securities	757	5.4%	8	4.7%	19	1.6%	5	5.3%
5	Credit Suisse First Boston	676	4.8%	2	7.6%	4	6.7%	8	3.9%
6	Nikko Securities	604	4.3%	3	6.0%	5	6.0%	14	3.0%
7	Morgan Stanley	553	3.9%	5	5.9%	1	10.2%	4	6.7%
8	Morgan Guaranty	459	3.3%	7	4.8%	3	7.8%	3	8.3%
9	Merrill Lynch	438	3.1%	21	1.1%	20	1.6%	10	3.6%
10	Industrial Bank of Japan	432	3.1%	9	4.5%	8	4.4%	19	1.3%
	Total Issues by Japanese Borrowers (U.S.$ millions)	$14,053		$9,719		$4,618		$2,110	
	Combined Share of 1985 Top Ten	49.4%		47.1%		55.3%		60.8%	

Lead Managers For All Euro-Yen Issues

1985 Rank		1985 Amount (U.S.$ M)	Share	1984 Rank	Share	1983 Rank	Share	1982 Rank	Share
1	Nomura Securities	980	13.9%	2	14.8%	3	12.6%	2	28.1%
2	Daiwa Securities	575	8.2%	1	30.4%	2	19.7%	1	43.3%
3	Merrill Lynch	327	4.7%	—	—	—	—	—	—
4	Mitsui Trust and Banking	325	4.6%	—	—	—	—	—	—
5	Morgan Guaranty	313	4.5%	10	1.4%	—	—	—	—
6	Nikko Securities	313	4.5%	3	7.9%	4	7.2%	3	14.9%
7	Bank of Tokyo	273	3.9%	—	—	—	—	—	—
8	Yamaichi Securities	264	3.8%	—	—	1	35.6%	—	—
9	Salomon Brothers	263	3.7%	5	4.9%	—	—	—	—
10	Industrial Bank of Japan	247	3.5%	15	1.5%	—	—	—	—
34	Morgan Stanley	58	0.8%	18	1.4%	—	—	—	—
	Total Euro-Yen Issues (U.S.$ Millions)	7,032		1,130		298		421	
	Combined Share of 1985 Top Ten	55.2%		60.8%		75.1%		86.2%	

Source: *Euromoney International Capital Markets Annual* 1986.

Exhibit 11

Euroyen and Japanese Bond Market: Value of Bond Issues (U.S.$ millions[1])

	1981	1982	1983	1984	1985	1986
Euroyen Bond Issues[2]	363	442	253	2,225	7,723	20,194
Total Bond Issues in Japan	174,411	180,608	201,563	212,156	258,950	376,717[3]
Government Bonds	36%	40%	39%	36%	37%	41%
Publicly Offered Corporate Bonds	5%	3%	3%	5%	4%	7%
Bank Debentures	38%	36%	39%	39%	43%	45%
Yen-Denominated Foreign Bonds[4]	2%	2%	2%	2%	2%	1%

[1]U.S.$ values computed based on average annual exchange rates.
[2]Publicly offered bonds issued by both Japanese and non-residents.
[3]Preliminary Estimate of 1986 Total Bond Issues.
[4]Publicly and Privately offered.
Source: *Manual of Securities Statistics 1987*, Nomura Research Institute. *International Financial Statistics Yearbook* 1986, IMF.

Exhibit 12

Commission Revenue of Securities Companies in Japan (Yen billions)

	1981	1982	1983	1984	1985	1986
Commission Revenue	1,044	849	1,243	1,523	1,940	3,055
Brokerage Commission	776	526	901	1,080	1,399	2,384
Exchange Rate[1]	220.54	249.08	237.51	237.52	238.54	168.52
			(U.S. $ millions)			
Commission Revenue	$4,735	$3,407	$5,234	$6,411	$8,135	$18,130
Brokerage Commission	3,521	2,110	3,794	4,548	5,865	14,147

[1]Average annual exchange rate.
Source: *Manual of Securities Statistics 1987*, Nomura Research Institute. *International Financial Statistics*, IMF.

Exhibit 13

Morgan Stanley Tokyo Branch:
Employees as of October 1987

Investment Banking		46
Sales and Trading		216
Equity	95	
Fixed Income	89	
Foreign Exchange	7	
Asset Management	5	
Research	18	
Market Admin.	2	
Finance, Admin. & Operation		179
Administration		5
Total Tokyo Branch		446

Source: Morgan Stanley.

Primerica
Corporation

In early May 1987, Gerald Tsai, chairman
and chief executive officer of Primerica Corporation, was mulling over the latest
opportunity available to the company to further its move into the financial services sector. It had been holding serious discussions with the stockholders and
management of Smith Barney & Company, an old and distinguished New York-
based investment bank, for the purchase of all of its equity by Primerica for
approximately $750 million in cash.

Mr. Tsai had been interested in gaining a more substantial foothold in the
investment banking business for some time and therefore was particularly interested in the Smith Barney opportunity. He knew that he would have to present his
company's board of directors with a persuasive case for going forward with the
acquisition, particularly since the financing to pay for it would increase Primerica's debt-to-capitalization percentage from less than 30% to more than 50% in one
leap. Standard and Poor's had indicated that, if the acquisition were undertaken,
a downgrade of the company's senior debt from its current BBB rating might have
to be considered. Given the rapid pace of change in the financial services sector in
general, and the securities sector in particular, he was sure that the board would
want to understand fully the reasoning behind this proposed move onto Wall
Street.

Background on Primerica

Primerica Corporation was the new name adopted in early 1987 for the American Can Company, which had long been an important factor in packaging products for U.S. food and other industries. It had, for many years, been designated as
one of the 30 companies whose common stock was included in the Dow Jones
Industrial Average. Beginning in the 1970s, the company began to scale back its
dependence on its traditional paper and packaging markets and undertook a program of diversification into other, largely unrelated businesses.

Initially, this diversification focused on the specialty retailing sector. In 1977

This case was prepared by Professor Samuel L. Hayes, III.
*Copyright © 1987 by the President and Fellows of Harvard College. Harvard Business School case
9-288-019.*

the company acquired Pickwick, the world's largest distributor of music records, and in 1978 it added Sam Goody, a chain of retail record stores. The company also acquired Fingerhut Corp. in 1978, one of the largest direct-mail marketers in the United States.

In response to an internal study in 1980 commissioned by William Woodside, the company's then chairman, American Can undertook to accelerate its asset redeployment. Divestment of more of the company's paper and can manufacturing business was recommended as a way of avoiding the very large fixed-asset investments required, and the volatile market for those products. The study reaffirmed the continuing attractiveness of the distribution and specialty retailing sector, but noted that the high price-earnings multiples then being attached to such companies made further acquisitions expensive. Therefore, the study recommended the identification of still another potential growth sector to complement American Can's position in specialty retailing. The key characteristics of such a new business sector, it suggested, would include a strong competitive position, a focus on specialized market segments where distribution was critical, low fixed-capital intensity and a preponderance of liquid assets. By 1981 the search for such a growth sector had singled out financial services as a particularly attractive target. It was viewed as a fragmented business with many marketing niche opportunities, particularly where distribution and information-based marketing (some of American Can's self-perceived strengths) were critical. And it was a business in a current state of upheaval, with a number of opportunities for entry.

Accordingly, in 1981, American Can decided to seek to sell 25% of its paper and packaging assets and also announced it was on the lookout for attractive acquisition candidates in the financial service sector. Soon after the announcement, Woodside received a letter from Gerald Tsai, Jr., owner of Associated Madison Companies, a life insurance holding company, congratulating him on American Can's redeployment strategy and inquiring about the possibility of a joint venture that would use Fingerhut's mailing system to sell Associated Madison's insurance. Tsai had acquired a national reputation in the early 1960s with the Fidelity mutual fund group as an astute stock picker and a master of market timing and then as founder of the ill-fated Manhattan Fund. After a long series of subsequent discussions, Woodside and Tsai developed the idea of using Tsai's expertise in the insurance business and his company, Associated Madison, as a possible vehicle for American Can's entry into financial services.

As Woodside described it later, "I was looking for a man more than a company. I needed someone who could take $500 million and quickly generate a presence in a new field." In April 1982, a deal was struck in which American Can acquired Madison for $127 million in stock and cash. Tsai was named executive vice president in charge of the financial services sector.

Under Tsai's direction, American Can actually ended up spending more than $1 billion during the next four years in acquiring financial service-related businesses. Transport Life Insurance Company was acquired in 1982, followed by another insurance company, PennCorp Financial, in early 1983. American Capital Corporation, a mutual fund manager and investment advisor, was acquired in September 1983. Voyager Group (credit insurance) and an indirect investment in Ticor (title and mortgage insurance) were also added in the following months. In May 1985 Berg Enterprises, a major mortgage originator, was added to American Can's growing financial service portfolio. American Can also bought a minority position in Jeffries Group, an institutional brokerage firm during 1985.

The funds to pay for this ambitious acquisition program came from a variety of sources. In addition to the company's annual net cash flow, the paper operations were sold to the James River Corporation for $423 million in July 1982. In November 1984 the Canadian packaging operations were sold for $190 million plus an equity position in the acquiring company. Further, the company's remaining packaging operations were sold in November 1986 to Triangle Industries for approximately $450 million in cash plus five million shares of Triangle stock; in the following month, the company sold its large headquarters complex in Greenwich, Connecticut for $170 million. In February 1987, the company sold 142,000 acres of timberlands for $69 million.

American Can also sought to raise funds by selling minority positions in several of its own subsidiaries to public investors. A plan to sell 20% of Fingerhut in a public offering in 1984 aborted because of unfavorable market conditions at the time. In March 1986, however, a public offering of 17% of American Capital common stock was successfully floated to yield net proceeds of $79 million to American Can. This was nearly twice what the company had paid for all of American Capital when it was acquired three years earlier. And in February 1987 the company, soon to change its name to Primerica Corporation, made a successful public offering of 18% of the Musicland Group's common stock for net proceeds of $38 million. The market value of Primerica's remaining shares in American Capital was currently $360 million and that of Musicland was $215 million.

The company also utilized borrowings as a means of financing acquisitions. While it had used a 35% total-debt-to-capitalization ratio as a capital structure target, the actual ratio had swung around that desired point with considerable variance. Financial leverage had reached a high of 42.8% at the end of 1983 and a low of 30.5% by the end of 1984. Standard and Poor's credit rating on the company's senior debt, BBB, was the highest risk category that was still considered to be of investment grade, and there were indications that if the company were to stray too far above its target debt ratio, that rating might have to be downgraded. Partially to forestall this, Primerica had raised additional equity in three separate offerings over the past several years—a total of six million shares that yielded $300 million in net proceeds to the company. Moreover, preferred stock (some of which was convertible into common) was also used as a means of raising additional funds during the same period. Balance sheets for 1985 and 1986 are presented in Exhibit 1.

Operating Results

Operating results for the company as it made this massive transition from traditional packager to specialty retailer and financial service vendor were impressive. Earnings from continuing operations rose from $71 million in 1983 to $192 million in 1986 (see Exhibit 2). Return on average book equity, which stood at 8.5% in 1983, had reached 12.7% in 1986. By 1986 the Financial Services sector had grown to $1.5 billion in revenues (see Exhibit 3) and $287 million in before-tax operating income. It currently accounted for more than 70% of the company's profits from continuing operations. Specialty Retailing's 1986 revenues of $1.4 billion represented a 19% increase over 1985. This sector's approximately $110 million of operating income constituted the balance of the company's income from ongoing operations. The following review of the two principal "legs" to the company's ongoing operations reveals the underpinnings of the business portfolio's success.

Financial Services

Insurance

By the beginning of 1987, Primerica had solidified its position as one of the nation's leading insurance underwriters. Total life insurance in force stood at $193 billion and the company, for the third consecutive year, produced more individual life than any other group in the United States. Primerica's principal life insurance operations, headquartered in Atlanta, included the PennCorp Financial Group's affiliate Massachusetts Indemnity & Life Insurance Company (Milico) and National Benefit Life Insurance Company (NBLIC). Milico's life products were sold exclusively by the A.L. Williams organization. NBLIC's products were sold via that company's network of general agents.

Primerica was also among the country's largest credit insurers, providing credit life as well as accident and health coverage to protect policy holders against loss of valuable possessions. Other insurance products included individual accident and health, group accident and health, mortgage redemption, disability income and extended warranty coverages. Transport Life (selling both casualty and credit insurance), Voyager Group (selling credit insurance), and Triad Life Insurance (underwriting mortgage redemption insurance) were the major conduits to this sector of the market.

Asset Management

American Capital Management and Research had nearly quadrupled its assets under management since being acquired by Primerica in 1983. Growing to $17 billion from $4.8 billion in three years, the Houston-based investment management and marketing firm provided investment advisory services to some 30 mutual funds.

In December 1986 the company formed a joint venture with the A.L. Williams Corporation. Beginning in April 1987, the venture would create, manage, administer and market a new group of mutual funds to be sold by the more than 24,000 licensed representatives of a subsidiary of Williams. This subsidiary had sold $1.3 billion in mutual funds in 1986, including $500 million of funds managed by American Capital. In addition, in 1986 American Capital had introduced a tax-exempt trust series of five funds as well as the American Capital Federal Mortgage Trust fund.

Broadening its asset management operations, Primerica had entered into a limited partnership agreement with Rosenberg Capital Management in 1986. The partnership encompassed Rosenberg's existing operations and called for Primerica to share in Rosenberg's profits. Headquartered in San Francisco, Rosenberg was a highly respected investment advisory firm that provided services principally for corporate retirement funds, institutional clients and high net worth individuals. Assets under management currently approached $10 billion.

Mortgage Banking

Mortgage Banking became a principal business within the Financial Services sector in May 1985 when American Can acquired Berg Enterprises, Inc., one of the leading mortgage originators in the United States for existing single-family homes. Favorable interest rates and demographic trends contributed to strong demand in 1986 for first mortgages and refinancings of existing mortgages. To take advantage of the favorable climate, Berg expanded its mortgage banking business dramatically in 1986; mortgage originations had totaled almost $2.5 billion, nearly double the 1985 level.

Berg pooled its mortgages and then sold them as mortgage-backed securities, primarily to institutional investors. For these investors, it serviced a portfolio in excess of $2.6 billion at the beginning of 1986, a 42% gain from the prior year. Berg had more than 60 mortgage loan offices in 15 states, nearly double the number of the previous year. In 1986, Berg also acquired four regional mortgage companies, including one of the largest mortgage originators in the Midwest.

Specialty Retailing

Direct Mail Marketing

Built around the Fingerhut Companies, one of the country's largest mail order businesses, Primerica's direct mail subsidiaries generated revenues of $904 million through a broad line of products to more than 15 million regular customers. Combining extensive customer profile and demographic information with rigorous product testing, Fingerhut's ongoing businesses in 1986 posted their eighth consecutive year of record revenues and operating profits. Fingerhut's skill and success in targeted marketing led the authors of the widely read book, *In Search of Excellence*, to describe it as "the ultimate niche company," in which "virtually every individual customer is a separate market segment."

Figi's, Inc., a direct mail marketer to upper middle income households offering specialty foods, had an excellent year in 1986. Michigan Bulb Company results were, however, adversely affected by weakness in the garden and nursery products industry.

At 1986 year end, Primerica further expanded its direct mail operations by acquiring Looart Press, Inc., and its operating subsidiary, Current, Inc., for $114 million. Current was one of the country's largest marketer of greeting cards, stationery and related products, with annual sales of more than $100 million.

Specialty Stores

The company's specialty stores business also experienced exceptional growth during 1986. As a result of greater productivity in existing operations and selective acquisitions, specialty stores revenues were up 29% to $476 million.

The Musicland Group, the largest chain of pre-recorded music and home entertainment stores in the United States, strengthened its market position by acquiring 60 additional retail outlets during 1986, bringing the total to 525 stores. Musicland's operating income rose 67% over the prior year. In addition, Dunham's sixteen Athleisure sporting goods and athletic apparel stores in four Midwest states doubled their operating income during 1986.

Background on Smith Barney & Company

Tsai and his staff had undertaken a considerable amount of research and investigation of the Smith Barney acquisition prospect. They knew that Smith Barney was a securities firm with a long and distinguished history. Founded in 1873, it had survived the market crash of 1929 and the ensuing Depression years and had grown substantially in the post-World War II U.S. economic expansion. It had a long record as a financial counselor and underwriter to corporations and municipalities and had enjoyed "major bracket" status among underwriting syndicates during all of the post-World War II period as a result of these ongoing corporate relationships. In more recent years it had expanded its presence in the retail and institutional brokerage areas. At the beginning of April 1987, Smith Barney had assets of approximately $6.7 billion, equity capital of $350 million and 6,319 employees.

Investment Banking

Smith Barney had a substantial and highly-regarded capability in both financing and providing counseling services to U.S. corporations and governmental units. Its business in this field had grown considerably and as a consequence the firm's professionals assigned to this sector had also increased from 80 in 1976 to 156 at the beginning of 1987. In the corporate sector, the firm had managed domestic issues worth some $5.6 billion in 1985 and almost $12 billion in 1986. Among their clients were such prominent names as Dow Chemical, Manufacturers Hanover and Chrysler Corporation. In the "league table" totals, Smith Barney ranked in eleventh position in the U.S. security industry in 1986 (see Exhibit 4).

This relative standing held consistently across a number of subcategories within the various other institutional investor "league tables." In 1986, for instance, Smith Barney ranked 12th in all negotiated debt and equity financings (their financing volume here was $7.4 billion), 12th in all negotiated debt financings ($4.8 billion), 15th in all negotiated equity financings ($2.6 billion), 6th in competitive securities offerings ($4.2 billion) and 15th in the volume of initial public offerings for U.S. companies ($1.2 billion for 30 issuers).

Overseas, Smith Barney had offices in Bahrain, Geneva, London, Lugano (Switzerland), Mexico City, Paris, Zurich and Tokyo (where the firm had been one of the first to enter the Tokyo market; it maintained a staff there of 70 professionals). Its overall presence abroad was, however, modest in comparison to some of its more important U.S. securities firm competitors. It did not appear among the top 25 firms in any of the "league tables" chronicling the activities of underwriters operating in various sectors of the London-based Euro-markets.

Smith Barney was also active in the area of mergers, acquisitions and leveraged buyouts. In 1986, the M&A group of 20 professionals completed 34 transactions with a total value of more than $3.4 billion. Six of these were leveraged buyouts. The firm was also an important factor in risk arbitrage.

Smith Barney had a substantial presence in the public finance sector. Its more than 121 professionals (compared to 24 in 1976) had managed tax-exempt financings in 1986 worth more than $27 billion. The relative strength of the firm in this municipal sector was reflected in the relevant "league tables" for such publicly issued debt instruments (Exhibit 5). In 1986, Smith Barney enjoyed 5th place ranking overall and exhibited particular strength in the areas of water and sewers, public power, "general obligation" bonds of municipalities as well as in taxable municipal issues, a category which was becoming increasingly important in light of recent changes in U.S. federal tax law.

Institutional Services

Smith Barney employed a 100-person sales force directed at some 1,600 institutional investors. These services were also extended to institutional investors abroad through the firm's branch offices in London and Tokyo.

Smith Barney's Equity Research Department provided technical market analysis as well as in-depth fundamental and quantitative analysis of 574 domestic and foreign companies in 42 industry groups. The firm placed 22 of its 34 equity research analysts on the 1986 Institutional Investor All-America Research Team. Overall, the firm ranked tenth in the number of first, second and third place choices both in 1985 and 1986. Greenwich Research Associates surveys ranked the firm seventh in overall research penetration.

In the fixed-income area, the research group provided broad coverage of the municipal bond market, particularly in power generation, "general obligation" and housing bonds and was currently strengthening its capabilities in industrial, utility, financial and high-yield issues.

Smith Barney had long been a major factor in equity block trading and consistently ranked among the top five U.S. securities firms in equity trading volume in a marketplace where an average of 70% of the secondary market activity was now institutional. In the over-the-counter market, the firm made markets in 350 securities. In this OTC market, the firm's trading volume was approximately 65% individual and 35% institutional. 1986 surveys by Greenwich Research Associates placed Smith Barney sixth in equity trade execution services.

Over the past few years, the firm had also expanded its capabilities in fixed-income securities markets, both in the domestic U.S. market and abroad, where the firm provided trading capabilities for U.S. government bonds, Eurobonds, yen and Euroyen bonds in its London and Tokyo offices. Staff in these cities had been expanded to provide for 24-hour trading in U.S. Treasury securities.

Retail Distribution

At the beginning of 1987, Smith Barney had approximately 100 retail branch offices. Ninety-four of these were located across the United States in 28 states and the others were situated in Japan, Great Britain, Switzerland, Mexico and Bahrain. The firm's 2,100 retail account executives serviced 500,000 investment accounts (averaging $125,000 in size) that were targeted at individual investors with relatively high net worths who could profitably use Smith Barney's sophisticated services. Gross production per experienced retail account executive had increased from $75,000 per salesperson in 1976 to $275,000 per salesperson in 1986.

Smith Barney retail salespeople sold more than $1 billion of mutual fund shares to their customers. In addition, they sold a number of specially-designed unit trust shares that were tailored to specific tax needs, as well as other direct investment tax shelters. The Vantage Account, which provided automatic reinvestment of free credit balances, sophisticated monthly statements, checkwriting privileges and an American Express Gold Card, was also marketed.

Investment and Financial Services

Through the activities of several of its units, Smith Barney managed money for both individuals and institutions. The Capital Management Department of 25 investment professionals, including nine portfolio managers, managed under contract $2.7 billion for more than 100 pension funds, endowment funds, charitable funds, and individual clients and had consistently achieved top-quartile performance results. The Mutual Fund Department managed more than $2.8 billion in money market funds, $500 million in equity and convertible bond funds, and a $500 million U.S. government securities fund.

Operating Results

Smith Barney had been consistently profitable over the past decade, with only one down year in 1984. With a 22% compound growth in annual revenues and a 29% annual compound growth in net income over the past ten years, return on book equity had generally ranged between 20% and 25%. For the securities firm's 1987 fiscal year, which ended in March 1987, revenues grew by $100 million to $1.1 billion and net income rose 32% from the 1986 fiscal level to $60.8 million. Both assets and capital had also grown dramatically over the same ten-year period. Total assets were $6.6 billion at the end of 1986 (see Exhibit 6) as compared with $443 million in 1976. Equity capital stood at $300 million at the end of 1986, compared to $35 million in 1976. During that period, the firm's mix of business had also undergone substantial change, notably in the growth of principal trading and financial services (see Exhibit 7).

These investment results were consistent with overall securities industry experience. As noted in Exhibit 8, Smith Barney's year-to-year operating profits compared favorably to the industry average. And the firm's capital size placed it in the sixteenth position among the top 25 U.S. securities firms (see Exhibit 9).

Primerica's Analysis of Smith Barney Opportunity

Primerica's management under the direction of Gerald Tsai, who succeeded William Woodside as Chairman and Chief Executive Officer in 1986, believed that several links were still missing in the company's objective for a financial services business portfolio. A desired addition would be one or more trust companies that could leverage off of the company's four million policy holders and 1.5 million mutual fund shareholders. Unfortunately, under U.S. regulations, such operations would require Primerica to register as a one-bank holding company and that, in turn, would preclude any of the firm's business units from selling insurance policies. Pension consulting and insurance brokerage were other niches which fit logically into Primerica's future vision of itself, and the company was actively looking for appropriate acquisitions in these areas.

Investment banking was yet another important "missing link" in Primerica's projected business portfolio. It was the company's view that financial services and investment banking were going "global" and that in the future the three major financial centers would be New York, London and Tokyo.

Tokyo was seen as having formidable barriers to entry because of the dominant position enjoyed by the four leading Japanese securities firms in that marketplace. Having one's own branch office there, however, was seen as an absolutely necessary starting point for any efforts to build a defensible niche in Tokyo.

Primerica had decided to initially focus on gaining an entrance into London, where the entry barriers were much less formidable. In 1985, the company purchased a 4.9% position in Kleinwort Benson, one of the largest British merchant banks in the city, with the thought of possibly increasing that ownership position in the future. Subsequently, however, the repercussions of "Big Bang" had driven the prices of London-based securities firms sharply higher and Primerica sold its equity position in Kleinwort at a substantial profit. Tsai reiterated his desire to acquire a London merchant bank but was content to bide his time until the right opportunity presented itself.

In Tsai's view, the "right opportunity" to acquire a New York-based investment bank had now surfaced. The price of publicly-owned securities firms had seriously lagged the rest of the U.S. stockmarket so that now they were at an all-

▼▼▼▼▼▼▼▼▼▼▼▼▼▼▼▼▼▼▼▼▼▼▼▼▼▼▼▼▼▼▼▼▼▼▼▼ ▪

time relative "low" to the market as a whole (see Exhibits 10 and 11). In fact, it was the first time that Tsai could recall when, during a bull market, brokerage stocks had not sold at a lofty P-E multiple either early *or* late in such a cycle. Consequently, he was convinced that in a market downturn, it was likely that the brokerage stocks would decline less relative to other groups of stocks, particularly since, in his view, the brokerage firms had been more successful in curbing their overhead during this current business expansion and were therefore better positioned to ride out a future downturn. Tsai saw it as his mandate "to weigh risks and to buy companies that appear to be relatively cheap."

Mr. Tsai believed that Smith Barney fit that profile. There were, he believed, a number of synergies between the two organizations that could be exploited. Although Smith Barney's more than 2,000 account executives were now selling about a billion dollars a year in mutual funds to their retail customers for such leading management companies as Fidelity and Keystone, they were annually selling only about $25 million of American Capital's various funds. He saw no reason why, with proper incentives, that number couldn't be expanded to $300–$400 million.

Further, Tsai believed that a variety of Primerica's insurance products could be channeled through this retail securities sales force for sale to their customers. He was aware that several other brokerage firms had experienced only mixed results in their own attempts to do this, but he knew that E.F. Hutton had apparently found a successful formula with single premium deferred annuities, thus avoiding some of the complexities of other insurance products.

While Tsai was attracted to the synergies of a brokerage firm, he did not want to acquire a very large one:

> I don't want to own a company like Merrill Lynch, because then Merrill would overshadow everything else we do. It would loom so large that swings in Merrill's business would whip around Primerica's results. Fortunately, Smith Barney's projected 1987 net operating income would constitute no more than 15–20% of Primerica's expected results for 1987.

Tsai did not want to wrap Primerica in the mantle of a brokerage firm in the eyes of the stock market, either. Both securities brokerage firms and life and casualty insurance companies carried multiples substantially lower than the diversified financial services with which Primerica was now identified in the market's eyes. A chart of Primerica's stock price performance is set forth in Exhibit 12.

As far as future plans for Smith Barney, if the acquisition were completed, Mr. Tsai foresaw opportunities growing out of cross-selling between institutional research and corporate finance. Since research analyst "stars" often had privileged access to the senior managements of the companies they followed, they were in a position to introduce Smith Barney's corporate finance teams and facilitate their new business efforts. Tsai was convinced that Smith Barney's corporate finance capability could be more effectively and profitably utilized in this manner, particularly by targeting medium-sized firms equivalent to the Fortune Second Five Hundred.

Actually, Tsai's interest in acquiring Smith Barney dated back to 1984 when he first contacted Robert Powell, CEO of Smith Barney, about acquiring all or part of the 22% stake in Smith Barney which a group of Gulf-area investors had acquired in 1982 for $40 million. In 1986, Smith Barney had discussed internally the idea of going public, partly in response to the Gulf investor group's desire to sell its shares for a targeted $160 million. The investment bank had not then (or subsequently) felt the need for any additional capital, given its business mix, and so the idea of a public offering had been shelved. Although no formal bid had yet been made, Primerica's tentative feelers suggested that a price of $750 million for 100% of the firm's equity would be favorably received by both the firm's active partnership and the minority stockholder group.

In the event that the Smith Barney acquisition proposal was approved, Tsai planned to raise the necessary funds to pay for the purchase through debt financing.

Exhibit 1

Comparative Balance Sheets ($ millions)

Assets	December 31, 1986	1985
Cash and short-term investments	$ 209	$ 273
Financial Services:		
Investments	1,670	1,456
Receivables, net	272	279
First mortgage loans held for sale	591	221
Value of insurance in force	219	238
Deferred policy acquisition costs	592	448
Property, equipment, and leasehold improvements, net	66	61
Other assets	276	247
Specialty Retailing:		
Receivables, net	352	272
Inventories	217	153
Property, equipment, and leasehold improvements, net	121	70
Other assets	107	72
Cost of acquired businesses in excess of net assets	387	329
Net assets of discontinued operation		447
Other assets	271	186
Total Assets	$5,350	$4,752

Liabilities

Policy liabilities and accruals	$1,124	$1,111
Accounts payable and other liabilities	1,271	926
Debt obligations	665	864
Notes payable collateralized by first mortgage loans	574	207
Deferred income taxes	199	138
Redeemable preferred stock	163	200
Common Shareholders' Equity:		
Common stock	58	56
Capital in excess of par value	622	580
Net unrealized depreciation of equity securities	(8)	(11)
Cumulative translation adjustments	(2)	(4)
Earnings reinvested	824	728
	1,494	1,349
Treasury stock, at cost	(140)	(43)
Net Equity	1,354	1,306
Total Liabilities and Stockholders' Equity	$5,350	$4,752

Source: Primerica Corp.

Exhibit 2

Summary of Operations, Years Ended December 31
($ millions, except per-share amounts)

	1986	1985	1984	1983	1982
REVENUES					
Financial services	$1,465	$1,280	$1,045	$ 750	$ 108
Specialty retailing	1,380	1,156	995	848	754
Other businesses	42	39	313	557	1,098
Total Revenues	$2,887	$2,475	$2,353	$2,155	$1,960
OPERATING COSTS AND EXPENSES					
Financial services	1,178	1,100	888	610	92
Specialty retailing	1,270	1,056	923	800	724
Other businesses	30	29	312	553	1,286
Total Operating Costs and Expenses	$2,478	$2,185	$2,123	$1,963	$2,102
Business operating income	409	290	230	192	(142)
Corporate expenses	(91)	(68)	(70)	(60)	(57)
Interest expense and other, net	(99)	(82)	(81)	(69)	(50)
Operating profit	219	140	79	63	(249)
Gain on sale of stock of subsidiary and equity and investor	70	33	—	10	—
Gain (loss) on issuance of stock by equity investor	—	—	(1)	10	—
Income (loss) from continuing operations before income taxes and minority interest	289	173	78	83	(249)
Provision (benefit) for income taxes	97	71	(9)	12	(108)
Income (loss) from continuing operations before minority taxes	192	102	87	71	(141)
Minority interest, net of income taxes	(5)	—	—	—	—
Discontinued operation, extraordinary items net of income taxes	9	47	49	29	8
Net income (loss)	$ 196	$ 149	$ 136	$ 100	$ (132)
Dividends on preferred stock	21	25	26	25	4
Income (loss) applicable to common stock	$ 175	$ 123	$ 110	$ 75	$ (136)
Average number of common shares outstanding (in thousands)	54,570	48,822	45,092	40,032	37,400
Earnings per share of common stock					
Income (loss) from continuing operations	$3.04	$1.57	$1.35	$1.16	$(3.88)
Discontinued operations	.60	.96	1.02	.58	.22
Extraordinary items	(.43)	—	.08	.14	—
Net Income	$3.21	$2.53	$2.45	$1.88	$ 3.66

Source: Primerica Corp.

Exhibit 3

Financial Services Sector Revenues by Source ($ millions)

Financial Services	1986	1985	1984
Insurance premiums			
Individual life	$ 390.0	$ 370.9	$ 305.0
Individual accident and health	234.6	212.0	194.2
Credit	112.1	101.4	96.4
Group	255.6	290.5	226.0
Warranty, property and casualty	61.0	45.7	35.2
Total	$1,053.3	$1,020.5	$ 856.8
Net investment income	156.6	108.6	130.9
Mutual fund management fees and sales commissions	118.6	89.0	43.5
Mortgage banking and other	136.3	62.0	13.9
Total	$1,464.8	$1,280.1	$1,045.1
Specialty Retailing			
Direct mail marketing	$ 904.6	$ 785.4	$ 637.5
Retail stores	475.7	370.3	306.4
Other			51.3
Total	$1,380.3	$1,155.7	$995.2

Asset Composition	Total Assets			Depreciation			Additions to Property, Equipment and Leasehold Improvements		
	1986	1985	1984	1986	1985	1984	1986	1985	1984
Financial services	$3,940.4	$3,212.4	$2,445.4	$12.8	$7.0	$3.4	$17.2	$13.0	$12.1
Specialty retailing	929.1	681.3	512.0	12.9	11.2	10.7	19.3	26.9	14.2
Other businesses	39.2	81.4	85.5	3.5	5.3	16.5	.8	1.2	4.4
Corporate	441.4	329.4	338.3	5.6	6.6	4.0	11.8	3.3	5.9
Discontinued operations[a]		447.1	430.8						
Total	$5,350.1	$4751.6	$3,812.0	$34.8	$30.1	$34.6	$49.1	$44.4	$36.6

[a]Depreciation and additions to property, equipment, and leasehold improvements do not include the discontinued operation.

Source: Primerica Corp.

Exhibit 4

Total Corporate Securities

Bonus Credit to Lead Manager

1985	1986		$ Volume (millions)	No. of Issues
1	1	Salomon Brothers	$47,717.6	767
2	2	First Boston	41,818.4	705
3	3	Merrill Lynch	31,341.0	570
4	4	Goldman Sachs	29,894.9	523
5	5	Drexel Burnham Lambert	27,577.3	355
6	6	Morgan Stanley	26,547.6	458
7	7	Shearson Lehman Bros.	16,760.2	475
8	8	Kidder, Peabody	10,866.0	304
13	9	Bear Stearns	5,740.3	176
9*	10	Paine Webber	4,668.4	179
11	11	Prudential-Bache	4,615.7	140
12	12	E.F. Hutton	4,058.2	129
10	13	Smith Barney	3,895.2	149
14	14	Dean Witter Reynolds	2,914.2	94
16	15	Lazard Freres	2,451.2	48
15	16	Dillon Read	2,313.2	52
18	17	Donaldson, Lufkin & Jenrette	2,072.8	84
19	18	Alex. Brown & Sons	1,643.2	95
25	19	Rothschild, Unterberg, Towbin	1,443.5	61
17	20	Allen & Co. Inc.	1,006.8	14
20	21	Daiwa Securities	772.0	26
24	22	Wertheim	634.4	27
23	23	Wheat, First Securities	618.4	52
22	24	Nomura Securities	586.5	13
—	25	Thomson McKinnon	567.4	29

Full Credit to Lead Manager

1985	1986		$ Volume (millions)	No. of Issues
1	1	Salomon Brothers	$50,867.1	446
2	2	First Boston	45,054.1	408
6	3	Morgan Stanley	32,180.3	280
4	4	Merrill Lynch	30,367.8	309
5	5	Drexel Burnham Lambert	30,354.8	268
3	6	Goldman Sachs	30,179.8	265
7	7	Shearson Lehman Bros.	17,256.1	268
8	8	Kidder, Peabody	10,289.2	193
9*	9	Paine Webber	4,975.3	119
14	10	Bear Stearns	4,168.2	86
13	11	Prudential-Bache	4,080.3	77
10	12	Smith Barney	3,315.4	56
15	13	E.F. Hutton	2,564.4	44
17	14	Lazard Freres	2,201.9	15
12	15	Dillon Read	2,184.5	26
11	16	Dean Witter Reynolds	2,171.0	42
21	17	Donaldson, Lufkin & Jenrette	1,389.2	39
18	18	Alex. Brown & Sons	1,340.2	47
25	19	Allen & Co. Inc.	1,276.7	10
16	20	Rothschild, Unterberg, Towbin	1,263.7	31
20	21	Wheat, First Securities	735.8	27
—	22	Thomson McKinnon	480.4	19
23	23	Wertheim	468.6	9
22	24	B.C. Ziegler	458.7	45
—	25	Keefe, Bruyette & Woods	367.8	13

Full Credit to Each Manager

1985	1986		$ Volume (millions)	No. of Issues
1	1	Salomon Brothers	$99,650.3	767
2	2	First Boston	85,663.0	705
3	3	Merrill Lynch	72,833.3	570
4	4	Goldman Sachs	60,095.4	523
5	5	Morgan Stanley	58,487.7	458
6	6	Shearson Lehman Bros.	42,677.8	475
7	7	Drexel Burnham Lambert	40,341.0	355
8	8	Kidder, Peabody	25,707.9	304
14	9	Bear Stearns	14,616.5	176
11	10	E.F. Hutton	12,947.3	129
10	11	Smith Barney	11,663.0	149
9*	12	Paine Webber	10,944.4	179
12	13	Prudential-Bache	10,138.7	140
13	14	Dean Witter Reynolds	8,765.8	94
18	15	Donaldson, Lufkin & Jenrette	7,018.4	84
15	16	Lazard Freres	6,883.2	48
16	17	Dillon Read	6,234.3	52
21	18	Alex. Brown & Sons	4,637.9	95
20	19	Rothschild, Unterberg, Towbin	4,069.7	61
—	20	Daiwa Securities	3,987.2	26
21	21	Nikko Securities	3,100.0	11
—	22	Allen & Co. Inc.	2,658.7	14
—	23	Nomura Securities	2,580.3	13
24	24	Wertheim	2,144.7	27
23	25	Wheat, First Securities	1,931.2	52

*Includes Rotan Mosie.

Source: *Institutional Investor.*

Exhibit 5

Total Public Finance Issues

Bonus Credit to Lead Manager

1985	1986		$ Volume (millions)	No. of Issues
1	1	Merrill Lynch	$7,148.1	270
2	2	Goldman Sachs	7,009.5	202
6	3	Salomon Brothers	6,426.7	212
7	4	Shearson Lehman Bros.	6,005.7	175
8	5	Smith Barney	5,541.9	212
3	6	First Boston	5,160.1	129
5	7	E.F. Hutton	4,998.1	203
9*	8	Paine Webber	3,655.1	140
11	9	Drexel Burnham Lambert	3,278.7	122
4	10	Kidder, Peabody	3,216.1	131
13	11	Prudential-Bache	2,801.3	127
12	12	Bear Stearns	2,588.3	92
16	13	Rothschild, Unterberg, Towbin	2,217.9	82
20	14	Dillon Read	1,774.0	53
19	15	Donaldson, Lufkin & Jenrette	1,689.8	58
10	16	Morgan Stanley	1,642.6	59
22	17	Howard, Weil	1,442.0	42
14	18	Rauscher Pierce Refsnes	1,433.7	57
—	19	Morgan Guaranty	1,191.7	52
23	20	Citicorp	1,149.9	38
17	21	Dean Witter Reynolds	1,099.3	63
—	22	Lazard Freres	1,098.5	33
18	23	John Nuveen	881.5	56
25	24	Russell, Ree & Zappala	848.2	19
—	25	Stone & Youngberg	684.2	17

Full Credit to Lead Manager

1985	1986		$ Volume (millions)	No. of Issues
6	1	Salomon Brothers	$11,602.1	85
1	2	Goldman Sachs	10,768.4	88
2	3	Merrill Lynch	10,553.6	92
3	4	Smith Barney	6,610.2	93
8	5	Shearson Lehman Bros.	6,257.4	59
5	6	First Boston	5,276.6	41
7	7	E.F. Hutton	4,033.4	65
9*	8	Paine Webber	3,465.6	50
4	9	Kidder, Peabody	3,460.5	55
19	10	Dillon Read	2,904.6	21
10	11	Drexel Burnham Lambert	2,881.4	49
12	12	Prudential-Bache	2,576.6	40
11	13	Morgan Stanley	2,564.7	18
13	14	Bear Stearns	2,312.5	25
22	15	Rothschild, Unterberg, Towbin	2,278.7	25
14	16	Donaldson, Lufkin & Jenrette	1,781.5	19
16	17	Rauscher Pierce Refsnes	1,468.1	24
—	18	Citicorp	1,287.3	5
24	19	Morgan Guaranty	1,263.2	17
25	20	Howard, Weil	1,192.2	18
16	21	Dean Witter Reynolds	1,133.7	19
15	22	John Nuveen	932.4	35
20	23	Russell, Ree & Zappala	838.8	6
—	24	Lazard Freres	803.3	7
—	25	Stone & Youngberg	788.0	15

Full Credit to Each Manager

1985	1986		$ Volume (millions)	No. of Issues
1	1	Merrill Lynch	$41,438.1	270
2	2	Salomon Brothers	35,151.2	212
4	3	Goldman Sachs	29,632.8	202
5	4	Shearson Lehman Bros.	28,777.5	175
8	5	Smith Barney	27,452.5	212
6	6	E.F. Hutton	24,822.5	203
9	7	First Boston	22,990.0	129
3*	8	Paine Webber	20,864.6	140
10	9	Bear Stearns	17,852.4	92
13	10	Drexel Burnham Lambert	16,088.4	122
11	11	Prudential-Bache	15,542.2	127
14	12	Rothschild, Unterberg, Towbin	15,331.4	82
7	13	Kidder, Peabody	12,647.6	131
19	14	Morgan Guaranty	10,750.0	52
15	15	Dillon Read	10,531.4	53
12	16	Morgan Stanley	9,806.3	59
18	17	Donaldson, Lufkin & Jenrette	9,791.7	58
17	18	Citicorp	9,533.6	38
—	19	Lazard Freres	8,106.0	33
—	20	Daniels & Bell	6,631.3	37
16	21	Dean Witter Reynolds	5,771.1	63
20	22	Rauscher Pierce Refsnes	5,600.2	55
—	23	Chase Manhattan	5,357.8	22
23	24	Howard, Weil	4,737.4	42
22	25	Chemical Bank	4,247.4	24

*Includes Rotan Mosie.

Source: *Institutional Investors.*

Exhibit 6

Smith Barney, Inc. and Subsidiaries
Consolidated Statements of Financial Condition (unaudited)

ASSETS	Years Ended December 31,				
	1982	1983	1984	1985	1986
Cash	$ 20,328	$ 22,104	$ 22,168	$ 16,848	$ 63,505
Cash and securities segregated under federal and other regulations	10,950	10,155	9,112	34,693	43,524
Securities purchased under agreements to resell	711,309	811,251	2,060,979	1,251,909	1,371,402
Receivable from brokers and dealers	424,604	346,909	757,331	1,278,565	755,829
Receivable from customers	484,004	593,924	630,346	1,083,818	973,647
Trading securities owned, at market value	1,043,898	1,003,120	1,844,394	3,371,874	3,126,371
Memberships in exchange	1,990	1,977	2,118	2,118	2,118
Property, equipment, and leasehold improvements, at cost, less accumulated depreciation and amortization	45,992	51,767	61,621	68,368	74,337
Other assets	95,856	110,197	173,037	170,821	218,213
	$2,838,931	$2,951,404	$5,561,106	$7,279,284	$6,628,946
LIABILITIES AND STOCKHOLDERS' EQUITY					
General liabilities					
Short-term loans	$ 468,436	$ 435,649	$1,353,256	$1,539,270	$1,570,165
Securities sold under agreements to repurchase	970,543	971,036	1,579,288	2,497,030	1,995,333
Payable to brokers and dealers	501,910	446,069	760,974	1,244,423	963,873
Payable to customers	236,712	186,065	287,262	485,812	568,143
Trading securities sold not yet purchased, at market value	223,421	342,972	999,082	713,370	567,099
Notes payable	15,978	127,148	33,928	52,919	73,800
Accounts payable and accrued liabilities	254,157	239,717	340,410	461,038	477,005
Total General Liabilities	$2,671,157	$2,748,656	$5,354,200	$6,993,862	$6,224,418
Subordinated liabilities and stockholders' equity					
Stockholders' liability	33,162	37,154	23,020	59,929	104,486
Stockholders' equity	134,612	165,594	183,886	225,493	300,042
Total subordinates' liabilities and stockholders' equity	167,774	202,748	206,906	285,422	404,528
	$2,838,931	$2,951,404	$5,561,106	$7,279,284	$6,628,946

Source: Primerica Corp.

Exhibit 7
Changing Revenue Mix—Smith Barney, Inc.

	Percent of Total Revenues		Compound Growth Rate
	1976	1986	
Commissions	55%	35%	15%
Investment banking	26	21	18
Principal trading	11	23	30
Financial services	5	18	28

Source: Primerica Corp.

Exhibit 8
Return on Equity—Securities Industry vs. Forbes 1000 Median

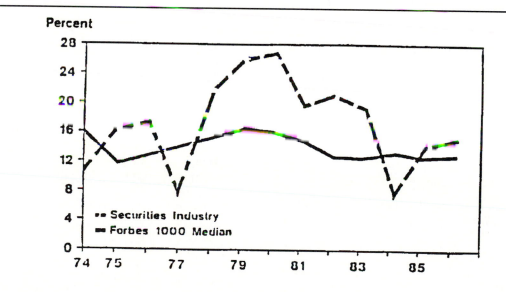

Source: Primerica Corp.

Exhibit 9

Top U.S. Securities Firms ($ millions)

1986 Rank	1987 Rank	Name of Firm	Total Capital	Equity Capital	Subordinated Debt	Total Assets
1	1	Salomon Brothers	$3,209.2	$2,090.4	$1,118.8	$88,979
2	2	Shearson Lehman Brothers	3,122.0	1,495.0	1,627.0	38,945
3	3	Merrill Lynch, Pierce, Fenner & Smith	2,864.8	2,014.8	850.0	50,256
5	4	Goldman, Sachs & Company	1,951.0	1,529.0	422.0	—
7	5	Drexel Burnham Lambert	1,870.5	1,289.2	581.3	35,903
6	6	First Boston	1,363.8	958.8	405.0	44,628
4	7	Prudential-Bache Securities	1,288.7	1,031.3	257.4	—
8	8	Dean Witter Reynolds	1,213.6	683.2	530.4	—
9	9	Bear, Stearns & Co.	1,057.2	709.7	347.5	31,914
10	10	E. F. Hutton & Co.	986.4	601.8	384.6	22,514
13	11	Morgan Stanley & Co.	901.2	576.2	325.0	20,540
12	12	Donaldson, Lufkin & Jenrette	766.1	246.0	520.1	—
11	13	Paine Webber	635.1	414.1	221.0	14,157
15	14	Kidder, Peabody & Co.	595.5	358.4	237.1	—
14	15	Stephens	418.8	418.8	—	—
17	16	Smith Barney, Harris Upham & Co.	407.9	283.4	124.5	—
16	17	Shelby Cullom Davis & Co.	366.6	366.6	—	—
18	18	Allen & Co.	359.5	359.5	—	—
19	19	Thomson McKinnon Securities	298.0	208.0	90.0	—
23	20	L. F. Rothschild, Unterberg, Towbin	289.3	201.1	88.2	—
22	21	Van Kampen Merritt	236.5	236.5	—	—
20	22	Spear, Leeds & Kellogg	234.0	147.0	87.0	—
21	23	A. G. Edwards & Sons	231.0	231.0	—	—
25	24	Oppenheimer & Co.	211.0	134.2	76.8	—
32	25	Dillon, Read & Co.	190.9	164.6	26.3	—

Source: Primerica Corp.

Exhibit 10

Merrill Lynch Price/Book Relative to the S&P 500

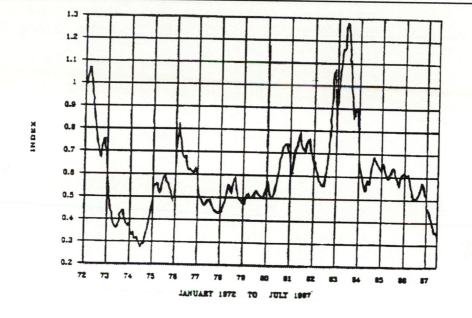

Merrill Lynch P/E Ratio Relative to S&P 500

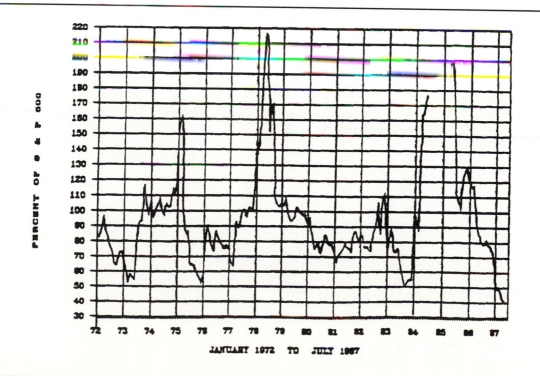

Source: Primerica Corp.

Exhibit 11

Securities Firms Market and Operating Statistics

Summary Page	Smith Barney	Alexander Brown	Bear Stearns	First Boston	Merrill Lynch	Morgan Stanley	Paine Webber	Averages
Price/latest 12-month earnings ratio[a]	12.5x	14.5x	8.7x	9.2x	9.0x	8.5x	13.6x	10.6x
Market-to-book ratio[a]	2.5x	2.7x	2.0x	1.6x	1.5x	2.3x	1.6x	1.9x
Market as a percent of revenues[a]	67.6%	123.0%	60.3%	114.4%	44.9%	72.6%	43.2%	76.4%
Market as a percent of assets[a]	11.3%	42.5%	3.9%	3.1%	8.1%	6.1%	6.6%	11.7%
Asset-to-equity ratio[b]	15.4x	4.2x	29.1x	25.6x	12.5x	16.8x	13.1x	16.7x
Return on sales	5.4%	8.4%	7.3%	11.8%	4.9%	8.2%	3.1%	7.0%
3-year average ROS	NA	NA	NA	16.2%	2.9%	5.5%	2.8%	6.1%
5-year average ROS	NA	NA	NA	16.5%	4.0%	6.2%	2.7%	6.5%
Return on average equity	22.0%	25.4%	32.4%	18.6%	18.0%	36.6%	15.0%	24.0%
3-year average ROE	NA	NA	NA	21.8%	9.6%	31.0%	17.7%	18.7%
5-year average ROE	NA	NA	NA	26.3%	14.3%	25.4%	18.8%	20.0%
Return on average assets	0.8%	2.9%	0.6%	0.3%	0.9%	0.9%	0.5%	1.0%
3-year average ROA	NA	NA	NA	0.4%	0.6%	0.7%	0.7%	0.6%
5-year average ROA	NA	NA	NA	0.5%	1.0%	0.7%	0.7%	0.7%
Net income 3-year growth rate	NA	NA	NA	9.0%	26.8%	57.9%	−7.5%	29.6%
Net income 5-year growth rate	NA	NA	NA	17.6%	18.3%	33.3%	35.1%	30.5%
Revenue 3-year growth rate	18.7%	NA	24.7%	36.5%	19.1%	42.0%	15.7%	26.1%
Revenue 5-year growth rate	20.5%	NA	NA	35.1%	18.9%	31.1%	18.3%	24.8%
Common equity 3-year growth rate	18.1%	NA	40.5%	35.5%	15.1%	56.1%	19.7%	30.8%
Common equity 5-year growth rate	33.8%	NA	NA	37.0%	19.8%	43.5%	33.7%	33.6%
Asset 3-year growth rate	43.3%	NA	40.3%	30.2%	26.6%	57.7%	25.0%	38.2%
Asset 5-year growth rate	25.7%	NA	NA	36.4%	24.6%	NA	35.7%	30.6%

[a]Based on purchase price of $750 million.
[b]After netting resale and repurchase agreements.
Source: Primerica Corp.

Exhibit 12

American Can is a Big Hit on Wall Street

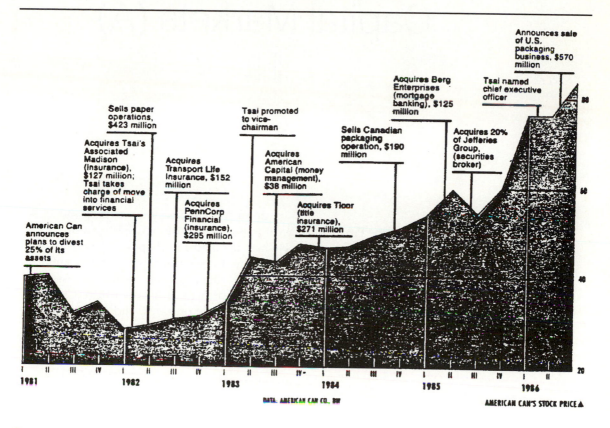

Announces sale of U.S. packaging business, $570 million

Tsai named chief executive officer

Acquires Berg Enterprises (mortgage banking), $125 million

Acquires 20% of Jefferies Group, (securities broker)

Sells Canadian packaging operation, $190 million

Sells paper operations, $423 million

Tsai promoted to vice-chairman

Acquires Tsai's Associated Madison (insurance), $127 million; Tsai takes charge of move into financial services

Acquires American Capital (money management), $38 million

Acquires Transport Life Insurance, $152 million

Acquires Ticor (title insurance), $271 million

Acquires PennCorp Financial (insurance), $295 million

American Can announces plans to divest 25% of its assets

DATA: AMERICAN CAN CO., BW

AMERICAN CAN'S STOCK PRICE▲

1981   1982   1983   1984   1985   1986

Note: American Can made a $50 million investment to fund a buyout of Ticor. Stock prices do not reflect a 2-for-1 split that has been applied in Exhibit 2.

Source: *Business Week*, August 18, 1986.

CSFB and the International Capital Markets (A)

John M. Hennessy, president and chief executive officer of the Financiere Credit Suisse First Boston (CSFB), put down the May 16, 1987 issue of *The Economist*. He had just read a fairly pessimistic survey of the future of the Euro-markets (or of the international capital markets, as Hennessy preferred to call them). Despite the negative overall assessment, Hennessy felt pleased with the magazine's treatment of his own firm, CSFB. Its position of leadership was acknowledged a couple of times, and CSFB received notice as one of the few firms "brave enough to publish meaningful profit figures." Indeed, in every year of its existence CSFB had been profitable, and more than that—profits had grown rapidly from Sfr20 million in 1979 ($12 million) to Sfr226 in 1986 ($126 million).

His firm's performance pleased Hennessy; but he also knew that major changes in the markets were occurring and that CSFB had to respond. Here, one passage in *The Economist*'s comprehensive review of the international capital markets seemed to reflect the thinking of top management at CSFB:

> "The bear market in profitability began in 1986 and the markets will be even less profitable this year," predicts Mr. Hans Joerg Rudloff, deputy chairman of CSFB, which is probably the most profitable Euromarket firm. . . . "With dozens of new mice nibbling at a cake which is getting smaller, you have to be a pretty crafty rat to get a good slice."

Overall *The Economist* article pointed to many strengths in CSFB. Yet Hennessy recalled that an earlier article in *Business Week* had raised doubts about CSFB. Citing the firm's unusual structure and a changing business environment, *Business Week* had noted the "persistent competitive frictions between [CSFB] and its two owners."[1] Such skepticism proved difficult to dispel, because CSFB was unusual and difficult for outsiders to understand. At the same time, the structure of the firm also made it possible for CSFB to be so successful.

This case was prepared by Assistant Professor David M. Meerschwam.
Copyright © 1990 by the President and Fellows of Harvard College. Harvard Business School case N9-290-029.

Financiere Credit Suisse First Boston

Origin

The Financiere Credit Suisse First Boston was created in 1978. At that time Credit Suisse, one of Switzerland's three dominant banks, held sole ownership of another unusual venture: Credit Suisse White Weld (CSWW). (During the late 1960s Credit Suisse and the New York investment bank, White Weld, a powerful presence in the Euro-markets from its earliest days, entered into this joint venture, and in 1973 both placed their Euro-securities activities in CSWW.) In 1978 CSWW was fully acquired by Credit Suisse.

Credit Suisse bought White Weld's share of the joint venture because at that time White Weld (NY) was acquired by Merrill Lynch. According to press reports Credit Suisse did not want to enter into a joint venture with Merrill Lynch (at the time the largest securities firm in the world), which seemed too large for comfort. After attaining full ownership of CSWW, Credit Suisse looked to replace the U.S. investment banking partner. Rumor insisted that the then-CEO of CSWW, John Craven, preferred an alliance with Dillon Read, but that the chairman of Credit Suisse, Rainer Gut, considered Dillon Read too small. Another possible partner, Morgan Stanley, was said to be not interested in an alliance, since it was planning to build its own Euro-bond activities. Yet another candidate, Salomon Brothers, appeared too strong; it did not need a partner. Goldman Sachs seemed unattractive because there were no "vibes" between it and CSWW, according to one manager of CSWW.[2]

Finally, First Boston emerged as the most attractive candidate. It was an old line firm, with a strong reputation and a good client base in the U.S. Still, John Craven had his doubts. Reportedly he believed that the basic structure of CSWW or of a CSFB—with pressure from both parents—would prove too weak to survive bad times. For First Boston, however, the deal seemed attractive, especially since recent results looked disappointing for the publicly owned firm. Where 1976 had shown record profits of almost $20 million, profits dropped to $1 million in 1978.

Credit Suisse offered First Boston a 40% stake in the joint venture, to be called Financiere Credit Suisse First Boston. In return First Boston transferred 40% of its ownership to the new firm. Financiere paid $28 million for these First Boston shares (@ $28 per share, when the current market value was $17 per share). First Boston paid $18 million for its share of Financiere. Thus a cash infusion from Credit Suisse to First Boston took place and Credit Suisse held a 60% ownership in CSFB. Both the cash infusion and stock ownership by Credit Suisse proved attractive to First Boston, as William E. Mayer, chairman of its Executive Committee noted: "This was a very vulnerable place in 1978. . . . [The cash infusion from, and stock deal with, Credit Suisse] saved our business and made it takeover-proof."[3]

Consortium Banks

CSFB was not the only financial service firm created by existing banks. In 1970, banks such as Chase Manhattan, Royal Bank of Canada, National-Westminster Bank and the Westdeutsche Landesbank acted together to organize The Orion group. Similar efforts resulted in the formation of Becker-Paribas and the European American Bank. In addition, various take-overs and mergers produced other new cross-national entities. During the 1980s, especially because of the Big Bang in London in 1986, many new industry groupings occurred. Even earlier, within the U.S. investment banking industry, significant consolidation had taken place.

In general, market analysts agreed that international consortium banks and joint banking ventures seemed destined to be unsuccessful. The Orion group, for example—although formed especially to enter the syndicated Euro-lending market, and later the Euro-bond market—made it more difficult to assure that its parents would not try to increase market shares of their own Euro-market operations at the cost of their new consortium bank. In particular, Chase Manhattan's London-based Euro-bond group increasingly emerged as a competitor for Orion, and not as an ally.

CSFB: Activities

In contrast to many other consortium banks, CSFB functioned very well. Revenue rose from $53 million in 1979 to $280 million in 1986, and profits increased from $20 to $126 million. Total equity rose from $102 million to $466 million; while total assets employed stood at $569 million in 1979, and at $2.9 billion in 1986. The firm also grew from 361 employees (1978) to 1,023 (1986). In fact, throughout the 1980s, CSFB played the role of market leader in the Euro-market.

CSFB's revenues of $280 million in 1986 were generated through three main businesses. The first of these, underwriting of securities in the Euro-market, extended, by 1986, well beyond the form of straight bond issues, which earlier had dominated the Euro-markets. Instead, in 1986, a large number of different securities were offered, as CSFB underwrote a broad product line and generated "investment banking" revenue of $84 million. Most of this investment banking revenue came from underwriting, although marginal revenues were derived from other activities. A second business made the largest contribution to revenues: trading activities. Here, revenues generated in brokerage as well as in principal transactions contributed—with the former producing more revenue than the latter for a total of $105 million. The third business, investment management, provided the firm with a contribution to total revenue of $25 million. (The remaining revenue of $66 million came from interest revenues and income from investments, such as the investment in First Boston Inc., which generated income of $54 million in 1986.)

CSFB: Organization

CSFB was divided into a number of companies, all wholly owned by CSFB and its branches. A few of these companies require comment: CSFB Limited served as the London-based *investment banking arm* of the firm. Here, most activity involved issuing securities, while some M&A deals were done in partnership with First Boston. Outside the London-based capital market, capital was raised through CSFB-EffectenBank in Frankfort (acquired in 1985), CSFB Nederland N.V. in Amsterdam (acquired in 1987) and CSFB (Asia) Limited based in Singapore. CSFB also had a branch in Tokyo.

CSFB Securities represented the *trading arm* of the parent; in Europe it traded many Euro-securities, as well as such new instruments as gold and foreign exchange options. It was organized as a branch of CSFB. Separate companies involved in trading were CSFB Futures Trading (Geneva) and CSFB (GILTS) Limited (London), which emerged as soon as Great Britain allowed foreign banks to operate in this fashion. Both companies specialized in derivative securities.

Meanwhile, Clariden Bank, operating out of Zug, Switzerland, became active in investment management, as did CSFB Investment Management Limited and CSFB Asset Management Limited (both operating out of London).

In general, the "holding company" structure of CSFB tended to exaggerate the physical barriers that existed between the various parts of the firm. For example, in London CSFB occupied one office building, which housed traders, investment bankers, and investment management specialists. Even some employees from First Boston Inc.'s London branch shared the premises. Again, directors and officers of various companies owned by CSFB sat on each other's boards. For example, Oswald J. Grubel, Financiere Credit Suisse First Boston's executive vice president served as a director of CSFB Limited, a director of CSFB Management Limited, a director of CSFB (GILTS) Limited, chairman of CSFB (Asia) Limited, chairman of CSFB Futures Trading, and a member of the supervisory board of CSFB Nederland N.V. Grubel was primarily responsible for all trading activities of CSFB, as well as for supervising CSFB Securities.

John Hennessy himself was actively involved with CSFB from the time of its formation. Earlier, in 1974, he joined First Boston after a career in banking and consulting and after serving as deputy assistant secretary of the Treasury. Then, when CSFB was organized, he accepted responsibility for its management and strategic planning, and its enormous success must, at least in part, be attributed to him. But now, with the market undergoing change, Hennessy would have to reassess his strategy. Already he had shown himself able to change course when required to do so. For example, in 1984 his management restructuring caused 3 top executives and 10 traders to defect. "We had to let these people vote with their feet or encourage them to do so," said Mr. Hennessy.[4]

CSFB's Position in the Euro-Market

Euromoney, in its annual review of the various league tables in the Euro-markets, called 1986 *The Year of the Yen*; the same year could have been called *Another Year of CSFB*.[5] For, although competition did increase and the composition of issuers and issues did change and some instruments did disappear, CSFB once again led the overall issue table.[6] The firm's share of the market (SoM) stood at 11.2% and CSFB's total issue volume represented $20.5 billion. Compared to 1985, however, CSFB clearly did worse. In that year the gap between CSFB's 14.1% SoM and second-placed Merrill's 5.7% had been very substantial. In 1986 the runner-up in the overall table was Nomura Securities, which more than doubled its market share, to reach 7.9%.

Fixed Rate Market

In fact, Nomura's spectacular success largely derived from an explosion of Japanese yen issues, for both Japanese (90%) and non-Japanese (10%) issuers. While in 1985 only $6.3 billion yen issues were brought to the market, 1986 saw issue volume of $16.3 billion. Since Nomura captured a 42.5% share of all yen issues, its overall standing also rose. Most of the yen issues were fixed rate issues (some with equity warrants attached); accordingly, Nomura captured first place in the fixed rate market.

In 1986 the fixed rate market had total issue volume of $125.9 billion, up from $78.9 billion in 1985. Nomura held market share of 10.7%, Deutsche Bank, 8.6%; Daiwa Securities, 6.5%. CSFB's 1986 share of this market fell to 5.5% (down from 6.6% the previous year) for a total issue volume of $7.0 billion. (In 1985 CSFB's share won it second rank, while Deutsche Bank led the table with 8.8%.)

Floating Rate Issues

The "rise of the yen" proved less important in the floating rate note (FRN) market, where, in 1986, total issue volume was $47 billion, and CSFB was by far the dominant player. Its market share of 23.5% gave it more than twice the share of number two on the league table, Morgan Guaranty. Still, after a continuous rise since its birth in 1970, the overall size of the FRN market began to decline after reaching a peak issue volume of $55 billion in 1985.

This decline of the entire FRN market imposed on CSFB—with its stable market share and leadership—an issue volume decline of $1.7 billion in 1986. Even more troublesome for the firm, prospects for the future health of this market seemed poor. One new instrument, for example, the perpetual floating rate note, became the first instrument to fail in the Euro-markets. While in 1986 perpetual FRNs had accounted for 46% of all FRNs ($21.6 billion), during 1987 no issues were possible in the first six months, while ordinary FRN issue volume stood at less than $6.6 billion, in a nonseasonal market.

Convertible Bonds

CSFB also dominated the small convertible bond issue market. Through such issues, it raised $2.1 billion for clients and won a 24% share of total market. Increasingly, however, so-called synthetic convertibles became an attractive alternative; these consisted of packages of straight, fixed rate bonds, together with equity warrants. Since after the package was purchased its warrants could be sold separately, such synthetic convertibles could trade as bonds, warrants, or convertible bonds.

Japanese firms, in particular, were attracted by the synthetic convertibles. Bonds-cum-equity warrants were included, for tabulation purposes, in the fixed rate tables. Still the Japanese firms did enter occasionally into ordinary convertible issues. With a market share of 2.1%, Sumitomo Trust and Banking company was the most active issuer of convertible bonds of the Japanese firms.

Currency Composition

In 1986, the preferred currency remained the U.S. dollar; nonetheless the dollar's market share of all issues declined to 62.8% (down from 70.3% in 1985). As could be expected, the Japanese yen showed the greatest gain; its share increased to 9.9%, which pushed the German DM out of second place. The yen's 9.9% represented a near doubling of the 5.5% share attained in 1985.

In dollar issues, CSFB dominated the markets for the third consecutive year with 15.6% share. However, the American-Swiss combination lost share for the third consecutive year to Japanese firms. The yen issue market was entirely locked up by Japanese firms, while Deutsche Bank ruled the DM market, with a 45% share.

Issuer Characteristics

For the public sector issuer, CSFB proved the favorite underwriter. While its dominance of this market declined from 23% in 1985 to 17% in 1986, it still raised more than $9 billion. Firms numbered 2 to 5 in the rankings all had shares between 6-7% but among these the performance of Nomura and Salomon Brothers seemed impressive: Both went from no issues to $3 billion. All issues underwritten by Nomura were yen-denominated.

For corporate issues, most borrowers came from both the U.S. and Japan. For the former, CSFB was the preferred manager, while the latter stayed with Japanese firms. But once again, in this corporate sector, the relative importance of the two countries was shifting to the disadvantage of the U.S. and, therefore, of

CSFB. In 1985 Salomon Brothers and CSFB each held a 16% U.S. corporate market share ($3.5 billion). In 1986 each held 12% of the market, but this share amounted to only $1.5 billion in issues. Japanese corporate borrowers, on the other hand, increased their activity and Nomura's $1.3 billion in 1985 in yen issues (20% SoM) rose in 1986 to $4.4 billion (31% SoM).

International Equities

After 1983 international equity issues represented an important part of the international capital markets. In such issues, equities were placed in various countries, mostly through "local" underwriters that participated in the underwriting syndicates. Some of the equities "migrated" back to the "home" country of the issuer, even though most securities firms tried hard to avoid such "repatriation." Deutsche Bank took leadership in this market in 1986 with $4.4 billion of issues. CSFB stood at second place, in 1986, with $1.6 billion in a $11.2 billion dollar market.

Euro-Commercial Paper

CSFB also attained a solid position in the Euro commercial paper (CP) market, with $13.1 billion of Euro CP "arrangements." Here, the firm held fourth place (14.34%), competing against several firms that were not major players in the other Euro products. Citicorp Investment Bank, for example, placed first in the Euro CP market (18.8%). Still, rapid growth in the CP market seemed a thing of the past and only a few new market opportunities appeared, such as the incipient Euro-yen CP market, which the Japanese Ministry of Finance approved as of 1986.

CSFB's Competitive Environment

Annual Report 1986

In its annual report for 1986, CSFB paid particular attention to continued innovation and deregulation in the financial markets. The most important changes it attributed to an increased use of swaps and other innovative financing techniques:

> In the past, new issue activity was substantially dependent on the net financing needs of the borrowers. Today, the swap-induced active management of assets and liabilities triggers capital markets' new issue volume which is independent of borrowers' net financing needs. Effectively the refinancing and arbitrage of past obligations occur on an ongoing basis. . . .

> As a consequence of product innovation, financial intermediaries (particularly the traditional investment and merchant banks) have seen their historical roles altered. In the past they served as direct intermediaries between borrowers and investors and were rewarded with commissions; in general they did not take a principal risk. . . .

The annual report also described ongoing financial deregulation. While strict national regulation had worked to create the Euro-markets, deregulation now was taking place in most major capital markets:

> While many obstacles to free capital flows still exist, it nevertheless can be stated that the liberalization of the past three years has radically altered the forum in which issuers, investors and financial institutions conduct their respective businesses. For the most part, investors now can satisfy their desires to achieve the highest risk-adjusted return. And borrowers are unrestrained in their freedom to seek the lowest risk-adjusted cost of money.

As a result of all these changes, according to the annual report, financial institutions would increasingly have to go beyond their local markets and into the global arena. The annual report warned that not all institutions would be able to adjust to this new world: "Not all will succeed." Yet here the implicit assumption remained that CSFB surely would.

Geographic Diversification

CSFB met the increasing need for participation in various capital markets by actively developing its international network. With principal offices located in London, CSFB established an important subsidiary in the CSFB-Effectenbank (Frankfurt), purchased in 1986. Clariden Bank in Zurich and Geneva belonged to the CSFB networks as did local offices in Singapore [through CSFB (Asia) Limited], New York and Tokyo. The acquisition of a Dutch bank served to make CSFB "a major participant in the Dutch guilder capital market," according to the annual report. Yearly issue volume in guilders represented $2.2 billion, but more importantly, CSFB's acquisition of a small bank in the Netherlands underscored the firm's belief in broad, diversified presence. At the same time, CSFB paid particular attention to each country's specifics and to their impact on overall opportunities for the firm. For example, the Netherlands, which accounted for almost 40% of all pension funds in continental Europe, could easily become a powerful absorption base for new issues.[7]

Other banks followed similar strategies, although often with an important difference: Some banks tried to stay as much as possible in the main financial centers (such as London, Tokyo, New York and Hong Kong), while others also attempted to penetrate much smaller markets. For example, the Swiss Banking Corporation set up banking presences in Germany and Spain (as did banks like Morgan Guaranty and Citicorp). U.S. investment banks, such as Morgan Stanley, First Boston and Goldman Sachs, eschewed these "secondary markets," however.

Merchant Banking

In general, the 1986 annual report of CSFB indicated that the increased tendency towards capital commitments of investment banks was changing the business environment:

> In the past [the investment and merchant banks] served as direct intermediaries and were rewarded with commissions; in general they did not take principal risk. In short, it was a relatively simple business.

Here, the increasing importance of principal transactions was related to the dwindling margins available in the underwriting business. Also, traders suggested that trading profits in the Euro-market would be more difficult to come by. With more competition in the primary markets, informational advantages had to be "bought" at higher prices. Traditionally, profits were generated by the biggest players because of their better market information. Furthermore, since the Euro-bond issues had usually been small, and since the bought deal gave the issuer a lot of information about the placement of the issue, profitable trading opportunities did exist.

The new prominence of "merchant banking" and especially of principal transactions in response to falling profits in the traditional business was not limited to the Euro-market; in the U.S. a similar change occurred as investment banks started to rely increasingly on advisory fees from mergers and acquisitions and principal transactions to generate income.

Now, opportunities for high-risk principal transaction banking were explored both domestically by such banks as Morgan Stanley in the U.S. and S.G. Warburg in the U.K., and in international markets. For CSFB, this notion of increasing the risk of business transactions was not new; the firm had pioneered the "bought deal." However, in advisory services and principal transactions CSFB could only claim less experience, since these activities had largely been taken care of by the firm's parents, while CSFB made its mark in underwriting and trading.

Secondary Market Trading

At CSFB trading accounted for 37% of total revenues; it was considered to be more profitable than investment banking, because the cost structure was different. Trading volume in the Euro-markets remained hard to measure; the issues did not have to be registered and there was no central institution that compiled all issue information, let alone trading statistics. Still, 1986 volume could be estimated at between $3 trillion and $3.5 trillion. For 1981 the figure stood at approximately $0.5 trillion. Earlier trading volume estimates were not available, partly because small issues held to maturity by retail investors were not actively traded. In fact, many bonds ended up in fiduciary accounts held at Swiss banks.

CSFB organized one of the largest and most efficient trading operations in the business. While outsiders mostly marvelled at the spectacular success of the firm in the new issue market (easily documented through the standings in the league tables), trading more than held its own. Looking at Swiss franc results (to avoid dollar valuation problems), issue revenues grew from Sfr40 million in 1981 to Sfr151 million in 1986. Trading revenues grew even faster; from Sfr49 million to Sfr190 million over the same period.

However, the trading activities of CSFB experienced the same problems that affected the issuing side. Competition drove trading spreads down, new institutions appeared (such as market brokers in 1980) and information flowed ever more swiftly through the markets to the detriment of the larger firms. Technological change also occurred. Originally, the trading market used cables and telegrams, but later a telephone market developed in which two prices could be quoted over the phone in response to a particular client. Monitors displayed a variety of bonds and prices, but these could only be interpreted as *indicative* prices rather than as *firm commitment*.

Before entering into a transaction, traders in the markets typically placed some calls (sometimes as many as a dozen or more). This process slowed the flow of information significantly, and it allowed those traders with the highest volume to capitalize on their "superior" information. By 1986, however, the belief prevailed that the introduction of a screen market was inevitable. With that system in place, one party would enter firm prices (i.e., the price at which it was committed to trade) on the screen, and then a second party would look at the screen and press buttons to execute trades.

For the largest firms in the secondary market, such screen trades could be costly, especially in contrast to the current system. For not only do firm prices reflect a lot of information about seasoned issues, but the screens would also allow smaller players to infer from those prices what the big firms thought about newly traded issues. Under the current system, the big issue houses supplied their own traders with special information. Since typically only a small percentage traded, such information has been very valuable.

A screen system would mean that all issues listed were actually tradeable and that all required automatic execution. Finally, a screen market would change the minimum efficient size for a trading floor. With screens, only a trader and his screen with a couple of buttons would be needed, as opposed to a large number of traders making many phone calls to ferret out information. Smaller firms, therefore, should benefit from screen trades, but for large firms, screen trading would require some reconsideration of their expansion plans. CSFB (like Morgan Stanley), for example, would have to reconsider their need for a huge trading floor, planned to be built outside the City of London. As one trader noted: "If screen trading is adopted Cox [the senior managing director of Morgan Stanley] and Hennessy can rip up their plans. [With screen trading] you could fit the number of traders in a decent size classroom."[8]

Strategic Evaluation: 1987

In 1987, CSFB could look back upon a highly successful past. The firm was born amid doubts about the feasibility of its structure, and several management difficulties made observers repeatedly ask whether or not the firm could survive.[9] Then as the firm began to show formidable strength, new competitors aggressively attacked its leadership position, especially when the basic character of the market responded to the maturity of the Euro-markets. Other changes ensued, as deregulation in many national markets offered traditional Euro-market issuers new alternatives, and for the first time a Japanese firm (Nomura) was ranked as the number one overall lead issuer for the first 6 months of 1987. Despite all this, CSFB closed its books for 1986 with record profits.

Still, Hennessy had the responsibility for making a general strategic evaluation. This required him to review the entire product line offered by the firm and also those new products or businesses which CSFB might enter into. Even more than that, Hennessy would have to calibrate each such decision with the desires and aspirations of the two parent firms.

Of these, First Boston represented one of the premier investment banks in the U.S. After a difficult period in the late 1970s, the firm was able to position itself very strongly in the 1980s. One major reason for success was the performance of First Boston's M&A financial advisory services. In 1986, net income of $180 million (including a contribution of $32 million from CSFB) was generated, while total assets stood at $48 billion and total equity at $1 billion. Given average compensation of $157,000 per employee, the firm seemed very profitable. Like other U.S. investment banks, First Boston had set up an international network. Its London office had grown rapidly, as had the Tokyo presence, where 150 were working for First Boston in July 1987, a doubling of employees within a year.

The other parent, Credit Suisse, represented one of the three large Swiss banks. In 1986 it held total assets of $64 billion, deposits of $60 billion, bank capital of $3.7 billion, and claimed net earnings $469 million. Like other large Swiss banks, Credit Suisse was known for its strong retail placement power. The bank's investment in CSFB and, indirectly, in First Boston had been completed under the direct supervision of the chairman ("spokesman") Rainer Gut.

Hennessy looked at the articles in *The Economist* and *BusinessWeek*, and he realized that CSFB's success had made the firm highly visible in the industry. His firm's strategy would be evaluated not only by the parents of the firm, but also by countless U.S. investment banks, U.S. commercial banks, Japanese securities firms and city banks, German and Swiss universal banks, as well as by all the other participants in the international capital markets. These players, moreover, would surely attempt to respond to the moves made by CSFB. With a glance at the two globes that stood in his office, Hennessy began to formulate a strategy for CSFB in the increasingly internationalized capital markets.

▶ Endnotes

1. *BusinessWeek*, February 2, 1987.

2. See *Euromoney*, March 1979, p. 80.

3. See *Wall Street Journal*, April 22, 1987.

4. *Wall Street Journal*, February 14, 1986.

5. This section relies on *Euromoney*, Annual Financing Report 1987, a supplement to the March 1987 issue of *Euromoney*.

6. All league tables use the full credit to lead-manager (or book runner) method.

7. See *Euromoney*, December 1986, p. 33.

8. See *Euromoney*, Annual Financing Report 1987, supplement to the March 1987 issue of *Euromoney*.

9. The most notable of these occurred in 1986 when Michael Von Clemm decided to leave the firm. Many participants in the markets considered Von Clemm the most brilliant "client-man" in the business. Von Clemm had formed, together with John Hennessy and Hans-Joerg Rudloff, the leadership of the firm.

Exhibit 1

Financiere Credit Suisse-First Boston
Consolidated Income Statement
(Sfr. Thousands)

	1986	1985	1984	1983	1982	1981	1980	1979	1978
REVENUES									
Inv. Banking	151,367	125,495	108,090	86,266	60,235	39,670	10,912	17,199	5,037
Trading Ops.—net	190,008	175,343	119,675	95,223	87,536	48,742	73,279	46,340	17,037
Inv. Mgt.	44,936	36,704	25,704	22,771	17,939	14,665	16,033	9,695	4,597
Inv. & Int. Inc.[1]	117,450	110,897	78,462	58,757	61,158	47,323	35,032	15,624	3,895
Total Rev.	503,762	448,440	331,931	263,017	226,868	150,399	135,256	88,857	30,565
EXPENSES									
Personnel	152,833	122,281	88,883	69,661	58,533	44,176	37,605	30,895	13,700
Gen. & Adm.	94,816	67,220	46,516	46,137	40,436	33,320	20,511	21,430	9,022
Provisions	664	25,557	21,735	15,656	21,197	15,265	6,369	(1,284)	(2,191)
Exch. Adj.	359	15,631	8,430	(2,414)	2,409	(2,065)	1,823	4,608	4,138
Other[2]	—	—	—	—	—	—	11,391	6,242	2,102
Total Exp.	248,673	230,689	165,564	129,041	122,575	90,696	77,699	61,891	26,770
Gross Income	255,089	217,751	166,368	133,976	104,293	59,703	57,557	26,966	3,795
Taxes	29,240	30,192	26,259	17,802	12,146	6,997	12,971	7,080	3,724
Net Income	225,848	187,559	140,109	116,174	92,147	52,707	44,586	19,887	71

[1] The major part of investment and interest income consists of equity in undistributed earnings of First Boston, Inc. in the amount of Sfr. 97 m and Sfr. 81.5 m in 1986 and 1985 respectively.

[2] Includes the items "Transfers to Operating Revenues" and "Interest Paid." After 1981, revenue and expense figures were reclassified.

Source: Financiere CSFB Annual Report, various issues.

Exhibit 2

Financiere Credit Suisse-First Boston
Consolidated Balance Sheet
(Sfr. Millions)

	1986	1985	1984	1983	1982	1981	1980	1979	1978
ASSETS									
Cash With Banks	844	253	442	224	285	170	144	113	67
Negotiable CDs	162	993	842	366	303	391	220	60	170
Marketable Sec.'s & Pr. Metals	2,164	1,418	1,423	502	356	230	352	245	131
Accts. Rec. for Sec.'s Sold	876	581	1,230	163	365	166	134	111	114
Loans and Notes	408	251	211	237	252	292	348	276	217
Investments in Assoc. Co's	547	520	318	195	141	108	96	83	56
Other	263	306	108	96	93	69	69	58	59
Total Assets	5,263	4,323	4,574	1,784	1,794	1,426	1,362	947	814
LIABILITIES AND SH. EQUITY									
Demand Deposits	700	657	471	467	395	292	210	101	98
Time Deposits	2,377	1,820	1,946	548	560	667	560	427	432
Accts. Pay. for Sec.'s Purchased	663	696	1,329	119	339	62	167	116	90
Sundry Creditors	270	285	272	204	135	104	144	64	41
Long-Term Debt	414	170	70	70	70	70	70	70	—
Total Liabilities[1]	4,424	3,629	4,089	1,408	1,499	1,194	1,151	778	661
Shareholders' Equity	840	694	485	377	295	232	211	169	153
Total Liabilities and Sh. Equity	5,263	4,323	4,574	1,784	1,794	1,426	1,362	947	814

[1]Contingent Liabilities were Sfr. 389 m., 94 m., and 54 m., respectively for 1986, 1985, and 1984.
Source: Financiere CSFB Annual Report, various issues.

Exhibit 3

Exchange Rates: Swiss Francs per U.S. Dollar
(Average Exchange Rate)

Year	Rate
1978	1.7880
1979	1.6627
1980	1.6757
1981	1.9642
1982	2.0303
1983	2.0991
1984	2.3497
1985	2.4571
1986	1.7989
1987	1.5184[1]

[1]Average of first and second quarter of 1987.
Source: International Financial Statistics, IMF; various issues.

Exhibit 4

First Boston, Inc.
Consolidated Income Statement
(U.S. $ Millions)

	1986	1985	1984	1983	1982	1981	1980	1979	1978
REVENUES									
Principal Transactions	397	312	196	177	235	111	99	62	20
Investment Banking	670	383	220	198	150	119	66	51	53
Commissions	123	85	75	72	47	35	32	21	21
Net Interest Income	107	97	59	43	56	23	5	(1)	(7)
Other	12	11	16	26	11	4	12	8	7
Total	1,310	888	566	515	499	292	214	140	94
Total Expenses	1,065	706	448	407	345	216	163	114	90
Income Before Income Taxes and Equity in Earnings of Affiliate	245	182	117	108	154	76	51	26	4
Income Taxes	97	73	53	42	73	36	23	12	2
Income Before Equity in Earnings of Affiliate	148	109	64	66	81	40	28	14	2
Equity in Earnings of Affiliate[1]	32	22	15	14	12	7	6	3	(0.25)
Net Income	181	130	80	80	93	46	34	17	2

[1]Net of Deferred Taxes
Source: First Boston, Inc. Annual Reports; various issues.

Exhibit 5

Credit Suisse: Income Statement
(Sfr. millions)

	1985	1986
Revenue		
Interest and Discount Business	808	829
Commissions	888	1,035
Foreign Exchange and Precious Metals	300	323
Securities Revenue	402	486
Long-term Holdings Revenue	56	60
Miscellaneous	59	71
Total Revenues	2,513	2,804
Expenses		
Personnel	874	979
General	397	454
Depreciation and Provisions	554	609
Total Expenses	1,825	2,042
Gross Income	688	762
Taxes	181	195
Net Income	507	566

Source: Credit Suisse Annual Reports.

Exhibit 6

Eurobond Yearly Issue Volume: Breakdown by Instrument
(U.S. $ Millions)

Year	Total	Fixed Rate		Floating Rate		Equity Convertible And Warrants	
1963	148	128	86%	—	—	20	14%
1964	681	623	91%	—	—	58	9%
1965	810	750	93%	—	—	60	7%
1966	1,343	1,146	85%	—	—	197	15%
1967	1,774	1,547	87%	—	—	227	13%
1968	3,085	1,366	44%	—	—	1,719	56%
1969	2,876	2,042	71%	—	—	834	29%
1970	2,762	2,273	82%	300	11%	189	7%
1971	3,289	3,044	93%	—	—	245	7%
1972	5,508	4,397	80%	60	1%	1,051	19%
1973	3,709	3,199	86%	40	1%	470	13%
1974	1,937	1,707	88%	145	7%	85	4%
1975	7,282	6,987	96%	215	3%	80	1%
1976	12,915	11,021	85%	1,100	9%	794	6%
1977	15,742	13,254	84%	1,595	10%	893	6%
1978	12,254	8,910	73%	2,300	19%	1,044	9%
1979	14,487	9,244	64%	4,058	28%	1,185	8%
1980	18,828	12,224	65%	4,129	22%	2,475	13%
1981	26,084	16,761	64%	6,700	26%	2,623	10%
1982	47,266	34,770	74%	11,197	24%	1,299	3%
1983	47,251	30,492	65%	14,960	32%	1,799	4%
1984	79,424	43,579	55%	31,684	40%	4,161	5%
1985	135,760	72,460	53%	55,460	41%	7,840	6%
1986	175,946	107,371	61%	46,879	27%	21,696	12%
1987[1]	86,613	60,973	70%	4,596	5%	21,044	24%

[1]January to June 1987.

Source: Philip Hubbard, "A History of Eurobonds," Harvard Business School Working Paper, 1987. *Euromoney*, September 1987.

Exhibit 7

Average Gross Spread per Eurobond Issue
(Percentage)

	1980	1981	1982	1983	1984	1985	1986
Fixed Rate Issues	2.014	1.920	1.930	2.000	1.906	1.926	1.146
Floating Rate Issues	2.043	1.878	1.500	1.366	0.821	0.551	0.487

Notes: Gross Spread includes underwriting and management fees, selling concession, and reallowance. Value is the unweighted average of spreads.

Source: *Euromoney* and Securities Data Corp.

Exhibit 8

Eurobond and U.S. Domestic Bond Market:
New Issue Volume
(U.S.$ million equivalents)

Year	Eurobond Issues			Bond Issues in U.S.	
	Total	U.S. $ (%)	Yen (%)	Total (Gross)	Foreign (%)
1963	148	61%		29,114	5%
1964	681	83%		29,420	4%
1965	810	75%		33,350	5%
1966	1,343	64%		37,642	4%
1967	1,774	89%		60,691	3%
1968	3,085	73%		56,006	4%
1969	2,876	57%		39,409	4%
1970	2,762	62%		74,054	2%
1971	3,289	58%		86,069	3%
1972	5,508	57%		76,123	2%
1973	3,709	52%		83,119	2%
1974	1,937	54%		114,720	3%
1975	7,282	46%		164,942	4%
1976	12,915	67%		194,479	5%
1977	15,742	65%	0.6%	201,399	4%
1978	12,254	46%	0.5%	212,070	3%
1979	14,487	67%	0.7%	214,900	3%
1980	18,828	69%	1.5%	272,400	2%
1981	26,084	85%	1.3%	283,700	2%
1982	47,266	85%	1.2%	369,600	2%
1983	47,251	79%	0.5%	416,900	1%
1984	79,424	80%	1.5%	527,800	1%
1985	135,760	72%	4.8%	708,200	1%
1986	175,946	63%	9.9%	750,300	1%
1987[1]	86,613	39%	18.6%	NA	NA

[1] January to June 1987.

Sources: Eurodollar data 1963–1978 from *The Eurodollar Bond Market*, Euromoney Publications 1979; 1978–1986 from World Financial Markets, Morgan Guaranty Trust Co.; 1987 from *Euromoney*.

U.S. Domestic and Foreign Bonds data from *OECD Financial Statistics* and *OECD Financial Statistics Monthly;* various issues.

Euroyen data 1977–1986 from OECD; 1987 from *Euromoney* 9/1987.

Eurobond totals from Philip Hubbard, "A History of Eurobonds," Harvard Business School Working Paper, 1987.

Exhibit 9

Eurobond Secondary Market Turnover
(U.S.$ billion equivalents)

Year	Euro-Clear	Cedel	Total[1]
1974	8	8	13
1975	14	15	23
1876	37	30	54
1977	65	39	83
1978	77	39	93
1979	101	55	125
1980	161	79	192
1981[2]	300	200	400
1982	520	350	696
1983	632	406	830
1984	1,022	524	1,237
1985	1,460	768	1,783
1986	2,336	958	2,635

[1] To eliminate double-counting, this total represents 80% of the sum.

[2] Turnover in 1981 and 1982 estimated.

Sources: Euromoney Capital Markets 1982, Orion Royal Bank Ltd. *Euromoney,* various issues.

Exhibit 10

Eurobond Issues: Bookrunner and Lead Manager Rankings[1]

(U.S. $ millions)

	January–June 1987			1986		1985		1984		1983		1982	
	Rank	Amount (US $M)	Mkt. Share	Rank	Mkt. Share	Rank	Mkt. Share	Rank	Mkt. Share	Rank	Mkt. Share	Rank	Mkt. Share
Nomura Securities	1	$11,469	13.0%	2	7.9%	8	3.7%	7	3.5%	9	2.3%	13	2.0%
CSFB	2	4,948	5.6%	1	11.2%	1	14.1%	1	16.6%	1	21.6%	2	12.2%
Daiwa Securities	3	4,889	5.6%	5	4.8%	12	2.2%	13	1.8%	22	1.1%	17	1.5%
Deutsche Bank	4	4,637	5.3%	3	6.7%	6	5.7%	3	7.3%	2	16.2%	1	15.3%
Yamaichi Secur's	5	4,430	5.0%	12	2.4%	20	1.7%	23	1.2%	49	0.3%	55	0.2%
Nikko Securities	6	3,982	4.5%	10	2.8%	25	1.4%	19	1.4%	27	0.9%	43	0.3%
Morgan Guaranty	7	3,431	3.9%	4	5.4%	7	5.8%	2	7.7%	6	3.0%	8	2.8%
Salomon Brothers	8	3,036	3.5%	7	4.6%	5	5.8%	5	6.0%	15	1.7%	4	4.6%
S. G. Warburg	9	2,917	3.3%	19	1.5%	13	2.1%	9	2.4%	6	4.5%	5	3.2%
Ind. Bk. of Japan	10	2,754	3.1%	18	1.5%	5	0.6%	39	0.6%	35	0.6%	—	—
Combined Share of Top Ten[2]			53%		55%		56%		61%		62%		59%

	1981–1978				1977–1973			1972–1968			1967–1963		
	Rank	Amount	Mkt. Share		Rank	Amount	Mkt. Share	Rank	Amount	Mkt. Share	Rank	Amount	Mkt. Share
CSFB	1	$7,655	10.7%	Deutsche Bank	1	$6,505	16%	1	$2,163	12%	1	$665	14%
Deutsche Bank	2	7,385	10.3%	CSWW	2	3,379	8%	2	1,771	10%	2	420	9%
Morgan Stanley	3	3,743	5.2%	S. G. Warburg	3	3,104	7%	3	941	5%	3	394	8%
S. G. Warburg	4	3,378	4.7%	Morgan & Cie	4	2,876	7%	4	925	5%	4	368	8%
WestLB	5	2,705	3.8%	WestLB	5	2,571	6%	5	912	5%	5	350	7%
Societe Generale	6	2,005	2.8%	UBS	6	2,113	5%	6	800	5%	6	238	5%
RBC/Orion Royal	7	1,711	2.4%	Dresdner Bank	7	2,008	5%	7	800	5%	7	236	5%
Goldman Sachs	8	1,608	2.2%	Commerzbank	8	1,492	4%	8	743	4%	8	215	4%
UBS	9	1,565	2.2%	Paribas	9	1,480	4%	9	697	4%	9	213	4%
BNP	10	1,541	2.2%	First Boston	10	1,470	4%	10	668	4%	10	141	3%
Combined Share of Top Ten			46%				65%			59%			68%

Firm names for lower tables (rows 1972–1968 and 1967–1963):

1972–1968: Deutsche Bank, Morgan and Cie, White Weld, S. G. Warburg, Dresdner Bank, Kuhn Loeb, Lehman Brothers, WestLB, Amro, Commerzbank

1967–1963: Deutsche Bank, Kuhn Loeb, S. G. Warburg, Hambros Bank, Morgan & Cie, First Boston, N. M. Rothschild, White Weld, BCI, Dillon Read

[1] Rankings for 1982 to 1987 are by bookrunner (bookrunner receives full amount); rankings for 1963 to 1981 are by lead manager (sole lead managers receive full amounts, co-lead managers receive apportioned amounts).

[2] Represents share of top ten in each year.

Sources: *Euromoney,* various issues. Euromoney International Capital Markets Annual 1986. Ian Kerr, *A History of the Eurobond Markets—The First Twenty-One Years;* Euromoney Publications, 1984.

Exhibit 11

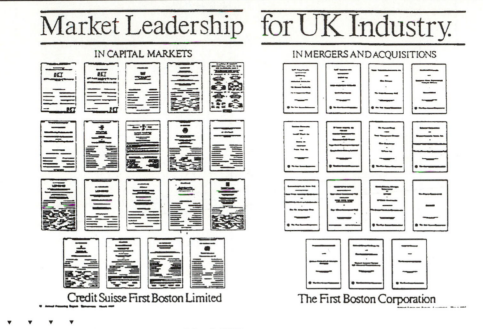

Source: Euromoney Annual Financing Report, March 1987.

Exhibit 12

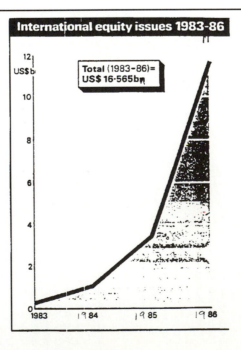

Source: Euromoney Annual Financing Report, March 1987.

Cumberland National Corporation

As of mid-1988, Cumberland National Corporation had grown to be a major banking company with almost $40 billion in assets, including six banking subsidiaries in four neighboring Southeastern states. The organization was performing well with a return on assets of 1.1 percent and a return on equity of almost 18 percent. Cumberland National was being rewarded for this performance by favorable treatment from the stock market.

Thomas Heyward, president and CEO of Cumberland National Corporation, was pleased with the corporate performance, but was considering ways to fine-tune the organization. There were several issues on his agenda, but key among them was the issue of how and where to strengthen the coordination among the banking company subsidiaries, while retaining a high degree of initiative and responsibility at each of these subsidiaries, called bank affiliates by the corporation. Heyward had pushed hard for individual bank performance in the early years of the firm. A coordinated strategy was encouraged during this period, but the affiliates operated relatively independently.

As the organization grew to encompass six major affiliates in four states, Heyward recognized the need for increased integration. Some efforts to increase this integration had occurred over the last several months, but Heyward was still seeking to find the right mix of integration and affiliate independence and marketing power.

History of Cumberland National Corporation

Cumberland National Corporation was formed in the early 1980s with the interstate merger of two banks with strong earnings records, Columbia Central Bank and Peoples Commerce Bank. According to William Fenner, chairman of Peoples Commerce, the series of discussions leading to the merger began one evening as he leaned across the dinner table at a bankers' conference and said to Thomas Heyward, chairman of Columbia Central, "Tom, if they change the law, let's get together." Fenner wanted Peoples Commerce to take advantage of the opportunities which were opening up with the adoption of interstate banking laws in several states. He realized, however, that if Peoples Commerce were to

This case was prepared by Paige Manning under the supervision of Professor Dwight B. Crane.
Copyright © 1988 by the President and Fellows of Harvard College. Harvard Business School case 9-288-064.

start an acquisition program, it could have a deleterious effect on earnings. On the other hand, he did not believe that an acquisition of Peoples Commerce by a dominant bank holding company would be in its best interests.

With this knowledge, Fenner examined the banking companies having a potential interest in a partnership with Peoples Commerce. Of the banking companies he observed, Fenner believed that Columbia Central was the best candidate with which to merge even though it had almost twice the assets of Peoples Commerce ($7 billion versus $4 billion). Based upon his knowledge of Heyward and of Columbia Central, Fenner felt that Heyward would desire a partnership more than a relationship in which his bank would be dominant.

Heyward viewed Peoples Commerce as a good merger candidate because, like Columbia Central, it had a regional focus. Both banks concentrated on their own regions, for example, focusing their corporate lending primarily on medium-sized firms. Heyward also felt that the banks would fit well together because they had complementary strengths. The fact that Peoples Commerce had strong management made the merger all the more attractive to Heyward.

After the merger was finalized, management moved quickly to coordinate the activities of the two banks, but did little in the way of consolidating their back office operations and systems. Committees were formed in each of the various banking functional areas, such as trust and retail banking, to determine how the two banks would work together. For example, in corporate banking decisions were quickly made to resolve any problem of overlapping calling territories. To facilitate this process of bringing the two banks together, business line coordinators were appointed in each of the functional areas to help the banks work together and to plan for the future.

During this period of consolidation, Cumberland National expanded its presence in its two home states by acquiring another bank in each state. Both acquired banks had a strong presence in their marketplace and had assets between $1 billion and $2 billion. These two high-quality banks were acquired to expand the corporation's retail network to areas not serviced by the banks of the initial merger.

As other state laws changed and interstate banking heated up, Cumberland National began targeting banks in neighboring states for acquisition. Within a two-year period, the corporation made two large acquisitions of bank holding companies. The first, which occurred in 1987, was Union South Financial Corporation, an eight-bank holding company having assets of $5 billion and located in an adjacent state. With the acquisition of this banking company, Heyward adopted a more formalized approach to the management of the holding company. He formed a senior management committee, consisting of himself and the CEOs from Columbia Central, Peoples Commerce and Union South, to direct the broad policy and strategic issues affecting the corporation.

In 1988, Cumberland National acted as a white knight and acquired a $5 billion seven-bank holding company, Gulf States Bancorp, located in another adjacent state. One advantage accruing to the corporation from the acquisition of these bank holding companies was that in addition to acquiring strong individual banking firms, the corporation also acquired the solid multi-bank networks built up by these holding companies in each of their states.

Corporate Banking

As the multi-state banking structure evolved, the coordination of corporate banking across the system proved to be less complicated than the coordination of a number of the other business areas. A relatively straightforward coordination process was possible because each affiliate serviced a natural geographic calling territory with little or no direct competition from the other system affiliates. The decisions to split the calling territory were, for the most part, made grographically. In some cases they were made by industry when the industry had a particular geographic concentration or when a bank affiliate had a particularly strong position in an industry.

The head of corporate banking at Columbia Central, Ronald Paige, was the business line coordinator for corporate banking. He reported to the CEO of Columbia Central in his role as head of corporate banking, and reported to the management committee in his role as line coordinator for corporate banking. The corporate banking coordinator helped to resolve any turf issues which were raised by the splitting of the calling territory among the affiliates. Where two banks did call on the same customer, most of the cases were resolved by assigning the customer to the closest affiliate. When this geographic assignment did not work, however, the corporate banking coordinator and the affiliates worked to determine which affiliate had the more important relationship and what preferences, if any, the customer had. With this information, the coordinator determined the calling responsibility.

While the corporate banking area was, for the most part, organized according to geography, there was a need for specialized concentration at headquarters for some corporate banking services. For example, Cumberland had some "national accounts" that were large corporations. These were serviced by the multinational group at Columbia Central or by loan production offices (located in six major U.S. cities), which reported to Paige as head of corporate banking. The relatively small international banking department, the merchant banking group, and the corporate cash management group were also based at Columbia Central and reported to Paige. To service the various geographic regions, the merchant banking and cash management groups also had representatives in each of the four largest affiliates.

As a result of the corporate banking areas of the affiliates working together, the roles of the corporate account officers across the Cumberland National system were standardized. For example, corporate account officers were all considered relationship managers and were required to prepare a yearly marketing plan which specified the amount of time to spend and the possible goals to achieve with each customer. Corporate account officers were also required to gain familiarity with all the products in corporate banking and in other functional areas so that they would be able to cross-sell products. (Some common training programs helped with this objective.) They were rewarded for their cross-selling efforts, especially by the merchant banking group which paid fees to corporate account officers who referred deals.

Although the functions of the corporate account officers were coordinated across the affiliates, substantial authority remained with the affiliates. For example, the affiliates were allowed the freedom to price their own products and to develop their own credit policy. Although there were no corporate policies on pricing, there was communication about pricing and other loan terms because each affiliate's senior loan officer held a seat on the credit policy committee, which reviewed all major credits. The credit policy committee, which met quarterly, was also responsible for setting corporate policies where needed. It reviewed, for example, the total corporate exposure to industry groups. In addition, the credit policy committee established a house lending limit for each bank affiliate, tied to the amount of its capital. Loans exceeding this house limit required corporate credit policy approval.

Trust

Unlike corporate banking, the business line coordinator for trust was based at Peoples Commerce Bank rather than at headquarters. Peoples Commerce had built a national reputation for its money management and trust activities, and had considerable experience and expertise in these areas. The trust coordinator was head of trust at Peoples Commerce. He reported to the CEO of Peoples Trust as the head of its trust department, and reported to the management committee as the trust coordinator.

Although each affiliate maintained its own trust department, several trust activities were being consolidated and run out of Peoples Commerce. Investment research was one example of a centralized trust activity; the investment research group at Peoples Commerce provided the affiliates with regular research on a list of companies for their use in portfolio management. The affiliates were not tied to this list, however, and were free to augment it with their own research of local companies. Another centralized activity performed at Peoples Commerce was the management of all of Cumberland National's commingled funds, that is, portfolios that were pools of smaller trust funds.

Other examples of the consolidation movement within trust included the initiative of Richard Askew, the trust coordinator, to install a common trust information system in the affiliates to improve the quality of their service and to achieve better performance measurement and reporting. In addition, Askew was pursuing the possibility of consolidating all trading activity. Within the affiliates there was some concern about this centralization trend. One such concern focused on the fact that as Cumberland National was becoming more sophisticated, the costs of this sophistication were being passed along to the affiliates. For example, Jeffrey Sutton, president and CEO of Gulf States Bancorp, remarked that the new trust information system was a better system than the one currently operated by Gulf States, but that the costs of the new system would very likely be higher than the expense Gulf States was currently bearing.

Another concern held by a number of the affiliates was that the centralization of certain trust activities would lead to the breakdown of some local relationships with securities firms. As explained by Charles Hardison, chairman and CEO of Union South Financial Corporation, the maintenance of ties with the local brokerage community was important because these firms provided key information about local companies. If trading were centralized, the affiliates felt they might lose this information stream because they would not be able to keep the local securities firms interested in servicing them.

Operations

Development of common systems like the new trust information system required an integrated approach to operations. During Cumberland National's early years, Columbia Central Bank and Peoples Commerce Bank coordinated their operations activities, but did little in the way of consolidating operations systems. As new banking companies were acquired, however, the need to develop a strategic plan for the consolidation of operations became more important. With each new acquisition, Cumberland National gained about sixty new operations systems and associated employees. According to one of the affiliate bank CEOs, the affiliates backed the consolidation of operations because they felt that the largest source of cost savings from the mergers would be found in this consolidation. In order to capture these cost savings and to plan for the future,

Cumberland National hired Robert Griffin to develop a global operations strategy. Griffin, who was located at Peoples Commerce rather than headquarters, was hired away from a large West Coast bank where he had gained a reputation for his ability to manage large operations functions.

Griffin's strategy for the consolidation of Cumberland National's operations called for the formation of three corporate data centers with identical operating environments. The data center operating environments were identical so that applications could be run in any of the three data centers. However, some systems were run only in the data center geographically closest to their applications. For example, the new trust information system was run in the data center closest to Peoples Commerce. Other applications characterized by high transaction volume, such as retail, were run in all of the data centers.

While centralizing operations was critical, Griffin could not pin down the dollar value of the economies of scale associated with the consolidation of operations. The process of calculating the savings from consolidation, both to the corporation and to the affiliates, was difficult because the allocation of costs could not be determined until the corporate systems were up and running in all of the affiliates. Furthermore, products and services were being improved as part of the consolidation process.

As Griffin implemented his overall strategy, his role evolved from that of operations coordinator to that of the line manager in charge of operations; the senior operations officers of all of the affiliates reported directly to him. As head of operations, Griffin was working to formalize the operation reporting relationships by establishing both functional and regional reporting networks. He anticipated a time when Cumberland National would have an operations reporting structure comprised of functional managers for each of the various operations systems and line managers for each affiliate.

Once Griffin's strategy had been implemented, the task of coordinating the operations of a new acquisition with those of Cumberland National became much easier and less complicated. The effectiveness of Griffin's overall strategy was demonstrated by the ease with which Cumberland National converted Gulf States Bancorp, the most recent of the Cumberland National acquisitions, to the corporate systems and centralized data centers.

A senior executive of Gulf States Bancorp described the straightforward plan that had been involved in converting Gulf States to Cumberland National's structure and systems:

> The plan calls for Gulf States to move its data processing hardware to the nearest data center over the course of a year. Over the following few years all of Gulf State's applications will be converted to the corporate systems, and we will reduce staff here. Gulf States will interact with the data center as a remote-site data center after the completion of the conversion process, and we will keep some key systems here because of our strong position in electronic funds transfer.

While the benefits of consolidating operations included capturing economies of scale and facilitating the integration of new acquisitions, these benefits came at a cost—the cost of losing the flexibility to accommodate all of the individual needs of the affiliates. Considerable time and effort was spent designing systems which met the dual objectives of meeting the affiliate needs and achieving economies of scale. Griffin and his group worked to satisfy both objectives in the design of a new branch automation system, the Enhanced Retail System (ERS). This system was to be used with tellers, loan officers and other "platform" people who worked with customers. ERS provided fast access to customer information, enabling the teller to deal with the customer needs faster, and the system also provided fast access to terms available on various banking products enabling the platform people to better sell products to customers.

Griffin described the difficulty encountered in developing a design which pleased all the affiliates:

> A committee was formed to design an automated system which would conform to the requirements of the various affiliates. The initial ERS design presented to the corporate management committee for approval was rejected because of its prohibitive cost. The committee went back to the affiliates to convince them to reduce their requirements. By going back to the affiliates the committee was able to reduce the cost of ERS by 36 percent, but the savings were achieved at the cost of time.

According to one bank affiliate, the final product will be helpful, but too much democracy was involved in the ERS design process.

Retail

While recognizing the need to work together on issues such as the design for ERS, the Cumberland National affiliates believed strongly in the philosophy of owning their individual retail customers and having the independence to deal with their own retail markets. This philosophy, coupled with the fact that retail was more segmented than the other banking functions, served to make retail the most difficult function to integrate, as noted by Carl Stone, the retail banking coordinator, located at corporate headquarters. Appreciating the need for affiliate independence in the retail marketplace, the bank affiliates retained all decision-making authority pertaining to the number and location of branches, ATM placement, pricing of consumer deposit and loan products, and the choice of products to market. Affiliates also retained their names. Most of the affiliates' retail customers were oblivious to the fact that their bank had joined an interstate bank holding company.

The retail coordinating committee, made up of the senior retail banking people at each affiliate, met every 60 days to exchange and share ideas about issues which impacted their marketplaces, such as marketing. For example, all the affiliates had worked together on a corporate image campaign. This coordination was not formalized, however, because no affiliate was bound to participate in the campaign if unsatisfied with the final product. In fact, one affiliate did choose to drop out, believing that the campaign would not work in its marketplace.

Cumberland National and the affiliates recognized the need for more formal coordination and consolidation of some activities, such as the Enhanced Retail System. In addition, Cumberland National had identified product areas such as consumer mortgages, student loans and credit cards, which should be centralized and run as one business. Cumberland National had, in fact, already begun its efforts to centralize credit card operations in an effort to capture the potential economies from the centralization of credit card processing. Cumberland National formed a new bank subsidiary to manage its centralized credit card business. Once on the system, the affiliated banks transferred their credit card assets to the credit card bank subsidiary. This bank passed along to the affiliates all the net income received from the credit card operations less a small fee fixed as a percent of assets.

At the corporate level, the consolidation of the credit card business was expected to improve profitability and some of the affiliates expected improved returns. Other affiliates, however, were concerned that the movement of these assets would lead to a reduction in profitability because the funding costs of the credit card bank would be higher than their funding costs. Another affiliate, Gulf States Bancorp, stood to take a large reduction in revenues from the centralization of credit card processing because it had been very active in credit card processing for its correspondent banks. An executive there commented:

> If they take way our revenue stream, I hope Cumberland National plans to replace the revenue stream with something else or allows us to lop off the entire expense. Lots or negotiation still must be done in this area.

Like some of the affiliates, the head of the credit card bank subsidiary also had concerns about the profitability of centralized credit card operations. In his case, because the profitability of the credit card bank was fixed by formula, and was therefore unchanging, he raised the question of how his performance and that of his subsidiary would be evaluated, particularly since the return on assets he was allowed was below the corporate target.

Carl Stone, executive vice president of Columbia Central Bank and the coordinator for retail banking, believed that there was much more to do in the retail area:

> We have made a lot of progress with the branch automation system and we have begun to put in place a back office system for consumer deposits. We hope to also put in place a new back office system for consumer loans, and we are looking to reduce costs through the centralized purchasing of products like travelers checks and credit life insurance. Furthermore, we are looking forward to the day when the repeal of Glass-Steagall will allow us to distribute securities; we have formed a task force to help us plan for this event.

Asset and Liability Management

A second area in which each affiliate felt strongly about maintaining its independence was that of asset and liability management. Each of the affiliates was responsible for its own asset and liability management. Thus, each affiliate not only managed its own securities portfolio, but also set its own policies with regard to its liquidity position and interest rate risk. The importance of having local control over asset and liability management was illustrated by William Fenner, CEO of Peoples Commerce, who explained that his bank chose to operate with ample liquidity and capital so that the bank could jump into new opportunities as they became available.

John Andersen, the coordinator for asset and liability management, explained that while decisions were made by the individual affiliates, these decisions were made within guidelines established by the corporation. For example, there were policy limits on the amount of interest rate risk that each affiliate could take. These limits were relatively strict in order to keep the corporation as a whole within its established limits, even if all the affiliates were to "bet" in concert on an interest rate move.

Cumberland National developed these policy limits in conjunction with the affiliates. Jeffrey Sutton, President and CEO of Gulf States Bancorp, explained that because Gulf States felt strongly about controlling its own asset and liability management, the Gulf States representative on the committee took an active part in developing the corporate guidelines to ensure that Gulf States would have sufficient flexibility.

Although these guidelines somewhat restricted the affiliates' freedom to manage their own assets and liabilities, one affiliate president noted that the policy limits were useful because they encouraged the affiliates to share information. For example, the affiliates were encouraged to share information about their asset and liability management strategy and their view of the future direction of interest rates and the economy.

Human Resource Management

Consistent with the corporation's philosophy, each of the bank affiliates had a high degree of autonomy with regard to hiring, firing and salary decisions. All of the affiliates, however, were on a common payroll system and some corporatewide policies were in place. As explained by David Scott, senior vice president-Human Resources for Cumberland National, all employees were part of the corporate benefit programs including pension, health benefits and profit sharing, and some common policies had been adopted. For example, there were Cumberland National policies for employee transfers and displaced employees. Finally, the top sixty or so officers in the corporation were part of a corporatewide compensation program so that the senior people in each affiliate were treated in a consistent manner.

Recent Moves Towards Consolidation

In an effort to increase integration and to encourage the senior officers to work together for the good of the corporation, Heyward, Cumberland's CEO, put in place a new approach to compensation for the top sixty people in the organization. Their compensation in the new program consisted of a base salary, cash bonus, and stock incentives. The base salary for each individual was based on the size and performance of the banking company with which he or she was affiliated. For example, a senior officer from a $5 billion affiliate would receive a base salary competitive with that of comparable officers from other $5 billion banks. The annual cash bonuses, however, were tied to total corporate performance only, including the growth of Cumberland National's earnings per share, return on equity, and return on assets. The stock incentive, which was designed to place a significant amount of Cumberland National stock in the hands of the officers to promote their long-term interest in the performance of the corporation and to promote a Cumberland National culture, was based on the three-year performance of the firm.

Another move Heyward made to increase integration was to alter the reporting relationships of the retail coordinator and the head of operations so that they both reported to the same member of the senior management committee. With this move he hoped to strengthen the linkage between retail and operations throughout the system.

Over the past several months Heyward and his colleagues had been carefully considering areas of the corporation where stronger integration was needed, and where it should be avoided. This led, for example, to the appointment of Griffin as the line manager for operations and the shift in reporting relationships. Heyward was now considering what other changes, if any, should be made or encouraged to evolve over time. One issue was the role of the business line coordinator. Heyward viewed this role as a continuum; at one end of the spectrum the role took the form of a facilitator who improved the coordination among the affiliates, and at the other end of the spectrum the role took the form of a line manager for each function. His task was to determine now where on the continuum the Cumberland National business coordinators should lie.

Citicorp's Investment Bank and Vickers da Costa

MEMORANDUM

Negotiations for the acquisitions of Vickers are close to completion, and our letter of offer will be submitted to the Vickers Board and shareholders, during the next few days. This memorandum provides summary background on the transaction.

The Company

Vickers is a London-based stock brokerage firm (founded some 95 years ago), which, more recently, has established a successful niche position in Asian securities servicing U.K., European, and United States' institutional investors. Its principal offices are located in London, Tokyo, and Hong Kong, with smaller activities in Singapore and New York.

The Transaction

It is proposed that Citicorp acquire 100% of Vickers and spin out the London Stock Exchange Business into a new company to be owned 70.1% by the current management shareholders, and 29.9% by us. This structure is required by the current London Stock Exchange limitations on ownership.

Business Rationale

Vickers is one of a limited number of foreign firms holding a securities license in Japan, the others being Merrill, Salomon, Bache, Hutton, Smith Barney, Jardine Fleming, and Kidder. Obtaining a license by direct application is regarded as impossible for the foreseeable future. However, acquisition of an existing license has some prospect of success. Due to their character, none of the other license holders could be acquired by Citicorp. Thus, Vickers provides a unique, but unassured, opportunity to enter the Japanese securities market.

Vickers' existing overseas business is healthy and is projected to remain so. The U.K. vehicle faces the uncertainty of the advent of negotiated commissions in the London market. In aggregate, the financial prospects and product diversification aspects are attractive, especially in light of the unique Japanese opportunity.

This case was prepared by Assistant Professor David M. Meerschwam.
Copyright © 1987 by the President and Fellows of Harvard College. Harvard Business School case 9-288-025.

This internal memorandum was circulated to senior management at Citicorp in late 1983. If the acquisition were completed, it would expand Citicorp's presence in the investment banking field; thus it could represent a major step toward fulfilling management's goal for Citicorp to make it the preeminent international investment bank.

Citicorp's possible acquisition of Vickers (and the effect it would have on Citicorp's approach to global investment banking) raised serious challenges. Yet the size of the expected transaction was not a major concern. The financial press estimated that Citicorp would pay $20 million to $30 million — a manageable sum for a company with $5.8 billion in equity capital. The real challenge was to decide whether Vickers fit with Citicorp's overall strategy. Here, serious questions had to be asked: Would the purchase of Vickers force Citicorp into additional purchases, or could the project stand on its own? Which parts of Vickers would prove most valuable to Citicorp, and how could they be fit together with Citicorp's existing businesses? Would the purchase primarily strengthen specific weaknesses in the existing organization, or would it simply create new opportunities? The very possibility of acquiring Vickers served by itself to highlight the changing nature of investment and commercial banking, as the largest U.S. commercial bank found itself debating the purchase of a London securities broker which had attractive operations in Japan.

Paul J. Collins, Citicorp's senior executive in charge of the Investment Bank, contemplated these issues as he reviewed the briefing books prepared by his staff on Citicorp's Investment Bank and Vickers da Costa. He also considered the role of the Investment Bank and its relationships with other parts of the corporation, because Vickers da Costa might set a new direction in the development of the Investment Bank. Top management, Collins thought, would have to make broad strategy decisions as the corporation pursued a field where strong, experienced, highly profitable players already operated, such as Salomon Brothers, Nomura, and S. G. Warburg. In order to set strategy, Citicorp first would need to evaluate its current businesses and its rationale for entering the investment banking business. Earlier, management had articulated its willingness to commit Citicorp's formidable resources to building its Investment Bank into the preeminent global investment bank; now, Collins must set the strategy to achieve this goal.

Citicorp's Banking Business in 1983

In 1983, Citicorp was the largest banking organization in the world, with 63,700 employees, 1,603 offices in 94 countries, $135 billion in assets, and $860 million of net income. In contrast to many other large U.S. banks, Citicorp's net income derived primarily from outside the U.S.: North America contributed 38%; the Caribbean, Central, and South America, 26%; Europe, the Middle East, and Africa, 19%; and Asia/Pacific, 17%.

Apart from its broad geographical distribution, Citicorp offered a broadly diversified product portfolio. In 1983, three "banks" made up Citicorp: The Institutional Bank, the Individual Bank, and the Investment Bank. They contributed 70%, 19%, and 11%, respectively, of total income, with ROE of 22%, 18%, and 32%. (The Investment Bank was officially known as the Capital Markets Group. See Appendix A.)

The Institutional Bank offered services to corporate clients, the Individual Bank to retail customers. The Investment Bank serviced institutions and individuals with products not offered by the other two banks. Foreign exchange and money market transactions for institutional clients accounted for almost 45% of the net income of the Institutional Bank.

Citicorp's broad geographic and product market portfolio put it in a unique position in the context of capital transactions, which were becoming increasingly international. For example, international banking claims (i.e., Eurocurrency transactions and local currency transactions for nonresidents) grew from $20 billion in 1964 to $208 billion in 1972, and to $2,553 billion in 1983. Similarly, international banking assets also grew until they comprised 72% of total bank assets in the U.K., 8% in Germany, 11% in Japan, and 17% in the U.S.

U.S. holdings of foreign assets also grew from $23 billion in 1952, to $60 billion in 1962, to $149 billion in 1972; in 1983, of $761 billion in foreign assets, $84 billion consisted of securities. Even faster growth had taken place in the international liabilities of the U.S., as countries such as Japan rapidly expanded their international net asset position. Portfolio diversification, international capital market deregulation, and current account imbalances were partly responsible for these developments.

Citicorp stood as an acknowledged leader in international banking. In 1983, the bank's largest business group, the Institutional Bank, had $37 billion in non-U.S. loans outstanding, out of $60 billion of commercial loans. While the Institutional Bank dominated Citicorp's net income, the relative profit performances of the three banks in the organization did shift over time:

Net Income ($ millions)

	Institutional Banking	Individual Banking	Investment Banking
1979	521	0	69
1980	665	−79	100
1981	669	−42	118
1982	751	66	119
1983	758	202	128

Note: Values exclude corporate and other overhead, which amounted to $228 million in 1983.

These results reflected the changing environment in which Citicorp operated. While the bank had been a leader in the innovation of many banking products, such as the negotiable certificate of deposit and interest rate swaps, traditional loan products—especially standard loans to the largest corporations—became less popular. As a response, Citicorp developed in the U.S. a carefully targeted and highly successful middle-market strategy, especially in areas such as real estate and leveraged finance. Still, one senior executive noted:

> I know that some say that the standard loan-to-large-corporations business is going to be tough and is never going to come back, but just wait. Some of the newer ways in which "securitization" takes place might become difficult if the overall optimism in the securities markets dies down. The Commercial Paper market could dry up. It happened before and could happen again. Then you will see how many are going to come back to us to ask for simple loans.

Meanwhile, the liabilities side of the bank's balance sheet was also undergoing change. With many new interest-paying deposit-like instruments available, noninterest-bearing demand deposits were losing their importance as the major source of funds. Here, one option for Citicorp (and other banks) was to purchase funds in the Certificate of Deposit market and the Euromarkets, thus making the bank "independent" of a stable retail deposit base. Using these funding vehicles, other banks had executed strategies of rapid growth to become aggressive lenders through traditional loan origination, loan participation, or loan purchases. Citicorp, in contrast, preferred to rely on an aggressive diversified funding strategy. Some other banks followed a different route, with a less diversified funding base, and they got into trouble; of these, Continental Illinois Bank from Chicago represented the largest casualty so far. Yet other banks had turned away from the lending and deposit business entirely, transforming themselves into merchant banks. As one senior banker at such a bank noted: "The risks are simply no longer commensurate with the rewards in traditional banking. Actually, that is precisely the case because there is no longer any 'traditional' banking."

New Competition and Financial Supermarkets

Apart from the changing importance of the traditional loan product, Citicorp also faced challenges from new competitors. In the U.S., the development of the Commercial Paper (CP) market, the advent of Rule 415, and the spectacular growth of the high yield market — all heightened the possible threat represented by investment banking houses. During the second half of both the 1970s and 1980s, many investment banks expanded rapidly, and remuneration escalated at all professional levels within those organizations. High profits, often driven by advisory services and principal transactions, made all this possible. As a result, an intense competition for highly qualified personnel soon developed.

Meanwhile, the international environment was also changing. The remarkable success of the Japanese economy and the overall organization of the Japanese financial system had created large banks in their home country. In Germany, universal banks operated unhindered by any such separation between investment and commercial banking as that which existed in both the U.S. and Japan. In the U.K. during the 1980s, a reorganization of the financial system allowed for stronger, better-capitalized players in the investment banking sector, while large, nationwide commercial banks continued to operate. Most important, across the world a notion of "global financial markets" was gaining in popularity, and new "financial supermarkets" appeared under the sponsorship of several industry participants presented by some as the only way into the future.

Those who endorsed financial supermarkets believed that only large, broadly diversified financial institutions, offering all products to all clients, would remain viable organizations in the future. As new financial products were developed, to create attractive substitutes for traditional instruments, competition across products and institutions would intensify. Continuation of this trend would make it necessary for the financial institution of the future to offer all kinds of products. Yet other observers argued that the concept of a financial supermarket remained ill-defined while any alleged economics of scope seemed impossible to demonstrate.

The supermarket concept itself was not new. In the early 1920s, National City Bank—Citicorp's predecessor—stood as a strong wholesale and investment bank. Services to individuals were only added on later. Also, National City Bank maintained an international network with branches in 21 countries. By 1929, the bank was the largest in the U.S. and the second largest in the world, behind only the British Midland Bank. It was also the largest distributor of securities and a leading underwriter.[1] After the financial dislocations and instability of the 1930s, however, the few financial supermarkets that existed in the U.S. soon disappeared from public view, only to be discussed again in the financial press during the 1970s—now as a partial result of regulatory change.

By 1983, various reorganizations at Citicorp had created the Institutional Bank, the Individual Bank, and the Investment Bank. These "Three I's" made a potential "financial supermarket" out of Citicorp; but in 1983, the "Third I" had not yet fully developed. Management expected, however, to grow the Investment Bank rapidly. As one senior manager in the Investment Bank noted:

> There is no doubt that we are going to be a major investment bank. The whole separation between investment and commercial banking no longer makes sense. Look at what investment banks do; they commit their own capital in deals, they provide bridge financing. They can't expect to expand their reach while we sit back and wait to see our business disappear with our hands tied by the Glass-Steagall Act. It's just a matter of time until Glass-Steagall goes, and then you will see Article 65 in Japan follow. In London we can already enter into the business. Once we are able to play in all three places, we are going to be a formidable player. We are much better prepared than the others to manage a large global organization. We have name recognition in more places than the others. In building a global investment bank, Citicorp has as good a chance as anyone else. Actually, we have a better shot at it!

Citicorp's Investment Bank

After the reorganization of 1982, which had formed the Investment Bank by combining the Investment Management Group, the Merchant Banking Group and the Financial Markets Group, Citicorp separated the activities of the Investment Bank into investment banking, investment management, and international private banking. The Investment Bank's approximately 5,000 employees represented 8% of total employment at Citicorp. Net income of $128 million, which did not include the investment banking income of the Institutional Bank, accounted for 11% of total income of Citicorp; it could be defined as follows: 60% of the $128 million was from "investment banking" (50% origination and distribution, and 50% trading and positioning); 20% was from investment management and other services; and 20% was from international private banking. Net income which excluded foreign exchange revenues still placed Citicorp's investment bank among the top earners in the U.S. investment banking industry.

Investment Banking

Citicorp's investment banking activities were organized by three geographic areas. Business plans were produced by the U.S.; Europe, the Middle East, Africa and Asia (EMEAA); and the Western Hemisphere. This geographic distribution seemed consistent with many of Citicorp's other businesses. Within the various geographies, trading and positioning, distribution, origination, and mergers and acquisitions were segmented.

Citicorp estimated the U.S. origination market to have an issue volume of $1,200–$1,300 billion. Within this market, Citicorp was excluded from certain municipal underwritings and from all corporate equities and bond issues. Within the markets in which Citicorp participated, its share of Eurosecurities was falling: In 1977, Citicorp underwrote $235 million; in 1982, while volume rose to $485 million, Citicorp's place in the league tables fell from sixteenth to thirty-fifth. In the market for private placements, Citicorp remained a marginal player; while the top six firms accounted for 60% of the total market, and the top 15 for 90%, Citicorp did not rank among them. In eligible municipal notes and bonds (approximately 45% of the total municipal market) Citicorp did stand among the top 10 issuers. In the Commercial Paper market, Citicorp was mainly active in Citicorp's own issues. Finally, in mortgage-backed securities, Citicorp had not yet developed a major presence.

Citicorp considered its U.S. distribution weak, in contrast to that of its entrenched investment banking competitors, in all four segments: banks, insurance companies, investment counselors and mutual funds. Although the quality of its sales force had been upgraded over time, Citicorp still considered it low when compared to the forces of its top competitors.

In U.S. trading and positioning, Citicorp's government securities trading operations stood as the largest of any commercial bank. Since the U.S. government market was the deepest homogeneous market in the world, Citicorp's very strong position here held great importance. Still, its market share declined from 12.5% in 1979 to 6.5% in 1982, as aggressive competitors continued to enter the market. In municipal securities trading, Citicorp maintained only a small presence, as less than 10% of the total trading profits were generated here. Trading in money market instruments was also much smaller than the government securities operations. Citicorp actively positioned in all areas in which it traded securities. Still, 1982 profit center earnings from positioning represented less than 10% of the total Investment Bank.

Meanwhile, the total U.S. Mergers and Acquisitions and Divestitures (M&A) market grew from a total of $22 billion in 1977 to $83 billion in 1981. Here, Citicorp's presence was primarily in smaller M&A transactions, in management buyouts, and in cross border M&A. While the largest U.S. investment banks generated $15-$25 billion each in M&A transactions, Citicorp established activity in transactions with a total value of $1.5 billion. (A total of 18 deals were made by the firm in 1983, compared to an average of 50 deals each by the four largest participants: Goldman Sachs, First Boston, Lazard Freres, and Morgan Stanley. At Citibank, the average size of the deals stood at $81 million, compared to $323 million at each of the top five.)

All U.S. investment banking activities described above, with net income of $38 million, contributed approximately 30% of the total net income of Citicorp's Investment Bank. Activities of the EMEAA added another 18%, and the Western Hemisphere added 12%.

EMEAA contributions were divided according to both geography and products. Fifty percent of all activities were considered mainstream products; of these, 27% was generated in Asia, 50% in the U.K., 11% in Switzerland, 8% in Germany, and 4% in other locations. Using a product distribution, 38% resulted from currency hedging and swaps, 25% from securities trading and positioning, 24% from loans syndication, and 13% from other businesses. In all, EMEAA contributed $23 million to net income.

In the Western Hemisphere outside the U.S., Citicorp was active in a host of different countries, with different products generating net income of $15 million.

Investment Management

In 1983, Citicorp managed over $36 billion in assets. It offered a global investment portfolio consisting of equities, debt, and real estate securities. Included were both general and specialty funds, such as a venture capital fund, an emerging growth fund, and a high-yield fund. Net income was approximately $25 million.

International Private Banking

After the reorganization of 1982, International Private Banking (IPB) reported as a profit center within the Investment Bank. During the 1970s, and especially after the oil shock of 1973, IPB experienced success in attracting funds to manage. Many of the products that were offered relied on U.S. government securities, especially where clients seemed primarily concerned about safety. Furthermore, in dealing with high net worth individuals, the group noted that a substantial float was often available when clients did not rapidly reinvest their funds, so long as interest rates remained high.

During the late 1970s and early 1980s, the profitability of IPB was put at risk. Less float became available, while demand for private security transactions by increasingly sophisticated investors, who often showed interest in non-U.S. securities, increased. Still, the IPB was regarded, inside and outside of Citicorp, as a highly successful institution in terms of both profitability and professionalism. By early 1982, the Investment Management Group (IMG) and IPB had emerged as the driving forces in establishing a truly international securities business. So when it appeared that a British broker, W.I. Carr, who operated mostly in the Hong Kong market, would be available for sale, IPB and IMG sought approval to attempt an acquisition. Before Citicorp could enter into negotiations, however, W.I. Carr was purchased by another firm.

Opportunities for the Investment Bank

By building a strong worldwide investment banking presence, Citicorp established various potential advantages over its competitors. As a senior executive in the Investment Bank noted, its foreign exchange capabilities had become formidable, and these could be used to get access to new clients and to aid related investment banking activities. Also, the international securities business would provide additional opportunities, since Citicorp already had the resources to build a worldwide network. Several executives at the bank also believed that the popular trend toward financial "globalization" might work in Citicorp's particular favor because the firm could demonstrate vast international experience. Yet, another possible advantage could result from Citicorp's comparable experience with complex organizations and management structures. (See Appendix B for Citicorp's internal summary assessment of the Investment Bank's competitive position.)

FOREIGN EXCHANGE By 1983, Citicorp's investment banking-related businesses were uneven in relative importance. Most successful were the trading functions in the deep U.S. government security and foreign exchange markets. In 1980, foreign exchange transactions generated revenues of $164 million; in 1981, $265 million; in 1983, $241 million; and in 1984, $274 million. All the while, the foreign exchange business was principally located in the Institutional Bank. Some Citicorp managers argued, however, that the foreign exchange function should be consolidated into the Investment Bank, along with those other investment banking-related activities currently located in the Institutional Bank. In fact, a strong foreign exchange group might benefit the whole Investment Bank. A strategy document noted:

> From one perspective, the existing business, with its successful trading and positioning activities (foreign exchange, hedging products, government bonds) can buy us time and pay for the development of other products. At the same time, it provides a skill basis which can be valuable in developing new products and penetrating the mar-

kets for investment banking services. From a second perspective, our trading and positioning activities may be viewed as a core business that will continue to generate the largest share of revenues and profits. From a third perspective, our FX, hedging and government bond trading units are such an enormously successful proposition that their very success can, maybe even justifiably, absorb the bulk of management attention.

CORPORATE SECURITIES   For Citicorp the rewards for running a global securities business could be very large. While in 1982, worldwide equity turnover was only $745 billion, by the end of the decade this number was expected to grow to $3,500 billion. Profitability in this segment would result from increases in equity prices, volume, and commission rates, which, according to forecast might well in 1990 provide $7-$17 billion in total commissions. Also it was expected that the current trend toward institutional equity holdings would continue. Citicorp noted in a strategy discussion that the securities business "could be dominated by a very few major firms."

> The combination of institutionalization of stock ownership, the growth in cross-border investment, and deregulation of fixed commissions could change stockbroking from a relatively fragmented to a highly concentrated business.

> This is made even more likely because of the increasing importance of market making as a factor on which institutional investors choose between stockbroking firms, and which inevitably means that large global firms have an inherent competitive advantage.

GLOBAL BANKING   Given its difficulty in entering the U.S. investment banking field—at least so long as the Glass-Steagall Act remained effective—Citicorp faced the need to build its investment banking capability from a non-U.S. perspective. Because of the trend toward more international financial transactions, this need could actually create an advantage for Citicorp. Still, several major U.S. investment banks already had started to expand outside the U.S., especially into the U.K. and Japan, from their strong domestic positions. Since Citicorp had no strong position in any one particular investment banking product, it would have to decide whether to expand across a broad range of products, or with only a few. Thus, Citicorp was forced to integrate, from the beginning, both a product and a geographic market strategy. At its Investment Bank one executive declared:

> If you think about Citicorp with an Investment Bank, an Institutional Bank and an Individual Bank, it's clear that we are uniquely positioned to offer a wide product line. Citicorp can build on experience in one bank to help the others. Not only can clients move between banks, within the banks they can move between products. The problem with a wide product line is of course that you can't concentrate your efforts and you can't lever your position in new products from a spectacularly well-established one. Also we have the problem that regulation is national. How can you develop a broad line if you can't do one thing in country A and another in country B? If regulation is national, can markets be global?

Already during the 1980s "globalization" of finance had emerged as a buzzword, with popularity second only to "securitization." Nevertheless, some managers at Citicorp felt that this intriguing concept was being adopted all too easily. An executive in charge of foreign exchange activities remarked:

People are getting carried away with this notion of global everything. Take investment banking. It is not quite clear where many of the presumed global advantages lie. One way to describe the world is by thinking of three markets. One is the "time-zone market." There, truly global products are transacted. That's really in New York, Tokyo and London. The second consists of developed national centers. Zurich, Amsterdam, and Sydney are examples. Finally, you have the developing places.

Now, you can also divide the product sector. There are strategic financial services. From there you get to institutional securities. These are company-specific. Another sector consists of the financial markets for deep, internationally homogeneous products. There are really very few of these. Investment management services obviously need competence in the three areas I just described. But ask yourself, how much of all this is really globalized, and where are the huge economies of scope and scale everybody is so excited about?

You see, in the various types of markets, we can do different things in terms of product sectors, and we have to use different feed-in mechanisms to get the business. In many of the developed national center markets, we have a good shot at doing the institutional securities business. Few companies there know that we don't do origination, market-making, and positioning in the United States. We have a great name in those markets and, if the larger companies there do "traditional" business with Citi, the Investment Bank can get in too.

In the various national markets, and especially in the three central ones, change was occurring. For Citicorp specific changes in the investment banking industry, as well as the effects of those changes on the established local players added up to new opportunities. As one senior executive noted:

We shouldn't fool ourselves. Citicorp was not a real competitor for investment banking services during the 1970s or 1980s. But that's going to change. If you want to make a presence in a market, none is better than the one in which the entrenched players are experiencing lots of change. We have to decide in this changing market what to do; how to create opportunities out of globalization. Think of a simple matrix. Vertically the investment banking products. Horizontally, the countries. Now think of the lines; do you draw product lines vertically, horizontally or diagonally? Which products are global and which are local? All investment banks are trying to figure this out. We have more experience than anyone at juggling such a task. Also, we have the organizational structure.

ORGANIZATIONAL CHALLENGES AND OPPORTUNITIES Rapid growth among investment banks, together with their entry into foreign markets forced them to pay increased attention to "management issues." Citicorp, for example, declared in its annual report for 1979:

As we continue to grow, it is imperative that we resist the historical tendency of large institutions to become institutionalized—that is to say, "bureaucratized"—with added layers of management separating those who make decisions from those who provide services. Such layering of management invariably leads to hardening of the intellectual arteries in any organization and tends to quench entrepreneurial incentive.

Another adverse consequence of rapid business growth around the world is the tendency to Balkanize what is essentially one business into separate components occasionally striving at cross-purposes. Such Balkanization sacrifices the economies of scale that otherwise would be available to us and to our customers if we integrated these fragments of the same business on a global basis.

While in the past, it had often been suggested that a bank like Citicorp would not be able to compete with much more flatly organized U.S. investment banks, where "producers" rather than "managers" stood at the center, now Citicorp's formidable experience in managing large organizations appeared to offer a competitive advantage (rather than a disadvantage) in a world increasingly dominated by a few large banks. These international banks would be differently managed and controlled—run in a way quite different from the "nonmanaged" style of the presently dominant local investment banks. In the future, then, Citicorp's acknowledged management expertise might provide new opportunities. Traditionally in Citicorp, local organizations experienced a lot of freedom, but they also reported upward through a well-established management hierarchy. In the words of one vice president:

> To understand Citi's success, you have to understand the importance of local autonomy in managing and controlling large complex organizations. Local organizations had their own responsibility. They did their loan origination, they had their treasury function, and they financed themselves. The great thing was that all the local autonomy didn't matter that much from a risk perspective. We were in so many places that the portfolio was diversified. Local independence was essential. You just can't run a bank as big as this one without local autonomy. Citicorp is outstanding at combining the local autonomy with overall control and management.

Vickers da Costa (Holdings plc.)

When IPB and IMG continued to search for a broker, Vickers da Costa (Vickers), a British securities broker, became the most interesting candidate. In the U.K., financial markets were changing, and the old system of "single capacity" dealing was abolished so that brokers and market makers could be combined into a single function. Also, the fixed commission structure was replaced with negotiated commissions. Finally, the restrictions on outside ownership of stock exchange members was due to change: the old limit declared that no more than 30% interest could be acquired; but that limit was expected to be increased to 100%.

All this change led experts to anticipate the appearance of many new entities in London markets. Clearing banks, merchant banks, and foreign banks—all were looking to purchase British financial institutions. For Citicorp, one of the first firms to actively pursue a possible acquisition after the announcements of regulatory change on the London Stock Exchange, Vickers seemed attractive.

Already Vickers operated out of London, Hong Kong, Tokyo, and New York. It had secondary operations in Singapore, Taiwan, and the Philippines. At all locations, Vickers was a full service broker with strong research competence in Far Eastern stocks. In the London market, Vickers (VCL) accounted for 1% of the total value of equity transactions, and its research department covered industry sectors that accounted for 35% of market turnover. Apart from brokerage activity, the 245 employees offered few additional products. Net brokerage income represented approximately $5 million in London, $2 million in Japan, and $2.1 million in Hong Kong.

In Hong Kong, Vickers (VCHK) obtained virtually all of its income from securities brokerage activities. Market share there had risen to 6.3% of turnover at the local stock exchanges, in 1983, and internal management expected the upward trend to continue. VCHK was the third largest broker in Hong Kong, after Jardine Fleming Securities Limited and Sun Hung Kai Investment Services Limited. Of the $2.1 million of net income generated in Hong Kong, 90% derived from activities carried out through Tokyo. Sixty-five employees worked for VCHK.

Vickers also had a U.S. presence (VCUS)—a member firm of the National Association of Securities Dealers. Of the total commission earnings of that company, less than 1% was generated in the U.S. Still, growth remained strong, with revenues tripling between 1981 and 1982 and doubling between 1982 and 1983. Only six people worked for VCUS.

In Tokyo, Vickers (VCT) was active mostly in dealing for non-Japanese residents, although it did participate in underwriting of yen-dominated international bond issues and a few equity issues. The largest client of VCT was VCHK, which accounted for almost 70% of all commissions generated in Tokyo. Twenty-eight people formed the staff in the Tokyo office, which had opened in 1972. In 1978, the office became a registered branch, and it was issued a security dealing license, as the third non-Japanese firm to qualify. This license allowed the firm to enter into a variety of investment banking activities (excluding foreign exchange transactions, which, in Japan, can only be executed by commercial banks). At that time, 248 such licensed securities dealers operated in Japan; 83 were members of the Tokyo Stock Exchange (TSE).

The TSE, the largest of Japan's eight exchanges, accounted for more than 80% of all equity transactions in the country. The TSE listed 1,430 companies and had capitalization of ¥98 trillion in 1983. Of the 83 members of the TSE, four giants dominated the market: Daiwa, Nikko, Nomura, and Yamaichi, which together accounted for over 50% of all transactions. Non-Japanese held 5% of Japanese securities and accounted for 17% of all turnover.

The non-Japanese security license holders were: Merrill Lynch (with 131 employees); Jardine Fleming (42); Smith Barney, Harris Upham (40); Vickers (31); Prudential Bache (31); Salomon (25); Kidder Peabody (25); and Goldman Sachs (which only recently entered the market and had few employees). When Prudential Insurance Corporation purchased Bache Securities, it eagerly awaited the reaction of the Japanese Ministry of Finance (MoF). In Japan, insurance companies could not enter into the securities business. However, the MoF appeared satisfied that sufficient distance would remain between Prudential and Bache, and Bache retained its license.

For Vickers, the Japanese license proved particularly valuable because of its transactions on behalf of Hong Kong operations. Furthermore, the abolition of foreign exchange controls in the U.K., fueled the appetite of British investors for foreign securities. In servicing these investors, Vickers held an advantage because of its highly esteemed research division; its coverage of Japanese securities was broad and effectively directed at investors in foreign stocks.

A Japanese license could be lost by violating any one of the many rules that the organization was subject to. A typical violation involved a company carrying out some business which

> under Japanese legislation would be incompatible with the securities business, or the carrying on of such activity by a closely related party. Incompatible activities include those of a bank, trust company. . . .

Strategic Options

Most investment banking industry observers and participants expected the future investment banking world to be very different from the present. Almost every observer foresaw a small group of internationally active, dominant firms.

Here, Citicorp was uniformly expected to be among these ultimate survivors. In order to claim its place, by building a major investment banking presence, Citicorp considered four strategic options:

1. **Global Focus**—serving all clients in all geographic markets, in all product markets.

2. **Product Focus**—serving all clients, in all geographic markets, with only restricted products.

3. **Geographic Focus**—serving clients in one geographic market with all products.

4. **Local Focus**—serving clients in different geographic markets with different products.

In 1983, it became clear that Citicorp's Investment Bank was "local." Depending on where the corporation wanted to be in the future, it would have to take action in pursuing one of the four options that had been formulated. Yet all four options posed some problems for Citicorp, especially when that firm compared itself to those U.S. and Japanese investment banks which had substantial domestic businesses and still were actively building international activities. Citicorp, in contrast, held no natural advantage in any domestic market, and thus no base on which to build a global presence.

For Citicorp, the possible acquisition of Vickers da Costa offered an intriguing opportunity, even though the acquisition itself was small and, in absolute size, not all that important. Still, Vickers offered a window of opportunity on entering new markets by strengthening Citicorp's intentions of building a global investment bank—one that would compete with the best U.S. and Japanese institutions, which presently dominated the market. At the same time, however, the acquisition of Vickers could represent no more than a step toward Citicorp's ultimate goal. And even worse, if Vickers did not form a strategic fit, it might actually be a costly mistake especially in terms of organizational confusion and misdirected energy, at a crucial time in the development of the Investment Bank at Citicorp.

Appendix A
Citicorp's Investment Bank and Vickers da Costa

Citicorp's Organizational Structure: Evolution Since 1978

The present structure of the bank and of investment banking at Citicorp can be understood by looking back at 1978. At that time, seven business groups existed, each led by an executive vice president. By 1983, the corporation consisted of three banks: the Institutional Bank, the Individual Bank, and the Investment Bank. The Investment Bank's business was divided into three parts: investment banking, investment management, and international private banking.

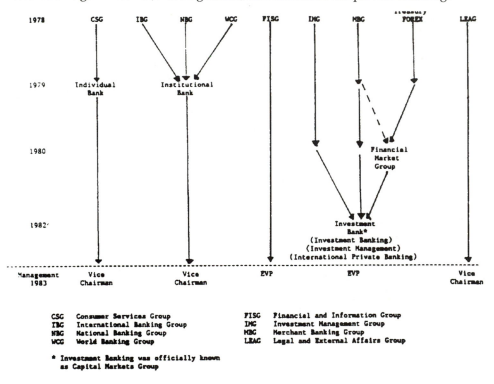

1. Consumer Services Group (CSG). This group dealt with the financing needs of individuals in the U.S. (mostly in New York City and parts of New York State) and abroad.

2. International Banking Group (IBG). IBG was responsible for institutional banking activities in 92 countries, except for those activities that were the specific territory of another group. The individual countries' operating and treasury functions were overseen by this group.

3. National Banking Group (NBG). U.S. corporations other than multinational corporations were serviced through this group.

4. World Corporation Group (WCG). This group offered credit and financial services to the largest multinational corporations. Using both industry and geographic segmentation, the group managed each company's account from the country in which the company was headquartered.

5. Financial and Information Services Group (FISG). FISG maintained delivery of credit, treasury, money market, fiduciary, operational, and informational services to correspondent banks, thrift institutions, and federal, state, and municipal entities.

6. Investment Management Group (IMG). IMG handled all investment-related activities for high net worth individuals and institutions from around the world.

7. Merchant Banking Group (MBG). MBG offered fee-based financial advice and funding, fundraising for the public sector, and venture capital activities. In the non-U.S. sector, activity centered in the London and Hong Kong offices. The international group participated in international loan syndication, underwriting and distributing international securities, and international corporate finance.

In 1979, the bank reorganized around two core businesses: Institutional Banking and Individual Banking. At this time, FISG, IMG, MBG, Legal and External Affairs (LEAG), and Treasury and Foreign Exchange were described as "other businesses." Three senior executive vice presidents were appointed: Hans H. Angermueller (LEAG), John S. Reed (Individual Banking), and Thomas C. Theobald (Institutional Banking). All three were considered potential successors to Mr. Wriston, chairman of Citicorp. In 1980, a Financial Markets Group was created; in 1982 the Capital Markets Group was formed and became unofficially known as the Investment Bank. Messrs. Angermueller, Reed, and Theobald were, in 1982, appointed vice chairmen of Citicorp, with responsibility for the LEAG, the Individual Bank, and the Institutional Bank, respectively.

Appendix B
Citicorp's Investment Bank and Vickers da Costa

Citicorp's Competitive Analysis of its Investment Bank

1. Investment Banking

► Continued trend of industry consolidation into large diversified institutions.

► Large U.S. commercial banks attempting to enter.

► Commercial banks dominate in products required for global reach, such as foreign exchange and loan syndication.

► U.S. investment banks dominate U.S. and European corporate securities.

► European markets have major presences of big Swiss, German, and other European banks.

► Increased competition for U.S.-based clients from foreign banks.

► Citicorp has no dominant local market position. Citicorp is the most broadly based global merchant bank.

► Citicorp is a leader in product development, i.e., swaps, hedges, and counter trade.

2. Investment Management

▶ U.S. market highly competitive and low fee.

▶ Large U.S. investors have increasingly used small boutiques.

▶ U.K. merchant banks have excellent reputation and market share for international investment management.

▶ U.S. investment managers are not known for international expertise.

▶ Citicorp's competitive advantage lies in high reputation as U.S. investment manager and leading participant in foreign exchange.

3. International Private Banking

▶ Increased competition from U.S. commercial banks following Citicorp.

▶ Major Swiss banks hold dominant positions due to established presence and regulatory advantages.

▶ Major market share in many geographic areas controlled by local competitors. Hard for multinational banks like Citicorp to enter.

▶ Citicorp has no exclusive franchise in any single sector.

▶ No single competitor can match Citicorp's product and geographic range.

▶ Endnotes

1. See Harold B. van Cleveland and Thomas F. Huertas, *Citibank 1812–1970*, Cambridge, MA: Harvard University Press, 1985, p. 157.

Exhibit 1

Consolidated Balance Sheet of Citicorp and Subsidiaries
(Percentages)

ASSETS	1983	1982	1981	1980	1975	1970	1960
Cash and Due from Banks[1]	3.1%	3.6%	3.3%	6.0%	8.6%	18.9%	23.4%
Deposits at Interest with Banks	8.4%	8.9%	9.7%	11.0%	11.5%	—	—
Investment Securities	4.3%	3.7%	5.5%	5.8%	7.4%	11.2%	23.4%
Loans and Lease Financing[1]							
Commercial	44.3%	48.3%	49.3%	47.2%	53.6%	58.0%	49.1%
Consumer	21.4%	17.7%	15.4%	13.6%	8.2%	—	—
Lease Financing	1.3%	1.4%	1.6%	1.6%	1.8%	0.9%	—
Other Assets	17.2%	16.4%	15.2%	14.8%	8.9%	10.9%	4.1%
Total Assets ($ billions)	$134.66	$130.00	$119.23	$114.92	$ 57.85	$ 25.75	$ 8.67
LIABILITIES							
Deposits							
Domestic Demand[2]	5.8%	5.5%	6.3%	8.8%	16.3%	29.1%	88.2%
Time	15.7%	14.2%	10.5%	8.7%	17.4%	18.8%	—
Overseas	37.8%	39.2%	43.7%	45.0%	43.5%	33.8%	—
Purchased Funds and Other							
Borrowings	16.6%	17.6%	18.8%	19.6%	8.1%	8.4%	0.0%
Long-Term Debt	8.8%	1.9%	2.1%	1.9%	—	1.0%	—
Other Liabilities	11.1%	17.9%	15.1%	12.6%	10.6%	4.2%	3.0%
Total Liabilities	95.7%	96.3%	96.4%	96.6%	95.9%	95.2%	91.2%
STOCKHOLDERS' EQUITY							
Preferred Stock	0.4%					—	—
Common Stock	0.4%	0.4%	0.4%	0.5%	0.9%	1.4%	2.8%
Surplus	0.7%	0.7%	0.7%	0.7%	1.2%	2.1%	4.4%
Retained Earnings	3.1%	2.8%	2.6%	2.4%	1.9%	0.9%	1.6%
Total Stock.'s Equity[3]	4.3%	3.7%	3.6%	3.4%	4.1%	4.8%	8.8%
Total Liabilities plus Equity							
($ billions)	$134.66	$130.00	$119.23	$114.92	$ 57.85	$ 25.75	$ 8.67

[1]For 1960 and 1970, "Cash and Due from Banks" and Deposits at Interest with banks are lumped together. Also, loans are not disaggregated.

[2]1960 Deposits are lumped together.

[3]Total includes items not specifically shown.

Source: Citicorp Annual Report, various issues.

Exhibit 2

Consolidated Income Statement of Citicorp and Subsidiaries
($ millions)

	1983	1982	1981	1980	1975	1970	1960
INTEREST REVENUE							
Interest & Fees on Loans	79%	78%	76%	76%	78%	81%	66%
Deposit with Banks	7%	10%	11%	14%	12%	7%	15%
Federal Funds Sold and Repos	5%	3%	3%	3%	0%	2%	NA
Investment Securities	3%	3%	4%	4%	6%	10%	19%
Trading Accounts	3%	3%	3%	1%	1%	1%	NA
Lease Financing[1]	2%	2%	2%	2%	2%	NA	NA
Total Interest Revenue	$15,197	$16,173	$16,658	$13,040	$ 4,569	$ 1,499	$ 288
INTEREST EXPENSE							
Deposits	62%	67%	68%	71%	83%	83%	NA
Other Borrowed Money	36%	30%	30%	27%	17%	17%	NA
LT Debt and Conv. Notes[2]	2%	2%	2%	2%	0.33%	NA	NA
Total Interest Expense	11,154	12,647	14,179	10,495	2,850	944	41
Net Interest Revenue	4,043	3,526	2,479	2,545	1,720	555	247
Loan Loss Expense	520	473	305	298	327	24	NA
Net Interest After Loan Loss Expense	3,523	3,053	2,174	2,247	1,392	531	247
Fees, Commission, and Other Revenue							
Fees and Comm's	70%	70%	64%	63%	69%	49%	NA
Foreign Exchange	15%	15%	17%	14%	7%	11%	NA
Other[3]	15%	15%	21%	23%	23%	40%	NA
Total Fees	1,840	1,595	1,574	1,171	367	207	NA
Other Operating Expenses	3,757	3,398	2,936	2,574	1,148	507	110
Income Before Taxes	1,606	1,250	812	844	611	231	137
Income Taxes	746	527	281	337	263	86	66
Net Income[3]	$ 860	$ 723	$ 531	$ 499	$ 350	$ 141	$ 71

[1]1970 Lease Financing is included in other revenue and foreign exchange.

[2]1970 Long-term Debt included in Other Borrowed Money.

[3]Net income is adjusted for the after-tax effect of securities transactions by $(8) million in 1980, $(1.687) million in 1975, and $(4.487) million in 1970.

Source: Citicorp Annual Reports, various issues.

Exhibit 3

Ranking of Banks by Assets (1983)

	Assets (U.S. $ bill) 1983	Rank by Assets 1983	1980	1976	Net Income[1] (U.S. $ mill) 1983	Rank
World						
Citicorp	$126	1	5	2	$860	1
BankAmerica	115	2	3	1	390	8
Dai-Ichi Kangyo Bank	110	3	10	6	181	35
Fuji Bank	103	4	12	10	269	17
Sumitomo Bank	101	5	14	12	295	15
Banque Nationale de Paris	100	6	1	7	204	27
Barclays Group	93	7	7	15	419	6
Mitsubishi Bank	99	8	13	23	195	30
Sanwa Bank	91	9	15	14	180	36
Credit Agricole	89	10	2	3	194	31
United States						
Citicorp	126	1	2	2	860	1
BankAmerica	115	2	1	1	390	8
Chase Manhattan	73	3	3	3	430	5
Manufacturers Hanover	65	4	4	4	337	11
J. P. Morgan & Co.	56	5	5	5	460	4
Chemical New York	48	6	6	6	306	14
First Interstate Bancorp	44	7	12	NA	247	20
Continental Illinois	41	8	7	8	108	82
Bankers Trust	38	9	8	7	261	21
Security Pacific Natl. Bk.	34	10	10	10	264	18

[1]Net income ranks for both World and United States are absolute world rank.
Sources: *Institutional Investor,* various issues (for assets rank); *Euromoney,* various issues (for net income rank). Moody's Bank and Finance Manual 1984.

Exhibit 4

Selected Assets of Commercial Banks (as a percentage of total assets)

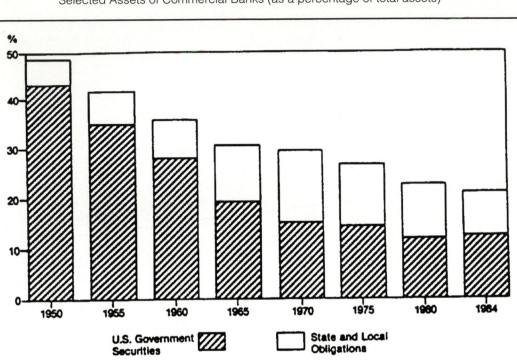

Demand Deposits at Commercial Banks (as a percentage of total liabilities)

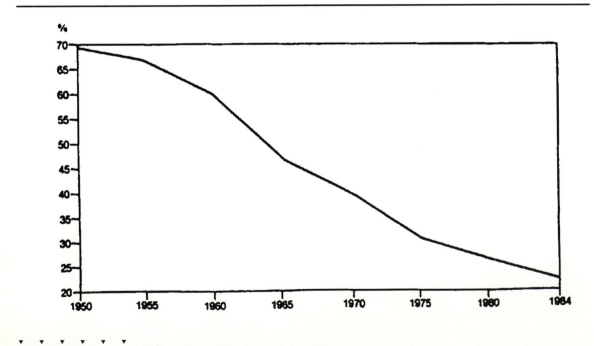

Source: The Board of Governors of the Federal Reserve System, *Flow of Funds Accounts*.

Exhibit 5

Investment Banks: Selected Data for 1983

	Merrill Lynch	First Boston	Shearson Lehman	Morgan Stanley	Nomura Securities	Daiwa Securities
No. of Employees	44,000	2,700	16,900	NA	8,372	6,828
Gross Revenue (U.S. $ millions)	$ 5,687	$ 515	$ 1,811	$ 860	$ 1,555	$ 884
Net Income (U.S. $ millions)	$ 230	$ 80	$ 174	$ 51	$ 292	$ 105
Comp/Employee (U.S. $ thousands)	51,507	104,926	48,499	NA	38,828	NA
Total Assets (U.S. $ millions)	$26,139	$ 22,003	$ 9,045	$7,442	$ 5,725	$4,197

Source: Moody's Bank and Finance Manual, various issues. Tables in Ernest Bloch, "Inside Investment Banking" (Illinois: Dow Jones-Irwin, 1986).

Exhibit 6

New York, London, and Tokyo Stock Exchanges: Comparative Statistics

	(U. S. $ billions)[1]				
	1983	1980	1975	1970	1965
Market Value of Listed Shares					
NYSE	$1,584	$1,243	$ 685	$ 636	$ 537
TSE	534	340	146	45	24
LSE	976	629	477	226	NA
Stock Trading Volume (Annual)					
NYSE	775	382	132	102	73
TSE	231	161	52	25	11
LSE	85	72	39	21	10
Exchange Rates (Yearly Average)					
UK/US	0.6592	0.4299	0.4501	0.4167	0.3571
Japan/US	237.51	226.74	296.79	360	360

[1]Dollar value computed from local currency value and given exchange rates.
Sources: "Fact Book" published by each Stock Exchange. International Financial Statistics, Yearbook 1986; IMF, for exchange rates.

Exhibit 7

Top Foreign Exchange Dealers

	Rank		Est. Market Share	
	1983	1980	1983	1980
Citibank	1	1	8.1%	11.4%
Bank of America	2	2	5.2%	6.1%
Chase Manhattan	3	5	3.4%	4.5%
Morgan Guaranty	4	3	3.0%	5.2%
Bankers Trust	5	7	2.9%	3.8%
Royal Bank of Canada	6	18	2.2%	0.5%
Banque Nationale de Paris	7	10	2.0%	2.0%
Barclays	8	16	2.0%	0.6%
Dresdner	9	—	2.0%	—
Swiss Bank Corp	10	4	1.9%	4.5%
Continental Illinois	11	11	1.7%	1.3%
National Westminster	12	15	1.6%	0.6%
Harris	13	13	1.6%	0.8%
Amsterdam-Rotterdam	14	—	1.5%	—
Skandinaviska-Enskilda	15	14	1.4%	0.7%
First Chicago	16	—	1.4%	—
Bank of Tokyo	17	20	1.4%	0.4%
Toronto-Dominion	18	—	1.3%	—
Bank of Montreal	19	—	1.3%	—
Chemical	20	12	1.2%	0.9%
Share of Top Twenty[1]			47.1%	51.7%

[1]Share of top twenty in each year.

Source: *Euromoney,* May 1983.

Exhibit 8

Lead Manager Rankings of Eurobond Issues[1]

	1983			1982		1981		1980		1979		1978	
	Rank	Amount (US$ millions)	Market Share	Rank	Market Share	Rank	Market Share	Rank	Market Share	Rank	Market Share	Rank	Market Share
CSFB	1	$7,763	16.4%	1	15.2%	1	13.6%	1	9.9%	1	11.7%	4	4.4%
Deutsche Bank	2	5,241	11.1%	2	11.3%	3	6.0%	2	8.9%	2	8.9%	1	23.3%
Merrill Lynch	3	2,061	4.4%	6	3.6%	5	4.7%	—	—	—	—	18	1.4%
S. G. Marburg	4	1,810	3.8%	8	3.3%	4	5.9%	4	4.5%	5	3.8%	5	3.6%
Morgan Guaranty	5	1,786	3.8%	4	3.8%	12	2.3%	—	—	—	—	—	—
Morgan Stanley	6	1,628	3.4%	3	7.8%	2	6.6%	3	7.0%	3	4.9%	—	—
BNP	7	1,502	3.2%	—	—	15	2.0%	15	1.8%	9	3.0%	10	2.1%
Dresdner	8	1,279	2.7%	12	1.6%	—	—	7	3.4%	7	3.5%	3	5.6%
Nomura	9	1,110	2.4%	14	1.5%	7	2.9%	—	—	16	2.0%	12	1.9%
Salomon Brothers	10	1,070	2.3%	5	3.8%	6	4.5%	13	1.9%	—	—	—	—
Citicorp	17	814	1.7%	17	1.4%	—	—	12	2.0%	11	2.3%	—	—
Total Issues (US$ millions)		47,251			47,266		26,084		18,828		14,487		12,254
Share of Top 10[2]		53.4%			57.0%		52.3%		48.9%		50.2%		58.9%

[1]Sole lead managers receive full amounts; co-lead managers receive apportioned amounts.

[2]Combined share of each year's top ten issuers.

Source: Ian Kerr, *A History of the Eurobond Markets—The First Twenty-One Years,* Euromoney Publications, 1984.

PART 3

Financing Strategy

Continental Illinois
and the F.D.I.C. (A)

It came perhaps as a surprise to Roger Anderson, the former chairman of the Continental Illinois Corporation, when he saw his portrait and the words "Banker of the Year" on the cover of a major financial magazine in August 1984. But after reading the accompanying article in which the editors of *Institutional Investor* explained their choice, his surprise surely must have turned to anger. The article's headline noted that "the excesses of his regime brought America's eighth largest bank to the brink of collapse—and symbolizes all that has gone wrong with banking today."

In the article the editors noted an "irony,"

[As] recently as three years ago, Anderson and Continental were viewed as paragons by the banking world. Continental was often described as the best run bank in the country, the most feared bank, the most dynamic. It was doing all those things that analysts and the media prize: posting steadily increasing earnings, a burgeoning return on equity and a rapidly expanding share of the commercial and industrial loan market. In fact, from 1975 to 1980 those loans expanded from $4.9 billion to $9.6 billion....

Ultimately, of course, Anderson's approach backfired. In its zeal to build up its oil and gas portfolio, Continental purchased some $1 billion in energy-related loans from Penn Square Bank in Oklahoma City.

When Penn Square failed in July 1982 and other energy loans came a cropper, Continental found itself with a staggering $1.9 billion in non-performing loans....[1]

These nonperforming loans led Continental Illinois to the brink of collapse in May 1984. If the bank were indeed to fail the rest of the U.S. banking system was sure to suffer too. In the banking industry, with its many interbank transactions, trouble at one bank easily spreads to others. Not only do equity holders lose if a bank fails but creditors (such as other banks) may have to write off part of their assets related to the failed institution. As these other banks lose part of their assets, the collapse, or at least the destabilization, of the banking system could occur as a result of even one major bank being forced to close.

Various safeguards exist to prevent such scenarios. One of the foremost in the

This case was prepared by Assistant Professor David M. Meerschwam.
Copyright © 1985 by the President and Fellows of Harvard College. Harvard Business School case 9-385-296.

U.S. is the Federal Deposit Insurance Corporation (F.D.I.C.), whose task it is to insure deposits at member banks, to monitor their behavior, and, in case of possible failure, to minimize the disruptions of the financial system.

In May and June 1984 the attention of the F.D.I.C. was fully focused on Continental. It had become clear that, without assistance, the bank would fail; and the F.D.I.C. had to decide what action to take. It could try to facilitate a merger between Continental and another bank by purchasing or guaranteeing some of Continental's loans. It could also serve as receiver of the bank, selling off its assets to pay the liabilities. The F.D.I.C. would immediately pay the insured deposits or assure that another bank would assume responsibility for them. Finally the F.D.I.C. could manage the bank itself. In that case the bank would issue preferred stock to the F.D.I.C. in return for a capital infusion.

While pondering which avenue to pursue, William Isaac, the chairman of the F.D.I.C., wondered about the implied signals to the rest of the banking sector of any action.

Banking in the U.S.A.

The Dual System

It is difficult to trace the first forms of regular banking, since society created institutions that perform banking services from early time. Banks, in the modern sense of the word, emerged in the U.S. shortly after the Declaration of Independence. They were either state-chartered or non-chartered financial institutions, and operated within state borders only, until in 1791 the first federally chartered bank came into existence. Since that year the U.S. has had a dual banking system,[2] wherein state and federally chartered banks coexist.

Because of the dual nature of the banking system, some national banks started to develop interstate networks (mostly in the form of bank holding companies). In 1927, however, the McFadden Act forced national banks to adhere to the branching regulations of the individual states in which they operated. As a result, interstate banking did not develop in the U.S., but for a few interstate banks that were allowed to continue to operate across state borders due to a "grandfather" clause in the McFadden Act. Within states, regulation often restricted branch banking. The banking system in the U.S. became therefore highly fragmented compared to most others (see Exhibit 1B).[3]

Bank Failures and Government Action

The great multitude of individual banks was reflected in the large number of failures that came about. Between 1921 and 1929 more than 5,500 banks failed. The Great Depression added another 5,000 failures between 1929 and 1933. In fact, the failure rate became so large that "bank holidays" (closing all banks for several days) were imposed in various states to help troubled institutions fend off bank runs. In the late 1920s and early 1930s the situation became so unstable that the authorities decided to take action.

By 1932 Congress established the Reconstruction Finance Corporation (RFC) which helped to restore confidence in the banking sector. The RFC was authorized to purchase preferred stock, notes or debt of troubled banks.[4] It turned out that the scope of the RFC was not large enough to calm the markets. During the last months of President Hoover's administration the banking problems deepened. By March 4, 1933, the day Franklin D. Roosevelt was inaugurated, banks in

38 states were facing "bank holidays" imposed either by themselves or by the authorities. Roosevelt immediately proclaimed a nationwide bank holiday and called a special session of Congress on March 8 to pass emergency legislation. On March 9 this legislation was passed without debate, granting the president power to extend the bank holiday. Within a week the crisis passed and by March 15 13,000 banks that were considered solvent by the authorities were licensed to reopen, while 4,200 banks were denied licenses.

In the months following the crisis Congress worked on a new banking bill, and in June 1933 a Banking Act was passed that expanded the powers of the Board of Governors of the Federal Reserve System and that created the F.D.I.C. Since the RFC had not been sufficiently powerful to restore stability, it was hoped that deposit insurance would give the depositors the confidence needed to restore a properly functioning financial system. The reason why deposit insurance seemed important was that small depositors were often the cause for a run on a bank. If rumors started to circulate that a bank was "in trouble," many depositors decided to take their deposits out of the bank. And even if there were only a liquidity problem at the bank that might be explained to the larger (corporate) clients, small depositors had little incentive to wait and see what would happen. For them, transferring their deposits to another bank or holding cash seemed much better. It was hoped that deposit insurance for small depositors would, therefore, solve the problem.

The F.D.I.C.

The section of the Banking Act that referred to the F.D.I.C. made the basic objectives of the corporation clear:

> There is hereby created a Federal Deposit Insurance Corporation . . . whose duty it shall be to purchase, hold and liquidate . . . the assets of national banks which have been closed by action of the Comptroller of the Currency, or by vote of their directors, and the assets of the State member banks, which have been closed by actions of the appropriate State authorities, or by vote of their directors; and to insure . . . the deposits of all banks which are entitled to the benefits of insurance under this section.[5]

The creation of the F.D.I.C. established the third federal regulator of commercial banks. The comptroller of the currency is concerned with national banks only—chartering, supervising and examining them. The Federal Reserve System supervises all member banks. National banks have to belong to the system, state banks can elect to do so. The F.D.I.C. regulates all member banks of the Federal Reserve System while any other bank can apply for membership.

Insurance through the F.D.I.C. was, therefore, required for all member banks of the Federal Reserve System. Other non-Fed banks could apply for federal deposit insurance. If accepted by the F.D.I.C. they paid the same insurance premium: a fixed percentage of the deposit liabilities of the bank charged uniformly for all member banks. In the early years the maximum deposit insurance was set by Congress at $5,000 per account. Over time the figure has risen to $100,000.

Since the F.D.I.C. was created to instill confidence into a badly shaken system, it offered not only insurance but was also given the right of supervision over the member banks. Only after F.D.I.C. review of the financial history, the capital adequacy, the future earnings prospects, the general character of the management, and the community needs served by the bank, could (and can) membership be granted. Once the bank joined, the F.D.I.C. held various powers over it. Among them were the power to examine the bank, to terminate membership, to approve mergers and acquisitions, to approve branching decisions, and to oversee the aftermath of a failure. It was clear that the F.D.I.C. was to play a major regulatory role in the banking industry.

Of all the powers given to the F.D.I.C., the most important seemed the one that gave the corporation the right to deal with potential bank failures. The actual costs for the F.D.I.C. of overseeing the aftermath of a closure depended on the quality of the assets that were held by the bank in question. Suppose, as noted earlier, a bank faced a run and could not honor its deposits because of the maturity structure of its assets. In that case it was only a liquidity problem with which the F.D.I.C. had to deal. If, on the other hand, the quality of the assets of the bank were poor and a solvency problem existed, it was likely that the options mentioned before would carry costs for the F.D.I.C.

If costs were to occur, they would be financed through the "Fund" of the F.D.I.C., which had to be sufficiently large to make the market participants believe that the F.D.I.C. could avoid a possible string of failures. Referring to the adequacy of the Fund, the chairman of the F.D.I.C. stated in 1975 that:

> The ultimate question is whether the F.D.I.C. could cope with a wave of large bank failures or a general banking emergency. While I have indicated my belief that the F.D.I.C. has adequate financial resources to handle even within a single year, failures [of significant size] . . . a massive breakdown of our entire banking system, which I do not believe is even remotely possible, could be a different story. Were that nevertheless ever to happen, or were the F.D.I.C. ever to exhaust the funds available to it for insurance purposes, I have no doubt that Congress would act promptly to provide the F.D.I.C. with such additional borrowing authority or funds as might be needed to honor the government's commitment to insured depositors.[6]

1983: 50 Years of Confidence

The annual report of the F.D.I.C. in 1983 celebrated the 50th anniversary of the corporation with a logo on the cover that read, "50 Years of Confidence." The report noted that:

> The Federal Deposit Insurance Corporation has served as an integral part of the nation's financial system for 50 years. Established by the Banking Act of 1933 at the depth of the most severe banking crisis in the nation's history, its immediate contribution was the restoration of public confidence in banks. While the agency has grown and modified its operations in response to changing economic conditions and shifts in the banking environment, the mission of the F.D.I.C. over the past five decades has remained unchanged: to insure bank deposits and reduce economic disruptions caused by bank failures.

In the same report William Isaac wrote in his "Chairman's Statement":

> Although the anniversary was observed in a festive atmosphere, 1983 was a year of serious and intensive activity for the F.D.I.C. There were 48 bank failures, which was a post-depression record, including several large institutions.

> The Division of Liquidation's strategic plan aims at keeping pace with a continued high rate of bank failures, and the adaptation of innovative means of handling failed banks and liquidating their assets.[7]

It is unlikely that Mr. Isaac quite foresaw how innovative the F.D.I.C. had to become in 1984.

Banking in a Changing Environment: The 1970s

While bank failures never exceeded 10 per year during the first 30 years after the Second World War, they increased to 14 in 1975 and 17 during 1976. Between 1976 and 1981 the number of failures fell again, but in 1982, 42 banks had to be closed by the F.D.I.C. and in 1983, 48 (see Exhibit 1A). It was clear that a "new instability" had come about.

During the 1970s important changes took place in the regulatory environment. Regulation of the banking sector had been a feature of the system even before the Banking Act of 1933, but became especially important thereafter. While the F.D.I.C. supervised the banking behavior of the member institutions, the interest rates banks could offer on deposits were also regulated. Regulation Q was the strongest weapon and was imposed by the Federal Reserve Board. Since 1934 the Fed, under Regulation Q, set interest rate ceilings for all time and saving deposits. These interest rate ceilings were, however, not binding constraints. Between 1933 and 1956, the average interest rate paid was 1%, less than half the ceiling. In 1957, however, as market pressure drove, for the first time, rates to the limits allowed by Regulation Q, the ceilings were adjusted upward for savings and time deposits with a maturity of more than 90 days. The rationale was given by the Federal Reserve in its annual report for 1956:

> . . . The maxima [in the past] were well above the rates actually paid, and only recently did the demand for credit begin to bring rates up to the ceiling....[I]t would be desirable to permit individual member banks greater flexibility to encourage the accumulation of savings than was available under the existing maximum permissible rates.[8]

Between 1957 and 1966 the maximum rates were regularly altered. New legislation passed in 1966 made regulation more flexible as it broadened the classifications of time deposits; still, many interest rate ceilings became effective as market rates rose above them.

While the actions of the Federal Reserve Board were aimed at enhancing the ability of the banks to compete for deposits, some of the largest banks started to look for markets where they could do business outside the jurisdiction of the regulators. Not only were these banks concerned about the interest rate regulations; for some of them it had become difficult to keep the relationships they had established with some of their customers because, as businesses and individuals moved and relocated, branching and interstate restrictions made it difficult for banks to follow their clients. These banks, eager to grow and to compete on price in an environment where relationships mattered less, now turned to the so-called Euro-currency market.

In these markets, banks competed for funds outside their home country. A Euro-dollar loan was defined as a dollar loan made outside the U.S. Similarly a Euro-deposit was a deposit where the denomination of the currency of deposit was different from the one used in the country where the bank that took the deposit was located. The origin of this market could be traced to the 1950s, when dollar deposits were made by Eastern-bloc countries to banks in western Europe, because they were concerned about the power the Federal Reserve held over deposits in the U.S. Furthermore, U.S. balance of payments deficits during the 1950s resulted in foreign holdings of dollars. In addition, the financial transactions of the multinational corporation helped the Euro-currency markets to grow.

As Euro-deposits grew rapidly (see Exhibit 4) a market came into existence in which banks competed on price unhindered by regulators.

While in the early stages of the Euro-markets only the largest banks participated, smaller banks entered increasingly during the 1970s and interbank loans grew rapidly. Thus, it became clear that U.S. banks now had an opportunity to buy and sell funds, if there was a willingness to pay the required prices, without having to pay much attention to the relationships that had been fostered earlier by branching prohibition and geographical market segmentation. A shift from "relationship" to "price" banking had taken place.

But the Euro-currency market was not the only one in which "price banking" developed. In June of 1970, the authorities suspended Regulation Q for single maturity (30–89 days) deposits of $100,000 or more. This action was taken for two reasons. First, it would allow banks to recoup part of the deposit market. Since the rate ceilings had been below interest rates offered on other financial instruments in 1969, "disintermediation" had taken place: rather than using the banks as the financial intermediaries, savers had invested directly in various assets. Secondly, the failure of the Penn Central railroad had further worsened the position of the commercial banks. When the Penn Central railroad failed, commercial paper issued by Penn Central was not honored and holders of other commercial paper became nervous about the quality of their assets. As a result the commercial paper market dried up, and companies that typically relied on this market for their funds had to turn to commercial banks. Since most of these companies had back-up credit lines, the sudden call for funds severely depleted the liquidity of the banks and new means of funding became important for these banks. The crisis in the commercial paper market thus hastened the change in regulation. As interest rate ceilings for the large deposits were suspended, the so-called negotiable Certificate of Deposit (CD) became increasingly popular. These negotiable CDs were first introduced by Citibank in 1961, and were precisely what their name suggested. They were certificates issued by a bank (with the bank's name printed on them) that acknowledged a deposit and stated an interest rate for the particular maturity of the CD. After purchasing a CD, the depositor could sell his CD in an active secondary market. Typically, these CDs were for deposits of $1 million or more; but some smaller CDs were also issued. When Regulation Q was suspended for deposits of $100,000 and more, the rate that could be paid for "negotiable" CDs could truly be negotiated. In fact negotiable CDs increased by $2.2 billion in the two weeks following the suspension of Regulation Q.[9] (See Exhibit 3.) Again it became possible for banks to enter a market in which the relationship value of transactions was low and where prices (i.e., interest rates) were the main tool for competition.

Apart from the growing importance of the CD and Euro-currency markets, another change took place that further reduced the value of relationships in financial transactions. New financial instruments were developed, such as "Pass-Through Mortgages." For the traditional mortgage the relationship between the home buyer and the bank is fundamental. The bank evaluates the property and the ability of the buyer to generate enough income to make the required payments. Only after the bank is satisfied with both will it provide the mortgage. Both the client and the bank then enter into a relationship that might last for over 20 years. The Pass-Through, however, operated differently. Private institutions assembled mortgages that were guaranteed by GNMA, a government-owned corporation. Securities were then issued and sold that were backed by these mortgages.

The bank that originated the mortgages thus had to be concerned about its ability to sell the package at an attractive price. Depending on the desires of other banks to grow the asset side of their balance sheet, the market mechanism determined a price at which the transaction took place. Other very similar instruments were invented that all allowed for price competition.

Risks and Opportunities

The changing banking environment in the U.S. provided both risks and opportunities to bankers. While it became possible to "buy and sell" money, it also became more likely that the costs of funds in a vigorously competitive market could rise sharply if the market became suspicious of an institution or, worse than that, large deposits or loans could simply be withdrawn. A scenario that could easily develop under these circumstances would show a rapidly growing bank, funding itself with large quantities of "purchased," as opposed to "relationship," money and buying high yielding but risky assets (i.e. loans). In such a situation, bad loans could lead to much higher funding costs, withdrawals, or both. Whether insurance for deposits up to $100,000 would then be an effective safeguard against possible failure seemed extremely doubtful.

The Summer of 1982

The 42 bank failures in 1982 made it an unusual year. But the problems lay not only in the failure rate itself. The kinds of institutions that got into trouble and their relationships to some of the largest banks in the U.S. also caused concern. Two incidents in particular during the summer of that year helped concentrate the minds of those involved with the financial system of the U.S.

The Drysdale Problem

In May of 1982, Drysdale Government Securities failed. Drysdale had only been established as an independent company in January of that year,[10] and was very active in the so-called "RePo" (repurchase agreement) business. A RePo is an agreement between a holder of securities to sell them currently and to buy them back at a specified future date for a particular price. The difference between the two prices is the implicit interest rate the holder of the original securities has to pay for the use of the liquid funds over the time period.

Drysdale engaged in government securities RePo's with various dealers, and its main supplier of these securities became Chase Manhattan Bank which sold government securities with RePo to Drysdale. Chase obtained its securities in turn through RePo's from the government securities brokers, such as Merrill Lynch and Goldman Sachs. Using a fairly complicated financial mechanism, Drysdale sold the securities to others, allegedly profiting from a timing difference between the coupon payment to the final holder by the government and the coupon payment that had to be made to the originator of the RePo. When, on May 17, it became clear that Drysdale could not fulfill the obligations to the originators of the RePo's (a total of $160 million seemed at stake), Chase argued that it was not responsible, as it had only acted as an agent for the government securities brokers (i.e., Merrill, Goldman, and others), and that they should have to carry the losses. After a few days of negotiations Chase changed its position and decided to take responsibility for the losses, which by then were estimated to total a quarter of a billion dollars.

What worried many was not so much the fact that Drysdale had gotten into trouble. The real reason for concern was that Chase Manhattan was so deeply involved with Drysdale and also that Chase was initially unwilling to finance the losses associated with Drysdale.

The Penn Square Bank of Oklahoma City

Another bank that got into deep trouble during that summer was Penn Square. This bank, located in a shopping mall in Oklahoma City, had been active in making energy-related loans. In order to grow rapidly (total assets grew more than five-fold between 1975 and 1981, while many more loans were made and sold off) it had to make risky loans. One strategy used by Penn Square was to sell some of their loans to other institutions. Still, in July 1982 Penn Square had to be closed by the regulators; too many of its "assets" were bad loans. Their high risk strategy had clearly not worked. Yet this was not what concerned the bank regulators and the analysts of the banking sector most. The failure of a small, unimportant bank in Oklahoma City was hardly an indication of problems with the U.S. financial system. What was troublesome was that again a major bank was directly involved. This time it was primarily the Continental Illinois Bank of Chicago. Like many other financial institutions Continental had bought loans from Penn Square. The quality of these loans ($1 billion in total) seemed at best debatable. How was it possible, it was asked, that the 8th largest bank in the U.S. could be so deeply involved with a bank of the status of Penn Square, especially since Continental's professed expertise was precisely in energy-related loans?

Confidence Regained?

And thus while in the summer of 1982 serious questions could be raised about the strategies and stability of some of the largest U.S. banks, no crisis developed. Chase Manhattan did eventually honor the Drysdale obligations and Continental seemed large enough to absorb the potential losses associated with Penn Square.

Continental Illinois

The 1983 Annual Report

Continental's very size helped it overcome its immediate problems in the summer of 1982. The new banking environment had allowed Continental to grow rapidly. Its 1983 annual report contained the farewell comments of Roger Anderson, the outgoing chairman of the bank, to his stockholders. Mr. Anderson wrote that during the eleven years in which he had led the bank to become the seventh largest banking corporation in the U.S., it had not always been a smooth ride. Two energy crises, severe inflation, and recession had plagued the 1970s and early 1980s. Yet, the chairman noted, "earnings had been up every year until 1982." Severe setbacks encountered in that year would, Anderson believed, be overcome by his 54-year-old successor as chairman, David J. Taylor, who had served for 26 years with the bank. The new president, Edward Bottum, had also been with the bank for almost a quarter of a century. Anderson assured the stockholders that he was "completely confident of their ability to manage Continental."

In the same annual report David Taylor presented some comments of his own. He referred to the recent problems at the bank, but continued to note that:

> As we move towards a brighter future, we are dealing directly and firmly with the realities of today. . . . The problems the organization has been grappling with since July 1982 are substantial. They arise from a group of credits in our loan portfolio

primarily related to the loan participation purchased from the Penn Square Bank and a few other large energy-related credits. The balance of our loan portfolio has some problems, but I do not feel that these are out of line with other major banks. . . . While aware of the difficulties, we are proceeding confidently. We have sound strategies and programs to position Continental for the future and for the vigorous pursuit of profitable opportunities.[11]

History

In an official bank publication "A Brief History," the antecedents of the present Continental Bank are set in 1932. The brochure does not mention that it was only in 1939 that the then-chairman Walter Cummings was able to buy back preferred stock that had been held by the RFC. The RFC had obtained this stock in 1932 in return for a $50 million capital infusion to help the severely troubled bank. Between 1959 and 1969 David Kennedy, who became Secretary of the Treasury, led the bank. Under his leadership Continental was the "second bank" in Chicago. Many considered First Chicago the dominant bank in Illinois. "The University of Minnesota graduates went to Continental, the Harvard MBAs to First Chicago,"[12] recalled an officer at First Chicago. During the 1970s, Continental and First Chicago both grew and in 1975 both banks held around $20 billion in assets. Chairman Roger Anderson, who had taken the helm in 1973, described Continental's strategy as "conservative but aggressive."[13] And indeed the 17% earnings and assets growth shown by the bank between 1975 and 1980 seemed most impressive. In 1980, *Dun's Review*, a financial magazine, ranked Continental as one of the five best-run companies in the U.S. In that year Continental had $42 billion assets, First Chicago $29 billion.

In order to produce this asset growth, Continental had to look aggressively for lending opportunities, since it could use the CD and Euro-markets for funding. Energy-related loans were a specialty. Continental's association with energy went back to the middle 1950s. It had been one of the few banks to hire energy specialists, and, as the oil price increases of the 1970s whetted the investment appetite of independent oil producers in the U.S., many turned to Continental. For some of the most risk-prone entrepreneurs, however, Continental was "too conservative." They looked for more aggressive lenders, such as the Penn Square Bank, which established a close relationship with Continental. This relationship became so close that in early 1982, a senior lending officer at Continental was moved out of energy lending when it was discovered that he had received personal loans from Penn Square. By that time Continental held $1 billion of Penn Square loans. When, in July 1982, bank regulators closed Penn Square, Continental was left with a troublesome legacy. Not only was the quality of the loans at best debatable, but the ease with which Penn Square had shed them to Continental amazed many. Lee Iacocca, chairman of the recently bailed out Chrysler Corporation, was reported to have said that he would not have asked the government for money had he known how easy Continental was!

While the asset side of the bank's balance sheet did not look very good, funding problems also occurred. Since the bank was not allowed by Illinois banking laws to operate a network of branches, its deposit base of funding could not grow rapidly and the bank had turned to the markets where relationships did not matter but where prices were preeminent. In those markets the costs of funds, if available at all, rise sharply if lenders are concerned about the quality of the assets of a bank. Still, chairman-to-be David Taylor wrote in February 1984 that "aware of the difficulties, we are proceeding confidently."[14]

When, in March 1984, almost two years after the Penn Square disaster, David Taylor succeeded Roger Anderson, he must have hoped that Continental was "safe" again. Nine weeks later the crisis came.

May 7–17, 1984: Can Continental Survive?[15]

On Monday, May 7, unusual activity started to take place at Continental. As in most cases of a potential bank failure, it was not clear what set off the chain of events that led people to think that the bank had serious problems. What is clear is that on that Monday rumors were circulating in the financial markets that foreign bankers had gotten "nervous" about their deposits at Continental and that they no longer offered funds, or at least increased the rates they charged to the bank. It was rumored that the bank's own estimate of $2.3 billion of problem loans was an underestimate. By Tuesday, May 8, Chairman Taylor tried to formally dispel these rumors. And even though he knew that the unusual nature of such a statement might upset the markets even further, he thought it was necessary. The treasurer of Continental was given the task of making the announcement and described the rumors to the press as "totally preposterous." Still, the problems did not go away, and on Thursday, the Comptroller of the Currency, C. Todd Conover, denied the rumors too. Mr. Conover also contacted Paul Volcker, the chairman of the Federal Reserve Board, and William Isaac, the chairman of the F.D.I.C., to request a meeting to discuss the situation at Continental. Isaac seemed prepared:

> We had a contingency plan for this kind of circumstance and decided it ought to be implemented if the situation continued to deteriorate. The F.D.I.C. could infuse a substantial amount of money on an interim base. We felt the number had to be large enough to restore confidence in the institution. At least $1 billion but no more than $2 billion. The plan included the F.D.I.C.'s promise to protect all depositors, however big. We even had the documents ready without names and amounts. I called Continental to say we would be prepared to implement steps to begin the capital infusion.[16]

Yet Continental did not seem ready to accept direct intervention by the F.D.I.C. It wanted to explore the "private solution." Under the leadership of Morgan Guaranty, 15 banks negotiated a temporary $4.5 billion loan package for Continental over the weekend of May 12. But, when this package was announced, it was not sufficient to calm the markets. Even domestic correspondent banks of Continental started to withdraw their funds. By Tuesday, May 15, David Taylor asked Goldman Sachs, Continental's investment banker, to look for a possible merger partner. On that same day, Volcker, Isaac, and Conover met in Washington. They decided that if the assistance of the F.D.I.C. was required, the Morgan-led banks should contribute $500 million of the $2 billion infusion suggested by Isaac. This would bring the total involvement of these banks to $5 billion. As it became clear during the day that Continental needed the infusion, lawyers from the banks and the F.D.I.C. started to meet. On Thursday, May 17, an agreement was in place; the F.D.I.C. announced that it guaranteed all deposits and Continental was out of immediate danger.

Saving Continental

After announcing the temporary rescue package on May 15, the three parties involved (Continental, the other banks and the F.D.I.C.) started to look for a more permanent solution. David Taylor preferred one that would allow his bank to remain independent. In a May 21 memo, he told his staff that "the search for a solution that will avoid our merging with another institution is our number one priority."[17] At the same time, however, Goldman Sachs was sending out information packages to prospective buyers. These buyers (the Chemical Corporation, Citicorp and First Chicago were rumored to be interested) had to read through the thick folders sent by Goldman Sachs. They had to evaluate precisely what it was they might be buying, which meant that they had to evaluate the quality of the asset portfolio of Continental. Furthermore, they had to find out what the possible reaction of the Illinois legislature would be if an out-of-state holding company tried to acquire Continental. Also, the potential buyers wanted to know to what extent the F.D.I.C. would be willing to purchase the "bad loans." If the F.D.I.C. were to do this it would effectively infuse new capital into the bank. Finally, these banks had to assess how their own competitive environment would change if one of them merged with the eighth largest bank in the U.S.

As the banks tried to formulate their strategies, William Isaac had to decide what role the F.D.I.C. was to play. Too early a commitment could lead to the "F.D.I.C. being taken to the cleaners."[18] On the other hand if no private solution were to be found, the F.D.I.C. might have to deal with Continental all alone.

▶ Endnotes

1. *Institutional Investor*, August 1984.
2. During the period between 1836 and 1863 only state-chartered banks operated, since Congress failed to renew the charter of the only nationally chartered bank.
3. For a description of the development of commercial banking in the U.S., see *Money and Banking in the United States Economy*, H. D. Hutchinson, Prentice-Hall, 1984.
4. One of the banks that was assisted by the RFC was Continental Illinois. In 1932 the RFC bought preferred stock of the bank.
5. Banking Act 1933, Section 8 and Federal Reserve Act 1916, Section 12a.
6. Speech by Frank Wille, chairman F.D.I.C., quoted in: *The Federal Deposit Insurance Fund: Is It Adequate?* D.C. Bregenzer, New Brunswick, Unpublished, Stonier thesis.
7. F.D.I.C., Annual Report, 1983.
8. Federal Reserve Board Annual Report, 1956.
9. See *Regulation Q and Monetary Policy*, C.F. Haywood, Association of Reserve City Bankers, 1971.
10. Until January 1982, Drysdale Government Securities had been a part of Drysdale Securities. But as the dealings in government securities grew rapidly a separate company was set up.
11. Continental Illinois, Annual Report, 1983.
12. Quoted in *Wall Street Journal*, July 30, 1984.
13. Ibid.
14. Continental Illinois, Annual Report, 1983.
15. For a description of the crisis, see *Wall Street Journal*, July 30, 1984.
16. Quoted in *New York Times*, May 21, 1984.
17. Quoted in *New York Times*, May 22, 1984.
18. Quoted in *Wall Street Journal*, May 22, 1984.

Exhibit 1A

U.S. Bank Data

Year	Deposit Insurance Losses (F.D.I.C.) ($ millions)	Number of Closed Banks	Deposits of Closed Banks ($)	Deposits in Commercial Banks ($ billions)	
				Total	Insured
1983	834	48	5442	1690	1268
1982	870	42	9908	1545	1134
1981	721	10	3826	1409	989
1980	−35	10	216	1324	949
1975–79	119	54	2377	5241	3460
1970–74	181	27	2833	3453	2131
1965–69	9	33	226	2215	1315
1960–64	4	24	69	1501	849
1955–59	0	23	48	1147	644
1950–54	2	23	63	931	506
1945–49	1	21	34	769	368
1940–44	6	95	206	473	192
1935–39	20	341	299	251	113
1933–34	0	54	35	40	18

Source: F.D.I.C. Annual Reports.

Exhibit 1B

Number of Commercial Banks in the U.S.

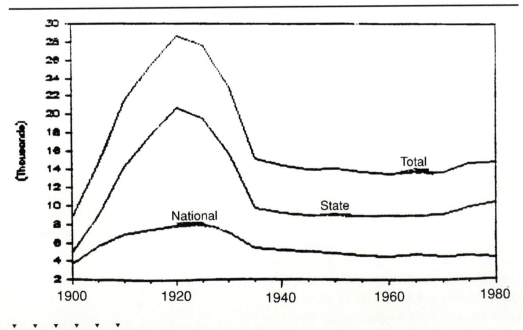

Source: Federal Reserve System.

Exhibit 2

Employment at the F.D.I.C.

	1983	1982	1981	1980
Total	3846	3504	3394	3644
Legal Division	103	105	106	107
Division of Liquidation*	1153	778	429	460
Division of Supervision	2053	2129	2359	2544

*Includes temporary employees related to bank failures.

Source: F.D.I.C. Annual Reports.

Exhibit 3

Domestic CDs Outstanding

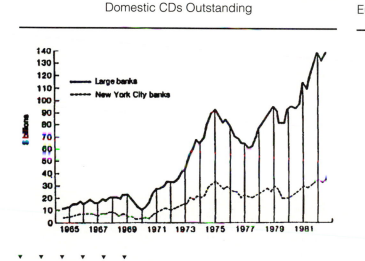

Source: *Federal Reserve Bulletin.*

Euro-dollar CDs Outstanding (U.S. $ billions)

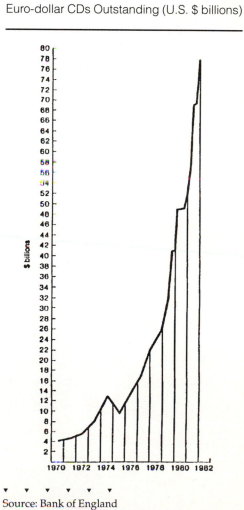

Source: Bank of England

Exhibit 4

Euro-Currency Market

Year	World Market Size ($ billions)	Eurodollars as % of Gross
1983	2148	80
1982	2038	79
1981	1814	77
1980	1538	74
1979	1245	72
1978	946	73
1977*	748	75
1976	565	79
1975	460	78
1974	375	77
1973	305	73
1972	200	78
1971	145	76

*Change in series, old series

1977	700	76

▼ ▼ ▼ ▼ ▼ ▼

Source: Morgan Guaranty, World Financial Markets.

Exhibit 5

Top Ten U. S. Commercial Banks
Ranked by Assets ($ billions)

	1983*	1982*	1970**
Citicorp	$126	$121	$26
Bank America	115	115	30
Chase Manhattan Bank	73	75	25
Manufacturers Hanover	65	64	13
J. P. Morgan & Co.	56	55	12
Chemical New York	47	45	11
First Interstate Bancorp	44	41	11
Continental Illinois	41	42	9
Bankers Trust	38	37	10
Security Pacific National	34	31	8

▼ ▼ ▼ ▼ ▼ ▼

Source: *Moody's Financial. **Institutional Investor*, June 1984.

Exhibit 6

Penn Square Bank
($ millions)

	Loans and Discounts	Total Assets
1980	$198	$288
1979	106	160
1976	34	59
1973	17	31
1970	15	24

▼ ▼ ▼ ▼ ▼ ▼

Source: Moody's Financial.

Exhibit 7

Consolidated Balance Sheet of Continental Illinois Banking Corporation
(U.S.$ billions)

	1983	1982	1981	1980	1979	1978	1977	1976	1975	1974	1973	1972	1971
ASSETS													
Cash and due from depository institutions													
Cash and non-interest bearing deposits	2.570	2.199	2.513	4.362	3.367	3.897	2.879	1.524	1.761	1.906	1.557	1.780	1.341
Interest bearing deposits	3.587	1.881	5.083	4.294	4.035	3.837	3.933	*	*	*	a	a	a
Investment securities	1.762	2.064	2.169	2.506	2.226	2.174	2.501	2.364	2.281	1.774	2.070	1.803	1.708
Loans and lease receivables													
Loans	30.390	32.870	32.175	26.910	23.182	18.462	14.863	12.904	12.038	12.655	9.994	7.120	4.896
Lease receivables	1.038	1.172	1.123	0.720	0.610	0.432	0.400	0.273	0.230	**	b	b	b
Less													
Unearned income	-0.270	-0.323	-0.423	-0.263	-0.215	-0.139	-0.121	**	**	**	b	b	b
Reserve for credit losses	-0.383	-0.381	-0.289	-0.246	-0.212	-0.191	-0.168	-0.163	-0.161	-0.157	b	b	b
Other Assets	3.402	3.415	4.620	3.806	2.797	2.586	1.513	5.074	4.067	3.463	3.250	2.126	2.136
Total Assets	42.096	42.897	46.971	42.089	35.790	31.058	25.800	21.976	20.216	19.641	16.871	12.829	10.081
LIABILITIES													
Deposits													
Domestic Demand	4.281	4.205	4.839	5.231	5.216	4.926	4.429	3.538	3.674	3.663	3.638	3.341	3.194
Time	9.246	8.485	10.125	8.349	7.301	7.216	5.661	5.170	5.677	6.090	4.939	3.595	2.570
Foreign	15.903	15.485	14.631	13.734	11.490	9.018	8.664	7.108	5.938	5.716	4.021	3.064	2.692
Federal funds purchased and securities sold under agreements to repurchase	4.831	5.920	11.013	9.565	7.767	8.673	6.034	5.244	4.100	3.421	3.595	2.190	1.040
Other borrowings	2.677	4.029	a	a	a	a	a	a	a	a	a	a	a
Long-term debt	1.256	1.272	0.862	0.676	0.530	a	a	a	a	a	a	a	a
Other liabilities	2.081	1.793	3.792	3.010	2.123	a	a	a	a	a	a	a	a
Total liabilities	40.275	41.189	45.262	40.565	34.427	29.833	24.788	21.060	19.389	18.890	16.193	12.190	9.496
Shareholders' Equity													
Common Stock	0.290	0.200	0.198	0.197	0.196	0.196	0.178	0.177	0.174	0.174	0.173	0.172	0.171
Capital Surplus	0.527	0.525	0.523	0.518	0.510	0.509	0.428	0.427	0.429	0.425	0.421	0.394	0.317
Retained Earnings	1.005	0.985	0.990	0.810	0.656	0.521	0.406	0.309	0.222	0.152	0.082	0.072	0.095
Total Shareholders' Equity	1.822	1.710	1.713	1.525	1.362	1.226	1.012	0.913	0.825	0.751	0.676	0.638	0.583
Total Liabilities and Equity ***	42.097	42.899	46.973	42.090	35.789	31.059	25.800	21.973	20.214	19.641	16.869	12.828	10.079
¹Domestic CDs		6.082	6.431	5.533	4.145	3.540	2.196	2.294	2.481	2.413	1.769	0.955	0.725

a Included in line above.
b Not Available.

* Included in "Other Assets.." ** Included in "Lease Financing." *** Differences between total assets and liabilities due to rounding errors.

Source: Continental Illinois Annual Reports.

Exhibit 8

CONT'L ILL. HLDG. NYSE-CIH	RECENT PRICE	1.5	P/E RATIO	See Text	Trailing: NMF Median: 6.5	RELATIVE P/E RATIO	See Text	DIV'D YLD	See Text	648

Source: Value Line Investment Survey, Part 3, February 1985, p. 648. Copyright © 1991 by Value Line Publishing, Inc.; used by permission.

Restructuring
the Mellon Bank

On Sunday, July 24, 1988, the Board of Directors of the Mellon Bank Corporation met to discuss a restructuring plan proposed by Mellon's top management. The plan, which would substantially alter the bank's balance sheet, called for Mellon to spin off a billion dollars worth of problem assets into a new bank. The ambitious and unusual plan was the latest in a series of actions designed to extract Mellon from the troubles that had plagued it during the past few years.

As the directors met, Wall Street was buzzing with rumors. Some of the details of the plan had been leaked to the *Wall Street Journal* on Thursday, July 21. Investors seemed to react positively. On July 21, Mellon's common stock closed at 32.75, up .875 from the previous day. On Friday, July 22, the stock gained an additional 0.125. The Standard and Poor's 500, meanwhile, lost 3.34 on Thursday and 3.16 on Friday, to finish the week at 263.50.

The Mellon Bank

The Mellon Bank traces its roots back to the 1840s when Thomas Mellon, a young Pittsburgh lawyer, began lending funds earned in his law practice. Mellon prospered as a lawyer and investor, but the practice of law eventually palled, and in 1859 he became a judge on the Allegheny Court of Common Pleas. The attractions of the bench also faded, and Judge Mellon stepped down in 1869 to found the T. Mellon and Sons' Bank. In 1874, Judge Mellon was joined by his son Andrew W. Mellon. Eight years later, impressed by his son's abilities, Judge Mellon put the 26-year-old Andrew in charge of the bank. In 1887, Andrew was joined at the bank by his brother Richard, and the two ran the bank as partners until Andrew became Secretary of the Treasury in 1921.

Pittsburgh and the Mellons prospered together. The family operated as much like "venture capitalists" as traditional bankers. By the time Andrew left for the Treasury, the Mellons had obtained large interests in many firms, the most prominent of which were Alcoa, Gulf, Carborundum, and Koppers. The Mellons' bank

---

This case was prepared by Michael Baldwin under the supervision of Assistant Professor David M. Meerschwam.

Copyright © 1989 by the President and Fellows of Harvard College. Harvard Business School case 9-289-036.

became the dominant bank in Pittsburgh, and one of the most important banks in the country. It would continue in that role for most of the twentieth century.

The Mellon family maintained a large equity and management interest in the bank, which by 1984 had evolved into the Mellon Bank Corporation. The bank's single largest shareholder was Andrew's son Paul, who remained on the board until 1976. As of late April 1987, the Mellon family owned 13.6% of the bank's 28 million shares of common stock, and was represented by three of the bank's 25 directors.

By the mid-1970s the Mellon Bank was one of the oldest and largest banks in the U.S. In 1974, Mellon ranked 13th in terms of total assets. In terms of profitability, however, Mellon lagged most of its major competitors. Mellon returned 10.3% on common equity in the year that ended in June 1974. Of the nation's 25 largest banks, only Crocker National provided a lower return. Customers, competitors, and analysts described Mellon with phrases like "arrogant and conservative," and "solid but dull." As one analyst remarked: "Its principal strength is its strong capital position. It's the Morgan of the Midwest. If they'd only do something."[1]

"Doing something" was exactly what Mellon's management had in mind. In the words of James Higgins, who became Mellon's chairman in 1974: "This bank has been superbly managed by my predecessors over the years and they have built a foundation for further building domestically and internationally."[2] Mellon expanded nationally and internationally as it opened new overseas branches and lending offices throughout the U.S.

The pace of change accelerated under J. David Barnes, who became president of the bank in January 1980, and chairman and CEO in 1981. Barnes, a Harvard Law School graduate who had spent most of his career in staff jobs, was faced with a changing lending environment and a stagnant Pittsburgh economy. Under his leadership, Mellon stepped up the national and international expansion efforts his predecessors had begun. The bank moved aggressively into high growth areas like international lending, real estate lending, and energy lending. Exhibit 4 details the growth of Mellon's loan portfolio.

Some of Mellon's initiatives quickly turned sour. Mellon, along with many other large banks, found that its international loans were becoming increasingly troublesome as the 1980s wore on. The bank's international business seemed solidly profitable in the early 1980s, but by 1986 it was losing money (in part because it had accumulated almost $900 million of Brazilian and Mexican debt). Domestic initiatives fared no better. Mellon opened an energy lending department, complete with a loan office in Dallas, in 1982. It purchased a Houston mortgage banking firm, and increased its real estate and construction lending by almost 50% in 1984.

Analysts and competitors found Mellon's efforts to expand its lending business easy to criticize, at least in retrospect. One Southwest energy banker commented: "They were just too aggressive for a bank removed from the oil patch. They offered cheaper pricing than we would consider just to get their foot in the door."[3] Others flayed Mellon's expansion into Latin American lending. One analyst said: "They went into Mexico in a big way in recent years because it seemed an easy way to get loan volume. Like a lot of big banks, they got too greedy."[4]

Mellon's efforts to compete with the money center banks in domestic and international lending were accompanied by an attempt to broaden its presence in the mid-Atlantic area. Pennsylvania's banking laws, which had previously restricted Mellon to the Pittsburgh area, were modified to allow statewide branching in 1982. Mellon purchased several smaller Pennsylvania banks, along with a small savings and loan in Maryland. The acquisition program was designed to increase Mellon's base of consumer deposits (as opposed to the corporate and institutional deposits which Mellon had traditionally relied upon), and to improve the firm's access to small and medium-size customers.

The firm's acquisition efforts were also troubled. The most notable problems stemmed from the 1983 acquisition of Philadelphia's Girard Bank. Girard, a venerable firm with a strong retail business and a specialization in serving small to medium-size businesses, represented a toehold in a market segment and a geographic area that Mellon wanted to develop. Girard had accumulated a large number of problem loans (partly as a result of an abortive move into international lending) and Mellon was able to buy the firm for 75% of its book value. Once the merger was completed, however, Mellon executives seemed surprised by the full extent of Girard's problems. Barnes quickly moved to tighten control over the loosely managed firm. Many of Girard's top executives were removed or reassigned. Girard's lending officers were restricted to the Philadelphia market and much decision-making authority was transferred to Mellon in Pittsburgh. Girard was renamed Mellon Bank (East).

The changes extended to Girard's areas of strength. Mellon contended that Girard's retail banking systems were outdated, and replaced them with its own. Some observers argued that the lending approach Mellon imposed on Girard was not suitable to small customers. As one former Girard employee put it: "They don't understand small business. They took the same criteria in judging a small company as they did toward A.T.&T. Lots of companies didn't like that and went elsewhere."[5] In fact, many of Girard's customers and employees left for other firms.

From Barnes's perspective, Mellon's imposition of its culture and technology on Girard and the other acquisitions was a painful necessity: "Up front it's expensive, but over the long haul economical. We're trying to evolve to where we can support any bank with one uniform package of products and support services."[6] Barnes felt that Mellon was being criticized for dealing with issues that other banks expanding through mergers and acquisitions would also have to face. He commented: "It's the pioneers who always get the arrows in the back."[7]

While some areas of the bank struggled, others flourished. Mellon's revenues from fee-based services expanded throughout Barnes's tenure as CEO. Mellon was widely recognized as a leading supplier of personal and corporate trust services, investment management, cash management for businesses, and data processing services for other financial institutions. These service businesses played an important part in the bank's overall strategy, not least because they were perceived as being relatively immune to business cycles, credit risk, and trading risk. They were also less capital-intensive than more traditional banking businesses.

Mellon's capital markets area also had some very good years. In 1985 the firm earned $50 million aftertax on gains from securities sales (almost 25% of net income). In 1986 aftertax gains on securities sales amounted to $73 million (almost 40% of net income). The bank's income from securities trading, however, was volatile.

Some contended that Mellon faced deep-seated organizational problems. One former manager complained about Barnes's sense of priorities, saying: "He'd spend an hour discussing the design of an internal company publication, but he didn't seem to care or realize that the bank was assigning 23-year-olds just out of school to be loan investigators in Latin America."[8] Others complained that the bank was too hierarchical and bureaucratic. An international lending officer remarked that "we're overburdened with bureaucracy. For every customer I call on, I have to write at least two reports. Paperwork takes a third of my time."[9]

One of the most serious organizational criticisms centered upon what some called Mellon's arrogance and clubby culture. In the words of securities analyst Nancy Bush:

> Rumblings that there were problems were passed up the chain, but each level watered down recommendations coming from below. The admonitions got weaker. The message didn't get across. No one wanted to be the bearer of bad news. . . . When things began to deteriorate, the bank made a serious error, circling the wagons. They began to rely on the name and mystique of Mellon; everybody in management put blinders on. They went too far in pumping the cachet. A name is important but it doesn't excuse you from looking rigorously at a loan. . . . They always took the best case scenario, not the worst. The results would have been the same, but it wouldn't have been so traumatic or surprising."[10]

The Management Change

Mellon expanded rapidly in the 1980s. Assets doubled from $16 billion in 1980 to $34 billion in 1986. Net interest revenue before provisions for loan losses rose from $327 million in 1980 to $941 in 1986. Service and trading revenue rose from $103 million to $706 million (with gains on securities sales accounting for almost $137 million of the increase). The bank's problems, however, grew with it. The annual provision for loan losses rose from $29 million in 1980 to $316 million in 1986, while operating expenses rose from $259 million to $1,145 million. If gains from securities sales were excluded, the bank's income in 1986 was lower than in 1980.

As problems mounted, Barnes began efforts to contain the damage. In October 1986 he hired Richard Daniel, a highly regarded loan workout expert from Security Pacific and Crocker National. Daniel, who joined Mellon as a vice chairman, quickly formed a loan workout group and stepped up efforts to identify and collect problem loans. Barnes also began cutting salaries and bonuses.

The problems came to a head when the results for the first quarter of 1987 were reported. In early April, Barnes acknowledged that the bank's management had made an "error in judgment" with the aggressive lending policies of earlier in the decade. He conceded: "We don't know when we will get our full momentum back."[11] The admissions were accompanied by the first quarterly loss in the bank's history. Mellon reported a first-quarter loss of $59.8 million, and a $76 million increase in provisions for credit losses (from $99 million the previous quarter to $175 million). In another first, the quarterly dividend was slashed from $0.69 to $0.35 per share.

After the extent of the losses became apparent, Barnes met with Nathan Pearson and Andrew Mathieson. Pearson, the senior member of the bank's board of directors, was an adviser to Paul Mellon. Mathieson was also a director and adviser to the Mellon family. Shortly after the meeting, Barnes resigned. The board selected Pearson to act as chairman and CEO on a temporary basis, while Mathieson headed the effort to locate a permanent replacement.

The search led to Frank Cahouet (pronounced COW-et). Cahouet had worked at Security Pacific for 24 years before leaving the vice chairman's position in 1984 to head a successful turnaround effort at Crocker National, which had been purchased by Britain's Midland Bank. During his two-year tenure at Crocker, which had been plagued by bad loans, Cahouet replaced the management team, cut the firm's staff by over 25%, sold the headquarters building for a $188 million profit, and consolidated operations. After Midland Bank unexpectedly sold Crocker to Wells Fargo in 1986, Cahouet left to become president and CEO of the Federal National Mortgage Association. He was the first outsider ever selected to head Mellon. Pearson commented: "Crocker's situation has a great deal of similarity to ours here."[12]

The news of Cahouet's appointment was accompanied by an announcement that Mellon expected to add another $415 million to its loan loss reserves and experience an operating loss of about $85 million in the second quarter, producing an expected quarterly loss of $500 million.

The Turnaround

Cahouet started work on June 22, 1987, the same day he moved to Pittsburgh. In early July he froze hiring and salaries and warned of impending layoffs. Several top managers were among the first to go as he brought in a new management team from money-center banks in New York and Los Angeles.

One of Cahouet's first moves was to hire Anthony Terracciano, a 23-year veteran of Chase Manhattan, as Mellon's new president and chief operating officer. Terracciano was a hard-driving executive who, as vice chairman in charge of global banking, had been considered a strong candidate for the presidency of Chase. Cahouet also hired Keith Smith, a former colleague at Crocker National, to serve as Mellon's chief financial officer.

The new team set out to redefine Mellon's strategy. Cahouet summarized the bank's strategy for the shareholders in the 1987 annual report:

> We have a clear sense of our strategic focus and direction. Mellon is a well-balanced superregional bank holding company, with an excellent franchise both nationally and within the Central Atlantic region. We will not overconcentrate on any one business, product line or market. The Corporation intends to maintain its blend of wholesale, retail and fee-generating service businesses. The Mellon concept of a superregional stresses that the Corporation maintain a leadership position in serving both the national wholesale market and our multi-state retail market. And, while we do not intend to be a major participant in international markets, Mellon will continue to maintain a presence in the world's key money centers.[13]

With Cahouet doing the long-range planning and Terracciano handling day-to-day operations, the new team proceeded to shake up the bank. The work force was cut 15%, to 16,000 workers, for planned savings of $65 million. Management overhauled the corporate banking area, which had failed to keep up with modern product developments and had been troubled by political infighting. Terracciano began efforts to improve communication and coordination between different product groups. On a broader scale, Cahouet and Terracciano began flattening and simplifying Mellon's organizational structure, with the objective of creating closer linkages between groups which served the same customers or offered related products. In early 1988, Mellon moved to rationalize its regional banking business, establishing central or regional transaction processing centers and placing more reliance on the regional banks for product distribution.

A year after Cahouet began the turnaround effort, the results seemed positive. Mellon earned $53 million in the first six months of 1988, compared with a $626 million loss in the first six months of 1987. (Exhibits 1, 2, and 3 provide summary financial information for Mellon.) Nevertheless, the vigorous effort to revitalize Mellon was not without its costs. Many Mellon veterans were unprepared for the style of the new management team. One summed up the new attitude when he commented: "The old, conservative Mellon banker who quietly did his job is out. Now you have to have the killer instinct to succeed."[14] Another lamented: "Obviously we needed something to change. But some of us wonder if it's been a little too fast."[15] Mellon suffered what the *Wall Street Journal* termed "massive defections" among old-style managers.[16] At one point Florida's Barnett Banks actually set up a recruiting office in Pittsburgh.

Some industry observers wondered if Mellon would be able to recover its regional dominance. During the years when Mellon was expanding nationally and internationally, local rivals had been developing the middle-market business that Mellon now hoped to capture. Some of the most formidable competition would come from Pittsburgh-based PNC Financial, which had conducted an aggressive expansion campaign in the Middle Atlantic region. PNC had attained returns that were far superior to Mellon's, and by the end of 1987 it had also accumulated more assets. Exhibit 5 shows selected statistics for Mellon and its competitors.

A number of Cahouet's actions were inspired by the troubled state of Mellon's loan portfolio. The credit approval process was made more rigorous, and efforts were made to expand the accountability of individual credit officers. Cahouet continued to make aggressive provisions for credit losses. He also moved to improve Mellon's weakened capital base. In September 1987 Mellon issued $150 million in stated rate auction preferred stock and $270 million in subordinated capital notes. In mid-1988, however, Mellon still had an ample supply of problem loans which posed a potential threat to its capital base.

Strategies for Troubled Loans

Mellon was not the only bank with troubled loans. When Mexico suspended principal repayments on its $80 billion of foreign debt in 1982, many banks that had rushed to develop international business in the 1970s were forced to review the growing problems in their international loan portfolios. The problems worsened as the decade progressed. In 1985 Peru announced that it would limit principal and interest payments to 10% of its export earnings. By February 1987, when Brazil suspended interest payments on its foreign bank debt, the need to recognize the extent of losses and develop strategies for recovery had become pressing.

Citicorp's Approach

In the 1970s, Citicorp had been one of the pioneers in lending to developing countries in the aftermath of the oil shock. Citicorp had a long history of dealing with many of these countries, dating back to the late 1800s when it had been a major underwriter of bonds issued by Latin American nations. Later, in the 1960s, when countries like Brazil embarked on rapid growth strategies, several U.S. banks had been actively involved in funding those strategies. In the mid-1970s the lending opportunities to the Latin American countries increased, often for reasons having to do with the countries' balance of payments. In evaluating the credit worthiness of the borrowers, banks seemed to hold different criteria than for ordinary industrial customers. Walter Wriston, Citicorp's chairman, was widely quoted as saying: "Countries don't go bankrupt." By the end of 1986, Citicorp's loans to Mexico and Brazil alone amounted to $7.4 billion. (The bank's primary capital was approximately $13.5 billion.) Citicorp's total exposure to countries engaged in some form of debt refinancing was $14.9 billion.

John Reed, Wriston's successor, was a pioneer in another sort of effort. On

Tuesday, May 19, 1987, Reed announced that Citicorp would add $3 billion to its loan loss reserve, increasing its total loan loss reserve to about $4.9 billion. The increase in reserves reduced Citicorp's equity base and put the book value of the firm's net assets more closely in line with the market value of its international portfolio. (Most Third World debt traded at about 65% of face value.) The addition to reserves caused Citicorp to record a quarterly loss of $2.5 billion, the largest in the history of U.S. banking. Investors seemed to react positively to the announcement. The closing price of Citicorp common stock rose from 52.25 on May 18 to 55.375 at the end of the week. Citicorp's actions set an example for the industry, and in the following weeks several other banks also increased reserves to more closely reflect the true value of their international loans.

Reed also moved to replace some of the equity that had been transferred to the loan loss reserve. On September 16, Citicorp sold 20 million common shares at $58.25 to raise $1.14 billion. The equity sale increased the number of shares outstanding to approximately 158 million. It also seemed to depress the stock price, which had reached a high of 68.375 on August 13. Citicorp's stock fell 1.375 to close at 65.625 when the stock issue was announced on August 18, and it continued to fall in the following weeks.

Reed believed that recognizing the loan losses up front would give Citicorp more flexibility to reduce its loan exposure (perhaps by as much as $5 billion) through mechanisms such as debt-equity swaps and loan sales. "Liquification will be the game for the next few years," he commented.[17]

Repackaging International Debt

Many borrowers and lenders shared Reed's hope that new financial techniques could be used to alleviate the burden of the $1.2 trillion of Third World debt outstanding at the end of 1987. Much of the hope centered upon debt-equity swaps. Another school of thought focused upon more general techniques of securitization.

A number of bankers were interested in transforming the loans into a combination of bonds and equity. A typical plan called for the loans to be repackaged into senior bonds (which would mature in five years), junior bonds (which would mature in 20 years), and equity (which would share in any remaining loan repayments).

Michael Milken, a senior banker at Drexel Burnham Lambert and the developer of the high-yield bond market, was one of the best known exponents of international debt repackaging. Milken spoke enthusiastically of the opportunities in the LDC debt market: "You have to recapitalize some of these countries, the way you had to recapitalize some companies in the 1970s. . . . The opportunities are enormous. This is a trillion-dollar market, ten times the size of the high-yield [bond] market. The potential payoff is so much bigger."

One of Milken's projects was reportedly the creation of a "conversion fund" which would engage in debt-equity swaps. Investors would pool their money to buy Latin American loans at a discount on the open market. Local governments would buy back the loans with their own currencies, which the fund would then use to purchase equity stakes in local businesses.[18]

Drexel was far from being the most active participant in debt-equity swaps. Banks and multinationals had been doing debt-equity swaps for some time, and other investment firms had made their own plans for conversion funds. A number of Drexel's competitors seemed to believe that the firm's Third World debt efforts were designed to divert attention from government investigations that had been directed at Drexel and Milken. One managing director of First Boston dismissed Milken's efforts as "good public relations."[19]

Loan Losses and Regulation

Given an environment where many banks were increasing their loan loss reserves and examining options involving debt-equity conversions and high yield finance, Cahouet and Terracciano had to reconsider Mellon's asset policies as they worked to formulate and implement an overall strategy. One thing, however, was clear. Regulatory constraints and accounting conventions would play an important role in any possible solution to Mellon's loan problems. In particular, Mellon needed to consider a number of recent changes in tax law, accounting standards, and bank capital requirements.

Capital Requirements, Loan Loss Reserves, and Taxes

Banks in the U.S. were required by their regulators to obey certain capital requirements. The rules were complex and differed between various types of institutions. Until new international capital requirements were adopted in 1988, however, nationally chartered banks typically had to fund 6% of their assets with primary capital. Primary capital consisted mainly of common stock and retained earnings, certain forms of preferred stock and subordinated debt, and loan loss reserves. Additions to loan loss reserves were charged against equity, but did not reduce a bank's primary capital.

Before the Tax Reform Act of 1986, banks were permitted to deduct additions to loan loss reserves from their taxable income. In general, the annual tax deduction was limited to either (1) the amount required to bring the loan loss reserve up to the average percentage of loans written off during the current year and the last five years, or (2) 20% of the amount required to bring the loan loss reserve up to 0.6% of outstanding loans.

The Tax Reform Act of 1986 prohibited banks with over $500 million in assets from recognizing additions to loan loss reserves as a deductible expense. Loan losses could only be recognized for tax purposes when the loans themselves were written down.

New International Capital Requirements

On July 11, 1988, the United States and 11 other leading industrial nations agreed to adopt common capital guidelines for international banks. The Federal Reserve Board had still not stated exactly how the guidelines would be adapted for U.S. banks, but the general thrust of the requirements was clear. By the end of 1990, U.S. banks would have to maintain two "tiers" of capital worth a combined total of at least 7.25% of risk-adjusted assets. The minimum capital level would rise to 8% of risk-adjusted assets at the end of 1992. In the meantime, banks would have to maintain existing capital levels.

The agreement divided capital into two "tiers." The first tier included common stock, retained earnings, and a limited amount of some forms of preferred stock. At least 50% of the required capital had to consist of first tier capital, and no more than 25% of first tier capital could consist of preferred stock. The second tier included loan loss reserves, eligible preferred stock not included in first tier capital, certain long-term unsecured debt, and certain hybrid securities that (among other things) could not be converted at the option of the holder. The amount of loan loss reserves that could be included in second tier capital was limited to 1.5% of risk-adjusted assets, and this limit would be reduced to 1.25% at the end of 1992.

The Restructuring Plan

After months of effort, Mellon's management knew what to do with the bad loans. The latest element of the bank's recovery program centered upon an ambitious *good bank/bad bank* restructuring plan designed by Mellon and Drexel Burnham Lambert. The plan called for Mellon (the "good bank") to spin off about a billion dollars' worth of problem assets to a new bank (the "bad bank") which Mellon would create and capitalize. The new bank would be known as the Grant Street National Bank (in liquidation), and would carry out a plan of liquidation approved by the Comptroller of the Currency.

The restructuring plan involved new financing for both Mellon and Grant Street. Mellon would sell the problem assets to Grant Street for their estimated market value of approximately $575 million. Grant Street would finance about $130 million of the purchase price by issuing common stock, junior preferred stock, and senior preferred stock to Mellon. The rest of the purchase would be financed by issuing bonds. Although the details of the plan were not absolutely final, one or more bond issues totaling $425–450 million were planned.

Mellon would also need to raise money. The assets it planned to sell to Grant Street had a face value of approximately $975 million, and the $400 million difference between their face value and their sale price posed a problem. Mellon planned to write off about $200 million against the bank's existing loan loss reserves. The remaining $200 million would, in effect, be written off directly against equity. Mellon would need to replace the equity that was lost (if only to comply with the provisions of the recent central bank agreement), and it planned to raise some additional equity to further improve its capital position.

Grant Street National Bank and the Financing Plan

The sole function of the Grant Street National Bank would be to liquidate the portfolio of problem assets that it purchased from Mellon. It would not take deposits, would not belong to the Federal Reserve System, and would not be insured by the FDIC. It would only make new loans if such loans were legally or economically necessary for the management of its existing asset portfolio. Any changes to the original plan of liquidation would need to be approved by the Comptroller of the Currency and two-thirds of all voting shares.

Grant Street would stay in business only for as long as it took to liquidate the assets it purchased from Mellon. Leslie Hannafey, the Drexel banker in charge of analyzing the cash flows associated with the asset portfolio, expected that Grant Street would exist for less than ten years.[20] Projected cash flows are given in Exhibit 8.

Grant Street would be independent of Mellon. The two banks would, however, have close ties. Grant Street's officers and directors were nominated by Mellon. William B. Eagleson, a retired chairman of the Mellon Bank Corporation, would serve as Grant Street's chairman, president, CEO, and liquidating agent. (A national bank in liquidation is required to have a liquidating agent to supervise the realization of its assets.) Various provisions of the firm's by-laws and articles of association worked to impede changes in the firm's management. (Many changes, for example, had to be approved by two-thirds of all voting shares.)

Grant Street would oversee, but not actually manage, the business of liquidating its asset portfolio. The portfolio would be managed by Collection Services Corporation (CSC), a new subsidiary of Mellon run by Richard Daniel. CSC would perform numerous services on behalf of Grant Street. The services would include collecting loans, selling loans and assets acquired in connection with loans, and engaging in litigation. Grant Street would pay CSC's expenses plus 3% of net cash flow (defined as the excess of Grant Street's receipts over asset-related operating expenses). Grant Street could replace CSC under certain conditions.

The plan's architects believed that Grant Street would be able to deal with the problem assets more effectively than a traditional bank such as Mellon. Drexel's Michael Milken remarked: "If you have to produce quarterly earnings and maximize quick principal paydowns, you reduce your ultimate recoveries. The 'developing' bank [Grant Street] should be in a better position to maximize the final return on its loans."[21]

The restructuring plan called for Grant Street to purchase substantially all of Mellon's problem assets, with the exception of its troubled international loan portfolio. Mellon had rejected the idea of selling its international loans because of the difficulty of valuing LDC debt. In Cahouet's words: "We couldn't figure out how to do it. . . . If you do LDCs on a cash-flow basis, it gets to be impossible."[22] The composition of Grant Street's loan portfolio, which consisted largely of real estate loans and related assets, is detailed in Exhibit 7.

Grant Street would be funded with several classes of equity and debt. Mellon would purchase and retain about $90 million of senior preferred stock. Mellon would also purchase $2.6 million of junior preferred stock. This stock would be distributed to Grant Street's directors. Finally, Mellon would purchase $35 million of Grant Street common stock, which would be distributed to Mellon's shareholders as a special dividend. One share of Grant Street common stock would be distributed for each common share of Mellon. Grant Street's equity securities are detailed in Appendix A.

The bulk of Grant Street's funding would consist of debt. Drexel planned to raise $425–450 million by issuing two classes of collateralized pay-through notes in late October 1988. The principal of the senior notes would be repaid as quickly as Grant Street's cash flow permitted, while principal payments on the junior notes would commence after the senior notes were repaid. The senior notes would have an estimated lifespan of 1.3 years, while the junior notes would have an estimated lifespan of 3.3 years. Mellon had also arranged for Grant Street to have access to a $30 million revolving credit facility (which would initially be provided by Continental Illinois) in case it needed additional funds for working out the problem loans. Borrowings made under the revolving credit facility would be senior to the pay-through notes. Grant Street's debt securities are detailed in Appendix B.

Mellon Bank and the Financing Plan

The plan called for Mellon to raise additional equity immediately with two private placements of three new classes of preferred stock. The largest stock sale would be to E.M. Warburg, Pincus & Company, a New York venture capital firm. The transaction would make Warburg Mellon's largest investor, with holdings equivalent to 18.4% of Mellon's common stock. Both the conditions of the transaction and an agreement with bank regulators, however, placed strict limits on Warburg's voice in Mellon's management.

The first private placement involved $75 million of Series D preferred stock and $100 million in Series F preferred stock. The principal buyer would be Warburg, Pincus. The sale had not been widely circulated among institutional investors. Warburg agreed not to exercise more than 19.9% of the voting power in corporate elections. It also agreed not to acquire more than 24.9% of Mellon's outstanding voting securities. It agreed to vote in favor of management's nominees for the board of directors, and to vote no less favorably than other shareholders upon proposals advanced by the board of directors. It agreed that, if a tender offer were made for Mellon, it would not tender its shares unless the offer were approved by the board of directors. Finally, Warburg agreed to limitations upon its ability to sell its Series D and F shares (or any common stock obtained through the conversion of those shares) for five years after the placement. It also agreed that, if it chose to sell its shares in the sixth through tenth years after the placement, the shares would be broadly distributed.

The standstill restrictions upon Warburg's actions would generally last for ten years. Warburg could terminate them earlier, however, if Mellon failed certain financial requirements, or if another party acquired over 50% of Mellon's voting securities or replaced a majority of Mellon's board. Warburg could also terminate the restrictions upon the departure of Mellon's current CEO (Cahouet), and either the current COO (Terracciano) or the current CFO (Keith Smith).

The second private placement involved $100 million of Series E convertible preferred stock. The Series E stock would essentially amount to a bridge loan from a group of institutional investors. If the stock was still outstanding in August 1989, it would automatically be converted into common stock at 85% of the market price. Mellon's management did not plan to leave the Series E stock outstanding for a full year: it hoped to redeem it with $100 million raised in a common stock offering in the near future. The Series E stock would have no voting rights except those conferred by Pennsylvania law.

Mellon planned to bolster its capital position still further with later offerings of another $250 million in common stock. A combination of puts and warrants would be used to assist in raising this additional $250 million. Drexel and other institutional investors would commit to purchasing 12 million shares of Mellon stock at $22 per share on or about September 1, 1989 if Mellon had not been able to raise equity on more advantageous terms beforehand. As compensation for the purchase commitments, Drexel and the other investors would receive 3 million warrants which entitled them to purchase 3 million shares of Mellon stock at $25 per share. The warrants could be exercised between August 1, 1989 and August 1, 1994.

The new securities proposed for Mellon are detailed in Appendixes C and D.

The Decision

As the board meeting began on Sunday, July 24, 1988, the directors took their seats. Several of them leafed through the large binders of documents they had been given. Some pondered the particular securities and prices that had been proposed, while others tried to evaluate the effects of the transaction on the operations and strategy of the bank. Since the plan involved the first application of the good bank/bad bank strategy for a bank that wasn't on the brink of failure, some wondered if Mellon should not try more conventional means of solving its problems. Still others tried to see how Mellon, once a pillar of banking conservatism, had ever reached such a state. As the meeting came to order, board members and management resolved to make the right decision.

Appendix A
Grant Street's Equity Securities

This appendix presents, in simplified form, the equity securities issued for the capitalization of Grant Street.

Senior Preferred Stock

1. 900,000 shares with 2 votes per share. To be purchased by Mellon Bank Corporation at $100 per share. Cumulative dividends at 2.75% over the

rate on the A-2 notes (see Appendix B for a description of the Debt Securities), to be paid in additional preferreds until all A-1 and A-2 notes have been redeemed. Preferred stock is to be redeemed at par at six month intervals as soon as the A-1 and A-2 notes have been fully paid.

Junior Preferred Stock

2. 3,428,000 shares with 2.35 votes per share. To be purchased by Mellon Bank Corporation at $ 0.76 for distribution to Grant Street's directors. No annual dividends, but a liquidation distribution of $ 0.35 before any distribution to common shareholders can be made. After a liquidation distribution to common shareholders is made of $ 0.95, junior and common shareholders share in any remaining liquidation distribution on a pro share basis. After the A-1 and the A-2 notes have been paid, and after the senior preferred stock is redeemed, 40% of the junior preferred can be converted to common shares on a share-for-share basis.

Common Stock

3. 29,000,000 shares with one vote per share. To be purchased by Mellon Bank Corporation for $1.21 per share. No annual dividends, but to receive a liquidating distribution of $0.95 per share after liquidating distribution of $0.35 per share is made to junior preferred shareholders. Common shareholders and junior preferred holders share on a pro share basis in any remaining distribution.

Appendix B
Grant Street's Debt Securities

This appendix presents, in simplified form, the debt securities issued by Grant Street.

A-1 Notes

1. Issue $198 million in notes. Stated maturity is November 1, 1991, but can be extended at Grant Street's option for one year. Principal repayment is subordinated to interest payments on the A-2 notes. Interest rate is 10.25% until November 1, 1991, and 10.75% thereafter.

A-2 Notes

2. Issue $252 million in notes. Stated maturity is November 1, 1993, but can be extended at Grant Street's option for one year. Principal repayment is subordinated to repayment of principal of A-1 notes and would gradually rise to 103.00% of the face value by November 1983. Interest rate is 14.25% until May 1, 1991, rises to 14.50% thereafter until November 1, 1993, and 15.00% thereafter until November 1, 1994.

Appendix C
Mellon Bank's Equity Securities

This appendix presents, in simplified form, the equity securities issued for the recapitalization of Mellon Bank Corporation.

Series D Junior Convertible Preferred Stock

1. Issue 4,285,714 voting shares at $17.50 each, to be purchased by Warburg Pincus. Noncumulative dividends at 115% of those on common stock. 60% of dividends must be used to purchase additional Series D stock, but Warburg's total voting rights are not to exceed 19.9% of total voting stock of Mellon. Stock carries subscription rights to purchase 3,143,000 additional shares at $17.50. Each Series D preferred is, after five years, convertible into .7609 common shares. Conversion is automatic after five years have passed and all subscription rights have been exercised. After eight years, any remaining Series D stock is converted automatically. Under certain circumstances, such as a change in control, the Series D shares (including those converted from Series F) can be converted into common stock on a one-for-one basis, but not into more than 10 million common shares minus any earlier conversions.

Series F Junior Convertible Preferred Stock

2. Issue 571,429 non-voting shares at $175 each, to be purchased by Warburg Pincus. Noncumulative dividends at 1150% of those on common stock. 60% of dividends must be used to purchase Series D stock. Each share will automatically convert into 10 shares of Series D stock on September 30, 1988, or upon regulatory approval, whichever comes later.

Series E Mandatory Convertible Preferred Stock

3. Issue 1,000,000 non-voting shares at $100 each. Cumulative dividends at the greater of LIBOR + 3.5% or 11% at the date of sale and increasing by 0.5% at the end of each succeeding three month period. Automatically convertible into common stock at 85% of market price 12 months from sale if not redeemed earlier at $100 plus accrued dividends.

Appendix D
Options and Warrants

This appendix presents, in simplified form, options and warrants related to the recapitalization of Mellon Bank Corporation.

Option

1. Mellon buys a put for 12,000,000 shares, exercisable for one week starting September 1, 1989. The exercise price is approximately $22 per share. After Series E preferred is redeemed, the funds that can be raised by selling stock into the put will be reduced on a dollar for dollar basis by any further issues of common stock or securities convertible into common stock, thus reducing the number of shares subject to the put agreement.

Warrant

2. In payment for the put, 3,000,000 warrants are provided to purchase shares at approximately $25 per share exercisable between August 1, 1989 and August 1, 1994.

▶ **Endnotes**

1. *New York Times,* September 29, 1974, p. III 7.

2. Ibid.

3. *New York Times,* April 13, 1987, p. D3.

4. *Wall Street Journal,* March 26, 1987, p. 6.

5. *New York Times,* March 9, 1986, p. III 33.

6. *Wall Street Journal,* March 2, 1984, p. 29.

7. *New York Times,* March 9, 1986, p. III 33.

8. *Wall Street Journal,* April 10, 1987, p. 27.

9. *Wall Street Journal,* March 26, 1987, p. 6.

10. *Bankers Monthly,* August 1987, p. 40.

11. *New York Times,* April 13, 1987, p. D1.

12. *Wall Street Journal,* June 16, 1987, p. 36.

13. Mellon Bank Corporation, 1987 Annual Report, p. 10.

14. *Wall Street Journal,* August 9, 1988, p. 30.

15. *Institutional Investor,* January 1988, p. 70.

16. *Wall Street Journal,* August 9, 1988, p. 30.

17. *Business Week,* June 15, 1987, p. 31.

18. *Wall Street Journal,* September 14, 1987, p. 6.

19. Ibid.

20. *Barron's,* August 15, 1988, p. 11.

21. Ibid.

22. *American Banker,* September 1, 1988, p. 14.

Exhibit 1

Summary of Financial Information
($ millions, except per share amounts)

	Year Ended December 31					
	1987	1986	1985	1984	1983	1982
Net interest revenue	$ 823	$ 941	$ 872	$ 747	$ 615	$ 446
Provision for credit losses	1,056	316	148	117	52	68
Service revenue	616	525	365	302	230	131
Trading revenue	(12)	24	23	5	12	21
Gain on sale of investment securities*	13	135	93	4	11	(15)
Gain on settlement of pension obligations	126	—	—	—	—	—
Other revenue	47	22	12	26	34	11
Operating expense	1,403	1,145	966	815	631	382
Provision for income taxes	(2)	3	49	(7)	35	10
Net income (loss)	(844)	183	202	159	184	134
Net income (loss)						
Domestic	(361)	213	198	160	151	91
International	(483)	(30)	4	(1)	33	43
Per common share						
Net income (loss)	(31.19)	6.20	7.13	5.64	7.44	6.83
Dividends	1.74	2.76	2.68	2.60	2.44	2.24
Average balances						
Money market investments	3,641	2,565	3,072	3,634	4,298	4,183
Investment securities	4,023	3,868	2,113	1,378	1,672	1,298
Loans	21,471	22,704	20,082	17,347	13,935	10,886
Interest-earning assets	29,381	29,629	25,667	22,821	20,345	16,653
Total assets	32,565	33,834	30,246	27,601	24,232	19,539
Deposits	21,881	20,006	18,250	17,009	14,579	12,280
Notes and debentures	1,843	1,430	1,058	610	565	417
Redeemable preferred stock	94	94	93	89	48	—
Common shareholders equity	1,361	1,716	1,562	1,438	1,253	1,018
Total shareholders equity	1,474	1,768	1,562	1,438	1,253	1,018
Key ratios (based on average balances)						
Return on assets	—	.54%	.67%	.57%	.76%	.69%
Return on common equity	—	9.88	12.26	10.35	14.25	13.21
Net interest margin	3.15%	3.70	3.81	3.80	3.57	3.29
Capital ratios (based on year-end figures)						
Common equity to assets	2.82%	5.08%	4.90%	4.90%	5.23%	5.26%
Total equity to assets	3.53	5.27	4.90	4.90	5.23	5.26
Primary capital ratio	8.48	7.23	6.62	6.64	6.09	6.04
Total capital ratio	10.08	8.66	7.92	7.71	7.28	6.83
*After tax gain on sales of investment securities	$ 13	$ 73	$ 50	$ 2	$ 6	$ (8)

Source: Mellon Bank Corporation, 1987 Annual Report, page 20.

▪ ▼

Exhibit 2

Recent Statements of Financial Position
($ millions)

	June 30, 1988	December 31, 1987
ASSETS		
Cash and due from banks	$ 1,952	$ 1,879
Interest-bearing bank deposits	2,695	2,136
Federal funds sold and securities purchased under agreements to resell	2,070	1,215
Other money market investments	61	43
Trading account securities	14	77
Investment securities	3,483	3,783
Loans	19,843	20,199
Reserve for credit losses	(1,130)	(1,130)
Net loans	18,713	19,069
Other	2,246	2,323
Total assets	$31,234	$30,525
LIABILITIES AND STOCKHOLDERS' EQUITY		
Deposits in domestic offices	$17,830	$18,732
Deposits in foreign offices	3,341	2,816
Federal funds sold and securities sold under agreements to repurchase	4,836	4,057
Commercial paper	548	427
Other	3,479	3,321
Total liabilities	30,034	29,353
Redeemable preferred stock	94	94
Convertible preferred stock	68	68
Stated rate auction preferred stock	150	150
Common equity	888	860
Total shareholders' equity	1,200	1,172
Total liabilities and shareholders' equity	$31,234	$30,525

▼ ▼ ▼ ▼ ▼ ▼

Source: Mellon Bank Corporation, 1988 Second Quarter Report, page 15.

Exhibit 3

Recent Six-Month Income Statements
($ millions, except per share amounts)

	Six months ended	
	June 30, 1988	June 30, 1987
Interest revenue	$1,197	$1,269
Interest expense	809	842
Net interest revenue	388	427
Provision for credit losses	85	708
Net interest revenue after provision for credit losses	303	(281)
Service and other revenue		
Service revenue	319	301
Trading revenue	5	(9)
Gains on sale of investment securities	4	2
Gain on settlement of pension obligations	—	—
Other revenue	43	18
Total service and other revenue	371	312
Operating expense		
Salaries	222	266
Employee benefits	33	55
Other expense	352	355
Total operating expense	607	676
Income before income taxes	67	(645)
Provision for income taxes	14	(19)
Net income (loss)	53	(626)
Dividends on preferred stock	13	8
Net income (loss) applicable to common stock	40	(634)
Net income per common share	$1.40	$(22.98)
Average common shares outstanding	28,467,058	27,571,562

Source: Mellon Bank Corporation, 1988 Second Quarter Report, page 16.

Exhibit 4

Composition of Mellon's Loan Portfolio
($ millions)

						December 31,							
	1987	1986	1985	1984	1983	1982	1981	1980	1979	1978	1977	1976	1975
DOMESTIC OPERATIONS													
Commercial and financial	$ 9,324	$11,352	$11,593	$ 9,877	$ 7,215	$ 5,744	$ 4,834	$3,725	$3,156	$2,676	$2,399	$2,120	$2,309
Real estate	4,895	5,640	4,303	3,651	2,995	2,033	1,765	1,473	1,329	970	781	713	705
Consumer credit	2,766	2,696	2,227	2,014	1,500	907	955	952	992	856	737	646	502
Lease finance assets	443	413	387	289	237	198	184	170	139	123	107	105	95
Total domestic operations	17,428	20,101	18,510	15,831	11,947	8,882	7,738	6,320	5,616	4,625	4,024	3,584	3,611
International operations	2,771	3,428	3,809	3,856	3,542	2,681	2,370	1,832	1,410	1,520	1,433	1,345	1,165
Total loans and leases	20,199	23,529	22,319	19,687	15,489	11,563	10,108	8,152	7,026	6,145	5,457	4,929	4,776
NONPERFORMING ASSETS													
Nonaccrual and restructured loans													
Domestic	848	671	386	310	256	206	126	73	73	†	†	†	†
International	407	227	191	214	198	116	47	21	8	†	†	†	†
Total problem loans	1,255	898	577	524	454	322	173	94	81	83	110	188	220
Other problem assets*	394	180	57	28	29	24	23	32	52	67	105	105	69
Total nonperforming assets	1,649	1,078	634	552	483	346	196	126	133	150	215	293	289
Nonperforming assets as % of total loans and leases	8.2	4.6	2.8	2.8	3.1	3.0	1.9	1.5	1.9	2.4	3.9	5.9	6.1
Nonperforming assets as % of total assets	5.4	3.1	1.9	1.8	1.8	1.7	1.1	0.8	1.0	1.3	2.2	3.1	3.2

*Almost entirely composed of real estate acquired in connection with loan settlements.
†National and international problem loans are not reported separately for 1975–78.

Source: Mellon Bank Corporation, various Annual Reports.

Exhibit 5

Comparison of Mellon and Selected Competitors

	1983	1984	1985	1986	1987
Total year-end assets ($ billion)					
Mellon	$26.4	$30.6	$33.4	$34.5	$30.5
PNC	17.7	21.3	26.6	31.4	36.5
Money center average	55.1	61.0	66.4	72.1	76.3
Return on average assets (%)					
Mellon	0.76	0.57	0.67	0.54	−2.59
PNC	1.02	1.09	1.11	1.23	0.79
Money center average	0.64	0.60	0.69	0.70	−0.65
Return on average equity (%)					
Mellon	14.25	10.35	12.26	9.79	−58.01
PNC	15.72	16.34	17.41	19.08	12.21
Money center average	14.31	12.95	14.02	13.58	−14.16
Nonperforming assets (% of total assets)					
Mellon	1.8	1.8	1.9	3.1	5.4
PNC	0.8	0.9	0.9	0.9	1.2
Money center average	1.8	2.1	1.8	1.9	3.5
Noninterest income (% of average assets)					
Mellon	1.19	1.22	1.63	2.09	2.43
PNC	1.44	1.64	1.62	1.90	1.54
Money center average	1.15	1.31	1.58	1.95	2.20
Noninterest expense excluding income taxes and loan loss provision (% of average assets)					
Mellon	2.61	2.95	3.19	3.39	4.31
PNC	3.04	3.11	3.01	2.87	2.60
Money center average	2.41	2.50	2.79	3.04	3.28
P/E ratios (based on operating earnings)					
Mellon	7.1	8.4	9.9	15.0	—
PNC	7.5	7.6	9.9	10.0	7.7
Money center average	5.5	5.9	7.3	7.4	4.8

Note: Money center average includes Bankers Trust, Chase Manhattan, Chemical, Citicorp, Manufacturers Hanover, J. P. Morgan, Republic NY, Bank of Boston, and First Chicago.
Source: Salomon Brothers, *A Review of Bank Performance: 1988 Edition.*

Exhibit 6

Mellon Common Stock Information, 1970–1988

Date	Stock Price at Month-end ($)	Shares Outstanding (millions)	P/E Ratio	Average Bank P/E Ratio
Dec. 1970	28	20	10.8	11.2
Dec. 1971	26	20	10.7	11.5
Dec. 1972	25	20	10.7	13.7
Dec. 1973	22	20	8.2	11.1
Dec. 1974	19	20	5.9	6.1
Dec. 1975	26	20	7.8	6.7
Dec. 1976	29	20	8.7	8.8
Dec. 1977	26	20	7.0	6.9
Dec. 1978	26	20	5.9	5.7
Dec. 1979	28	20	5.4	5.2
Dec. 1980	32	20	5.5	5.4
Dec. 1981	37	20	5.7	5.3
Dec. 1982	37	20	5.2	5.6
Dec. 1983	51	26	7.1	6.5
Mar. 1984	39	26	6.0	6.3
Jun. 1984	38	26	6.2	5.5
Sep. 1984	42	26	6.9	6.5
Dec. 1984	47	27	8.4	6.6
Mar. 1985	48	27	8.3	7.1
Jun. 1985	54	27	10.1	8.2
Sep. 1985	48	27	8.9	6.9
Dec. 1985	52	27	9.9	8.6
Mar. 1986	72	27	13.7	10.9
Jun. 1986	70	27	14.8	10.7
Sep. 1986	55	27	11.6	9.2
Dec. 1986	55	27	15.0	8.9
Mar. 1987	50	27	—	9.7
Jun. 1987	36	28	—	9.8
Sep. 1987	41	28	—	9.3
Dec. 1987	27	28	—	6.4
Jan. 1988	25	28	—	NA
Feb. 1988	27	28	—	NA
Mar. 1988	28	28	—	NA
Apr. 1988	28	29	—	NA
May 1988	28	29	—	NA
Jun. 1988	30	29	—	NA

Note: P/E ratios are based on operating earnings for previous 12 months. "Average bank P/E ratio" is average for 35 banks as defined by Salomon Brothers.

Source: P/E ratios are from Salomon Brothers, *A Review of Bank Performance: 1988 Edition*. Stock information is from Standard and Poor's, *Daily Stock Price Record* (NYSE), various editions.

Exhibit 7

Assets on Grant Street's Books after Asset Sale*

TYPE OF ASSET	Book Value ($ million)
Commercial and Industrial Loans and Leases	
Energy	$128.157
Consumer Products & Services	73.736
Industrial Manufacturing	43.477
Miscellaneous	13.770
Total Commercial and Industrial	$259.140
REAL ESTATE LOANS	
Housing and Land	119.194
Operating Properties	
Commercial	62.448
Hotel	7.135
Total Real Estate Loans	188.777
REAL ESTATE ASSETS	
Housing Units	$ 31.777
Land	25.198
Operating Properties	
Commercial	53.702
Hotel	2.380
Multi-Family	1.453
Total Real Estate Assets	114.510
Personal Property	14.217
OTHER ASSETS	
Cash	0.059
Other (organization cost)	0.902
Total Assets	$577.605

*The exhibit details Grant Street's balance sheet as it would have appeared on July 1, 1988.

Source: Adapted from Drexel Burnham Lambert's offering circular for Grant Street's Class A-1 and A-2 notes.

Exhibit 8

Grant Street National Bank (in Liquidation) Projected Cash Flows
($ million)

					Years Ending June 30,					
	1989	1990	1991	1992	1993	1994	1995	1996	1997	1998
CASH INFLOWS										
Real estate assets										
Operating properties										
Gross rental income	$ 12.6	$ 18.9	$ 21.6	$ 14.4	$ 9.0	$ 1.8	$ 0.0	$ 0.0	$ 0.0	$ 0.0
Operating expenses	(10.8)	(11.7)	(11.7)	(7.2)	(4.5)	(0.9)	0.0	0.0	0.0	0.0
Other expenditures	(9.0)	(6.3)	(0.9)	(2.7)	(0.9)	0.0	0.0	0.0	0.0	0.0
Sales and repayments	19.8	0.0	55.9	74.8	28.0	54.1	0.0	0.0	0.0	0.0
Total operating properties	12.6	0.9	64.9	79.3	31.6	55.0	0.0	0.0	0.0	0.0
Housing units and land										
Sales and loan proceeds	70.3	54.1	30.7	28.0	18.9	48.7	14.4	9.0	7.2	7.2
Other expenditures	(20.7)	(12.6)	(6.3)	(4.5)	(3.6)	(3.6)	(0.9)	(0.9)	(0.9)	(0.9)
Total housing units and land	49.6	41.5	24.4	23.5	15.3	45.1	13.5	8.1	6.3	6.3
Residential mortgages	8.1	14.4	11.7	9.9	8.1	37.0	0.9	0.9	0.0	0.0
Total real estate assets	70.3	56.8	101.0	112.7	55.0	137.1	14.4	9.0	6.3	6.3
Commercial and industrial loans:										
Gross receipts	117.2	111.8	88.4	74.8	23.4	20.7	18.9	12.6	9.9	29.8
Future advances	(18.9)	0.0	0.0	0.0	0.0	0.0	0.0	0.0	0.0	0.0
Total commercial and industrial loans	98.3	111.8	88.4	74.8	23.4	20.7	18.9	12.6	9.9	29.8
Interest on working capital	2.7	3.6	3.6	3.6	1.8	2.7	0.9	0.0	0.0	0.9
Gross cash inflow	171.3	172.2	193.0	191.1	80.2	160.5	34.2	21.6	16.2	37.0
CASH OUTFLOWS										
Bank operating expenses	21.6	18.9	16.2	13.5	10.8	9.9	8.1	6.3	5.4	5.4
Administrative fees	4.5	5.4	5.4	5.4	2.7	4.5	0.9	0.9	0.9	0.9
Income taxes	0.0	0.0	0.0	0.9	8.1	28.0	6.3	3.6	2.7	10.8
Total asset-related outflows	26.1	24.3	21.6	19.8	21.6	42.4	15.3	10.8	9.0	17.1
Net Cash Flow before Debt Service	$145.2	$147.9	$171.4	$171.3	$58.6	$118.1	$18.9	$10.8	$ 7.2	$19.9

Source: Adapted from Drexel Burnham Lambert's offering circular for Grant Street's Class A-1 and A-2 pay-through notes, page F-3.

Shearson Lehman Brothers and American Express: 1987

On Monday, March 23, 1987, the board of directors of the American Express Company (Amexco) met to consider a partial sale of Shearson Lehman Brothers, Amexco's wholly owned brokerage and investment banking subsidiary. Amexco's management proposed to sell about 18% of Shearson to the public, 8.5% to selected Shearson employees and an employee stock ownership plan, and 13% to the Nippon Life Insurance Company. The sale would be the latest step in a series of acquisitions and divestitures made over the last 20 years.

The stock market had reacted positively to the spinoff proposal. On February 26, when the public first learned that part of Shearson might be sold, Amexco's stock jumped from 68.625 to 72.75. (The rumors circulating on February 26 also concerned two other items which would be considered at the meeting on March 23. Amexco's management had proposed a 2-for-1 stock split and a $0.02 increase in the quarterly dividend.) On Friday, March 20, the stock closed at 77.25. The S&P 500, meanwhile, had advanced 5% from the close on February 25 to March 20.

American Express

The American Express Company was founded in 1850 when three express companies joined forces. They filled a profitable market niche between the mail and freight services. In 1882, American Express started its evolution into a financial services firm when it responded to the Post Office's introduction of the postal money order with an improved money order of its own. Sometime around 1890, Amexco invented the traveler's check, which proved immensely popular. Amexco's European offices began offering other travel-related services to the multitudes of American tourists who used traveler's checks, and in the early 1900s the firm developed a large European travel business. The firm obtained banking charters in a number of countries in order to support the money order and traveler's check businesses, whose "float" was recognized as a stable and important source of income.

This case was prepared by Michael Baldwin under the supervision of Assistant Professor David M. Meerschwam.
Copyright © 1989 by the President and Fellows of Harvard College. Harvard Business School case N9-290-002.

After World War II, Amexco's new president positioned the firm to capitalize on the great postwar travel boom. Amexco's float exploded, surpassing $250 million by the early 1950s. The firm also moved successfully to provide overseas banking services to military personnel. Earnings began rising in 1948 with a string of increases that remained unbroken until the 1980s. Following Diners Club's introduction of a restaurant charge card in 1950, Amexco introduced a travel and entertainment charge card in 1958.

In 1960, Howard L. Clark became president of Amexco and brought in a new manager for the charge card effort, which was experiencing major start-up difficulties. By 1967, over 2 million "cardmembers" were charging $1.1 billion annually, and Amexco was making profits of $6.5 million from the card. Clark also toyed with many acquisition ideas, but the only major deal he completed was the acquisition of Fireman's Fund, a California-based property and casualty insurer, in 1968. Fireman's Fund was generally viewed as a mediocre firm in a highly cyclical industry, and the acquisition puzzled many observers and Amexco executives. In 1972, Clark also acquired a 25% stake in Donaldson, Lufkin & Jenrette, Inc., for $15 per share. But anticipated synergies did not materialize, and the stake in DLJ was distributed to Amexco's shareholders in 1975, when it was valued at about $3 per share.

American Express in 1977

Having increased Amexco's net income 30-fold by 1977, Clark resigned. Robinson, a 41-year-old Harvard MBA who had worked at Morgan Guaranty and been a partner at White Weld before joining Amexco in 1970, would be the CEO. Morley, a 45-year-old Harvard MBA, would be the president.

The American Express that Robinson and Morley inherited consisted of three business units. *Travel Related Services* (TRS) handled traveler's checks, the American Express cards, and the travel business. $13 billion of checks were sold each year. Eight million cardholders charged over $10 billion a year, generating fees of over $160 million, revenue from discounts of about $375 million, and total profits of about $70 million. Analysts viewed both businesses as mature. They also noted that banks and Visa were cutting into Amexco's market share in the traveler's check and credit card businesses. In order to try to keep TRS growing in this environment, Robinson brought in Louis V. Gerstner, Jr., a 35-year-old Harvard MBA and former McKinsey consultant.

The *American Express International Banking Corporation* (AEIBC) handled a full range of international banking activities. It did not do any banking in the U.S., and was therefore not subject to U.S. banking regulations. An aggressive expansion program during the 1970s had increased assets from $1.8 billion in 1972 to $4 billion in 1977. Of these new assets, a substantial fraction were loans to Third World nations. Overall, the bank earned about 0.6% on its assets, and profits increased in 1977, but only with the assistance of a reduction in the loan loss reserve.

The *property and casualty insurance unit*, Amexco's third business line, had gone through difficult years in the mid-1970s. Operating earnings at Fireman's Fund fell 50% in both 1974 and 1975. Only the use of unorthodox accounting techniques involving Fireman's catastrophic loss reserve enabled Amexco to maintain its unbroken string of annual earnings increases. By the late 1970s, however, the property and casualty business was recovering, and Fireman's Fund was once again making a large contribution to Amexco's profits.

The Acquisition Trail

The new executive team soon began trying to add what Clark had called a "fourth leg" to Amexco. Companies such as Walt Disney, Book-of-the-Month Club, Philadelphia Life Insurance Company, and McGraw-Hill were considered, but transactions were not concluded. In two smaller deals, $175 million was spent for a 50% share in a cable TV venture with Warner Communications, and $50 million to acquire First Data Resources, which processed credit card transactions.

After considering and rejecting a merger proposal from Merrill Lynch (the largest brokerage firm), Amexco executives examined Shearson Loeb Rhoades and E. F. Hutton (the second and third largest firms). Robinson began talks with Sandy Weill, the head of Shearson, in the fall of 1980. While considering a deal with Shearson, Robinson acquired six additional firms, at a total cost of $100 million. When in March 1981 Prudential, with its $60 billion in assets, acquired Bache Halsey Stuart Shields for $385 million, Robinson and Weil immediately reopened their talks. Robinson remarked on "a rapid evolution taking place in the delivery of financial services." Changes in financial services were "inevitable, and those companies which act to guide change will flourish."[1] On April 21, 1981, Shearson and Amexco agreed to merge in a tax-free stock swap, valued at $1 billion.

Shearson Loeb Rhoades

Shearson had started in 1960 when four partners pooled their life savings of $215,000 to form Carter, Berlind, Potoma and Weill (CBWL after 1968). By the late 1960s the partners anticipated declining profits in institutional brokerage, their main business activity, and decided to redirect their efforts. The firm's first acquisition came in 1967, when it bought Bernstein Macauley, a money management firm. Weill recalled: "We felt it was important to have a recurring source of income, and not just income related to the exchange volume or the direction of the markets, but the kind of income you can earn at night and Saturday and Sunday."[2]

In 1969, CBWL laid the groundwork for a series of retail brokerage acquisitions. It created its own back office under the supervision of Frank Zarb, an operations expert hired away from Goodbody. In addition, a painful acquisition of the Beverly Hills office of McDonald & Company provided a thorough knowledge of what to expect when two brokerage firms merged.

In 1970, CBWL bought Hayden Stone, an old-line firm that was on the brink of failure. It was an ambitious acquisition. CBWL had two offices, 200 employees, and 5,000 accounts. Hayden Stone had 28 offices and 50,000 accounts. Weill recalled: "Frank and the rest of us came up with a system to bring those accounts in, process substantial added volume and keep it under control. We couldn't afford to lose, and I guess that first one really taught us how to do it right and created a lot of enthusiasm and tremendous pride among our people."[3] CBWL-Hayden Stone went public soon after Merrill Lynch in 1971, and the offering provided the capital for further expansion.

Weill became CEO in 1973, and Peter Cohen, a recent Columbia MBA, became his operations expert and right-hand man. By the time they bought Shearson Hammill in 1974 (after picking up two smaller firms along the way) they believed they had mastered the economies of scale involved in brokerage mergers. The Shearson acquisition was followed by the purchases of four additional brokerages and a 25% stake in a fifth, as well as a mortgage banking firm. The last merger that was actually completed before the Amexco deal was with Loeb Rhoades, Hornblower & Co. in 1979. It gave the firm a new name and doubled its size, to 9,000 employees and 268 offices. In 1981, before the agreement with Amexco, Shearson also agreed to acquire the Boston Company, a Boston trust concern.

Weill's expansion strategy involved fast and deep cost-cutting. The merger with Loeb Rhoades, for example, entailed the quick loss of 3,000 jobs. Weill commented: "It's stupid to take prisoners. If there's one thing I learned from my partnership days, it's that you can't have two people doing the same job."[4] The engine driving all the mergers was the efficiency of Shearson's back office. Marshall Cogan, who ran the firm until 1973, observed: "The strategy hasn't changed over the last seventeen years: It is to put more and more volume through an existing data-processing plant that is the state of the art."[5]

In 1981, Shearson was commonly regarded as one of the best-managed firms in the retail brokerage industry. It returned 62.8% on its equity in 1980, and averaged a 34% return on equity in the five years ending in 1980. Still, Weill saw the need for even more resources. He recalled: "By 1980 internationalization and securitization were beginning to make it clear that companies had to have access to a lot of capital and that technology was going to be key. . . . And then you had American Express sitting across the street, with a small corporate staff and an unbelievable reputation for quality and great technology."[6] In June 1981, the firm was merged into Amexco.

Shearson and American Express Together

Managers at Amexco and Shearson believed the combined firms could realize substantial synergies. In Weill's words: "We don't look at our company as a financial conglomerate with a holding company. It's one enterprise."[7] A new "Financial Management Account" (which had inspired the original talk of a joint venture) would allow customers to purchase financial services with their American Express cards. Shearson salespeople could sell Fireman's Fund insurance and annuities. The AEIBC, in turn, could sell Shearson products such as money management to its private banking customers. New products and cross-selling efforts, however, were only the start. Weill believed that Amexco, "one of the premier financial marketing companies," would provide invaluable marketing expertise to Shearson. In Weill's words, "The securities business is sales-oriented and not marketing-oriented, and that's got to change."[8]

Others, of course, saw pitfalls. One analyst commented: "I'd be surprised if Shearson's returns in the future will be as good as in the past. Larger organizations like American Express just can't make decisions as quickly, and the securities industry is an opportunistic business."[9] Some wondered if the Brooklyn-born Weill, who had started as a runner at Bear Stearns, would be happy working under Robinson, the scion of an Atlanta banking family.

Robinson acknowledged that there would be some clashes, but thought that they could be positive: "Putting the two cultures together, letting them learn from and complement each other, represented one of the hidden opportunities of this deal. Shearson people, on the one hand, are learning more about market concepts and market positioning and tactics, while on the other hand, the whole drumbeat of the decision process has been stepped up at American Express because of the Shearson culture."[10]

Remaking American Express

When the Shearson acquisition was made in 1981, AEIBC seemed to be Amexco's most troubled business unit. After unsuccessful efforts to sell the bank, a new group of managers shifted its focus to private banking and trade finance. Expenses were cut, and many bankers were fired. In early 1983, the move into private banking received a major boost: Amexco bought the non-U.S. businesses of Trade Development Bank Holding S.A., a Geneva-based institution with a large private-banking business and $5 billion in low-cost deposits.

AEIBC, Shearson, and the American Express cards gave Amexco a strong position serving what Robinson called "the affluent top" of financial service consumers.[11] Much of the middle market, which Amexco estimated at 34 million households spending $140 billion annually on financial services, remained untapped. To remedy this defect, Weill conducted negotiations with Alleghany Corp. aimed at acquiring Investors Diversified Services (IDS). IDS, a Minneapolis-based vendor of mutual funds, insurance, and financial planning, controlled $17.6 billion in assets and focused its marketing on the middle market. IDS customers were typically financially conservative Midwesterners earning between $30,000 and $65,000. Robinson remarked: "We think they have a unique franchise in this market."[12] In January 1984 Amexco bought IDS alone for about $775 million in cash, stock and notes.

At Fireman's, however, problems were accumulating. The property and casualty insurance industry entered another cyclical price war in 1979, and operating profits began to deteriorate. At first, however, the price war seemed to leave Fireman's untouched. Profits continued to rise, partly through deft manipulation of "special items" such as complicated reinsurance transactions and adjustments to loss reserve margins. The situation became worse in late 1982, when Fireman's management anticipated an industry turnaround and increased its sales efforts. As late as August 1983, the company anticipated reported earnings of $266 million. But the turnaround didn't materialize and the special items were exhausted. Fireman's management was faced with a fourth-quarter loss of $141 million and annual income of $30 million (down from $244 million the previous year). The drop in Fireman's earnings snapped Amexco's 35-year record of earnings growth. Moreover, Amexco had to inject $230 million into Fireman's to support its loss reserves.

As long as Fireman's had been a profitable investment, it had never really been integrated into Amexco. (As one Fireman's manager recalled: "Even when we asked for help from American Express on technical matters, they tended to ignore us."[13]) The hands-off approach, however, was now over. Weill and William McCormick, a former McKinsey consultant who had more recently served as vice-chairman of TRS under Gerstner, took command of the firm. In early 1984, they fired 1,140 of the firm's 13,000 workers and cut annual expenses by $60 million. Operations experts were brought in from Shearson and Amexco to rebuild Fireman's outdated computer systems, with the objective of saving another $70 to $80 million annually.

The turnaround seemed successful, but Robinson and Gerstner, over Weill's objections, decided to sell most of Amexco's holdings in Fireman's Fund. (Its small life insurance business, however, was merged into TRS.) Successive offerings in 1985 and 1986 reduced Amexco's stake in Fireman's to 27%, and raised over $1.2 billion for Amexco.

Fireman's was not the only business to be sold in 1985. Warner Amex, the cable TV venture, had finally become profitable after years of losses. Amexco sold its share for $450 million, saying that it "did not fulfill original expectations as a distribution channel for financial and travel services."[14]

While some of Amexco's acquisitions were troubled, Gerstner led TRS to far better results than many had expected. Gerstner applied an aggressive, growth-oriented philosophy to businesses that many had considered mature even in the 1970s. As he said in 1984: "We should all develop the mind-set, the orientation and the conviction that our current businesses are young, vigorous and ready to be grown, if only we have the continued imagination and will to do it."[15] Under Gerstner's leadership, TRS's net income increased from $145 million in 1978 to $599 million in 1986. Furthermore, in 1987, the new Optima card (Amexco's first true credit card) would bring the firm into direct competition with bank-sponsored credit cards.

As the fortunes of Amexco's businesses changed, the firm's executives jockeyed for position. Shearson executives began moving into top positions at American Express soon after the merger. Many observers thought Weill would eventually try for the top position at American Express. At the end of 1982, Peter Cohen became the CEO of Shearson, with Sandy Weill remaining as chairman but with increasingly few identifiable responsibilities. Weill slowly became what his old partner Roger Berlind called "an executive without portfolio."[16] Fireman's was taken public over his objections, and in spite of his efforts to do a leveraged buyout of it. In June 1985, Weill resigned. Lou Gerstner became the new president of Amexco, and Peter Cohen became the new chairman of Shearson.

The Question of Synergy

Throughout the 1980s, Robinson focused on developing synergies between the business units. Some of these synergies were to be a result of combining different corporate cultures at the headquarters level. As Robinson said: "Any Harvard-vs.-Yale kind of competitive vibrations are all to the good. The cultures are clashing just as I hoped they would."[17] Sometimes, of course, the clashes were not productive. TRS executives resisted the idea of letting Shearson advertise in their mailings. Jeffrey Lane, Shearson's COO, thought he understood why: "The card is an instrument of trust and not risk. There's risk in everything we do as brokers."[18] Shearson's ideas of selling products through TRS went largely unfulfilled: "Pre-merger, the great dream was that we would go from half a million brokerage clients to 15 million clients—the number of cardmembers at the time." But "we have found it more difficult to put the pieces together than we thought. The walls have broken down more slowly than we would have liked."[19]

In January 1985 Amexco changed its earlier strategy of placing the American Express name on all of its business units. IDS and Shearson were among the units to have their names changed. IDS/American Express became IDS Financial Services, and Shearson Lehman/American Express became Shearson Lehman Brothers. Gerstner explained: "That's an important marketing decision. Shearson Lehman does not want to have the same image as American Express. We want to use multiple brand names that have slightly different positions."[20]

In early 1987 Amexco estimated that, in spite of occasional problems, about 70% of the 260 different collaborative efforts it had launched had been successful. About half of these efforts used cross-selling, and the rest involved sharing other resources. Shearson and AEIBC worked jointly on 12 big financing efforts in 1986. (Relations between Shearson and AEIBC personnel, however, were tense.) IDS did as much business in Balcor real estate partnerships as Shearson, even though Balcor was a Shearson unit. Amexco was very successful selling life insurance to cardholders and to customers of Shearson and IDS. AEIBC was particularly assiduous in its efforts to sell products produced by other areas of Amexco. All senior managers were required to identify and pursue two or three synergy projects each year, and all professionals were evaluated on their contributions to the "One Enterprise" effort. Amexco estimated that about 10% of its 1986 income could be attributed to various synergies. In early 1987, however, the final verdict on synergy was still uncertain. In Robinson's words: "We've hit a home run or two, but mostly singles and doubles."[21]

Amexco's top managers periodically complained to stock analysts and others about something they considered negative synergy. Amexco's stock traded at a price-earnings multiple of around 14, compared to about 20 for the overall market. CFO Howard Clark, Jr., saw a possible explanation: "Most of the analysts who follow us come out of the insurance industry, because of our long association with Fireman's Fund. They believe that owning a brokerage business that contributes 25% to our earnings is a liability. They see the volatility of the market, and tend to ignore the fact that most of our money is made in fees from asset management."[22]

Expanding Shearson

Shearson continued to expand rapidly after its acquisition by Amexco. It completed the acquisition of the Boston Company and purchased Balcor, a Chicago real-estate firm. By the end of 1983 it had purchased four regional brokers in the Northwest, Southeast, Northern California, and the Midwest. The move that had the deepest impact, however, was the acquisition of Lehman Brothers Kuhn Loeb in 1984.

Lehman Brothers Kuhn Loeb, a loosely managed partnership which was one of the nation's leading investment banks, was suffering from the aftereffects of a bitter change in leadership in mid-1983. Torn by deep divisions within the firm and worried by mounting trading losses, the partners decided to seek a buyer. When Cohen was approached by a Lehman partner on March 31, 1984, he immediately recognized "a once-in-a-lifetime opportunity" to greatly strengthen Shearson's capabilities in trading and investment banking.[23] In May 1984, Amexco acquired Lehman for $380 million, mainly in bonds and notes. (The price was over three times Lehman's book value, which was somewhat higher than in other recent brokerage acquisitions.) The acquisition gave Shearson almost 3,000 new employees who had generated a total of $60 million in profits during the year ending in September 1983. Cohen moved quickly to consolidate operations, firing about 700 employees to generate annual savings of $75 million. At the same time, he obtained three-year non-compete agreements with the 57 Lehman partners he wanted to retain.

Many observers speculated that the cultural differences between the tightly managed, retail-oriented Shearson and the freewheeling, trading- and deal-oriented Lehman would doom the new firm. (One pessimist likened it to "McDonald's buying the 21 Club.") Lane admitted the difficulty of combining strong retail and wholesale operations: "Our challenge is to accomplish what no one else has ever accomplished."[24]

As one former Lehman partner recalled: "The guts of Lehman were screaming out for the organization and management Shearson possessed."[25] In the spring of 1985, Cohen forced the investment banking group to put together a long-term plan (a first for Lehman). The compensation system was changed so that bonuses would be awarded for new business, and the firm started aggressively soliciting large corporate clients. After several months, the new approach started yielding results. For example, a Lehman partner involved in one large underwriting commented: "Before the merger, Lehman Brothers would not have been invited to participate because it lacked a broad retail distribution system."[26] Thus, the newly merged firms seemed to be complementing each other, and while in 1985 about 135 investment bankers had left Shearson Lehman, by early 1986 the exodus of talented employees and loss of business seemed to be over, although there were still occasional signs of unrest.

The Lehman merger was not the only major initiative of the Cohen years. In 1983, Shearson began construction of a $209 million data center. When the center was completed in 1986, Shearson had the capacity to process 100,000 trades per day (compared to the 40,500 that it currently processed). Lenny Haynes, the firm's chief of operations, remarked: "Opening this facility was like giving Peter a checkbook. From that point on there was never a question that the firm would do a major acquisition."[27] For a brief time in the fall of 1986, it seemed like the major acquisition would be E.F. Hutton. Shearson made an informal cash offer of $1.55 billion ($50 per share) to buy Hutton, which had 6,400 brokers in 400 offices. Hutton's profit margins were below average, and it had recently brought in new top management after pleading guilty to 2,000 counts of wire fraud. A merger would have given Shearson a total of 12,100 brokers, close to Merrill Lynch's 12,400. Hutton's board, however, turned down the offer, reportedly because they were holding out for $1.7 billion ($55 per share, or about twice book value).

Another new operations facility was scheduled to begin construction in 1987. When the project was completed, at an estimated cost of $460 million, Shearson would be able to consolidate its back office operations at the site of the new data processing center.

Shearson was also expanding aggressively in Europe and Japan. In 1986 it acquired L. Messel & Co., a London brokerage firm it had bought a small stake in two years earlier. The number of employees in its London office had ballooned from 700 to 1,400 in only two years. Although Shearson was not yet a member of the Tokyo stock exchange, its 10-year-old Tokyo office had 100 employees.

Shearson in 1987

In early 1987, Shearson had 27,000 employees and slightly less than $1.4 billion in stockholders' equity. Its 1986 revenues had reached a record $4.1 billion, and net income was a record $316 million. Each of its five major business units had broken earnings records in 1986.

In 1986, the investment banking division underwrote 1,396 securities issues worth almost $95 billion, and advised on 188 mergers, acquisitions and divestitures worth $24 billion. About 69% of the equities it underwrote went to its retail customers. The firm was placing increasingly high emphasis on merchant banking, in an effort to provide what vice chairman George Sheinberg called a combination of "brains and brawn."[28] In 1986, the firm committed to providing a total of $4 billion in financing to support 15 transactions. Most of the financing was in the form of bridge loans, but the firm also made some equity investments.

The firm's capital markets division generated revenue of almost $1 billion in 1986, up almost 40% from 1985. The pace declined slightly in the first three months of 1987. The capital markets division was particularly strong in money markets, corporate bonds, and over-the-counter stocks. It made markets in about 2,650 over-the-counter-stocks. Efforts were underway to improve its research department, which had finished 15th in *Institutional Investor*'s 1986 polls. The firm still tended to minimize the risks it took in trading and arbitrage. It did, however, have to establish a $60 million reserve for losses it suffered when the price of tin plunged following the collapse of the international tin cartel.

Shearson's private client group had 5,700 brokers in 311 U.S. branches and 175 brokers in 22 overseas branches. Its 1986 revenues amounted to almost $1.5 billion, up 36% from 1985. It served 1.7 million active customers who held about $72 billion in assets through Shearson. Marketing studies indicated that its target market in the U.S. consisted of 10 to 12 million affluent households. In 1986, the average broker generated $260,000 in commissions, compared to $270,000 at Merrill Lynch and an industry average of $244,000. (In 1980, Shearson's 3,400 brokers had generated an average of $120,000 in commissions.) Most of the retail brokers were qualified to sell insurance (although they sold relatively little), and the firm had initiatives in the areas of mortgage and consumer lending. The private client group planned to grow by 500 brokers each year, not counting those gained through acquisitions.

The firm's eight asset management subsidiaries managed $60.4 billion and administered an additional $61.6 billion as of the end of 1986. Shearson's asset management subsidiaries generated $310 million in revenue in 1986, up from $210 million in 1985.

Shearson provided a number of other services. The Boston Company engaged in private banking as well as asset management. Boston Safe Deposit and Trust, a subsidiary of the Boston Company, also handled a $3 billion portfolio of mortgages and personal loans. Ayco, a financial planning subsidiary acquired in 1983, generated $20 million in fees in 1986. Balcor, the real estate subsidiary, had suffered because of real estate partnerships it had sponsored in the Southwest and tax reform that eliminated the basis for much of its business. It had responded with pushes into construction lending and property management.

The Common Stock Offering

In the fall of 1986, management at Shearson and Amexco began to consider a partial public offering of the firm. Amexco planned to sell 18 million shares of Shearson's new common stock to the public at $34. Each common share would initially pay a quarterly dividend of $0.1875. The proceeds from the public offering would go to Amexco. An additional five million shares would be given in exchange to certain Shearson employees who had participated in a special program which gave them a direct claim on Shearson's profits. (The program, which had accrued liabilities of $69.3 million, would then be terminated.) Another 2.5 million shares would be sold to Shearson employees for 60% of the initial offering price. Finally, one million shares would be sold to Shearson's employee stock ownership plan (ESOP) within 30 days of the offering. The ESOP would pay the initial offering price if the purchase was made on the offering date, or the fair market price if the purchase was made after the offering date. The proceeds from the 3.5 million shares sold to Shearson employees and the ESOP would go to Shearson.

After it was taken public, Amexco would retain 60.5 million common shares. Amexco did not, however, need to have a majority of the voting shares to retain control. Shearson's board would have three classes of directors. One of these classes would initially consist of past and current officers and directors of American Express. Until Amexco's stake in Shearson dropped below 40% for seven months, this special class of directors would be required to approve many important corporate actions. Examples of such actions included significant mergers, capital expenditures, stock issues, determination of dividends, selection of a CEO, and selection of directors.

Nippon Life

The Nippon Life Insurance Company was the largest life insurance company and the largest holder of securities in Japan. At the end of March 1987, Nippon Life had over $100 billion in assets. It had $1.253 trillion of life insurance in force at the end of 1986 (the most in the world). Its annual cash flow was about $18 billion. Nippon Life invested between $1 and $2 billion each year in foreign bonds, mostly in the U.S. It was also a large investor in U.S. stocks. It owned between 2 and 3 percent of each of the four largest Japanese securities firms.

The Nippon Life Deal

The final deal that Robinson and Cohen worked out with Nippon Life called for it to purchase 13% of Shearson for between $500 and $600 million. It would do so by buying 13 million shares of Series A Cumulative Convertible Voting Preferred Stock at 115% of the IPO price for the common stock (with dividends set at 5% of the purchase price). As long as Nippon Life retained two-thirds of the Series A stock, it would be entitled to two seats on Shearson's board of directors, and could also place an adviser on American Express's board. Nippon would also receive a five-year warrant for 1 million Amexco shares at $100 per share.

The investment agreement gave Amexco and Nippon Life numerous rights and obligations. Nippon Life agreed not to acquire more than 33.3% of Shearson's voting stock for 25 years. If Amexco retained at least a 5% share of Shearson, it could restrict Nippon's ability to transfer its shares for several years. Finally, as long as it retained two-thirds of its Series A stock, or an equivalent amount of common stock, Nippon Life had numerous protections against dilution of its holdings or abandonment by Amexco.

Kiyonobu Shimazu, a Shearson managing director, summed up the advantages of the deal: "We were given a huge missile base in Asia."[29] Robinson said it was "another important step forward in positioning American Express as the leader in worldwide financial services."[30]

► Endnotes

1. *Wall Street Journal*, April 28, 1981, p. 3.
2. *Institutional Investor*, June 1987, p. 83.
3. Ibid., p. 84.
4. *Institutional Investor*, May 1980, p. 143.
5. *Institutional Investor*, March 1988, p. 89.
6. *Institutional Investor*, June 1987, p. 87.
7. *Wall Street Journal*, August 15, 1984, p. 18.
8. *Business Week*, December 20, 1982, p. 53.
9. *Business Week*, May 18, 1981, p. 111.
10. *Financial World*, May 1, 1982, p. 30.
11. *Wall Street Journal*, July 13, 1983, p. 3.

12. Ibid.

13. *Euromoney,* July 1985, p. 49.

14. American Express 1986 Annual Report, p. 19.

15. *Euromoney,* July 1985, p. 41.

16. *Business Week,* July 8, 1985, p. 28.

17. *Business Week,* June 2, 1986, p. 79.

18. *Euromoney,* July 1985, p. 54.

19. Ibid.

20. Ibid., p. 41.

21. *Fortune,* Feb. 16, 1987, p. 79.

22. *Financial World,* May 5, 1987, p. 30.

23. *Fortune,* March 31, 1986, p. 33.

24. *Euromoney,* July 1985, p. 48.

25. *Institutional Investor,* December 1985, p. 59.

26. *Fortune,* May 31, 1986, p. 34.

27. *Institutional Investor,* March 1986, p. 93.

28. *Wall Street Journal,* March 27, 1986, p. 6.

29. *Business Week,* April 6, 1987, p. 36.

30. *Banker,* May 1987, p. 9.

Exhibit 1

Overview of American Express Bank
($ millions)

	1986	1985	1984	1983	1982	1981	1980	1979	1978
Net income	$ 175	$ 164	$ 156	$ 136	$ 60	$ 47	$ 41	$ 35	$ 32
Loans and discounts	7,401	6,671	6,124	6,373	4,474	3,942	3,771	3,446	3,377
Loan loss reserve	192	180	165	162	103	91	89	82	75
Total assets	17,313	15,276	13,688	13,309	7,715	7,100	6,954	6,321	5,535
Deposits and credit balances	13,406	11,675	10,517	10,505	5,723	5,336	5,259	4,880	4,290
Shareholders' equity	1,214	1,109	897	819	367	323	294	265	237
Return on average assets (%)	1.08	1.12	1.16	1.04	0.80	0.66	0.59	0.58	0.60
Return on average equity (%)	14.8	17.28	17.81	17.67	17.56	15.32	14.60	14.06	14.14

Note: Acquisition of TDBH became effective January 1, 1983.

Source: Annual reports, American Express.

Exhibit 2

Overview of Travel Related Services
($ millions)

	1986	1985	1984	1983	1982	1981	1980	1979	1978
Revenues	$ 5,951	$ 4,226	$ 3,620	$ 2,889	$ 2,516	$ 2,175	$ 1,661	$ 1,239	$ 993
Net income	599	461	387	301	247	209	177	151	145
Total assets	18,830	15,314	12,542	10,226	8,445	7,994	6,877	5,405	4,470
Charge volume	63,648	55,435	47,638	38,400	32,000	27,300	21,500	16,300	12,600
Average travelers checks outstanding	3,257	2,904	2,634	2,437	2,535	2,468	2,542	2,343	2,105
Cards in force (millions)	23.8	22.2	20.2	17.3	15.0	13.3	11.9	10.5	9.5
Return on average equity (%)	25.8	25.3	25.3						

Note: Merchants paid Amexco 3% to 5% of the value of goods and services charged on American Express cards. Cardholders paid Amexco an annual membership fee. Charge volumes for 1983 and earlier were estimated by the casewriter.

Source: Annual reports, American Express.

Exhibit 3

Overview of IDS Operations
($ millions)

	1986	1985	1984
Revenues	$ 2,395	$ 2,201	$ 1,576
Annuity premiums	949	843	709
Investment revenue	777	680	521
Net income	96	76	62
Life insurance in force	19,394	17,013	13,818
Assets owned and/or managed			
Assets managed for institutions	4,358	3,457	3,080
Assets owned & assets managed for individuals			
Owned assets	10,206	8,601	6,411
Managed assets	15,620	12,100	9,812
Financial planners (#)	5,567	5,021	4,500
Return on average equity (%)	10.4	9.2	8.1

Source: Annual reports, American Express.

Exhibit 4

Breakdown of American Express Operations

Net Income ($ millions)										
Business unit	1986	1985	1984	1983	1982	1981	1980	1979	1978	1977
Travel Related Services	$ 599	$461	$387	$301	$277	$209	$177	$151	$145	$129
Shearson Lehman Brothers	316	201	103	175	124	107	NA	NA	NA	NA
American Express Bank	175	164	156	136	60	47	41	35	32	20
IDS Financial Services	96	76	62	NA	NA	NA	NA	NA	NA	NA
Insurance Services	NA	1	43	30	244	231	210	186	163	130
Other and corporate	(67)	(80)	(125)	(117)	(94)	(76)	(52)	(27)	(26)	(21)
Adjustments and eliminations	(9)	(13)	(16)	(10)	0	0	0	0	0	0
Total	$1,110	$810	$610	$515	$581	$518	$376	$345	$314	$264

Assets ($ billions)										
Business unit	1986	1985	1984	1983	1982	1981	1980	1979	1978	1977
Travel Related Services	$18.8	$15.3	$12.5	$10.2	$ 8.4	$8.0	$ 6.9	$ 5.4	$ 4.5	$ 3.6
Shearson Lehman Brothers	54.0	34.9	22.7	9.1	6.4	4.1	NA	NA	NA	NA
American Express Bank	17.7	15.7	13.8	13.3	7.7	7.1	6.9	6.3	5.5	4.6
IDS Financial Services	10.2	8.6	6.4	NA	NA	NA	NA	NA	NA	NA
Insurance Services	NA	1.6	7.7	7.1	6.5	6.2	5.8	5.2	4.7	3.9
Other and corporate	1.6	2.0	1.2	1.1	0.8	0.5	0.5	0.6	0.4	0.4
Adjustments and eliminations	(2.8)	(3.3)	(2.6)	(2.2)	(1.5)	(0.8)	(0.4)	(0.4)	(0.3)	(0.2)
Total	$99.5	$74.8	$61.8	$38.5	$28.3	$25.1	$19.7	$17.1	$14.7	$12.3

Source: Annual reports, American Express.

Exhibit 5

Income Statements for Shearson Lehman Brothers
($ millions)

	1986	1985	1984	1983	1982	1981
REVENUES						
Commissions	$ 938	$ 713	$ 536	$ 598	$ 444	$ 364
Investment banking	890*	623	425	386	211	117
Market making and principal						
transactions	983	715	477	304	218	126
Interest and dividends	1,193	825	584	351	303	239
Investment advisory fees	310	230	145	110	89	NA
Mortgage banking	71	57	70	41	30	33
Other	215	83	25	21	23	57
Total revenues	4,600	3,246	2,262	1,811	1,318	936
EXPENSES						
Compensation and benefits	1,919	1,394	992	820	589	421
Interest	1,030	658	467	206	162	86
Communications	277	223	193	145	119	87
Occupancy and equipment	236	191	151	99	74	48
Advertising and market						
development	139	110	99	58	37	21
Brokerage, commissions and						
clearance fees	50	40	33	35	31	27
Professional services	112	76	53	23	28	NA
Other	349	204	105	100	50	40
Total expenses	4,112	2,896	2,093	1,486	1,090	729
Pretax income	488	350	169	325	228	207
Provision for income tax	172	149	64	151	104	101
Net income	$ 316	$ 201	$ 105	$ 174	$ 124	$105

*Underwriting, $465 million; Financial advisory, $427 million.

Note: Shearson's acquisition of Lehman Brothers became effective on May 11, 1984. Lehman's results prior to that date are not reflected in the income statements.

Source: Shearson prospectus (May 1987) and earlier Shearson 10-K reports.

Exhibit 6

Balance Sheets for Shearson Lehman Brothers
($ millions)

	March 31, 1987	December 31, 1986	1985	1984	1983	1982	1981	1980
ASSETS								
Cash	$ 366	$ 436	$ 116	$ 140	$ 147	$ 232	$ 122	$ 30
Time deposits	1,024	1,154	1,300	621	544	381	47	—
Segregated assets and deposits with clearing organizations	781	561	479	336	444	746	332	463
Receivables								
Brokers and dealers	5,988	6,198	4,318	2,200	1,879	1,508	1,066	747
Customers	4,193	4,449	3,588	2,314	1,954	1,285	1,155	1,121
Others, net	2,262	2,118	1,302	612	379	293	37	13
Securities purchased under agreements to resell	15,687	12,547	7,719	4,912	477	278	297	8
Securities & commodities owned	19,983	20,562	12,654	9,642	2,294	1,094	924	354
Mortgage & construction loans	4,212	3,763	1,837	767	389	161	75	76
Buildings & equipment, net	980	946	665	221	162	114	80	32
Deferred expenses and other	711	806	532	299	193	122	92	45
Goodwill	435	438	417	368	107	95	33	14
Investments in affiliates	—	—	—	77	75	43	10	3
Total assets	$56,622	$53,978	$34,927	$22,509	$9,044	$6,351	$4,270	$2,906

Notes: March 31,1987 balance sheet figures are estimates as of March 20, 1987. Shearson's acquisition of Lehman Brothers became effective on May 11, 1984. Balance sheets for prior periods do not reflect Lehman's financial position.

Source: Shearson prospectus (May 1987) and 10-K reports.

Exhibit 7

Balance Sheets for Shearson Lehman Brothers
($ millions)

	March 31,	December 31,						
	1987	1986	1985	1984	1983	1982	1981	1980
LIABILITIES								
Commercial paper and short-term debt	$ 9,041	$ 9,264	$ 5,633	$ 2,437	$1,392	$ 347	$ 156	$ 132
Advances from parent	—	—	—	1,005	—	—	—	—
Payables								
Brokers and dealers	5,894	5,070	5,476	2,075	2,224	2,102	1,277	942
Customers	2,144	2,358	1,630	1,098	831	887	679	693
Banks	606	180	98	487	591	532	350	275
Accrued liabilities and other payables	1,522	1,853	1,962	1,018	694	523	245	192
Deposit liabilities	7,456	7,151	3,143	1,679	1,367	466	373	—
Securities sold under agreement to repurchase	18,010	18,573	9,960	7,797	517	436	499	9
Securities and commodities sold but not yet purchased	6,417	4,835	4,529	2,998	353	197	124	166
Total	51,090	49,284	32,431	20,594	7,969	5,490	3,703	2,411
Collateralized mortgage obligations	1,341	677	—	—	—	—	—	—
Term notes	1,523	1,362	460	19	19	25	30	25
Subordinated indebtedness	1,305	1,297	859	867	346	284	165	166
Other liabilities	—	—	—	—	—	—	—	30
Total liabilities	55,259	52,620	33,750	21,480	8,334	5,799	3,898	2,632
Stockholders' equity								
Common stock	8	8	8	—	—	—	—	2
Additional paid-in capital	441	440	452	428	176	189	133	132
Retained earnings	914	910	717	601	534	364	240	144
Treasury stock	—	—	—	—	—	—	—	(4)
Total stockholders' equity	1,363	1,358	1,177	1,029	710	552	373	274
Total liabilities and stockholders' equity	$56,622	$53,978	$34,927	$22,509	$9,044	$6,351	$4,270	$2,906

Note: March 31,1987 balance sheet figures are estimates as of March 20, 1987. Shearson's acquisition of Lehman Brothers became effective on May 11, 1984. Balance sheets for prior periods do not reflect Lehman's financial position.

Source: Shearson prospectus (May 1987) and 10-K reports.

Exhibit 8

Balance Sheets for American Express
($ millions)

	Year Ended December 31,			
	1986	1985	1984	1983
ASSETS				
Cash	$ 2,650	$ 1,669	$ 2,020	$ 1,878
Time deposits	4,989	6,299	5,470	4,071
Investment securities:				
At cost	18,484	12,615	13,449	12,063
At lower of cost or market	1,396	627	315	211
At market	16,561	11,158	8,566	1,490
Total	36,441	24,400	22,330	13,764
Securities purchased under				
agreements to resell	12,626	7,745	4,915	534
Accounts receivable	22,685	18,140	14,802	11,497
Loans and discounts	11,634	9,152	7,089	7,564
Land, buildings & equipment (net)	2,172	1,682	858	860
Assets in segregated asset accounts	1,304	920	741	687
Other	4,975	4,770	3,623	3,126
Total assets	$99,476	$74,777	$61,848	$43,981
LIABILITIES				
Customers' deposits & credit balances	$22,446	$16,203	$13,262	$12,511
Travelers Cheques outstanding	2,990	2,679	2,454	2,362
Accounts payable	8,414	8,378	4,829	4,704
Securities sold under agreements				
to repurchase	18,573	9,960	7,797	530
Securities and commodities sold				
but not yet purchased	4,835	4,529	2,998	353
Insurance and annuity reserves:				
Fixed annuities	7,449	4,134	3,234	2,555
Life and disability policies	1,554	1,271	847	639
Unearned premiums	—	—	1,131	1,195
Property-liability losses	—	—	3,619	3,278
Investment certificate reserves	1,507	1,497	1,325	1,279
Short-term debt	14,620	10,401	7,941	4,585
Long-term debt	8,400	5,399	3,839	2,643
Liabilities related to segregated				
asset accounts	1,280	900	726	672
Other liabilities	4,282	4,057	3,239	2,984
Total liabilities	93,750	69,408	57,241	39,937
Shareholders' equity				
Money market preferred stock	300	300	225	—
Common stock	129	133	130	128
Capital surplus	1,603	1,483	1,224	1,130
Net unrealized securities gains (losses)	11	(9)	(23)	50
Foreign currency translation adjustment	46	(12)	(33)	(23)
Retained earnings	3,637	3,474	3,084	2,758
Total shareholders' equity	5,726	5,369	4,607	4,043
Total liabilities and shareholders' equity	$99,476	$74,777	$61,848	$43,981

Source: Annual reports, American Express.

Exhibit 9

Income Statements for American Express
($ millions, except per share amounts)

	Year Ended December 31,		
	1986	1985	1984
REVENUES			
Commissions and fees	$ 7,543	$ 6,108	$ 4,814
Interest and dividends, net	3,764	3,292	3,291
Life insurance premiums	1,149	1,059	798
Annuity premiums	967	860	739
Property-liability premiums	—	—	2,834
Other	1,229	530	419
Total revenues	14,652	11,849	12,895
EXPENSES			
Compensation and benefits	3,438	2,573	2,260
Interest	2,619	2,269	2,104
Provisions for losses & benefits:			
Annuities	1,371	1,238	1,018
Life insurance	941	860	609
Investment certificates	109	107	104
Banking, credit, financial			
paper & other	951	693	479
Occupancy and equipment	789	636	656
Commissions and brokerage	—	—	509
Advertising and promotion	696	528	490
Communications	472	415	383
Taxes other than income taxes	242	197	171
Miscellaneous printed matter	199	154	150
Other	1,212	930	815
Total expenses	13,039	10,600	12,159
Pretax income from continuing operations	1,613	1,249	736
Income tax provision	503	437	126
Income from continuing operations	1,110	812	610
Discontinued operations (net of taxes)			
Loss from operations	—	(2)	—
Gain on disposal	140	—	—
Net income	$ 1,250	$ 810	$ 610
Dividends on common stock	304	291	276
Net income per common share ($)	5.55	3.55	2.79
Dividends per common share ($)	1.38	1.32	1.28

Source: Annual reports, American Express.

Exhibit 10

American Express Common Stock History

Date	Price at month-end	Shares Outstanding (millions)	Earnings per share* ($)	NYSE Financials	S&P
Dec. 1977	18	143	1.73	100	100
Dec. 1978	15	143	2.08	103	98
Dec. 1979	15	143	2.36	111	105
Dec. 1980	20	143	2.56	116	121
Dec. 1981	22	186	2.81	133	131
Dec. 1982	32	186	2.92	130	122
Mar. 1983	41	186	3.02		
Jun. 1983	48	198	3.20		
Sep. 1983	37	200	3.42		
Dec. 1983	33	201	3.45	173	163
Mar. 1984	32	213	2.53		
Jun. 1984	29	214	2.27		
Sep. 1984	35	215	1.95		
Dec. 1984	38	216	1.92	162	164
Mar. 1985	41	216	2.79		
Jun. 1985	48	218	2.92		
Sep. 1985	42	222	2.89		
Dec. 1985	53	222	3.12	207	191
Mar. 1986	69	222	3.55		
Jun. 1986	63	222	4.28		
Sep. 1986	56	219	5.26		
Dec. 1986	57	215	5.49	266	242
Jan. 1987	68	215	5.55		
Feb. 1987	74	215	5.55		
Mar. 1987**	77	216	5.55		

*The table shows earnings per share for the most recently reported 12-month period (as opposed to earnings per share for the most recent 12 months).

**Closing price on March 20, 1987.

Note: American Express repurchased about 17.5 million shares (at an average price of $57.66) during 1985 and 1986. The net reduction in shares outstanding was smaller, however, since it also issued substantial amounts of stock in exchange for warrants and for a number of other purposes.

Sources: Standard & Poor's Corporation, *Daily Stock Price Record*, various editions. Information on shares outstanding in late 1986 and early 1987 is from American Express annual reports. NYSE Financials and S&P index from *Economic Report of the President*, 1989.

Exhibit 11

Underwriting Market Share of Shearson Lehman Brothers*

Domestic Offerings

Year	Rank* (as book manager)	Market share (%)	Rank (full credit to all managers)
1986	7	6.1	6
1985	7	6.9	6
1984	6	8.1	5
1983	6	8.1	5
1982	6	7.9	6
1981	6	6.8	6

Common Stock Offerings

Year	Rank** (as book manager)	Market share (%)	Rank (full credit to all managers)
1986	4	7.4	1
1985	6	7.1	5
1984	4	7.7	3
1983	5	7.2	4
1982	4	6.3	7
1981	4	8.0	4

Euro and Foreign Debt

Year	Rank*** (as book manager)	Market share (%)	Rank (full credit to all managers)
1986	15	2.0	Not in top 15

*Rankings from 1983 and earlier incorporate both Shearson/American Express and Lehman Brothers Kuhn Loeb.

**Rank is based on full credit to lead manager.

***Not in top 15 before 1986.

Source: First Boston Equity Research Report, August 6, 1987.

Exhibit 12

Market Information for Brokerage Stocks

Firm	Price	Yield (%)	P/E ratio	Book value	Beta
First Boston	$51.875	1.9	10.09	$30.39	1.45
E. F. Hutton	41.000	2.1	—	22.48	1.70
Merrill Lynch	45.750	1.7	10.30	26.56	1.75
Morgan Stanley	75.375	0.5	8.95	31.58	NA
Paine Webber	37.875	1.4	12.50	20.49	1.70
Salomon Brothers	40.750	1.6	11.81	22.72	1.80
American Express	77.250	1.9	14.07	12.60	1.50

Source: Barron's and Value Line.

Exhibit 13

Return on Average Common Equity for Brokerage Firms (%)

Firm	1986	1985	1984	1983	1982
First Boston	21.7	22.3	18.8	24.4	39.6
E. F. Hutton	—	1.6	8.6	22.1	22.7
Merrill Lynch	17.5	10.2	5.0	13.2	24.7
Morgan Stanley	36.8	38.0	27.5	27.1	33.8
Paine Webber	14.2	8.5	3.9	35.8	25.2
Salomon Inc.	16.1	20.8	9.1	23.4	20.7
Shearson Lehman	24.9	18.9	12.7	27.6	26.8

Exhibit 14

Return on Average Assets for Brokerage Firms (%)

Firm	1986	1985	1984	1983	1982
First Boston	0.3	0.4	0.4	0.4	0.7
E. F. Hutton	—	0.2	0.3	1.1	1.5
Merrill Lynch	0.9	0.6	0.3	1.0	1.6
Morgan Stanley	0.8	0.7	0.6	0.8	1.3
Paine Webber	0.5	0.3	0.1	1.5	0.9
Salomon Inc.	0.6	0.8	0.4	1.1	1.0
Shearson Lehman	0.7	0.7	0.7	2.3	2.3

Exhibit 15

Return on Revenue for Brokerage Firms (%)

Firm	1986	1985	1984	1983	1982
First Boston	5.5	5.3	4.0	5.4	6.7
E. F. Hutton	—	0.4	1.9	5.1	4.8
Merrill Lynch	4.7	3.1	1.6	1.0	5.9
Morgan Stanley	8.2	5.9	4.6	6.0	7.0
Paine Webber	3.0	1.8	0.8	5.9	3.0
Salomon Inc.	7.6	9.8	5.2	15.2	11.7
Shearson Lehman	6.9	6.2	4.6	9.6	9.4

Source: Exhibits 13–15 are taken from Standard & Poor's Insurance and Investment Industry Survey (December 31, 1987). The Salomon figures, however, have been adjusted to reflect the firm's 1986 change in accounting for commodity transactions. In addition, some other figures have been corrected using information in annual reports.

PART 4

Segments of the Financial Product Markets

J.P. Morgan's Mexican Bank Debt–Bond Swap

Rodney B. Wagner, vice-chairman of the credit-policy committee at J.P. Morgan, looked at various "bid-forms" that had arrived at the bank by Friday, February 26, 1988. The forms contained the bids of commercial banks from around the world to exchange holdings of Mexican loans for a new bond. Wagner and several colleagues at Morgan had been responsible for the development of a "debt-bond exchange" for Mexican loans, in which as much as $10 billion of new bonds were offered in exchange for existing bank debt. Morgan's plan had attained wide spread attention. Many acknowledged it as a major new way of dealing with the "debt crisis." But while Morgan scored high for its innovativeness and the bank's ability to design "investment-banking" type products, the actual amount of the bids was lower than anticipated. Slightly over $6.7 billion in face value of loans were tendered.

Even though the bid volume had been disappointing, Wagner was not unhappy with the attention Morgan and Mexico had gotten for structuring the transaction. J.P. Morgan (with principal subsidiary Morgan Guaranty Trust) had worked closely with Mexico in designing an innovative way to deal with the LDC-debt problem. Still, Wagner was concerned that a small transaction would not be conclusive in showing the value of the new approach. He had few doubts that the basics of the exchange made a lot of sense, but what worried him was that another bank might take basically the same idea, adjust it, and be more successful.

Wagner knew that the Mexican government (advised by Morgan) could not extend the deadline on the bids beyond February 26. Also he knew that several investment banks, competitors of J.P. Morgan, had valued the exchange significantly differently from what had been calculated by the bank's bond team. As he looked at the various bids, he wondered about Morgan's assessment. He decided to once again look at the proposal and value it. Wagner realized that the exchange offer had to be attractive to two parties: the Mexican government (Morgan's client), and current holders of eligible bank debt that could be exchanged for the new bonds.

This case was prepared by Assistant Professor David M. Meerschwam.
Copyright © 1988 by the President and Fellows of Harvard College. Harvard Business School case 9-289-013.

Mexican Debt

By the middle of 1987 Mexican international bank debt stood at $78 billion. Of the total, U.S. banks collectively owned $24 billion (face value) of Mexican loans. British banks reported holdings of $8 billion, German banks $4 billion. Japanese banks did not report their international debt exposure by individual country but it was generally estimated that they held approximately $15 billion. Mexico's total debt accounted for approximately 33% of total Latin American and Caribbean bank debt (total $260 billion). Newspaper attention had focussed on the Mexican debt problem since the summer of 1982 when "suddenly" the third-world debt problem was elevated to crisis proportions.

The debt crisis resulted in various attempts to deal with both Mexico's problems in servicing the debt as well as with the impact a possible write-down of the loans would have on the capital adequacy of the major lending banks. The stability of these banks could in turn have important repercussions on the stability of the financial systems of the countries in which they operated. In dealing with the Mexican debt problem, the principal strategy followed by the major banks was to gradually build up their capital position to minimize exposure. In May 1987 Citicorp's chairman John Reed announced an increase in Citicorp's loan-loss reserve of $3 billion (given a portfolio of third-world debt of $12 billion). This 25% ratio developed into an industry standard and implied that several banks acknowledged, for the first time, that the loans might be worth less than their face value.

A strategy to reduce exposure was debt-equity swaps. In principle such a transaction allowed the banks to sell their loans (at some discount so that a write-off did take place) to a foreign direct investor into Mexico. The investor would sell the loans to the Mexican government, receive Mexican pesos and invest them in Mexico. Depending on the prices charged at the various intermediate steps of the transaction such debt-equity transactions could be favorable for all parties. While banks typically kept the Mexican loans on their books at face value, a small but active secondary market valued most Mexican loans at approximately 50% of face value. On average these loans had a weighted average life of 14 years and paid LIBOR + 13/16. Most banks in the U.S. had not accumulated enough reserves to reflect the secondary market value.

For banks that had made loans to Mexico, the difference between the face (book) value of their loans and the fair market value was not the only cost associated with their exposure to Mexico. As a result of their holdings of loans and of Mexico's difficulty to earn the required foreign exchange for balance of payment transactions including interest payments, banks had been requested on three occasions to provide "new money." Typically they were, after some negotiations, honored. Furthermore, there was always the risk that regulatory reform would force a capital adjustment to adjust the value of the Mexican loan portfolio closer to the secondary market value. Under such a scenario banks would either have to find new capital or reduce the size of their existing loan portfolios.

In spite of the bank's strategies, the basic problems of Mexico remained significant in terms of fulfilling its debt obligations. This was well understood and frequent rescheduling of the debt took place prior to 1987. In these reschedulings typically the maturity of the debt was extended while the interest rates were revised downward. The rescheduling process was often painfully slow because agreement of all bank participants had to be obtained. Especially after 1987, it became more difficult to obtain new money commitments from some mostly smaller participants.

The Exchange Offer

The exchange offer, devised by Morgan working with Mexico, asked holders of eligible bank debt to submit bids at which they would be willing to exchange specified amounts of principal of bank debt for specified amounts of principal of a new 20-year bond. The new bonds were the obligation of the Mexican government. Mexico would collateralize the principal of the floating rate bonds. The bonds would carry a coupon of LIBOR + 1 5/8%.

The U.S. Treasury would sell special 20-year zero-coupon bonds to Mexico to collateralize the principal of the bonds. The zero-coupon bonds were to be held in a special account at the Federal Reserve Bank of New York. The collateral would secure the principal only at the stated maturity; non-payment of interest by Mexico before the stated maturity of the bond would not be a reason for the holders of the new bonds to claim the collateral before the stated maturity of 20 years.

The bonds were to be issued in registered form, in denominations of $250,000 and integral multiples of $1000 in excess of $250,000. The bonds were structured in such a way that it would be difficult to separate them into component parts. Interest and coupon would be paid in U.S. dollars.

The government of Mexico agreed that new bonds would not be subject to restructuring and that neither the new bonds nor the cancelled debt offered and accepted in exchange for the new bonds would be considered part of the base amount in any possible future request for new money by the Mexican government.

Mexico agreed that it would use its best efforts to obtain a listing for the bonds on the Luxembourg Stock exchange and that until the fifth anniversary of the bonds it would provide the fiscal agent for the bonds with annual information about Mexico's GNP, GDP, government expenditures and receipts, central and other bank reserves, balance of trade, balance of payments and foreign exchange controls.

The bonds would represent the direct, general and unconditional obligation of the Mexican government. They would rank at least *pari passu* in seniority with all other external indebtedness of the Mexican government.

Bid Procedure

Bids for the bond would be made through a bid ratio. The bid ratio would be equal to the principal amount of eligible debt a holder would be willing to exchange for $1.00 principal amount of the new bond. For bid ratios relating to non-U.S. dollar denominated eligible debt, foreign exchange rates would be set at market levels. With the bid ratio, the amount of tendered principal would have to be supplied.

Bids could be submitted until February 19, 4:00 p.m., unless the Mexican government decided to extend the bid period to February 26. All bids could be rejected by the Mexican government at its sole discretion. The Mexican government would review all bids after the bid deadline. Bids would be accepted starting from the highest bid ratio to the lowest bid ratio acceptable to the Mexican government. The Mexican government would be under no obligation to accept any or all of the bids.

Accounting Consequences

Tax consequences associated with the exchange were evaluated by Price Waterhouse. The opinion is summarized in Appendix 1.

Bank Regulatory Consequences

The Comptroller of the Currency and Administrator of National Banks opined on the consequences of the exchange for regulatory matters as relevant for a nationally chartered bank. The opinion is summarized in Appendix 2.

Considerations in Evaluating the Bonds

In designing the exchange and determining the possible attractiveness of the exchange for various parties, J.P. Morgan had stressed various issues, among them:

1. Mexico had met its foreign currency obligations (interest and principal) on all publicly issued external bonds since 1917.

2. While the bonds would be issued in registered form the bonds could be held through nominees so that ultimate ownership would not be known by the government of Mexico.

3. A successful exchange could create interest savings for Mexico which would in and of itself increase the likelihood of prompt interest payments.

4. A successful development of a secondary market for the bonds would significantly enhance the liquidity of the bonds compared to the secondary market trading in loan obligations.

5. The principal of the bond was effectively defeased through the U.S. government zero-coupon bonds.

Valuing the Exchange

As Wagner and other bankers at Morgan entered the building on Wall Street on Saturday morning to reevaluate the bond, they tried to determine not only what a reasonable bid ratio would be, but also what the cut-off ratio should be for Mexico. In particular they understood that the Mexican government was interested in finding what the impact of the exchange would be on their annual interest payments. Also, it was clear that domestic political consideration in Mexico would play a role in setting the acceptable exchange ratio.

Recent market conditions were such that 20-year U.S Treasury strips yielded 8.790%. Ordinary Treasury rates were at 8.29% for 10 years and 8.48% for 30 years. Interpolated yields were 8.32% for 14-year Treasuries and 8.39% for 20-year Treasuries. Swap quotes (floating to fixed) for Mexican loans were at 85 bp over Treasury for both 14-year and 20-year maturity. (Thus, a 14-year LIBOR obligation could be swapped to a 14-year fixed rate obligation at 9.170%.) LIBOR stood at 7.5%.

In valuing the offer Wagner made two different assumptions about the way in which current Mexican bank debt was priced in the secondary market (at 50%). One method was to assume that those debts could really be treated as perpetuities, since they could well be rolled over. Another way was to conservatively assume that the principal in year 14 would be close to zero.

Appendix I

Price Waterhouse informed Morgan Guaranty Trust Company among other matters that:

Due to the uniqueness of the exchange the act of tendering does not constitute a clear demonstration of intent to dispose of the existing loans and thus, if the tendered loans are not accepted there is no requirement to write the loans down to the market value at which they were tendered.

Appendix II

The Office of the Comptroller of the Currency, the F.D.I.C., and the Federal Reserve System informed Davis, Polk & Wardwell, counsel to J.P. Morgan, among other matters that:

1. Banks under its supervision could hold the new bonds under either (1) their lending authority (as an extension of the preexisting lending relationship) or (2) their investment authority, but not both.

Additional purchases of bonds would only be allowed under the banks' investment authority. Total holdings of investment securities were not to exceed 5% of bank capital. This limitation would not apply to a bank's holdings as a result of the exchange itself, but would apply to any additional purchases of bonds.

2. Banks would have to charge against loan losses the difference between the carrying value of the loans exchanged and the fair market value of the bonds.

Any loans tendered but not actually exchanged would: (1) have to be written down to a value not to exceed the value at which they were tendered in the exchange or (2) cause an obligation to increase, if necessary, the loan loss reserve to an amount that would ensure adequacy of the reserve given the difference between the tendered price and the carrying value.

Exhibit 1

External Debt of Ten Largest LDC Debtor Nations
(U.S. $ millions)

	1970	1975	1980	1981	1982	1983	1984	1985	1986	1987
Argentina										
Total External Debt	$ NA	$ NA	$27,157	$35,657	$43,634	$45,087	$46,828	$48,444	$48,908 $	NA
Long-Term Debt	5,182	6,581	16,774	22,736	27,113	35,838	37,086	40,179	43,012	NA
Debt to Banks	NA	3,185	18,942	22,939	22,168	23,357	26,131	28,966	32,404	33,264
Brazil										
Total External Debt	NA	NA	70,237	79,978	91,304	97,855	103,520	106,730	110,675	NA
Long-Term Debt	5,138	23,725	56,711	64,657	73,303	81,007	87,835	91,094	97,164	NA
Debt to Banks	NA	14,848	43,320	49,605	56,082	57,465	77,866	76,925	81,021	81,526
Chile										
Total External Debt	NA	NA	12,116	15,704	17,348	18,202	19,959	20,221	20,741	NA
Long-Term Debt	2,576	4,374	9,433	12,666	14,004	14,996	17,266	17,465	17,930	NA
Debt to Banks	NA	786	6,662	9,561	10,433	10,950	13,685	14,344	14,034	13,743
Colombia										
Total External Debt	NA	NA	6,936	8,713	10,302	11,423	12,285	14,044	14,619	NA
Long-Term Debt	1,582	2,744	4,599	5,939	7,178	8,163	9,417	10,945	13,022	NA
Debt to Banks	NA	1,579	4,261	4,868	5,541	5,926	6,993	6,565	6,637	6,464
Mexico										
Total External Debt	NA	NA	57,450	78,270	86,111	92,965	96,436	97,135	101,722	NA
Long-Term Debt	5,966	15,609	41,287	53,287	59,743	81,565	87,636	88,715	91,062	NA
Debt to Banks	NA	13,499	41,031	55,524	58,978	62,925	72,508	74,643	74,219	76,029
Ecuador										
Total External Debt	NA	NA	5,997	7,666	7,705	8,318	8,332	9,233	8,954	NA
Long-Term Debt	243	709	4,422	5,645	5,514	6,939	6,811	7,191	7,977	NA
Debt to Banks	NA	484	3,599	4,157	4,099	4,195	4,981	5,254	5,395	5,515
Peru										
Total External Debt	NA	NA	9,989	10,283	12,271	12,381	13,082	13,688	15,303	NA
Long-Term Debt	2,658	5,077	7,431	7,417	8,605	10,243	11,077	11,869	12,386	NA
Debt to Banks	NA	2,302	3,892	4,295	5,216	4,471	5,729	5,624	5,296	5,374
Venezuela										
Total External Debt	NA	NA	29,589	31,927	31,827	32,261	32,949	32,079	33,891	NA
Long-Term Debt	965	1,494	14,054	14,952	17,124	17,751	22,449	21,800	32,499	NA
Debt to Banks	NA	2,964	21,314	22,288	22,657	22,011	25,451	25,862	25,040	24,862
Nigeria										
Total External Debt	NA	NA	8,888	12,039	12,445	17,985	18,224	18,348	21,876	NA
Long-Term Debt	573	1,144	5,335	7,615	9,926	12,936	12,536	13,432	21,546	NA
Debt to Banks	NA	270	3,358	4,707	6,980	8,088	8,601	9,338	10,280	10,514
Philippines										
Total External Debt	NA	NA	17,458	20,817	24,316	24,049	24,571	26,184	28,173	NA
Long-Term Debt	1,495	2,805	9,049	10,438	12,158	13,704	14,323	16,559	21,622	NA
Debt to Banks	NA	2,036	6,977	7,245	8,329	8,055	13,852	13,414	14,176	13,842

1. Total External Debt does not include undisbursed debt.

2. Long-Term Debt includes private non-guaranteed debt, and both public and publicly-guaranteed debt.

3. During 1984 the BIS broadened its reporting coverage. As a result, the increase in Debt to Banks between 1983 and 1984 is in some cases disproportionately large.

Source: World Debt Tables, World Bank. International Banking Statistics, Bank for International Settlements (BIS). "Statistics on External Indebtedness: Bank and Trade-Related Non-Bank External Claims on Individual Borrowing Countries and Territories"; BIS/OECD; various issues.

Exhibit 2

Ten Largest U.S. Bank Exposures to Mexico in 1987
($ millions)

	Mexico —Exposure—	LDC	Loan Loss Reserve	Primary Capital	Assets	Net Income
Citicorp	$ 2,600	$ 13,300	$ 4,618	$ 16,771	$203,607	$(1,138)
BankAmerica Corp.	2,505	9,918	3,263	8,040	93,000	(955)
Manufacturers Hanover Corp.	1,927	8,900	2,652	6,138	73,348	(1,140)
Chemical New York Corp.	1,755	5,904	2,068	6,081	78,200	(854)
Chase Manhattan Corp.	1,670	8,600	2,720	7,648	81,400	(895)
Bankers Trust New York Corp.	1,302	4,006	1,298	5,000	56,500	1
J. P. Morgan & Co.	1,156	5,400	1,708	7,172	75,400	83
First Chicago Corp.	874	2,946	1,547	3,848	44,200	(571)
First Interstate Bancorp.	617	1,359	1,220	3,726	50,900	(565)
Wells Fargo & Co.	604	1,900	1,357	4,046	44,183	51
Total Top Ten	15,010	62,233	22,451	68,470	800,738	(5,983)
Total All U.S. Banks	$23,268	$102,701	$ NA	$127,700	$1,621,000	$ NA

Note: 1. All figures are $ millions at December 31, 1987.

2. Primary Capital equals Shareholders' Equity, Loan Loss Reserves, and certain Subordinated Debentures.

Source: Annual Reports 1987. *The Banker (U.K.)*, March 1988. "Country Exposure Lending Survey," Federal Financial Institutions Examination Council (Bd. of Governors of the Federal Reserve System).

Exhibit 3

Ratio of Exposure to Primary Capital
(U.S. Banks)

	6/83	6/84	6/85	6/86	9/87
All U.S. Banks					
L.D.C.	175%	156%	127%	102%	80%
Latin America	112%	102%	86%	72%	60%
Mexico	33%	30%	26%	22%	18%
Nine Money Center Banks					
L.D.C.	274%	246%	203%	167%	134%
Latin America	169%	158%	134%	117%	99%
Mexico	44%	42%	36%	31%	27%
All Others					
L.D.C.	108%	96%	77%	59%	45%
Latin America	73%	65%	54%	42%	34%
Mexico	24%	23%	19%	15%	13%
Primary Capital ($ millions)					
All U.S. Banks	$74,700	$84,760	$98,800	$110,700	$127,700
Nine M. C. Banks	30,200	34,100	39,300	44,200	50,900
All Others	44,500	50,660	59,500	66,500	76,800

Note: 1. Exposure equals cross-border and foreign office non-local currency claims adjusted for guarantees and external borrowing.

2. Primary Capital equals Shareholders' Equity, Loan Loss Reserves, and certain subordinated debentures.

Source: "Country Exposure Lending Survey," F.F.I.E.C. LDC exposure includes OPEC and non-oil Africa, Asia, and Latin America. Latin America exposure includes Venezuela and Ecuador, which CELS places in OPEC.

Exhibit 4

Secondary Market Price of Mexican Paper
(Cents on the Dollar)

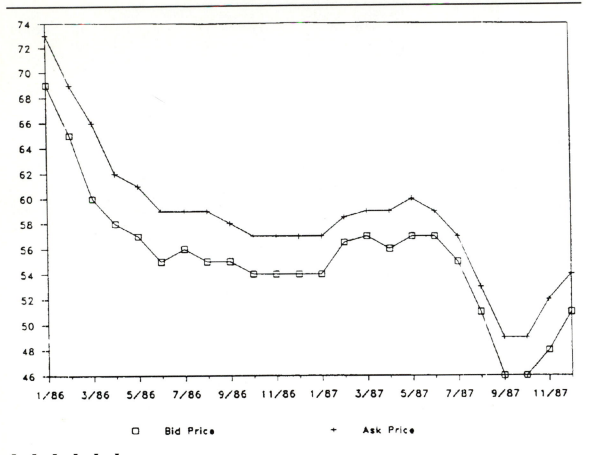

□ Bid Price   + Ask Price

Note: In July 1985, bid and ask prices were 80 and 82 cents on the dollar respectively.

Source: *Euromoney*, Special Supplement, January 1988.

Exhibit 5

Mexico Selected Economic Data
(U.S. $ millions)

	1970	1975	1980	1981	1982	1983	1984	1985	1986	1987
Gross National Product	$35,147	$86,710	$180,319	$230,120	$155,050	$133,127	$161,306	$169,047	$121,372	NA
Exports of G&S	2,935	6,365	24,637	30,415	27,723	28,635	32,460	29,744	23,762	NA
Current Acct. Balance	(1,123)	(4,195)	(8,436)	(14,312)	(6,347)	5,111	3,769	235	(1,760)	NA
International Reserves	756	1,869	4,176	4,971	1,778	4,794	8,019	5,679	6,674	12,464
Exchange Rate	13	13	23	26	96	144	193	372	924	2,210

Note: Pesos/US$ at end of period.

Source: World Debt Tables, World Bank. International Financial Statistics, IMF.

Exhibit 6

Mexico: Statistics Related to Production and Export of Oil

Year	Proven Reserves (Mill. Bbl.)	Oil Production (Th. Bbl./day)[1]	Exports of Crude Oil		
			Price ($ U.S./Bbl.)[2]	Value ($ U.S. Mill.)[3]	Volume (Mill. Bbl.)[4]
1970	3,200	NA	$ NA	$ NA	$ NA
1975	9,600	806	11.10	432	39
1980	44,000	2155	29.88	9,342	313
1981	57,000	2585	32.88	13,278	404
1982	48,300	3005	32.88	16,179	492
1983	48,000	2950	27.88	14,826	532
1984	48,600	3015	27.88	14,942	536
1985	49,300	3015	27.60	13,385	485
1986	54,700	2745	12.25	5,600	457
1987	48,600	2879	18.14	7,801	430

[1]Includes crude and shale oil, oil sands, and natural gas liquids.

[2]Official price of "Isthmus" on July 1 (1975–1985), and end-December (1986–1987).

[3]Computed from Peso value at average exchange rate.

[4]"Implicit" volume computed from dollar exports and price/barrel.

Sources: G. Jenkins, *Oil Economists' Handbook. Oil and Gas Journal*, year's final issue, 1985–1987.
BP Statistical Review of World Energy. *Petroleum Economist* (U. K.), various issues.

Schroders' Perpetual Floating Rate Note Exchange Offer

On July 22, 1987, Yoshiharu Yamamoto, Director and General Manager of the Maruzen Bank and Trust Company, looked at the telex his assistant had just handed him.[1] In it, the British merchant bank, J. Henry Schroder Wagg & Co. Limited ("Schroders"), offered an exchange. Selected perpetual floating rate notes plus specified amounts of cash could be exchanged for floating rate notes due in 2015, plus non-voting shares in a new company to be formed for the purpose of issuing the new floating rate notes and the non-voting shares.

For Yamamoto, the offer provided an opportunity to exchange the bank's holdings of perpetual floating rate notes ("perps"). Maruzen Bank held $1,000,000 face value of Bank of Ireland[2] perps. The perps had coupons of 3 month Libor + 25 basis points and were trading at 78% of face value in July 1987. Maruzen also held $1,000,000 face value of 6 month Limean + 25 bp Barclays perps, trading at 91.25%. Maruzen had invested in the perps when they were traded close to face value. For the exchange, Maruzen would have to add $217,600 in cash to the Bank of Ireland perps and $144,700 to the Barclays perps, according to the price-circular (see Exhibit 2).

Yamamoto had been concerned about his bank's perps holdings for some time. The discount on the perps seemed heavy and had not improved since the market turmoil that had started toward the end of 1986. Furthermore, Yamamoto was worried about his bank's capital position. There were persistent rumors in the financial district of Tokyo that the Japanese Ministry of Finance, like the Bank of England in the U.K. and the Federal Reserve in the U.S., would shortly require Japanese banks to write down primary bank capital on a one-for-one basis with their perp holdings.

When AAA, floating rate CMO's appeared in October 1986 at rates significantly above the rates on perps (Libor + 40 bp vs Libor + 25 bp), Maruzen had contemplated investing in them. However, the bank had not reshuffled its portfolio then. Now it wasn't certain that Yamamoto could still reorganize his investments, because liquidity for perps had dried up in some cases. Perhaps Schroders' offer

---

This case was prepared by Assistant Professor David M. Meerschwam.

presented a good opportunity. Yamamoto wondered how to evaluate the offer. He felt that the perps had given him more than enough problems so far; he didn't want to be wrong once again!

The Floating Rate Note Market

By the mid-1970s, the Floating Rate Note (FRN) market had grown to become a major part of the Euro securities markets. In response to increased interest rate volatility and with reference to the floating rate syndicated loan market, a new market developed for dated securities whose interest rate was linked to a widely available reference rate (such as Libor, Limean, U.S. Treasuries, etc.). While the first FRNs were issued as early as 1970, the instrument attained real importance later on. By 1985, almost half of all new issues in the international capital market were floating rate and $55.4 billion of FRNs were offered. *Perps were floating rate notes of infinite maturity.* They made up 29% of the total FRN market in 1985. In 1986, the overall floating rate market retracted (issue volume $48 billion), but the share of the perps continued to grow to 46%.

Most of the perps issued were callable and linked to Libor. Libor is the London Interbank Offer Rate, charged to the most credit worthy banks for borrowings. Two different Libor rates are often quoted; the 3-month and the 6-month Libor. Other rates that were used to base the perps on were Libid and Limean. Libid is the London Interbank Bid Rate with which banks in the Euromarket attract Euro-dollar deposits from their best customers. Limean is the mean of Libor and Libid. The coupon on floating rate note instruments could be reset at a different frequency, but typically the base rate period was used (i.e., once every six months for 6-month Libor).

Perps were issued by financial institutions such as U.S. thrifts and British building societies, and commercial banks. For many in the last category the perps could function as primary capital. The Bank of England (BoE) had been the first monetary authority to include perps in the calculation of bank primary capital. The BoE had taken its decision in November 1984 *after* the first perpetual issue in April 1984, by National Westminster Finance B.V. In the U.S., the Fed ruled on November 3, 1986 that perps could be included in the capital base of banks, since they were securities of infinite maturity. Citicorp entered the market on November 6 for $500 million, at 3-month Libid + 37.5 basis points.

Interest paid on the perps was deductible from profit before taxes in the U.K. and most other countries. In the U.S., the IRS would not allow tax deductibility for an instrument of infinite maturity. To overcome the objection the Citicorp perp carried a 30-year put provision. This satisfied the IRS. Permission to consider the perp primary bank capital in both the U.S. and the U.K. was important for the regulators since there was a professed attempt to harmonize bank capital requirements across the three primary capital markets: Tokyo, New York and London. Banks in the U.K. and in the U.S. that invested in perps were required to write their capital down (on a one-for-one basis). Also, many perps had a provision that under certain circumstances the interest would not be paid. Activation of such a clause would also imply that the dividend on preferred and common stock was omitted.

British Commercial Bank Issues

The four large British clearing banks used the perp market actively. The first issuer in the perp market was National Westminster Bank, through a finance subsidiary. NatWest Finance issued 500 6MLibor 0.375 (=$500 million at 6-month Libor + 37.5 bp) in April 1984. By October 1984 Barclays followed with a 600 6MLibor 0.250 issue. Lloyds entered the market in May 1985 with a 750 6MLibor 0.250 issue. Midland had an identical issue in May 1985. (Maruzen had invested in the "Barclays 1.")

Bank	Issue Date	Issue	
NatWest Finance	Apr 1984	500 6MLibor	0.375
NatWest A	May 1985	500 6MLimean	0.250
NatWest B	May 1985	500 6MLimean	0.250
NatWest C	Nov 1985	500 3MLibid	0.250
Barclays OIC B.V.	Oct 1984	600 6MLibor	0.250
Barclays 1	Jun 1985	600 6MLimean	0.250
Barclays 2	Jan 1986	750 6MLibid	0.250
Midland 1	May 1985	750 6MLibor	0.250
Midland 2	Aug 1985	500 6MLibor	0.250
Midland 3	Nov 1986	300 6MLibor	0.100
Lloyds Bank 1	May 1985	750 6MLibor	0.250
Lloyds Bank 2	Oct 1985	500 6MLibor	0.188
Lloyds Bank 3	Jul 1986	600 6MLibor	0.100

The Perp Crisis

It is difficult to date precisely the decline in the market for the perps. Also there is little agreement about what precisely caused the appearance of deep discounts on many perpetual instruments. What is clear is that until December 1986, perps typically traded within half a point of their face value, then several perps started to trade around the mid-1990s. By January the perps traded in the mid-1980s. While no one knew exactly what had caused the price decline it was believed that the behavior of Japanese investors must have been important.

Market participants estimated that, apart from significant dealer inventories which were rumored to exist, Japanese investors and especially banks had accounted for 80% of all purchases. Also it was rumored that a November 27, 1986, issue for Standard Charter, a highly rated U.K. bank at 6MLibor 0.150bp had put a lot of pressure on the market and the manager of the issue, CSFB, had not fully supported the issue. Still, the Standard issue seemed not that unusual; many issues had been priced at 6MLibor 0.100.

While there was uncertainty about the causes of the collapse of the perp market (with many issues losing up to 25% of their face value) there was also uncertainty about the appropriateness of the prices that resulted after the fall. Many investment bankers noted that it was difficult to price floating rate note instruments and that perps were even harder to value. By the summer of 1987—when perp prices had not recovered, liquidity in the market was debatable at best, and regulators displayed concern about the perps—several solutions to the perp problem were offered. Schroders' exchange offer was advertised as such a solution.

The Exchange Offer

THE EXCHANGE The offer proposed to exchange specified perpetuals and specified amounts of cash, for 28-year dated floating rate notes (at LIBOR + 30bp) and shares. Units of $1,000,000 face value of perps with the appropriate amounts of cash (see Exhibit 2) would be exchanged for $930,000 face value of FRNs and 50 B-shares. A new company Security Investment Holdings Limited (Company) was formed for this purpose.

ELIGIBILITY   Only specified series of perpetuals were eligible for exchange. The Company would determine which perps it would be willing to accept and what cash amounts were required.

INSURANCE   The FRNs that would be issued would be fully insured by Financial Security Assurance, and were expected to be rated AAA. Part of the cash proceeds [see Exhibit 2] associated with the exchange would be used to purchase the insurance.

COMPANY INVESTMENTS   The Company would use the cash proceeds of the offering to purchase 28-year zero coupon bonds (U.S. Treasury and World Bank)—to decrease the principal of the 28-year FRNs.

BANK OF ENGLAND   The BoE made it clear that for banks under its supervision it would not consider holdings of the FRNs to be issued by the Company as holdings of other bank capital.

THE B-SHARES   During years 1–28, the owners of the B-shares would have the right to all income of the Company after paying the interest on the FRNs and service costs of the company. After redemption in year 28 of the FRNs, the shares would be entitled to 90% of the assets and income (after service costs) of the Company.

SERVICE COSTS   During the first 28 years, service costs charged by the Company would be $1000 per year per $930,000 of new FRNs. After maturity of the FRNs $100 per year per 50 B-shares would be charged.

AUTHORIZED SHARE CAPITAL   300,000 B-class shares would be authorized. 100 A-class shares would be issued at par ($1) to an indirect, wholly owned subsidiary of the parent company of Schroders.

The Decision

Mr. Yamamoto considered the exchange offer. Maruzen's investment bankers in New York and London stated that LIBOR would be at 8% in the future and was expected to remain stable. 30-year U.S. Treasuries yielded 8.6%. Also they informed him that the average coupon on all the perps listed as eligible for exchange was Libor + 18.7 bp and that the average trading price was 88%. Yamamoto was also told that FRNs like the new ones to be issued were trading at LIBOR + 50 bp.

► Endnotes

[1]Maruzen Bank and Trust is a disguised Japanese bank.

[2]The Bank of Ireland is a commercial bank.

Exhibit 1

INFORMATION MEMORANDUM

EXCHANGE OFFER
by
SECURITY INVESTMENT HOLDINGS LIMITED
(Incorporated with limited liability in the Cayman Islands)

OF UP TO

U.S. $1,000,000,000
Guaranteed Secured Floating Rate Notes Due 2015
Comprising up to 29 Series
and
UP TO

53,763
Class B Non-voting Shares

The Notes will be Unconditionally and Irrevocably Guaranteed as to
Payment of Principal and Interest Pursuant to
a Surety Bond Issued by Financial Security Assurance Inc.

FINANCIAL
SECURITY
ASSURANCE.

This Information Memorandum relates to an offer by Security Investment Holdings Limited (the "Company") to exchange selected Perpetual Notes and specified Dollar Amounts (each as defined herein) for Guaranteed Secured Floating Rate Notes Due 2015 (the "Notes") and Class B Non-voting Shares (the "B Shares") at a rate of $930,000 of Notes and 50 B Shares for every $1,000,000 of Perpetual Notes tendered upon the terms and subject to the conditions set forth herein. The amount of the Notes and the number of the B Shares to be issued are subject to increase as described under "Terms and Conditions of the Exchange Offer".

The Notes will be issued in up to 29 series (each a "Series"), secured as described herein and unconditionally and irrevocably guaranteed as to payment of principal and interest pursuant to a surety bond issued by Financial Security Assurance Inc. ("Financial Security"). The Notes will initially be in bearer form but will be subject to mandatory conversion into Notes in registered form in the circumstances described in "Conditions of the Notes" and in "Registration".

Interest on each Series of the Notes is payable in arrears on Interest Payment Dates (as defined herein) falling 4 business days after the interest payment dates for the corresponding exchanged issue or issues of Perpetual Notes, at a rate of 0.30 of 1 per cent. per annum above London interbank offered rates determined as provided herein.

The Notes will mature at par on 20th November, 2015. The Notes of any Series may be redeemed prior to maturity in whole or in part at par on any Interest Payment Date by the Company at the direction of Financial Security. In addition, Notes of any Series will, in certain circumstances, be redeemed mandatorily at par prior to maturity on any Interest Payment Date.

The B Shares will be in bearer form and will be issued subject to the Memorandum and Articles of Association of the Company — see "Description of the Shares".

Application will be made to list the Notes and the B Shares on the Luxembourg Stock Exchange. If granted, the listing for the B Shares will not become effective until 120 days after completion of the distribution of all of the B Shares, as determined by J. Henry Schroder Wagg & Co. Limited ("Schroders").

The Notes are expected, on issue, to be assigned an AAA rating by Standard & Poor's Corporation and Nippon Investors Service Inc. and an Aaa rating by Moody's Investors Service, Inc. A credit rating is not a recommendation to buy, sell or hold securities and may be subject to revision or withdrawal at any time by the assigning rating organisation.

The Notes of each Series will be represented initially by a temporary Global Note to be deposited with a common depositary for Morgan Guaranty Trust Company of New York, as operator of the Euro-clear System ("Euro-clear") and CEDEL S.A. ("Cedel") on or about 13th August, 1987. Each temporary Global Note will be exchangeable for definitive Notes, in bearer form, with detachable coupons and talons, not earlier than 90 days after the completion of the distribution of all of the Notes, as determined by Schroders, upon certification that the beneficial owners thereof are not U.S. persons (as defined herein). The B Shares will be represented initially by a single bearer certificate which will be deposited with the common depositary in like manner. Such share certificate will be exchangeable for definitive bearer share certificates (in units of 5 B Shares or an integral multiple thereof), with coupons for dividends and other rights attached, not earlier than 120 days after completion of the distribution of all of the B Shares, as determined by Schroders, upon certification as aforesaid.

J. Henry Schroder Wagg & Co. Limited

**Salomon Brothers International
Limited**

**Nomura International
Limited**

Dated 22nd July, 1987

Exhibit 2

Cash Amounts Required for Each U.S. $1,000,000 Face Value of Eligible
Perpetual FRNs Until July 24, 1987, at 16:00 hours

Eligible Perpetuals	Additional Cash Required from Perp. Holder for Exchange (U.S. $)
<u>Bank of Ireland</u>	<u>$217,600</u>
Bank of Scotland	174,800
BNP	164,700
Banque Paribas	164,400
Banque Paribas	167,900
Barclays Overseas Investment Co. BV	139,900
<u>Barclays Bank plc</u>	<u>144,700</u>
Barclays Bank plc	144,100
Bergen Bank	177,600
CIBC	174,900
Commissioners of the State Bank of Victoria	142,800
Christiania Bank og Kreditkasse	174,300
Citicorp	142,500
Den Danske Bank af 1871 A/S	174,900
Den Norske Creditbank	174,600
Genossenschaftliche Zentralbank AG	175,200
HongKong & Shanghai Banking Corp.	187,700
HongKong & Shanghai Banking Corp.	192,200
HongKong & Shanghai Banking Corp.	197,300
Hydro Quebec	142,400
Lloyds Bank plc	152,600
Lloyds Bank plc	154,400
Lloyds Bank plc	157,900
Midland Bank plc	172,500
Midland Bank plc	172,500
Midland Bank plc	177,100
National Westminster Finance BV	139,900
National Westminster Bank plc	143,900
National Westminster Bank plc	143,900
National Westminster Bank plc	143,900
Republic New York Corp.	157,400
Royal Bank of Canada	172,400
Royal Bank of Scotland Group plc	174,700
Royal TrustCo. Ltd.	217,300
Societe Generale	167,400
Standard Chartered plc	197,400
Standard Chartered plc	197,400

Source: *International Financing Review*, July 1987.

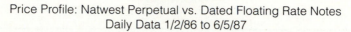

Exhibit 3

Price Profile: Natwest Perpetual vs. Dated Floating Rate Notes
Daily Data 1/2/86 to 6/5/87

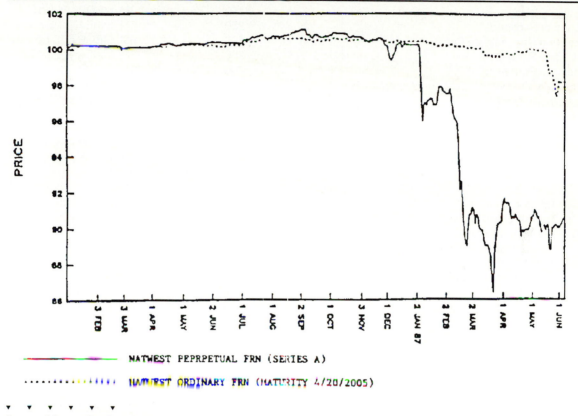

Source: Salomon Brothers Inc.

Exhibit 4

Selected Details of the Eligible Perpetual Note Issues

Issuer	Issue Amount ($ millions)	Coupon
Bank of Ireland	$150	3M LIBOR+25 bp
Bank of Scotland	250	6M LIMEAN+25 bp
Banque Nationale de Paris	500	6M LIBOR+7.5 bp
Banque Paribas	200	3M LIMEAN+37.5 bp
Banque Paribas	400	3M LIBOR+12.5 bp
Barclays Overseas Investment Company BV	600	6M LIBOR+25 bp
Barclays Bank Plc	600	6M LIMEAN+25 bp
Barclays Plc (Series 2)	750	6m LIBID+25 bp
Bergen Bank A/S	200	6M LIBOR+12.5 bp
CIBC	300	6M LIBOR+25 bp
Christinina Bank og Kreditkasse	200	6M LIBOR+18.75 bp
Citicorp	500	3M LIBID+37.5 bp
The Commissioners of the State Bank of Victoria	125	6M LIBOR+6.25 bp
Den Danske Bank of 1817 A/S	100	6M LIBOR+25 bp
Den Norske Creditbank	150	3M LIBOR+25 bp
Genossenschaftliche Zentralbank AG	100	6M LIBOR+25 bp
HongKong & Shanghai Banking Corp	400	6M LIBOR+25 bp
HongKong & Shanghai Banking Corp	400	3M LIMEAN+25 bp
HongKong & Shanghai Banking Corp	400	3M LIMEAN+18.75 bp
Hydro Quebec	400	6M LIBOR+6.25 bp
Lloyds Bank plc	750	6M LIBOR+25 bp
Lloyds Bank plc	500	3M LIBOR+18.75 bp
Lloyds Bank plc	600	6M LIBOR+10 bp
Midland Bank plc	750	6M LIBOR+25 bp
Midland Bank plc	500	6M LIBOR+25 bp
Midland Bank plc	300	6M LIBOR+10 bp
National Westminster Finance BV	500	6M LIBOR+12.5 bp
National Westminster Bank plc	500	6M LIMEAN+25 bp
National Westminster Bank plc	500	6M LIMEAN+25 bp
National Westminster Bank plc	500	3M LIBID+25 bp
Republic New York Corp	150	6M LIBOR+25 bp
Royal Bank of Canada	300	3M LIMEAN+25 bp
Royal Bank of Scotland Group plc	350	6M LIMEAN+25 bp
Royal TrustCo Ltd	150	6M LIBOR+15 bp
Societe Generale	300	6M LIBOR+7.5 bp
Standard Chartered plc	400	6M LIBOR+27.5 bp
Standard Chartered plc	300	6M LIBOR+15 bp

Source: Information Memorandum, Financial Security Assistance.

Tiffany & Company

On Friday, May 1, 1987, Mr. William Chaney and Mr. Thomas Andruskevich, chairman and senior vice president for finance, respectively, of Tiffany & Company, were meeting with representatives of two New York based investment banks, Shearson Lehman Brothers and Goldman Sachs, in connection with an impending 4.5 million share initial public offering of Tiffany's stock that was scheduled for early the following week. At issue was the price at which the shares should be offered to public investors and, secondarily, what the "gross spread" payment to the underwriters should be. An anticipated price in the range of $21–23 per share had been indicated in the preliminary documents filed with the Securities and Exchange Commission several weeks before. While there was no formal obligation to stick to that range, indications of interest had been solicited with this in mind. Not surprisingly, Messrs. Chaney and Andruskevich were convinced that, based on both the company's fundamentals as well as the very full "book" of investor indications of interest, a price of at least $25 was feasible and logical. The representatives of the two co-managing investment bankers were less sanguine and argued for a price at the mid to upper part of the indicated range. They were also wondering whether they should create a significant "short position" in the stock by initially selling more shares than were planned. It was important to reach a speedy resolution of the price and other terms so that the offering could go forward on schedule.

History

In 1837, two enterprising young New Englanders, Charles L. Tiffany and John Young, opened a "Stationery and Dry Goods" shop at 259 Broadway in New York, investing a thousand dollars borrowed from Tiffany's father. Gold jewelry was introduced in 1845 and Swiss watches, bronze statuary and jewelry set with precious stones were added in 1847. The following year a new Tiffany goldsmithing shop produced the first Tiffany-made jewelry. That same year a representative of the firm, on a trip to Paris, was able to purchase the jewels of Maria Amelia, wife

---

This case was prepared by Professor Samuel L. Hayes, III.
Copyright © 1987 by the President and Fellows of Harvard College. Harvard Business School case 9-288-022.

of the recently deposed French King, Louis Philippe. The New York press dubbed Tiffany "King of Diamonds" when he put the French crown jewels on display, and from that day forward, Tiffany's took its place as a premier American jeweler. This success allowed Tiffany to bring New York's leading silver manufacturer, John C. Moore, into the firm and thus assured its future world leadership in the silver industry as well.

In its first thirty years the firm grew from a modest boutique to a great retail emporium. At the Paris Exposition of 1867 it won the first medal ever awarded to an American silver maker. This period also saw the origin of the famous "Tiffany blue" packaging (the most fashionable decorating color of the period) and its logo, derived from the gilded wooden letters used on the firm's store-front.

In the last quarter of the 1800s, Tiffany outfitted America for the Gilded Age, that continuous celebration of its newfound prosperity. The great American families flocked to Tiffany's to order their jewels, the invitations to their social events, their private silver patterns and commemorative objects.

In this period, too, the most acclaimed American gemologist, George F. Kunz, joined Tiffany's. He began work at the firm in 1877, the year the 128.54 carat "Tiffany Diamond" was purchased. By 1899 he had assembled what many contemporary observers considered to be the finest collection of American gemstones, which Tiffany's exhibited at the Paris Exposition of 1889 and which J. Pierpont Morgan later purchased for the New York Museum of Natural History. By then, Tiffany's owned branches in London and Paris and held appointments as gold and silversmiths to every crowned head in Europe.

Charles Comfort Tiffany inherited the leadership from his father in 1902 and moved the store to a grandly scaled stone and steel palace on Fifth Avenue designed by Stanford White. He proved to be a shrewd merchant and promoter of Tiffany's image as the arbiter of good taste. Thirty-seven years later, concurrent with the opening of the New York World's Fair in 1939, Tiffany & Co. moved twenty blocks up Fifth Avenue to the current location of its flagship store at Fifty-Seventh Street and Fifth Avenue.

In the mid-1950s, Walter Hoving, another reknowned U.S. merchant, took over the leadership of Tiffany's and was responsible for the appointment of the designers who continued in 1987 as important mainstays to the company: Jean Schlumberger, Donald Claflin, Elsa Peretti, Angela Cummings, and Paloma Picasso, daughter of Pablo Picasso. Tiffany's precious gem department, headed by the first Tiffany's great-grandson, Henry B. Platt, introduced to the world two new gemstones, tanzanite and tsavorite, and popularized George Kunz's discovery, kunzite.

By the late 1970s, Tiffany's was some twenty times larger than when Hoving had first assumed leadership. Profits in 1978 were 8% on sales of $73 million. Asset turnover was an efficient 1.5 times; accounts receivable turnover was 5.2 times and inventory turnover was 1.3 times. The Company had, however, severely restricted its investment in accounts receivable and inventory management control systems, as well as in equipment, storage facilities and additional retail outlets. In fact, the firm had committed a total of only $5 million to capital expenditures in the five year period ending in 1978. Thus, although profitable, the firm was, in fact, severely stretched and reaching a crisis point. Inventory was difficult both to store and locate and, because of an antiquated manual accounts receivable system, accounts receivable were not monitored and collection efforts were minimal. Premises were also cramped and employee morale was low.

In 1979, Avon Products, Inc., which had gained a nationwide reputation as direct selling marketers through their door-to-door sales of cosmetics, bought Tiffany & Company from Hoving and other shareholders for $94 million. Acquired as part of its strategy for entering the specialty retail industry, Avon sought to build Tiffany's business by broadening the product line to reach beyond its traditional affluent customer base to the larger middle market. With an infusion of $53 million, substantial renovations were made in the New York, Chicago and Beverly Hills stores, new stores were opened in Dallas, Kansas City (closed in 1985) and Boston, and a modern distribution and office facility were opened in Parsippany, New Jersey. Additionally, new systems were developed and implemented, including a jewelry cost and locator system, a direct mail system, a corporate order processing system, and point-of-sale terminals in the branch stores. Employee training was introduced, and benefits and compensation packages were improved to enhance customer service. A Tiffany credit card was also inaugurated.

Sales grew steadily from $84 million in 1979 to $124 million in 1983. Operating expenses, however, also increased inordinately, reaching 43% of sales in 1983 as compared to 34% in 1978. Despite the investments in internal systems, the company's ability to manage its assets did not improve. Accounts receivable turnover decreased from 5.2 times in 1978 to 3.5 times in 1983, while inventory turnover declined from 1.3 times to 1.1 times during that same period.

By mid-1984 the management of Avon had concluded that Tiffany's would not make a good fit with the parent's long-range strategy and consequently put the company up for sale. Through its investment banker, Morgan Stanley, it began to solicit indications of interest from a wide variety of outside parties. Literally dozens of potential buyers investigated the possibility of purchasing the company, but in the end only two serious offers were forthcoming. Of the two, Avon's management determined that the more attractive purchase proposition had been made by Tiffany's own management, backed by a London-based merchant bank, Investcorp.

In the latter part of 1984 this group purchased from Avon for $135.5 million all of the equity of Tiffany (for $87.1 million) and the Fifth Avenue store building (for $48.4 million) in what was ultimately structured as a leveraged buyout. In a second step, the new ownership group refinanced a substantial portion of the purchase price through an $85 million arrangement with General Electric Credit Corporation (GECC); this included a $75 million secured revolving credit facility, a $10 million, 16% subordinated note due in 1992, and common stock warrants to purchase approximately 25% of the company's equity on a fully diluted basis. Additionally, the New York store building was sold and leased back under a 35-year agreement, thus raising $48 million. The company's distribution center in New Jersey was also sold and leased back while its manufacturing facility in Newark was shut down and put up for sale.

Tiffany's management ended up purchasing approximately 20% of the equity shares, with that ownership spread out among some 28 people within the top and upper management ranks of the company. Investcorp owned 49.8% and GECC held 25.7% of the equity. The balance was purchased by other collaborating investors, including a 1% ownership by Shearson Lehman Brothers, which had assisted in the negotiations that led to the buyout.

Tiffany under Independent Ownership

The newly independent Tiffany's sold through three principal channels of distribution in 1985. "United States Retail," which consisted of Tiffany's New

York and branch stores as well as the network of selected independent retailers authorized under Tiffany's wholesale trade program, accounted for approximately 72% of sales. "Direct Marketing" consisted of both sales by a group of specialized sales personnel to corporate customers as well as that volume generated through Tiffany's direct mail catalogues. These channels accounted for approximately 25% of sales. "International Retail," which at that point consisted of sales to the Mitsukoshi department store chain in Japan, accounted for the remaining 3%.

In the aftermath of the leveraged buyout, the company's financial situation was very tight (see Exhibits 1 and 2). The Tiffany management therefore worked assiduously both to lower costs and to improve sales in each sector of the business. Through public and private information channels, they signaled their intention to refocus attention on the affluent customers who had long been the focus prior to Avon's ownership.

Strenuous efforts were made to increase the turnover of inventory and accounts receivable as a means of generating additional cash and reducing working capital carrying costs. A new internal security control system was put in place to reduce inventory loss through pilferage. Outside consultants were brought in to help management to identify excess costs in all areas of the business and, in the course of the cost saving implementation, some 138 positions were eliminated to give a total employee headcount of 1,250 by the end of 1985.

Additional senior management resources were also added in the areas of retail store, international and trade, and corporate sales; plans were formulated for a further push into retail markets abroad. A site for a new branch in London was identified and duly opened in September 1986, thus returning Tiffany to the London scene after an absence of some 35 years. This new branch was established as a joint venture with European retailing interests so as to both minimize capital calls on Tiffany and to insulate its profit and loss statement from any adverse early operating results of the branch. Under the agreement, Tiffany started out with a minority share of the branch's equity but had the option to acquire a majority position. Other European branch store sites were being sought in West Germany and Switzerland. In Asia, the company was exploring the possibilities of a retail branch in Hong Kong.

Management also formulated a master plan for the introduction of the first Tiffany fragrance, whose launching was timed to coincide with the planned celebration of the company's 150th anniversary in 1987. Initially to be sold only in Tiffany stores and through direct marketing channels, it would subsequently be offered through other prestigious retail "doors" in the United States and abroad. While each of these growth opportunities held considerable promise, they were also capital absorbing. Given Tiffany's post-LBO financial position, this presented a special concern to management. The company had finished the fiscal year ending in January 1986 with a considerable loss and a nominal net worth.

Thus, each month's operating results were intently examined for signs of improvement. While some early indications of the positive impact of the cost reduction program had been noted by early 1985, the sales picture was much less encouraging. Month after month, retail sales in the New York flagship store and in the seven branches were below expectations, thus depressing the profit-and-loss results inordinately. Tiffany broke with long tradition and held a sale in January 1985 in an attempt to clear away certain categories of slow-moving inventory. Nonetheless, the disappointing sales figures continued during 1985 and, most importantly, into the crucial 1985 Christmas selling season, when almost

40% of annual sales were typically generated. Only the sales picture in Japan exhibited any material improvement during this period.

Although the sales trend was proving disheartening to Tiffany's management, the effectiveness of the cost reduction program was increasingly evident with each passing month. Improved purchasing procedures were producing materially better gross margins, and overhead expense reduction, reflected in the selling, general, and administrative expenses category, was also encouraging. Further, the general decline in interest rates during 1985 and 1986 was significantly reducing the carrying costs of the heavy debt burden the company had incurred in the leveraged purchase from Avon:

	Fiscal Year Ended January 31,		
	1985	1986	1987
Net sales	100.0%	100.0%	100.0%
Cost of sales	57.8	53.3	52.7
Gross profit	42.2%	46.7%	47.3%
Selling, general and administrative expenses, including occupancy expense	44.7	41.3	35.3
Income/(loss) from operations	(2.5)%	5.4%	12.0%
Interest expense	5.4	8.7	4.9
Other income/(deductions)	0.1	0.2	(0.1)
Income/(loss) before income taxes and extraordinary item	(7.8)%	(3.1%)	7.0%

Finally, in March 1986, an improvement in retail sales was noted, and similar advances were soon thereafter noted in the corporate and in the direct mail parts of the business as well. Steady, above-budget sales advances continued in all categories for the balance of 1986 so that the sales results for the fiscal year ending January 31, 1987 were gratifying, particularly on a comparative basis:

	Fiscal Year Ended January 31,		
	1985 Sales	1986 Sales	1987 Sales
		($ millions)	
U.S. retail	$ 97.5	$ 99.3	$124.9
Direct marketing	33.7	36.1	44.0
International retail	4.1	6.4	13.6
Total	$135.3	$141.8	$182.5

As calendar year 1986 monthly operating results continued to present a consistently positive trend, management began to review its financing arrangements. Under the terms of the GECC revolving credit agreement by which the company's working capital needs were met, Tiffany was required to maintain certain coverages with respect to eligible accounts receivable and inventory. Because of the tightness of that coverage requirement and despite the company's strenuous efforts to reduce its net working capital needs, Tiffany had had to call upon Investcorp to extend a $13 million letter of credit guarantee from Investcorp that would permit borrowing under the GECC revolving credit arrangement to rise to required levels. As operating results improved, Investcorp had on several occasions expressed its hope that this capital guarantee could be eliminated.

Further, although the general decline in interest rates had yielded significant savings to Tiffany on the carrying cost of the GECC floating rate loan, the improved operating picture made it increasingly likely that the company would be able to negotiate a more favorable short-term financing arrangement with another lender. When initial efforts to renegotiate the terms of the GECC revolving credit were not encouraging, management began to think of the possibility of a more comprehensive refinancing that could repay GECC completely and free the company to make alternative lender arrangements.

With the encouragement of Tiffany's five person board, Messrs. Chaney and Andruskevich began in the autumn of 1986 to explore the refinancing options which might be open to the company during the year ahead. A great deal obviously depended on a continuation of the favorable operating results, and so each month's figures continued to be scrutinized closely. Among the options which management identified, one obvious possibility was to pursue more vigorously with GECC the renegotiation of some of the terms of the current financing agreement, including a reduction in the interest rate as well as a relaxation in the borrowing limits such that the Investcorp letter of credit could be eliminated.

A second possibility was the substitution of another lender in the place of GECC, presumably on considerably better terms to reflect Tiffany's improved operating results. Preliminary conversations with several New York City banks suggested that this was a good possibility.

A third option was to seek to sell shares to the public in an initial public offering. This had, from the beginning, been a longer-term goal for the management and other investors participating in the leveraged buyout; no one, however, had expected that it would be able to be seriously considered so soon after the change of ownership. Mr. Andruskevich made inquiries with several people familiar with the public equity markets, including William Shutzer, a partner in the investment banking firm of Shearson Lehman Brothers and a member of Tiffany's board of directors. Mr. Shutzer advised that with a minimum six months of additional positive operating results, a public offering could indeed be considered, particularly if the current bullish mood of the U.S. stock markets sustained itself until then.

Preparations for a Public Offering

After much discussion among Tiffany's top management and board of directors, it was decided in October 1986 to aim for an initial public offering sometime during the first half of 1987, assuming that both Tiffany's upbeat operating results and the favorable U.S. market for equities continued. From that point on, a number of preparatory steps to "going public" were instituted by Mr. Chaney, Mr. Andruskevich, and other members of Tiffany's management.

One important task was to prepare a prospectus laying out the company's financial history and current operations as required by the Securities Act of 1933. The first draft of this document was prepared by Patrick Dorsey, Tiffany's vice president and general counsel, in close cooperation with both the company's public accountants and outside law firm.

Another concern was the selection of an investment bank or banks to manage the public offering. Although Shearson Lehman was represented on the board of directors, Tiffany's management and board had determined not to automatically award the lead managership to that investment bank. Instead, the company would cast a wider net among U.S. investment banks in search of the securities firm that could best serve Tiffany in this important role. After considerable preliminary investigation, it was decided to invite three leading underwriters to make serious presentations to the company as finalist candidates for the lead managership. In their written and oral presentations, the three finalists—Shearson Lehman, Morgan Stanley and Goldman Sachs—addressed themselves to the general market outlook for new equities, the pricing considerations that would influence the offering price that Tiffany could obtain, and the special resources of their own firms that made them particularly qualified to serve as lead manager.

Serving in the "lead" management position on an underwriting carried important benefits for the designated securities firm. The management fee was typically 20% of the "gross spread" and, while it was commonly split evenly with any other co-managers that might be included, the sums could be sizeable. The position also permitted a great deal of control over how the securities were actually distributed. The lead manager typically recommended to the issuer the composition of the syndicate of securities firms that would underwrite and distribute the securities. Equally important, the lead manager "ran the books"; that is, determined which members of the syndicate would get what proportion of the offering to sell to its customers. A large part (typically 60%) of the "gross spread" paid to the syndicate was in the form of the "selling concession" paid to the firms that actually sold the securities to investors. Thus, having the power to dictate which firms got how many securities carried great weight, particularly in the way the lead manager was reciprocally treated in other underwritings in which it participated. The underwriting part of the fee, 20%, was usually eaten up by the syndicate's out-of-pocket expenses. Finally, because of the real power and influence exercised by the lead manager, the offering was considered to be "its deal" both within and outside the investment community. There was also a presumption that the lead manager would have some sort of an ongoing relationship with the issuing company after the public offering, although in recent years such relationships had become somewhat looser.

Thus, because of the global importance of the Tiffany brand image and the benefits that would accrue as the retailer's lead manager on this offering, each of the three firms mobilized their most senior officials in an effort to convince Tiffany of its merits for this assignment. Each firm made numerous informal contacts with Tiffany's management and board members over a number of weeks as the company considered its choice.

In January, 1987, with the reassurance of monthly operating results continuing to exceed expectations by 20–30% through the end of the 1986 Christmas selling season, Tiffany's management recommended to its board that Shearson Lehman be named as the lead underwriter and that Goldman Sachs serve as co-manager. The selection of Shearson Lehman reflected not only that firm's excellent record with similar initial public offerings and high level of familiarity with Tiffany's affairs, but also its large retail network of some 6,000 account executives in 311 branch offices in the United States and abroad. It was felt that this in-house retail selling power could help ensure a successful placement of the Tiffany shares even if institutional interest were not to live up to current expectations. Goldman Sachs edged out Morgan Stanley for the co-managership in part because of Goldman's very highly regarded retail analyst whose endorsement of the Tiffany stock could be an important support both to the public offering and to the performance of the shares in the aftermarket.

With the naming of the lead and co-managers, preparation for the public offering accelerated. Shearson Lehman's William Shutzer and Charles Marquis of the company's attorneys, Gibson, Dunn & Crutcher, collaborated with Tiffany's general counsel in further refining the initial draft of the prospectus, which would ultimately have to be cleared by the Securities and Exchange Commission and which would serve as the principal source of information to investors contemplating purchase of the new common shares. They were, of course, critically dependent on the financial data being audited and reviewed by Tiffany's independent accountants, Coopers & Lybrand. Under SEC rules, a full three years of previous operating history must be presented and, given the change in ownership and the accompanying radical change in the firm's capital and asset structure, assembling that on a comparative basis was a demanding task.

It was also necessary for the lead investment bank, in consultation with co-manager Goldman Sachs, to put together a syndicate of securities firms to underwrite the new offering. Mr. Greg Sacco, Shearson Lehman's syndicate manager, was central in this process. He found wide interest among other firms in participating in the public offering, even though a firm price would not be established until the eve of the offering. A total of 75 U.S. securities firms were eventually signed on, including all of the "major bracket" New York-based firms and some 50 regional firms. These syndicate members would share, in four diminishing brackets of participation, 3.5 million of the 4.5 million shares to be offered.

In addition, Shearson Lehman and Goldman Sachs had recommended to Tiffany that there be a "foreign tranche" of off-shore securities firms to sell the remaining 1.0 million shares of the offering. Although it was expected that Shearson and Goldman would underwrite approximately three-quarters of this amount through their foreign affiliates, thirteen other firms were signed on, including British, Swiss, German, and French merchant banks as well as two of the largest Japanese securities firms. One U.S. commercial bank's off-shore affiliate was also included.

Tiffany's Messrs. Chaney and Andruskevich were also preparing themselves for the meetings with prospective investors and their brokers that were mandated by the Securities Act of 1933. Colloquially known as "road shows," they were presented in major cities in the United States and abroad in the three weeks or so preceding the planned offering, now tentatively set for early May 1987. The schedule called for them to make such presentations in New York, Chicago, San Francisco, Boston, Los Angeles, Houston, Minneapolis, and Toronto. In Europe, they would visit London, Zurich, Geneva, Frankfurt, Milan, and Edinburgh. Hopefully, the SEC's comments and reactions to the company's preliminary prospectus would be received during the course of these selling meetings such that the offering would "become effective" (i.e. cleared for sale to investors) just as the meetings were concluding.

Pricing and Terms of the Offering

Threading its way through the discussions and dialogue between executives of Tiffany and its investment bankers was the subject of the pricing of the issue. Each of the "finalist" candidates for lead manager had, of course, presented statistical evidence to suggest the probable general range of the price, assuming that the tone of the markets did not change materially by the time of the actual offering. As they explained it, a number of factors were germane to the pricing decision, including profit margins, growth rates in both sales and earnings, capital structure, dividend policy and book value. While conceptually these and other considerations should be reducible to an estimate of future earnings and dividends, discounted by the appropriate annual investment return for that class of risk, in practice the securities firms looked to the market valuations of companies in comparable businesses for clues as to the price at which a newly issued security such as the Tiffany common stock would sell.

Shearson Lehman and Goldman Sachs identified three groups of publicly owned companies with which they believed that Tiffany was in one way or another comparable: jewelry retailers, such as Jewelcor, specialty retailers, such as The Limited and diversified retailers, such as Federated Department Stores. Financial information on these groups of companies is presented in Exhibits 3–6.

In conversations with Tiffany's management, Shearson Lehman's syndicate manager, Mr. Sacco, explained that one of the most difficult aspects of the valuation analysis was determining what the Tiffany "franchise" was worth. Brand names with immediate recognition often obtained a valuation premium over and above that which could be defended strictly on the basis of the financial results. He cautioned, however, against attempting to stretch too far to exploit that franchise value in the initial offering price. A recent initial public offering for shares of Coca-Cola Enterprises, a unit of Coca-Cola, had been tentatively priced inordinately high in the eyes of a number of market participants and had triggered a somewhat hostile reaction from the financial community. Some investors and their financial advisors had apparently attributed to the issuer the attitude that the market needed its paper and should be prepared to pay whatever Coca-Cola deemed satisfactory. Coca-Cola Enterprises had had to lower its indicated price range, had ultimately sold the shares at the lower end of that reduced range and had fared relatively poorly in the aftermarket.

In Tiffany's case, the investment bankers noted that the leveraged buyout was still very recent and quite visible in the highly leveraged capital structure that would have to be featured in the prospectus. Although the management's success in turning around the company was impressive, the period of positive results was nonetheless relatively short. Mr. Sacco was concerned that, in light of these factors, the size of the deal that could be sold to the marketplace might be limited. That, in turn, could have an impact on the stock's valuation, since there might not be sufficient shares introduced into the publicly traded "float" so that substantial positions could be acquired by large and sophisticated institutional investors.

Further, a number of Tiffany's current investors wanted to participate in the public offering by selling part of their own holdings, perhaps as much as 25%. It had therefore been initially anticipated that 2 million of the originally planned 4.0 million share offering would actually be a "secondary" sale of shares already in the hands of the original LBO investors. The net proceeds of those shares would go to them. The 2.0 million offering balance would constitute "primary" shares; that is, shares that had not been previously issued to other investors. The sale proceeds of these shares would go to Tiffany to provide additional capital to permit the company to re-balance its capital structure into a more conservative—and less costly—form. Shortly before the date of the planned Tiffany stock offering, two substantial foreign investors had indicated an interest in buying 500,000 shares and the "secondary" part of the offering had consequently been increased to 2.5 million, since Tiffany's management did not anticipate an internal need for the additional capital.

It was the investment bankers' recommendation that no dividend be paid on the common shares for the present. Given Tiffany's continuing profitable uses for additional capital, it was felt that this would be acceptable to many prospective investors.

Contrary to the usual practice with I.P.O.'s, it was also recommended that Tiffany's immediately list on the New York Stock Exchange. Typically, a new offering was first traded in the over-the-counter market where the managing underwriters could directly participate in the market-making activity and thus help to dampen any untoward volatility in the shares' price once the "stabilization" period for the new shares had ended and the stock had been allowed to trade on its own. This had particularly been the practice with issuers unfamiliar to the market. Since Tiffany enjoyed instant name recognition within the financial community, no "seasoning" period seemed required.

In setting the initial offering price, the investment bankers also stressed the importance of "leaving something on the table" so that, when left entirely to market forces, the shares would trade at a modest premium from their offering price. As an example, if the shares were offered at $21 to $22 each, then the underwriters would hope to see them trade on their own at the $24 to $25 level. They had warned against putting too high a price range in the preliminary prospectus for fear that, if the general tone of the market were to soften, the adverse psychological impact of having to subsequently backtrack on the price could actually push the ultimate offering price inordinately lower.

The general tone of the equity markets was somewhat volatile at the end of April (see Exhibit 7). After an impressive upward advance through the first quarter of 1987, the Dow Jones Industrial Average had lost some ground during April, although it had closed up 45 points for the week ending May 1, at 2280. Bond prices had also recovered somewhat from their recent bearish levels and the Dow Jones Industrial's price-earnings multiple, which had been at 14X several months before, now stood at 16X.

The "roadshows" had also gone very well, both in the United States and in Europe. As a result, the current "book" on the offering was approaching 16 million shares, almost 4 times the number of shares that would be available for sale. Mr. Sacco was leery of depending on these "indications of interest" among investors, however. From past experience, he knew that such preliminary enthusiasm should evaporate when the actual time to make a firm purchase commitment arrived. He was also concerned that some of these interested investors would turn out to be "flippers," people who buy stock in the expectation of a quick run-up and then "flip" out of the stock, dumping their shares on the aftermarket in favor of something else that is "hot." Of course, if the shares were to fail to rise quickly in the aftermarket, these short-term speculators would be even quicker to cut and run, thus pouring a quantity of unwanted shares into the marketplace just as the underwriting syndicate was attempting to complete the share placement.

As a means of better managing the distribution of new shares, underwriters were permitted to "stabilize" the aftermarket for the shares during the offering, a period which might run from a few hours to several days. The lead manager was responsible for entering a "syndicate bid" at the offering price in the aftermarket, thus assuring the price would go no lower and providing a means for gathering in shares that had been poorly placed initially so that they could be resold.

The lead manager could, of course, "go long" on the stock as a means of supporting the price; that is, buy the offered shares with its own capital. There was a risk to "going long," however. Should either the general market or the market's response to these newly issued shares turn negative, the manager might find itself unable to find new buyers for the temporarily inventoried securities at or near the offering price. That would force the sale at depressed prices, incur a loss, and thus wreck efforts to maintain an orderly market during the distribution.

To avoid that situation, underwriting syndicates were usually permitted to create a "short position" in the shares they were selling. In the Tiffany example, they would be permitted to initially sell more than the 4.5 million shares formally being offered by the company. By selling, say, 5 million shares initially, the syndicate would have a short position of 500,000 shares that it could draw upon to support the immediate aftermarket price of the shares. The very presence of such a position would have an upward bias on the price because the market would expect additional purchasing power to be in evidence in the aftermarket as a consequence of the short position.

The risky aspect of that maneuver, however, was the possibility that the new shares would immediately jump to a premium and the syndicate would be unable to cover its over-sales except at a premium price. To avoid this risk, there had grown up a practice first used in an offering by the Green Shoe Company (now the Stride Rite Corporation) by which the issuer agrees to increase the size of the offering in the event that the underwriters find themselves with a short position which can't be covered at or near the offering price. This so-called "Green Shoe" provision had removed much of the price movement risk.

Thus, as Tiffany's management and its underwriting managers were working towards a final new issue pricing strategy, the possible use and the size of a short position was one of the factors under consideration.

Finally, there was the question of the gross spread to be charged by the underwriters. Gross spreads on recent initial public offerings varied from approximately 5 1/2% to 8% (see Exhibit 8). The size of the gross spread was usually a function of the anticipated difficulty of the deal. The general level of market uncertainty was obviously one factor. The other important consideration was the expected investor reception for the specific offering. To the extent that it was anticipated that a large retail sales component would be required, a larger gross spread would be called for because the retail account executives needed to be well compensated to enhance their enthusiasm for the deal. In this case, Tiffany's investment bankers felt that a gross spread of 6 1/4% was called for, particularly given the pressures to price the offering as fully as possible. A higher price, they pointed out, would be likely to meet investor resistance and would therefore require more sales effort to successfully place the deal.

As the Tiffany executives and their investment bankers began their final pricing discussions on May Day, 1987, they knew that the foregoing array of factors would have to be carefully weighed as they sought a final set of offering terms that would meet both the needs of the company as well as those of the underwriting syndicate and public investors.

Exhibit 1

Consolidated Balance Sheets ($ millions)

	June 30, 1986	January 31, 1987
ASSETS		
Current Assets		
Cash	$ 1.1	$ 1.9
Accounts receivable, less allowances of $2.6 and $2.8, respectively	14.7	21.2
Inventories	63.0	58.0
Prepaid expenses	3.9	4.4
Total	$82.7	$85.5
Property and equipment	11.2	11.2
Other assets, net	1.4	2.0
Total	$95.3	$98.7
LIABILITIES AND STOCKHOLDERS' EQUITY		
Current Liabilities		
Accounts payable and accrued liabilities	$23.0	$23.9
Current maturities of long-term notes	2.0	—
Merchandise and other customer credits	4.9	5.0
Total current liabilities	$29.9	$28.9
Deferred income taxes	—	5.4
Revolving credit loan-related party	36.4	34.6
Subordinated notes-related parties	23.0	15.0
Other long-term liabilities	1.7	1.9
Stockholders' equity		
Common stock $.01 par value; authorized 15,000,000 shares, issued 5,996,000	.1	.1
Additional paid-in capital	7.5	7.6
Retained earnings/(deficit)	(3.2)	5.3
Total	$ 4.4	$13.0
Less: Treasury stock 183,200 and 199,200 shares at cost, respectively	(.1)	(.1)
Total stockholders' equity	4.3	12.9
Total	$95.3	$98.7

Exhibit 2

Supplemental Selected Financial Data ($ thousands, except per share data)

	Fiscal Year Ended January 31, 1985			Fiscal Year Ended		Pro Forma (Unaudited)
	Eight Months Ended Sept. 30, 198- (Pre-Acquisition)	Four Months Ended Jan. 31, 1985 (Unaudited)	Combined (Unaudited)	Jan. 31, 1986 (Unaudited)	Jan. 31, 1987	Fiscal Year Ended Jan. 31, 1987
INCOME STATEMENT DATA						
Net sales	$ 70,945	$64,384	$135,329	$141,849	$182,527	$182,527
Cost of goods sold	43,482	34,760	78,242	75,548	96,124	96,124
Gross profit	$ 27,463	$29,624	$ 57,087	$ 66,301	$ 86,403	$ 86,403
Selling, general and administrative expenses	35,982	24,567	60,549	58,700	64,486	64,486
Income/(loss) from operations	$ (8,519)	$ 5,047	$ (3,462)	$ 7,601	$ 21,917	$ 21,917
Interest expense	3,110	4,221	7,331	12,298	8,921	1,595
Other income/(deductions)	(102)	330	228	237	(228)	(228)
Income/(loss) before income taxes and extraordinary item	$(11,731)	$ 1,166	$(10,565)	$ (4,460)	$ 12,768	$ 20,094
Charge equivalent to and provision/(benefit) for income taxes	(6,013)	597	(5,421)	(1,855)	5,986	9,796
Income/(loss) before extraordinary item	$ (5,718)	$ 569	$ (5,144)	$ (2,605)	$ 6,782	$ 10,298
Extraordinary item resulting from utilization of net operating loss carryforward	—	—	—	—	608	—
Net income/(loss)	$ (5,718)	$ 569	$ (5,144)	$ (2,605)	$ 7,390	$ 10,298
Per Share Data:						
Net income/(loss) per common share						
Primary						
Income/(loss) before extraordinary item				$(0.41)	$0.84	$1.01
Extraordinary item				—	—	—
Net income/(loss)				$(0.41)	$0.92	$1.01
Fully diluted:						
Income/(loss) before extraordinary item				$(0.41)	$0.83	$1.01
Extraordinary item				—	—	—
Net income/(loss)				$(0.41)	$0.90	$1.01
Weighted average number of common shares						
Primary				6,394,936	8,078,080	10,221,392
Fully diluted				6,394,936	8,221,392	10,221,392

	Sept. 30, 1984 (Unaudited)	Jan. 31, 1985 (Unaudited)	Jan. 31, 1986 (Unaudited)	Jan. 31, 1987	As Adjusted (Unaudited) Jan. 31, 1987
Balance Sheet Data					
Working capital	$ 80,302	$ 89,453	$62,138	$56,508	$56,108
Total assets	133,937	123,458	99,255	98,731	97,431
Long-term debt	57,433	87,535	67,629	49,568	8,618
Stockholders' equity	48,462	10,653	5,548	12,862	53,188

Exhibit 3

Summary Market Data for Selected Retailers (April 30, 1987)

Value[b]	Latest Twelve Months' E.P.S.	1987 Estimated E.P.S.[a]	Current Stock Price (4/30/87)	Current Market Price as a Multiple of:		
				LTM E.P.S.	1987 E.P.S.	Book
Jewelry Retailers						
Barry's Jewelers, Inc.	$0.69	$1.10	$ 7.750	11.2x	7.0x	1.7x
Gordon Jewelry Corporation	(0.61)	1.40	18.000	NM	12.9x	0.8x
Jewelcor, Inc.	2.44	NA	12.500	5.1x	NA	0.9x
Kay Jewelers, Inc.	1.52	1.85	19.250	12.7x	10.4x	3.7x
Sterling, Inc.	1.42	1.78	19.750	13.9x	11.1x	3.5x
Weisfields, Inc.	1.19	1.50	18.000	15.1x	12.0x	1.0x
			Range	5.1x – 15.1x	7.0x – 12.9x	0.8x – 3.7x
			Mean	11.6x	10.7x	1.9x
			Median	12.7x	11.1x	1.4x
Specialty Retailers						
Charming Shoppes	$0.81	$1.09	$25.625	31.8x	23.5x	9.2x
The Dress Barn, Inc.	1.01	1.11	32.000	31.7x	28.8x	10.8x
The Gap Inc.	1.93	2.32	57.500	29.8x	24.8x	10.6x
Lands' End, Inc.	1.46	1.82	37.250	25.5x	20.5x	12.7x
The Limited, Inc.	1.21	1.73	41.125	34.0x	23.8x	11.1x
Pep Boys=Manny, Moe and Jack	1.55	1.98	43.375	28.0x	21.9x	4.0x
Toys 'R Us, Inc.	1.17	1.60	35.875	30.7x	22.4x	5.8x
Williams-Sonoma, Inc.	0.45	1.21	19.000	42.2x	15.7x	4.2x
Louis Vuitton	1.55	1.92[c]	45.875	29.8x	23.9x	13.9x
			Range	25.5x – 42.2x	15.7x – 28.8x	4.0x – 13.9x
			Mean	31.5x	22.8x	9.1x
			Median	30.7x	23.5x	10.6x
Diversified Retailers						
Carter Hawley Hale Stores	$0.87	$3.17	$62.875	NM	NM	3.4x
Dayton-Hudson Corp.	2.65	3.39	43.125	16.3x	12.7x	2.1x
Federated Department Stores Inc.	6.44	7.51	92.500	14.4x	12.3x	1.7x
May Department Stores Co.	2.44	2.97	44.750	18.3x	15.1x	2.8x
			Range	14.4x – 18.3x	12.3x – 15.1x	1.7x – 3.4x
			Mean	16.3x	13.4x	2.5x
			Median	16.3x	12.7x	2.5x

LTM = latest twelve months.

[a] All estimates based on Institutional Brokers Estimate System (IBES) projections dated March 19, 1987, unless otherwise noted.

[b] As of most recent financial reporting period.

[c] Estimate based on Drexel Burnham research report dated January 6, 1987.

Exhibit 4

Historical Market Data for Selected Jewelry Retailers ($ millions, except per share data)

	Barry's Jewelers, Inc.	Gordon Jewelry Corp.	Jewelcor, Inc.	Kay Jewelers, Inc.	Weisfields, Inc.	Sterling, Inc.
Ticker Symbol	BARY	GOR	JC	KJI	WEIS	STRL
Exchange Traded on	OTC	NYSE	NYSE	AMEX	OTC	OTC
Price per Share						
Current (4/30/87)	$7.750	$18.000	$12.500	$19.250	$18.000	$19.750
YTD range[a]	5.75–10.50	18.13–20.75	10.00–13.63	14.63–22.75	17.50–20.50	13.50–23.75
1985 range	NA–NA	15.13–18.38	4.50–13.33	8.30–13.70	11.00–17.25	— –NA
1984 range	NA–NA	13.75–21.66	3.92–5.33	13.79–21.66	10.75–13.75	— –NA
1983 range	NA–NA	12.56–22.88	3.33–6.67	12.56–22.88	8.13–13.88	— –NA
1982 range	NA–NA	9.28–15.75	2.25–4.67	9.28–15.75	5.81–8.50	— –NA
Earnings per Share						
1988 estimated[b,c]	NA	NA	NA	$2.05	NA	NA
1987 estimated[b,d]	$1.10	$1.40	NA	1.85	$1.50	$1.78
Latest 12 months	0.69	(0.61)	$2.44	1.52	1.19	1.42
1985	0.87	0.72	0.32	0.89	1.39	NA
1984	NA	2.32	0.34	0.67	1.62	NA
1983	NA	1.70	0.26	(0.01)	1.20	NA
Ratio of Current Price to						
1988 estimated EPS	NAx	NAx	NAx	9.4x	NAx	NAx
1987 estimated EPS	7.0x	12.9x	NAx	10.4x	12.0x	11.1x
Latest 12 months' EPS	11.2x	NAx	5.1x	12.7x	15.1x	13.9x
Book value per share	1.7x	0.8x	0.9x	3.7x	1.0x	3.5x
Price-Earnings Ratio						
1985	NA–NA	12.2–14.8	5.2–15.3	6.9–11.4	7.2–11.3	NA–NA
1984	NA–NA	19.1–30.1	12.2–16.7	15.4–24.3	7.7–9.9	NA–NA
1983	NA–NA	5.4–9.9	9.8–19.6	18.8–34.1	5.0–8.6	NA–NA
1982	NA–NA	5.5–9.3	8.7–18.0	NA–NA	4.8–7.1	NA–NA
Dividend Data						
Current indicated annual	$0.00	$0.52	$0.00	$0.32	$0.50	$0.00
Current yield	NA	2.89%	NA	1.66%	2.78%	NA
Book value per share	$4.58	$21.72	$13.41	$5.21	$17.87	$5.72
Shares outstanding (thousands)	4,587	10,504	3,260	6,375	1,096	3,905
Aggregate market value (millions)	$35.5	$189.1	$40.8	$122.7	$19.7	$77.1

[a]Latest fiscal year.
[b]Estimates based on Institutional Broker Estimates System (IBES) projections dated March 19, 1987.
[c]Next fiscal year.
[d]Current fiscal year.

Exhibit 4 continued on page 302.

Exhibit 4 (continued)

Historical Operating Data for Selected Jewelry Retailers ($ millions, except per share data)

Most Recent Fiscal Year Ending	Tiffany & Co. 1/31/87	Barry's Jewelers, Inc. 5/31/86	Gordon Jewelry Corp. 8/31/86	Jewelcor, Inc. 1/31/86	Kay Jewelers, Inc. 12/31/85	Weisfields, Inc. 1/31/86	Sterling, Inc. 1/25/86
Net Sales							
Latest 12 months	$182.5	$83.7	$501.6	$235.5	$276.5	$50.5	$84.6
1985	182.5	69.3	489.0	251.8	230.4	48.7	70.1
1984	141.8	63.0	501.7	229.4	206.7	45.9	59.3
1983	135.3	49.7	506.4	195.7	182.0	45.0	46.9
1982	124.4	39.4	474.9	182.1	158.0	40.0	37.1
1981	115.8	20.6	489.8	165.3	137.4	42.0	36.7
Compound growth	12.0%	35.4%	0.0%	11.1%	13.8%	3.8%	17.6%
Gross Profit and Margins							
1985	$86.4 47.3%	$34.2 49.4%	$211.2 43.2%	$59.8 23.7%	$130.2 56.5%	$27.8 57.1%	$41.0 58.5%
1984	66.3 46.7	29.9 47.5	194.3 38.7	54.6 23.8	114.1 55.2	26.4 57.5	32.9 55.5
1983	57.1 42.2	23.5 47.3	210.5 41.6	49.6 25.3	99.9 54.9	25.7 57.1	26.0 55.3
1982	52.6 42.2	18.8 47.7	200.9 42.3	44.3 24.3	83.9 53.1	24.1 60.3	20.1 54.3
1981	47.0 40.6	9.6 46.6	224.0 45.7	41.3 25.0	71.3 51.9	24.5 58.3	20.1 55.0
Compound Growth	16.4%	37.4%	-1.5%	9.7%	16.2%	3.2%	19.5%
Operating Income and Margins							
1985	$21.9 12.0%	$4.0 5.8%	$32.7 6.7%	$12.8 5.1%	$22.4 9.7%	$3.8 7.8%	$9.9 14.1%
1984	7.6 5.4	3.3 5.2	19.1 3.8	10.0 4.4	20.2 9.8	3.7 8.1	7.6 12.8
1983	(3.5) -2.6	3.5 7.0	43.2 8.5	8.1 4.1	16.0 8.8	4.1 9.1	4.7 10.0
1982	5.6 4.5	1.4 3.6	45.3 9.5	6.8 3.7	9.5 6.0	3.4 8.5	1.9 5.1
1981	7.2 6.2	(0.7) -3.4	52.2 10.7	8.1 4.9	5.2 3.8	4.2 10.0	1.9 5.1
Compound growth	32.2%	NA	-11.1%	12.1%	44.1%	-2.5%	51.7%
Pretax Income and Margins							
1985	$20.1 11.0%	$5.5 7.9%	$25.0 5.1%	$6.2 2.5%	$15.0 6.5%	$3.4 7.0%	$7.9 11.2%
1984	(4.5) -3.1	3.8 6.0	14.2 2.8	3.1 1.4	11.0 5.3	3.3 7.2	5.6 9.4
1983	(10.6) -7.8	3.0 6.0	38.9 7.7a	2.9 1.5	8.2 4.5	3.9 8.7	3.5 7.4
1982	2.0 1.6	(0.1) -0.3	37.8 8.0	1.9 1.0	(0.3) -0.2	2.8 7.0	(0.3) -0.7
1981	5.5 4.7	(1.0) -4.9	40.5 8.3	1.8 1.1	(4.2) -3.1	3.7 8.8	(0.2) -0.5
Compound growth	38.3%	NA	-11.4%	36.2%	NA	-2.1%	NA

Exhibit 4 (continued)

Most Recent Fiscal Year Ending	Tiffany & Co. 1/31/87		Barry's Jewelers, Inc. 5/31/86		Gordon Jewelry Corp. 8/31/86		Jewelcor, Inc. 1/31/86		Kay Jewelers, Inc. 12/31/85		Weisfields, Inc. 1/31/86		Sterling, Inc. 1/25/86	
Net Income and Margins														
1985	$10.3	5.6%	$3.3	4.8%	$13.4	2.8%	$3.1	1.2%	$7.5	3.3%	$1.8	3.7%	$4.2	6.0%
1984	(2.6)	−1.8	2.1	3.3	8.5	1.7	1.3	0.6	5.4	2.6	1.8	3.9	3.2	5.3
1983	(5.1)	−3.8	1.9	3.8	22.0	4.3a	1.5	0.8	4.1	2.3	2.1	4.7	2.1	4.5
1982	1.0	0.8	(0.6)	−1.5	19.8	4.2	1.1	0.6	(0.1)	−0.1	1.5	3.8	(0.1)	−0.2
1981	2.7	2.3	(1.0)	−4.9	21.7	4.4	0.8	0.5	(1.9)	−1.4	2.0	4.8	0.0	0.0
Compound growth	39.6%		NA		−11.3%		40.3%		NA		−2.6%		510.8%	
Earnings per Share														
Latest 12 months	$1.01		$0.69		($0.61)		$2.44		$1.52		$1.19		$1.42	
1985	1.01		0.87		1.24		0.87		1.20		1.52		1.03	
1984	(0.41)		NA		0.72		0.32		0.89		1.39		NA	
1983	(0.65)		NA		2.32		0.34		0.67		1.62		NA	
1982	NA		NA		1.70		0.26		(0.01)		1.20		NA	
1981	NA		NA		1.85		0.11		(0.32)		1.60		NA	
Compound growth	NA		NA		−9.5%		67.7%		NA		−1.3%		NA	
Interim Operating Data	NA		9 Mo. to 2/87		6 Mo. to 2/87		12 Mo. to 1/87		12 Mo. to 12/86		12 Mo. to 1/87		12 Mo. to 1/87	
Sales														
1986	NA		$69.1		$223.4		$235.5		$278.1		$50.5		$55.5	
1985	NA		54.7		210.8		251.8		232.0		48.7		41.1	
% change	NA		26.3%		6.0%		−6.5%		19.9%		3.7%		35.2%	
Earnings per Share														
1986	NA		$0.63		($0.43)		$2.44		$1.52		$1.19		$1.42	
1985	NA		0.81		1.42		0.87		1.20		1.52		1.05	
% change	NA		−22.2%c		NA		180.5%		26.7%		−21.7%		37.9	

a Does not include gain on sale of assets of $9.5 million pretax or $5.3 million after tax.

Exhibit 4 continued on page 304.

Exhibit 4 (continued)

Comparative Capitalization Profile for Selected Jewelry Retailers ($ millions, except per share data)

As of	Tiffany & Co. 1/31/87[a]		Barry's Jewelers, Inc. 11/30/86		Gordon Jewelry Corp. 11/30/86		Jewelcor, Inc. 10/31/86		Kay Jewelers, Inc. 9/30/86		Weisfields, Inc. 10/31/86		Sterling, Inc. 10/25/86	
NET ASSETS														
Cash and short-term investments	$ 1.9		$10.6		$ 2.1		$ 4.6		$ 0.5		$ 0.1		$ 0.1	
Other current assets	82.3		66.2		374.8		160.1		166.9		33.1		62.0	
Total current assets	$84.2		$76.9		$376.9		$164.7		$167.4		$33.2		$62.1	
Short-term debt	0.0		0.6		94.6		23.9		72.8		6.9		0.5	
Other current liabilities	35.6		17.1		94.0		98.4		48.1		11.2		27.6	
Net working capital	$48.6		$59.1		$188.3		$ 42.4		$ 46.6		$15.1		$34.0	
Net plant, property and equipment	11.2		11.8		60.1		29.6		24.9		8.4		17.4	
Other tangible assets	2.0		2.6		14.8		4.2		0.0		0.0		1.9	
Net tangible assets	$61.8		$73.6		$263.3		$ 76.1		$ 71.4		$23.5		$53.3	
Intangibles	0.0		0.0		8.1		1.6		2.2		0.0		2.7	
Net assets	$61.8		$73.6		$271.4		$ 77.7		$ 73.6		$23.5		$56.0	
CAPITALIZATION														
Long-term debt	$ 8.6	13.9%	$50.0	67.9%	$43.1	15.9%	$19.1	24.6%	$ 37.4	50.8%	$ 3.9	16.7%	$33.0	58.9%
Other liabilities, deferred items, and min. int.	0.0	0.0	2.6	3.5	0.0	0.0	14.9	19.2	3.0	4.1	0.0	0.0	0.6	1.2
Preferred stock at liquidating value	0.0	0.0	0.0	0.0	0.0	0.0	0.0	0.0	0.0	0.0	0.0	0.0	0.0	0.0
Common equity	53.2	86.1	21.0	28.5	228.3	84.1	43.7	56.3	33.2	45.1	19.6	83.3	22.3	39.9
Total Capitalization	$61.8	100.0%	$73.6	100.0%	$271.4	100.0%	$ 77.7	100.0%	$ 73.6	100.0%	$23.5	100.0%	$56.0	100.0%
Common shares outstanding (thousands)	8,297		4,587		10,504		3,260		6,375		1,096		3,905	
Book value per share	$6.41		$4.58		$21.74		$13.41		$5.21		$17.87		$5.72	
Tangible book value per share	$6.41		$4.58		$20.97		$12.93		$4.87		$17.87		$5.03	

[a]Pro forma capitalization assuming an initial public offering with a primary component of $40 million applied to paydown of debt.

Exhibit 5

Comparative Market Data for Selected Specialty Retailers ($ millions, except per share data)

	Charming Shoppes Inc.	The Dress Barn Inc.	The Gap, Inc.	Lands' End, Inc.	The Limited, Inc.	Pep Boys Manny-Moe-Jack	Toys 'R Us, Inc.	Williams-Sonoma Inc.	Louis Vuitton
Ticker Symbol	CHRS	DBRN	GPS	LEYS	LTD	PBY	TOY	WSGC	LVTNY[e]
Exchange Traded on	OTC	OTC	NYSE	OTC	NYSE	NYSE	NYSE	OTC	OTC
Price Per Share									
Current (4/30/87)	$25.625	$32.000	$57.500	$37.250	$41.125	$43.375	$35.875	$19.000	$45.875
YTD Range	19.75 — 30.13	22.50 — 37.75	36.00 — 62.50	24.24 — 39.25	32.00 — 48.75	41.75 — 53.00	29.00 — 39.75	17.75 — 27.50	39.38 — 47.00
1985 Range[a]	10.25 — 18.42	4.10 — 15.40	5.13 — 15.94	NA — NA	8.67 — 21.25	14.81 — 28.75	16.83 — 27.50	9.00 — 13.00	16.50 — 32.63
1984 Range	6.83 — 11.92	2.55 — 4.40	4.44 — 5.94	NA — NA	5.08 — 9.33	11.63 — 16.56	14.08 — 23.50	5.83 — 9.83	14.44 — 17.81
1983 Range	12.58 — 13.67	3.60 — 5.15	4.06 — 11.31	NA — NA	3.83 — 10.33	9.27 — 17.06	11.58 — 21.67	8.92 — 23.00	NA — NA
1982 Range	3.17 — 6.67	NA — NA	1.63 — 4.81	NA — NA	1.17 — 4.17	4.88 — 10.06	5.67 — 16.58	NA — NA	NA — NA
Earnings Per Share									
1988 Estimated[b,c]	$1.40	$1.47	$2.55	NA	$2.30	NA	NA	NA	NA
1987 Estimated[b,d]	1.09	1.11	2.32	$1.82	1.73	$1.98	$1.60	$1.21	$1.92[f]
Latest 12 Months	0.81	1.01	1.93	1.46	1.21	1.55	1.17	0.45	1.55
1985	0.59	0.83	1.01	NA	0.80	1.29	0.93	0.62	1.15
1984	0.42	0.48	0.38	NA	0.51	1.17	0.87	0.05	0.82
1983	0.37	0.26	0.63	NA	0.39	1.00	0.72	0.12	0.79
1982	0.26	0.16	0.58	NA	0.19	0.81	0.52	0.48	NA
Ratio of Current Price to									
1988 Estimated EPS	18.3x	21.8x	22.5x	NAx	17.9x	NAx	NAx	NAx	NAx
1987 Estimated EPS	23.5x	28.8x	24.8x	20.5x	23.8x	21.9x	22.4x	15.7x	23.9x
Latest 12 Months EPS	31.8x	31.7x	29.8x	25.5x	34.0x	28.0x	30.7x	42.2x	29.6x
Book Value Per Share	9.2x	10.8x	10.6x	12.7x	11.1x	4.0x	5.8x	4.2x	13.9x
Price-Earnings Ratio									
1985	17.5 — 31.4	4.9 — 18.6	5.1 — 15.8	NA — NA	10.8 — 26.6	11.5 — 22.3	18.1 — 29.6	14.5 — 21.0	14.3 — 28.4
1984	16.3 — 28.4	5.3 — 9.2	11.7 — 15.6	NA — NA	10.0 — 18.3	9.9 — 14.2	16.2 — 27.0	NA — NA	17.6 — 21.7
1983	34.3 — 37.3	13.8 — 19.8	6.4 — 18.0	NA — NA	9.8 — 26.5	9.3 — 17.1	16.1 — 30.1	NA — NA	NA — NA
1982	12.2 — 25.6	NA — NA	2.8 — 8.3	NA — NA	6.1 — 21.9	6.0 — 12.4	10.9 — 31.9	NA — NA	NA — NA
Dividend Data									
Current Indicated Annual	$0.12	$0.00	$0.50	$0.00	$0.24	$0.24	$0.00	$0.00	$0.00
Current Yield	0.47%	NA	0.87%	NA	0.58%	0.55%	NA	NA	NA
Book Value Per Share	$2.79	$2.98	$5.41	$2.94	$3.71	$10.96	$6.23	$4.49	$3.31
Shares Outstanding (thousands)	50,044	11,086	35,455	10,020	188,649	18,037	124,464	3,937	24,900
Aggregate Market Value (millions)	$1,282.4	$354.7	$2,038.6	$373.3	$7,758.2	$782.3	$4,465.1	$74.8	$1,142.3

► a Latest fiscal year.

► b Estimates based on Institutional Broker Estimates System (IBES) projections dated March 19, 1987.

► c Next fiscal year.

► d Current fiscal year.

► e ADR's represent 1/4 of each ordinary share outstanding.

► f Estimate based on Drexel Burnham research report dated 1/6/87.

Exhibit 5 continued on page 306.

Exhibit 5 (continued)

Comparative Operating Data for Selected Specialty Retailers ($ millions, except per share data)

	Tiffany & Co. 1/31/87	Charming Shoppes Inc. 2/1/86	The Dress Barn Inc. 7/31/86	The Gap, Inc. 2/1/86	Lands' Ends, Inc. 1/31/86	The Limited, Inc. 2/1/86	Pep Boys Manny-Moe-Jack 2/1/86	Toys 'R Us, Inc. 2/2/86	Williams-Sonoma Inc. 2/2/86	Louis Vuitton 12/31/85
Most Recent Fiscal Year Ending										
Net Sales										
Latest 12 Months	$182.5	$521.2	$156.0	$848.0	$265.1	$3,142.7	$485.9	$2,444.9	$100.4	$274.8
1985	182.5	391.6	135.8	647.3	227.2	2,387.1	388.9	1,976.1	68.3	186.2
1984	141.8	297.3	103.0	518.2	172.2	1,343.1	348.4	1,701.7	44.4	148.8
1983	135.3	238.4	61.6	480.5	123.4	1,085.9	305.8	1,319.6	44.5	110.9
1982	124.4	174.3	43.7	444.9	72.1	721.4	265.4	1,041.7	35.0	NA
1981	115.8	143.9	32.5	417.4	32.8	364.9	233.5	783.3	23.0	NA
Compound Growth	12.0%	28.4%	43.0%	11.6%	62.2%	59.9%	13.6%	26.0%	31.3%	NA
Gross Profit and Margins										
1985	$86.4 47.3%	$135.5 34.6%	$52.6 38.7%	$250.2 38.7%	$91.5 40.3%	$718.8 30.1%	$137.0 35.2%	$653.2 33.1%	$30.6 44.8%	$122.3 65.6%
1984	66.3 46.7%	103.5 34.8%	37.9 36.8%	162.9 31.4%	70.4 40.9%	404.3 30.1%	122.1 35.1%	562.8 33.1%	21.0 47.3%	97.0 65.2%
1983	57.1 42.2%	85.5 35.9%	21.8 35.4%	166.3 34.6%	51.9 42.1%	327.6 30.2%	108.2 35.4%	438.3 33.2%	21.9 49.1%	71.1 64.1%
1982	52.6 42.2%	58.3 33.4%	15.0 34.3%	155.4 34.9%	30.1 41.7%	209.4 29.0%	89.4 33.7%	336.4 32.3%	17.2 49.2%	NA NA
1981	47.0 40.6%	46.7 32.5%	10.6 32.6%	137.1 32.8%	13.6 41.4%	109.2 29.9%	78.8 33.7%	260.5 33.3%	NA NA	NA NA
Compound Growth	16.4%	30.5%	49.3%	16.2%	61.1%	60.2%	14.8%	25.8%	NA	NA
Operating Income and Margins										
1985	$21.9 12.0%	$50.7 12.9%	$16.8 12.4%	$71.3 11.0%	$21.8 9.6%	$276.2 11.6%	$48.0 12.3%	$218.7 11.1%	$4.4 6.4%	$67.1 36.1%
1984	7.6 5.4%	34.1 11.5%	10.0 9.7%	25.8 5.0%	13.6 7.9%	173.1 12.9%	39.5 11.3%	200.2 11.8%	(0.4) -0.9%	53.0 35.6%
1983	(3.5) -2.6%	28.9 12.1%	4.9 8.0%	42.9 8.9%	13.0 10.5%	135.4 12.5%	32.8 10.7%	170.5 12.9%	0.2 0.4%	40.5 36.6%
1982	5.6 4.5%	19.0 10.9%	3.1 7.1%	41.8 9.4%	NA NA	70.9 9.8%	24.5 9.2%	120.1 11.5%	3.1 8.9%	NA NA
1981	7.2 6.2%	16.3 11.3%	1.4 4.3%	29.6 7.1%	NA NA	38.4 10.5%	21.0 9.0%	84.6 10.8%	1.1 4.8%	NA NA
Compound Growth	32.2%	32.8%	86.1%	24.6%	NA	63.8%	23.0%	26.8%	41.4%	NA
Pretax Income and Margins										
1985	$20.1 11.0%	$53.0 13.5%	$17.7 13.0%	$67.9 10.5%	$21.6 9.5%	$239.3 10.0%	$38.9 10.0%	$219.8 11.1%	$4.3 6.3%	$68.0 36.5%
1984	(4.5) -3.1%	36.0 12.1%	10.6 10.3%	22.1 4.3%	12.8 7.4%	157.5 11.7%	34.9 10.0%	206.2 12.1%	(0.3) -0.7%	50.4 33.8%
1983	(10.6) -7.8%	31.2 13.1%	5.3 8.6%	41.7 8.7%	12.5 10.1%	134.9 12.4%	28.9 9.5%	178.2 13.5%	0.5 1.1%	41.0 37.0%
1982	2.0 1.6%	21.1 12.1%	3.2 7.3%	35.0 7.9%	6.2 8.6%	60.6 8.4%	22.9 8.6%	124.3 11.9%	2.8 8.0%	NA NA
1981	5.5 4.7%	18.3 12.7%	1.4 4.3%	22.8 5.5%	1.5 4.6%	38.5 10.6%	21.0 9.0%	94.1 12.0%	0.9 3.9%	NA NA
Compound Growth	38.6%	30.5%	88.6%	31.4%	94.8%	57.9%	16.7%	23.6%	47.8%	NA
Net Income and Margins										
1985	$(10.3) 5.6%	$28.7 7.3%	$9.2 6.8%	$34.4 5.3%	$11.3 5.0%	$145.3 6.1%	$21.1 5.4%	$119.8 6.1%	$2.4 3.5%	$30.0 16.1%
1984	(2.6) -1.8%	20.2 6.8%	5.3 5.1%	13.0 2.5%	6.7 3.9%	92.5 6.9%	18.3 5.1%	111.4 6.5%	0.2 0.5%	22.0 14.8%
1983	(5.1) -3.8%	17.3 7.3%	2.8 4.5%	21.6 4.5%	7.3 5.9%	70.9 6.5%	15.5 5.1%	92.3 7.0%	0.4 0.9%	18.2 16.4%
1982	1.0 0.8%	12.1 6.9%	1.7 3.9%	18.2 4.1%	3.4 4.7%	33.6 4.7%	12.1 4.6%	64.2 6.2%	1.5 4.3%	NA NA
1981	2.7 2.3%	10.9 7.6%	0.7 2.2%	11.8 2.8%	1.5 4.6%	22.4 6.1%	11.2 4.8%	48.9 6.2%	0.5 2.2%	NA NA
Compound Growth	39.6%	27.4%	90.4%	30.7%	65.7%	59.6%	17.2%	25.1%	48.0%	NA
Earnings Per Share										
Latest 12 Months	$1.01	$0.81	$1.01	$1.93	$1.46	$1.21	$1.55	$1.17	$0.45	$1.55 [a]
1985	1.01	0.59	0.83	1.01	1.13	0.80	1.29	0.93	0.62	1.15
1984	(0.41)	0.42	0.48	0.38	NA	0.51	1.17	0.87	0.05	0.82
1983	NA	0.37	0.26	0.63	NA	0.39	1.00	0.72	0.12	0.79
1982	NA	0.26	0.16	0.58	NA	0.19	0.81	0.52	0.48	NA
1981	NA	0.23	0.08	0.39	NA	0.13	0.75	0.42	0.17	NA
Compound Growth	NA	25.9%	79.5%	26.9%	NA	57.5%	14.5%	22.0%	38.2%	NA
Interim Operating Data:		12 mo. to 1/87	6 mo. to 1/87	12 mo. to 1/87	12 mo. to 1/87	12 mo. to 1/87	12 mo. to 1/87	12 mo. to 1/87	12 mo. to 1/87	12 mo. to 12/86
Sales 1986	NA	$521.2	$86.6	$848.0	$265.1	$3,142.7	$485.9	$2,444.9	$100.4	$274.7
1985	NA	391.6	66.4	647.3	227.2	2,387.1	388.9	1,976.1	68.3	186.2
% Change	NA	33.1%	30.5%	31.0%	16.7%	31.7%	24.9%	23.7%	47.0%	47.5%
Earnings Per Share										
1986	NA	$0.81	$0.60	$1.93	$1.46	$1.21	$1.55	$1.17	$0.45	$1.55 [a]
1985	NA	0.59	0.42	1.01	1.13	0.80	1.29	0.93	0.62	1.15
% Change	NA	37.3%	42.9%	91.1%	29.2%	51.2%	20.2%	25.8%	-27.4%	34.8%

[a] Company has reported an estimate of net income for the year. Actual figure not yet available.

Exhibit 5 (continued)

Comparative Capitalization Profile for Selected Specialty Retailers ($ millions, except per share data)

As of	Tiffany & Co. 1/31/87[a]	Charming Shoppes Inc. 11/1/86	The Dress Barn Inc. 1/24/87	The Gap, Inc. 11/4/86	Lands' End, Inc. 10/31/86	The Limited, Inc. 11/1/86	Pep Boys Manny-Moe-Jack 11/1/86	Toys 'R Us, Inc. 11/2/86	Williams-Sonoma Inc. 11/2/86	Louis Vuitton 12/31/85
NET ASSETS										
Cash and Short-Term Investments	$1.9	$26.9	$17.7	$35.4	$1.4	$14.0	$0.2	$30.7	$1.0	$22.0
Other Current Assets	82.3	107.6	16.4	172.4	50.1	546.9	68.4	920.1	33.1	87.2
Total Current Assets	$84.2	$134.4	$34.1	$207.8	$51.4	$560.8	$68.6	$950.8	$34.1	$109.3
Short-Term Debt	0.0	0.0	0.0	14.6	9.6	0.0	1.6	260.9	7.0	6.9
Other Current Liabilities	35.6	72.6	14.0	82.4	25.7	414.2	50.6	594.3	16.4	37.9
Net Working Capital	$48.6	$61.8	$20.1	$110.7	$16.1	$146.6	$16.4	$95.6	$10.6	$64.5
Net Plant, Property and Equipment	11.2	84.2	13.1	113.5	26.7	700.7	209.4	784.0	14.0	27.3
Other Tangible Assets	2.0	7.4	0.5	10.2	0.0	165.0	2.8	16.6	0.4	0.8
Net Tangible Assets	$61.8	$153.5	$33.7	$224.4	$42.8	$1,012.3	$228.7	$896.2	$25.0	$92.5
Intangibles	0.0	0.0	0.0	1.3	0.0	0.0	0.0	0.0	0.0	5.2
Net Assets	$61.8	$153.5	$33.7	$225.7	$42.8	$1,012.3	$228.7	$896.2	$25.0	$97.8
CAPITALIZATION										
Long-Term Debt	$8.6 / 13.9%	$1.4 / 0.9%	$0.0 / 0.0%	$13.5 / 6.0%	$10.6 / 24.9%	$214.7 / 21.2%	$22.5 / 9.8%	$83.2 / 9.3%	$7.3 / 29.3%	$3.4 / 3.5%
Other Liab., Def. Items & Min. Int.	0.0 / 0.0%	12.5 / 8.1%	0.7 / 2.2%	20.3 / 9.0%	2.7 / 6.4%	96.8 / 9.6%	8.5 / 3.7%	37.5 / 4.2%	0.0 / 0.0%	11.9 / 12.2%
Preferred Stock at Liquidating Value	0.0 / 0.0%	0.0 / 0.0%	0.0 / 0.0%	0.0 / 0.0%	0.0 / 0.0%	0.0 / 0.0%	0.0 / 0.0%	0.0 / 0.0%	0.0 / 0.0%	0.0 / 0.0%
Common Equity	53.2 / 86.1%	139.7 / 91.0%	33.0 / 97.8%	191.9 / 85.0%	29.4 / 68.8%	700.7 / 69.2%	197.7 / 86.4%	775.5 / 86.5%	17.7 / 70.7%	82.5 / 84.4%
Total Capitalization	$61.8 / 100.0%	$153.5 / 100.0%	$33.7 / 100.0%	$225.7 / 100.0%	$42.8 / 100.0%	$1,012.3 / 100.0%	$228.7 / 100.0%	$896.2 / 100.0%	$25.0 / 100.0%	$97.8 / 100.0%
Common Shares Outstanding (000)	8,298	50,044	11,086	35,455	10,020	188,649	18,037	124,464	3,937	24,900
Book Value Per Share	$6.41	$2.79	$2.95	$5.41	$2.94	$3.71	$10.96	$6.23	$4.49	$3.31
Tangible Book Value Per Share	$6.41	$2.79	$2.98	$5.38	$2.94	$3.71	$10.96	$6.23	$4.49	$3.10

[a] Pro forma assuming an initial public offering with a primary component of $40 million and paydown of long term debt.

Exhibit 6

Comparative Market Data for Selected Diversified Retail Companies ($ millions, except per share data)

	Carter Hawley Hale Stores	Dayton-Hudson Corp.	Federated Department Stores, Inc.	May Department Stores Co.
Ticker Symbol	CHH	DH	FDS	MA
Exchange Traded on	NYSE	NYSE	NYSE	NYSE
Price per Share				
Current (4/30/87)	$62.875	$43.125	$92.500	$44.750
YTD range	48.00 – 62.88	38.75 – 48.50	83.13 – 104.0	35.38 – 49.88
1985 range[a]	22.63 – 31.25	29.38 – 48.75	50.50 – 71.7	19.13 – 32.50
1984 range	18.25 – 32.25	26.13 – 37.25	42.63 – 55.7	15.25 – 21.63
1983 range	15.13 – 24.75	25.00 – 40.63	44.00 – 69.0	13.50 – 21.00
1982 range	10.50 – 17.25	13.19 – 32.13	33.13 – 54.2	7.75 – 16.50
Earnings per Share				
1988 estimated[b,c]	$3.17	$4.35	$8.62	NA
1987 estimated[b,d]	2.35	3.39	7.51	$2.97
Latest 12 months	0.87	2.65	6.44	2.44
1985	0.92	2.92	6.09	2.20
1984	0.83	2.68	5.76	NA
1983	1.56	2.54	6.26	NA
1982	1.27	2.15	4.67	NA
Ratio of Current Price to:				
1988 estimated EPS	19.8x	9.9x	10.7x	NAx
1987 estimated EPS	26.8x	12.7x	12.3x	15.1x
Latest 12 months' EPS	72.3x	16.3x	14.4x	18.3x
Book value per share	3.4x	2.1x	1.7x	2.8x
Price-Earnings Ratio				
1985	24.6 – 34.0	10.1 – 16.7	8.3 – 11.8	8.7 – 14.8
1984	22.0 – 38.9	9.7 – 13.9	7.4 – 9.7	NA – NA
1983	9.7 – 15.9	9.8 – 16.0	7.0 – 11.0	NA – NA
1982	8.3 – 13.6	6.1 – 14.9	7.1 – 11.6	NA – NA
Dividend Data				
Current indicated annual	$1.22	$0.92	$2.96	$1.14
Current yield	1.94%	2.13%	3.20%	2.55%
Book value per share	$18.63	$20.51	$55.72	$16.06
Shares outstanding (thousands)	19,923	97,340	48,853	153,566
Aggregate market value (millions)	$1,252.7	$4,197.8	$4,518.9	$6,872.1

[a] Latest fiscal year.

[b] Estimates based on Institutional Broker Estimates System (IBES) projections dated March 19, 1987.

[c] Next fiscal year.

[d] Current fiscal year.

Exhibit 6 continued on page 309.

Exhibit 6 (continued)

Comparative Operating Data for Selected Diversified Retail Companies ($ millions, except per share data)

Most Recent Fiscal Year Ending	Tiffany & Co. 1/31/87	Carter Hawley Hale Stores 2/1/86	Dayton-Hudson Corp 2/1/86	Federated Department Stores, Inc. 2/1/86	May Department Stores Co. 2/1/86
Net Sales					
Latest 12 months	$182.5	$4,089.8	$9,797.1	$10,512.4	$10,328.0
1985	182.5	3,977.9	8,793.3	9,978.0	9,490.0
1984	141.8	3,724.3	8,009.0	9,672.3	8,769.5
1983	135.3	3,101.7	6,963.3	8,689.6	7,811.3
1982	124.4	2,590.6	5,660.7	7,698.9	6,734.3
1981	115.8	2,485.7	4,942.9	7,067.6	6,046.3
Compound Growth	12.0%	12.5%	15.5%	9.0%	11.9%
Gross Profit and Margins					
1985	$ 86.4	$1,127.3	$2,515.0	$2,663.3	$2,535.6
	47.3%	28.3%	28.6%	26.7%	26.7%
1984	66.3	1,022.2	2,299.5	2,574.6	2,371.1
	46.7	27.4	28.7	26.6	27.0
1983	57.1	861.3	2,038.4	2,420.7	2,129.5
	42.2	27.8	29.3	27.9	27.3
1982	52.6	739.0	1,702.8	2,080.4	1,804.7
	42.2	28.5	30.1	27.0	26.8
1981	47.0	729.9	1,460.9	1,955.5	1,633.2
	40.6	29.4	29.6	27.7	27.0
Compound Growth	16.4%	11.5%	14.5%	8.0%	11.6%
Operating Income and Margins					
1985	$ 21.9	$ 203.8	$ 632.3	$ 655.2	$ 765.3
	12.0%	5.1%	7.2%	6.6%	8.1%
1984	7.6	160.0	585.1	647.1	722.4
	5.4	4.3	7.3	6.7	8.2
1983	(3.5)	154.9	544.5	688.2	665.7
	(2.6)	5.0	7.8	7.9	8.5
1982	5.6	139.6	457.5	518.5	519.2
	4.5	5.4	8.1	6.7	7.7
1981	7.2	136.5	342.6	540.0	460.3
	6.2	5.5	6.9	7.6	7.6
Compound Growth	32.1%	10.5%	16.6%	5.0%	13.6%
Pretax Income and Margins					
1985	$ 20.1	$ 70.1	$ 524.6	$ 533.7	$ 657.5
	11.0%	1.8%	6.0%	5.3%	6.9%
1984	(4.5)	35.6	479.3	573.4	625.2
	(3.2)	1.0	6.0	5.9	7.1
1983	(10.6)	79.6	450.7	601.0	561.8
	(7.8)	2.6	6.5	6.9	7.2
1982	2.0	52.2	384.8	421.7	407.5
	1.6	2.0	6.8	5.5	6.1
1981	5.5	55.7	287.5	473.0	363.6
	4.7	2.2	5.8	6.7	6.0
Compound Growth	38.3%	5.9%	16.2%	3.1%	16.0%

Exhibit 6 continued on page 310.

Exhibit 6 (continued)

Most Recent Fiscal Year Ending	Tiffany & Co. 1/31/87		Carter Hawley Hale Stores 2/1/86		Dayton-Hudson Corp. 2/1/86		Federated Department Stores, Inc. 2/1/86		May Department Stores Co. 2/1/86	
Net Income and Margins										
1985	$10.3	5.6%	$48.0	1.2%	$283.6	3.2%	$303.9	3.0%	$347.0	3.7%
1984	(2.6)	−1.8	27.1	0.7	259.3	3.2	286.7	3.0	334.8	3.8
1983	(5.1)	−3.8	55.4	1.8	245.5	3.5	311.7	3.6	302.5	3.9
1982	1.0	0.8	40.5	1.6	206.7	3.7	232.8	3.0	220.1	3.3
1981	2.7	2.3	39.3	1.6	159.5	3.2	258.3	3.7	196.0	3.2
Compound growth		39.6%		5.1%		15.5%		4.1%		15.4%
Earnings per Share										
Latest 12 months	$1.01		$0.87		$2.65		$6.44		$2.44	
1985	1.01		0.92		2.92		6.09a		2.20	
1984	(0.41)		0.83		2.68		5.76b		NAd	
1983	(0.65)		1.56		2.54		6.26c		NAd	
1982	NA		1.27		2.15		4.67		NAd	
1981	NA		1.33		1.67		5.17		NAd	
Compound growth		NA		−8.8%		15.0%		4.2%		NA
Interim Operating Data	NA		12 Mo. to 1/87		12Mo. to 1/87		12 Mo. to 1/87		12 Mo. to 1/87	
Sales										
1986	NA		$4,089.8		$9,259.1		$10,512.4		$10,328.0	
1985	NA		3,977.9		8,255.3		9,978.0		9,490.0	
% change	NA		2.8%		12.2%		5.4%		8.8%	
Earnings per Share										
1986	NA		$0.87		$2.62		$6.23		$2.44	
1985	NA		0.92		2.89		5.88		2.20	
% change	NA		−5.4%		−9.3%		6.0%		10.9%	

[a] Excludes gain of $13.1 million from sale of Boston store division and reorganization expense of $48.2 million, or $0.34 per share.

[b] Excludes gain on sale of shopping centers of $42.6 million or $0.85 per share net of taxes.

[c] Excludes gain on sale of shopping centers of $40.1 million, loss for liquidation of Bullock's Northern California division of $12.0 million, and capital contribution of $15.0 million, or $0.85 per share.

[d] Earnings per share figures on a consolidated basis to reflect pooling of interest with Associated Dry Goods not yet available.

Exhibit 6 continued on page 311.

Exhibit 6 (continued)

As of	Tiffany & Co. 1/31/87[a]		Carter Hawley Hale Stores 11/1/86		Dayton-Hudson Corp 11/1/86		Federated Department Stores, Inc. 11/1/86		May Department Stores Co. 11/1/86	
Net Assets										
Cash and short-term investments	$ 1.9		$ 22.5		$ 120.8		$ 99.2		$ 239.0	
Other current assets	82.3		1,410.0		2,799.5		3,381.4		3,432.9	
Total current assets	$84.2		$1,432.6		$2,920.3		$3,480.6		$3,671.9	
Short-term debt	0.0		185.1		287.6		472.6		464.9	
Other current liabilities	35.6		783.6		1,682.6		1,791.5		1,811.5	
Net working capital	$48.6		$ 463.8		$ 950.1		$1,216.6		$1,395.5	
Net plant, property and equipment	11.2		872.4		2,168.3		2,427.0		2,511.8	
Other tangible assets	2.0		182.3		189.3		74.6		331.6	
Net tangible assets	$61.8		$1,518.4		$3,307.7		$3,718.2		$4,238.9	
Intangibles	0.0		0.0		0.0		0.0		0.0	
Net assets	$61.8		$1,518.4		$3,307.7		$3,718.2		$4,238.9	
Capitalization										
Long-term debt	$8.6	13.9%	$ 679.3	44.7%	$1,159.4	35.1%	$ 597.8	16.1%	$1,122.8	26.5%
Other liabilities, deferred items, and min. int.	0.0	0.0	167.9	11.1	152.1	4.6	398.3	10.7	547.5	12.9
Preferred stock at liquidating value	0.0	0.0	300.0	19.8	0.0	0.0	0.0	0.0	102.8	2.4
Common equity	53.2	86.1	371.2	24.5	1,996.2	60.4	2,722.0	73.2	2,465.8	58.2
Total Capitalization	$61.8	100.0%	$1,518.4	100.0%	$3,307.7	100.0%	$3,718.2	100.0%	$4,238.9	100.0%
Common shares outstanding (000)	8,297		19,923		97,430		48,853		153,566	
Book value per share	$6.41		$18.63		$20.51		$55.72		$16.06	
Tangible book value per share	$6.41		$18.63		$20.51		$55.72		$16.06	

[a]Pro forma capitalization assuming an initial public offering with a $40 million primary component.

Exhibit 7

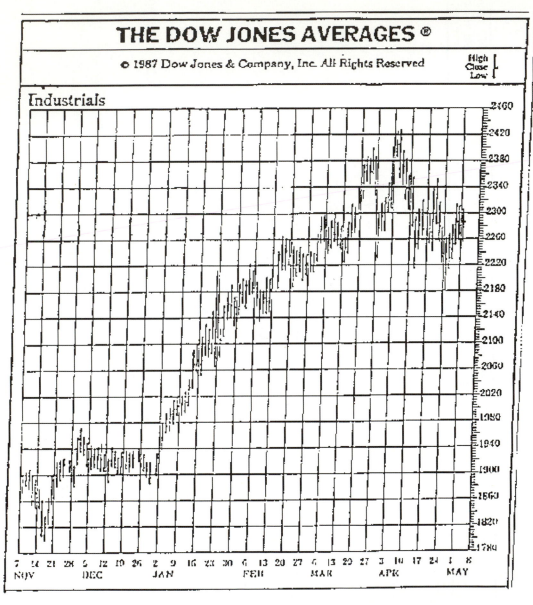

Source: *Wall Street Journal*, May 1, 1987.

Exhibit 8

Initial Public Offerings of Common Stock by Industrial Issuers—Offering Size $70–$130 Million (1/1/84 to present)

Date	Issuer	Amount ($ million)	Price per Share	Total Shares Offered (000)	Primary Shares as a % Offered	Secondary Shares as a % Offered	Gross Spread as a % Price	Syndicated	Managers
8/10/84	MTV Networks	$ 76.9	$15.00	5,125,000	100.0%	—	7.00	Yes	SLAE/SAL/DBL
8/14/84	Entex Energy Development	90.0	20.00	4,500,000	100.0	—	7.50	Yes	MLCM
3/22/85	Herman's Sporting Goods	75.9	16.50	4,600,000	28.3	71.7	6.06	Yes	MLCM/BEAR
4/19/85	Freeport-McMoran Energy	121.0	22.00	5,500,000	—	100.0	7.27	Yes	LAZ/DWR(BOOKS)/FBC/EFH
5/09/85	Highland Superstores	103.6	18.50	5,600,000	48.7	51.3	5.50	Yes	GS/EFH
8/15/85	Alco Health Services	75.2	16.00	4,700,000	100.0	—	6.00	Yes	KP/DBL
8/29/85	Diamond Shamrock Offshore	102.5	20.50	5,000,000	100.0	—	7.32	Yes	GS/SLB/KP
10/08/85	Vestron	70.2	13.00	5,400,000	100.0	—	5.77	Yes	MLCM/SBH
11/12/85	Rayonier Timberlands L P	88.0	20.00	4,400,000	—	100.0	7.00	Yes	LAZ/EFH
1/14/86	Santa Fe Energy Partners	100.0	20.00	5,000,000	100.0	—	7.50	Yes	KSA/EFH/DWR
1/17/86	Cablevision Systems	90.6	14.50	6,250,000	100.0	—	6.55	Yes	DBL/DWR
2/20/86	Burger King Investors Master	81.4	20.00	4,070,000	100.0	—	6.90	Yes	MLCM/SBH/BOET/BRAD/DA
5/19/86	Genetics Institute	74.4	29.75	2,500,000	100.0	—	6.75	Yes	MS/ROBERTSON
5/21/86	Prospect Group	73.1	9.75	7,500,000	100.0	—	7.18	Yes	SLB
6/10/86	Pannill Knitting	126.0	21.00	6,000,000	—	100.0	6.19	Yes	MLCM/BEAR
6/20/86	Worlds of Wonder	108.0	18.00	6,000,000	66.7	33.3	6.28	Yes	SBH/DWR
7/09/86	Bernard Chaus	76.5	17.00	4,500,000	25.0	75.0	6.18	Yes	MLCM/BEAR
8/01/86	Aaron Spelling Productions	77.0	14.00	5,500,000	18.0	81.8	6.79	Yes	DBL/BEAR
8/01/86	Leslie Fay Companies	72.0	18.00	4,000,000	100.0	—	5.50	Yes	MLCM/BEAR
8/21/86	Watts Industries	74.3	16.50	4,500,000	22.2	77.8	5.45	Yes	SLB/DLJ
10/15/86	La Quinta Motor Inns L P	79.5	20.00	3,975,000	100.0	—	7.00	No	MLCM/DLJ/SBH
10/23/86	Fred Meyer	96.2	14.25	6,750,000	66.7	33.3	5.96	Yes	GS/SLB
10/31/86	Motel 6 L P	81.0	13.50	6,000,000	100.0	—	7.00	Yes	DBL/SLB
12/11/86	Vista Chemical	75.6	17.00	4,448,000	90.7	9.3	6.06	Yes	EFH
12/17/86	Georgia Gulf	78.0	19.50	4,000,000	17.5	82.5	6.51	Yes	GS
12/17/86	Prime Motor Inns L P	70.0	20.00	3,500,000	100.0	—	7.00	Yes	SBH/EFH/SAL/DWR/MONT
12/19/86	Winchell's Donut Houses L P	90.0	18.00	5,000,000	—	100.0	7.00	Yes	MLCM/DWR
12/23/86	Falcon Cable Systems L P	80.0	20.00	4,000,000	100.0	—	8.00	Yes	MS/Paine-W/DWR/BEAR
2/05/87	Sun Distributors L P	96.9	5.00	19,380,000	—	100.0	7.50	Yes	SLB/DWR
3/27/87	Allstar Inns L P	72.9	12.50	5,832,137	100.0	—	7.04	Yes	DBL/DWR/BATEMAN
4/07/87	Maritrans Partners L P	119.4	9.75	12,250,000	100.0	—	6.97	Yes	GS/DWR/WHEAT
4/07/87	Red Lion Inns L P	98.8	20.00	4,940,000	100.0	—	7.00	Yes	MLCM/SBH

Average Gross Spread: All deals   6.68%

Non-limited Partnership Deals   6.18%

Source: Shearson Lehman.

John Case Company

||||||

In March 1985, Anthony W. Johnson was working on a proposal to purchase his employer, the John Case Company. The Case company, with corporate headquarters in Dover, Delaware, was a leading manufacturer of commercial desk calendars. Mr. Johnson, vice president of finance and administration, considered the company an excellent acquisition opportunity, provided he should conclude that the owner's asking price was acceptable, and provided he could arrange satisfactory financing for the transaction.

Background

A few weeks earlier John M. Case, board chairman, president and sole owner of John Case Company, had informed his senior management group that he intended to retire from business and was about to initiate a campaign to sell the company. For several years his physician had been urging him to avoid all stress and strain; now Mr. Case had decided to sever his business connections and devote his time to travel and a developing interest in art history and collection.

On the basis of previous offers for the company, Mr. Case had decided to ask for $20 million, with a minimum of $16 million immediately payable in cash. He thought acquisitive corporations should find this price attractive, and he believed it would be easy to dispose of the business.

Mr. Case had assured the management group that their jobs and benefits would be well protected by the terms of any sale contract that he might negotiate. Despite his faith in Mr. Case's good intentions, Mr. Johnson had been quite apprehensive about the prospect of having his career placed in the hands of an unknown outsider. However, after some reflection, Mr. Johnson had concluded that the sale decision should be viewed as an opportunity to acquire control of a highly profitable enterprise. Purchase of John Case Company would not only assure career continuity but also provide a chance to turn a profit in the company's equity. Mr. Johnson had realized that his personal financial resources were far too limited to allow him to bid alone for control of Case. Consequently, he had persuaded August Haffenreffer, vice president of marketing, William Wright, vice president of manu-

This case was prepared by Professor Samuel L. Hayes, III.

facturing, and Richard Bennink, the controller, to join him in trying to buy the corporation, rather than standing by while control passed to an outsider. In response to Mr. Johnson's request, Mr. Case had agreed to defer all steps to merchandise the company until he had accepted or rejected a purchase proposal from the management group, provided this proposal was submitted within six weeks.

Because of his background in finance and his role in initiating the project, Mr. Johnson had assumed primary responsibility for assessing the profit potential of the opportunity and for structuring a workable financial plan for the acquisition. Since Mr. Case had not yet solicited bids from other potential purchasers, Mr. Johnson believed that it would be most realistic to regard Mr. Case's stated sale terms as fixed and nonnegotiable.

Mr. Johnson, then, needed to determine whether he could meet the asking price and still realize a profit commensurate with the risk in this purchase. Moreover, he needed to figure out how the management group, with roughly a half a million dollars between them, could finance the purchase and at the same time obtain voting control of the corporation.

Thus far, Mr. Johnson had managed to obtain a tentative commitment for a $6 million unsecured bank term loan, and he had persuaded Mr. Case to accept unsecured notes for the noncash portion of the purchase price. He was still faced with the problem of raising close to $10 million on an equity base of $500,000 without giving up control to outsiders.

Mr. Johnson now had three weeks in which to come up with a workable financial plan or lose the deal. He was acutely aware that the life savings of his associates and himself would ride on his judgment and ingenuity.

The Company

The John Case Company was the leading producer of business calendars in the United States. The company was established in 1920 by Uriah Case (Mr. Case's paternal grandfather) to do contract printing of commercial calendars. Mr. Case had joined the organization in 1946 upon graduation from college, and in 1951 he had inherited the company.

Under Mr. Case's leadership, primary emphasis was placed on controlled expansion in the established line of business. By 1984 Case, with an estimated 60–65% share of its market, had been for over a decade the largest company in a small but lucrative industry. Operations had been profitable in every year since 1932, and sales had increased in every year since 1955. In 1984, the most recently completed fiscal year, earnings had amounted to $1,966,000 on sales of approximately $15.3 million. The return on average invested capital in 1984 was around 20%. Over the past five years, sales had increased at a 7% compound rate, while earnings, benefiting from substantial cost reductions, had more than doubled. Exhibits 1 through 3 present recent financial figures for the company.

Products

As noted above, Case's principal products were commercial desk calendars. The company designed and manufactured disposable-page and flipover-page desk calendar pads in a variety of sizes. The company also sold desk calendar bases, which were purchased from outside suppliers who manufactured to Case's specifications. In 1984, standard desk calendar pads had contributed approximately 80% of net sales and 90% of earnings before taxes. Bases accounted for 10% of sales, and miscellaneous merchandise, chiefly wall calendars, accounted for the rest.

Sales were highly seasonal. Most final consumers did not start using calendars for the forthcoming year until November or December of the current year. In consequence, about 90% of Case's total shipments typically took place between June and December, with about 60% of shipments concentrated in the third quarter and 25% in the fourth quarter. Since calendar pads were dated, any merchandise remaining in stock at the end of the selling season was subject to rapid obsolescence.

Manufacturing

The production process was relatively simple, employing widely available skills and technology. High-speed offset presses were used to print appropriate dates on paper purchased in bulk from outside suppliers; the printed sheets were then trimmed to the required sizes and stored for shipment. The entire process was highly automated and was characterized by high fixed costs, high set-up costs, and low variable costs.

In spite of highly seasonal sales, Case operated on level production schedules. Since the product lines were for all practical purposes undifferentiated from competing lines and the relevant production technology was well known, the capacity to sell on the basis of price, while achieving a good return on invested capital, was regarded by management as a critical success factor in the industry. Minimum production costs were therefore imperative.

Level production enabled the company to take advantage of extremely long production runs and thus to minimize down time, the investment in equipment, expensive setups, and the use of transient labor. Level production in conjunction with the company's dominant market share provided scale economies well beyond the reach of any competitor.

The combination of seasonal sales and level production resulted in the accumulation of large seasonal stocks. However, by concentrating the sales effort in the middle six months of the year, Case was able to circumvent most of the risk usually connected with level production in a seasonal company in return for modest purchase discounts. Since customers could easily predict their needs for Case products as their budgets for the forthcoming year took shape, they were willing to place their orders well in advance of shipment. As a result, Case could manufacture against a firm backlog in the last few months of the year and thus circumvent the risk of overproducing and ending the year with large stocks of outdated finished goods.

Case maintained production facilities in nearby Wilmington, Delaware and, through a wholly owned subsidiary, in Puerto Rico. Earnings of the Puerto Rican subsidiary, which sold all its output to the U.S. parent, were entirely exempt from U.S. taxes and until 1992 would be exempt from all Puerto Rican taxes. The tax exemption on Puerto Rican production accounted for Case's unusually low income tax rate. All Case plants and equipment were modern and excellently maintained. A major capital expenditures program, completed in 1983, had resulted in Case having the most up-to-date facilities in the industry. At the predicted rate of future sales growth, Mr. Wright, the chief production officer, did not anticipate any need for substantial capital expenditures for at least five or six years. None of the company's work force was represented by labor unions.

Marketing

As its products were nondifferentiable, Case's marketing program concentrated on providing high-quality customer service and a uniformly high-quality product. Case products were sold nationwide. Geographically, the company was strongest in the Northeast, the Southwest, and the far West. Large accounts were handled by the company's five-man sales force, and smaller accounts were serviced by office supply wholesalers. Roughly 10% of sales had historically gone to the federal government.

Even though the product was undifferentiated, Mr. Haffenreffer, the marketing vice president, believed that it did have some significant advantages from a marketing viewpoint. Selling costs were extremely low, as consumption of the product over the course of a year automatically generated a large replacement demand without any effort on the part of Case. About 95% of total sales generally consisted of reorders from the existing customer base, with only 5% of sales going to new customers. Historically over 98% of the customer base annually reordered Case pads and, as needed, additional Case bases. By dealing with only one source of supply, the customer was able to take maximum advantage of discounts for volume purchases. As the product was virtually immune to malfunction and the resultant customer dissatisfaction, once Case bases had been installed the typical buyer never received any incentive to spend time and money on a search for alternative sources. Consumption of Case products was, in addition, extremely insensitive to budget cuts, economy drives, consumer whims, and the like. The desk calendar was a small-ticket but high-priority item. It was an essential in the work routines of most of its end users, and it was not expensive enough to yield a meaningful reward in savings to would-be budget cutters. As a dated product, the desk calendar, unlike many other office products, represented a nondeferrable purchase.

Finances

The dominant influence on Case company's financial policy was Mr. Case's still-vivid perspective of the Great Depression as imparted by his father and grandfather. Mr. Case steadfastly refused to consider levering his equity in the company. Accordingly, Case operated with an all-equity capitalization. The size of the capital budget was determined by the volume of internally generated funds in conjunction with Mr. Case's decision on how much to withdraw in the form of dividends. Dividend payments had sometimes been sharply contracted to accommodate capital investment opportunities. Over the past three years, however, internally generated funds had been plentiful, and dividends had averaged 70% of net earnings.

Like the capital budget, the seasonal accumulation of inventories and receivables was financed from internal sources. To minimize warehousing expenses for finished goods, Case provided generous credit terms to customers who accepted early shipments. Payments for June through October shipments were not due until the end of November, although substantial discounts were offered for earlier payment. The collection period averaged 60 days. Credit experience was excellent, and generous credit terms were considered a key factor in the company's competitive success.

Although the company had not resorted to seasonal borrowing in close to 10 years, it maintained for emergency purposes two $2 million lines of credit at major Eastern banks. Exhibit 4 shows 1984 working capital balances by month.

Case's credit record with suppliers was excellent. All trade obligations were promptly paid when due.

Management

The senior management team consisted of Mr. Case plus the four individuals interested in buying the corporation. Transfer of ownership to the latter would not occasion much change in the *de facto* management of the organization. Although Mr. Case continued to exercise the final authority on all major issues of policy and strategy, over the past few years he had gradually withdrawn from day-to-day affairs and now spent much of his time in Europe and Puerto Rico. As Mr. Case had relaxed his grip on Case Company's affairs, he had increasingly delegated the general management of the firm to Mr. Johnson.

Compensation was generous at the senior executive level. Mr. Case drew an annual salary of $400,000, his four key subordinates received an average salary of $90,000. In addition, the four senior executives received annual bonuses which aggregated 10% of earnings before taxes and bonuses.

Apart from Mr. Johnson, the members of the purchasing group were all in their late 30s and early 40s and between them represented more than 50 years' experience in the business. After being graduated from a leading graduate school of business administration, Mr. Johnson, age 40, had worked for five years in the venture capital department of a large eastern city bank and for two years in his own management consulting firm before joining the Case Company.

Company Prospects

The overall prospect was for continued growth at a steady, though unspectacular, pace. The rate of Case sales growth, management believed, was closely correlated with the rate of growth in the size of the domestic white collar work force. Given expectations of a continuing shift of labor out of agricultural and blue collar occupations and into white collar positions, this suggested that the company should grow somewhat faster than the economy as a whole. Assuming no material changes in product lines or market share, management thought sales growth would average about 5–6% per annum in the foreseeable future. Profit margins were expected to improve somewhat over the next few years, as volume expanded and an increasing proportion of new production was directed to the tax-exempt Puerto Rican facility.

Competition

Although the commercial desk calendar industry was profitable indeed for its leading participant, it was not, in the opinion of Case management, an attractive area for potential new competitors. At present, the industry was divided between Case with roughly a 60–65% share of market and Watts Corporation, a privately held company, with an estimated 20–25% share. Watts' strength was concentrated in the Midwest and Southeast. The remainder of industry sales was fragmented among a host of small, financially weak printing shops. Case management found it difficult to imagine how a potential competitor could arrive at an economically justifiable decision to enter their market. Price was the only conceivable basis on which a new entrant could compete, but, lacking the scale economies available to Case, a new entrant would necessarily be a high-cost competitor. Mr. Haffenreffer estimated that it would take a new entrant at least 3–5 years to reach break-even, assuming no retaliatory price cuts by Case. Furthermore, entering this market would necessitate a minimum capital investment of $2–$4 million plus the working capital needed to support seasonal sales. On balance, it seemed unlikely that a potential competitor would brave these obstacles in the hope of grabbing a share of a $25–$30 million industry with mediocre growth prospects.

Mr. Case judged that Case Company's financial strength, relative cost advantages, and entrenched distribution system had served to deter Watts from trying

▾ ■

to invade any of Case's prime market areas. Likewise, he thought Case could not take away a substantial market share from Watts without risking a price war that might seriously impair margins for a protracted period.

Unexploited Opportunities

The business plan finally approved by Mr. Case had not incorporated a diversification scheme vigorously advanced by the other members of senior management. The vice presidents had contended that Case could significantly boost both the rate of growth and level of earnings by using its cash flow and its production and distribution strengths to expand into related product lines. The proposal had called for expansion into other dated products, such as appointment books, planning books, and the like, imprinted with the name, logo, or other message of the customer, and into desk calendars similarly imprinted. Mr. Johnson had estimated that this project would require an initial capital investment of $200,000 and special product development and merchandising expenses of $900,000 spread over the first two years of the undertaking. It had been estimated that the new line should yield sales of approximately $1 million in the first full year of operation with a growth rate of about 40% per annum in years 2 through 4, as the line achieved nationwide distribution and recognition. A 12–15% growth rate was anticipated in subsequent years. It was thought that this type of product line would have a profit margin before taxes of about 6%. The management group believed that the proposed line could serve as a profitable first step toward developing a full line of desk top products for commercial, industrial, and government markets.

Mr. Case had rejected the proposal on several grounds. He had observed that the proposal advocated entering a riskier line of business in which none of the management group had experience. In the proposed line of business the customer could choose among a variety of competing designs, and manufacturers had to actively generate repeat sales. He had also pointed out that the project would require a substantial investment in working capital for seasonal sales, if the new line grew as predicted. Finally, he had stated that he was quite content with his present income and, at his age, unwilling to reinvest earnings in the hope of achieving a strong position in a more competitive and less profitable business than the present one.

With Mr. Case out of the picture, the management group would have the freedom to pursue its growth program. Mr. Johnson believed that over a period of years Case's growth rate could be improved significantly if earnings were reinvested in related businesses rather than disbursed as dividends. The higher growth rate would be translated into profits for management if, for instance, the faster growth allowed them to take the company public at a relatively high price-earnings ratio.

The Purchase Proposal

Mr. Johnson recognized that a successful proposal would have to blend and reconcile the interests and goals of all parties to the transaction: the seller, the buyers, and external suppliers of finance.

The management group had determined that between them they could raise at most about $500,000 for investment in Case. Raising this amount would necessitate drawing down savings accounts, refinancing home mortgages, and liquidating positions in the stock market. Mr. Johnson was prepared to commit $160,000, Mr. Haffenreffer $140,000, and Messrs. Wright and Bennink $100,000 apiece. It had been tentatively agreed that all members of the management group would buy stock at the same price. It had also been tentatively concluded that the group would not accept a proposal that left them with less than 51% of the shares. With less than 51% of the stock the management group might not achieve the autonomy to establish corporate policy or to dispose of the company where and as they chose.

Valuation

As pointed out above, Mr. Johnson believed that Mr. Case's asking terms of $20 million with a minimum of $16 million in cash would remain fixed, at least until the company had been shown to a number of prospective buyers. In the past year, Mr. Case had held discussions with two companies that had made unsolicited bids to purchase Case. The first offer, $15 million in cash, had come from a medium-sized firm with a diversified line of office products. It had been rejected by Mr. Case on the basis of price. The second offer had come from a highly diversified medium-sized company sporting a price-earnings ratio of more than 20x and seeking to establish a position in office products through a series of acquisitions. The final offer had come to $32 million in letter stock[1] of the acquirer. Mr. Case had found this bid extremely tempting, but had been unwilling to tie up his wealth in unmarketable shares of a company with which he was not intimately familiar. The acquirer, lacking excess debt capacity and unwilling to float new stock to raise cash, had backed out of the discussions.

Mr. Johnson had, in addition, assembled financial figures on the publicly traded companies he thought most comparable to Case company. These data are presented in Exhibit 5.

Financing

In terms of the mechanics of the transaction, Mr. Johnson planned to effect the purchase through a new corporation in which the management group would buy 500,000 common shares at $1.00 a share. Given the management group's $500,000 compared to the $20 million asking price, the biggest problem facing Mr. Johnson was how to fund the new company at all, not to mention the objective of keeping control in the management group. Mr. Johnson had managed to obtain tentative commitments for $10.5 million, including the management group's $500,000. Prior to submitting a purchase proposal to Mr. Case, however, he would have to line up commitments for the entire $20 million funds needed.

It was clear that the noncash component of the purchase price would have to be met by issuing notes with a market value of $4 million to Mr. Case. In order to maintain the maximum amount of flexibility and borrowing capacity for raising financing from outsiders, Mr. Johnson had proposed that Mr. Case take 4%, junior subordinated, nonamortizing notes. After some negotiation, Mr. Case had expressed his willingness to accept a $6 million nonamortizing, 4% five-year note which would be junior to all other debt obligations of the newly formed corporation. The members of the management group as well as the corporate acquirer would have to endorse the note. It was agreed that covenants on the note would include: (1) no additional debt or leases except debt incurred in the acquisition of the Case Company, short-term seasonal borrowings, or debt incurred to retire the five-year note; (2) no dividends and maintenance of at least $3.0 million in working capital; (3) no changes in management or increases in management compensation; (4) no sale of Case shares by Messrs. Johnson, Haffenreffer, Wright, or Bennink so long as the five-year note was outstanding. If the borrower should default on any terms of this note or of any other indebtedness, the junior subordinated

▾ ■

notes would become immediately due and payable. If not promptly paid, ownership of the shares held by the management group would revert to Mr. Case. The note could be retired before maturity in whole or in part in accord with the following schedule of discounts:

Year	Percent of Face Value
1	58%
2	71
3	81
4	96
5	100

In his efforts to line up financing from outside sources, Mr. Johnson had succeeded in obtaining a tentative commitment for a $6 million term loan from a large Philadelphia bank known for its aggressive lending policies. This loan would be amortized over a maximum period of six years through annual installments. The rate would be two points above floating prime, and the borrower would have to maintain average compensating balances of 10% of the outstanding principal amount of the loan. The amount of $6 million was the maximum the bank would commit for on a term basis. Lending officers of the bank had emphasized that any additional term indebtedness incurred in the acquisition of Case would have to be effectively subordinated to this loan. Exhibit 6 presents an abstract of the provisions that the bank term loan would bear. Exhibit 7 presents Mr. Johnson's forecast of Case's cash flows over the next six years.

Having negotiated the bank commitment, Mr. Johnson was still left with the problem of raising an additional $9.5 million. He thought that he would have to turn to venture capital sources to raise the rest of the funds needed. Based on his experience in venture finance, Mr. Johnson knew that a venture capitalist would be targeting a return of about 20–25% on his/her funds. He also knew that most venture capitalists preferred to place their funds in the form of debt securities rather than common stock. The venture capitalist could generally exercise more effective control over his/her investment through the covenants on a debt obligation than through the voting power on stock. Principal repayment on debt also provided a mechanism for a tax-free recovery of capital; this might not be possible with stock until the company had gone public. Mr. Johnson expected to have to pay an 8–9% coupon rate on any debt funds obtained from a venture capital source. The venture capitalist would probably attempt to realize the rest of his/her return by taking warrants to buy shares in the new corporation at $1.00, the same price initially paid by the management group. The venture capitalist would probably insist on having the option of exercising the warrants in either cash or Case debentures.

▶ **Endnote**

1. Letter stock is unregistered stock. Such stock may not be sold to the public without registration under the Securities Act of 1933, a costly and time-consuming process. Because letter stock is restricted in its transferability, it represents a relatively illiquid investment and generally sells at a discount below the price that registered stock would command in the public securities markets. When letter stock is issued in an acquisition, the acquiring company issuing the stock generally specifies that the stock cannot be registered for a certain period of time.

Exhibit 1

Consolidated Income Statements ($ thousands)

	1980	1981	1982	1983	1984
Net sales	$9,740	$10,044	$11,948	$13,970	$15,260
Cost of sales	5,836	5,648	6,994	8,304	9,298
Gross profit on sales	$3,904	$ 4,396	$ 4,954	$ 5,666	$ 5,962
Selling and administrative expenses	2,216	2,072	2,470	3,022	3,274
Other income and (expense)=net	40	108	70	128	120
Profit before income taxes	$1,728	$ 2,432	$ 2,554	$ 2,772	$ 2,808
Federal income taxes	816	972	920	942	842
Net profit	$ 912	$ 1,460	$ 1,634	$ 1,830	$ 1,966

Exhibit 2

Consolidated Balance Sheet as of December 31, 1984 ($ thousands)

Assets		Liabilities and Shareholders' Equity	
Current assets		Current liabilities	
Cash and marketable securities	$ 5,762	Accounts payable	$ 654
Accounts receivable	2,540	Accrued expenses	366
Inventories at lower of cost or market	588	Accrued income taxes	246
Prepaid expenses	108		
Total current assets	$ 8,998	Total current liabilities	$ 1,266
Property, plant, and equipment=net	2,110	Shareholders' equity	
Miscellaneous assets	74	Common stock ($1.00 par value)	200
		Retained profits	9,716
		Total liabilities and	
Total assets	$11,182	shareholders' equity	$11,182

Exhibit 3

Ten-Year Summary of Operations ($ thousands, except per share data)

	1975	1976	1977	1978	1979	1980	1981	1982	1983	1984
Net sales	$7,688	$8,356	$8,526	$8,790	$9,350	$9,740	$10,044	$11,948	$13,970	$15,260
Net profit	638	668	742	748	758	912	1,460	1,634	1,830	1,966
Dividends	600	200	280	280	440	440	480	1,220	1,374	1,480
Earnings per share	3.19	3.34	3.71	3.74	3.79	4.56	7.30	8.17	9.15	9.83
Net profit margin	8.3%	8.0%	8.7%	8.5%	8.1%	9.4%	14.5%	13.7%	13.1%	12.9%

Exhibit 4

Monthly Working Capital Balances—1984 ($ thousands)

	Jan	Feb	Mar	Apr	May	Jun	Jul	Aug	Sep	Oct	Nov	Dec
Cash	$5,536	$5,714	$5,396	$4,784	$4,328	$4,098	$2,354	$766	$2,050	$3,830	$5,734	$5,762
Accounts receivable	1,480	760	734	804	718	604	3,432	6,104	6,164	4,322	2,398	2,540
Inventories	1,124	1,666	2,210	2,752	3,294	3,838	2,754	1,670	526	588	608	588
Current liabilities	(1,186)	(1,220)	(1,242)	(1,146)	(1,422)	(1,344)	(1,072)	(1,216)	(1,174)	(1,384)	(1,340)	(1,266)
Net working capital	$6,954	$6,920	$7,098	$7,194	$6,918	$7,196	$7,468	$7,324	$7,566	$7,356	$7,400	$7,624

Exhibit 5

Comparative Data on Selected Companies in Related Lines of Business

	Standard & Poor's 425 Industrial Stocks	Standard & Poor's Publishing Averages	DeLuther, Inc.[a]	Wakefield Co.[b]	Officomp, Inc.[c]	John Case Company
Trading market			OTC	OTC	OTC	— —
Current market price			$22.25	$14	$29.25	—
Indicated dividend yield			5.5%	8.7%	3.7%	—
Price-earnings ratio						
1984	9.9	14.6	8.7	7.2	10.5	
1983	11.8	19.6	6.4	5.0	10.2	
1982	10.4	14.4	10.8	11.9	13.8	
Price range						
1984			24.625–16.250	14.875–8.125	33.125–26.500	
1983			18.500–12.125	11.500–5.125	19.000–12.875	
Earnings per share (E) and Index (I)						
1984			(E) $2.48 / (I) 110	(E) $1.62 / (I) 82	(E) $2.98 / (I) 177	(E) $9.83 / (I) 216
1980			2.26 / 100	1.97 / 100	1.68 / 100	4.56 / 100
Sales (S) ($ thousands) and Index (I)						
1984			(S) $16,427 / (I) 142	(S) $12,223 / (I) 108	(S) $18,608 / (I) 160	(S) $15,260 / (I) 157
1980			11,568 / 100	11,317 / 100	11,630 / 100	9,740 / 100
Net earnings (N) ($ thousands) and Index (I)						
1984			(N) $1,051 / (I) 117	(N) $501 / (I) 84	(N) $1,656 / (I) 178	(N) $1,966 / (I) 216
1980			902 / 100	600 / 100	930 / 100	912 / 100
Net profit margins						
1984			6.4%	4.1%	8.9%	12.9%
1980			7.8	5.3	8.0	9.4
Profit/net worth						
1984			16.6%	6.0%	16.9%	19.8%
1983			14.2	5.7	15.0	19.0
1982			15.4	8.8	14.7	19.2
Book capitalization ($ thousands)			12/31/70	12/31/70	12/31/70	12/31/70
Long-term debt			$ 3,995 / 38.7%	$ 1,822 / 18.0%	$ 4,173 / 29.9%	— / —
Common stock and surplus			6,318 / 61.3	8,298 / 82.0	9,783 / 70.1	$ 9,916 / 100.0
Total			$10,313 / 100.0%	$10,120 / 100.0%	$13,956 / 100.0%	$ 9,916 / 100.0%
Total market value ($ thousands)			$ 9,456	$ 4,573	$16,234	—
Shares outstanding ($ thousands)			425	310	555	200

▸ ▸ ▸ ▸

[a]Producer of desk-top accessories, advertising specialty calendars, office stationery.

[b]Producer of advertising specialty calendars.

[c]Producer of broad line of office paper products and desk accessories.

Exhibit 6

Excerpts from Summary of Loan Agreement for Bank Term Loan

Description of the Loan

AMOUNT $6 million

RATE   Prime rate plus 2%, floating[a]

TERM   6 years

REPAYMENT   Annual payments equal to the greater of $1 million or the sum of net profit plus amortization of goodwill and debt discounts less $200,000.

PREPAYMENT   Permitted in whole or in part at any time without penalty. All prepayments to be applied to the outstanding principal balance of the loan in inverse order of maturity.

COMPENSATING BALANCES   Borrower must maintain average annual deposit balances equal to at least 10% of the outstanding principal amount of the loan.

Conditions Precedent

Prior to the making of the loan described above, borrower must have satisfied the following terms and conditions:

INCORPORATION   Borrower must be a duly incorporated corporation authorized to undertake this borrowing and all other transactions associated with this borrowing.

PURCHASE AGREEMENT   Borrower must have entered a contract to purchase 100% of the John Case Company.

FINANCING   Borrower must have arranged firm commitments for the financing of this transaction in a manner consistent with the terms of this loan agreement.

EQUITY PURCHASE   Messrs. Johnson, Haffenreffer, Wright, and Bennink must have committed not less than $500,000 in aggregate to the purchase of common stock in the newly formed corporation which will purchase John Case Company.

Affirmative Covenants

During the life of this loan, borrower will adhere to the following terms and conditions:

FINANCIAL STATEMENTS   Quarterly financial statements must be provided within 60 days of the end of the first three quarters. Audited financial statements bearing an unqualified opinion from a public accounting firm must be provided within 90 days of the end of borrower's fiscal year.

ACCOUNTING CHANGES   Borrower will make no changes in its method of accounting.

Negative Covenants

During the life of this loan, borrower will not do any of the following without written consent of the lender:

Exhibit 6 continued on page 326.

Exhibit 6 (continued)

CONTINUATION OF MANAGEMENT   No changes in management. Aggregate compensation to Messrs. Johnson, Haffenreffer, Wright, and Bennink not to be increased by more than 5% in any year, present compensation to serve as a base for this computation.

NEGATIVE PLEDGE   No assets to be pledged or otherwise used as collateral for any indebtedness.

SALE OF ASSETS   No sale of a substantial portion of the assets of the borrower. Borrower will not merge with or be acquired by any other entity.

ACQUISITIONS   Borrower will not acquire any other entity.

CAPITAL EXPENDITURES   Not to exceed $300,000 in any one year.

DIVIDENDS   In any one year restricted to after-tax profits minus all principal repayments on outstanding indebtedness.

WORKING CAPITAL   Not to decline below $3 million.

ADDITIONAL INDEBTEDNESS   No additional debt (including leases) with a term exceeding one year, unless subordinated to this loan. Any short-term debt must be retired for a period of at least 30 consecutive days in every year.

SENIOR DEBT   Senior debt, including all short-term indebtedness, may not exceed $10 million plus all earnings retained in the business after December 30, 1985.

Events of Default

In the event of default, this loan plus accrued interest will become immediately due and payable. The following will constitute events of default:

▶ Failure to pay interest or principal when due.

▶ Violation of any affirmative or negative covenant on this loan.

▶ Bankruptcy, reorganization, receivership, liquidation.

▶ Commission of an event of default on any other indebtedness.

[a]At the time of the case, the prime rate was 10.00%.

Exhibit 7

Cash Flow Forecasts ($ thousands)

	1985	1986	1987	1988	1989	1990
Net sales	$16,024	$16,844	$17,686	$18,570	$19,498	$20,472
Earnings before interest and taxes[a]	3,433	3,640	3,757	3,608	3,788	3,976
Interest expense[b]	1,675	1,538	1,369	908	800	800
Profit before tax	$ 1,758	$ 2,102	$ 2,388	$ 2,700	$ 2,988	$ 3,176
Taxes	274	364	440	556	660	714
Profit after tax	$ 1,484	$ 1,738	$ 1,948	$ 2,114	$ 2,328	$ 2,462
Add back noncash charges	240	260	284	300	310	340
Cash flow from operations	$ 1,724	$ 1,998	$ 2,232	$ 2,444	$ 2,638	$ 2,802
Less: increase in working capital	156	162	170	180	190	200
Less: capital expenditures	120	134	142	150	466	600
Available for debt retirement	$ 1,448	$ 1,702	$ 1,920	$ 2,114	$ 1,982	$ 2,002
Planned debt retirement:						
Bank loan	$ 1,448	$ 1,702	$ 1,920	$ 930	$ 0	$ 2,002
Case's loan	0	0	0	1,184	4,766[c]	0
Subordinated loan	0	0	0	0	0	0
Debt as % of total capital	89%	80%	70%	58%	47%	35%

[a]Reflects elimination of J. M. Case's salary.

[b]Nine percent coupon on subordinated loan of $6 million; 4% coupon on seller's note of $6 million; 12% rate on bank term loan; 10% rate on seasonal loan.

[c]J. M. Case's note is retired from cash flow and a $2.8 million new bank term loan in 1989.

Consolidated Equipment Company

Consolidated Equipment Company was a large producer of heavy industry equipment and manufactured control devices, with its main headquarters and production facilities located in the Philadelphia area. The company had grown over a long period of years. Its principal sales volume was in a specialized line of industrial equipment, accounting for more than half of its 1988 sales volume. Technological developments had limited sales of new equipment in this major line of the company's production in recent years, and it seemed unlikely that original equipment sales would expand beyond their 1989 volume. While the demand for replacement parts would remain high for several years to come, it would eventually be limited by the cessation of growth and possible decline in the sale of new equipment.

The management of Consolidated was thus confronted with the difficult task of maintaining a satisfactory rate of growth in the overall volume of the company's sales and earnings. Two main strategies were adopted. One was to intensify the company's research and development efforts in product lines that had previously accounted for a relatively small portion of Consolidated's total volume but seemed to offer more promising opportunities for long-term growth than its main line of industrial equipment. The second was to inaugurate a vigorous search for companies Consolidated might acquire in industries other than its main product line. The successful implementation of these strategies explains in part the growth of Consolidated in recent years (Exhibit 1) and its sound financial position at the end of 1988 (Exhibit 2).

Consolidated was particularly interested in acquiring small companies with promising products and management personnel but without established growth records. The management of Consolidated hoped to be able to acquire several such companies each year, preferably before their earning capacity had been sufficiently well established to command a premium price. In this way Consolidated hoped over a period of years to build a broad base for expansion and diversification.

The management of Consolidated was aware of the fact that the potential rate of growth of many small companies was limited by inadequate capital resources and distribution systems. It was convinced that Consolidated's abundant capital resources and nationwide distribution system could greatly facilitate the growth of many such companies. Consequently, it hoped that Consolidated would be able to acquire promising small companies on terms that would be mutually attractive because of the complementary character of the contributions that Consolidated and any potential small companies it might acquire could make to the combined enterprise.

There would be, of course, many facets to any decision concerning a potential acquisition. Among the most important was the caliber of the management of the company to be acquired, provided that the old management would be expected to remain. Likewise, the quality of the company's product line, research capabilities, and patent position, if any, was a prime consideration. Others were the degree to which the products of the two companies would mesh and the extent to which the value of the acquired company would be enhanced by an association with an established company.

Because of the desire to seek out companies that were poised for high growth but as yet undiscovered by the markets, most of the acquisitions were expected to be relatively small firms. Consequently, if these acquisitions were to have a significant impact on the growth rate of Consolidated, it was important that wise decisions be made in selecting the companies to be purchased from the many potentially available for acquisition. The management of Consolidated anticipated that for each company it should attempt to acquire, many companies might have to be screened.

Even after a prospective acquisition had passed the preliminary screening tests established by the management of Consolidated, there still remained the difficult task of determining the maximum offering price to be placed on the stock or assets of the company to be acquired. Until such an evaluation was made, serious negotiations with the potential sellers could not commence.

In order to apply consistent standards and to minimize the work load, the financial staff of Consolidated had been requested by its top management to work out a standardized procedure to be used in evaluating potential acquisitions. The method used in evaluating the Wellesley Machinery Company, discussed below, is typical of that ordinarily used by Consolidated.

The remainder of the case will describe very briefly the Wellesley Machinery Company and then discuss in more detail the method by which the financial staff arrived at a figure to recommend to management as a possible maximum purchase price. Not all the members of the management were convinced of the validity of the method of evaluation currently being used by Consolidated. The final section of the case outlines briefly the doubts expressed by these members.

Wellesley Machinery Company

Wellesley Machinery Company was a relatively small privately owned Massachusetts company with a diversified line of precision machinery products. It had a plant with approximately 500,000 square feet and employed about 350 persons. Its sales organization was rudimentary. In the opinion of both the Wellesley and Consolidated managements, this was one of the explanations for Wellesley's relatively low volume of sales and profits.

Consolidated had an interest in acquiring Wellesley, if a satisfactory price could be agreed on, because Consolidated was favorably impressed by the quality of Wellesley's management and by its product lines. Wellesley manufactured various precision machine products for which competition was severe and the prospects for growth limited. It also had several proprietary products on which it earned a much higher rate of profit and from which it expected to achieve substantial growth. In addition, Wellesley had several promising products scheduled to be put on the market in the near future. These items, several of which were revolutionary by industry standards, were expected to make a major contribution to Wellesley's future growth. The management of Wellesley also anticipated improvements in its production processes that would increase its gross margin on sales above the levels then prevailing.

Preliminary negotiations concerning an acquisition of Wellesley by Consolidated were begun in mid-1989. The management of Consolidated had considerable confidence in the quality of Wellesley's management and shared its hopes that Wellesley would be successful in developing new and improved products. Both managements believed that Wellesley's products could be marketed much more successfully by the combined organization than by Wellesley acting alone.

Consolidated's information as to other aspects of Wellesley's operations was much more scanty. Wellesley had furnished Consolidated with audited financial statements only for the year ending December 31, 1988 (Exhibits 3 and 4). The financial staff of Consolidated was informed that the deficit in the retained earnings account (Exhibit 4) and the negligible charge against net income for income tax accruals (Exhibit 3) resulted from operating losses incurred in 1985 and 1986. These losses, however, were attributed to temporary conditions and were not regarded by the management of either company as indicative of Wellesley's potential earning capacity. Preliminary unaudited statements for the first seven months of 1989 showed sales of approximately $5,500,000 and profits before taxes of about $1,000,000.

The management of Consolidated recognized that a much more thorough examination would have to be made before a firm offer could be made to Wellesley for the acquisition of its stock or assets. Among other things, much more detailed financial information would be needed for the years preceding 1988 and for the first part of 1989. Other aspects of Wellesley's operations, such as the strength of its patent position, would also have to be subjected to detailed scrutiny by Consolidated. Meanwhile, however, preliminary negotiations were instituted. In connection with these negotiations, the financial staff of Consolidated was requested by its top management to prepare an estimate of the maximum price at which Consolidated might consider acquiring Wellesley, based on the limited information then available. Such an estimate might help to determine whether the probability that a deal could be worked out was high enough to justify the detailed examination of Wellesley that would have to be undertaken before Consolidated could make a firm offer.

Consolidated's Method of Evaluating Acquisitions

Basic Approach

As previously noted, Consolidated's financial staff had worked out a fairly standardized method of evaluating potential acquisitions. This value was calculated by discounting at Consolidated's cost of capital the future cash flow to be derived from the acquisition. The present worth of this future cash flow was the maximum price that Consolidated would be willing to pay for an acquisition.

The future cash flow of a potential acquisition was obtained by forecasting the future profits, working capital, capital expenditures, depreciation, and other items affecting the cash flow to be derived from the acquisition. These forecasts were reviewed by the financial staff with other Consolidated personnel who were familiar with the products and with the industry of the company under consideration.

Forecast of Future Cash Flows

Typically, three forecasts were considered in evaluating a company: an optimistic forecast (quite often this was the forecast submitted by the company to be purchased); a "most likely" forecast (the one that qualified Consolidated personnel believed most likely to be realized); and finally, a minimum forecast (reflecting the minimum growth reasonably to be expected from the potential acquisition). The cash flows resulting from each of these forecasts were then discounted at Consolidated's cost of capital to arrive at a range of values for the company.

Although these three sets of forecasts were normally prepared, the management usually decided upon the terms to be offered for a potential acquisition on the basis of the minimum forecast. This procedure was used because management had found that very frequently the *actual* growth rate of its acquisitions had not been as rapid as the minimum forecast.

As an illustration of the divergence that was often reflected in these forecasts, the president of Wellesley estimated that the annual increase in sales would be about $4,000,000 a year for the next three years under *Wellesley's* management but that the annual rate of growth could be considerably greater than that if Consolidated were to acquire Wellesley. The forecast made by Consolidated's staff for the same three years, shown in Exhibit 5, assumes that Consolidated would acquire Wellesley at the beginning of 1990.

Consolidated's normal procedure was to forecast the cash flows to be used in its evaluation for a five-year period. It then held constant the cash flow predicted for years 6 to 10. The staff preparing the forecasts recognized that this procedure introduced a conservative factor in its evaluation, but this element of conservatism was thought desirable as a means of counterbalancing the tendency cited above to overestimate the growth rate for the first five years. Finally, in year 10 a terminal value was placed on the company to be acquired. In effect, then, Consolidated's procedure valued a potential acquisition as the sum of the present worth of the cash flow to be realized over the next 10 years plus the present worth of the terminal value at the end of the tenth year.

Assignment of Terminal Value

The decision to use a terminal value at the end of the tenth year was prompted by two factors. First, it was recognized that in the normal case Consolidated would still own a company from which cash flows would be derived, and the company would, therefore, be of value to Consolidated at the end of the 10-year period. Second, it seemed impractical to Consolidated to attempt to forecast cash flows for longer than 10 years.

In the past Consolidated had used several different approaches to set a terminal value on a potential acquisition at the end of the tenth year. These approaches included (1) the book value of the acquired company at this date, and (2) its liquidating value at this date, that is, an estimate of the sale price of the acquired company, based on a specified multiple of earnings at the end of the tenth year.

However, Consolidated's staff recognized that each of these procedures had serious limitations. Book value and liquidating value often would not reflect the worth of a company based on its present and potential earnings. The sale of a company at a specified multiple of 10-year earnings was regarded as a more adequate reflection of the value of the company in that year. The possible tax adjustments resulting from capital gains or losses arising from the sale, as well as the appropriate price-earnings multiplier for each company, were recognized as presenting additional complications for this method of determining a terminal value. Furthermore, Consolidated's staff was concerned about a possible internal contradiction in this approach to the problem. It reasoned that to value the company in the tenth year at a specified price-earnings multiplier would be somewhat unrealistic: if the company's performance were satisfactory, Consolidated probably would not be willing to sell; and if its performance were poor, Consolidated probably would not be able to obtain the value indicated by the price-earnings multiplier.

At the time of the Wellesley evaluation Consolidated's staff was using a somewhat different approach. The terminal value of the company in year 10 was assumed to be the present worth of 20 years of additional cash flow. The annual rate of cash flow for years 11 through 30 was normally assumed to be equal to that for years 6 to 10, with the possible exception of adjustments for certain noncash expenses such as are shown in Exhibit 5. This procedure was believed to reflect more satisfactorily Consolidated's intention in making an acquisition, that is, to realize a satisfactory cash flow over the long run.

Obviously, an assignment of a terminal value based on a discounting of the estimated cash flows (or earnings) from years 11 through 30 would not necessarily require Consolidated to retain the company for 30 years in order for the acquisition to be profitable. For example, if Consolidated could sell an acquisition at the end of the tenth year for the calculated terminal value, then, disregarding possible capital gains taxes, the investment would be just as profitable as if the assumed 20 years of additional earnings were realized in years 11–30. The Consolidated procedure ignored years beyond year 30 because their contribution to the present worth of the terminal value with a discount rate of 15%, or thereabouts, would be negligible.

Working Capital and Capital Expenditures

In determining the cash flows that would be caused by an acquisition, estimates also had to be made of changes in working capital requirements and of prospective capital outlays. If no better evidence was available, working capital requirements for a proposed acquisition were based on a historical analysis of relevant financial ratios of the company or industry for previous years. Expenditures on fixed assets were estimated at a level designed to maintain physical facilities in good working order and to handle the projected increases in sales volume.

Since sales volume was estimated to increase only for the first five years, as noted above, working capital requirements were generally considered to remain constant after year 5. A typical assumption with respect to capital expenditures was that they would be equal to depreciation outlays after year 5. The Wellesley evaluation was made in this manner (Exhibit 5).

Treatment of Debt

The financial staff of Consolidated eliminated debt from the capital structure of potential acquisitions by assuming in its cash flow estimates that this debt would be paid off in full in year zero. As a corollary, interest charges associated with this debt were also eliminated from the estimates of cash outflows for subsequent years. The rationale for this treatment of debt and associated interest charges was that the future earnings of an acquisition should not be benefitted by the use of leverage in the capital structure. This treatment was designed to permit all potential acquisitions to be evaluated on a comparable basis.

Estimate of Cost of Capital

Consolidated's practice at the time of the Wellesley acquisition was to discount its cash flow estimates for future years at a rate of 15%. This figure was assumed to be an approximation of Consolidated's cost of equity capital. As Exhibit 2 indicates, Consolidated's capital structure consisted almost entirely of common equity. Management, however, was not committed to such a capital structure as a matter of company policy; it was, in fact, actively considering the possible benefits to be derived from having a larger proportion of senior debt capital in its capital structure. It had determined that such long-term funds could be obtained at a fixed annual interest cost of approximately 10%.

Application of Above Procedure to Wellesley

Exhibit 5 shows in detail how Consolidated's procedure was applied in the evaluation of Wellesley. The cash flow from Wellesley was calculated first by estimating after-tax profits in years 1 to 10 and then adding back noncash expenses such as depreciation and amortization. From this sum the cash required for additions to working capital and new capital expenditures was subtracted. In addition, all long-term debt was assumed to be retired at the beginning of 1990 and was shown as an initial outlay. The resulting total represents the estimated cash contribution to be derived from Wellesley over the 10-year period beginning January 1, 1990. The cash contribution of each year was then discounted at 15% to obtain an estimate of the present worth of contributions from operations over that 10 years. The estimated terminal value of Wellesley at the end of year 10 was then computed as the present worth of 20 additional years of earnings, that is, the earnings of years 11–30 discounted to year zero at 15%. The sum of the estimated present worth of the contribution from operations for the first 10 years and of the present worth of the terminal value assigned to Wellesley represents Consolidated's estimate of the purchase price that it would be justified in paying for all the outstanding stock of Wellesley. This sum amounted to $28,820,000 for Wellesley (Exhibit 5).

Views of Other Members of Consolidated Management

Although the evaluation procedure described in the preceding section was currently being used by Consolidated, its merits were still under active debate within the company. Some members of management, for example, thought that more emphasis should be placed on the effect a potential acquisition would have on Consolidated's earnings per share. Ms. D. Luther, a company director who was especially interested in Consolidated's acquisition program, shared this view and contended vigorously that the $28,820,000 price for Wellesley, as calculated in Exhibit 5, was far too high. She prepared the illustrative data in Table A to support her position.

Ms. Luther pointed out that even if Wellesley's profits after taxes were assumed to expand to $2,500,000, far in excess of its 1988 or probable 1989 level, the acquisition would result in a dilution of Consolidated's earnings per share. In no circumstances, she contended, could Wellesley's earnings expand sufficiently to overcome this dilution in earnings per share for at least several years. While

Ms. Luther did not deny that Wellesley was a promising young company, she argued that no one could foresee the future well enough to predict with confidence that Wellesley's profits after taxes would soon reach or exceed a level of $2,500,000 to $3,000,000, the minimum range needed to prevent a dilution in Consolidated's earnings per share.

Table A

Ms. Luther's Illustrative Data

Hypothetical levels of profits after taxes to be derived from Wellesley	$ 2,000,000	$ 2,500,000	$ 3,000,000	$ 3,500,000	$4,000,000
Approximate earnings per share of Consolidated without acquisition of Wellesley	$ 5	$ 5	$ 5	$ 5	$ 5
Number of shares of Consolidated's stock which could be exchanged for all outstanding shares of Wellesley without diluting Consolidated's earnings per share	400,000	500,000	600,000	700,000	800,000
Approximate market value of Consolidated's common stock at time of contemplated acquisition	$ 50	$ 50	$ 50	$ 50	$ 50
Implicit value placed on Wellesley by earnings-per-share criterion	$20,000,000	$25,000,000	$30,000,000	$35,000,000	$40,000,000

In this connection, Ms. Luther urged that her numerical illustration was highly conservative in that it assumed no growth in Consolidated's own future earnings per share. In fact, the $5 figure understated reported earnings in 1988 and even more so the projected earnings for 1989. A reasonable allowance for the growth in Consolidated's earnings per share over the next several years, she pointed out, would require that Wellesley's profits after taxes be substantially larger than the top figure of $4,000,000 shown in her numerical illustration, to prevent a dilution in Consolidated's earnings per share for an indefinite and possibly permanent period.

The proponents of the discounted cash flow method of evaluating acquisitions such as Wellesley conceded to Ms. Luther that it would be preferable for Consolidated to acquire Wellesley for cash rather than by an exchange of stock. But they pointed out to her that since Consolidated was in a highly liquid position, an outright purchase for cash was feasible. Thus Consolidated's earnings per share would increase provided that the return on Consolidated's investment in Wellesley exceeded what was available from money market securities.

Ms. Luther responded that she recognized the validity of this argument if the Wellesley acquisition were viewed in isolation. As a general principle, however, she stated, Wellesley should be considered as one of a series of companies that Consolidated hoped to acquire each year. Ms. Luther pointed out that, although Consolidated could probably acquire Wellesley without resorting to outside financing, such financing would be required if Consolidated were to press vigorously its planned program of acquisitions. She concluded, therefore, that the Wellesley acquisition should be required to pass the same earnings-per-share hurdle that she felt would have to be applied to subsequent acquisitions. In summary, then, Ms. Luther continued to press her original contentions, namely, that Wellesley should be acquired only if the price were such that no dilution in earnings per share would result if the acquisition were made by an exchange of stock. The most she would concede was that a reasonable time should be allowed so that Wellesley's profits would reflect the anticipated benefits from the combined operation before calculating the effect on Consolidated's earnings per share of acquiring or not acquiring Wellesley.

Other influential members of Consolidated's management were concerned about the impact of the Wellesley acquisition on Consolidated's return on its book investment. They pointed out that Consolidated was currently earning approximately 8% on the book value of its equity capital. If Wellesley were to be acquired for $28.8 million, it would have to earn about $2.3 million after taxes to match this rate of return. At best, they contended, several years would pass before earnings of this amount could be reasonably anticipated. Meanwhile the acquisition of Wellesley would dilute Consolidated's return on its book investment.

With these widely conflicting views regarding the appropriate means of evaluating potential acquisitions, all parties concerned were anxious to arrive at a consensus as to the best procedure as soon as possible. Without such a consensus, continuing differences of judgment were bound to occur. These differences would inevitably slow down the company's acquisition program. In addition, favorable opportunities might be rejected and poor ones accepted unless a consistent and defensible method of valuing potential acquisitions could be agreed upon as company policy.

Exhibit 1

Selected Operating Data, 1984–1988 ($ millions)

Year	Net Sales	Income after Taxes	Earnings per Common Share	Dividends per Common Share	Market Price of Common Stock
1984	$ 946.8	$54.0	$3.87	$2.20	$33–57
1985	950.4	51.6	3.62	2.00	38–45
1986	1,002.0	49.2	3.41	2.00	38–54
1987	1,099.8	62.4	4.50	2.00	45–55
1988	1,203.6	70.8	5.11	2.00	45–55

Exhibit 2

Balance Sheet as of December 31, 1988
($ thousands)

ASSETS	
Current assets	
Cash	$ 32,064
Marketable securities	52,512
Accounts and notes receivable	193,824
Inventories	292,044
Total current assets	$ 570,444
Net fixed assets	621,222
Patent rights and other intangibles	18,516
Other assets	13,824
Total assets	$1,224,006
LIABILITIES AND STOCKHOLDERS' EQUITY	
Current liabilities	
Accounts and notes payable	$80,748
Income taxes payable	57,894
Accrued expenses and other liabilities	27,174
Total current liabilities	$ 165,816
Other liabilities (provision for pensions; various reserve accounts; and minority interest)	121,548
Mortgage notes and other noncurrent liabilities	17,562
Total liabilities	$ 304,926
Capital stock	
Preferred stock	50,868
Common stock	283,914
Retained earnings	584,298
Total stockholders' equity	$ 919,080
Total liabilities and stockholders' equity	$1,224,006

Exhibit 3

Wellesley Machinery Company, Income Statement
for Year Ending December 31, 1988
($ thousands)

Net sales	$7,294
Deduct: Cost of goods sold	3,348
Gross profit on sales	$3,946
Deduct: Selling and administrative expenses	2,526
Net operating income	$1,420
Other income less other deductions	142
Net profit before income taxes	$1,562
Provision for income taxes	78
Net income	$1,484

Exhibit 4

Wellesley Machinery Company,
Balance Sheet as of December 31, 1988
($ thousands)

ASSETS

Current assets	
Cash	$ 1,090
Accounts receivable	1,300
Inventory	4,840
Prepaid expenses	370
Total current assets	7,600
Net plant and equipment	4,560
Patents and other intangibles	2,300
Miscellaneous other assets (including	
large fire loss claim)	2,180
Total assets	$16,640

LIABILITIES AND STOCKHOLDERS' EQUITY

Current liabilities	
Accounts payable	$ 880
Advances from officers	840
Notes payable	1,160
Accrued expenses	190
Accrued taxes	260
Total current liabilities	3,330
Debentures payable	2,730
Total liabilities	$ 6,060
Stockholders' equity	
Common stock	1,540
Paid-in capital	12,600
Retained earnings (deficit)	(3,560)
Total equity	$10,580
Total liabilities and equity	$16,640

Exhibit 5

Wellesley Acquisition Study, Evaluation of Company ($ thousands)

	Initial Outlay	1990	1991	1992	1993	1994	1995	1996	1997	1998	1999	Total
I. Operating Statement												
Net sales		$18,660	$25,000	$32,000	$38,000	$44,000	$44,000	$44,000	$44,000	$44,000	$44,000	$377,660
Cost of sales		8,400	10,500	12,800	14,440	16,720	16,720	16,720	16,720	16,720	16,720	146,460
Gross profit		$10,260	$14,500	$19,200	$23,560	$27,280	$27,280	$27,280	$27,280	$27,280	$27,280	$231,200
Deduct												
Selling, gen. & admin.		5,600	7,500	9,600	11,400	13,200	13,200	13,200	13,200	13,200	13,200	113,300
Research and development		940	1,260	1,600	1,900	2,200	2,200	2,200	2,200	2,200	2,200	18,900
Net profit before tax		$ 3,720	$ 5,740	$ 8,000	$10,260	$11,880	$11,880	$11,880	$11,880	$11,880	$11,880	$ 99,000
Tax at 50%		1,860	2,860	4,000	5,140	5,940	5,940	5,940	5,940	5,940	5,940	49,500
Net profit after tax		$ 1,860	$ 2,880	$ 4,000	$ 5,120	$ 5,940	$ 5,940	$ 5,940	$ 5,940	$ 5,940	$ 5,940	$ 49,500
Cash flow												
Add:												
Depreciation		880	960	960	960	1,200	—	—	—	—	—	4,960
Other noncash charges against income		280	280	280	280	280	280	280	280	280	200	2,720
Deduct:												
Increase in working capital		—	—	1,600	1,800	1,800	—	—	—	—	—	5,200
Capital expenditures		840	—	—	2,600	—	—	—	—	—	—	3,440
Long-term debt	$2,180[a]											2,180
Mortgages	220[a]											220
Cash contribution from 10 years' operations	$(2,400)	$ 2,180	$ 4,120	$ 3,640	$ 1,960	$ 5,620	$ 6,220	$ 6,220	$ 6,220	$ 6,220	$ 6,140	$ 46,140
Present worth Contribution at 15%	(2,400)	1,896	3,115	2,393	1,121	2,804	2,687	2,339	2,034	1,766	1,518	19,327

II. Total Present Worth Value of Company at a 10% Discount Factor

Present worth contribution from operations	$19,327
Terminal value—present worth of 20 add. yrs. of earnings	9,493
Total present worth value of company	$28,820

[a]Outlays assumed to be made on January 1, 1990.

Philip Morris
Companies, Inc. (A)

Late in the afternoon of June 26, 1989, the staff leader for corporate financing at Philip Morris Companies, Inc., reflected on the recommendation to be made to Hans G. Storr, executive vice president and chief financial officer, concerning the company's next step in issuing debt securities under its $5.0 billion shelf registration. Philip Morris had filed the shelf to permit the refinancing of short-term debt arising from its $12.9 billion purchase of Kraft, Inc. Since December 13, 1988, the date that the SEC declared the registration statement effective, the company had issued $1.5 billion in public debt securities (see Exhibit 1).

Mr. Storr's staff monitored the markets continually. They kept track of the Treasury markets, new issues of investment-grade fixed-income securities, and trading in the company's paper, among other things. On a daily basis, they polled the investment banks to determine what rates the company could attain at various maturities. Recently, they had begun to hear from market sources that Philip Morris would find the market particularly receptive to a medium-term offering. With characteristic bravado, several underwriters had suggested that the company could successfully sell as much as $500 million in 5–7 year debt securities (more than three times the size of the average shelf debt issue, but equal to the company's first offering under its shelf registration).

Most of the investment banks had recommended that the company pursue a negotiated transaction, selecting a lead manager to assemble the underwriting group and then pricing the issue according to market interest. However, Mr. Storr's staff knew from experience that investment banks almost always recommended negotiated deals because they were easier to execute and carried less risk. A few had boldly offered to buy the securities outright in competition with the others. The expressions of interest were strong enough and the pricing indications attractive enough to lead the Philip Morris staff to conclude that they should act now.

Before the staff went to Mr. Storr, however, there were other factors to consider. The fixed income markets had rallied since May and it was believed that the rally would continue, hopefully allowing the company to refinance more short-term debt in the coming months. While obtaining the best terms on each issue was

This case was prepared by Professor Samuel L. Hayes, III.
Copyright © 1991 by the President and Fellows of Harvard College. Harvard Business School case N9-292-005.

always an important consideration, the staff had to have confidence in the underwriter's ability to execute the transaction smoothly in the market. If the offering size was too big, or if priced too aggressively, it could create an overhang that might sour the market's attitude toward the company and negatively influence future issuances. Also, the staff recognized that the distribution of these securities would influence future trading in the secondary market. Where should these securities be distributed? Could Philip Morris influence the distribution of the securities by the underwriter? If so, how?

History of Philip Morris Companies, Inc.

The Philip Morris organization dated back to 1850 in Great Britain under a grant from Queen Victoria. Its emergence as a distinct U.S. entity followed the 1911 breakup of the American Tobacco Trust, led by its legendary chairman, James B. (Buck) Duke. Armed with a superior cost advantage gained from exclusive contract rights to the industry's most efficient cigarette-making machine, the young Duke forced the larger cigarette producers to sell out to him and drove the smaller producers out of business. At its peak, the Trust accounted for over 90% of the cigarettes sold in the United States.

Following the dissolution of the Trust, four major competitors emerged, each with its own flagship brand: RJ Reynolds with Camel, Liggett and Myers with Chesterfield, Lorillard with Old Gold, and a scaled-down American Tobacco with Lucky Strike. Of the four competitors, all except American were previously owned by the Trust through Continental Tobacco, Duke's holding company for "plug" or chewing tobacco firms. In 1919, Philip Morris and Company, Ltd., would list among its assets Continental Tobacco, by then a manufacturer of English-style cigarettes, including Marlboro, Dunhill, English Ovals, and others. At this time, Philip Morris also imported other brands into the United States and maintained a marketing arrangement for private label brands with Stephano Brothers.

With these seemingly modest beginnings, Philip Morris gradually began to grow. Targeting different market segments, the company established itself first with the low-priced Paul Jones brand in the 1930s, and then more decisively with the upscale Philip Morris English Blend as the country moved into World War II and economic recovery. Finally, in 1954, the company repositioned Marlboro, previously marketed as a women's cigarette, by adopting the cowboy as its symbol. According to company Chairman George Weissman, "We chose the cowboy because he's close to the earth. He's an authentic American hero. Probably the only one. And it worked."[1] Through the consistent and frequent advertising of its new symbol, Marlboro began a steady march to become, by 1980, the best-selling cigarette in the world.

The tobacco companies had wrestled with anti-smoking lobbyists since the beginning of the century. In 1966, the lobbyists scored a victory when the Cigarette Advertising and Labeling Act was passed requiring all cigarette packages after January 1, 1966, to bear the message: "Caution—Cigarette Smoking May Be Hazardous To Your Health."

In the 1980s, the Surgeon-General stepped up the campaign to eradicate smoking. Lawsuits pending against the major tobacco companies were also on the rise. The tobacco companies saw other threats, as well, to the growth of their primary businesses. With the pressure upon the U.S. government to find ways to reduce the federal budget deficit, it was possible that subsidies might be reduced and excise taxes increased which would lower the profit margins of tobacco companies.

Initial Diversification

Coincident with the rise of publicly expressed concerns over the health effects of smoking in the early 1950s was the movement by many tobacco companies to begin to diversify operations. In 1957, Philip Morris completed its first acquisition, Milprint, a manufacturer of packaging products, followed the next year by Polymer International, a chemical company. Both companies had few direct ties to cigarette manufacturing. The American Safety Razor Company was acquired in 1960, a relatively large acquisition for the company at that point. In 1969, Philip Morris made its first foray into a different consumer product business with the acquisition of Miller Brewing Company, then the eighth but now the second largest U.S. brewer. During this period the company also purchased a number of companies related to the paper, packaging and industrial adhesives businesses. It purchased the Seven-Up Company in 1978 (and subsequently sold it in 1986). Finally, in 1982, under the leadership of CFO Storr, Philip Morris formed Philip Morris Credit Corporation as a vehicle to shelter income by investing in leveraged leases and to manage its investment in Mission Viejo, a California-based real estate development firm. By the end of 1988, the Credit Corporation had grown to nearly $3.3 billion in assets.

Even though the company was diversifying its product lines, it was also growing its existing businesses, particularly in the international area. In 1979, it acquired the international business of the Liggett Group, Inc. (formerly Liggett and Myers), adding Chesterfield and Lark. In 1981, it added a 26% equity interest in Rothmans International, a leading British-based international cigarette and luxury goods manufacturer and marketer. In the same year, the company stepped up its capital expenditures to more than $1 billion, outspending its cash flow by $140 million. By 1984, however, the company had completed most of its major expansion programs and was able to reduce its capital spending to $300 million; this left it with a substantial positive cash flow.

At the end of 1984, with the company now generating excess cash flow, predominantly from its tobacco business, it faced an important decision: it could either increase its payout to shareholders through increased dividends and share repurchases (perhaps even by taking the company private), or it could continue to seek out acquisitions.

The Beginning of the Maxwell Era

Shortly after assuming the post of chairman and CEO of Philip Morris, Inc., in 1984, Hamish Maxwell began to look for acquisitions in the food industry, aided by the substantial positive cash flow now being generated. To support his acquisition strategy, he formed Philip Morris Companies, Inc., a holding company for its tobacco as well as its nontobacco interests (see organizational structure in Exhibit 2). The net result of the reorganization was to create a holding company with a series of sister companies reporting to it. This gave the organization greater flexibility in pursuing further diversification.

Maxwell agreed late in 1985 to acquire all of the outstanding stock of General Foods Corporation for $5.6 billion. With General Foods, Philip Morris acquired a host of well-established brand names, including Maxwell House, Sanka and Brim coffees, Kool-Aid, Tang, Crystal Light and Country Time powdered beverages, Jell-O gelatins and puddings, Post cereals, Oscar Mayer meats, Birds Eye frozen foods, and Entenmann bakeries. The General Foods acquisition was initially financed by drawing on the company's revolving credit facility. Shortly thereafter, this bank debt was refinanced with a combination of commercial paper, supported by the revolving credit, and issuance of medium-term debt in both the U.S. domestic and Euro-bond markets. All financing was undertaken at the holding company level.

After the acquisition, Philip Morris undertook to restructure parts of General Foods and paid particular attention to bolstering the company's coffee business. General Foods was recast into three operating companies: General Foods USA; Worldwide Coffee & International; and Oscar Mayer Foods. Meanwhile, the tobacco business maintained its rapid and steady growth after 1985. Tobacco was generating over $3.2 billion annually in free cash flow by mid-year 1988, growing at 14% annually. With the completion of the General Foods restructuring and the continued growth in tobacco, the time was right to consider other acquisitions.

The Kraft Acquisition

By the fall of 1988, Maxwell and his management team had set its sights on Kraft, Inc. Fearful of a possible takeover move, Kraft's board of directors had already established various anti-takeover measures to protect management and its shareholders, including a "poison pill" and a "shareholders protection program," devices designed to make an unwelcome bid difficult to succeed. On October 18, Philip Morris initiated a "hostile" tender offer for Kraft at $90 per share. After reviewing the proposal, Kraft's board rejected it as inadequate, proposing instead to recapitalize the company with a special dividend of cash and securities which it valued at $110 per share. Ultimately, the market did not view that proposal as worth its claimed value and Philip Morris was able to negotiate a purchase price of $106 in cash for all of the shares of Kraft. On December 7, Philip Morris completed the acquisition, making Kraft one of its subsidiaries. In total, it paid about $12.9 billion. In the history of acquisitions of U.S. companies up until that time, the Kraft purchase was exceeded only by the purchase of Gulf Oil by Chevron for $13.2 billion in 1984.

The Kraft acquisition greatly expanded Philip Morris' scope of operations within the food industry. Philip Morris picked up such well-known products as Velveeta cheese spread, Parkay margarine, Miracle Whip salad dressings, Philadelphia brand cream cheese and a variety of items under the Kraft name, including mayonnaise and macaroni and cheese. Kraft's distribution system, organized according to dry, frozen, and refrigerated products, complemented those of General Foods very well. As one of the world's largest advertisers, Philip Morris would likely be able to reduce its media and promotional costs significantly by obtaining greater volume discounts. All factors considered, Kraft gave Philip Morris critical mass upon which a truly global consumer food products company could be built.

For Philip Morris, however, the acquisition did not come cheaply. Wall Street analysts calculated that the roughly $13 billion purchase price was equal to about 1.1 times Kraft's 1988 sales, 15.5 times its operating income, and nearly 13.0 times operating cash flow.[2] The justification for such a high purchase price could only come from expected significant cost savings, continued revenue growth and low financing costs.

Philip Morris's strategy for financing its purchase of Kraft was patterned after the General Foods acquisition. The initial financing requirements were met temporarily with a $12 billion bank revolving credit and internally generated funds. After the closing, Philip Morris would issue medium-term debt in the public markets to refinance the bank debt. On December 8, 1988, a day after closing the Kraft purchase, the company filed a shelf registration statement under Rule 415 of the Securities and Exchange Commission (SEC) to issue $5 billion in debt securities and currency and debt warrants over the following two years. The SEC declared the registration statement effective five days later. Shortly after going effective, Philip Morris sought to issue the first notes from the shelf.

Issuance under Shelf Registrations

In 1982, the SEC enacted Rule 415, establishing a streamlined process to allow larger, well-known corporations to avoid bureaucratic delays in securities registration. Instead of separately registering each securities offering, companies would be allowed to register a large amount of securities which could be issued in segments at any time during the two year period following approval by the SEC. In this way, shelf registrants could take advantage of "windows of opportunity" in the capital markets and thereby obtain lower cost financing.

The change in procedures put additional pressure on investment banks in an already competitive business. Under the new procedures, it was customary for issuers to designate "underwriter's counsel," an outside law firm who would participate in the preparation of the basic documents forming part of the initial registration statement and also review the periodic filings under the Securities Exchange Act of 1934 which were incorporated by reference into the registration statement and offering prospectus.

The issuer would also designate certain investment banks who would be candidates for managing the securities distribution. These designated investment banks would either contact the issuer or be contacted by the issuer if a favorable opening in the market appeared. The investment bank was expected to provide a pricing proposal to the issuer within a matter of a few minutes or hours. Once a lead manager for the issue had been selected, that investment bank would have to decide whether and how large a syndicate of cooperating securities firms should be gathered. Once that determination had been made, the lead manager along with underwriters' counsel would conduct a due diligence session with the issuer,[3] almost always by phone, where the latest developments affecting the issuer would be reviewed. If the underwriters found everything to be in order, they effectively became the owner of the securities and were obligated to deliver the agreed-upon financing proceeds to the issuer when the transaction was settled five business days later.

Each underwriter's bid would reflect an assessment of not only the issuer's value in the eyes of the market (e.g., "we think your securities should 'clear' the market at about 85 basis points over Treasuries of comparable maturity") but also a projection of the market's immediate future direction. Thus, an investment bank might bid aggressively if it believed the market would rally. In addition, the underwriter could hedge the purchase of the issuer's securities by shorting U.S. Treasury securities with a similar maturity. In this way, its exposure would be limited to the spread over Treasuries.[4] As long as this spread remained fixed, the underwriter could lock in its fee, regardless of changes in interest rates.

From the SEC's perspective, the rationale for Rule 415 was based upon its perception of the market's knowledge of these well-known companies. Shelf registrations would in principle be limited to those companies who had a wide following by investors and research analysts. The SEC believed that the marketplace could effectively evaluate these companies' current circumstances and future prospects over the two-year life of the shelf. Underwriters would not be relieved of their due diligence responsibility; they would continue to bear liability for unexpected losses to investors for one year from the date of issuance. Nevertheless, under Rule 415, more of the burden for judging creditworthiness and value would now clearly fall away from underwriters and upon investors and research analysts. (A list of SEC filings by Philip Morris Companies, Inc., and Philip Morris, Inc., is given in Exhibit 3.) More than a few experts, however, questioned whether the due diligence function would be compromised under this rule.[5]

After the Kraft acquisition, Philip Morris invited all of the six designated underwriters[6] with which it would expect to do business after the registration statement became effective to participate in a detailed due diligence meeting. Representatives of the underwriters listened to company presentations on the Kraft acquisition, financing strategy, and tobacco product liability. They were also invited to ask questions of management at the end of the meeting.

Market Concerns over Kraft and the Leveraged Buyout of RJR Nabisco

The markets' reactions to the news of the takeover of Kraft was not positive for Philip Morris. Within two days after announcing the bid, the price of Philip Morris common stock fell six points to 94, reflecting the high purchase price and what the media reported as "flak from investors over the company's track record with acquisitions."[7] In the debt markets, *The Wall Street Journal* reported that spreads above treasuries for Philip Morris paper had initially widened twenty basis points, from 75 to 95, upon the announcement of the tender offer.[8] Other observers reported that buyers for Philip Morris paper had largely disappeared and that only the bidding of several large investment banks kept levels up.

Shortly after the Kraft announcement, the markets were jolted with the announcement that F. Ross Johnson, CEO of RJR Nabisco, the chief rival of Philip Morris in the tobacco business, would pursue a leveraged buyout (LBO) of his company. The investment-grade fixed-income markets were hammered, particularly in Europe. With the prospect of massive amounts of additional debt being added to its balance sheet, holders of the unsecured debt of RJR Nabisco saw the value of their investments plummet with lower credit ratings. The issues of other investment-grade industrial companies traded off in sympathy—and fear. (However, the very largest investment grade industrial issues, considered immune to an LBO because of their size, were unaffected.) A movement began to protect bondholders from this type of "event risk" by adding covenants to new debt issues which would (among other things) limit releveraging. Philip Morris, however, was unswayed by these market developments and pushed ahead, as it had done in the past, with plans to issue senior unsecured debt with no protection in the indenture against such event risk.

First Issuance under the Shelf Registration

On December 1, 1988, Philip Morris selected Merrill Lynch as lead manager, with Goldman Sachs and Salomon Brothers as co-managers, to underwrite a $500 million offering of ten-year notes. Given the uncertainty of the marketplace, the company decided to pursue a negotiated transaction, rather than solicit competitive bids. The company took the unusual step of issuing a preliminary prospectus, which it dubbed a "pickled herring," presumably to provide investors with more information about the Kraft acquisition. On December 20, one day after issuing the preliminary prospectus, the issue was priced. The new 10-year notes carried a coupon of 9.80% and were offered to the public at 98.334% of face value to yield 10.087%.

The company was well satisfied with the issue's reception by the market. At this point, most portfolio managers had already "closed" their portfolios for year-end valuation and it took a special opportunity to induce them to reopen for further purchases prior to January 1. The fact that a half-billion-dollar issue was placed (mainly with institutions) and that in the secondary market the notes traded within two or three basis points of par was seen as a positive reflection on Philip Morris' credit standing and on the accuracy of the issue's pricing.

Events during the First Six Months of 1989

Shelf issuance by Philip Morris ceased for the two months following the offering of the 9.80s, in part because the general level of interest rates was rising. On March 1, 1989, the company issued its audited financial statements for the year ended December 31, 1988 (see Exhibits 4–7). Because Philip Morris had taken on an additional $11 billion in debt to finance the Kraft acquisition, fixed-charge coverage fell from 2.6 to 2.2 times. Nonetheless, in March the company raised $1.0 billion in fixed-rate, short-term, 12–18 month notes in four separate issues, which it promptly swapped into floating rate obligations at a net cost which was below that of the highest quality commercial paper. The proceeds from these financings were used to pay down bank debt.

In May, the company released its results for the quarter ended March 31, 1989 (Exhibit 4). Operating revenues had increased 45% to $10.8 billion and operating income had grown 40% to $1.5 billion. Earnings per share increased 23% from $2.08 to $2.55. If Kraft had been included in the results for the March 1988 quarter, sales and operating income would have risen 2% and 16%, respectively. Because the company was able to quickly pay down a substantial part of its Kraft-financing debt, the ratio of earnings to fixed charges increased to 3.0 times for the quarter.

Helped by this positive news and a rallying Treasury and short-term money market (see Exhibits 8 and 9), the company's share price increased from $120 in March to $141 in the beginning of June.

As Treasury yields began to decline in June, the company began to consider issuing additional medium-term notes. By the first week in June, it had refinanced all of its bank debt with commercial paper. Interest rates continued to fall. Other corporations had begun to take advantage of the lower rates (see Exhibit 10). The staff therefore made their final assessments and calculations before going into Mr. Storr's office to give him their recommendation.

▶ Endnotes

1. Cited in Peter Taylor's *The Smoke Ring* (New York: Pantheon Books, 1984).
2. Operating cash flow is defined as operating income before the deduction of depreciation and amortization.

3. Due diligence is the term applied to the procedures undertaken by an underwriter to thoroughly review the business, operations, management, and financial records of an issuer. Because the underwriters were liable under the Securities Act of 1933 for omissions or misstatements regarding the issuer's affairs, this process helped to protect investors against fraud.

4. The spread is defined as the difference between the yield-to-maturity (after the underwriting discount) on the issuer's securities and the yield on the Treasury security with a comparable maturity.

5. See for example, Joseph Auerbach and Samuel L. Hayes, III, *Investment Banking and Diligence: What Price Deregulation?* (Boston: Harvard Business School Press, 1986).

6. Those underwriters were Merrill Lynch, Goldman Sachs, Salomon Brothers, Shearson, Morgan Stanley, and First Boston. These six firms were generally acknowledged to be the most powerful underwriting and trading firms on Wall Street.

7. *Wall Street Journal*, October 20, 1988.

8. *Wall Street Journal*, October 19, 1988.

Exhibit 1

Securities Issuance under Shelf Number 33-25906 (December 1988–June 1989)

Ratings:	Standard and Poor's	A			
	Moody's	Baa1			
Issue Date	12/20/88	03/02/89	03/09/89	03/20/89	03/29/89
Size ($ million)	500.0	250.0	150.0	300.0	300.0
Coupon	9.80%	10.15%	10.20%	10.85%	10.50%
Description	Notes	Notes	Notes	Notes	Notes
Maturity	12/15/98	03/09/90	09/15/90	12/28/90	04/05/90
Price to public	98.336%	100.00%	100.00%	100.00%	99.975%
Discount	.600%	.125%	.150%	.150%	.125%
Net to company	97.736%	99.875%	99.85%	99.85%	99.85%
Underwriters[a]	ML, GS, SAL	FBC	ML	MS	SLH
Effective yield	10.087%	10.15%	10.20%	10.85%	10.50%
Spread	100	56	70	99	55

[a]ML - Merrill Lynch
 GS - Goldman Sachs
 SAL - Salomon Brothers
 FBC - First Boston Corporation
 MS - Morgan Stanley
 SLH - Shearson, Lehman, Hutton

Source: Prospectuses and *Corporate Financing Week.*

Exhibit 2

Corporate Organization Chart—Major Subsidiaries (June 1989)

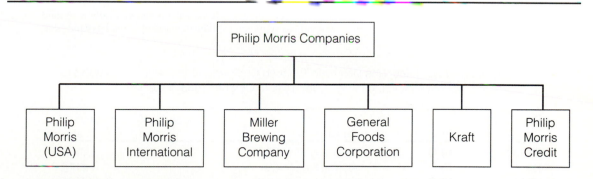

Note: Kraft and General Foods are now operated as a single unit called Kraft/General Foods. Philip Morris Credit Corporation is now called Philip Morris Capital.

Source: Company annual reports.

Exhibit 3

Document Filings by Philip Morris Companies with the Securities and Exchange Commission
(October 1988–June 1989)

Document Date	Type	Description	Amd	Entered Date
09/30/88	10-Q	Quarterly Financials		11/18/88
12/31/88	10-K	Annual Financials		04/12/89
12/31/88	10-K	Amendment (1)	A01	05/22/89
03/31/89	10-Q	Quarterly Financials		05/16/89
12/02/88	8-K		27	12/16/88
12/02/88	8-K	Amendment (2)	A01	03/10/89
12/07/88	8-K		27	12/27/88
03/01/89	8-K		57	03/10/89
03/30/89	12-K-SEª			04/10/89
12/07/88	12-K-SE			12/08/88
12/31/88	ARS			3/21/89
03/10/89	Proxy			3/23/89
12/07/88	S-3	Reg Stmt #33-25906		12/21/88
12/07/88	S-3	Reg Stmt #33-21033	A01	12/21/88
12/20/88	Prospectus	9.80% Notes Due 1988		01/05/89
03/02/89	Prospectus	10.15% Notes Due 1990		03/17/89
03/09/89	Prospectus	10.20% Notes Due 1990		03/23/89
03/20/89	Prospectus	10.85% Notes Due 1990		03/30/89
03/29/89	Prospectus	10.5% Notes Due 1990		04/10/89
04/27/89	8-B		A01	05/12/89
06/09/89	S-8 POS	33-13210	A	
06/09/89	S-8 POS	33-10218	A	
06/23/89	S-8 POS	33-14561	A	

ªFor users of the SEC's EDGAR system, which allows companies to file statements electronically with the SEC (i.e., by computer via modem), 12-K-SE documents represent exhibits in hard copy that have not been filed electronically.

Philip Morris (USA), Inc. (the Domestic Tobacco Company) Document Filings with the Securities and Exchange Commission (October 1988–June 1989)

Document Date	Type	Description	Amd	Entered Date
09/30/88	10-Q	Quarterly Financials		11/18/88
12/31/88	10-K	Annual Financials		04/11/89
03/31/89	10-Q	Quarterly Financials		05/16/89
05/13/88	12-K-SE			02/09/89

A01 - Amendment number one

ARS - Annual Reports

S-3 - Shelf registration statement filed with the SEC

8-B

S-8 POS - Amendment to stock purchase or profit sharing plan

12-K-SE

Exhibit 4

Consolidated Statements of Earnings ($ millions—except as otherwise indicated)

	3 Months 3/31/88	3 Months 6/30/88	3 Months 9/30/88	3 Months 12/31/88	3 Months 3/31/89
Operating revenues	$7,421	$7,944	$7,737	$8,640	$10,770
Less: Cost of sales	3,131	3,337	3,215	3,855	5,326
Excise taxes on products sold	1,542	1,492	1,451	1,397	1,419
Gross profit	2,748	3,115	3,071	3,388	4,025
Less: Marketing, admin., & research	1,688	1,847	1,801	2,484	2,459
Amortization of goodwill	31	24	25	45	96
Operating income	1,029	1,244	1,245	859	1,470
Less: Interest and other debt expense	170	151	133	216	451
Earnings before taxes and accounting change	859	1,093	1,112	643	1,019
Less: Income taxes	389	482	491	301	429
Earnings before effect of accounting change	470	611	621	342	590
Accounting change	(273)	0	0	0	0
Net income	$ 763	$ 611	$ 621	$ 242	$ 590
Weighted average number of shares	236.0	235.0	233.8	233.0	231.0
Earnings per share-continuing	$2.08	$2.60	$2.66	$1.47	$2.55
-accounting change	$1.16	—	—	—	—
Dividends declared per share	$0.90	$0.90	$1.13	$1.13	$1.13
Payout ratio	43.3%	34.6%	42.3%	76.6%	44.0%

Exhibit 5

Consolidated Balance Sheets ($ millions)

	12/31/87	3/31/88[a]	6/30/88[a]	9/30/88[a]	12/31/88	3/31/89
ASSETS						
Consumer products						
Cash and cash equivalents	$ 90	$ 395	$ 770	$ 1,503	$ 168	$ 160
Receivables, net	2,065	2,466	2,351	2,222	2,222	3,233
Inventories						
Leaf tobacco	2,008	1,795	1,531	1,623	1,873	1,780
Other raw materials	840	823	800	819	1,540	1,563
Finished product	1,306	1,551	1,511	1,495	1,971	2,162
Other current assets	245	174	177	173	377	415
Total current assets	6,554	7,204	7,140	7,835	8,151	9,313
Property, plant and equipment						
Land and land improvements	494				612	
Buildings and building equipment	2,800				3,422	
Machinery and machinery equipment	5,678				7,137	
Construction in progress	426				761	
Total property, plant and equipment	9,398	9,579	9,668	9,796	11,932	12,099
Less accumulated depreciation	(2,816)	(2,951)	(3,022)	(3,119)	(3,284)	(3,391)
Net property, plant and equipment	6,582	6,628	6,646	6,677	8,648	8,708
Goodwill and other tangible assets	4,052	4,025	4,001	3,971	15,071	15,001
Other assets	1,359	670	621	596	1,921	1,843
Total consumer product assets	18,547	18,527	18,408	19,079	33,791	34,865
Financial services and real estate[a]						
Finance assets, net	2,185				2,578	2,548
Real estate held for sale/investment	482				379	368
Other assets	223				212	243
Total financial services and real estate	2,890	1,194	1,193	1,216	3,169	3,159
Total assets	$21,437	$19,721	$19,601	$20,295	$36,960	$38,024

[a]For balance sheet dates 3/31/88, 6/30/88, and 9/30/88 Financial Services and Real Estate Assets are reported net of Liabilities.

Exhibit 5 (continued)

	12/31/87	3/31/88[a]	6/30/88[a]	9/30/88[a]	12/31/88	3/31/89
LIABILITIES						
Consumer Products						
Short-term borrowings	$ 691	$ 831	$ 373	$ 243	$ 433	$ 263
Current portion of long-term debt	465	774	783	586	127	863
Accounts payable	791	771	881	1,029	1,777	1,567
Payable for untendered Kraft shares					435	96
Accrued liabilities						
Taxes, except income taxes	537	843	696	675	595	778
Employment cost	453				697	
Other	1,287	1,634	1,874	1,978	2,556	3,147
Income taxes	727	946	776	983	1,089	1,120
Dividends payable	213	212	209	260	260	260
Total current liabilities	5,164	6,011	5,592	5,754	7,969	8,094
Long-term debt	5,199	4,770	4,989	5,203	15,882	16,545
Deferred income taxes	1,288	1,314	1,385	1,428	825	898
Other liabilities	633	600	599	591	1,988	2,017
Total consumer products liabilities	12,284	12,695	12,565	12,976	26,664	27,554
FINANCIAL SERVICES AND REAL ESTATE						
Short-term borrowings	284				264	152
Long-term debt	1,094				1,240	1,178
Deferred income taxes	756				894	949
Other liabilities	196				219	206
Total financial services & real estate liabilities	2,330	0	0	0	2,617	2,485
Total liabilities	14,614	12,695	12,565	12,976	29,281	30,039
Common stock	240	240	240	240	240	240
Additional paid-in capital	272	257	255	253	252	235
Earnings reinvested in the business	6,437	6,727	7,145	7,523	7,833	8,163
Currency translation adjustment	146	163	122	72	117	84
Less treasury stock	(272)	(361)	(726)	(769)	(763)	(737)
Total stockholders' equity	6,823	7,026	7,036	7,319	7,679	7,985
Total liabilities and stockholders' equity	$21,437	$19,721	$19,601	$20,295	$36,960	$38,024

[a]For balance sheet dates 3/31/88, 6/30/88 and 9/30/88 Financial Services and Real Estate Assets are reported net of Liabilities.

Exhibit 6

Calendar Years Ended December 31 ($ millions)

	1986	1987	1988
REVENUES			
Tobacco	$12,691	$14,644	$16,586
Food	9,664	9,946	11,265
Beer	2,054	3,105	3,262
Financial services and real estate	474	488	629
Total	25,883	28,183	31,742
OPERATING PROFIT			
Tobacco	2,848	3,290	3,846
Food	639	605	392
Beer	154	170	190
Financial services and real estate	31	68	162
Other	(9)	19	0
Total operating profit	3,663	4,152	4,590
Unallocated corporate expenses	(126)	(162)	(193)
Total operating income	3,537	3,990	4,397
DEPRECIATION			
Tobacco	200	214	237
Food	167	201	221
Beer	136	137	136
Financial services and real estate	3	4	4
Total	506	556	598
OPERATING CASH FLOW			
Tobacco	3,048	3,504	4,083
Food	806	806	613
Beer	290	307	326
Financial services and RE	34	72	166
Total segments	4,178	4,689	5,188
Unallocated corporate expenses	(126)	(162)	(193)
Total operating cash flow	4,052	4,527	4,995
CAPITAL EXPENDITURES			
Tobacco	191	246	467
Food	395	402	466
Beer	80	57	86
Financial services and real estate	12	2	
Total	678	707	1,019
FREE CASH FLOW			
Tobacco	2,857	3,258	3,616
Food	411	404	147
Beer	210	250	240
Financial services and real estate	22	70	166
Total segments	3,500	3,982	4,169
Unallocated corporate expenses	(126)	(162)	(193)
Total free cash flow	3,374	3,820	3,976
ASSETS			
Tobacco	5,808	4,467	6,001
Food	8,629	9,125	24,870
Beer	1,736	1,680	1,623
Financial services and real estate	2,276	2,890	3,169
Total segments	18,449	20,162	35,663
Corporate assets	1,033	1,275	1,297
Total assets	$19,482	$21,437	$36,960

Exhibit 7

Consolidated Statements of Cash Flows ($ millions)

	12 Months 12/31/87	3 Months 3/31/88	6 Months 6/30/88	9 Months 9/30/88	12 Months 12/31/88	3 Months 3/31/89
CASH FLOWS FROM OPERATING ACTIVITIES						
Net earnings-consumer products	$1,770	$ 694	$1,281	$1,857	$ 2,173	$ 551
-financial services & real estate	72	69	93	138	164	39
Net earnings	1,842	763	1,374	1,995	2,337	590
Consumer products						
Depreciation and amortization	704	191	367	546	779	306
Deferred income tax provision	338	34	77	97	(43)	78
Restructuring charges	71				348	
Gain on sale of Rothman's Int'l						
Cumulative effect of accounting change		(232)	(232)	(232)	(232)	
Cash effects of changes in						
Receivables, net	(117)	(375)	(136)	(242)	601	(1,034)
Inventories	(52)	(8)	224	67	2	(210)
Accounts payable	(101)	(23)	122	183	408	(203)
Income taxes	52	223			556	47
Other		258	509	910	(7)	62
Financial services and real estate						
Deferred income tax provision	231	53	92	158	178	56
Cumulative effect of accounting change		(41)	(41)	(41)	(41)	
Increase in real estate receivables	(92)	(28)	(44)	(62)	(81)	(14)
Decrease in real estate held for sale	(14)	44	93	92	108	10
Other	19	4	87	116	85	7
Net cash from operating activities	2,881	863	2,492	3,587	4,998	(305)
CASH FLOWS FROM INVESTING ACTIVITIES						
Consumer products						
Capital expenditures	(235)	(211)	(427)	(671)	(1,024)	(319)
Purchase of Kraft, Inc.	73				(11,363)	(339)
Purchase of other businesses	(718)			72		
Proceeds from sales of assets					44	
Other	117	(4)	25		52	(20)
Financial services and real estate						
Investments in finance assets	(624)	(10)	(181)	(275)	(481)	(43)
Finance assets proceeds	147	22	64	120	133	62
Other	(2)	11	11	11	1	
Net cash from investing activities	$(1,242)	$(192)	$(508)	$(743)	$(12,638)	$ (659)

Exhibit 7 continued on page 354.

Exhibit 7 (continued)

	12 Months 12/31/87	3 Months 3/31/88	6 Months 6/30/88	9 Months 9/30/88	12 Months 12/31/88	3 Months 3/31/89
CASH FROM FINANCING ACTIVITIES						
Consumer Products						
Short-term borrowings	$(219)	$137	$(324)	$(411)	$8,761	$893
Long-term debt proceeds	484		494	741	1,212	700
Long-term debt repaid	(1,177)	(144)	(358)	(561)	(881)	(259)
Purchase of treasury stock	(200)	(116)	(486)	(539)	(539)	
Dividends paid	(714)	(212)	(425)	(635)	(895)	(260)
Issuance of shares	26	13	15	23	28	9
Other	9	(5)	35	(6)	(85)	3
Financial Services and Real Estate						
Short-term borrowings	109	(36)	(184)	(155)	(20)	(112)
Long-term debt proceeds	438			201	201	
Long-term debt proceeds	(482)				(32)	
Other	(9)		(30)	(28)	12	2
Net cash from financing activities	(1,735)	(363)	(1,263)	(1,370)	7,762	976
Effect of exchange rates on cash	113	(3)	(41)	(61)	(44)	(20)
Increase (decrease) in cash	17	305	680	1,413	78	(8)
Beginning cash	73	90	90	90	90	168
Ending cash	90	395	770	1,503	168	160
Cash paid:						
Interest-consumer product	690	161	289	374	589	387
Interest-financial services	112	13	44	72	88	19
Income taxes	641	136	566	808	1,088	267

▼ ■

Exhibit 8

Selected Interest Rates (Yields in percent per annum)

Instruments	June 2	June 9	June 16	Week Ending June 23	June 30	May	June
Federal funds (effective)[a]	9.84%	9.68%	9.35%	9.48%	9.58%	9.81%	9.53%
Commercial paper[b,c]							
1-month	9.51	9.32	9.28	9.35	9.35	9.58	9.34
3-month	9.31	9.05	9.04	9.16	9.10	9.47	9.11
6-month	9.05	8.71	8.74	8.92	8.73	9.29	8.80
Finance paper placed directly[b]							
1-month	9.39	9.21	9.17	9.28	9.27	9.48	9.24
3-month	9.04	8.71	8.73	8.77	8.77	9.27	8.77
6-month	8.69	8.25	8.11	8.19	8.15	8.97	8.22
Bankers acceptances (top rated)[b]							
3-month	9.16	8.88	8.95	9.05	8.94	9.35	8.97
6-month	8.88	8.56	8.66	8.81	8.55	9.15	8.66
CDS (secondary market)							
1-month	9.52	9.36	9.27	9.36	9.35	9.61	9.35
3-month	9.39	9.15	9.13	9.29	9.16	9.59	9.20
6-month	9.33	9.02	9.02	9.24	8.98	9.60	9.09
Bank prime loan[a,d]	11.50	11.29	11.00	11.00	11.00	11.50	11.07
Discount window borrowing[a,e]	7.00	7.00	7.00	7.00	7.00	7.00	7.00
U.S. government securities							
Treasury bills							
Auction average[b,f]							
3-month	8.50	8.17	8.13	8.22	8.07	8.40	8.22
6-month	8.36	7.99	7.79	8.08	7.78	8.39	8.00
1-year	—	8.18	—	—	—	8.44	8.18
Auction average (investment)[f]							
3-month	8.81	8.46	8.42	8.51	8.35	8.70	8.51
6-month	8.85	8.44	8.22	8.54	8.21	8.88	8.45
Secondary market[b]							
3-month	8.54	8.18	8.14	8.13	8.03	8.43	8.15
6-month	8.33	7.89	7.87	8.05	7.79	8.41	7.93
1-year	8.16	7.79	7.84	7.92	7.71	8.31	7.84
Treasury constant maturities[g]							
1-year	8.80	8.40	8.45	8.53	8.28	8.98	8.44
2-year	8.76	8.38	8.41	8.50	8.23	9.02	8.41
3-year	8.71	8.33	8.38	8.45	8.20	8.98	8.37
5-year	8.60	8.28	8.30	8.37	8.13	8.91	8.29
7-year	8.61	8.31	8.30	8.38	8.16	8.88	8.31
10-year	8.57	8.28	8.26	8.34	8.14	8.86	8.28
30-year	8.58	8.33	8.22	8.30	8.10	8.83	8.27
Composite							
Over 10 years (long-term)[h]	8.70	8.45	8.36	9.44	8.25	8.95	8.40
Corporate bonds							
Moody's seasoned							
AAA	9.37	9.16	9.02	9.09	9.02	9.57	9.10
BAA	10.27	10.06	9.98	10.05	9.97	10.46	10.03
A-Utility[i]	9.80	9.63	9.70	9.59	9.49	10.09	9.65
State & local bonds[j]	7.15	6.95	6.88	7.08	7.02	7.25	7.02
Conventional mortgages[k]	10.48	10.20	10.04	10.19	10.07	10.77	10.20

Exhibit 8 continued on page 356.

Exhibit 8 (continued)

Note: Weekly and monthly figures are averages of daily rates, except for state and local bonds, which are based on Thursday figures, and conventional mortgages and A-utility bonds, both of which are based on Friday figures.

[a]Weekly figures are averages of seven calendar days ending on Wednesday of the current week; monthly figures include each calendar day in the month.

[b]Quoted on bank-discount basis.

[c]Rates on commercial paper placed for firms whose bond rating is AA or the equivalent.

[d]One of several base rates used by banks to place short-term business loans.

[e]Rate for the Federal Reserve Bank of New York.

[f]Rates on issue-date basis.

[g]Yields on activity traded issues adjusted to constant maturities. Source: U.S. Treasury.

[h]Unweighted average of all issues outstanding of bonds neither due nor callable in less than 10 years, including one very low yielding "flower" bond.

[i]Estimate of the yield on the recently offered, A-rated utility bond with a maturity of 30 years and called protection of 5 years; Friday quotations.

[j]Bond Buyer Index, general obligation 20 years to maturity, mixed quality; Thursday quotations.

[k]Contract interest rates on commitments for fixed-rate first mortgages. Source: FHLMC.

Source: Federal Reserve statistical release. These data are scheduled for release on the first Tuesday of each month. The availability of the release will be announced when the information is available.

Exhibit 9

Prices on Various Philip Morris Debt Securities and Yields on U.S. Treasury Securities
(Weeks ended November 18, 1988, through June 23, 1989)

Week Ended	Philip Morris, Inc. PMI[a] 9.125%	Philip Morris, Inc. PMI[a] 9.125%	Philip Morris Companies, Inc. PMCI 9.80%	Philip Morris Companies, Inc. PMCI 10.85%	1 Year GOVTS	7 Year GOVTS	10 Year GOVTS
11/18/88	92.8	93.0			8.55%	8.92%	8.99%
11/25/88	91.8	94.0			8.71	9.05	9.10
12/02/88	91.4	93.4			8.75	9.08	9.11
12/09/88	92.2	89.5			8.89	9.04	9.03
12/16/88	91.2	89.5			9.10	9.19	9.16
12/23/88	91.8	89.5			9.00	9.12	9.08
12/30/88	91.2	89.5			9.07	9.22	9.17
01/06/89	90.8	89.6			9.17	9.31	9.24
01/13/89	91.4	89.8	97.8		9.11	9.25	9.18
01/20/89	92.1	92.1	98.4		8.96	9.97	9.02
01/27/89	93.4	93.6	99.0		8.97	9.02	8.97
02/03/89	92.7	92.8	98.4		9.05	9.04	9.00
02/10/89	91.9	92.8	97.8		9.15	9.11	9.05
02/17/89	91.6	92.8	97.5		9.27	9.28	9.21
02/24/89	90.6	92.8	96.6		9.41	9.38	9.31
03/03/89	90.6	92.0	96.6		9.40	9.39	9.33
03/10/89	90.6	92.0	96.6		9.39	9.32	9.27
03/17/89	90.2	92.0	96.3		9.56	9.42	9.35
03/24/89	89.9	92.0	96.0		9.78	9.58	9.49
03/31/89	90.3	91.6	96.3	100.1	9.71	9.47	9.37
04/07/89	91.6	92.0	97.5	100.4	9.47	9.29	9.20
04/14/89	91.6	91.0	97.5	100.5	9.48	9.36	9.27
04/21/89	92.0	90.0	97.8	100.8	9.28	9.19	9.14
04/28/89	92.3	90.0	98.2	100.8	9.22	9.13	9.09
05/05/89	92.3	90.0	98.2	101.1	9.16	9.07	9.07
05/12/89	92.1	90.0	98.2	101.2	9.05	9.06	9.05
05/19/89	93.2	91.0	99.1	101.4	8.89	8.81	8.79
05/26/89	94.3	91.1	100.0	101.4	8.86	8.67	8.63
06/02/89	95.0	91.1	100.6	101.5	8.80	8.61	8.57
06/09/89	97.0	91.4	102.6	102.0	8.40	8.31	8.28
06/16/89	97.0	96.0	102.6	101.9	8.45	8.30	8.26
06/23/89	97.7	98.5	102.6	101.8	8.53	8.38	8.34

[a]For these Philip Morris, Inc. 9-1/8s due 7/15/2003 prices listed are dealer quote.

Sources: For Philip Morris Securities—Dow Jones News Retrieval. These represent dealer quotes only and may not be reflective of actual trading. For Treasury Securities—Federal Reserve Statistical Release.

Exhibit 10

Corporate Financing Record (Friday—Thursday)

Company and Date to Market	Total Offering ($ millions)	Terms of Offer	Call Prot. (yrs.)	Spread over Treas.	M	S&P	Manager	Underwriting Spread	Underwriting Fee (per 1,000)	Management Fee
DEBT NEGOTIATED										
New Zealand 6/15	$ 90	9.5% notes/00 at 99.798% Y: 9.53%	5	120	Aa3	AA	MS	.651%	$1.20	$1.30
Dr. Pepper/Seven Up Companies 6/15	93	0% sr. sub. disc. notes/98 at 53.5%. Rate to reset on 10/92 at 15.50%.	3	N/A	B3	CCC+	PB	3.50	—	—
Detroit Edison 6/20	300	9.875% gen'l and ref. mtge bonds 19 at 98.82% Y: 9.999%	5	170	Baa2	BBB	MS	.885	2.00	1.75
Sterling Electronics 6/20	10	10.75% conv. sub. debs/09 at 100% Conv. into com. at $5.125. Prem: 32.26%	3	—	—	—	RM	5.75	16.00	11.50
Western Financial Auto Loans 2/6/20	100	9.15% auto loan ctfs. at 99.938% Y: 9.30%	N/C	70	Aaa	AAA	DBL	n/a	—	—
Alaska Air Group 6/21	75	6.875% conv. sub debs/ 14 at 100%. Conv. into com. at $33.60. Prem: 22.74%. Puttable upon changes in mgmt. control.	3	—	Ba3	BB+	FB, ML	—	1.50	3.00
Magma Copper 6/21	100	14.5% sub. reset notes/01 at 100%. Rate to reset 6/92 600 basis points over 3 Treasury indices through '94 when it will reset a final time via the same formula.	3	—	B2	BB-	DBL	3.50		
Nova Scotia 6/21	200	8.875% debt/19 at 100%.	N/C	62.5	A2	A-	ML, WG	.875	2.00	1.75
Big Bear Stores 6/22	150	12.75% sr. notes/97 at 100%.	4	—	B1	B-	SAL	3.00	—	—
INCO 6/22	150	9.875% s.f. debs./19 at 97.40% Y: 15.2%. Rate to reset as if the price were at par for the first five years in the case of a downgrade or a change in control.	10	185	Baa2	BBB-	MS	.898	2.00	1.75
Weingarten Realty Investors 6/22	40	8% conv. cap debs./0.9 at 100%. Conv. into shs. of beneficial interest at $33.50. Prem: 18.06%. Puttable commencing 5/91. Contains event-risk protections.	5	—	—	A+	EDJ	4.50	5.00	10.00
COMPETITIVE										
Philadelphia Electric 6/21	175	10% 1st and ref. mtge. bonds/19 at 98.59%. Y: 10.15%	5	185	Baa3	BBB-	SLH, SAL	.579	—	—
Consolidated Natural Gas 6/22	100	8.75% debs./99 at 99.661% Y: 8.80%	N/C	47	Aa2	AA	SLH	.361	—	—
Virginia Electric & Power 6/22	100	8.75% 1st and ref. mtge. bonds/99 at 99.75% Y: 8.91%.	N/C	57	A1	A+	FB, SAL	.432	—	—

Rating Code

M - Moody's

S&P - Standard & Poor's

MS - Morgan Stanley

PB - Prudential Bache

RM - Rotan Moseley

DBL - Drexel Burham Lambert

FB - First Boston

ML - Merrill Lynch

WG - Wood Gundy

SAL - Salomon Bros.

EDJ - Edward D. Jones

SLH - Shearson Lehman Hutton

Source: *Corporate Financing Week,* June 26, 1989.

Philip Morris Companies, Inc. (B)

Early in the afternoon of Monday, June 26, 1989, Jessica Palmer, managing director for Capital Markets at Salomon Brothers placed the telephone receiver back in its cradle and stared for a moment at the lights on the panel that flashed incessantly. She had just received a call from Nancy De Lisi, assistant treasurer for Corporate Financing at Philip Morris asking Salomon to bid in competition with five other investment banks for $500 million of seven-year securities to be issued by Philip Morris Companies, Inc. Ms. De Lisi would expect Salomon's response within the next fifteen minutes.

Background of Salomon Brothers

Salomon Brothers was one of the six largest, full-service investment banks on Wall Street. It served institutional firms almost exclusively, developing perhaps the strongest institutional distribution base among securities firms. Its primary strength was in the trading of government, corporate, and mortgage-backed bonds. Its institutional focus, trading expertise, and willingness to take risks propelled it into underwriting leadership in the 1980s. By 1989, however, its dominance was beginning to slip, as other firms, most notably Merrill Lynch, began to outperform it in the annual underwriting totals.

Relationship with Philip Morris

Salomon had built its leadership position in the transaction-driven environment of the late 1970s and throughout the 1980s. Many of the relationships that it had formed with issuers were initiated by "buying" the business—that is, by offering companies financing at levels and spreads that many other firms would be unwilling to match. Through a combination of market savvy and risk-management techniques, Salomon had proved itself capable of managing this risky business profitably. Its relationship with Philip Morris provided a typical example of how Salomon worked to expand its corporate relationships.

Prior to 1985, Salomon had had few direct dealings with Philip Morris. Until

---

This case was prepared by Professor Samuel L. Hayes, III.
Copyright © 1991 by the President and Fellows of Harvard College. Harvard Business School case N9-292-006.

that time, Philip Morris had been served almost exclusively by Goldman Sachs and Lehman Brothers. With the acquisition of General Foods in 1985, Hans G. Storr, the chief financial officer of Philip Morris, worked to broaden his company's relationships among other selected Wall Street firms in an effort to obtain the cheapest financing possible. While Salomon had gained an entry to the company's business by this time, it was clearly interested in developing an even more important relationship.

After Philip Morris announced its acquisition of Kraft in October 1988, Salomon was one of the leading securities firms which continued to make markets in PM's securities despite the market's initially adverse reaction to the move. The research analyst covering PM expressed an optimistic outlook for Philip Morris's prospects (see Exhibit 1). Because of its demonstrated bond trading and distribution capabilities, Salomon won a place in the manager's group for the first post-Kraft offering, $500 million of 9.80% notes due in 1998, along with Merrill Lynch, the lead manager, and Goldman Sachs. Salomon skipped the bidding for $1 billion in 12–18 month notes that took place in March 1989, ostensibly because it was not interested in the swap business that accompanied these issues.[1] In June, with interest rates well off their April peaks and expected to decline still further, both Philip Morris and Salomon turned their attention to medium-term issues once again.

The Mechanics of the Bid

According to well-established market procedures, the investment banks would bid for $500 million of seven-year notes according to an "all-in" spread over treasuries. To illustrate this concept, consider the example illustrated in Table A:

Table A

"All-In" Spread Concept

	As % of Face Value	Yield-to Maturity
Coupon: 10.00%		
Maturity: 7 Years		
Sinking Fund: None		
Price to Public (a)	100.000%	10.00%
Underwriting Discount	.500%	.10%
Net Proceeds to Company (b)	99.500%	10.10%
All-in Cost		10.10%
On-the-run Treasury[2] (c)		9.00%
Spread (before discount) (a)-(c)	100 basis pts.	
All-in Spread (b)-(c)	110 basis pts.	

In this example, a 10% seven-year note, priced to the public at 100% of its face value, has a yield-to maturity of 10.00%. The cost to the issuer, however, must reflect the full effect of the underwriting discount.[3] At an assumed discount of .500% of face value, the issuer pays an effective rate, known as its "all-in cost," of

10.10%. (In a seven-year note, every one-tenth of one percent of underwriting discount—expressed as a percentage of the face value of the notes—adds two basis points to the all-in spread.) The all-in spread is the difference between the all-in cost to the company of the issue and the yield on the "on-the-run" treasury security with an equivalent maturity. In the example given above, if an underwriter believed that it could sell a seven-year, 10% issue to investors at a spread of 100 basis points over the corresponding treasury security and it required an underwriting discount of .500%, it would bid a spread of 110 basis points "all-in."

In June 1989, typical gross spreads for ten-year issues trading in the secondary market ranged from 90 basis points for issues rated "A" by the rating agencies to 130 basis points for issues rated "BBB." The most recently issued Philip Morris notes, the 9.80s of 1988, had just traded at 102 39/64 bid to yield 9.38%, a spread of about 112 basis points.

After winning the bid, the lead manager and the company determined the all-in cost by adding the bid spread to the yield on the "on-the-run" treasury at an agreed-upon time. Then they negotiated to determine the coupon on the issue.

After the issue had been priced, it was customary for the issuer to specify to the lead manager which investment banking firms should be invited to be co-managers. On negotiated deals, the members of the syndicate would be chosen prior to the pricing decision. On competitive deals, the group would typically be formed within a half hour of the pricing decision (unlike a number of other issuers, PM did not offer recommendations for inclusion in syndicates of its competitively won deals, preferring to leave that entirely to the lead manager's discretion). Depending on prevailing market conditions, the syndicate might be quite small, often made up of only major bracket firms. Frequently, only the lead manager and co-managers made up the syndicate.

Next, the lead manager organized a due diligence session, often by telephone conference call, where each of the managers' representatives heard a brief update from the company's financial officers and corporate counsel. At this time, they were invited to ask questions of the company. A typical due diligence conference call lasted for perhaps thirty minutes or more. In a Rule 415 issue, the ongoing work of securities analysts was relied upon more than the due diligence process and the prospectus to keep the market up to date on any developments with the issuer. Exhibit 2 presents the perspectives of several leading analysts on the industry outlook at the time of this financing.

When needed, the lead manager would also organize a "selling group" of securities dealers who received a selling commission but carried no underwriting risk. Within approximately 24 hours of the pricing decision, all of the issue was typically sold, the syndicate disbanded, and the securities free to trade at the market-determined reoffered price in the secondary market. The syndicate was expected to deliver the net proceeds of the offering to the issuer five business days after pricing.

Current Market Conditions

After bottoming out in mid-June, interest rates had begun rising on the weakness of the dollar and fears of inflation. However, on Friday, June 23, with the news that durable goods orders had declined 4.2% for the month of May, fears of recession began to influence investor psychology. As a result, the bond markets rallied on expectations of further easing of interest rates by the Federal Reserve.

Some analysts, however, were quick to point out that the Fed would probably approach the easing with caution, so that any decline in rates was likely to be modest.

In contrast, the corporate bond market seemed lackluster. Most of the trading by investors focused on the Treasury market. Consequently, corporate spreads widened slightly. Comments from both *Barron's* and *The Wall Street Journal* highlighting these influences on the treasury and corporate bond markets are excerpted in Exhibit 3.

Hedging

If successful in its bid, Salomon could protect itself from rising interest rates by shorting some or all of the comparable maturity treasury securities. In this way, it would only be exposed to changes in the spread above treasuries. As long as it was able to sell its Philip Morris bonds at the same spread, Salomon was assured that it would realize its underwriting discount, no matter which direction interest rates moved. If the spread widened, Salomon would lose money, since losses on its short position would exceed any gains on its long position. On the other hand, if spreads narrowed, Salomon would make money in excess of the underwriting discount.

To illustrate this concept, consider the following example:

Table B

Illustration of Hedging Concept

	Case 1	Case 2	Case 3
Yield on new notes (long)	10.00	10.35	9.75
Yield on Treasury (short)	9.00	9.25	8.85
Spread in basis points	100	110	90
Gain (loss) in basis points[4]			
Notes	None	(35)	25
Treasury	None	25	(15)
Net gain or loss	None	(10)	10

Case 1 gives the yield levels at which the hedge was locked in. As long as the spread remains fixed at 100 basis points, Salomon will realize the full amount of its underwriting commission. In Case 2, with fixed income yields rising, Salomon draws a loss on the hedge as the spread widens. This results from a greater loss (35 basis points) on its long position in the notes than its 25 basis-point gain on the short position in treasuries. In Case 3, when yields decline, a narrower spread produces a net 10 basis-point gain on the hedge, since the profit on the long position exceeds the loss on the short.

The Decision

Ms. Palmer walked over to Salomon's Syndicate Desk, which was headed by Robert Kleinert, a managing director, to formulate the firm's bid on the $500 million issue. The Syndicate Desk was responsible for pricing and managing the selling process for all new issues. Ms. Palmer's Capital Markets group managed Salomon's relationship with Philip Morris, providing the issuer with market intelligence and new ideas. The input of Capital Markets was important, but ultimately the Syndicate Desk would make the final decision on the bid. Mr. Kleinert considered all of the factors discussed above in framing his bid for the new note offering. The Treasury market was working in his favor, as the yield on the benchmark seven-year notes had declined from 8.27% to 8.22%. He and his associates would have to work quickly to formulate a bid and decide whether, and at what level, to hedge the new issue if their bid was accepted.

▶ Endnotes

1. At that time, spreads in the swap market were being influenced by the efforts of both Black and Decker and RJR Nabisco to swap floating-rate bank debt into fixed-rate obligations. Many investment grade issuers rushed to obtain the unusually attractive floating rates that could be created using this obvious credit mismatch.

2. An "on-the-run" treasury security is one that has been recently issued and consequently is likely to be the most actively traded and efficiently priced for any given maturity. Pricing on these securities is readily available to everyone in the investment community through services such as Telerate.

3. An underwriting discount is equal to the difference between the "net price to the public" of the issue and the "net proceeds to the company." It represents the compensation to the investment banks for underwriting and guaranteeing the placement of the issue.

4. If yields increase on a long position, a loss results. On a short position, an increase in yield produces a gain. Likewise, if yields decline, a long position will show a gain, a short position a loss.

Exhibit 1

Stock Research: Tobacco—Diana K. Temple, Salomon Brothers, November 8, 1988

. . . On October 30, Kraft agreed to be acquired by Philip Morris for $106 per share—a total of $13 billion. . . .

For 1988, Philip Morris management has indicated that earnings will equal approximately $10.15 per share, $0.10 less than our prior estimate because of increased marketing expenses. Given the $106 per share purchase of Kraft, we are reducing our 1989 estimate of Philip Morris's 1989 earnings from $12.25 per share to $11.50 per share, which would represent a 13% growth rate. Cash flow should rise to $18.80 per share in 1989.

We continue to recommend purchase of Philip Morris shares given the 4.8% current yield and prospects for 19% annual earnings growth after 1989. Philip Morris shares are now selling at 5.2 times cash flow, toward the low end of its 4.6–11.0 range of recent years. . . .

During the next five years, Philip Morris could repay $11 billion in acquisition debt. In addition, Kraft will generate $300–$400 million in excess cash annually, which could be used for share repurchase. With the acquisition of Kraft, Philip Morris nontobacco profits will rise to $2.4 billion—35% of the total, up from 25%.

Philip Morris will become the world's largest consumer company. . . . The advertising budget for the combined companies is $2.2 billion, compared with $2.4 billion for advertising and promotion for the first-ranked advertiser, Unilever.

Comparison of Leading Consumer Companies (dollars in millions)[a]

	1989E Sales	1989E Net Income	1987E Advertising	1989E EPS	Price (7 Nov)	1989E P/E	Estimated Five-Year Earnings Growth
Philip Morris	$45,510	$2,641	$2,200	11.50	$94	8.2	19%
RJR Nabisco	21,730	1,519	1,600[b]	6.75	87	12.9	14
Proctor & Gamble	21,000	1,126	1,600	7.10	82	11.5	14
Unilever	35,000	1,700	2,400[b]	6.13	59	9.6	14

▼ ▼ ▼ ▼ ▼ ▼

[a]Except per-share amounts

[b]Includes promotion

E = Estimate

Earnings Growth at 19% Projected Beyond 1989

We calculate Philip Morris earnings growth at 19% annually during the next several years based on the following assumptions:

► U.S. cigarette earnings will grow by 12% annually on flat to slightly lower unit sales, in the context of a 2% decline in industry sales. Prices will rise by 8–10% annually.

► International cigarette earnings will expand by 15–20% annually given 5%

or better unit gains because of solid unit growth in European and Asian markets. After a 12% price hike in 1988, prices will rise by 8–10%.

▶ Miller Brewing profits will rise by 10–12% with 2–3% unit growth because of continuing strength in Genuine Draft.

▶ General Foods profits will grow by 10%, better than our previous 8–10% projection because of some marketing savings. Unit growth will be 3% with negligible growth in coffee.

▶ Kraft operating profits will rise by 10% annually, assuming 4–5% tonnage gains and 7–9% revenue gains.

▶ Interest expense will decline from $1.5 billion in 1989 to $510 million in 1994 with the repayment of $11 billion in acquisition debt.

▶ Amortization will rise to $370 million in 1989 from $106 million in 1988, but will be stable thereafter.

▶ The tax rate will fall from 43.3% in 1989 to 41.4% in 1994 because of the declining importance of goodwill.

Exhibit 2

Excerpts from Wall Street Transcript

Excerpts from June 5, 1989 *Wall Street Transcript* roundtable discussion by three tobacco analysts on the Tobacco Industry.

Kurt Feurman (Drexel Burnham Lambert):

. . . five basic points: (1) litigation is fading; (2) the Kraft deal will (after much trepidation) not be very dilutive . . . (3) earnings momentum at Philip Morris is absolutely astounding . . . (4) investor psychology [is up] . . . (5) the RJR Nabisco deal is probably just as important as any of the other factors. . . . In 1988, the industry lost its first [litigation] case ever, won a case and a third ended in a mistrial. That is not exactly a stellar record. But two months after "losing" the Cipollone trial, [Philip] Morris raised its dividend 25 percent. The earnings and cash flow just keep rolling in.

Emanuel Goldman (Paine Webber):

. . . the investor perception sees the litigation risk petering out. The issue of pre-emption (that is, if you smoke and get sick, that's your problem because you should have known better in the first place) . . . the other issue is one of punitive damages, or I should say, the lack thereof—even with the Cipollone case where Mrs. Cipollone's estate where her husband, I think maybe out of sympathy more than anything, was awarded $400,000. In no case with anything, were there any punitive damages. . . .

Roy D. Burry (Kidder Peabody):

. . . I think the [tobacco] industry is growing worldwide, and certainly the market share growth of the companies we're talking about allows their unit volumes to increase significantly almost every year.

Exhibit 3

Excerpts from the Financial Press

Barron's, June 26, 1989, page 50
Current Yield . . . by Randall W. Forsyth

Hope of Fed Easing Sparks Rally

. . . Rumors of a pact among the U.S., Japanese, and West German authorities to ratchet down the dollar back to its levels of several weeks ago accelerated the currency's skid that began the week before last. The story, combined with further signs of a U.S. slowdown, fanned market speculation that the Federal Reserve was planning to take further steps to loosen monetary policy, including a possible cut in the discount rate. Such a move could help ease the upward pressure on the greenback and forestall any further softening in the domestic economy.

The prospect of easy money sent prices soaring across markets Friday, with bonds, stocks, precious metals and foreign currencies mounting spirited rallies. . . .

Notwithstanding market speculation of a cut in the discount rate from its current 7%, any easing decided by the FOMC (Federal Open Market Committee-added) is apt to be less dramatic. . . . In any case, the Greenspan Fed has preferred to move in small measured steps.

The Wall Street Journal, June 26, 1989

Indicators Could Feed Recession Whispers

Listen for whispers of "recession" to mount if economists are right in forecasting a drop in the May index of leading economic indicators . . .

"The economy is showing considerable weakness in a variety of places," said Lawrence A. Kudlow, chief economist with Bear, Stearns & Co., New York. Consumer spending has slowed, as evidenced recently by weak retail sales and auto sales, and Mr. Kudlow thinks that manufacturing may be weakening, too, "and that's a newer wrinkle." Friday's steep 4.2% drop in May durable goods orders only added to worries over weakness.

U.S. Auto Sales Fell 9.8% in Mid-June as Incentives Failed to Offset Weakness

Second Half Slowdown Is Predicted for Stocks

. . . But what worries strategists is that the dollar's rise has helped distract investors from a nagging problem: Although the economy is slowing, inflation isn't. As recently as a few weeks ago, the principal measures of retail and wholesale prices were showing alarmingly big gains. . . . [A.C. Moore, head of research at Argus Research says] "The Fed isn't going to be able to ease anytime soon, and that's going to make everybody a little more pessimistic."

Exhibit 3 continued on page 368.

Friday's Market Activity

Bond prices surged as the latest economic reports provided fresh evidence that the economy is slowing down. The reports fueled speculation that interest rates may be heading lower. The Treasury's benchmark 30-year bond was quoted late at 107 15/32, compared with 105 30/32 Thursday. The Treasury's latest 10-year note rose 7/8 point to 105 27/32, compared with 104 31/32 Thursday; its yield fell to 8.23% from 8.37%.

The surge in bond prices began Friday morning, shortly after the durable-goods report was released. Prices eased higher when the nation's auto makers reported weak auto sales in mid-June despite heavy dealer incentives.

But bond prices got a bigger boost in afternoon trading on rumors that the Federal Reserve was preparing to cut the discount rate to 7% . . . . Although many observers doubted the central bank would act so quickly, the rumors moved the market higher.

In the corporate sector . . . trading was light . . . many investors have concentrated on Treasury securities rather than corporate bonds. Reflecting the lack of demand, yield spreads between corporate bonds and comparable Treasuries have widened.

Eaton Vance and Prime Rate Reserves

"We don't like it, we don't want it and we don't need it." This was the concluding sentence of Jim Hawkes' conversation with a senior manager of one of the largest retail brokers in the U.S. and Hawkes was appalled. It was early September 1988, and clear that after months of talks Loeb White had decided not to introduce the new mutual fund suggested by Eaton Vance, Prime Rate Reserves. Hawkes (MBA, 1970), a VP and Director at Eaton Vance, was convinced that the product made sense and would be good for investors, good for the brokers and good for Eaton Vance. Now, he had to decide what to do next. Should he drop the idea, try to change it, look for mistakes, look for other brokers? Each route could be defended, but which was the best?

Prime Rate Reserves was designed to be a closed-end mutual fund. Its assets would be invested in senior bank loans made in highly leveraged transactions. The fund would pay a yield expected to be close to prime, with an underwriting discount of 4%. In Hawkes' thinking Prime Rate Reserves would fulfill a real investor need and could significantly extend Eaton Vance's total fund base. Since the firm's funds growth had slowed this would make Prime Rate Reserves an attractive addition to the various investment products offered by Eaton Vance. Actually, Hawkes was so convinced of the value of the product that he worried that if he would not be able to get it to the investor in the near future, others would bring substantially the same idea to the market; with a limited investor base, Eaton Vance could be in effect excluded, especially since Prime Rate Reserves would need at least $200–300 million worth of assets to "get off the ground."

For Hawkes, one of the seven directors of Eaton Vance, Prime Rate Reserves mattered. He had invested a major part of almost a year of his time to get the product to the stage where it was now. And while he was convinced that the product made good sense, he realized that actual success depended on many more factors. To manage the whole product introduction process was the real challenge.

Eaton Vance

Eaton Vance Corporation was formed in 1979 through the merger of Eaton & Howard and Vance-Sanders Company. The company, located in Boston's financial

---

This case was prepared by Assistant Professor David M. Meerschwam.
Copyright © 1990 by the President and Fellows of Harvard College. Harvard Business School case N9-290-020.

district, was a holding company of several subsidiaries, of which Eaton Vance Management was the most important. Through the company, $4.9 billion of assets were managed in October 1988. Other subsidiaries included Eaton Vance Distributors, which was a marketer of the company's mutual funds, and Investors Bank & Trust Company, a provider of fiduciary and related banking services. Several specialized subsidiaries that had real estate, oil and gas, and precious minerals mining portfolios also formed part of Eaton Vance.

Eaton Vance's main business activity in 1988 consisted of the introduction and management of mutual funds. In 1988, 22 such funds were offered (all of them open-ended funds, which meant that the funds stood ready to redeem shares). The firm also engaged in investment advice for individual clients, mostly through its Investment Counsel division. Management of mutual funds generated approximately 70% of total revenue in 1988.

The consolidated balance sheet showed $77 million in assets for the company itself. Of Eaton Vance's $4.9 billion of manager assets, $3.1 billion was held in its 22 continuously offered funds. Another $1.8 billion of assets were managed through the Investment Counsel division. High net-worth individuals and pension funds were typical clients of this group.

Through its various activities Eaton Vance generated $10.7 million in net income on an equity base of $37.4 million (return on ending assets of 13.9%). Furthermore, the 3.9 million shares and an average stock price of $19 per share for the final fiscal quarter of 1988 gave the firm a market value of $74 million. Of the 3.9 million shares, managers and officers at the firm held 38%.

Eaton Vance had 214 employees, whose average compensation was $64,000. Of the 214, most worked in managing the firm's funds, 15 were regional field marketing representatives and 14 were telemarketing specialists who supported the field representatives from the Boston office. Overall, 82 investment professionals were employed. Marketing, operations and administrative services employed 52, 24 and 58 respectively.

Both Landon Clay, the chairman, and Dozier Gardner, the president, of Eaton Vance, had backgrounds in investment management. This investment focus related to both main activities of the firm—investment management for individual accounts (such as pension funds) and mutual fund organization and management. Gardner, (MBA, 1959) noted that: "The industry is obviously changing. There is this trend to more and more specialized funds and I am not sure that I am all that comfortable with it."

The mutual funds were more labor intensive than the investment counseling business (the individual investment management sales force consisted of 3 sales representatives; for mutual funds 15 sales executives were employed). But the funds also yielded a higher management fee—approximately 65 basis points for the mutual funds versus 25bp for the individual investment counseling services.

The sales representatives had various backgrounds. Typically they had not been to graduate school programs but instead had worked for several years as brokers or as sales executives in other industries. While they were very familiar with the various products, they had little explicit investment management expertise. The investment executives in the firm, on the other hand, had little sales experience but many had graduate business degrees.

Compensation for the sales representatives consisted of a base salary (typically on par with the starting MBA salary) and a bonus related to the sales performance, which could be multiples of the base. The sales representatives (wholesaler, as they were known in the mutual fund industry) dealt with the brokers at the retail brokerage firms—these in turn sold the funds at the retail level. Most at Eaton Vance, and at other firms, regarded Eaton Vance's sales force highly.

The Mutual Fund Industry

Mutual funds grew rapidly in the U.S. during the last decade. While the first fund was organized in Boston in 1924, it was the popularity of the money market mutual fund, developed in the early 1970s, that propelled the mutual fund industry to high visibility. While total assets stood at $450 million in 1940, when Congress enacted the Investment Company Act, by 1977 total assets had grown to approximately $50 billion. The compound growth rate (CGR) of 13.6% for this period contrasted to a CGR of 34.2% during the period 1978–1988, at the end of which slightly over $800 billion in assets were under fund management.

Mutual funds were all predicated on the idea that they would offer retail investors some of the advantages available to the larger (institutional) investor. Thus, by buying a share in a pool of money (the fund) the investors could benefit from professional research, diversification and specialized portfolios. Furthermore, when in the 1970s interest rates started to rise and regulations in effect discriminated against the small retail investor, money market mutual funds allowed smaller investors to share in the higher returns available to wholesale investors in deregulated markets.

A mutual fund would sell shares to the public and invest the proceeds on behalf of the investors. Typically a management company would be responsible for the investments and would be compensated by the fund. Independent fund trustees would approve of the management charges and investments policies and practices.

The funds could be distinguished along various dimensions. One relates to the sales of shares held by investors. In the open-end mutual fund, the fund stands ready to redeem shares; as a result the amount of assets it deploys varies according to net sales or redemptions to the fund. In contrast, closed-end funds are defined as all funds that are not open-ended, and thus all funds that do not redeem shares. Investors in closed-end funds would only be able to sell the shares to other investors interested in buying.

Closed-end funds (which were listed on stock exchanges) were always underwritten. The underwriting fee consisted of two parts. One went to the brokers (400–450bp) with the remainder to the selling group (typically 150-250bp) as a sales discount. For many brokerage firms, the closed-end funds were handled by the same departments that dealt with the underwriting of ordinary corporate equity securities. These groups were in different departments of brokerage firms from the ones that dealt with the open-end funds.

Another distinction could be found in the way in which the funds were sold to the investors. Traditionally load funds immediately charged the investor the underwriting costs as an up-front fee (load). No-load funds did not explicitly charge such compensation up-front.

Furthermore direct sales funds existed. They were sold directly to the public, typically using marketing devices such as television commercials and newspaper advertisements. Broker/dealer funds, on the other hand, relied on traditional retail brokers to sell the funds to their customers. Broker/dealer funds typically compensated the brokers with a commission. Only money market mutual funds did not pay such commissions to the brokers—they were offered as a "service."

Various other special features existed and innovations kept occurring in the mutual fund market. For example, in 1980 experimentation had started with so-called 12b-1 open-end funds. These funds would be sold to investors at their net asset value, like no-load funds, but would carry annual charges (separate and in addition to the ordinary management fee) for "distribution" costs. Distribution costs were the costs incurred in selling the fund to the investor. Such a charge was novel and represented a change from the SEC's traditional view. Traditionally the SEC had argued that since the trustees should guard the interest of the existing shareholders of the fund they could not approve of charges related to the distribution charges of the fund. Furthermore, some feared potential conflicts of interest; with compensation to the management company typically related to the net asset value of the fund, the distribution charge could skew the fund's emphasis to growth through sales of new shares. Still, in 1980 Rule 12b-1 was adopted which allowed trustees each year to approve distribution charges for open-end mutual funds.

Given the structure of a particular fund, the major distinguishing characteristic was the types of investments it made. Bond and stock funds competed with money market funds and within the general categories many specialized funds were found. For example, municipal bond funds only invested in certain tax-free municipals, income-stock funds in high dividend-paying equity securities. With an increasing array of possible investment securities available the number of specialized funds grew rapidly. Also, until October 1987, the overall gains of the stock market helped the rapid growth of the industry. After October 1987, many investors shifted their investments from equity mutual funds into money market mutual funds. Since many fund management companies offer "families of funds" within which investors can switch (exchange) at low or no costs, the last quarter of 1987 saw a vast increase in such exchanges. In 1988, net sales (i.e., sales minus redemptions) to the equity, bond, and income funds was $19 billion; net sales to the money market funds stood at $28 billion.

Eaton Vance and Product Innovation

Eaton Vance, like other mutual fund management companies, had introduced different funds over time. The process of introduction was an informal one. While the firm was a well-known player in the industry, it was small enough to allow for an informal structure. Its most recent important product introduction had been the Marathon Group, a family of funds that had first been marketed in 1985.

By 1985, Eaton Vance had undergone change in its mutual fund offerings. It no longer offered any closed-end funds. It transformed its last remaining closed-end fund, Nautilus Fund, which had made investments in venture capital firms such as Apple Computers, into a continuously offered (open-end) fund. Also, in December of that year two new municipal bond funds were introduced. Both were Eaton Vance's first "deferred sales charges" funds (12b-1), and had sales of $24 million in their first month of existence. Eaton Vance borrowed money from banks to pay the brokers up front, but only charged investors over time. As the 1985 Annual Report stated:

> The new products . . . appear to have a large and ready market. If successful, they will contribute to earnings but will also require a substantial commitment of capital. With a strong balance sheet, Eaton Vance is in a comfortable position to make the necessary commitments to these products.

And the products were successful indeed. By year end 1986, a total of $707 million was invested in them. Eaton Vance noted in that year's Annual Report:

> The successful offering of deferred sales commission funds has important consequences for the future earnings of Eaton Vance and a significant impact on the Company's current balance sheet. When these funds are sold, Eaton Vance compensates the brokers with a 4% commission and establishes a balance sheet asset, deferred sales commissions. Fund shares incur no initial sales charge, but distribution plan payments of 1% per year of average net assets are charged to the Fund and paid to Eaton Vance. . . .
>
> Eaton Vance . . . also receives contingent deferred sales commissions from shareholders redeeming their shares within six years of their purchase. Other investment management firms market funds with deferred sales commission structures. However, none, to our knowledge, terminate charges against fund assets when payments have compensated the fund's distributor for its expenses and a reasonable profit as do Eaton Vance funds.

In the recent past, the firm had introduced three to five funds a year (which meant an increase from what had been done before). Some of these funds had been suggested by the sales force. However, it was always difficult for the sales people to accurately forecast the possible demand for the funds. Another way in which funds were introduced was for someone else in the organization to come up with an idea. Often industry statistics were studied to identify possible lacunae in Eaton Vance's family of funds. For example, it could become clear that single state municipal funds were selling well in the Northeast and that Eaton Vance primarily offered national funds. After several discussions a decision would be made whether or not to try to go ahead with a new product.

In general, ideas for new funds could be generated at different levels in the firm. They would "filter up" to senior management. And while the firm had created a "New Product Committee," it hardly ever met in a formal setting. Gardner, the president, explained that,

> Eaton Vance doesn't need too many formal structures. In the course of a day I presumably talk to Jim (Hawkes) four to five times and to the others as well. There are actually almost too many ideas—the real question is how do you determine which lead to take? The idea of the New Product Committee was quite useful to focus everyone on the importance of new funds, but you don't need such a formal setting at Eaton Vance. Different firms manage this in different ways, but I think we have the process under control. We have Jim Hawkes, one of the seven directors pretty much fully dedicated to this issue, and we all understand its importance.

In the first phase of a possible new product development, Eaton Vance would have to spend some resources to do research, file with the SEC, talk to the possibly interested brokers, etc. In the second stage, more would be spent on producing sales literature, road shows and other promotional items. Introduction costs could vary between $150,000 to several hundred thousand for a totally new, innovative fund.

Eaton Vance Dollar Funds

While Eaton Vance had been successful in several of its product offerings, there were always risks involved that the product may not sell well or that, if successful, others would quickly imitate a fund. In fact such imitation was quite easy. One manager noted:

Often imitation is really easy. Especially the big distributors see that a particular product goes well and they will very shortly thereafter come out with a similar product. There is very little you can do about it—it is the cost of being the first. For example, we came out with a couple of really smart and innovative prospectuses. You know, we had done our homework, the lawyers had set up a good structure, there was an innovative distribution plan and a couple of months later an identical prospectus was produced by someone else, they even forgot to take the typos out!

Another problem for Eaton Vance was to judge the potential of the funds. While "pricing" issues existed, in particular the expected yield calculations, the appeal of potential products was mostly hard to judge. The difficulty in judging market potential was exemplified by two new Eaton Vance funds; Eaton Vance Government Income Dollar Fund, L.P., and Eaton Vance Corporate High Income Dollar Fund, L.P. The funds would invest in U.S. government (guaranteed) securities and in high yield bonds, respectively. Both funds were designed to take advantage of the 1984 repeal of the U.S. interest withholding tax on bonds for non-U.S. residents. The sales department, in conjunction with several brokers, had suggested the product. Eaton Vance introduced the two funds that were exclusively designed for non-resident aliens in the U.S.

At Eaton Vance a manager much involved with the development of the product remembered that when the funds were designed Eaton Vance had gotten much information that:

There were a lot of investors out in the market who really wanted this type of product. We were told by a lot of contacts that something like this would go very well. These were investors who preferred to keep their investment in the U.S. and did not want to invest in, for example, the Euro-market. Also, the fund would offer diversification, high yield and high safety in the government sector.

When the two dollar funds were designed they were made into open-end, load (4.75%) funds, with a small (0.25%) 12b-1 expected annual distribution charge for continuing compensation to the selling brokers. The shares were sold through Eaton Vance Distributors, Inc., as principal underwriter of the fund. Still, most of the funds would be sold through the large national retail brokers.

After all the preparations were completed, the Dollar Funds were offered and turned out to be much less successful than Eaton Vance had hoped. At the end of 1988, more than one and a half years after its introduction, the Government Fund had just under $3.7 million in net asset value. The High Income fund fared better but still not nearly up to expectation—it had under $22 million in net assets. And while the performance of the funds had been as expected in yield terms (8.83% in net investment income to average net assets in the Government fund and 11.8% in the High Yield fund), most at Eaton Vance considered the product a disappointment.

Duane Waldenburg, vice-president and director, was in charge of the sales force. He considered the disappointing Dollar funds as representing an almost inevitable outcome of new product introductions:

Actually, some of the sales people had really strong indications that this would be a great product. We did our part—we carefully educated the wholesalers, showed why the product would make sense, wrote the right literature, but you never really know what will sell. . . .

Once, when we were really successful in selling KEOGH plans to companies, one of the strongest helps in selling was the idea of laying out the basic issues on a small

card that could fit in your shirt pocket. Doesn't sound really important, does it? . . .
But it worked!

Prime Rate Reserves

Jim Hawkes had become Eaton Vance's Chief Investment Officer in 1985. He
had been one of the firm's seven directors since 1982. After graduating from the
Harvard Business School in 1970, he had joined Eaton Vance as an investment
executive and had been responsible for various funds. When Hawkes was
appointed Chief Investment Officer he saw his role not only in terms of "supervising" the various investment activities:

> We have a very good group of fund managers and, since we only have 214 employ-
> ees, you really are in close contact with a lot of people. We meet daily with the senior
> professional people. Our chief economist may make a general presentation of recent
> economic events and then some other topics will come up. Someone from the
> government research group could present the way the current thinking is going, or
> someone from the portfolio model group can present the changes they have made.
> Someone from equity research could speak about a particular stock and at the end
> anyone can ask pretty much any question. I think it is all very informal, professional
> and actually quite informative—we all have a sense of what is going on.

> The actual portfolio managers really manage their own portfolios. I get little involved.
> I will talk to them and make sure that I understand what is going on but I am not
> really a Chief Investment Officer who decides what we buy today for a particular fund.
> But I do get involved with some of the general management issues. For example,
> around year end when performance evaluations are made.

Hawkes had gotten much involved in the product development process:

> I don't know why I have gotten involved in it. It is not some formal position or role that
> comes with my "title." I always found it quite interesting and as you think about the
> various issues that face Eaton Vance, someone has to make it a primary responsibil-
> ity to think about this. It really is my main task and I think that almost everyone at
> Eaton Vance takes new product development really seriously.

Hawkes had gotten interested in the possibilities of a new fund specially
designed around senior bank loans in highly leveraged transactions that had been
"sold down" by the bank originators. Such loans had burgeoned as many leveraged buy-out transactions had taken place. Banks that originated the loans (typically at prime plus 150bp) were rewarded with origination fees of up to 200bp.
For various reasons many banks decided to sell the loans to other banks. Such
down selling often reduced the original position of the originator to less than 5%
of the original issue:

> When I first thought about this it was around early 1988. I really didn't know much
> about the loans. I served on the high yield fund investment committee and started to
> realize that in all the documents we reviewed for the high yield bonds, there was
> always this large chunk of high yield, floating rate, senior bank debt. Also, I realized
> that retail investors had almost no way to share in this part of the financing. You
> know, a lot of the high yield bonds have ended up with retail investors—people like
> high yields, but retail investors could not participate in the bank tranche.

After spending several months talking to many bankers in New York,
Hawkes felt that he had attained a fairly good understanding of the loans. He

thought that since the loans were originated at prime plus a spread, a mutual fund that bought such loans could expect to yield prime to investors. Hawkes considered money market funds the basic alternative for investors who did not want to be exposed to interest rate risk. Such funds paid rates close to CDs and Hawkes thought that investors would compare Prime to CD and money market fund rates—Prime looked very favorable in such a comparison with rates between 1983 and 1988 on average 200bp above money market rates.

> Once we had the basic concept we figured it was all doable. First we realized that it would have to be a closed-end fund—our legal people saw no alternative, given the types of assets that would be held by the fund. Also, we wanted to raise a fair bit of money. Most of these loans participations are for $5–10 million minimum, and with a bit of diversification you are going to need $200–250 million. But that shouldn't be a problem. I think that the demand for something like this could easily be $400–500 million—that is, if you market it right.

A closed-end fund would typically be an underwritten fund, and it was clear that due to the illiquid nature of the assets Prime Rate Reserves would hold, regulation required it to be a closed-end fund. Normally, this meant that the brokerage houses would form a syndicate and charge an underwriting discount of 700–800bp. The discount would be divided into a selling discount (220–300bp) and a broker's commission (400–500bp). Thus most closed-end mutual funds were sold with total upfront loads of 700–800bp. For Prime Rate Reserve Hawkes considered a different structure—an underwriting discount of approximately 400bp. It seemed that this was the most that could be charged if the product would stand a good chance with the investors. The fee would mean that the selling concession (for the syndicate) would be around 150bp, while a broker's commission of 200–250bp could be offered. With such a pricing structure and a management fee of approximately 65bp, Eaton Vance calculated the Prime yield to the investor. Exhibit 9 provides a letter from Hawkes to Loeb White and an outline of the product.

Hawkes now figured that all was ready to go. Conversations with Loeb White were progressing and he foresaw a good demand for Prime Rate Reserves if only Eaton Vance could get it to the investors. Against this background Loeb White's "we don't like it, we don't want it and we don't need it," was highly unpleasant for Hawkes. He wondered whether it was now possible to make the product into a success after all.

Exhibit 1

Mutual Fund Assets

Year	Mutual Funds (A)	Money Market Funds (B)	(B) as percent of (A)
1970	47.6	NA	NA
1971	55.0	NA	NA
1972	59.8	NA	NA
1973	46.5	NA	NA
1974	35.8	1.7	4.7%
1975	45.9	3.7	8.1%
1976	51.3	3.7	7.2%
1977	48.9	3.9	8.0%
1978	55.9	10.9	19.5%
1979	94.2	45.2	48.0%
1980	134.7	74.4	55.2%
1981	241.3	181.9	75.4%
1982	296.6	206.6	69.7%
1983	292.9	162.5	55.5%
1984	370.6	209.7	56.6%
1985	495.5	207.5	41.9%
1986	716.3	228.3	31.9%
1987	769.9	254.7	33.1%
1988	810.3	278.4	34.4%
1989	995.1	360.2	36.2%

Source: *Wall Street Journal,* various issues; Investment Company Institute.

Exhibit 2

CD and Prime Rates

Quarter		CD Rate	Prime Rate
1985	Q1	10.65	10.50
	Q2	8.36	9.50
	Q3	8.52	9.50
	Q4	8.19	9.50
1986	Q1	7.80	9.00
	Q2	7.18	8.50
	Q3	5.65	7.50
	Q4	5.96	7.50
1987	Q1	6.32	8.25
	Q2	7.85	8.75
	Q3	7.90	8.75
	Q4	8.05	8.50
1988	Q1	7.10	9.00
	Q2	8.15	10.00
	Q3	9.10	10.00
	Q4	9.20	11.50
1989	Q1	8.71	11.00
	Q2	8.50	11.00
	Q3	8.59	11.00
	Q4	7.71	10.50

Source: *Wall Street Journal; Federal Reserve Bulletin.*

Exhibit 3

Annual Performance Indicators

Year	CPI	S&P 500	Money Market	Mutual Funds
1979	11.2	12.3	9.2	16.7
1980	13.5	25.8	12.0	28.5
1981	10.4	−9.7	16.0	−2.2
1982	6.1	14.5	12.0	20.3
1983	3.2	18.2	8.7	23.2
1984	4.3	6.1	10.0	2.6
1985	3.5	31.6	7.6	26.8
1986	2.0	15.3	6.2	14.8
1987	3.6	5.2	6.1	3.2
1988	4.4	17.1	7.1	19.5
1989	4.8	31.5	8.9	21.6

Source: *Wall Street Journal* and Barron's; Mutual fund return is the Lipper growth & income index.

Exhibit 4A

Funds under Management at Eaton Vance ($ million)

	1985	1986	1987	1988
Open-End Mutual Funds*				
High Current Return	$ 504	$ 717	$ 936	$ 879
Growth & Current Income	909	910	860	756
Long-Term Growth	126	124	115	117
Maximum Capital Appreciation	167	132	91	87
Tax Advantaged	83	925	1,126	1,218
Total Open-Ended Funds	1,789	2,808	3,128	3,057
Exchange Funds	473	519	494	490
Investment Counsel Division				
Total Funds Under Management	1,590	2,078	1,782	1,329
Total	$3,852	$5,405	$5,404	$4,876
Counselled as % of Total	41.3%	38.4%	33.0%	27.3%

*As of year end.

Exhibit 4B

Funds under Management at Eaton Vance* ($ million)

	1981	1982	1983	1984	1985
Open-Ended Funds	$ 701	$1,159	$1,479	$1,321	$1,710
Exchange Funds	425	434	489	449	473
Closed-End Funds	100	20	24	19	—
Total Mutual Funds	1,226	1,613	1,992	1,789	2,183
Counsel Assets	421	673	938	1,178	1,590
Total	$1,647	$2,286	$2,930	$2,967	$3,773
Counselled as % of Total	25.6%	29.4%	32.0%	39.7%	42.1%

*As of Oct. 31.

Exhibit 5

Income Statement ($ thousands)

	1984	1985	1986	1987	1988
INCOME					
Invest. Adviser Fees	$16,111	$18,537	$25,016	$32,812	$29,371
Underwriting Comm.	944	2,642	2,142	2,524	485
Distrb. Plan Payments	—	—	3,529	14,165	14,780
Other	770	944	976	1,058	1,468
Total Income	17,825	22,123	31,663	50,559	46,104
EXPENSES					
Compensation Empl.	6,341	7,780	10,536	14,810	13,741
Amort. Def. Commissions	—	—	2,169	7,489	6,902
Other	5,377	5,753	7,325	7,902	7,821
Total Expense	11,718	13,533	20,030	30,201	28,464
Operating Income	6,107	8,590	11,633	20,358	17,640
Other Income/Expenses					
Net Interest and Share of Partner Income	93	(57)	(188)	(79)	(603)
Income Before Tax Provision	6,200	8,533	11,445	20,279	17,037
Tax Provision	3,038	4,341	5,734	9,582	6,633
Income from Uncon. Subs.	906	596	687	853	337
Net Income	$ 4,068	$ 4,788	$ 6,398	$11,550	$10,741

Exhibit 6

Balance Sheet ($ thousands)

	1984	1985	1986	1987	1988
ASSETS					
Current Assets	$12,243	$14,624	$23,961	$10,442	$13,222
Investments to Subs. and Partnerships	13,079	15,931	15,860	19,059	19,870
Net Plant and Equip.	2,091	2,386	2,697	2,731	3,025
Notes from Officers	281	459	857	977	888
Goodwill	2,963	2,854	2,746	2,637	2,528
Def. Sales Commissions	—	—	30,852	45,057	37,862
Other Def. Charges	181	—	—	—	—
Total	30,657	36,254	76,973	80,903	77,395
LIABILITIES					
Current	7,204	8,789	14,650	10,249	7,442
Various Debentures	6,422	6,412	900	—	14,169
Note to Bank	—	—	15,000	7,500	—
Deferred Taxes	—	—	14,589	21,350	18,428
Total	13,626	15,201	45,139	39,099	40,039
Equity					
Total Shareholders'	17,031	21,053	31,834	41,804	37,356
Total Liabilities + Equity	$30,657	$36,254	$76,973	$80,903	$77,395

Exhibit 7

Financial Highlights
($ million except for per-share data)

	1984	1985	1986	1987	1988
Assets under Management	$3,000	$3,800	$5,400	$5,400	$4,900
Sales of Mutual Funds	173	413	1,204	1,062	280
Net Income	4.1	4.8	6.4	11.6	10.7
Total Assets	30.7	36.3	77.0	80.9	77.4
Total Equity	17.0	21.1	31.8	41.8	37.4
Per Share Data					
Fully Diluted Shares (x1000)	4,233	4,276	4,077	4,276	3,916
Book Value	$4.60	$5.63	$7.66	$9.91	$10.12
eps	$1.04	$1.20	$1.59	$2.70	$ 2.74
dps	$0.20	$0.22	$0.25	$0.30	$ 0.37
Return data					
RoE	24.1%	22.7%	20.1%	27.8%	28.6%
RoA	13.4%	13.2%	8.3%	14.3%	13.8%
RoManagedAssets	0.14%	0.13%	0.12%	0.21%	0.22%

Exhibit 8

Stock Performance by Quarter

	High	Low	S&P
1984	13	10	100.0
	12	10	96.4
	10	8	90.3
	10	8	100.6
1985	12	9	108.5
	14	11	110.3
	17	13	115.2
	21	15	115.2
1986	25	20	127.3
	30	21	143.0
	22	16	143.6
	21	16	146.1
1987	31	19	166.7
	33	24	173.9
	28	21	187.3
	27	13	141.2
1988	19	13	155.8
	24	18	158.2
	22	19	164.8
	21	19	169.1

▼ ■

Exhibit 9

Eaton Vance Management, Inc.

24 Federal Street
Boston, MA 02110

James B. Hawkes
Vice President
Chief Investment Officer

August 18, 1988

Ms. Margaret DuBois
Managing Director
Loeb White, Inc.
12 Wall Street
New York, NY 10285

Dear Maggie:

I'd like to bring you and your associates up to date on our progress with Eaton Vance Prime Rate Reserves (PRR). Please distribute the extra copies of this letter and associated material to Bob Patterson, George Carter and others as appropriate. A copy was given to John Francis at our recent meeting in Boston.

First, a summary of the work since our initial meeting with Loeb White on July 14. It's now clear that our basic idea—a fund with a yield equal to and adjusting with the bank prime rate and exhibiting a stable NAV as interest rates change—is sound. There will be credit quality risk since the portfolio will consist of corporate loans, including loans to below investment grade borrowers. However, credit risks will be minimized by careful selection, broad diversification, the senior position of PRR's holdings, restrictive covenants on the borrower, and a reserve for credit losses. A revised Concept Summary for PRR is included as Enclosure 1.

We have explored the market for higher-yielding bank loans in some depth, talking to many of the banks who originate these loans and visiting with the three largest factors (Bankers Trust, Citibank, and Manufacturers Hanover) in New York. Availability of these loans is much greater than we had thought, and there should be no problem in purchasing participations even if the fund is large. We estimate approximately three months to invest the proceeds of a sizeable underwriting. Please refer to Enclosure 2, "The Bank Loan Participation Market," for detailed information. A section on credit quality and liquidity has been included in response to Bob Patterson's request.

We have constructed a financial model (Enclosure 3) of PRR using Lotus 1-2-3. The model validates our concept and is useful in answering "what-if" questions. All items in the "assumption" section can be varied and will flow through to the estimated results. The enclosed example represents our view of the most likely case in terms of portfolio earnings, loan mix, and expected credit losses. Our goal is to pay investors the prime rate on their gross investment and have sufficient excess return to mod-

Exhibit 9 continued on page 382.

Exhibit 9 (continued)

estly increase NAV over time as a reserve for credit losses. By keeping fees (mainly our management fee) low, no more than 1% total, we're able to cover a 4% underwriting spread—at the high end of what was discussed at the July 14 meeting. I can provide additional runs with changed assumptions or the model on a floppy disk for use at Loeb White if you like.

Enclosure 4 is the first draft of a prospectus for Prime Rate Reserves. I emphasize that the prospectus is rough and needs work, but we thought it important to begin the drafting process. We would expect PRR's underwriters to contribute significantly to the final version. You'll note that the prospectus reflects a standard closed-end structure without the continuous offering/tender-to-redeem features originally contemplated. Assuming this fund is successful, we would expect to meet market demand with follow-on products.

Our enthusiasm for Prime Rate Reserves continues to grow as our research progresses. The fund offers that rare combination of innovation, investment merit, and marketing appeal and seems truly an ideal product for the current environment. We hope you agree.

With kind regards.

Sincerely,

James B. Hawkes, C.F.A.

JBH:ar
Enclosures

Exhibit 9 (continued)

<table>
<tr><td>Concept Summary
Eaton Vance Prime Rate Reserves
August 18, 1988</td><td>Margaret DuBois
Enclosure 1</td></tr>
</table>

Investment Objective:

- High income: Compound Income Yield (net of all expenses) equal to and adjusting with the bank prime rate—to be paid on gross investment in PRR.
- Stable NAV: All portfolio investments to be adjustable rate so as to minimize NAV sensitivity to interest rate changes.

Yield Comparisons:

Eaton Vance Prime Rate Reserves		10.00%	
Money Funds		7.30%	
6-month CD	(Retail)	7.34%	
1-year CD	(Retail)	7.71%	
2.5-year CD	(Retail)	7.85%	
5-year CD	(Retail)	8.37%	
Government Funds		8.67%	(SEC yield)
High Yield Bond Funds		11.85%	(SEC yield)

Investment Portfolio:

Trust will invest in a widely diversified portfolio of participation interests in senior fully collaterized floating rate corporate loans.

Fund Structure:

Closed-end non-diversified management investment company.
NYSE listing for investor liquidity.

Special Features:

- Monthly income distribution.
- Dividend reinvestment at NAV.
- Dividends reinvested via market purchase to support NAV and minimize discount.
- Reserve to cover possible loan defaults.

Miscellaneous:

- Expense ratio of 1% or less.
- Underwriting commission of 4%.

Exhibit 9 continued on page 384.

Exhibit 9 (continued)

Eaton Vance Prime Rate Reserves
The Bank Loan Participation Market

Margaret DuBois
Enclosure 2

Summary

Eaton Vance Prime Rate Reserves (PRR) will invest in loan participations which are portions of credit facilities syndicated and sold by large money center banks and insurance companies to investors, primarily other banks. PRR's portfolio will consist mainly of participations derived from secured term loans and bridge loans which arise chiefly in corporate restructurings, leveraged buyouts and recapitalizations, and revolving credit facilities. These loans are senior to all other debt, are fully collateralized and are structured with restrictive covenants. Over the last 12 months, it is estimated that $54 billion in bank loans for these purposes have been made, with participations of these loans representing a substantial amount. On these facilities, the borrower typically pays interest at a floating rate, with the participation-purchaser receiving a spread over the money market benchmark rate.

General Terms of Participations

Interest Rates

Borrowers typically have the option of choosing the applicable interest rate on their credit facilities. Three options are generally offered: Prime plus 1–1/2%, London InterBank Offered Rate (LIBOR) plus 2–1/2%, and Certificate of Deposit (CD) rate plus 2–3/4%.

Institutions which purchase participations typically receive a slightly lower interest rate than is paid by the borrower, with the difference retained by the originating bank(s). For example, the above options might lead to the participation-purchaser receiving Prime rate plus 1-1/4%, LIBOR plus 2-1/4%, or CD rate plus 2-1/2%.

The borrower also determines the length of the period for which the selected rate formula is to be applied. For example, in addition to the floating prime rate, the borrower may choose rates set for 30-day, 60-day, 90-day or 180-day periods. The participation-purchaser receives its applicable interest rate based on the same time period chosen by the borrower.

Maturity and Prepayment of Principal

Typically, revolving credit facilities mature in three years and term loans in seven years. Bridge loans often mature in nine months to a year.

The terms of the Loan Agreement between the borrower and the underwriting bank syndicate prescribe contractual repayments of term loans and annual cleanups of revolving credits, and also frequently require excess cash flow, as defined in the agreement, to be used to retire outstanding debt under the facilities. Recent prepayment experience of the largest lenders indicates that faster reduction in outstanding balances occurs.

Fees

The borrower typically pays various fees to the underwriting banks. A facility fee is received by the underwriting syndicate of banks which generally passes through to the participation-purchaser a portion of this fee.

For example, a facility fee of 50 basis points of the credit facilities may be paid by the borrower to the underwriting syndicate of banks. A participation-purchaser may receive as its up-front fee at the time of purchase a fee of 37-1/2 basis points.

Exhibit 9 (continued)

Eaton Vance Prime Rate Reserves
The Bank Loan Participation Market (continued)

Margaret DuBois
Enclosure 2

Security and Covenants

The credit agreement between the borrower and the underwriting syndicate usually contains definitive security provisions. Frequently, the accounts receivable, inventory and machinery and equipment of the borrower, or its operating subsidiaries, if applicable, are pledged as collateral for the revolving credit facility. Term loans frequently are secured by a pledge of stock in operating subsidiaries, if applicable, and a lien on significant assets.

The credit agreement also includes numerous convenants strictly proscribing the activities of the management. These include covenants prohibiting: additional indebtedness, mergers, asset sales, transactions with affiliates, dividends to shareholders, etc.

Major Participation Syndicators

The nation's largest commercial banks have demonstrated significant commitment to the growth of the bank participation market through the involvement of institutional investors. Frequent syndicators of these loans include: Manufacturers Hanover, Bankers Trust, Citibank, Morgan Guaranty, Wells Fargo, Security Pacific and Bank of America. These institutions, along with a few foreign banks, are also, not coincidentally, active lenders as agent banks in corporate restructurings, leveraged buyouts and recapitalizations.

These institutions generate in their lending efforts numerous credit facilities which they subsequently apportion and sell as participations. To supplement this activity in newly established credit facilities, these banks also act as middlemen or brokers of participations in existing credits, primarily those in which they acted as agent. A de facto secondary market exists as a result of the activity in the informal trading market.

Liquidity

The market for loan participations is rapidly developing, and sufficient liquidity exists to manage PRR in closed-end form. The volume of newly originated loans is substantial, and a large supply of purchased participations exists in the hands of financial institutions, primarily banks. There is a growing demand for participations, both in seasoned credits and new credits, by certain non-bank financial institutions. As the demand by these non-bank institutional investors grows in importance to the aggregate supply of participations, an active secondary market can be supported.

At present, effecting a purchase or sale of a participation frequently involves the use of the original agent bank of the credit as a broker in the transaction. The agent/broker attempts to match an offsetting seller or buyer for the trade. As non-bank financial institutions become more active, the secondary market will become more formalized. Bankers Trust, a leader in this niche, has currently dedicated three traders to the full-time brokerage of participations. In 1987, their trading volume was $750 million and in the first six months of 1988 was $688 million.

Exhibit 9 continued on page 386.

Exhibit 9 (continued)

Eaton Vance Prime Rate Reserves
The Bank Loan Participation Market (continued)

Credit Quality and Risk

Senior credit represents the highest level of credit worthiness of a borrower. As a financial instrument it reflects the most secure, least sensitive to general business cycle obligations of the borrower. For borrowers with less than investment grade securities outstanding, the senior credit is generally supported by a credit agreement which contains numerous convenants governing the activities of the borrower and restrictions on their ability to take action with the corporate assets.

The participation-purchaser's exposure to the initial high leverage is generally rapidly decreased. In certain situations the borrower is obligated to expeditiously dispose of identified assets or businesses. In most cases the credit agreements contain 'excess cash flow' tests which require the borrower to repay principal to the extent incremental free cash flow is generated. The following time frame reflects an example of the combined effect of both scheduled repayments and incremental prepayments: 40% of the credit is repaid in year 1, 30% in year 2, 10% in year 3, 10% in year 4, and 10% in year 5.

In circumstances where the underlying credit has been impaired, the borrower typically restructures the terms of the subordinated debt (e.g., offering equity) without materially changing the terms of the senior debt credit agreement. In a worst case, bankruptcy, the senior lenders often emerge from Chapter XI with the highest value and in the interim receive timely interest payments. There is some marketability of credit-impaired participations to bank work-out units and special situation investors, but at an appropriate discount to par.

Eaton Vance Prime Rate Reserves will retain excess earnings over prime to provide a cushion for credit losses.

PART 5

Managing Corporate Responsibility

Cash Management at Cameron Company

It was February 1981, and Graham Farrell, manager of the New Orleans branch of Cameron Company, a major stock brokerage firm, knew he had to do something to improve his branch's performance. He had just finished reading a memo from John Layton, the company money mobilizer (Exhibit 1). This was Layton's second memo in three months on maximizing branch interest income (Exhibit 2). Having missed Layton's special meeting on the subject the week before, Farrell paid special attention to the latest memo. He was conscious that despite his best efforts, the New Orleans branch had not advanced from the company's "Fair" category into the "Good" category for monthly profit performance (Exhibit 3). This was largely due to the difficulty he was having in boosting the branch's interest income to the levels achieved at other branches.

Company Background and Leadership

Established in 1904, Cameron Company had operated as a partnership until founder Ben Wright's death in 1962. At that time it was incorporated. By the time the company went public in 1972 it ranked eighth among 593 in New York Stock Exchange (NYSE) commissions. Within two years of going public it became the second largest NYSE member in terms of total revenue, and the fourth, based on total capital position.

John Mason, the current CEO, had been selected in 1970 after a bitter struggle with the other main contender, who had only recently left the company to take a major political position. Mason had been responsible for Cameron's growth from 95 branches and 1,250 account executives in 1972 to 400 offices worldwide and 6,600 account executives by the mid-1980s. He proudly claimed that the company's strengths lay in its retail sales force and distribution system, and its encouragement of an independent, entrepreneurial spirit among staff. He created a

This case was prepared by Research Assistant Brownwyn Halliday under the supervision of Professor Lynn Sharp Paine of the Harvard Business School (and formerly of Georgetown) and with the help of Professor Pietra Rivoli of the Georgetown Business School. Georgetown University School of Business Administration supported the development of this case. Although based on actual events as reported in public documents, all names have been changed and much of the case is fictional. *Copyright © 1991 by the President and Fellows of Harvard College and Georgetown University. Harvard Business School case N9-391-293.*

tough-guy image for himself and demanded that staff look aggressive and accept risks. He advocated aggressive selling and earning policies.

Mason did not allow the board to constrain his management of the company. Without board approval, he hired high-level staff with unusually generous compensation packages and authorized the expensive refurbishment of new office buildings. He believed that bureaucratic concerns should take a back seat to expediency. When the interests of the company demanded that he move quickly to make a deal or take advantage of a situation, he would do so. Despite his success, Mason was regarded as aloof and hard to get to know. Most people preferred to deal with the president of Cameron, Fred Cox.

Management Structure

Cameron's management structure was loose. There was considerable overlap of functions and responsibilities between Max Harris, the executive vice president and managing director who served as de facto chief financial officer; Don Bruff, the head of corporate planning and control to whom the controller and accounting department reported; and Tom Brown, the head of operations. However, Mason would intervene at any time on matters which were important to him, such as business negotiations with companies or industries with which he had decided Cameron should not deal. In addition, Cox, as president, was a dominant figure in the company. He had a dynamic personality, endless energy and a contagious enthusiasm. Layton, the money mobilizer, reported to three people: Harris, Brown, and George Penner, the senior vice president and cashier, on an "as necessary" basis. (See Exhibit 4 for a simplified organization chart.)

Company operations were divided into ten regions—nine domestic and one international—each headed by a regional vice president concerned with staffing branch offices and creating new business. All regional offices reported to Cox.

Interest Income

Since the beginning of 1980, Cox and Layton had encouraged branches to increase profits by generating interest income. This encouragement had been in the form of memos (Exhibits 1 and 2), correspondence, branch profit and loss statements, reports rating the performance of regions and branches in interest income (Exhibits 3 and 5), and the identification of "Office of the Month." Generating interest was also a frequent topic at regional meetings.

Other executive staff had also encouraged offices to increase their interest income. The 1981 Christmas letter from Max Harris, the executive vice president, had stressed the earnings potential of 18% interest rates. Careful cash management was an easy way for Cameron to make money without a lot of effort beyond keeping an eye on where the money was and moving it judiciously to ensure that it earned the maximum amount of interest possible.

Cameron's chief accountant, on his visit to the New Orleans branch in November, had also gone to some length to describe the aggressive approach that Cox was expecting branches to use to generate interest income. The accountant explained that setting up branches on a competitive basis for this purpose, something that Cox had suggested, made good sense in terms of the culture of the company. "We're aggressive, not only externally to our clients but also internally within the company. That's why we are so successful," he had said.

Cash Management at Cameron

Like other major stock-brokerage companies, Cameron had an extensive cash management system. On a daily basis, each branch deposited in its local bank the money it received from clients that day. Local deposits would then be transferred to a regional bank serving a group of Cameron branches, and ultimately into a central concentration bank account which deposited the funds to an account used to make disbursements. Many large companies used concentration banking to control the movement of funds and minimize idle cash balances. Concentration banks reported average daily balances so that firms could take maximum advantage of investment opportunities.

Cameron's cash management system was designed to generate interest income by: (1) transferring funds from the local banks to the central interest-paying bank as soon as possible; and (2) deliberately over-drafting accounts at the local banks to "recapture" lost interest income.

The over-draft system was based on Cameron's belief that it was entitled to interest on cash deposits from the moment of deposit. Since cash deposited in local noninterest-bearing accounts was not transferred to the interest-paying central account until the following day, Cameron lost overnight interest on those amounts. The over-draft system allowed Cameron to "recapture" this lost interest.

The over-draft system worked like this:

Monday

1. The branch deposits the day's receipts from the local bank. Suppose these receipts consist of $10,000 in cash and $5,000 in checks. The checks will clear on Tuesday.

$10,000 cash
$5,000 check

Cameron Branch Office

2. On instructions from the branch office, Cameron's regional office writes a check for $25,000 on the local bank to the regional bank. The check will clear Tuesday. The $10,000 overdraft is for the purpose of recapturing interest on the $10,000 cash deposit.

$25,000 check

Local Bank

3. Cameron headquarters writes a check for $25,000 on the regional bank for deposit into the central interest-paying account. The check will clear Tuesday.

$25,000 check

Regional Bank
Central Bank

Tuesday

All checks clear and the banks show the following balances:

Local Bank	Regional Bank	Central Bank
−10,000	0	25,000

On Wednesday, the Cameron branch office deposits customer receipts to cover the overdraft and the cycle begins again. By Wednesday, Cameron has earned one day's interest on $25,000. Cameron management thought the over-drafting practice was reasonable since the banks had the use of $10,000 in cash for two days and the use of $5,000 for one day. Since 2(10,000) + 5,000 = 25,000, this was the equivalent of $25,000 for one day.

This practice was common among corporate customers of banks. While it was not a written part of any contract or even explicitly discussed by banks and their customers, it was an accepted part of business. Banks did not necessarily like it, but they accepted it.

Relationship with Banks

Within the stock-brokerage industry, a company's relationship with its banks was crucial. Cameron, like most large corporations, had a cash management system that made use of two distinct categories of banking services. The first, depository accounts, were used to collect checks, process them quickly and make funds available to the firm. Disbursement accounts, in contrast, were used to ensure that checks were properly covered when presented for payment.

In conformity with industry practices, Cameron generally remunerated its depository banks through the compensating balance system. The bank and Cameron would determine the amount to be left on deposit in a noninterest-earning account and the time period of the arrangement. At the end of this time the bank would review its situation. In theory, if the bank considered that the cost of its services was more than the compensation it was receiving, it might ask the customer to increase its compensating balance, request a direct fee payment, or charge the customer the difference. Alternatively, it might choose to do nothing if it was a large customer and its loss could be covered elsewhere.

Banks did not expect their corporate customers to draw against the compensating funds on deposit, although they realized that this might happen from time to time. However, there was little consensus among banks on their responses to drawing on the deposit. The absence of a uniform practice was due to the prevailing business climate as well as to differences in location, region and bank size, the purpose of the demand deposit, the nature of the customer's business, and the identity and stature of the customer.

Over time, large companies such as Cameron had developed expectations about their banking relationships. They expected banks to tell them how to operate their accounts in terms of compensation and available funds overdrafts. Companies assumed bank approval of the way they ran their accounts unless told otherwise. Banks, on the other hand, were sometimes unaware of their customers' over-drafting practices because they lacked a system to monitor and match deposits with collected funds. The net result was that some corporate customers used their demand deposit accounts as an extension of credit.

Check Clearing: The Float Issue

The over-draft system for recapturing interest was used by many cash managers besides those at Cameron. It was part of an approach to cash management called "target balancing," which involved a draw-down formula designed to keep compensating balances at a minimum target level. Target balancing, which had come to be widely used to avoid overcompensating banks, recognized that money movement involves time—lags and delays while checks move among banks and are cleared before the recipient has access to the money. Cameron's draw-down formula permitted it to recover funds lost to its banks because of float.

"Float" is the name given to the amount of money that is "floating" in the system before it is paid out, i.e., the difference between the balance shown in the payer's records and the amount understood by the bank to be in the payer's account at any one time.[1] One commentator has called the float the "bookkeeping netherworld" between the time checks are written and the time funds are actually collected. For example, if a company writes a check for $10,000 and it takes four days for the $10,000 to be deducted from the company's bank account, then the company balance will appear in its own records as $10,000 less than the bank's records show for that four-day period. Essentially this means that the bank will have use of the $10,000 for four days longer than the company. The bank will also earn interest on this money while the company receives nothing if the money is in a noninterest-bearing account. The float is $10,000.

Float can be attributed to either:

▶ delivery time, the time taken for a check to travel from the check writer to its destination (e.g., by post, messenger service or special delivery); or

▶ check processing, the time taken from the deposit of the check in the bank to the crediting of the funds in the receiver's account.

Long floats are to the advantage of check writers whose money will earn interest until their checks clear. They are to the disadvantage of depositors, who must wait for checks to clear before they have access to the funds. A firm's net float is a function of its ability to speed up collections on checks received and to slow down collection on checks written. Some firms go to considerable trouble to speed up the processing of incoming checks to enable them to put the funds to work quickly.

Conversation with Ian Walsh

Farrell reread the Layton memo he had just received and decided to make some telephone calls to find out how other managers were able to be so successful. His first call was to his old friend Ian Walsh, Memphis branch manager. Walsh and Farrell had both joined the company in 1969 and had become firm friends over the years by attending many of the same company meetings and conferences. Walsh was an outgoing person, alert, and highly successful at company politics. Farrell regretted missing the meeting the money mobilizer had organized the previous week as it would have been an opportunity to catch up with his old friend. Walsh was delighted to hear from Farrell and more than happy to fill him in on Layton's presentations.

According to Walsh, Layton had explained in great detail how individual branches could increase their interest income and thereby benefit not only the company but themselves as well. Layton had emphasized that branch managers could earn the coveted "Office of the Month" and the "Office of the Year" awards, and regions could receive the title of "Region of the Month." As he listened to Walsh, Farrell felt bad. He knew he was letting his region down.

Over the telephone Walsh explained how he determined the float for the Memphis office and offered to send Farrell a copy of his notes from the meeting. Walsh also recommended careful attention to the two memos from Layton about increasing net interest earnings (Exhibits 1 and 2).

Farrell listened carefully as Walsh explained how to boost interest income by increasing the amount added to the day's deposits for float. Instead of following the standard company draw-down formula, Walsh added half as much again to this amount. As he said, the amount of float was arbitrary and really did not matter very much because the company had the money to cover whatever amount was written.

Walsh told Farrell that the manager of the Orlando branch added a zero to the amount he calculated using the formula. At the meeting this manager had explained how his method generated substantial interest income while affecting the banks only minimally. He had gone on to say that the money was only out for three days at most, and this was over a weekend. Walsh reported that his informal poll during the happy hour after the meeting had convinced him that a lot of branches were using the float formula liberally.

"So, Graham," said Ian, "if it is interest income that you need to boost profits, I've given you a few ideas. You just need to be creative and more aggressive. Actually, there is another way to generate interest income which is a bit hard for me, but which you might be able to do. It involves working with another branch and drawing checks on each other's banks. Why don't you give Rosemary Craig in San Francisco a telephone call? I know she is looking for a branch to set up some sort of mutual arrangements for checking accounts."

Conversation with Rosemary Craig

Farrell was rather thoughtful after all of this. He had the utmost faith in his friend's capabilities. From the beginning, he had been impressed with Ian's astuteness and business sense. At the same time, Farrell was a little envious. After his last performance review, he had sensed he was out of step with the times and with the company's culture. It was, after all, the 1980s. Technology and management practices were advancing rapidly. He did not like to think that he might be jeopardizing his promotional opportunities by not becoming more "with it," and he certainly had his eye on a job in corporate headquarters in the next few years. He wanted that job badly, but more importantly, he needed it to put his three children through college.

Farrell decided to give Rosemary Craig a call. She might have some useful tips for him. Farrell had met Craig only once and remembered her as rather assertive and single-minded in her climb up the corporate ladder.

Craig had been with Cameron only two years but she was already making significant contributions. She had come from a small Wall Street firm where she had developed a reputation as someone who was going places. Although Farrell could not be certain, he seemed to remember that she had joined Cameron because she believed she would not face the same promotional discrimination in a large firm as she had found in smaller companies. An ambitious and accomplished account executive, Craig was being given an opportunity to prove herself in a busy and complex branch office where success would be twice as difficult to achieve as in a smaller, less cosmopolitan area.

Craig was very responsive when Farrell mentioned Walsh's suggestion. She had realized after talking with other managers at a regional meeting that she was in a perfect position to increase her branch's interest earnings by increasing the time it took for checks to clear. By writing checks drawn on banks on the other side of the country she could increase the amount of time it took for a bank to clear a check purely because of travel time. San Francisco to New Orleans was not exactly across the country but it was enough of a distance to make a difference.

Farrell could see the logic of Craig's plans. It made sense for Cameron to utilize its network of branches as strategically as possible. A quick calculation showed him that using Craig's bank in San Francisco to pay some of his out-of-town customers could help his interest position considerably. He rather liked this idea and it was very similar to something his branch cashier, Joyce Fraser, had been talking about last month. Fraser had returned from a regional meeting of cashiers full of an idea about joining up with the Arizona branches in a check exchanging deal. Absorbed in finishing the budget forecast for the next year, Farrell had dismissed the idea at the time. He had told Joyce he would give it more thought later. Perhaps he should start thinking about it now.

Conversation with Joyce Fraser

Farrell was interrupted in his thoughts by Fraser who wanted to discuss some incidental problems she was having with the checks supplied by central office. American National Bank was having difficulty processing them and had telephoned to ask that the situation be investigated. Apparently, faulty coding was causing Cameron's checks to be rejected by the bank's automatic processing system. "They are also reminding us to staple the checks to settlement statements in the top left corner not the top right corner," Joyce said. "By stapling them in the right hand corner, the checks have to be manually processed and the bank doesn't like that," Joyce added. Apparently the checks were fed into the computer scanner from the right and the prick marks left by the staples in the right corner forced the machine to reject the checks. She laughed and commented on the new clerical officer who had started only a month ago. "Kevin is trying so hard to do everything right. He will be upset when I tell him to staple checks on the left. He'll probably think this is the end of his career with Cameron. But the guy is left handed and it comes naturally to him to do it that way."

After Fraser left, Farrell began to think about the implications of her comments. If the bank had to process the checks manually, then the clearing time would be extended for Cameron. This would mean that the branch would be obtaining additional interest on this money. Here was another way to increase monthly income.

Farrell called Fraser back to his office. "Don't say anything to Kevin about the checks yet. I don't think we should upset him for the few checks that American National will have to process manually. But I want to talk with you about a few other things. We need to manage our cash to earn more interest. I have a few ideas and would like your reactions."

► Endnote

1. Brigham Eugene F. and Louis C. Gapenski, in their text, *Financial Management—Theory and Practice*, 5th ed. (New York: The Dryden Press, 1988), gives the following definition of float (p. 731): *Float is defined as the difference between the balance shown in a firm's (or individual's) checkbook and the balance on the bank's records.*

Exhibit 1

Inter-Office Memorandum

TO: All Branch and Satellite Managers
FROM: John Layton, Money Mobilizer
SUBJECT: Net Interest Profits
DATE: January 20, 1981

Net interest profits are a vital aspect of every branch's profitability. In leaner times they have sometimes represented the difference between a profit and a loss for a branch. Fortunately, this is not true today; however, net interest profits still account for approximately 50% of the average branch's profits. And by paying insufficient attention to net interest profits, a branch may be ignoring potential revenue that would be brought directly to the "bottom line."

This memo gives an overview of the primary ways that net interest profits are generated, and it provides a list of suggestions that could improve a branch's net interest profits. This list is by no means all inclusive, and it would be appreciated greatly if any additional suggestions could be sent to us.

Interest profits are derived from four main categories:

1. **Margin Accounts**   The branch is credited with the charge to the customer, minus the call rate cost of the money.

2. **Short Positions**   The branch receives the full call rate on both the proceeds of the short sale *and* the additional margin, if any, put up in cash by customers as a result of the short. There is *no charge* to the branch.

3. **Free Credit Balances**   The branch is credited with the call rate on free credit balances, and is charged with cash account debit balances after settlement date.

4. **Interest on General Ledger Balances**   The branch earns interest on all credit balances in its general ledger and is charged for all debit balances, both at the call rate. The lion's share of the interest profit generated in this category is due to the float earned on checks and over drafting the branch's bank account.

(Note—for the first nine months of 1980, the first three of the preceding categories accounted for approximately 55% and the fourth for approximately 45% of the company's net interest profits.)

The following are suggestions that could *increase* your interest profits:

1. *Develop short sales.*

2. *Develop more margin accounts.*

3. *Improve branch profitability.*

4. *Overdraft the branch's bank account* (a memo on this was sent to all branch office managers on 1/10/81).

5. *Ensure that cash reserve is liquidated on settlement date, not on the extension day.*

6. *Try to mail confirmations as early in the day as possible* (before 10:00 a.m.).

7. *Attempt to mail drafts late in the afternoon.* The branch may earn an extra day on float for doing this.

8. *Be judicious in adjusting interest on cash reserve orders.*

9. *Tell account executives not to mail out small credit balances at the end of the month unless the customer requests it. This will save on postage.*

Source: Company records.

▼ ■

Exhibit 2

Inter-Office Memorandum

TO: All Branch and Satellite Managers
FROM: John Layton, Money Mobilizer
SUBJECT: How to Increase Interest Income
DATE: October 23, 1980

Customer interest income for the average retail office for 1980 was earned as follows:

68% Free credits less the cost of cash debits 17% Margin debits
14% Short credits
 1% Interest charged to customers with cash debit balances

Interest Earned on Free Credits is combined with the Cost of Cash Debits on the P & L. Branches earn interest on free credits at the current call rate.

Free Credit Income can be increased by:

Expediting delivery of confirms to customers (nonmargin) to increase payments made prior to the settlement date; thus creating free credit balances.

Have large nonmargin funds picked up directly from customers.

Pick up mail (checks received) from post office more frequently.

Delay paying out customer credit balances; then suggest Money Market Fund (MMF).

Limit number of customers on automatic dividend.

Cost of Cash Debits can be reduced by:

Having Account Executive (AE) stress to cash customers that purchases must be paid for on time or they will incur an interest charge.

Charge interest to customers when they fail to send in funds on time.

Charge AE if he/she waives interest charge to customer or when AE is at fault.

Make sure MMF is sold on or as of settlement date to cover buy trades.

Interest on General Ledger Balances

On General Ledger Accounts branches are charged interest on debit balances and earn interest on credit balances at the call rate.

Interest on Bank Account:

A well-trained cashier can earn an office more than an Account Executive when the account is properly managed.

Use a bank that will give you next-day Federal funds on all customer check deposits.

Limit use of local bank checks.

Remember: the firm can increase its earnings considerably by carefully managing its bank accounts to earn the maximum amount of interest. Careful timing is crucial in this endeavor.
JL/AF

▼ ▼ ▼ ▼ ▼ ▼

Source: Company records.

Exhibit 3

Inter-Office Memorandum

TO: All South Central Region Managers
FROM: Fred Cox
SUBJECT: January Performance
DATE: February 4, 1981

In January your region stood third of the nine, excluding International. Noted below are my perceptions of the performance of your offices:

Excellent	*Good*
Atlanta	Dallas West
Dallas (North)	El Paso
Houston (Central)	Lincoln
Memphis	Longview
Omaha	

Fair	*Poor*
Fort Worth	Austin
New Orleans	Houston (Southern Vale)
Oklahoma City	

Strangely, the region was split between offices that had excellent months and those that had very poor ones. Happily though, the former predominated and the overall results were substantially better. Were there accounting adjustments that made Dallas (North) profits so extremely high? The same question could be asked about Memphis. Have we finalized a replacement for George Knight in Austin?

FSC/GG

Source: Company records.

Exhibit 4
Organizational Structure

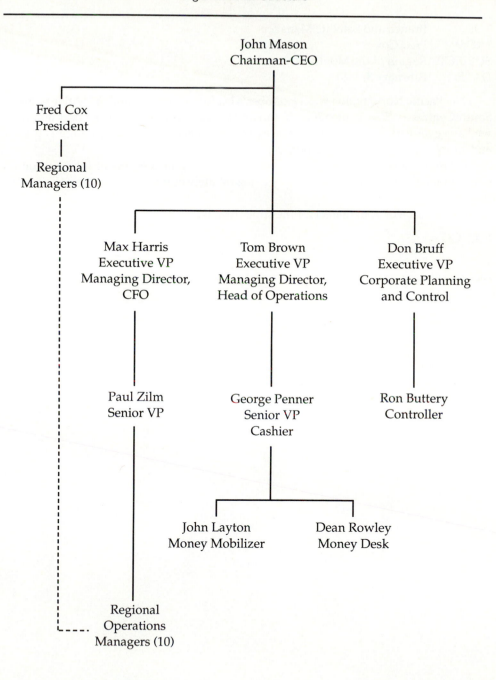

Exhibit 5

Inter-Office Memorandum

TO: Branch and Satellite Managers
FROM: Fred Cox
SUBJECT: Region of the Month—December
DATE: February 3, 1981

The Pacific North region was December's leader, with New England, Atlantic and South Central as close contenders. In the retail system it was one of the best months we have ever had, and in many instances, the difference between uncommonly great and simply great was interest profit.

Please be sure that you are all adhering to the sound precepts of John Layton's department. Interest is an excellent way to legitimately optimize a branch's or region's results.

And to each of you, thanks for the super results.

FSC/GG

Source: Company records.

Fairbanks, Perkins & Co., Inc.

On November 4, 1974, Mr. Duncan McFarland, a partner of the investment banking firm of McFarland, Paige & Co., received a phone call from the firm's vice president working at the printer on the Fairbanks, Perkins & Co., Inc. (hereinafter referred to as "FP") registration statement. The registration statement and exhibits for the FP exchange offer were ready for filing at the Securities and Exchange Commission. Mr. McFarland leaned back and wondered how successful the exchange offer would be. Would the shareholders find it attractive? Would the professional risk arbitragers participate? How appropriate was it for the company? It seemed not too long ago that Mr. McFarland had received a similar phone call advising him that the registration statement for the initial public offering, or IPO, of the common stock of FP was ready for filing.

Background of Fairbanks, Perkins & Co., Inc.

Fairbanks, Perkins & Co., Inc. commenced business in April 1966 as a full-service advertising agency. By its first 12-month fiscal year end, October 31, 1967, gross billings totaled $36.5 million, revenues from commissions were $5.5 million, and it had seven full-time employees. By fiscal year 1973 the firm had grown to a point where gross billings exceeded $185 million, revenues from commissions were $27.8 million and the firm employed 573 full-time people.

As a full-service advertising agency, FP attempted to increase the sales of its clients' products and services through the creation and execution of a complete advertising program. Typically an engagement by a client would begin with a study of the client's products or services to determine their present market and market potential, consistent with both the client's objectives and the constraints imposed by the available media. The firm would then create a total advertising program which embodied the agency's ideas with respect to the advertising "message," the media to be used, the packaging of the products, sales promotion materials, and possible fashion and style of personnel uniforms. After the client accepted the total program, the firm would write and produce the actual commer-

This case was prepared by Professor Samuel L. Hayes, III.
Copyright © 1975 by the President and Fellows of Harvard College. Harvard Business School case 9-276-003.

cials for television and radio and the written advertising for the printed media. The firm then arranged for the placement and distribution of the commercials and printed advertising with the various media organizations. Finally, follow-up studies of the results of the program were provided in order to assess the success or failure of the program as a whole or individual commercials or advertising within it.

According to published sources, FP in 1973 ranked 13th in the industry in gross billings and included among its clients many of the largest companies in a variety of industries.

The advertising industry had always been highly competitive and advertisers often switched accounts from one agency to another in order to maintain a constant flow of fresh ideas and assure the continued effectiveness of their advertising programs. Typically the larger marketing companies retained several agencies to do the advertising for their various products. Since creativity was the essence of successful advertising, the ability of an agency to attract and keep talented individuals was a key factor contributing to its relative success. Fairbanks, Perkins & Co. had been able to attract and keep talented people by paying substantial base salaries and offering employees opportunities to share in the growth of the firm through stock ownership (see Exhibit 1 for a partial list of officers and their remuneration). In order to make FP stock more attractive to its employees, as well as to make it an attractive vehicle for acquisitions, the firm undertook an IPO in 1968 of 409,000 shares of common stock at a price of $17.50 per share. In 1971, another public offering of 333,739 shares of common stock was made at a price of $21.75 per share. With the exception of 50,000 shares of the 1968 offering which were sold for the account of FP, both issues were secondary offerings, underwritten by McFarland, Paige & Co., in which officers, directors, and employees of FP sold substantial personal holdings of their stock. In order to broaden further the market for its shares and make them more attractive vehicles for acquisitions, FP listed its stock on the American Stock Exchange in 1970 and then moved on to the New York Stock Exchange in 1971.

In 1972, FP acquired an advertising agency which offered specialized advertising services to clients who did not wish complete advertising services. The acquisition was made through an exchange of shares in which FP issued 77,476 shares of its common stock for 100% of the stock of the acquired agency. Fairbanks, Perkins' stock was trading at $21.875 at the time of the acquisition.

Fairbanks, Perkins & Co. then made no further acquisitions up to the time of this 1974 proposed exchange offer. Its stock had traded lightly and had declined from a high closing price of $27.875 on January 31, 1972 to a low of $5.50 just prior to the announcement of the exchange offer. Although the stock market in general had also declined, FP's stock, as well as the equities of several other advertising agencies, had declined more drastically (see Exhibits 2, 3, and 4). This decline in the price of its stock had occurred despite increases in FP's revenues and net income (see Exhibits 5 and 6) and despite regular cash dividends since February 1971 which were now being paid at an annual rate of 71¢ per share.

Events Leading to the Exchange Offer

With its common stock selling at so low a price, FP was no longer able to accomplish what had been intended when its stock was originally offered to the public. The stock options granted to key employees were no longer valuable, and the common stock was no longer an attractive vehicle for acquisitions. Since there was no need for capital investment in plant or equipment, there was no convincing reason to maintain access to the public capital markets. In fact, there appeared to be some benefits associated with private ownership. There would be less emphasis placed on earnings per share, enabling the firm to give more generous remuneration to key employees. Since there would be no need for public disclosure of certain inside information, the agency could ensure a more confidential treatment of client information and acquisition plans. Thus there appeared to be good reasons for "going private."

Mrs. Judith Perkins, chairwoman of FP, had noticed that other public companies had made tender offers to their stockholders to purchase outstanding shares of stock in order to regain private status, and she therefore approached Mr. McFarland regarding the possibility of FP's making such a tender offer. Mr. McFarland knew that a substantial premium over the current market price of $5.50 would be required to purchase successfully most of the outstanding stock. He also knew that it would cause a strain on FP's cash position to repurchase the publicly held shares with 100% cash. He therefore suggested that some combination of cash and a fixed income security might make an attractive package for a shareholder since it would offer both current income and immediate cash in hand. Under any circumstances, Mr. McFarland and Mrs. Perkins would have wanted to construct a package that would be attractive to FP's shareholders. In this situation, however, they had an additional concern that the offer be "fair" because many of the shareholders had originally purchased their stock at much higher prices from "inside" shareholders in the secondary offerings managed by McFarland, Paige & Co.

In order to maximize the chances of success of an exchange offer of this magnitude, Mr. McFarland and Mrs. Perkins recognized that they not only needed to consider the interest of the shareholders, but they also required the active participation of the professional risk arbitragers. The risk arbitragers, who made up a small community on Wall Street, were highly sophisticated traders associated with securities firms that invested substantial capital in special situations such as announced mergers, exchange offers and tender offers. Having decided that there was a reasonably good probability that the announced offer would be consummated, the arbitragers would attempt to take advantage of the differences between the market prices of traded securities and their potential ultimate value. Risk arbitrage opportunities differed from riskless arbitrage situations where securities and their equivalents were simultaneously bought and sold with an assured spread. In the case of the exchange contemplated by FP, the arbitragers might buy at current market prices the common stock of FP in order to exchange it for the company's offer of cash and debentures. The arbitrager's hope was that the ultimate value of the cash and debentures would exceed the prices paid for the stock. In addition, the arbitragers would probably sell "short" on a "when-issued" basis the debentures to be received, covering their short position with the debentures actually received when the exchange offer was consummated. Through such short-selling, the arbitragers would be relieved of the risks of price fluctuations in the after-market for the debentures.

To attract the arbitragers into the market, Mr. McFarland knew that the offer should be structured so that the total potential principal amount of outstanding debentures to be issued would be large enough to assure a liquid secondary market in them. While the arbitragers tended to avoid situations with limited liquidity, a $10 million issue was considered sufficiently large to attract them. They could be further encouraged to participate in an exchange offer through the payment of fees for tendered shares. This would be accomplished by offering to pay "soliciting dealers" a fee for each share of stock exchanged through that dealer. Since an arbitrager, as a qualified broker-dealer, was eligible to receive that fee for each share it exchanged for its own account, the spread they could realize through the exchange would thus be enhanced.

The Exchange Offer

With the foregoing considerations in mind, it was finally decided to offer to purchase from all shareholders, other than the officers and directors, 1,405,008 shares of common stock in exchange for $3 cash and $8 principal amount of 10% subordinated sinking fund debentures due November 1, 1984, for each share of common stock tendered. FP would pay to McFarland, Paige & Co., as dealer-manager, a management fee of 12 ½¢ per share, and soliciting dealers 37 ½¢ per share, for all shares tendered. Other costs expected to be incurred by the firm were estimated at $215,000. In order to protect itself from possible contingencies, such as the institution of a lawsuit, the firm reserved the right to withdraw the offer at any time prior to the date on which it had to accept the shares tendered. If the offer were withdrawn, the firm could either accept the shares tendered or return them to their owners. For a description of the effects of the exchange offer on fixed charges, see Exhibit 7.

The debentures to be issued in exchange for the common stock would be subordinated, unsecured obligations of the firm and redeemable in whole or in part at the option of the firm at a price equal to their par value plus accrued interest. The debentures would also be subject to redemption through the operation of a sinking fund into which the firm was required to pay annually in cash an amount equal to 10% of the aggregate principal amount of the debentures originally issued. The firm could reduce the amount of required sinking fund payments through open market purchases of debentures by which it could gain credit for the actual funds expended for such purchases. It was expected that unless interest rates declined significantly, the firm would be able to acquire most or all of the debentures at a cost lower than par. Additional protection to debenture holders was provided by a covenant in the debenture agreement which limited common stock dividend payments to 10% of FP's earnings after the exchange offer had become effective.

While the debentures would not be rated by any of the rating agencies, the yields available on other publicly traded and rated debt instruments were useful for purposes of comparison to determine an approximate value for the FP debentures. Since yields on recently issued utility bonds with a quality rating of A were as high as 10% (see Exhibits 8 and 9), it was clear that the 10% subordinated debentures being offered would trade at a significant discount from par.

While Mr. McFarland expected that the debentures would initially be traded in the over-the-counter market, and that the company would subsequently apply for their listing on the American Stock Exchange, he recognized that if too few shares were tendered, the resultant amount of debentures and number of holders would not fulfill the listing requirements of the American Stock Exchange or support a liquid market in the debentures. In addition, shareholders might receive debentures in denominations of less than $1,000 which were not eligible for trading on the exchange and would have to be traded in the over-the-counter market, presumably at lower prices.

Possible Consequences of the Exchange Offer

As to the interests of the public shareholders, the offer presented an opportunity to dispose of what had become an unpromising investment at a value substantially above market price. Although the price of FP's stock currently stood at $8.125, the price on the day prior to the announcement of the exchange offer was $5.50. Assuming the tender of all shares owned, a shareholder would realize a taxable gain or loss on the transaction measured by the difference between (1) the shareholder's tax basis of the stock and (2) the amount of cash and fair market value of the debentures received. The fair market value of the debentures would be the price on the first day on which any debenture was traded on an established securities market following the company's acceptance of tendered shares.[1]

Should a shareholder decide not to tender his shares, it would be difficult to determine what value he might ultimately be able to receive for them. While a reduction in the number of shares outstanding would increase the agency's earnings-per-share, a significant reduction would also reduce the market "float" in the stock. This would reduce the liquidity in the market and increase the volatility of the stock price, resulting in a lower price earnings ratio for the stock. If a substantial number of shares were tendered and there was a large reduction in the number of shares outstanding and in the number of shareholders, the stock might no longer comply with the listing requirements of The New York Stock Exchange and be delisted. Similarly, the firm might no longer be required to fulfill some of the requirements of the federal securities laws regarding the solicitation of proxies and insider trading. In addition, if 1,291,583 shares or more were tendered, then the officers and board of directors of the firm would control 66 2/3% of the stock and would be able to effect a transaction by which the remaining publicly held shares could be retired at a price not necessarily the same as that represented in the current offer. Depending upon the relative success of the exchange offer, the FP officers might make additional offers for the remaining outstanding stock on different terms. The firm also might enter into agreements with its employees to repurchase stock from them at book value from time to time.

McFarland, Paige & Co. intended to maintain an orderly market for whatever common stock remained outstanding after the consummation of the exchange offer, and FP would continue to supply its shareholders and debenture holders with annual reports.

► Endnote

1. As to the accounting treatment for Fairbanks, Perkins & Co., no income, gain, or loss would be recognized upon the exchange. In computing its taxable income, the firm would deduct the interest payable on the debentures. If the "issue price" or fair market value of the debentures on the first day they were traded was 97.75% of their principal amount, or (as was expected) less, the debentures would be deemed to have been issued at an original issue discount in the amount of the difference between the market price and the principal amount of the debentures. In preparing its tax forms, FP would deduct annually an allocable portion of any original issue discount. The debenture holders would have to recognize a like amount as additional interest income.

Exhibit 1

Annual Remuneration of Certain Officers

Name	Title	Salary	Bonus
Judith Perkins	Chairwoman	$ 225,000	$186,000
John Fairbanks	President	130,000	30,000
William O. May	Executive Vice President	100,000	15,000
George C. Ash	Senior Vice President, Accounts Services	88,750	10,000
Paul G. Allen	Senior Vice President, Finance	75,000	15,000
Gary R. Fredericks	Senior Vice President, Administration	75,000	15,000
Mark Fields	Senior Vice President, Sales	70,000	10,000
Howard Stewart	Art Director	88,500	26,000
Arnold Stanley	President of Subsidiary	70,000	—
Jacob Carter	President of Subsidiary	89,000	—
All officers and directors including above		$2,773,000	$418,000

Exhibit 2

Monthly Closing Dow Jones Industrials

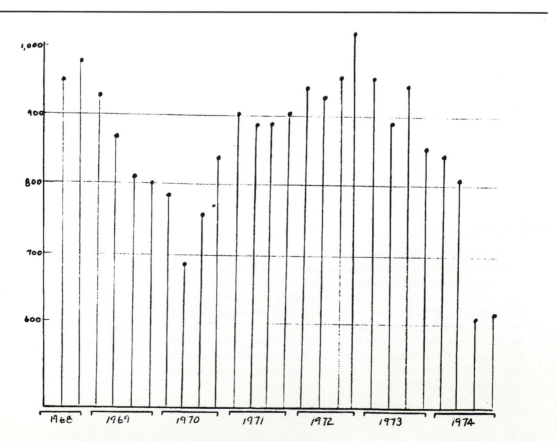

Exhibit 3

Selected Stock Price Ranges and Trading Volumes

	Stock Price Ranges				Quarterly Average Daily Volume	
	Fairbanks, Perkins		Dow Jones Industrials		Fairbanks, Perkins	All Registered Exchanges
Quarter Ending	High	Low	High	Low	(000)	(000,000)
1971						
First Quarter	25	15 ¾	916.8	830.6	9.0	564.3
Second Quarter	23 ⅞	17 ⅝	950.8	873.1	10.2	526.4
Third Quarter	22 ½	17 ⅝	920.9	839.6	5.9	420.7
Fourth Quarter	22 ¾	15 ⅞	901.8	798.0	6.0	460.6
1972						
First Quarter	27 ⅞	20 ⅛	950.2	889.2	12.8	605.8
Second Quarter	24 ¼	20	971.3	925.1	4.4	532.4
Third Quarter	23 ⅝	19 ¼	973.5	910.5	3.5	439.5
Fourth Quarter	21	16 ¾	1,036.3	921.7	3.8	522.1
1973						
First Quarter	21	14	1,051.7	922.7	2.6	510.3
Second Quarter	14	9 ¾	967.4	869.1	2.7	430.6
Third Quarter	14 ⅛	10 ¼	953.3	851.9	1.5	410.2
Fourth Quarter	13 ½	7 ¼	987.1	788.3	3.6	559.0
1974						
First Quarter	9 ⅝	7 ½	891.7	803.9	2.5	444.2
Second Quarter	9	7 ⅛	859.7	795.4	1.3	357.0
Third Quarter			677.9	757.4	—	372.2
(through September 4)	7 ⅛	5 ½			1.6	—
(through September 30)	7 ¾	7 ⅜			7.3	—
Fourth Quarter			616.2	577.6	—	439.7
(through November 1)	8 ¼	7 ½			12.4	—

Note: On September 4, 1974, the reported last sale price of the common stock on the New York Stock Exchange prior to the announcement of the Exchange Offer was 5 ½ per share. The closing price on November 1, 1974 was 8 ⅛.

Sources: The New York Stock Exchange, various *Fact Books*. Phyllis Pierce, *The Dow Jones Averages 1885–1985* (Homewood, Ill.: Dow Jones-Irwin).

Exhibit 4

Comparison of Several Advertising Agencies (aggregate dollar figures in millions)

	Fairbanks, Perkins & Co. 8/31/74	Doyle Dane and Bernbach 10/31/73	Foote Cone and Belding 12/31/73	Grey Advertising 12/31/73	Ogilvy & Mather 12/31/73	J. Walter Thompson 12/31/73
Capitalization						
Short-term debt	$ 0.1	$ 6.7	$ 1.7	$ 1.0	$ 6.0	$ 4.3
Long-term debt	$ 0.3	$ 1.8	$ 1.9	$ 0.9	$ 2.6	$ 5.1
Minority interest	—	0.1	—	—	0.5	—
Common	17.0	22.8	15.1	15.9	24.8	52.0
Shares outstanding	1,631,224	1,798,873	2,077,608	1,255,229	1,807,208	2,623,709
Net income[a]						
1973	$3.4	$3.6	$3.4	$2.5	$5.0	$4.3
1972	3.0	4.0	2.8	2.4	4.4	5.5
1971	2.6	3.8	1.8	1.6	3.4	7.7
1970	2.0	4.4	1.5	1.4	2.6	7.5
1969	1.6	3.9	2.3	1.6	2.3	6.6
EPS latest 12 months[b]	$2.09 (Aug.)	$1.53 (July)	$0.72 (Sept.)	$2.04 (Sept.)	$2.94 (Sept.)	$0.34 (Sept.)
1973	2.08	1.95	1.58	1.96	2.73	1.62
1972	1.90	2.10	0.87	1.92	2.43	2.05
1971	1.66	1.83	0.65	1.31	1.96	2.80
1970	1.25	1.96	(0.29)	1.14	1.60	2.66
1969	1.02	1.89	0.99	1.38	1.39	2.57
Price ranges						
1973	$21– 7	$24– 8	$13– 2	$17– 7	$34–13	$25– 8
1972	28–17	35–20	14–11	18–13	49–27	49–23
1971	25–16	25–19	13– 7	17– 9	28–16	60–35
1970	17– 6	25–14	12– 7	14– 6	17–10	36–21
1969	18– 9	33–19	16–11	19–12	23–11	41–24
Book value per share	$10.44	$12.70	$7.31	$12.64	$13.70	$19.80
Price 10/1/74	$8 1/8	$6 1/8 bid	$6 3/4	$6 3/8	$12	$6 3/4
P/E latest 12 months	3.89x	4.00x	9.38x	3.13x	4.08x	19.86
Price as % of book	77.8%	48.2%	92.3%	50.4%	87.6%	34.1%
Annual dividend per share	$0.71	$0.96	$0.80	$0.60	$0.90	$1.00
Yield on current price	8.7%	15.7%	11.9%	9.4%	7.5%	14.8%

[a]Before extraordinary items.

[b]Primary EPS after extraordinary items.

Exhibit 5

Statement of Consolidated Income (billings, revenues, and expenses—000,000 omitted)

	Seven Months Ending October 31, 1966	Year Ending October 31,							Ten Months Ending August 31,	
		1967	1968	1969	1970	1971	1972	1973	1973	1974
Gross billings[a]	$5.3	$36.5	$53.3	$77.4	$91.6	$108.0	$114.9	$185.3	$148.0	$152.7
Revenues										
Commissions and service fees[a]	0.8	5.5	8.0	11.6	13.7	16.1	17.2	27.8	22.1	22.9
Other income–net	—	—	0.1	0.2	0.2	0.1	0.2	0.7	0.5	0.4
Total	$0.8	$5.5	$8.1	$11.8	$13.9	$16.2	$17.4	$28.5	$22.6	$23.3
EXPENSES										
Salaries, wages and employee benefits	0.3	1.6	3.8	5.6	6.3	5.7	6.0	11.8	9.8	10.2
Other office and general expense	0.2	1.1	1.7	2.6	2.8	3.5	4.4	7.5	6.0	6.6
Amortization of motion picture, scripts, etc.	—	—	—	—	—	—	—	1.0	1.0	0.7
Amortization of deferred costs of advertising, etc.	0.0	0.1	0.4	0.6	0.5	0.6	0.5	0.6	0.5	0.7
Depreciation and amortization of property	0.0	0.0	0.1	0.1	0.2	0.3	0.4	0.6	0.5	0.5
Total expenses	0.5	2.8	6.0	8.9	9.8	10.1	11.3	21.5	17.8	18.7
Income before income taxes	0.3	2.6	2.1	2.9	4.1	6.1	6.1	7.0	4.8	4.6
Income taxes	0.2	1.4	1.2	1.3	2.2	3.5	3.1	3.6	2.5	2.2
Net income	$0.1	$1.2	$0.9	$1.6	$1.9	$2.6	$3.0	$3.4	$2.3	$2.4
Weighted average number of shares outstanding during each period	469.125	652.154	1,416.726	1,555.216	1,578.669	1,576.301	1,587.608	1,625.215	1,624.024	1,631.657
Per share of common stock										
Net income	NA	$1.21	$0.62	$1.02	$1.25	$1.66	$1.90	$2.08	$1.45	$1.46
Net income assuming full dilution	NA	$1.21	$0.62	$1.02	$1.24	$1.63	$1.83	$2.04	$1.43	$1.46
Cash dividends	NA	NA	NA	—	—	$0.60	$0.45	$0.80	$0.60	$0.51
Ratio of earnings to fixed charges	NA	NA	NA	13.67	17.72	26.05	25.70	10.48	9.15	8.46

▸   ▸   ▸   ▸   ▸

[a]Revenues from "Commissions and Service Fees" represent commissions earned from advertising placed with various forms of media, production commissions billed or accrued on expenditures incurred for clients, and fees derived from miscellaneous services. In accordance with prevailing industry practice "Gross Billings" are included for statistical purposes and are calculated by multiplying revenues from "Commissions and Service Fees" by 6.67, since these revenues generally amount to 15% of such billings.

Exhibit 6

Balance Sheet (000,000 omitted)[a]

	1969	1979	1971	1972	1973
CURRENT ASSETS					
Cash	$ 0.5	$ 1.4	$ 2.0	$ 3.1	$ 5.0
Marketable securities	0.3	0.7	0.1	0.1	1.0
Accounts receivable	8.6	13.0	13.6	10.3	17.3
Billable product expenses	1.2	1.3	1.3	1.3	2.3
Prepaid expense	0.1	0.1	0.1	0.2	0.5
Total current	$10.7	$16.5	$17.1	$15.0	$26.1
Property					
Leaseholds	1.9	2.7	2.7	3.3	4.2
Furniture and equipment	0.7	1.1	1.3	1.5	3.0
Subtotal	$ 2.6	$ 3.8	$ 4.0	$ 4.8	$ 7.2
Less: accumulated depreciation and amortization	0.2	0.4	0.7	1.0	2.1
Net property	$ 2.4	$ 3.4	$ 3.3	$ 3.7	$ 5.1
Investments in property	$ 0.9	$ 1.5	$ 1.4	$ 1.4	$ 1.2
Deferred charges and other assets	2.0	2.3	3.3	4.2	4.0
Total assets	$16.0	$23.7	$25.3	$24.3	$36.4
LIABILITIES AND SHAREHOLDERS' EQUITY					
Accounts payable	$ 8.7	$14.4	$14.0	$10.8	$18.6
Notes payable	—	—	—	—	0.4
Deferred taxes	0.8	0.8	1.0	1.2	1.5
Deferred compensation	0.1	0.2	0.2	0.3	0.4
Subtotal	$ 9.6	$15.4	$15.2	$12.3	$20.9
Common stock	1.6	1.6	1.6	1.6	1.7
Capital in excess of par	1.9	1.9	2.0	2.2	3.9
Retained earnings	2.9	4.9	6.6	8.9	10.9
	$ 6.4	$ 8.4	$10.2	$12.6	$16.5
Treasury stock	0.0	0.1	0.1	0.7	1.0
	$ 6.4	$ 8.3	$10.1	$12.0	$15.5
Total liabilities and shareholders' equity	$16.0	$23.7	$25.3	$24.3	$36.4

[a]Ending October 31.

▼ ■

Exhibit 7

Fixed Cash Payment Requirements

The following schedule sets forth certain of the company's estimated fixed cash payment requirements assuming the exchange offer is 100% successful. Payment requirements are based on the debt outstanding as of August 31, 1974 and on the estimated payment requirements for the debentures assuming that the exchange offer is 100% successful and that no debentures are purchased by the company in the open market or redeemed at the option of the company.

	September 1 to October 31, 1974	Year Ended October 31,			
		1975	1976	1977	1978
Rent	$252,000	$1,497,000	$1,521,000	$1,632,000	$1,619,000
Debt principal[a]	22,117	1,216,929	1,198,290	1,139,818	1,141,428
Debt interest[b]	6,128	1,164,455	1,040,301	922,506	808,453
Total	$280,245	$3,878,384	$3,759,591	$3,694,324	$3,568,881

▼   ▼   ▼   ▼   ▼   ▼

[a]Includes mandatory annual sinking fund installments of $1,124,006 representing 10% of the initial aggregate principal amount of the debentures assuming the exchange offer is 100% successful. No sinking fund installments are required to be made during the remainder of fiscal 1974. To the extent the company makes open market purchases of debentures at prices below their principal amount, the company will receive credits against the sinking fund payment obligations.

[b]Includes annual interest requirements of $1,124,006, $1,011,605, $899,205, and $786,804, in years 1975 through 1978 in the amount of 10% of the aggregate principal amount of the debentures outstanding assuming the exchange offer is 100% successful and 10% of the initial aggregate amount of the debentures is retired in each of the years.

Exhibit 8

Recent Debt Issues

Issue	Type	Amount	Date Due	Call Features	Ratings	Coupon (Percent)	Date of Offer in 1974	Offering Yield	Market Yield (Ask) 10/31
Abbott Labs	Debentures	$100,000,000	10/15/99	—	Aa(M)AA(S&P)(F)	9.20%	10/16	9.20%	9.25%
Beneficial Corp.	Debentures	100,000,000	10/15/79	N-C 10/15/79	Aa(M)AA(S&P)	9.75	10/08	9.75	9.77
Clark Equipment Credit Corp.	Debentures	50,000,000	1979	N-C 1979	A(M) (S&P)	10.25	10/24	10.25	10.27
Continental Oil Co.	Debentures	150,000,000	11/1/99	N-C 11/1/84	Aa(M)AA(S&P)	9.125	10/29	9.15	9.15
Dayton Power & Light Co.	Bonds	45,000,000	1981	N-C 10/1/80	A(M) BBB(S&P)	10.125	10/22	10.125	10.125
Exxon Pipeline Co.	Debentures	250,000,000	2004	N-C 10/15/2004	Aaa(M) AAA(S&P)	9	10/17	9.07	9.10
Idaho Power Co.	Bonds	50,000,000	2004	N-C 10/15/84	Aa(M) A(S&P)	10	10/24	10.00	10.00
Louisiana Power & Light Co.	Bonds	50,000,000	11/1/81	N-C 11/1/79	A(M)(S&P)	9.50	10/30	9.30	9.30
McDonalds Corp.	Notes	60,000,000	1982	N-C	A(M) (S&P)	9.625	10/16	9.72	9.75
National Rural Util. CFC	Bonds	100,000,000	1981	N-C 11/1/80	A(M) (S&P)	10.50	10/23	10.50	10.50
Niagara Mohawk Power Co.	Bonds	125,000,000	1981	N-C 1981	Aa(M)BBB(S&P)A(F)	12.60	10/08	12.60	12.60
Ohio Power Co.	Bonds	30,000,000	1981	—	Baa(M)BBB(S&P)	12.125	10/29	12.00	12.00
Pacific Gas & Elec. Co.	Bonds	150,000,000	6/1/82	N-C 12/1/81	Aa(M)AA(S&P)	9.85	10/09	9.85	9.87
Pacific Power Co.	Bonds	70,000,000	10/1/83	—	A(M)(S&P)(F)	9.875	10/23	9.92	9.96
Pacific Tel. & Tel. Co.	Notes	150,000,000	10/15/81	N-C 10/15/79	Aaa(M) AA(S&P)	9	10/16	9.05	9.07
Pacific Tel. & Tel. Co.	Notes	150,000,000	10/15/84	N-C 10/15/79	Aaa(M) AA(S&P)	9.10	10/16	9.10	9.10
Penny Financial Corp.	Debentures	100,000,000	1981	N-C 10/15/80	A(M) (S&P)	9.45	10/22	9.45	9.47
Penny Financial Corp.	Debentures	75,000,000	1984	N-C 10/15/84	A(M) (S&P)	10.20	10/22	10.20	10.22
Philadelphia Electric	Bonds	125,000,000	10/15/80	—	A(M)(S&P) AA(F)	11	10/17	11.00	11.00
Southern California Edison	Bonds	100,000,000	1981	N-C 11/1/79	As(M) AA(S&P)	9	10/31	9.00	9.00
Southern California Gas	Bonds	50,000,000	1981	N-C 10/1/80	As(M) A(S&P)	10.25	10/16	10.25	10.25
Weyerhauser Co.	Debentures	200,000,000	11/15/2004	N-C 11/15/84	As(M) AA(S&P)	8.90	10/31	8.90	8.90

N-C = Not callable.

M = Moody's

S&P = Standard & Poor's

F = Fitch's

Mebel, Doran & Company

It was Monday, February 23, 1987, and Harvey Hegarty, president and chief executive officer of Mebel, Doran & Company, a major investment banking firm based in New York, had been following the unfolding developments in the insider trading cases with a mixture of shock, fascination, and secret relief that, to the best of his knowledge, his firm was untouched by the spreading accusations of abuse. The revelations and charges had made him freshly aware of just how important an unimpeachable reputation was to a securities firm seeking to both maintain its current client and customer base as well as to pursue new business. He resolved that his firm would redouble its efforts to provide internal control procedures that would continue to protect Mebel Doran against abuses in the future.

At that point, Stephen Claire, one of Mr. Hegarty's partners, came into his office and informed Mr. Hegarty that he had just received a phone call from the Chairman of the Knox Corporation, one of Mebel Doran's oldest clients, voicing anger and alarm at the recent run-up in the share price of another company which Knox had secretly targeted for acquisition. Professionals in Mebel Doran's mergers and acquisitions group had been working with Knox on these takeover plans for some months and were well aware that management of the potential target, Power-Tie Corporation of Wilmington, Delaware, had publicly stated its hostility to any merger proposals that would threaten that company's independence.

The CEO of Knox had not-too-obliquely accused Mebel Doran of being the source of a leak of its plans. Mr. Claire had assured the client that this was highly unlikely, since the firm had devised elaborate procedures to assure the confidentiality of information entrusted to it by its clients and others. Nonetheless, he had promised to investigate immediately and report back to the client as soon as possible.

Mebel Doran and Company

Mebel Doran had been founded in Philadelphia in 1873 as merchants, importers and shippers. Over the years the company had gradually moved more and more heavily into financing operations, first as discounters of notes of local

This case was prepared by Professor Samuel L. Hayes, III.

tradesmen in the Philadelphia area and later as financial backers of fledgling manufacturing enterprises in the Delaware Valley. In 1913, shortly before the outbreak of World War I, the firm had sold its ocean shipping business, and in 1922 it had disposed of several textile mills that it had run since the late 1800s. This left it free to concentrate on the business of merchant banking, in which role it had raised funds for a broad variety of manufacturing and retailing businesses. It also had established several closed-end mutual funds during the 1920s that had been sold to retail investors through its small but effective cadre of salesmen operating out of the main Philadelphia office as well as offices in Pittsburgh and in Allentown, Pennsylvania. A New York office was also established after World War I to handle the clearing for an increasing volume of securities trades on the New York Stock Exchange and other exchanges. By the end of the 1920s, the New York branch had grown in size and scope of activities such that it began to rival in importance the main office in Philadelphia.

The stock market crash in 1929 and the malaise which subsequently beset the securities industry hit Mebel Doran with particular force. As prices fell, the firm sustained substantial losses on its securities positions, and the mutual funds which had been sponsored and managed by the firm saw values of their portfolios shrink by 85% between 1929 and 1932. Unwanted publicity had also dogged the firm as government hearings singled out Mebel Doran for particular censor for its alleged use of these captive mutual funds to purchase excess securities in slow-moving underwritings managed by the firm.

Sizeable losses were sustained from 1930 to 1933 and a number of the firm's partners sought to withdraw their remaining capital, thus threatening the very existence of the firm. It was only when a Boston-based manufacturer, John Hegarty, agreed to invest a substantial sum of additional capital in return for a controlling interest, that the firm's survival was assured.

Mebel Doran prospered in the post-World War II U.S. economy along with a number of other securities firms that had also suffered severe reverses during the Depression years of the 1930s. It participated as a "major bracket" underwriter in debt and equity underwritings and it enjoyed a substantial stable of client relationships that had either carried over from the pre-Depression period or had been cultivated since the end of the war. One of the firm's special strengths had been a nationwide network of branches catering to high net worth individuals. Although the center of the firm's operations had shifted to New York City, Philadelphia and the Delaware Valley area continued to be a region of special strength for the firm, both among investors as well as corporate and financial service clients.

Although initially slow to recognize the trend towards the institutionalization of savings, Mebel Doran had ultimately moved aggressively to establish itself as an important competitor in the institutional stock and bond marketplace. Its research analysts were usually prominently represented among Institutional Investor's *All American* list, and its institutional trading services were highly rated by portfolio managers, as reflected in several annual trade surveys, including the Greenwich Research polls.

As the nature and mix of the securities business shifted during the 1970s and early 1980s, Mebel Doran sought to maintain its competitive edge in the marketplace. Although not one of the "bulge group" of six leading investment banking firms, Mebel nonetheless occupied a respected niche in the group ranking just below those firms. It had been among the first to see the growing importance of

▼ ■

mergers and acquisitions as a source of revenue to securities firms (see Exhibit 1) and had what it believed was one of the most sophisticated and experienced groups of professionals available anywhere on Wall Street. It had also perceived that in the post-shelf registration era it would be important to be capable of bidding strictly on a price basis for underwriting business that offered little if any direct profit but which was an entre to other higher margin business. Partially in response to that, Mebel Doran had made the momentous decision to "go public" in 1984 as a means of raising a large amount of capital that would be permanently available to the firm in the future (see Exhibit 2).

Mebel Doran was proud of its long operating history and of the stature that had come to be attached to its name. Its reputation for excellence and integrity had been an effective calling card when approaching potential clients and investors, and had also enabled the firm to compete head-to-head with other leading securities firms for new employees at the top U.S. graduate business schools.

The Client Company

The Knox Corporation, a diversified manufacturing firm based in Philadelphia, had been a long-time client of Mebel Doran. The firm had brought Knox "public" in 1951 and had undertaken a number of financings for the company in succeeding years. Mebel Doran had also counseled the company in connection with its acquisition activities, which had been instrumental in the company's growth from sales of $75 million in 1960 to more than $1.7 billion in 1986 (see Exhibit 3). In late 1985, Knox had itself become the target of an outsider raid and, after several abortive attempts to find a friendly third-party merger partner, had implemented a public restructuring of its capitalization with the assistance of experts in Mebel Doran's mergers and acquisitions group. Some 43% of the company's common stock had been repurchased at a substantial premium above the prevailing market. The stock repurchase had been financed by drawing down Knox's cash reserves, selling off much of its real estate holdings and other redundant assets, and floating additional senior and junior debt securities such that the company's debt-to-capitalization ratio moved from 27% to almost 74% (see Exhibit 4). Coverage ratios had plummeted, not unexpectedly, from 8.4 times in 1984 to barely 2.0 times in 1986 (see Exhibit 2). The bond rating on the company's debt had also dropped from Baa to B, thus placing it in the "clearly speculative" category of investment risk.

In September 1986, a representative of Mebel Doran's M&A group had approached Knox with the idea of acquiring the Dover, Delaware-based Power-Tie Corporation, a publicly traded manufacturer with a product line which overlapped and extended that of one of the Knox divisions. Potential operating economies from the hoped-for combination were projected to boost Knox's operating income by approximately 15% even after the incremental financing costs had been deducted.

Power-Tie, which had been trading on the New York Stock Exchange in the $30 to $33 range for several months, had approximately 10 million shares outstanding which were fairly widely held. Historically, institutional interest in the company had been only modest. Knox had acquired 4.9% of the shares in carefully orchestrated open market purchases over the past month and a half and the confidential plan was to structure a tender offer that would seek a total of 51% of the outstanding equity in a cash transaction. This would then be followed by a merger in which the remaining shares of Power-Tie would be exchanged for a package of Knox securities, including high-yield debt instruments.

Mebel Doran's staff had been collaborating with Knox in arranging bridge financing for the proposed tender offer, even though they had not revealed the name of the potential target to the commercial bankers with whom they were talking. The net need for long-term funds would be somewhat reduced by the fact that Mebel Doran had identified substantial redundant assets at Power-Tie in addition to the fairly sizeable cash balances carried on the company's balance sheet.

Mebel Doran's arrangement with Knox called for a front-end fee of $2 million for its work in developing the strategy for acquiring Power-Tie. The agreement also called for payment of a contingent fee of 1% of the principal value of the merger transaction in the event that the acquisition was consummated, with the $2 million fee being credited against the total. The bulk of the preliminary preparation work was now completed and Mebel Doran was at the point in late February 1987 of sending an invoice to Knox for payment of the $2 million fee.

Further Inquiries

Mr. Hegarty was quite disturbed by the information that his partner had just related. A check of the trading volume and price action of Power-Tie's common stock confirmed that there had indeed been a sharp increase in share price, accompanied by heavy volume. He decided to go down and talk with the M&A professionals who had been working most closely on this deal.

In talking with an M&A vice president and two young associates who had been directly assigned to the project, he learned that in the course of their efforts to engineer a viable tender offer proposal, they had consulted with one of the traders in Mebel Doran's risk arbitrage group about the specifics of the Knox situation. Although Mebel Doran had always maintained a "Chinese Wall" between its M&A group and its risk arbitrage desk, there were situations in which the expertise and market savvy of these specialized traders constituted an important resource for the M&A specialists working to structure financial strategies on behalf of various of the firm's corporate clients. This type of contact between the two Mebel Doran entities had not been considered a real breach of the "Wall" because the securities of the companies in question were automatically placed on Mebel Doran's "restricted" list and therefore barred from trading by the firm's arbitrage desk. Further, the arbitrage personnel who were consulted in this capacity understood explicitly that the intra-firm inquiry was being made in the strictest confidence and that it constituted "insider information" in a legal sense of the term.

Mr. Hegarty next went down seven floors from the M&A headquarters to the offices of the risk arbitrage group to speak with the partner in charge of the unit, as well as with the trader with whom the M&A specialists had consulted. Mebel Doran's risk arbitrage activity was a profit center of long standing within the firm. It dated back to the days just before and after World War II when a large quantity of new securities were issued in various railroad reorganizations; this offered an attractive opportunity for "arbitraging" the newly issued securities against the old ones being surrendered. Over more than four decades, this arbitrage activity, almost completely financed with the firm's own capital, had been among the most profitable parts of the securities business. During the past several years, the amount of capital committed to arbitrage by Mebel Doran had grown enormously, so that in 1986 it was the largest capital commitment next to the firm's fixed income inventory. Moreover, the profitability of the arbitrage desk had grown so large that by 1986 it contributed more than a quarter of Mebel Doran's after-tax profits (versus the M&A group's contribution of 40% of the firm's profits).

When questioned, the arbitrageurs expressed puzzlement at the recent price and volume patterns in the Power-Tie stock and wondered if someone else was interested in taking over the company and had therefore caused the recent price run-up. Under further questioning, however, Mr. Hegarty learned that one of the group's arbitrageurs had gotten an inquiry about Power-Tie the week before from an arbitrageur at another securities firm. The caller from the other firm, with whom the Mebel Doran risk arbitrageur stood in frequent contact (they would typically call each other several times a day if deals seemed to be developing on the street), had asked, "Hey, I hear all these rumors about Power-Tie; do you know if anything is going on?" Mebel Doran's arbitrageur told Hegarty that he had tried to be noncommital, but did not remember exactly what he had replied.

Mr. Hegarty was angry and somewhat shaken at the way this inquiry had been handled and the implicit signal which it sent. He directed the partner in charge to initiate quiet inquiries to try to determine whether this particular arbitrageur who had contacted Mebel Doran for information had in fact been active in the Power-Tie stock trading. Three hours later, his partner reported back that, based on the bits and pieces that they had been able to put together, the arbitrageur in question had indeed been an active buyer of the Power-Tie shares over the past week. At this point, he was believed to be holding something just short of 5% of the company's outstanding equity in his inventory.

After directing his secretary to hold all his calls, he closed his office door and settled down to weigh just what he should do next.

Exhibit 1

Consolidated Statements of Income ($ thousands)

	Years Ended March 31,				
Assets	1982	1983	1984	1985	1986
REVENUES					
Commission	$114,673	$112,066	$ 166,468	$ 194,054	$ 182,193
Principal transactions	105,844	118,166	173,156	55,039	163,192
Investment banking	39,636	31,676	65,106	89,237	98,950
Interest and dividends	91,451	144,591	598,550	858,167	1,178,061
Other income	1,981	874	1,771	2,397	1,437
Total revenues	$353,584	$406,773	$1,005,051	$1,198,894	$1,623,833
EXPENSES					
Partner and employee compensation	$114,299	$121,839	$ 181,427	$ 205,205	$ 239,612
Interest	78,001	124,936	533,586	711,511	1,066,594
Floor brokerage, exchange and clearance fees	14,422	15,939	25,366	28,838	29,558
Communications	11,371	14,296	17,356	22,206	25,582
Professional fees	2,990	3,000	6,054	8,718	12,010
Depreciation and amortization	1,695	2,694	4,554	6,142	8,529
Taxes on income	117	1,343	2,606	1,962	1,710
Other taxes	3,784	4,963	6,079	7,966	10,129
Occupancy	5,357	7,173	9,254	11,641	19,390
Advertising and market development	5,588	7,150	9,292	11,707	14,324
Data processing and equipment	7,771	11,328	13,104	14,757	16,096
Other expenses	11,315	12,688	16,395	20,805	28,417
Total expenses	$256,700	$327,735	$825,073	$1,051,459	$1,471,981
Net income	$ 96,884	$ 79,421	$179,978	$ 147,435	$ 151,852

Exhibit 2

Consolidated Balance Sheets for Years Ended March 31,
($ thousands)

	1985	1986
ASSETS		
Cash and cash equivalent	$ 11,546	$ 692,000
Cash and securities deposited with clearing organizations or segregated in compliance with federal regulations (market value of securities $12,800 in 1984 and $46,378 in 1985)	63,911	116,299
Securities purchased under agreements to resell	5,750,843	8,153,585
Receivable from brokers, dealers and clearing organizations	856,622	1,651,709
Receivable from customers	1,388,622	1,663,508
Marketable securities and commodities owned at market value:		
United States Government	6,600,241	8,649,598
State and Municipal	62,606	106,705
Other	1,353,699	1,005,040
Furniture, equipment and leasehold improvements—at cost, less accumulated depreciation and amortization of $18,365 in 1984 and $26,895 in 1985	20,843	38,796
Other assets	49,000	71,821
Total assets	$16,158,085	$21,526,281
LIABILITIES AND EQUITY CAPITAL		
Money borrowed	$ 454,522	$ 564,711
Drafts payable	66,521	95,292
Installment sale notes payable	107,297	61,447
Securities sold under agreements to repurchase	6,440,523	12,295,771
Payable to brokers, dealers and clearing organizations	667,808	836,343
Payable to customers	1,016,806	2,109,001
Marketable securities and commodities sold, but not yet purchased– at market value		
United States Government	5,749,339	4,333,544
State and Municipal	7,165	10,299
Other	984,236	440,677
Accrued employee compensation and benefits	58,450	71,358
Other liabilities, accrued expenses, taxes and reserves	213,632	242,245
Senior subordinated notes	117,000	147,600
Other subordinated notes	2,993	2,993
Equity capital	271,800	315,000
Total liabilities and capital	$16,158,085	$21,526,281

Exhibit 3

Consolidated Statement of Earnings—The Knox Corporation and Subsidiaries
for the Twelve Months Ending December 31, 1986 ($ thousands)

Net sales revenue	$1,784,637
Expenses	
Cost of sales	1,356,230
Depreciation expense	35,737
Selling and administrative expense	212,004
Interest expense	64,287
Total expenses	$1,668,258
Earnings from continuing operations before income taxes	$ 116,379
Provision for income taxes	61,910
Earnings from continuing operations	54,469
Loss from discontinued operations	(80,272)
Net earnings (loss)	$ (25,803)

Exhibit 4

Consolidated Balance Sheet—The Knox Corporation December 31, 1986 ($ millions)

CURRENT ASSETS		CURRENT LIABILITIES	
Cash and marketable securities	$ 8	Notes payable to banks	$ 16
Accounts and notes receivable	241	Accounts payable	117
Inventories	346	Accrued expenses	182
Other current	129	Current portion of liabilities of discontinued operations	38
Total current assets	$ 724	Total current liabilities	$ 353
LONG-TERM ASSETS		LONG-TERM LIABILITIES	
Property, plant and equipment (net)	$ 336	Liabilities of discontinued operations	$23
		Long-term debt	570
Other Assets	30	Shareholders' Equity	152
Total Assets	$1,098	Total Liabilities, Shareholders' Equity	$1,098

A B C D E F G H I J
1 2 3 4 5 6 7 8 9 0